Lecture Notes in Computer Science 12779

More information about this subseries at http://www.springer.com/series/7409

Marcelo M. Soares · Elizabeth Rosenzweig ·
Aaron Marcus (Eds.)

Design, User Experience, and Usability

UX Research and Design

10th International Conference, DUXU 2021
Held as Part of the 23rd HCI International Conference, HCII 2021
Virtual Event, July 24–29, 2021
Proceedings, Part I

 Springer

Editors
Marcelo M. Soares
Hunan University, School of Design
Changsha, China

Department of Design
Federal University of Pernambuco
Recife, Brazil

Aaron Marcus
Aaron Marcus and Associates
Berkeley, CA, USA

Elizabeth Rosenzweig
World Usability Day and Rabb School
of Continuing Studies, Division of
Graduate Professional Studies
Brandeis University
Newton Center, MA, USA

ISSN 0302-9743   ISSN 1611-3349   (electronic)
Lecture Notes in Computer Science
ISBN 978-3-030-78220-7   ISBN 978-3-030-78221-4   (eBook)
https://doi.org/10.1007/978-3-030-78221-4

LNCS Sublibrary: SL3 – Information Systems and Applications, incl. Internet/Web, and HCI

This Springer imprint is published by the registered company Springer Nature Switzerland AG
The registered company address is: Gewerbestrasse 11, 6330 Cham, Switzerland

Foreword

Human-Computer Interaction (HCI) is acquiring an ever-increasing scientific and industrial importance, and having more impact on people's everyday life, as an ever-growing number of human activities are progressively moving from the physical to the digital world. This process, which has been ongoing for some time now, has been dramatically accelerated by the COVID-19 pandemic. The HCI International (HCII) conference series, held yearly, aims to respond to the compelling need to advance the exchange of knowledge and research and development efforts on the human aspects of design and use of computing systems.

The 23rd International Conference on Human-Computer Interaction, HCI International 2021 (HCII 2021), was planned to be held at the Washington Hilton Hotel, Washington DC, USA, during July 24–29, 2021. Due to the COVID-19 pandemic and with everyone's health and safety in mind, HCII 2021 was organized and run as a virtual conference. It incorporated the 21 thematic areas and affiliated conferences listed on the following page.

A total of 5222 individuals from academia, research institutes, industry, and governmental agencies from 81 countries submitted contributions, and 1276 papers and 241 posters were included in the proceedings to appear just before the start of the conference. The contributions thoroughly cover the entire field of HCI, addressing major advances in knowledge and effective use of computers in a variety of application areas. These papers provide academics, researchers, engineers, scientists, practitioners, and students with state-of-the-art information on the most recent advances in HCI. The volumes constituting the set of proceedings to appear before the start of the conference are listed in the following pages.

The HCI International (HCII) conference also offers the option of 'Late Breaking Work' which applies both for papers and posters, and the corresponding volume(s) of the proceedings will appear after the conference. Full papers will be included in the 'HCII 2021 - Late Breaking Papers' volumes of the proceedings to be published in the Springer LNCS series, while 'Poster Extended Abstracts' will be included as short research papers in the 'HCII 2021 - Late Breaking Posters' volumes to be published in the Springer CCIS series.

The present volume contains papers submitted and presented in the context of the 10th International Conference on Design, User Experience, and Usability (DUXU 2021), an affiliated conference to HCII 2021. I would like to thank the Co-chairs, Marcelo M. Soares, Elizabeth Rosenzweig, and Aaron Marcus, for their invaluable contribution to its organization and the preparation of the proceedings, as well as the members of the Program Board for their contributions and support. This year, the DUXU affiliated conference has focused on topics related to UX design and research methods and techniques, design education and practice, mobile UX, visual languages and information visualization, extended reality UX, and experience design across cultures, as well as UX design for inclusion and social development, health and well-being, and the creative industries.

I would also like to thank the Program Board Chairs and the members of the Program Boards of all thematic areas and affiliated conferences for their contribution towards the highest scientific quality and overall success of the HCI International 2021 conference.

This conference would not have been possible without the continuous and unwavering support and advice of Gavriel Salvendy, founder, General Chair Emeritus, and Scientific Advisor. For his outstanding efforts, I would like to express my appreciation to Abbas Moallem, Communications Chair and Editor of HCI International News.

July 2021   Constantine Stephanidis

HCI International 2021 Thematic Areas and Affiliated Conferences

Thematic Areas

- HCI: Human-Computer Interaction
- HIMI: Human Interface and the Management of Information

Affiliated Conferences

- EPCE: 18th International Conference on Engineering Psychology and Cognitive Ergonomics
- UAHCI: 15th International Conference on Universal Access in Human-Computer Interaction
- VAMR: 13th International Conference on Virtual, Augmented and Mixed Reality
- CCD: 13th International Conference on Cross-Cultural Design
- SCSM: 13th International Conference on Social Computing and Social Media
- AC: 15th International Conference on Augmented Cognition
- DHM: 12th International Conference on Digital Human Modeling and Applications in Health, Safety, Ergonomics and Risk Management
- DUXU: 10th International Conference on Design, User Experience, and Usability
- DAPI: 9th International Conference on Distributed, Ambient and Pervasive Interactions
- HCIBGO: 8th International Conference on HCI in Business, Government and Organizations
- LCT: 8th International Conference on Learning and Collaboration Technologies
- ITAP: 7th International Conference on Human Aspects of IT for the Aged Population
- HCI-CPT: 3rd International Conference on HCI for Cybersecurity, Privacy and Trust
- HCI-Games: 3rd International Conference on HCI in Games
- MobiTAS: 3rd International Conference on HCI in Mobility, Transport and Automotive Systems
- AIS: 3rd International Conference on Adaptive Instructional Systems
- C&C: 9th International Conference on Culture and Computing
- MOBILE: 2nd International Conference on Design, Operation and Evaluation of Mobile Communications
- AI-HCI: 2nd International Conference on Artificial Intelligence in HCI

List of Conference Proceedings Volumes Appearing Before the Conference

1. LNCS 12762, Human-Computer Interaction: Theory, Methods and Tools (Part I), edited by Masaaki Kurosu
2. LNCS 12763, Human-Computer Interaction: Interaction Techniques and Novel Applications (Part II), edited by Masaaki Kurosu
3. LNCS 12764, Human-Computer Interaction: Design and User Experience Case Studies (Part III), edited by Masaaki Kurosu
4. LNCS 12765, Human Interface and the Management of Information: Information Presentation and Visualization (Part I), edited by Sakae Yamamoto and Hirohiko Mori
5. LNCS 12766, Human Interface and the Management of Information: Information-rich and Intelligent Environments (Part II), edited by Sakae Yamamoto and Hirohiko Mori
6. LNAI 12767, Engineering Psychology and Cognitive Ergonomics, edited by Don Harris and Wen-Chin Li
7. LNCS 12768, Universal Access in Human-Computer Interaction: Design Methods and User Experience (Part I), edited by Margherita Antona and Constantine Stephanidis
8. LNCS 12769, Universal Access in Human-Computer Interaction: Access to Media, Learning and Assistive Environments (Part II), edited by Margherita Antona and Constantine Stephanidis
9. LNCS 12770, Virtual, Augmented and Mixed Reality, edited by Jessie Y. C. Chen and Gino Fragomeni
10. LNCS 12771, Cross-Cultural Design: Experience and Product Design Across Cultures (Part I), edited by P. L. Patrick Rau
11. LNCS 12772, Cross-Cultural Design: Applications in Arts, Learning, Well-being, and Social Development (Part II), edited by P. L. Patrick Rau
12. LNCS 12773, Cross-Cultural Design: Applications in Cultural Heritage, Tourism, Autonomous Vehicles, and Intelligent Agents (Part III), edited by P. L. Patrick Rau
13. LNCS 12774, Social Computing and Social Media: Experience Design and Social Network Analysis (Part I), edited by Gabriele Meiselwitz
14. LNCS 12775, Social Computing and Social Media: Applications in Marketing, Learning, and Health (Part II), edited by Gabriele Meiselwitz
15. LNAI 12776, Augmented Cognition, edited by Dylan D. Schmorrow and Cali M. Fidopiastis
16. LNCS 12777, Digital Human Modeling and Applications in Health, Safety, Ergonomics and Risk Management: Human Body, Motion and Behavior (Part I), edited by Vincent G. Duffy
17. LNCS 12778, Digital Human Modeling and Applications in Health, Safety, Ergonomics and Risk Management: AI, Product and Service (Part II), edited by Vincent G. Duffy

http://2021.hci.international/proceedings

10th International Conference on Design, User Experience, and Usability (DUXU 2021)

Program Board Chairs: **Marcelo M. Soares,** *Hunan University, China, and Federal University of Pernambuco, Brazil* **and Elizabeth Rosenzweig,** *World Usability Day and Brandeis University, USA* **and Aaron Marcus,** *Aaron Marcus and Associates, USA*

- Sisira Adikari, Australia
- Claire Ancient, UK
- Roger Ball, USA
- Eric Brangier, France
- Silvia de los Rios, Spain
- Marc Fabri, UK
- Ernesto Filgueiras, Portugal
- Josh A. Halstead, USA
- Chris Hass, USA
- Zhen Liu, China
- Wei Liu, China
- Martin Maguire, UK
- Judith Moldenhauer, USA
- Gunther Paul, Australia
- Francisco Rebelo, Portugal
- Christine Riedmann-Streitz, Germany
- Patricia Search, USA
- Dorothy Shamonsky, USA

The full list with the Program Board Chairs and the members of the Program Boards of all thematic areas and affiliated conferences is available online at:

http://www.hci.international/board-members-2021.php

HCI International 2022

The 24th International Conference on Human-Computer Interaction, HCI International 2022, will be held jointly with the affiliated conferences at the Gothia Towers Hotel and Swedish Exhibition & Congress Centre, Gothenburg, Sweden, June 26 – July 1, 2022. It will cover a broad spectrum of themes related to Human-Computer Interaction, including theoretical issues, methods, tools, processes, and case studies in HCI design, as well as novel interaction techniques, interfaces, and applications. The proceedings will be published by Springer. More information will be available on the conference website: http://2022.hci.international/:

General Chair
Prof. Constantine Stephanidis
University of Crete and ICS-FORTH
Heraklion, Crete, Greece
Email: general_chair@hcii2022.org

http://2022.hci.international/

Contents – Part I

Methods and Techniques for UX Research

Visual Languages and Information Visualization

Design Education and Practice

Contents – Part II

Design for Inclusion and Social Development

Design for Health and Well-Being

DUXU Case Studies

Contents – Part III

DUXU for Extended Reality

DUXU for the Creative Industries

Usability and UX Studies

UX Design Methods and Techniques

A Prototyping Framework
for Human-Centered Product Design:
Preliminary Validation Study

Salman Ahmed$^{(\boxtimes)}$ and H. Onan Demirel

Oregon State University, Corvallis, OR 97331, USA
{ahmedsal,onan.demirel}@oregonstate.edu

Abstract. Prototyping is a crucial aspect of the product design and development process. Successful development and deployment of products hinge on building correct prototypes. However, current prototyping frameworks often do not provide specific prototyping guidelines that are practical and readily applicable and do not consider Human Factors Engineering (HFE) design guidelines thoroughly. This paper presents a novel prototyping framework that integrates prototyping and HFE guidelines to address the research gap in the prototyping literature. The prototyping framework presents a database in the form of a graphical user interface (GUI), which contains userform data entry. The GUI userform helps the designer to develop prototyping strategies based on the prototyping best practices and HFE principles. Further, the GUI userform suggests tools and technologies that can be used to fabricate the prototype. Thus, the framework helps designers plan prototyping activities and reduces the reliance on intuition when fabricating prototypes. This paper also presents a preliminary validation study that focuses on exploring whether there is a statistical difference between the intervention and control group in developing prototyping strategies for various prototyping problems. The intervention and control group are tested using twelve prototyping problems, and the Prototyping Success score is measured for each group. An independent sample t-test is performed. From the statistical analysis, it can be inferred that the participants who use the prototyping framework produce mean Prototyping Success scores that are higher than that of the control group.

Keywords: Prototyping framework · Design · Human-centered design · Human factors engineering · Ergonomics · Validation · Digital human modeling

1 Introduction

Prototyping is a crucial aspect of the product design and development process [19]. Prototypes that can unveil the required information in a cost-effective and timely manner can help design high-quality products that are successful in the market. A comprehensive prototyping methodology can guide designers to build

© Springer Nature Switzerland AG 2021
M. M. Soares et al. (Eds.): HCII 2021, LNCS 12779, pp. 3–14, 2021.
https://doi.org/10.1007/978-3-030-78221-4_1

efficient and effective prototypes. However, prototyping is a complex activity, and the literature is scarce in presenting guidelines and frameworks that are comprehensive and widely accepted [3,14]. The current prototyping frameworks focus mainly on prototyping activity or hands-on prototyping experience [3]. Also, most of these frameworks rely on designers' intuition or experience rather than providing systematic guidelines and best practices to aid designers in their prototyping quest [12]. Another shortcoming of the existing prototyping framework is the lack of fabrication guidelines [3,12,14]. The absence of fabrication guidelines regarding what tools and technologies to use when building a prototype causes wide variation in the prototype quality even though designers use the same prototyping methods [14].

Further, the prototyping literature and methodologies within the human-centered product design domain are even more limited. The prototyping process for human-centered products is a subset of the general prototyping processes, which often require domain-specific knowledge (e.g., human factors engineering), human subject data collection, and user feedback. Also, the current prototyping frameworks do not consider human factor engineering (HFE) guidelines adequately [3,12,14]. The absence or partial consideration of HFE guidelines can result in products or workspaces that do not address human needs and limitations [7,10]. Another challenge in developing a widely accepted prototyping framework is proving the efficacy of the prototyping methodology. Prototyping activity is a blend of science and art, and there is no single definitive approach to define the best strategy in prototyping. Hence, validating a prototyping framework is taxing.

The purpose of the paper is twofold. First, the paper provides a brief overview of a novel prototyping framework that guides the designer to develop prototyping strategies for human-centered products by combining the principles and best practices of prototyping and human factors discipline. The second purpose is to present a validation methodology and a preliminary validation study based on the proposed prototyping framework.

2   Literature Review

Various definitions of the prototype, prototype taxonomy, and prototyping framework exists in the literature. Wickens et al. (1998) defined a prototype as an artifact that can be used to evaluate fit, form, or functional design representations that assist designers in communicating tests directly or validate design ideas [20]. Additionally, a prototype is defined as an artifact that approximates a feature (or multiple features) of a product, service, or system [15]. A recent definition proposed by Lauff et al. (2018) defines a prototype as a physical or digital embodiment of critical elements of the intended design and an iterative tool to enhance communication, enable learning and inform decision-making at any point in the design process [13].

Otto and Wood classified prototypes based on the evaluation of a concept. They divided prototypes into six classes: proof of concept, industrial design,

design of experiment, alpha, beta, and pre-production prototypes [15]. Proto-types are also classified with respect to the cost, stage of design, level of abstrac-tion or realism, intended evaluation purpose [15,16] in the literature. Another taxonomy of prototyping is based on the concept of *Prototyping Purpose* which was proposed by Petrakis et al. (2019) [17]. Petrakis et al. defines the *Prototyp-ing Purpose* as the actual reason for building a prototype to achieve explicit, already set objectives, then proposes 23 sub-roles of prototyping purpose [17].

A prototyping framework is a tool or platform created to generate strategies and guidelines for developing prototypes. Literature shows that widely accepted and comprehensive prototyping frameworks are scarce [3,4,14]. For example, Menold et al. (2017) developed The Prototype for X Framework (PFX) com-prised of three phases: Frame, Build and Test. Additionally, Menold et al. included three lenses, Feasibility, Viability, and Desirability, for designers to develop prototyping strategies [14]. Lauff et al. (2019) proposed a prototyping framework called Prototyping Canvas that is intended to be easy to use and practical so that designers can find it useful. The Prototyping Canvas leverages the prototyping principles of Purpose, Resource, and Strategy. The layout of the canvas is inspired by Business Model Canvas [12].

Camburn et al. (2015) proposed a framework that can assess and weigh out the different prototyping techniques and offer suitable strategies for building prototypes. The framework is developed by compiling the prototyping findings, best practices, and heuristics from the literature. The framework is validated by comparing prototypes created by the intervention and control group. More-over, Christie et al. (2012) developed a framework that has a prototyping strat-egy matrix, nine prototyping factors, and thirteen questionnaires. The thirteen questions are used to guide designers in selecting the right prototyping strategies and the matrix is used to evaluate different prototyping concepts and finalize the right one [4]. The literature review shows that no prototyping framework special-izes or even considers human-centered design requirements and characteristics explicitly by injecting HFE principles into prototype planning. Additionally, the existing frameworks are focus more on building better prototypes and hands-on activities within prototyping rather than providing a road-map to designers based on prototyping guidelines and best practices. Hence, even when following the same framework, intervention groups tend to create prototypes with vary-ing quality [14]. Further, the existing prototyping frameworks are not straight forward enough to be readily used by designers [12]. Therefore, the framework presented in this paper integrates HFE principles with prototyping factors to fill the knowledge gap. Additionally, it assists designers in planning prototyping activities and reduces the reliance on intuition when fabricating prototypes.

3   Methodology

The methodology of developing the proposed prototyping framework consists of five steps as shown in Fig. 1. The first step focuses on a thorough prototyping-related literature review that spans from human factors engineering, human-centered design, digital human modeling to human-machine interaction. The

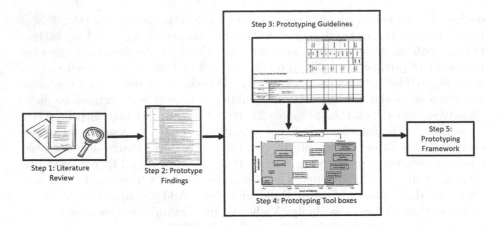

Fig. 1. Methodology to Build Prototyping Framework

best practices, guidelines, principles, and important factors from the literature are compiled into a summary table in the second step. The factors and guidelines crucial in developing prototyping strategies for human-centered products are then extracted from the summary table to form a matrix called House of Prototyping Guidelines (HOPG) in the third step. Similarly, the tools and technologies important for fabricating prototypes for human-centered products are extracted from the second step to create a Prototyping Toolbox. Finally, in the fifth step, the theories to strategize a prototype, as developed in the third step, and the practical tools to fabricate the prototype, as developed in the fourth step, are integrated and presented via a graphical user interface (GUI). The final step compiles the proposed prototyping framework that designers use in creating prototyping strategies for human-centered products. This paper also focuses on a preliminary validation of the proposed prototyping framework, so the methodology is only briefly described here. More details about the prototyping framework's building blocks can be found in our recent publications [1,2].

3.1 House of Prototyping Guidelines

House of Prototyping Guidelines (HOPG) brings the necessary guidelines and best practices together that are required to strategize prototypes theoretically. HOPG's structure is influenced by the structure of the House of Quality (HOQ) [8]. As shown in Fig. 2, HOPG has two sections: Prototyping Categories and Prototyping Dimensions. Similar to Customer Requirement in HOQ, Prototyping Categories tries to capture the need to build a prototype. A crucial part while building prototyping strategies is identifying the objective or the question the prototype will answer [9,12]. How many resources are available for prototyping? In addition to identifying purposes and resources in human-centered product prototyping, designers need to identify the type of ergonomic assessments and level of human-product interactions. The prototyping design problem will dictate

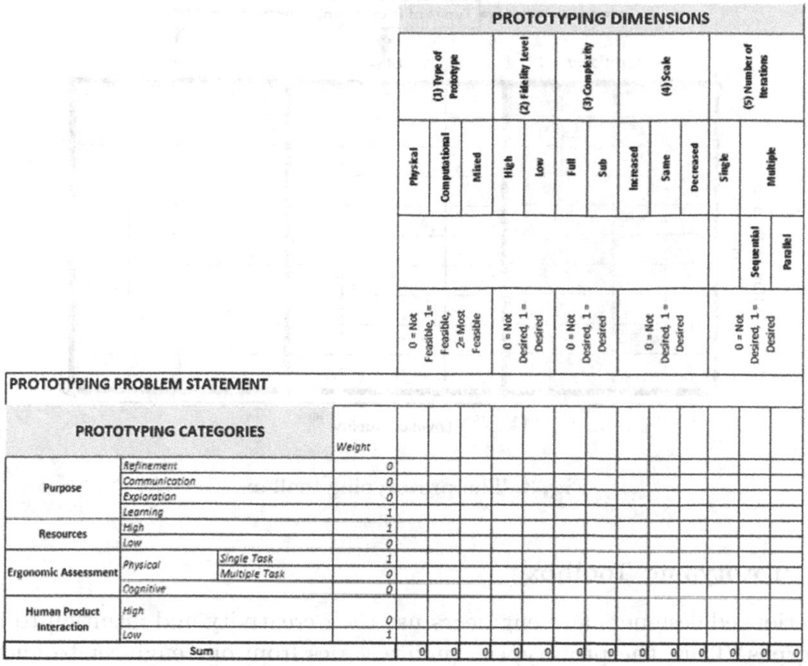

PROTOTYPING CATEGORIES		Weight	(1) Type of Prototype — Physical (0 = Not Feasible, 1 = Feasible, 2 = Most Feasible)	Computational	Mixed	(2) Fidelity Level — High (0 = Not Desired, 1 = Desired)	Low	(3) Complexity — Full (0 = Not Desired, 1 = Desired)	Sub	(4) Scale — Increased (0 = Not Desired, 1 = Desired)	Same	Decreased	(5) Number of Iterations — Single (0 = Not Desired, 1 = Desired)	Multiple — Sequential	Parallel
Purpose	Refinement	0													
	Communication	0													
	Exploration	0													
	Learning	1													
Resources	High	1													
	Low	0													
Ergonomic Assessment	Physical — Single Task	1													
	Physical — Multiple Task	0													
	Cognitive	0													
Human Product Interaction	High	0													
	Low	1													
Sum			0	0	0	0	0	0	0	0	0	0	0	0	0

Fig. 2. The house of prototyping guidelines (HOPG)

the designers to identify and weight the Prototyping Categories, i.e., the purpose, resource availability, type of ergonomic assessment, and interaction levels.

The next step in HOPG is to identify the Prototyping Dimensions. It is similar to the Engineering Specifications section found in HOQ. The Prototyping Dimensions consists of five dimensions: Type of Prototype, Fidelity Level, Complexity, Scale, and Number of Iterations. The Prototyping Categories, the embedded prototyping best practices, and the HFE principles will guide the designers to identify the Prototyping Dimensions. The designers will also rate the Prototyping Dimensions according to their relevance and capability of realizing the Prototyping Categories. Finally, the Prototyping Dimensions will be calculated using the given equation (See Eq. 1). The Prototyping Dimensions with the highest sum are the final Prototyping Dimensions chosen to strategize the prototype.

$$Sum = \text{Weight}(Prototyping\ Categories) \times \text{Rate}(Prototyping\ Dimensions) \quad (1)$$

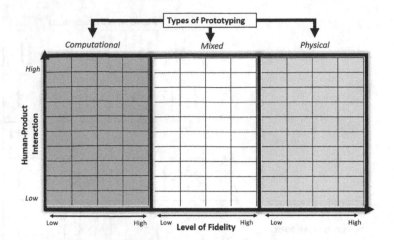

Fig. 3. The prototyping toolbox

3.2   Prototyping Toolbox

Inexperienced designers and engineers use their creativity and intuition to build prototypes. Thus, the prototypes' quality varies from one engineer to another, even when the same theoretical prototyping strategy is provided [5]. Thus, it is imperative to provide fabrication guidelines to ensure high-quality and consistency in prototyping. The fourth step of the prototyping framework contains the Prototyping Toolbox, which guides designers in the context of fabricating the prototype. Likewise, in the third step, designers are equipped with the theoretical knowledge required to strategize a prototype. The theoretical knowledge is mapped with the tools and technologies to identify the right fabrication guidelines within the Prototyping Toolbox. The Prototyping Toolbox contains three-axis: Type of Prototype, Fidelity Level, and Human-Product Interaction as shown in Fig. 3. The Human-Product Interaction Level is leveraged from Human Aspects of Design as proposed by Duffy (2007) [6]. The Type of Prototype and Fidelity Level of Prototype are leveraged from the Hierarchical Morphological Prototyping (HMP) Taxonomy [18].

Types of prototypes refer to the variety of prototypes. In this prototyping strategy, the variety is categorized into three types, which are Computational, Physical, and Mixed prototypes. The level of fidelity is classified into high and low fidelity. Though fidelity can be considered a continuum, only two levels are considered here due to the lack of proper classification found in the literature. Similar to the level of fidelity, the human-product interaction level is also a continuum. The human-product interaction can range from very-low to very-high. In this framework, the hierarchical task analysis (HTA) method is used to determine whether the human-product interaction is high or low [11]. The three-axis representation is then used to classify the tools and technologies used to fabricate the prototype. The Toolbox acts as an inventory of tools, and the theoretical strategies developed from HOPG are used to select the tools in the Toolbox.

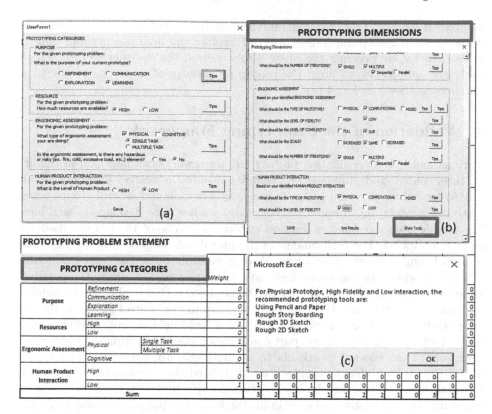

Fig. 4. The prototyping framework

3.3 Prototyping Framework

The fifth step and the final step of the methodology presents the Prototyping Framework. The final step is the culmination of all the previous steps, mainly focusing on the third and the fourth step. The prototyping framework combines the theoretical aspects of prototyping strategies from Step 3 and the practical fabrication guidelines from Step 4 to form the prototyping framework. Currently, it has a graphical user interface based on Microsoft Excel as shown in Fig. 4—the prototyping guidelines, HFE principles, tools, and technologies are all embedded into the interface. Figure 4 shows the snippets of the prototyping framework. The first step of the framework is to read and understand the prototyping problem. The second step is to identify the Prototyping Categories corresponding to the prototyping problem. The Prototyping Categories are shown in Fig. 4 (a). A designer can choose the Prototyping Categories based on the prototyping problems and the prototyping guidelines embedded as Tips. After identifying the prototyping categories and saving them within the framework (Microsoft Excel User Form), the designer should move on to the next step of selecting the Prototyping Dimensions, as shown in Fig. 4 (b). The prototyping guidelines are also embedded here as Tips. After going through the prototyping dimensions, the designer should save the framework and explore the final prototyping dimensions. Finally, by pressing the Show Tools button, the designer can see which tools are appropriate to build the prototype corresponding to the prototyping dimensions shown in Fig. 4 (c).

4   Validation of the Prototyping Framework

Various methods for validating prototyping frameworks can be found in the literature, and a gold standard or general guidelines is scarce. Camburn et al. (2015) looked for the comparison between intervention and control groups when testing a prototyping framework. Four case studies were developed, each having unique objectives and evaluation criteria [3]. Some of the criteria used for evaluation include the performance of the prototype, number of iterations, time to build, and number of concepts. Having multiple objectives and evaluation criteria improves the validation method's robustness and minimize the possibility of bias and skewness of the result. Menold et al. (2017) also used a similar approach via comparing the intervention group to the control group. Only one case study, converting a hand-held drill to a hand-held vacuum problem, was used. Technical quality, critical part count ratio, user satisfaction, and perceived user value were selected as criteria to evaluate the prototypes [14]. Christie et al. (2012) took a different approach and validated their prototyping framework by qualitatively assessing the intervention group's prototyping strategies only. Since no physical prototypes were built, the focus was put on the concept generation and analysis of the strategies that the participants used from the proposed prototyping framework. The goal was to see how well the participants use the prototyping framework to create the prototyping strategies [4]. Like Christie et al. (2012), Lauff et al. (2019) also carried out an intervention group only and qualitative analysis only of the prototyping canvas, as no physical prototype was built. 5-point-scale Likert questions were used to evaluate the prototyping canvas qualitatively [12].

The literature review shows that the validation approach can be performed either by comparing the intervention group with the control group or just by evaluating the intervention group. The evaluation criteria can be both quantitative and/or qualitative. Quantitative evaluation is usually done when physical prototypes are built, and qualitative evaluations are applied when there are only conceptual prototyping strategies and no physical prototypes are built. In this paper, a quantitative evaluation is performed to validate the framework objectively by comparing the intervention and control group. Though no physical prototypes are built, quantitative evaluations are done by measuring the Prototyping Success objectively. The Prototyping Success is measured as follows:

$$Prototyping\ Success = \text{Type of Prototype}(2) + \text{Level of Interaction}(1) \\ + \text{Level of Fidelity}(1) \tag{2}$$

The Prototyping Success evaluates the prototype by quantifying the prototyping strategies generated using the proposed Prototyping Framework. Type of Prototype, Level of Interaction, and Level of Fidelity are the toolbox's three axes, which guide designers to select the correct set of tools to fabricate the prototype. The designers can only select the correct set of tools from the toolbox to identify the correct prototyping strategies, i.e., the type of prototype, level of interaction, and level of fidelity. The HOPG guides the designers to identify the correct prototyping strategies by going through the Prototyping Categories and Prototyping Dimensions as shown in Fig. 2. The values in the parenthesis in Eq. 2 indicates the maximum value each axis can get. For example, the Type of Prototype has a maximum value of two (2) as there are only three types of the prototype available. Likewise, the Level of Interaction has a maximum value of one (1) as there are two levels of interaction possible. Moreover, the Level of Fidelity also has a maximum value of one (1) as there are only two levels of fidelity available. Hence, the maximum value of Prototyping Success is 4.

Table 1. Average prototyping success values

Prototyping success	
Intervention group	Control group
3.40	3.10
3.50	2.67
3.92	3.00
2.92	2.50
3.67	2.92

4.1   Prototyping Experiment Setup

In this experiment, twelve prototyping problems are used. More about the prototyping problems can be found in these papers [1,2]. These prototyping problems are adapted from the established prototyping literature. Hence, the correct prototyping strategy is known. Participants of these experiments are from an engineering background and are familiar with the concept of prototyping. The number of participants is ten, and they are randomly divided into either intervention or control group. Each participant is given twelve prototyping problems. The intervention group used the prototyping framework, and the control group used their own knowledge and experience to devise the prototyping strategies. The resulting prototyping strategies are evaluated against the known prototyping strategies from the literature, and the Prototyping Success is measured. An independent samples t-test is used to evaluate the Prototyping Success between the intervention and control group. The Prototyping Success values and the t-test results are given the Tables 1 and 2 respectively.

Table 2. Statistical analysis of prototyping success values

Mean	Intervention group	3.48
	Control group	2.83
Standard deviation	Intervention group	0.37
	Control group	0.24
p-value		0.012
95% CI		0.18 to 1.10

5   Discussion

In this paper, a novel prototyping framework is presented and validated. The framework bridges the prototyping research gap of how human-centered products can be designed and prototyped. The prototyping framework integrates the prototyping literature and HFE guidelines to develop a framework that provides theoretical guidelines for developing prototyping strategies and suggesting tools and technologies to fabricate the prototype. The existing prototyping framework rarely provides any guidelines to build prototypes for human-centered products by considering HFE. Further, existing prototypes often do not provide specific guidelines for strategizing and fabricating prototypes. The HOPG and Toolbox section of the proposed prototyping framework provides specific guidelines. Further, the GUI userform provides a user-friendly platform to access and use the prototyping framework to generate prototyping and fabricating strategies. Thus, this proposed prototyping framework bridges this gap and contributes to the literature.

The prototyping framework is validated by comparing the prototyping strategies between the intervention and the control group. Table 1 shows the average Prototyping Success values of each participant from both groups. An independent sample t-test is performed, and the results are given in Table 2. It is seen from Table 2 that the average Prototyping Success score is higher for the intervention group. Further, the p-value is less than 0.05, indicating a significant difference in the Prototyping Success score between the two groups. From this statistical analysis, it can be inferred that the participants who use the prototyping framework produce Prototyping Success scores that are higher than that of the control group.

6   Future Work

Several avenues can be explored in the future to improve the proposed prototyping framework. The prototyping and HFE guidelines embedded in the framework can be more exhaustive to cover broader prototyping aspects. In addition to increasing the general guideline database, specific guidelines and knowledge from different domains (e.g., healthcare, automotive, and aerospace) can be included to create a more domain focused prototyping framework. Another potential future work is to perform a comprehensive validation study by increasing the number of participants and prototyping problems. Additionally, a qualitative study in the form of a questionnaire can be conducted to understand the designers' thought processes and how they perceive the prototyping framework.

References

1. Ahmed, S., Demirel, H.O.: House of prototyping guidelines: a framework to develop theoretical prototyping strategies for human-centered design. In: Marcus, A., Rosenzweig, E. (eds.) HCII 2020. LNCS, vol. 12200, pp. 21–38. Springer, Cham (2020). https://doi.org/10.1007/978-3-030-49713-2_2
2. Ahmed, S., Demirel, H.O.: A pre-prototyping framework to explore human-centered prototyping strategies during early design. In: ASME 2020 International Design Engineering Technical Conferences and Computers and Information in Engineering Conference. American Society of Mechanical Engineers Digital Collection (2020)
3. Camburn, B., et al.: A systematic method for design prototyping. J. Mech. Des. **137**(8) (2015). 12 pages
4. Christie, E.J., et al.: Prototyping strategies: literature review and identification of critical variables. In: American Society for Engineering Education Conference (2012)
5. Deininger, M., Daly, S.R., Sienko, K.H., Lee, J.C.: Novice designers' use of prototypes in engineering design. Des. Stud. **51**, 25–65 (2017)
6. Duffy, V.G.: Modified virtual build methodology for computer-aided ergonomics and safety. Hum. Factors Ergon. Manuf. Serv. Ind. **17**(5), 413–422 (2007)
7. Gawron, V.J., Drury, C.G., Fairbanks, R.J., Berger, R.C.: Medical error and human factors engineering: where are we now? Am. J. Med. Qual. **21**(1), 57–67 (2006)
8. Hauser, J.R., Clausing, D., et al.: The house of quality. Harvard Bus. Rev. **66**, 63–73 (1988)
9. Hess, T., Summers, J.D.: Case study: evidence of prototyping roles in conceptual design. In: DS 75–1: Proceedings of the 19th International Conference on Engineering Design (ICED13), Design for Harmonies, vol. 1: Design Processes, Seoul, Korea, 19–22 August 2013 (2013)
10. Kantowitz, B.H., Sorkin, R.D.: Human Factors: Understanding People-system Relationships. Wiley, Hoboken (1983)
11. Kirwan, B., Ainsworth, L.K.: A Guide to Task Analysis: The Task Analysis Working Group. CRC Press, Boca Raton (1992)
12. Lauff, C., Menold, J., Wood, K.L.: Prototyping canvas: design tool for planning purposeful prototypes. In: Proceedings of the Design Society: International Conference on Engineering Design, vol. 1, pp. 1563–1572. Cambridge University Press (2019)
13. Lauff, C.A., Kotys-Schwartz, D., Rentschler, M.E.: What is a prototype? What are the roles of prototypes in companies? J. Mech. Des. **140**(6) (2018)
14. Menold, J., Jablokow, K., Simpson, T.: Prototype for X (PFX): a holistic framework for structuring prototyping methods to support engineering design. Des. Stud. **50**, 70–112 (2017)
15. Otto, K.N., et al.. Product Design. Techniques in Reverse Engineering and New Product Development. Tsinghua University Press Co. Ltd., Wuhan (2003)

16. Pahl, G., Beitz, W.: Engineering Design: A Systematic Approach. Springer, London (2013). https://doi.org/10.1007/978-1-84628-319-2
17. Petrakis, K., Hird, A., Wodehouse, A.: The concept of purposeful prototyping: towards a new kind of taxonomic classification. In: Proceedings of the Design Society: International Conference on Engineering Design, vol. 1, pp. 1643–1652. Cambridge University Press (2019)
18. Stowe, D.: Investigating the role of prototyping in mechanical design using case study validation. Master's thesis, Clemson University (2008)
19. Wall, M.B., Ulrich, K.T., Flowers, W.C.: Evaluating prototyping technologies for product design. Res. Eng. Des. **3**(3), 163–177 (1992)
20. Wickens, C.D., Gordon, S.E., Liu, Y., et al.: Longman New York (1998)

A Framework Based on UCD and Scrum for the Software Development Process

Daniela Argumanis(✉) ⓘ, Arturo Moquillaza ⓘ, and Freddy Paz ⓘ

Pontificia Universidad Católica del Perú, San Miguel, Lima 32, Peru
{daniela.argumanis,amoquillaza,fpaz}@pucp.pe

Abstract. This paper proposes a framework that successfully includes UCD techniques and roles into Scrum. A systematic literature review was previously developed with the purpose of defining the most relevant methodologies and techniques to overcome the challenges of integrating Scrum and UCD. Afterwards, the information gathered was complemented by interviews with HCI experts, designers and developers. The most relevant methodologies and techniques reported were further analyzed through a comparative analysis, after which one methodology and nine techniques were selected to be included in the Scrum-UCD framework. A first version of the proposal was developed, detailing phases, activities and roles that would work as a guide towards the development of small and large software development projects. This proposal was tested in a small software project that involved the redesign and improvement of a banking system, and results regarding the team experience, final product usability and resource efficiency were evaluated against previous projects' results of the same institution that followed Scrum without the integration of UCD. This comparison demonstrated that following the proposed framework improved the overall software development process, and the first version of the proposal was updated to solve the problems identified during the different stages of the project.

Keywords: Agile methodologies · Scrum · User-Centered Design · Usability · User experience · Human-computer interaction

1 Introduction

Nowadays, agile methodologies are widely used by software development teams because they allow continuous delivery of products and services with rapid response to changes. In addition, these methodologies facilitate prioritization and decision-making, while promoting collaborative work, fluid communication between teams and equitable participation of all parties towards a common, clear and concise objective [1]. However, the use of agile methodologies during the software development process does not ensure that the resulting information systems will satisfy the end user needs.

First, agile frameworks as Scrum do not describe the methods and techniques that should be employed in the design process in order to obtain intuitive, understandable and easy-to-use graphical user interfaces [2]. Likewise, these frameworks provide a higher

© Springer Nature Switzerland AG 2021
M. M. Soares et al. (Eds.): HCII 2021, LNCS 12779, pp. 15–33, 2021.
https://doi.org/10.1007/978-3-030-78221-4_2

priority to the development process, mainly focusing on the achievement of functional requirements. On the other hand, attributes such as usability and user experience are usually ignored, and minimum time and resources are allocated to the design phase [3]. Frequently, this situation results in a final product where users are unable to achieve their goals, and even if it meets the functional requirements, it may have a high risk of failure in the market.

This research addresses this problem through the proposal of a framework based on UCD and Scrum for the software development process. UCD is a methodology widely recognized and used by specialists in HCI to design usable and attractive products that meet the users' needs [4]. However, UCD does not define how software development teams should work or how they should be organized to achieve the promised software features.

Therefore, the purpose of this research is to develop a strategy that allows the integration of Scrum and User-Centered Design, allowing the incremental and synchronous development of the functionalities and usability of a software product. This paper is structured as follows: In Sect. 2, the Scrum and UCD concepts are described in detail. In Sect. 3, a comparative analysis was executed with the purpose of identifying the methodologies and techniques that are best suited to be included in the proposal. In Sect. 4, a formal framework was established that explicitly details the considerations to be taken when using both, Scrum and UCD, in software development. In Sect. 5, this framework was evaluated by being tested in a real software development project. In Sect. 6, taking into consideration the recommendations identified during the evaluation of the proposal, the framework was updated, and a final version was developed. Finally, the conclusions and future works are established in Sect. 7.

2 Main Concepts

2.1 Scrum

Scrum is one of the most popular agile frameworks, given that 70% of agile projects are based on Scrum [5]. It is adaptable, interactive, fast, flexible, effective and designed to offer considerable value in a quick way throughout the project. Teams are multifunctional, and work cycles (sprints) are short and concentrated.

2.2 User-Centered Design

User-Centered Design (UCD) is an iterative design process focused on user research, user interface design and usability evaluation to provide useful and usable software [6]. The purpose of this framework is to create an optimal product based on the user needs, rather than forcing users to adapt to the features of a product [7].

3 Selection of UCD Methodologies and Techniques

A systematic literature review was developed in a previous article [8] using the methodology proposed by Kitchenham, [9] with the purpose of defining the most relevant methodologies and techniques to overcome the challenges integrating Scrum and UCD. Afterwards, the information gathered was complemented with interviews with HCI experts, designers and developers, who gave great input based on their knowledge and experience. Finally, the results were analyzed through a comparison between the identified methodologies and techniques, selecting the ones to be included in the Scrum-UCD framework.

3.1 Comparative Analysis of the Investigation Results

The methodologies and techniques identified as most relevant during the investigation were further evaluated through a comparative analysis, considering their advantages, disadvantages, usage scenarios and associated costs. The comparative analysis is detailed in Table 1, Table 2, Table 3 and Table 4.

Table 1. Comparative analysis of methodologies

	Design in parallel to sprints	Design within sprints	*Lean UX*	*Design Thinking*
Advantage	Easier project planning	Design is validated by both designers and developers	Minimum resource waste	Better understanding of user needs
Disadvantage	Difficult team communication	Difficult to synchronize activities	High cost	Is only viable for innovation
Where to use	Big projects	Small projects	Totally new projects	Innovation projects
Where not to use	Small projects	Big projects	Project redesign or improvement	Project redesign or improvement

Table 2. Comparative analysis of techniques (part 1)

	Paper prototypes	Personas	*Sprint 0*	Pair designing
Advantage	Fast and economic proposals	Provides a clear knowledge of user needs	Provides space for user investigation and the elaboration of a global design vision	Provides a clear idea of technical restrictions to the designers
Disadvantage	Designs are too abstract	Not necessary for all project types	Waste of time if decisions are not implemented	Does not improve performance on small tasks
Investment	Low	Low	Average	Low
Project stage	Iterative	Preliminary	Preliminary	Iterative
Where to use	Any project	Projects with unknown users	Projects with little initial vision	Complex projects
Where not to use	–	Projects with known users	Projects with great initial vision	Small projects

3.2 Selected Methodology

Out of the four methodologies evaluated, the design in parallel to sprints was selected because it facilitates the planning of the iterations and can be adapted to almost every

Table 3. Comparative analysis of techniques (part 2)

	Card sorting	Heuristic evaluation	Big design upfront	Contextual inquiry
Advantage	Provides knowledge on the user's way of thinking	Helps to identify most design problems	Easier project synchronization	Provides knowledge on the user's context
Disadvantage	It is difficult to sort many cards	High cost	Changes are expensive	Great dependency on third parties
Investment	High	High	Average	Average
Project stage	Preliminary	Final	Preliminary	Preliminary
Where to use	Projects involving a lot of structured information	Project redesign or improvement	Projects with great initial vision	Any project
Where not to use	Projects involving little structured information	Totally new projects	Projects with little initial vision	–

Table 4. Comparative analysis of techniques (part 3)

	Design conducted by developers	Thinking aloud	Scenarios	Customer journey map
Advantage	Relieve the designers' overload of work	Provides a precise idea on the product's UX	Easier definition of the project's structured vision	Provides knowledge on users' process to achieve goals
Disadvantage	Developers are unmotivated to work with the design	Requires great planification to be effective	The information retrieved is undetailed	Does not provide information on functionality
Investment	High	Average	Average	Average
Project stage	Preliminary (developers' training), iterative	Iterative	Preliminary	Preliminary
Where to use	Small projects	Any project	Any project	Any project
Where not to use	Big projects	–	–	–

project. However, it was considered that the developers must participate in the validation of prototypes, and that both teams should participate together in every Scrum ceremony. This is necessary to improve communication between both parties, especially in small projects.

3.3 Selected Techniques

Out of the twelve techniques evaluated, the following nine techniques were selected:

- **Paper prototypes:** It was selected because it facilitates iterative prototype design and evaluation, minimizing time and resources.
- **Personas:** It was selected to make sure the whole team has a clear idea of the users. In totally new projects, Personas will be created from scratch, and for project redesigns, the existing Personas will be updated.

- **Sprint 0:** It was selected due to the designers' necessity of a space to understand user needs and define a global vision of the interfaces. Developers can use this space to define the system's architecture and the tools they will use, while they help the designers in their UCD activities.
- **Pair designing:** It was selected in order to make design sprints more efficient, as the developers will be able to validate if the design meets the technical restrictions of the project, and they will be able to help in the design improvement if necessary.
- **Card sorting:** It was selected only for projects that require structured information, because it facilitates the structure definition process.
- **Heuristic evaluation:** It was selected only for redesign projects, in order to allow the HCI expert to identify most problems of an existing design.
- **Contextual inquiry:** It was selected to gather knowledge of the user's activities, which is important for the requirement definition process.
- **Thinking aloud:** It was selected because it is effective to obtain information about the user experience when using the system.
- **Customer journey map:** It was selected because it is effective to obtain an idea of the business process the users are going to follow, and therefore identifying user needs in detail.

4 Design of the SCRUM-UCD Framework

To develop the framework, BPMN notation was selected to be able to detail the phases, activities and roles that would work as a guide towards the development of small and large Scrum-UCD software development projects. The workflow was divided into three phases: Initiation, planning and implementation.

4.1 Initiation Phase (Sprint 0)

The first phase of the framework starts with the declaration of the vision of the project based on the business case. The Product Owner creates a document defining the project's vision, which is improved after a contextual inquiry process that allows the Scrum-UCD team to meet the real users and their context, in order to be able to identify their needs in a transparent manner.

Afterwards, if the project is totally new, the UCD specialists create Personas, elaborating user profiles with the information gathered during the contextual inquiry. On the other hand, if it is a redesign project, the UCD specialists execute a heuristic evaluation of the previous design, with the purpose of identifying the design problems they must solve. Also, they update the existing Personas taking into consideration the new user needs identified, and in case the project does not have Personas, they create them from scratch.

Finally, the product backlog is created listing the project requirements, after which it is validated by users and improved iteratively. Once the requirements are accepted, the planning phase starts.

4.2 Planning Phase (Sprint 0)

The second phase of the framework involves the planning of the project. In case the project involves the creation or redefinition of the information structure of a system, the UCD specialists use the card sorting technique with users. Afterwards, regardless of the software type, the UCD specialists develop a customer journey map, with the purpose to define in detail the workflow the users are going to follow when using the system.

With the help of these techniques, the user stories are created and estimated, and the team starts the design of paper prototypes along with the Product Owner and stakeholders, defining a global vision of the system. Finally, the tasks are identified and included in the sprint backlog, which is created for the design and development sprints.

Before the implementation starts, the developers explain the technical restrictions of the project to the UCD specialists, so they can be considered during the design of prototypes. These restrictions are defined by the platforms in which the product will be developed, by the time and money limitations and by the capacities of the development team.

4.3 Implementation

The design sprint starts with the creation of paper prototypes. Afterwards, a designer and the developer seat together with the purpose of evaluating the design through the pair designing process. In case the developer identifies a design feature that cannot be implemented by the developers, he works together with the designer to improve the prototypes so they can be aligned with the technical restrictions of the project. Then, the UCD specialists reunite with the Product Owner to validate and improve the prototypes. Next, they start creating low fidelity prototypes, which are later validated by users using the technique the team identifies as the most efficient taking into consideration the limitations of time and resources (thinking aloud is recommended for most projects).

In case the project involves the development of a big system, the previous process is repeated iteratively until the prototypes are successfully validated by users. The smaller the project, the smaller the risk of wasted resources in case a change is requested in later stages of the implementation, so small projects can execute this validation only once and start to develop the high fidelity prototypes, taking into consideration the user observations that were pointed out during the low fidelity prototype testing.

In parallel to the design sprints, the development sprints are executed. Developers take advantage of the first sprint to define the architecture of the system and the tools they will use (frameworks, development environment, databases, etc.), while the UCD specialists start with the initial designs. During the next sprints (sprint i), the developers focus on the development of the deliverables, implementing the prototypes designed by the UCD specialists in the previous sprints (sprint i-1). Therefore, the design sprints are always ahead of the development sprints by one iteration.

At the end of the sprint, the deliverables provided by the UCD specialists (high fidelity prototypes) and the developers (implemented software) are validated with the Product Owner and stakeholders, and they go through one last user validation. The results help to identify the changes that the team needs to make, and these changes are included in the new version of the sprint backlog. Finally, the sprint concludes with the retrospective meeting.

5   Framework Evaluation

The framework detailed in the previous section was tested in a software development project involving the redesign and improvement of a banking system. Results regarding the team experience, final product usability and resource efficiency were evaluated against previous projects' results of the same institution that followed Scrum without the integration of UCD.

5.1   Implementing Scrum-UCD in a Real Software Development Project

The project was executed in four 1-week sprints (including sprint 0), and involved the following roles:

- 1 Product Owner/Scrum Master
- 1 UCD Specialist
- 2 developers
- 2 stakeholders

During the different phases of the project, the Scrum-UCD team communicated the following recommendations to improve the framework:

1. There should be more parallelism in the activities during the sprint 0, so time can be optimized.
2. The framework should have the flexibility to allow team members to decide whether they should execute a heuristic evaluation of the design, or if other guidelines are better suited to identify issues in the design.
3. The requirements should only be validated by the users in totally new projects, as in projects involving the redesign or improvement of a previous system, the requirements are already well stablished.
4. The design of the system's architecture and the configuration of the development tools should be included in parallel with the UCD activities during the sprint 0.
5. The Scrum ceremonies should be included explicitly in the framework.
6. The Scrum and UCD activities should be clearly distinguished.

5.2   Team Experience

After the project was completed, the Scrum-UCD team completed a questionary, with the purpose of evaluating if the proposed framework effectively improved the team's satisfaction and performance. The team members of a previous project executed following Scrum without UCD also completed the questionary, and the results were compared. The questionary was developed following the Technology Acceptance Model (TAM), where each participant defined a score, from 1 to 7, for each of the dimensions selected. The average score for each dimension of the questionary is presented in Table 5.

The participants from both teams also went through an interview, where they answered questions about their experience working with the framework and identified recommendations to improve the Scrum-UCD framework. The experiences of both teams are compared in detail in Table 6.

Table 5. TAM questionary results

Dimension	Scrum-UCD team	Scrum team
Perceived ease of use	5.9	5.3
Perceived usefulness	5.6	4.9
Anticipated use	5.3	4.9
Perceived characteristics of the results	6	5.3
Perceived satisfaction	5.3	4.8

Table 6. Comparative analysis of the team experience

	Scrum-UCD team	Scrum team
Working together	There was mutual support during the design, where developers even shared some ideas and suggestions. However, there was distance during the project implementation, as the developers did not participate during the design of high fidelity prototypes or during the prototype validation with the stakeholders. Moreover, in later stages of development their only interaction with the UCD specialist was to ask questions about the prototypes	The designers participated in multiple projects at the same time, so they were not explicitly part of a Scrum team. Therefore, they only interacted with developers during meetings, where they planned improvements. Also, the designers participated in the daily meetings about 3 times a week
Technical restrictions	The technical restrictions were mostly clear, and the developers' participation in the paper prototype validation saved a lot of time. However, some technical restrictions were not considered due to lack of time or lack of experience from the developers	When developers identified a technical limitation in the prototypes, they communicated with the designers and the prototypes were updated. However, due to the high rotation of the designers between projects, a knowledge transfer process was required each time a new designer entered the project. Also, sometimes it was necessary to redesign interfaces that were already implemented due to technical restrictions that depended on other work areas
Understanding the user needs	The developers always had in mind the real users, and their recommendations were always based on the user needs. They were able to identify design problems and notify them to the UCD specialist	The developers did not understand the importance of usability, and only though about the code while developing the system's features

(continued)

Table 6. (*continued*)

	Scrum-UCD team	Scrum team
Complications regarding the stakeholder's requests	At first, the team was synchronized, as the developers worked with back-end features that did not depend on the prototypes. When the developers started to implement the prototypes, the stakeholders requested changes, and there were not enough user tests to confront these requests. In consequence, the developers had to wait until the new prototypes were ready to continue with the implementation	The stakeholders requested last minute changes, which complicated the completion of the development within deadlines. Also, the stakeholders did not give enough importance to user testing. Moreover, the changes requested by the stakeholders were executed immediately, without redesigning the prototypes to avoid wasting time
User involvement	Only five users participated in the testing, as sprints had a duration of only one week and there was not enough time. Also, the framework did not recommend a minimum quantity of users. The prototypes were validated with users from the beginning, but after executing the changes requested by the stakeholders, these new prototypes were not tested	User testing was scheduled after finishing the first half of the project and at the end of the project, involving ten participants each time. After implementing the changes requested by the stakeholders, these new prototypes were not tested
Framework effectiveness in guaranteeing a usable product	The framework had a positive impact in the final product's usability, as the developers were more compromised to satisfy the user needs. However, there is need for an agreement where the final prototype satisfies both the stakeholder's requests and the user needs	With only Scrum, the final product can be of quality, but following the design guidelines of the institution is necessary to guarantee a good user experience. In the worst-case scenario where the final product does not satisfy the users, the workflow can be modified. It is important that the stakeholders understand the workflow of the product

After the interviews, the team members identified the following recommendations to improve the Scrum-UCD framework:

1. Specify the designer's activities during the final sprint.
2. Developers should participate in the design of high fidelity prototypes, as paper prototypes do not give a clear idea of the final interface.
3. Developers should participate during the validation of prototypes with the stakeholders.
4. It is necessary to stablish a minimum quantity of users for testing.
5. The analysis of test results must become a user story, as it provides evidence of the prototype's effectiveness during the validation with the stakeholders.

6. The prototypes must be tested with users after adding the changes requested by the stakeholders.
7. The user stories that do not depend on the design should be prioritized, in order to avoid waste of time while the developers wait until the design is ready.
8. One-week sprints are too short to complete all the required UCD activities.
9. The stakeholders should be more involved during the design sprints, instead of participating only in the sprint review.

5.3 Final product's Usability

The final product was evaluated for both the Scrum-UCD project and the Scrum without UCD project using the thinking aloud technique with five different users, who executed a list of tasks to evaluate the usability of each system. The users were all aged between 22 and 23 years old, and they all had an occupation related to computer engineering. The results of both tests, considering the tasks completed successfully and the overall score (out of five) given to each interface in a post-test questionary are detailed in Table 7.

Table 7. Results regarding the usability of the final product

User	Scrum-UCD: tasks completed successfully	Scrum: tasks completed	Scrum-UCD: average user satisfaction	Scrum: average user satisfaction
User 1	11/12	9/9	4.4	5.0
User 2	12/12	6/9	4.2	1.8
User 3	11/12	9/9	5.0	4.0
User 4	12/12	8/9	5.0	4.0
User 5	11/12	9/9	3.4	3.6
Average	95%	91%	4.4	3.7

5.4 Scope, Time and Cost

The scope, time and cost of both the Scrum-UCD project and the Scrum without UCD project were evaluated through a comparative analysis, which is detailed in Table 8.

The results show that the cost of the Scrum project was about three times the cost of the Scrum-UCD project. However, the scope (referenced by the number of views) of the first project is twice as large as the scope of the second project. Therefore, we can conclude that for each view developed, the Scrum project spent 150% of the cost that the Scrum-UCD would have spent for a similar view.

Table 8. Comparison of the scope, time and cost of the projects

Project	Scrum-UCD	Scrum
Time	3.5 FTE 4 weeks 4 sprints	4.25 FTE 10 weeks 5 sprints
Scope	7 views 4 people involved	12 views 5 people involved
Cost	69,600 PEN	219,000 PEN

6 Changes on the Scrum-UCD Framework

Taking into consideration the recommendations listed in Sect. 4.4 and 4.5, the framework was updated, and a final version was developed.

6.1 Initiation Phase (Sprint 0)

The initiation phase of the framework was updated, considering the following changes:

1. The heuristic evaluation technique was replaced by design evaluation using previously established guidelines, where the team should decide the most appropriate guidelines for the project.
2. If the project is focused on a redesign, the design evaluation using previously established guidelines should be executed in parallel to the contextual research and the creation or update of Personas.
3. If the project is not totally new, it will not be necessary to validate with users the requirements of the Product Backlog.

The final version of the initiation phase is shown in Fig. 1 and Fig. 2.

6.2 Planning Phase (Sprint 0)

The planning phase of the framework was updated, considering the following changes:

1. The development team should define the architecture of the system and configure the development tools in parallel to the elaboration of the customer journey map and the creation and refinement of user stories.
2. The technical restrictions of the project should be explained to the UCD specialists before the identification and estimation of tasks, in order to ensure a more precise estimation of the design tasks.
3. The creation of the sprint backlog was moved to the sprint planning ceremony of the implementation phase.
4. The sprint retrospective ceremony was aggregated for sprint 0.

The final version of the planning phase is shown in Fig. 3 and Fig. 4.

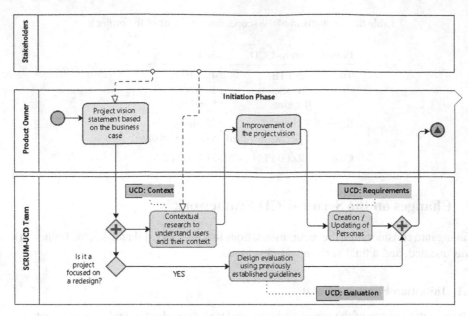

Fig. 1. Initiation phase of the project – Final version

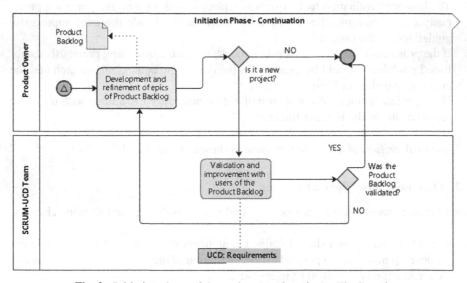

Fig. 2. Initiation phase of the project (continuation) – Final version

6.3 Implementation Phase

The implementation phase of the framework was updated, considering the following changes:

1. Every sprint will start with the sprint planning ceremony.

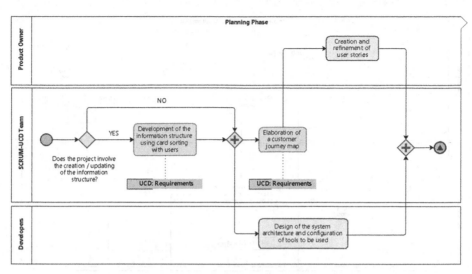

Fig. 3. Planning phase of the project – Final version

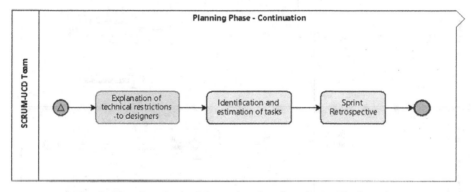

Fig. 4. Planning phase of the project (continuation) – Final version

2. During the sprint 1, the developers will now develop backend features and the system's database, as the architecture and development tools were already defined during the planning phase.
3. The pair design technique will be executed to validate and improve not only the low fidelity prototypes, but also the high fidelity prototypes.
4. The validation of the design and development sprints with the stakeholders will take place during the sprint review ceremony.
5. For the user tests, at least 5 users will be required, and the results must be processed to be presented to the stakeholders during the sprint review.
6. Each sprint will have a duration of at least two weeks.

The final version of the implementation phase is shown in Fig. 5 and Fig. 6 for small projects, and in Fig. 7 and Fig. 8 for large projects.

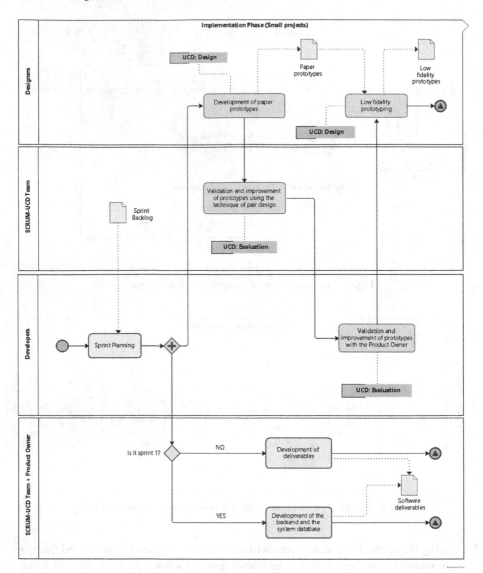

Fig. 5. Implementation phase for small projects – Final version

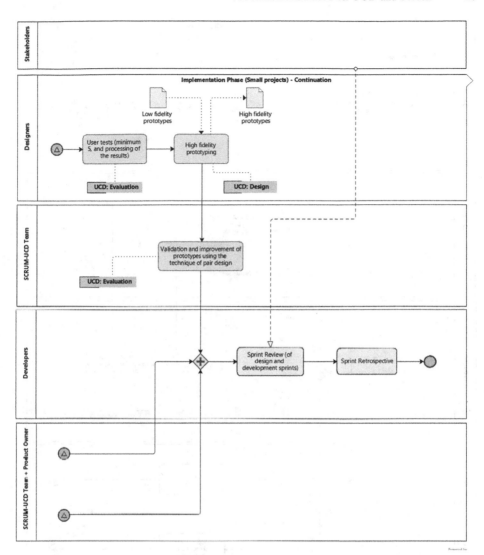

Fig. 6. Implementation phase for small projects (continuation) – Final version

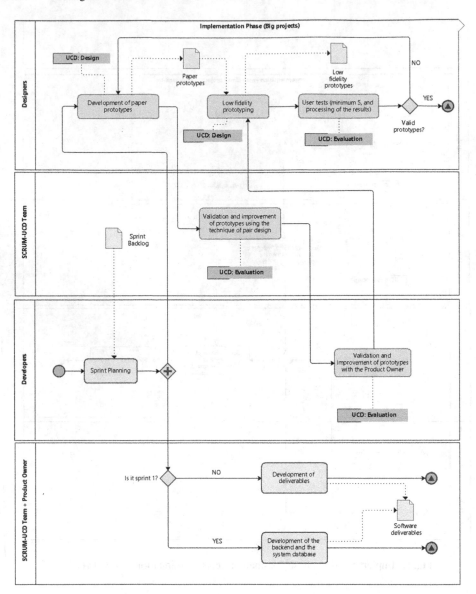

Fig. 7. Implementation phase for big projects – Final version

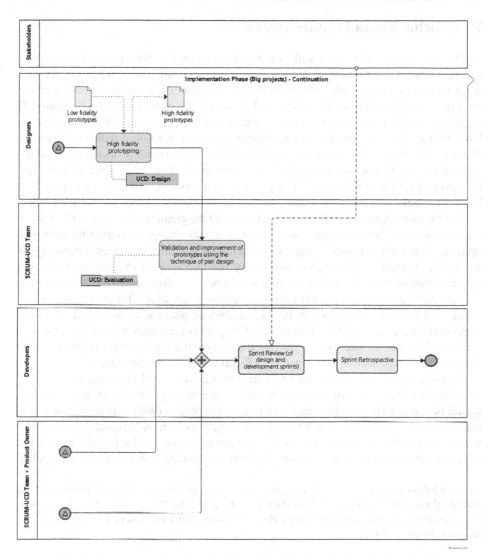

Fig. 8. Implementation phase for big projects (continuation) – Final version

7 Conclusions and Future Works

Applying the proposal in a real software development project demonstrated that following the Scrum-UCD framework helps to improve team equity, communication between team members, the overall software development experience and the usability of the final product. Also, the results in Sect. 4.7 show that the overall cost of a Scrum-UCD project is less than the cost of a project with a similar scope that follows only Scrum. Even though the framework requires a higher inversion of resources during the initial phases of the project, this is compensated with the reduction of costs in later stages of the project, as there is less risk of finding design issues on an already implemented interface. However, due to the inclusion UCD activities, each sprint should have a duration of at least two weeks in order to be able to successfully complete every user-centered task.

On the other hand, the stakeholders represented the greatest challenge of the Scrum-UCD project, as they frequently requested last minute changes, prioritizing their own opinions over the input given by real users. Therefore, it is necessary to test the prototypes with enough users and to process adequately the results, with the purpose of having evidence that will help the stakeholders make the best decision. Moreover, it is important to mention that there is a need to make stakeholders aware of the importance of the user experience of the final product. If the stakeholders do not provide enough resources to execute the necessary UCD techniques, or if they do not consider the results of the user testing when making decisions regarding the design, the final product might meet the stakeholders' expectations, but it can be difficult to use for the final users.

Finally, given that the Scrum-UCD framework was tested by using it in a small software development project that consisted of the redesign of an existing system, it would be valuable to test the framework in a bigger project (with a sprint duration of at least 3 weeks), and to test it in a totally new project as well. Additionally, it will be of interest to test the improved version of the framework in a similar project, to verify if the complications that emerged during the software development process were avoided.

Acknowledgement. This research is highly supported by the *Department of Engineering* of the *Pontifical Catholic University of Peru* (PUCP) in Peru and the *HCI, Design, User Experience, Accessibility and Innovation Technology Research Group* (HCI-DUXAIT). HCI-DUXAIT is a research group of PUCP.

References

1. Sacolick, I.: What is agile methodology? Modern software development explained | InfoWorld. https://www.infoworld.com/article/3237508/what-is-agile-methodology-modern-softwaredevelopment-explained.html. Accessed 05 June 2020
2. Teka, D., Dittrich, Y., Kifle, M.: Adapting lightweight user-centered design with the Scrum-based development process. In: Proceedings of the 2018 International Conference on Software Engineering in Africa - SEiA 2018, pp. 35–42 (2018). https://doi.org/10.1145/3195528.3195530
3. Lunström, M., Åberg, J., Blomkvist, J.: Perceptions of software developers' empathy with designers. In: Proceedings of the 2015 British HCI Conference on - British HCI 2015, pp. 239–246 (2015). https://doi.org/10.1145/2783446.2783563

4. Magües, D.A., Castro, J.W., Acuña, S.T.: Requirements engineering related usability techniques adopted in agile development processes. In: Proceedings of the International Conference on Software Engineering and Knowledge Engineering, SEKE, 2016-January, pp. 537–542. (2016). https://doi.org/10.18293/SEKE2016-057
5. CollabNet: 12th Annual State of Agile Report. Technical report, CollabNet VersionOne, Brisbane, CA, USA (2018)
6. Teka, D., Dittrich, Y., Kifle, M.: Adapting lightweight user-centered design with the Scrum-based development process. In: 2018 IEEE/ACM Symposium on Software Engineering in Africa (SEiA), pp. 35–42 (2018). https://doi.org/10.1145/3195528.3195530
7. Almughram, O., Alyahya, S.: Coordination support for integrating user centered design in distributed agile projects. In: 2017 IEEE 15th International Conference on Software Engineering Research, Management and Applications (SERA), pp. 229–238 (2017) https://doi.org/10.1109/SERA.2017.7965732
8. Argumanis, D., Moquillaza, A., Paz, F.: Challenges in integrating SCRUM and the user-centered design framework: a systematic review. In: Agredo-Delgado, V., Ruiz, P.H., Villalba-Condori, K.O. (eds.) HCI-COLLAB 2020. CCIS, vol. 1334, pp. 52–62. Springer, Cham (2020). https://doi.org/10.1007/978-3-030-66919-5_6
9. Kitchenham, B., Charters, S.: Guidelines for performing systematic literature reviews in software engineering. Technical report EBSE 2007–001, Keele University and Durham University (2007)

Science Fiction—An Untapped Opportunity in HCI Research and Education

Philipp Jordan[1]([⊠]) and Paula Alexandra Silva[2]

[1] Communication and Information Sciences, University of Hawaii at Manoa,
Honolulu, USA
philippj@hawaii.edu

[2] Department of Informatics Engineering, Center for Informatics and Systems,
University of Coimbra, Coimbra, Portugal
paulasilva@dei.uc.pt

Abstract. This work open up a conversation about the opportunities that Science Fiction offers to Human-Computer Interaction (HCI) and Design research. In doing so, first, it briefly challenges the term Design Fiction, an emerging concept with increasing popularity in HCI and Design research. Design Fictions are either, manifest design propositions, or intangible, imagined future interfaces, speculative interactions and would-be environments. Design Fictions as useful as they are, however, are not necessarily something new nor innovative in themselves. Speculative design and evaluation methods all have been staple methods of Computer Science research since the establishment of HCI as a discrete field sometime in the 1980s. Second, the paper proceeds to propose that the domain of Science Fiction could not only be useful, but rightly considered, as a legitimate field of creative inquire in HCI and Design education. By reframing the notion of Science Fiction from an 'anecdotal gimmick' toward an 'area of study' a novel, wide-ranging space for design inspiration, ingenuity and creativity opens up for conceptual exploration. We believe that such an elevation of Science Fiction as a serious research topic has strong potential to inform the Computer Science, HCI and Design research application and education endeavours of the future.

Keywords: Computer science research and education · Design Fiction · Speculative future studies · Popular culture in science · Science Fiction

1 Introduction

The interlinks of Science Fiction to the fields of Computer Science (CS), Human-Computer Interaction (HCI) and Design have long been recognized and discussed (e.g. [39,40,51,54]), however, it seems their full potentials remain largely untapped. While real-world scientific progress has been linked to Science Fiction, for example in the works of Ferro and Swedin [15,16] or Dourish [13], only a few, concrete examples can be identified, which:

© Springer Nature Switzerland AG 2021
M. M. Soares et al. (Eds.): HCII 2021, LNCS 12779, pp. 34–47, 2021.
https://doi.org/10.1007/978-3-030-78221-4_3

- use Science Fiction as a direct source of inspiration (for instance Schmitz, Endres and Butz [52]);
- incorporate Science Fiction as component of a Design curriculum (case in point Brueckner and Novy's *Science Fiction to Science Fabrication* course [6]) or;
- discuss Science Fiction potentials with a broader audience (e.g. in the context the User Experience Professionals Association [59]).

One may attribute a possible disregard of the implicit value proposition of Science Fiction (for CS, HCI and/or Design research) as a combination of a lack of understanding and acceptance as well as restraint toward—and stigmatization of—the topic in research communities with a predominantly, technical orientation.

Conversely, the nascent concept of Design Fiction has become increasingly popular in the HCI and Design research and education communities in recent years (e.g. [21,48]), among which Design Fiction methods and approaches seem to be gaining terrain. This, however, has not happened without hurdles, as the community still struggles to fully:

- understand and develop a shared vision of the concept and method [45] and;
- understand how to measure the outcomes it produces [3].

This denotes that Design Fiction is still in its infancy, which in turn urges discussion around how to correctly frame, define and use it.

This paper intends to contribute to the discussion of the topics above by presenting an argument for the integration of Science Fiction as a discipline for creative enquiry that should be brought further into HCI and Design research and application, than it has been in the past.

In doing so, the paper presents a schematic, but wide-scoping review of the previous contributions of Science Fiction to science in addition to a discussion, that contrasts Science Fiction with Design Fiction, wherein Design Fiction seems to appear as an evolution of Science Fiction and other well-established, speculative design methods in HCI.

Thus, the paper attempts to frame Science Fiction as an equal opportunity to advance CS, HCI and Design research as Design Fiction appears to be. In conclusion, the authors gauge and elicit potential advantages of an integration and usage of Science Fiction in future Computer Science education, research and practice.

2   Science Fiction

Science Fiction, Science and Visions of Computing. Studies located in the Science, Technology, Society (STS) context found rather extensive collaboration schemes between real-world scientists and movie-makers (see e.g. Kirby's work [27,28] on researchers, who act as scientific advisors on movie productions).

These collaborations are also manifest in unique initiatives bridging both domains, among those, the National Science Foundation-sponsored Science and

Entertainment Exchange, a one-of-its-kind endeavour with regards to academic movie consulting [47].

The intersection of Science Fiction and real-world scientific progress in Computer Science research has as well been noted by many in techno-philosophical and theoretical works, among those:

- Westfahl et al. [61], whose works explore conceptual linkages of Science Fiction and futurism;
- Doctorow et al. [12], who propose the usage of written, short Science Fiction stories or scenarios, with a substantial degree of scientific veracity, as innovation vehicles in a variety of contexts (Science Fiction Prototyping) or;
- Clarke and Stork [10], who explore the implications of the famous, artificial intelligence *HAL in 2001: A space Odyssey* (HAL's legacy).

Although useful, hardly any conceptual models exist, which fully describe the assemblage of Science Fiction and Computer Science research through either, unidirectional or multi-directional relations between both domains (e.g. [25,29, 43,52]).

Science Fiction in Contemporary Computer Science and HCI Research. A historical analysis of a subset of Science Fiction movies by Larson [32]) found a mirroring of the presentation of eleven computer technology trends, as depicted in ten Science Fiction films (in comparison to CS real-world innovation), contrasting popular assumptions that Science Fiction always 'leaps ahead' and envisions technological utopias.

More HCI-focused studies were able to elicit rather concrete Science Fiction affordances for forthcoming interaction paradigms:

- Troiano, Tiab and Lim [57] elicit, based on an analysis of 340 Science Fiction films, future interactions of shape-changing interfaces, including a set of general, behavioural patterns of these types of input/output user contexts.
- Figueiredo et al. [17] create a catalog of hand gestures, based of Science Fiction movies, while explicitly stating that Science Fiction props (e.g. movies, fictional devices, made-up environments, etc.) are valid targets of research.
- Shedroff and Noessel [53], published a larger book with a comprehensive review of user interfaces, including categorical areas of affordances and constraints of future HCI technology found in Science Fiction Film (e.g. user interfaces, devices, areas of applications).

Using science communication, in particular the Institute of Electrical and Electronics Engineers (IEEE) *Xplore* Digital Library as a reference repository, prior research [23] has found that the popular Science Fiction franchise *Star Trek* indeed inspired researchers working in areas of emerging information and communication technologies, among those as mobile and ubiquitous communication devices.

More related studies [44] surveyed the utilization of twenty different Science Fiction robots in the Association of Computing Machinery (ACM) Digital

Library, a study which provided similar results as Larson [32] did—a mirroring of the 'personality attributes' (e.g. utopian versus dystopian characterizations) of Science Fiction robots in computing research literature in a similar fashion as these attributes are depicted in Science Fiction Film and Movies.

Lastly, by means of spanning more than three decades of computing research in the ACM Digital Library, prior work also identified five contemporary HCI research themes, including theoretical design research, which are linked with Science Fiction referrals found in a sample of 83 scientific publications [24].

Science Fiction in Education. Science Fiction can also stimulate creativity of students in Computer Science and a diversity of other Science, Technology, Engineering and Mathematics (STEM) fields [60], such as computer ethics [7,8] or security [31], through an alternative viewpoint extending traditional technical foci in computing education.

As a matter of fact, as early as in the 1970s, the value of Science Fiction literature for educational purposes has been discussed in, for instance, Michalsky's essay [42] on the integration of Science Fiction into formal education, which presents an early notion of speculative fiction as a means to benefit student creativity.

While the topic lately gained traction (see e.g. [1,2,22,41,50,58]), Science Fiction in educational settings seems to be a double-edged sword, as has been viewed critically as well [46]—an indicator for a mindful integration of these materials in classroom and educational contexts in the time to come.

3 Design Fiction

Design Fiction—Definition and Tools. The origin of Design Fiction is opaque. According to Lindley and Coulton [35], the concept had its inception in 2005 via renowned Science Fiction author Bruce Sterling. However, its genesis may go back as early as 2003, as reviewed by Baumer, Blythe and Tanenbaum [3]. Julian Bleecker's 2009 essay [4] is often seen as a catalyst for popularizing the concept outside of academic niche circles.

Likewise, the epistemological meaning of the concept 'Design Fiction' is still in limbo and debated [3,35]. A number of definitions has been provided to define the method (for a list of works refer to [3]), however, in spite of those definitions, the concept, method, what it entails and produces as well as how its outcomes may be evaluated is still a hot topic of debate, where the community continues to strive for coherent and articulated understanding of Design Fiction (see for e.g. [3,45]).

Regardless of aforementioned growing pains, Design Fiction is an emerging method and nascent field in HCI and design research, that, in the last decade, has been popularized by a number of design researchers and labs in HCI and CS research (e.g. [5,14,34,55,56]).

In the authors view, Design Fictions are closely related to film theory fundamentals, such as Kirby's [30] 'diegetic prototypes' or Frank's [18] notions of 'perceived and referential realities'. In 2012, in an interview with slate.com[1], Bruce Sterling concurred with the notion that Design Fictions refer to *"... the deliberate use of diegetic prototypes to suspend disbelief about change"* (see also [34]). Sterling further explains that Design Fiction is *"... an approach to design that speculates about new ideas through prototyping and storytelling"*.

In Design Fiction, diegetic prototypes are placed within narrative elements and scenarios, to envision and explain possible futures for Design. The scenarios created have Design at their core and once created can be used as a lens for exploring the social implications of design practice and technology and in turn, as a lens for informing the creation of designed futures.

To our knowledge, there is not a specific or definite list of tools that Design Fiction uses/could use, nor how Design Fictions can specifically support the activities of 'prototyping' and/or 'storytelling', still the tools used in Design Fiction could include [3]: stories, pastiche scenarios, futuristic autobiographies, artifacts, probes and dramas.

To put it simply, Design Fictions are very often a tangible, non-functional prototype of some sorts, which are embedded in a story with the goal to start a discussion about Design, life and socio-technical alternatives. Design Fictions can, however, as well represent non-tangible outcomes, such as fictional research papers [36] and made-up job ads [19].

Design Fictions – as a research tool – can help to elicit affordances and requirements, through the creation of imaginative future interfaces, speculative interactions and would-be environments while (temporarily) disregarding their technological feasibility. Design Fictions also have the potential to inspire discussions with the wider public and civic society about the futures of computing, and, in the process of doing so, affording us with the possibility of tapping into the understanding of our social and cultural expectations and beliefs.

Design Fiction—Speculative Design Research Rebranded? While often seen as an avant-garde concept and progressive method in HCI and specifically Design research, Design Fictions are not new. Design Fictions, at least in Bruce Sterling's purview (see e.g. [34]) and have been *implicitly* used in speculative design research[2] as an integral part of the field in the last three decades.

To exemplify, past research (e.g. [11,26]) evidently shows that both, Computer Science scholars and HCI practitioners (and vice versa) have successfully developed, applied and established speculative design research methods, such as the wizard-of-oz technique, as early as 1983—approximately 40 years ago.

For instance, in 1983 Gould [20, 295], using the wizard-of-oz technique, introduced the idea of a fictional *"listening typewriter"* as a potentially:

> *"... valuable aid in composing letters, memos and documents. Indeed, it might be a revolutionary office tool, just as the typewriter, telephone and computer have been. With a listening typewriter, an author could [...]"*.

---

[1] https://slate.com/technology/2012/03/bruce-sterling-on-design-fictions.html.
[2] And its many derivatives, among those discursive, critical or reflective design etc. pp.

In 1983, a *"listening typewriter"* was clearly a technological impossibility and, by today's standards, a Design Fiction—a diegetic prototype to suspend disbelief about change and elicit future design affordances, requirements and constraints.

Likewise, as noted prior, many staple methods have been introduced to the field long before Design Fiction emerged as a novel, elusive and trendy concept, among those:

- cognitive walkthroughs of possible and hypothetical interfaces and dialogue systems [33];
- scenario-based design techniques with a focus on possible contexts and narratives [9] or;
- personas and storyboards [49].

Thus, we believe Design Fictions can conceptually be framed as 'rebranding' or 'rejuvinating' longstanding, established design research methods. Therefore, Design Fiction can be viewed as an 'evolution' or 'explicitation' of already existing design research approaches in HCI.

Arguably, 'earlier' Science Fiction materials have inspired and evolved into 'newer' concepts and methods, that have since moved towards HCI and Design and as a result developed into more tailored, fitting and applied HCI and Design methods.

Speculation about futuristic technological possibilities are well documented, whether in early Science Fiction, or in scientific literature. The act of speculating, imagining, play-acting is intrinsic to any design process and this is a well-understood phenomenon.

4   Rethinking the Role of Science Fiction in HCI

Science Fiction—A Means of Speculative Design Research. As outlined above, Design Fiction has been implicitly used in the past decades of Computer Science research and is therefore, a useful concept and evolution, but nothing new *per se*, nor as disruptive as it may seem to some.

Still, the term has grabbed both attention and momentum and, as a result, the method is growing in popularity and application. Design Fiction then might have the potential to mature into a distinctive practice and ultimately, into a coherent subdiscipline of HCI—as the field of modern Futures Studies did as a subdiscipline of Science, Technology and Society Studies.

Science Fiction, in contrast, with both, a long and rich history[3] and great capacity to influence the world is at a halt or downright forgotten as a valid contributor to the research and practice of the futures of Computing, HCI and

---

[3] According to some sources, Science Fiction dates back as early as 2AD with the Greek travel tale *"A True Story"*, a work consensually accepted as the first known writing with basic fictional elements, for example outer space travel and interstellar conflicts.

Design, or at least, it seems heavily underutilized playing a 'second fiddle' to Design Fiction.

Speculation about futuristic technological possibilities are common both in early Science Fiction, scientific literature and Design Fiction. The presence of *diegesis* is critical in all of them, as one cannot just describe an imaginary future technology and present that idea as a Design Fiction; the fiction requires a setting, a story and other things that help *"suspend disbelief about change"*, as Sterling asserted in his interview to the Slate in 2012 (see above).

Both Science Fiction and Design Fictions involve a narrative, a story, a *diegesis* and not just an idea of a fictional product. It is the elements surrounding the (future) artifact that help prompt conversation, debate and reflection and encourage dialogue about the wider implications of the emerging technological landscape.

Regardless of being/becoming a real technological artifact used in a real context, when those narratives are used with the purpose of deliberately triggering reflection, both Science Fiction and Design Fiction are valid and valuable methods. The objects prompting debate and reflection, those can be part of a Science Fiction film, novel, as well as custom-made Design Fiction artifact, installation, or exhibition.

So, how come the community so quickly proposed and adopted a 'new buzzword', leaving Science Fiction 'standing in the rain', where at least historically, we have been using—and being inspired by it—since hundreds of years. In this paper, we propose to use Science Fiction movies and shows as a means of speculative design research in Computer Science research, education and application. To this extends that Science Fiction materials may afford HCI and design researchers and practitioners with ways of stimulating creativity, exploring critical perspectives and inspiring new kinds of alternative imaginaries.

Not to Integrate Science Fiction in Computer Science, HCI, Design, or STEM Education—A Missed Opportunity. Science Fiction movies and shows have driven Computer Science research, education and application in an array of domains in an interdisciplinary manner, across time, extending into STEM education and studies of Science, Technology and Society. However, it seems that the use of Science Fiction is not considered a viable component in Computer Science, HCI, Design, or STEM research, application and education, it rather appears exotic.

We have identified in this paper selected examples, which do successfully bridge both domains, but overwhelmingly survey fractured efforts by unique individuals [38], professional associations [59] or singular, academic pilot courses [6]. We therefore argue that not including Science Fiction in the study of Computer Science, HCI and Design is a missed opportunity:

There is a more than 100 years and growing-old repository of Science Fiction cinematography available right now. This ample material encompasses a wide range and diversity of audiovisual use cases, product visions, future interactions and socio-technical exemplars at hand to be explored and studied—systematically and seriously.

Some might interpret Science Fiction movies and shows as Design Fictions themselves, in our opinion, a reasonable appropriation and reframing of cultural artifacts as research spaces. Therefore, we argue to integrate Science Fiction into Computer Science and STEM education, research and application as a serious, wide-ranging and integral addition.

Past and contemporary Science Fiction films and shows inevitable focus— to a lesser or larger extent—on yet-to-come HCI, speculative intelligent user interfaces and future human-machine integration. Science Fiction movies and shows can further provide visual use cases and compelling scenarios, allowing conjecture on technological foresight of beneficial and detrimental technology outcomes of our (future) society.

In addition, this genre of contemporary cinematography, in a compelling audio-visual format, can as well expose important ethical questions and dilemmas for the general public – from the role and agency of technology in our lives, to the moral utilization of autonomous robots; or as well highlight the conflict zone of technology, privacy and security in the 21st century.

When Integrating Science Fiction in Computer Science, HCI, Design, or STEM Education—Exercise Caution. While pledging for a more substantial use of Science Fiction in CS, HCI and Design education practice, it is important to highlight that the Science Fiction featured both, in entertainment and research, tends to be biased towards a mostly western selection of Science Fiction materials (e.g. [37, 44]).

Thus, it must be acknowledged that Science Fiction material can be an imbalanced resource that lacks the necessary diversity which, in turn, can possibly portray misleading representations of society and of peoples use of technology. Furthermore, typically utopian Science Fiction materials, where all people use, have access to, and are empowered by technology may blur any critical discussion or interpretation of whether a technological innovation is beneficial or detrimental. Lastly, in situations where gendered, undiverse and mostly Western-originated Science Fiction materials are utilized, discussions and learnings might be based on incorrect facts or misrepresentations of society.

A conscious and unbiased integration of Science Fiction materials in Computer Science and STEM domains is not only important, it is a necessary condition for the success of the proposed integration. Science Fiction materials for Computer Science education should represent diverse, equitable, inclusive and differentiated cultural, social and technological aspects. Importantly, the same prerequisites should apply to the curators and educators of these respective Science Fiction materials as well.

To resort to Science Fiction materials to inspire and support research and practice would also require academics to possess skills in a more humanities/arts and interdisciplinary style of educational delivery, which could be quite a substantial challenge for a significant share of current educators.

5   Conclusions and Future Work

Yesterday, we were frightened or scared by Science Fiction movies, such as *Metropolis, 2001: A Space Odyssey, The Terminator* or *Nineteen Eighty-Four*. Today, we wonder if we can ever wear an *Iron Man* suit[4], experience a *Star Trek* Holodeck[5] or survive on Mars, as depicted in the movie *The Martian*[6]. Tomorrow, we might want to explore a relationship with a machine instead of a human being, or experiment with inserting technology in our bodies or wonder about how to live a life completely embedded in virtual reality.

The relationship between Science Fiction and real-world science is closer than we think it is, as outlined in this paper to the extent possible. Computer Science, HCI, Design, or STEM Education and Science Fiction meet on academic, professional, educational and cultural domains in society, across cultures, languages and geographies. However, Science Fiction is not the speculative Design panacea.

Science Fiction is a repository and an artifact of both, the wonders and fears of socio-technological futures and it can very effectively trigger these visions, through powerful narratives and stories, through characters, diegetic prototypes, computer-generated imaginary and global movie production and distribution, accessibly to most of the global populace with a broadband connection.

In this paper, we attempted to show the concrete applicability and value proposition Science Fiction can offer in CS research, education and in the creation of future visions of society using diegetic prototypes in Science Fiction film and shows:

- Design researchers and HCI experts have moved towards using Science Fiction movies to derive new HCI interactions or explore the role and agency of robots in our lives.
- Science Fiction materials are piloted in Computer Science and HCI courses across innovative universities and departments.
- Computer science experts collaborate regularly with Science Fiction moviemakers in order to present more believable interactions and interfaces to the general public audience.

We conclude that Design Fiction is a valid and evolving method, with the potential to bring clarity to the field of speculative design research in HCI. At the same time, Design Fiction, can be viewed as prototyping and storytelling together, inspired by imagination, play-act and Science Fiction.

By reframing the notion of Science Fiction from an anecdotal gimmick toward an area of study, a novel, wide-ranging space for design inspiration, ingenuity and creativity opens up for conceptual exploration. We believe that such an elevation of Science Fiction as a 'serious research topic' has strong potential to inform the Computer Science, HCI and Design research, application and education endeavours of the future.

---

[4] https://news.clemson.edu/tiktok-sensation-learned-some-of-her-iron-man-building-skills-at-clemson-university.

[5] https://news.microsoft.com/innovation-stories/microsoft-mesh/.

[6] https://physicstoday.scitation.org/do/10.1063/pt.5.9047/full/.

References

1. Barnett, M., Wagner, H., Gatling, A., Anderson, J., Houle, M., Kafka, A.: The impact of science fiction film on student understanding of science. J. Sci. Educ. Technol. **15**(2), 179–191 (2006). https://doi.org/10.1007/s10956-006-9001-y
2. Bates, R., Goldsmith, J., Berne, R., Summet, V., Veilleux, N.: Science fiction in computer science education. In: Proceedings of the 43rd ACM Technical Symposium on Computer Science Education, SIGCSE 2012, New York, NY, USA, pp. 161–162. Association for Computing Machinery (2012). https://doi.org/10.1145/2157136.2157184
3. Baumer, E.P.S., Blythe, M., Tanenbaum, T.J.: Evaluating design fiction: the right tool for the job. In: Proceedings of the 2020 ACM Designing Interactive Systems Conference, DIS 2020, New York, NY, USA, pp. 1901–1913. Association for Computing Machinery (2020). https://doi.org/10.1145/3357236.3395464
4. Bleecker, J.: Design fiction: a short essay on design, science, fact and fiction (2009). https://blog.nearfuturelaboratory.com/2009/03/17/design-fiction-a-short-essay-on-design-science-fact-and-fiction/
5. Blythe, M., Encinas, E.: Research Fiction and Thought Experiments in Design. Now Publishers Inc., Hanover (2018)
6. Brueckner, S., Novy, D.: Syllabus | MAS S65: Science Fiction to Science Fabrication (2013). http://scifi2scifab.media.mit.edu/syllabus-3/
7. Burton, E., Goldsmith, J., Koenig, S., Kuipers, B., Mattei, N., Walsh, T.: Ethical considerations in artificial intelligence courses. AI Mag. **38**(2), 22–34 (2017). https://doi.org/10.1609/aimag.v38i2.2731
8. Burton, E., Goldsmith, J., Mattei, N.: How to teach computer ethics through science fiction. Commun. ACM **61**(8), 54–64 (2018). https://doi.org/10.1145/3154485
9. Carroll, J.M. (ed.): Scenario-Based Design: Envisioning Work and Technology in System Development. Wiley, New York (1995). https://doi.org/10.5555/209227
10. Clarke, A.C., Stork, D.G.: HAL's legacy: 2001's computer as dream and reality. MIT Press, Cambridge (2000). https://mitpress.mit.edu/books/hals-legacy
11. Dahlbäck, N., Jönsson, A., Ahrenberg, L.: Wizard of Oz Studies – Why and How. Know. Based Syst. **6**(4), 258–266 (1993).https://doi.org/10.1016/0950-7051(93)90017-N
12. Doctorow, C., Warner, C., Perkowitz, S., Johnson, B.D.: Science Fiction Prototyping: Designing the Future with Science Fiction (Synthesis Lectures on Computer Science). Morgan & Claypool Publishers (2011). https://www.morganclaypool.com/doi/abs/10.2200/S00336ED1V01Y201102CSL003
13. Dourish, P., Bell, G.: "Resistance is futile": reading science fiction alongside ubiquitous computing. Personal Ubiquitous Comput. **18**(4), 769–778 (2014).https://doi.org/10.1007/s00779-013-0678-7
14. Dunne, A.: Speculative Everything : Design, Fiction, and Social Dreaming. The MIT Press, Cambridge (2013). https://mitpress.mit.edu/books/speculative-everything
15. Ferro, D., Swedin, E.: Computer fiction: "a logic named Joe". In: Impagliazzo, J., Järvi, T., Paju, P. (eds.) HiNC 2007. IAICT, vol. 303, pp. 84–94. Springer, Heidelberg (2009). https://doi.org/10.1007/978-3-642-03757-3_9
16. Ferro, D.L., Swedin, E.G.: Science Fiction and Computing: Essays on Interlinked Domains. McFarland & Co, Jefferson, NC, online-ausg edn. (2011). https://airandspace.si.edu/research/publications/science-fiction-and-computing-essays-interlinked-domains

17. Figueiredo, L.S., Gonçalves Maciel Pinheiro, M.G., Vilar Neto, E.X., Teichrieb, V.: An open catalog of hand gestures from Sci-Fi movies. In: Proceedings of the 33rd Annual ACM Conference Extended Abstracts on Human Factors in Computing Systems, CHI EA 2015, New York, NY, USA, pp. 1319–1324. Association for Computing Machinery (2015). https://doi.org/10.1145/2702613.2732888

18. Frank, S.: Real reality: science consultants in hollywood. Sci. Cult. **12**(4), 427–469 (2003). https://doi.org/10.1080/0950543032000150319

19. Fuchsberger, V., Meneweger, T., Wurhofer, D., Tscheligi, M.: Apply now! fictional job postings as an instrument to discuss interactive futures of work. In: Proceedings of the 2017 Conference on Designing Interactive Systems, DIS 2017, New York, NY, USA, pp. 581–586. Association for Computing Machinery (2017). https://doi.org/10.1145/3064663.3064750

20. Gould, J.D., Conti, J., Hovanyecz, T.: Composing letters with a simulated listening typewriter. Commun. ACM **26**(4), 295–308 (1983). https://doi.acm.org/10.1145/2163.358100

21. Helgason, I., Smyth, M., Encinas, E., Mitrović, I.: Speculative and critical design in education: practice and perspectives. In: Companion Publication of the 2020 ACM Designing Interactive Systems Conference, DIS 2020, New York, NY, USA, pp. 385–388. Companion, Association for Computing Machinery (2020). https://doi.org/10.1145/3393914.3395907

22. Jeon, M.: Analyzing novel interactions in science fiction movies in human factors and HCI courses. Proc. Hum. Factors Ergon. Soc. Ann. Meet. **62**(1), 336–340 (2018). https://doi.org/10.1177/1541931218621078

23. Jordan, P., Auernheimer, B.: The fiction in computer science: a qualitative data analysis of the ACM digital library for traces of star trek. In: Ahram, T., Falcão, C. (eds.) AHFE 2017. AISC, vol. 607, pp. 508–520. Springer, Cham (2018). https://doi.org/10.1007/978-3-319-60492-3_48

24. Jordan, P., Mubin, O., Obaid, M., Silva, P.A.: Exploring the referral and usage of science fiction in HCI literature. In: Marcus, A., Wang, W. (eds.) DUXU 2018. LNCS, vol. 10919, pp. 19–38. Springer, Cham (2018). https://doi.org/10.1007/978-3-319-91803-7_2

25. Jordan, P., Mubin, O., Silva, P.A.: A conceptual research agenda and quantification framework for the relationship between science-fiction media and human-computer interaction. In: Stephanidis, C. (ed.) HCI 2016. CCIS, vol. 617, pp. 52–57. Springer, Cham (2016). https://doi.org/10.1007/978-3-319-40548-3_9

26. Kelley, J.F.: An empirical methodology for writing user-friendly natural language computer applications. In: Proceedings of the SIGCHI Conference on Human Factors in Computing Systems, CHI 1983, New York, NY, USA, pp. 193–196. ACM (1983). https://doi.org/10.1145/800045.801609

27. Kirby, D.A.: Science consultants, fictional films, and scientific practice. Soc. Stud. Sci. **33**(2), 231–268 (2003). https://doi.org/10.1177/03063127030332015

28. Kirby, D.A.: Scientists on the set: science consultants and the communication of science in visual fiction. Public Underst. Sci. **12**(3), 261–278 (2003). https://doi.org/10.1177/0963662503123005

29. Kirby, D.A.: Lab coats in Hollywood: Science, scientists, and cinema. MIT Press, Cambridge, Mass., first mit press paperback edition edn. (2010). https://mitpress.mit.edu/books/lab-coats-hollywood

30. Kirby, D.A.: The future is now: diegetic prototypes and the role of popular films in generating real-world technological development. Soc. Stud. Sci. **40**(1), 41–70 (2010). https://doi.org/10.1177/0306312709338325

31. Kohno, T., Johnson, B.D.: Science fiction prototyping and security education: cultivating contextual and societal thinking in computer security education and beyond. In: Proceedings of the 42nd ACM Technical Symposium on Computer Science Education, SIGCSE 2011, pp. 9–14, New York, NY, USA. Association for Computing Machinery (2011). https://doi.org/10.1145/1953163.1953173

32. Larson, J.: Limited imagination: depictions of computers in science fiction film. Futures **40**(3), 293–299 (2008). https://www.sciencedirect.com/science/article/pii/S0016328707001127

33. Lewis, C., Polson, P.G., Wharton, C., Rieman, J.: Testing a walkthrough methodology for theory-based design of walk-up-and-use interfaces. In: Proceedings of the SIGCHI Conference on Human Factors in Computing Systems, CHI 1990, New York, NY, USA, pp. 235–242. ACM (1990). https://doi.org/10.1145/97243.97279

34. Lindley, J.: A pragmatics framework for design fiction. In: 11th EAD Conference Proceedings: The Value of Design Research. Sheffield Hallam University (2016). https://doi.org/10.7190/ead/2015/69

35. Lindley, J., Coulton, P.: Back to the future: 10 years of design fiction. In: Proceedings of the 2015 British HCI Conference, British HCI 2015, New York, NY, USA, pp. 210–211. Association for Computing Machinery (2015). https://doi.org/10.1145/2783446.2783592

36. Lindley, J., Coulton, P.: Pushing the limits of design fiction: the case for fictional research papers. In: Proceedings of the 2016 CHI Conference on Human Factors in Computing Systems, CHI 2016, New York, NY, USA, pp. 4032–4043. Association for Computing Machinery (2016). https://doi.org/10.1145/2858036.2858446

37. Marcus, A.: HCI/CHI/UX and science fiction: A progress report (2013). http://interactions.acm.org/blog/view/hci-chi-ux-and-science-fiction-a-progress-report

38. Marcus, A.: The past 100 years of the future: HCI and user-experience design in science-fiction movies and television. In: SIGGRAPH Asia 2015 Courses, SA 2015, New York, NY, USA. Association for Computing Machinery (2015). https://doi.org/10.1145/2818143.2818151

39. Marcus, A., Soloway, E., Sterling, B., Swanwick, M., Vinge, V.: Opening Pleanary: Sci-Fi @ CHI-99: Science-Fiction Authors Predict Future User Interfaces. In: CHI 1999 Extended Abstracts on Human Factors in Computing Systems. Association for Computing Machinery, New York, NY, USA (1999). https://doi.org/10.1145/632716.632775

40. Marcus, A., Norman, D.A., Rucker, R., Sterling, B., Vinge, V.: Sci-Fi at CHI: Cyberpunk novelists predict future user interfaces. In: Proceedings of the SIGCHI Conference on Human Factors in Computing Systems, CHI 1992, New York, NY, USA pp. 435–437. Association for Computing Machinery (1992). https://doi.org/10.1145/142750.142892

41. Matuk, C., Hurwich, T., Amato, A.: How science fiction world building supports students' scientific explanation. In: Proceedings of FabLearn 2019, FL 2019, New York, NY, USA, pp. 193–196. Association for Computing Machinery (2019). https://doi.org/10.1145/3311890.3311925

42. Michalsky, M.W.: Manipulating our futures: the role of science fiction in education. Clear. House J. Educ. Strat. Issues Ideas **52**(6), 246–249 (1979). https://doi.org/10.1080/00098655.1979.10113595

43. Mubin, O., et al.: Towards an agenda for Sci-Fi inspired HCI research. In: Proceedings of the 13th International Conference on Advances in Computer Entertainment Technology, ACE 2016, New York, NY, USA. Association for Computing Machinery (2016). https://doi.org/10.1145/3001773.3001786

44. Mubin, O., Wadibhasme, K., Jordan, P., Obaid, M.: Reflecting on the presence of science fiction robots in computing literature. J. Hum. Robot Interact. **8**(1) (2019). https://doi.org/10.1145/3303706

45. Muller, M., et al.: Understanding the past, present, and future of design fictions. In: Extended Abstracts of the 2020 CHI Conference on Human Factors in Computing Systems, CHI EA 2020, New York, NY, USA, pp. 1–8. Association for Computing Machinery (2020). https://doi.org/10.1145/3334480.3375168

46. Myers, J.Y., Abd-El-Khalick, F.: "A ton of faith in science!" Nature and role of assumptions in, and ideas about, science and epistemology generated upon watching a sci-fi film. Journal of Research in Science Teaching 53(8), 1143–1171 (2016), https://onlinelibrary.wiley.com/doi/abs/10.1002/tea.21324

47. National Academy of Sciences: The Science & Entertainment Exchange (2021). http://scienceandentertainmentexchange.org/

48. Pillai, A.G., et al.: Communicate, critique and co-create (CCC) future technologies through design fictions in VR environment. In: Companion Publication of the 2020 ACM Designing Interactive Systems Conference, DIS 2020 Companion, New York, NY, USA, pp. 413–416. Association for Computing Machinery (2020). https://doi.org/10.1145/3393914.3395917

49. Pruitt, J., Grudin, J.: Personas: practice and theory. In: Proceedings of the 2003 Conference on Designing for User Experiences, DUX 2003, New York, NY, USA, pp. 1–15. Association for Computing Machinery (2003). https://doi.org/10.1145/997078.997089

50. Rogers, M.L.: Teaching HCI design principles using culturally current media. Proc. Hum. Factors Ergon. Soc. Ann. Meet. **54**(8), 677–680 (2010).https://doi.org/10.1177/154193121005400806

51. Samuelson, D.N.: Modes of extrapolation: the formulas of hard SF. Sci. Fict. Stud. **20**(2), 191–232 (1993). http://www.jstor.org/stable/4240249

52. Schmitz, M., Endres, C., Butz, A.: A survey of human-computer interaction design in science fiction movies. In: Proceedings of the 2nd International Conference on INtelligent TEchnologies for Interactive EnterTAINment, INTETAIN 2008, ICST (Institute for Computer Sciences, Social-Informatics and Telecommunications Engineering), Brussels, BEL (2008). https://doi.org/10.5555/1363200.1363210

53. Shedroff, N., Noessel, C.: Make it so: Interaction Design Lessons from Science Fiction. Rosenfeld Media, Brooklyn N.Y. USA (2012). https://rosenfeldmedia.com/books/make-it-so/

54. Stork, D.G.: From HAL to Office Appliances: Human-Machine Interfaces in Science Fiction and Reality. In: Proceedings of the 3rd International Conference on Intelligent User Interfaces, IUI 1998, New York, NY, USA, p. 181. Association for Computing Machinery (1998). https://doi.org/10.1145/268389.295093

55. Tanenbaum, T.J.: Design fictional interactions: why HCI should care about stories. Interact. **21**(5), 22–23 (2014). https://doi.org/10.1145/2648414

56. Tanenbaum, T.J., Tanenbaum, K., Wakkary, R.: Steampunk as design fiction. In: Proceedings of the SIGCHI Conference on Human Factors in Computing Systems, CHI 2012, New York, NY, USA, pp. 1583–1592. Association for Computing Machinery (2012). https://doi.org/10.1145/2207676.2208279

57. Troiano, G.M., Tiab, J., Lim, Y.K.: SCI-FI: shape-changing interfaces, future interactions. In: Proceedings of the 9th Nordic Conference on Human-Computer Interaction. NordiCHI 2016, New York, NY, USA. Association for Computing Machinery (2016). https://doi.org/10.1145/2971485.2971489

58. Tsai, F.H., Lin, K.Y., Chien, H.M., Chang, L.T.: Effects of a science fiction film on the technological creativity of middle school students. EURASIA J. Math. Sci. Technol. Educ. **9**(2) (2013).https://doi.org/10.12973/eurasia.2013.929a
59. UXPA: User Experience Magazine Issue 13.2. User Experience Magazine **13**(2) (2013). https://uxpamagazine.org/issue/13-2
60. Vrasidas, C., Avraamidou, L., Theodoridou, K., Themistokleous, S., Panaou, P.: Science fiction in education: case studies from classroom implementations. Educ. Media Int. **52**(3), 201–215 (2015). https://doi.org/10.1080/09523987.2015.1075102
61. Westfahl, G., Yuen, W.K., Chan, A.K.S.: Science Fiction and the Prediction of the Future: Essays on Foresight and Fallacy, Critical explorations in science fiction and fantasy, vol. 27. McFarland, Jefferson, N.C. (2011). https://searchworks.stanford.edu/view/9142260

To What Extent is Gamification an Effective Tool for Onboarding Users into a DHM Tool

Ari Kolbeinsson[1]([✉]) [iD], Adam Palmquist[2] [iD], Jessica Lindblom[3] [iD],
and Juan Luis Jiménez Sánchez[4]

[1] School of Engineering, University of Skövde, Högskolevägen 1, Skövde, Sweden
`ari.kolbeinsson@his.se`
[2] Department of Applied IT, University of Gothenburg, Forskningsgången 6,
417 56 Gothenburg, Sweden
[3] School of Informatics, University of Skövde, Högskolevägen 1, Skövde, Sweden
[4] Scania Sverige AB, Box 900, 127 29 Stockholm, Sweden

Abstract. Applying game like elements to tasks or computer systems meant for serious, non-game, activities is becoming more common, and is seen as a way to support users in learning a system or to support users in performing tasks better. Applying game like elements requires an understanding of users, the target task, and what can motivate the target users in their tasks. As in any system development, the success of the design requires validating, and this may be done multiple times in the development cycle. Some concepts, such as usability or user experience have well established testing methods, while gamification is still a relatively immature field and evaluation methods are still being developed. This paper follows the first evaluation of a gamification system to aid with onboarding new users into the IPS IMMA digital human modelling system, offering details on the heuristic evaluation method. So early in the process it is inevitable that problems were found, largely to do with how motivation of users was handled, and multiple suggestions for improvements are offered.

Keywords: Gamification · Digital human modelling · DHM · Onboarding · Evaluation

1 Introduction

This paper details a study that explores the effects of gamification on a digital human modelling (DHM) system called IPS-IMMA (hereafter Imma, see Fig. 1) for assisting new users in learning the system, or onboarding. An early gamification prototype/technical demonstrator is explored through a heuristic analysis to find what is required to support new users learning the Imma software. As gamification is a developing field it is necessary to start with an exploration of literature on the gamification of complex professional software, as well as possible evaluation methods for analysing such gamification efforts. This literature study identified potentially useful theories, as well as a collection of heuristics designed specifically for examining gamified systems. An evaluation was conducted, results analysed, and routes for improvement identified.

© Springer Nature Switzerland AG 2021
M. M. Soares et al. (Eds.): HCII 2021, LNCS 12779, pp. 48–66, 2021.
https://doi.org/10.1007/978-3-030-78221-4_4

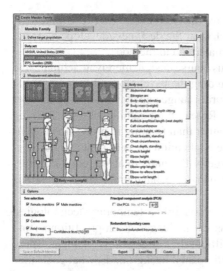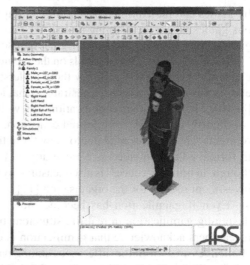

Fig. 1. The Imma interface, showing an interface for creating manikin families (left) and the Imma main interface after creating a manikin family (right)

2 Background

2.1 Gamification at Work

Traditionally, work and play have been viewed as two distinct arenas, focusing on seriousness and playfulness respectively, but nowadays these arenas are moving closer toward each other, highlighting the idea of introducing elements from gamification into the work domain [1]. According to Dale [2], the core purpose of introducing gamification in any context is to engage and encourage participation, which means that gamification is about understanding and utilising the triggers that affect human behaviour. Hence, gamification is the application of motivational psychology to influence the outcome. In other words, gamification aims at engaging humans on the emotional level and motivating them to achieve their goals. A commonly used definition of gamification is "the use of game design elements in nongame contexts" [3, p. 2], which has been broadened to encompass "the use of game mechanics and experience design to digitally engage and motivate people to achieve their goals" (Gartner, in [2], p. 84). Notably, this definition distinguishes gamification from serious games, which use "complete games for non-entertainment purposes" [4]. Broadly speaking, workplace gamification could be characterised "as the adaptation and application of game design principles and game interaction elements to workplace processes and behaviours" [5, p. 1]. Although the proliferation of gamification in the workplace has been around for a time, there are currently several knowledge gaps considering whether and in what ways it may contribute to increased efficacy, productivity, extrinsic motivation, worker engagement and well-being [e.g., 1; 2; 5; 6].

Research on game-based employee training is often concerned with serious games, not with gamification [7]. In contrast to serious games, gamification does not per se incorporate complete or actual games. Gamification uses a variety of design choices inspired by games and motivational psychology to improve different outcomes [8]. Unlike serious games where the learning material is part of what the designers/developers create, gamification depends upon the original course material and method.

Because gamification depends on the previous course design, merely attaching game elements in employee training without understanding the psychological impacts on the end-user is unlikely to enact a desirable behavioural change and may even harm the user [8–10]. There are other complications, as well. Research on gamification for learning is primarily concerned with formal education, rather than training in professional environments [7]. It is essential not to view these the application areas as synonymous: e.g. in formal education, success is generally an issue of the individual student's learning, though, in training, success is also measured by employee behavioural change that brings investment returns for the organisation [11].

Even if gamification has become more common in contemporary technologies, designing gamification in real-life situations has its challenges. Both practitioners and researchers acknowledge that gamification is difficult to design and implement. These challenges arise from the differences among participants' backgrounds, what goals they have, and their understanding of gamification [12]. There is no coherent design method for gamification, and existing methods tell little or nothing about how to design gamification [13]. To design meaningful gamified products the designers have to take into consideration three main topics:

1. Games are composed of many interconnected parts and therefore complicated to transfer from one context to another;
2. Gamification involves motivational information system design that entails an understanding of motivational psychology;
3. The goal of gamifying is to affect behaviour, which adds a layer to the scope of the design [14].

The design should appeal to the user's intrinsic or internalised motivations rather than solely relying on extrinsically motivating game elements. Meaningful gamification should underscore a clear connection to the end-users [15]. In addition to highlighting the lack of solid field case studies on how to design gamification for training situations, studies suggest that the field of gamification design needs multidisciplinary research methods with a variety of approaches to grasp the overall comprehension of the gamification business [7, 8, 12]. Due to the lack of solid case studies on how to design gamification for training situations, researchers suggest that the field of gamification design needs multidisciplinary research methods with a variety of approaches to grasp the overall comprehension of the gamification business [7, 8, 12].

2.2 Issues to Consider Before Gamifying the Workplace

Several frameworks exist on how to implement gamification, some aimed at practitioners and some aimed at researchers (For a synthesis see [16]). However, when it comes to gamifying the workplace there are several advantages as well as pitfalls to consider. The first take-home message stressed by Dale [2] is to carefully plan the gamification before the implementation, gaining a deeper understanding of 'why', 'what', and 'how' you should gamify the workplace. The following issues should be considered in the planning phase, slightly modified from Dale [2]:

- Identifying and formulating the organisation's purpose and goals for implementing gamification
- Carefully considering the company culture, asking questions about what kinds of rewards or benefits that motivate the workers, and how should these be incorporated and recognised within the gamification
- Identifying and staying focused on the kinds of behaviours that should be encouraged (or discouraged initially), and then work systematically backwards from these key behaviours. This is preferably achieved by identifying the main activities and triggers that most likely influence the envisioned behaviour.
- Updating the reward system regularly, ensuring that the workers persist to stay engaged and not getting uninterested with the older options.
- Avoiding game mechanisms that spread out points and badges like "sugar pellets" every time the user hits the right level.
- Sidestepping the idea to 'game' the workers, which means that the gamification should enhance work instead of exploiting their workers.
- Avoiding the usage of money as a motivator as that will weaken intrinsic motivational factors such as taking pride in doing a task well done or collaborating as part of a team. Instead, the focus should be on aspects that intrinsically value such as demonstrating their ability to acquire skills, mastering challenges, and accomplishing goals.
- Making it "look and feel" professional, although gamification borrows game design techniques, it does not have to look like a game. Instead, the focus should be on visualising accomplishments, setting milestones, and communicating added value.
- Respecting existing programs and work practices, do not confuse the workers with new processes and incentives that outrank more senior workers by junior workers solely because the juniors are better to handle the gamification itself rather than the work practice being gamified.
- Applying appropriate motivators. Humans want to feel that they are making progress and develop, which can be supported by presenting structure and task completion that encourage the workers to experience that they are making progress, while at the same time avoiding micromanaging through gamification.

To summarise, the ambition to trigger worker motivations by providing rewards via the implementation of gamification could result in so-called *gamification backlash*, which means that the usage of extrinsic motivations (e.g., points, badges, prizes, penalties, and progress bars) will decrease the workers' intrinsic motivations (e.g., recognition, personal achievement, responsibility, and mastery) [2]. This highlights the importance of being honest with the user and avoiding elements that contribute to the feeling of being tricked or taken advantage of, as that is not a feeling that users associate with a positive experience. Another major pitfall is the tendency to pay more attention on the technology side of gamification application and the game mechanics ('bells and whistles') rather than on the quest of engaging with as well as understanding and analysing the potential end-users of the application. In the very end, technology is the simpler task to accomplish whereas humans' underlying needs, emotions, and motivations are harder to grasp and are more complex. Dale's [2] major take-home message is that failed gamification projects often are the outcome from the tendency to put technology first and the users second.

However, as have been acknowledged from the field of Human-Computer Interaction (HCI) and User Experience (UX), it is a major mistake to ignore the users [17]. User involvement and an iterative user-centred design approach is likewise vital for a successful gamification strategy. Accordingly, any organisation that consider to implement a gamification strategy must therefore put emphasis on:

- Gaining a deep understanding of the primary and secondary user groups they intend to engage, including various skills and competence in their professional roles,
- Recognising the behaviours they intend to change in the users,
- Grasping what motivates the users as well as what aspects that maintain their, and engagement
- Characterising how to measure success.

Dale [2] presents the following intended benefits of implementing gamification at work, which could be achieved by following a systematic implementation of the gamification strategy:

- Increased motivation and productivity of workers,
- A better alignment of workers' goals and expectations as well as the company's/organisation's goals with stakeholders and customers/clients,
- Workers are to a larger extent engaged with new initiatives in the company/organisations, and
- Workers are to a larger extent transformed into advocates of the company/organisation.

Hence, it appears that the gamified workplace is becoming an increased trend. For example, Oprescu, Jones & Katsikitis [5] present ten gaming principles that are feasible to implement in the workplace in order to be beneficial for both the workers and the employer with a focus on productivity and wellbeing.

2.3   10 Gaming Principles that Focus on Productivity and Well-Being in the Workplace

The ten principles suggested for gamifying work processes formulated by Oprescu, Jones & Katsikitis [5] have been structured under the mnemonic *I play at work*. Their principles are motivated from theoretical bases, suggested approaches, and expected benefits.

I Orientation considers using processes that put the worker at the centre of the game experience, by engaging the users with a focus on cognitive and emotional outcomes. They point out that prior research has shown that successful games include personally relevant, carefully designed and progressively difficult challenges, in which the users have to increase their cognitive efforts to accomplish skill development. This means that a gamified work process may encourage users to progress through increasingly difficult tasks. Dale [2] similarly proposes a user-centred approach. The expected benefits are increased engagement and sense of control as well as self-efficacy.

Persuasive Elements considers the inclusion of persuasive elements that are based on psychological and behavioural theories that are encouraging the users to a larger extent to explore and learn more in ways that are beneficial to both the users and the company/organisation. The expected benefits are adoption of novel initiatives as well as increased satisfaction of internal communication.

Learning orientation considers skill development, knowledge acquisition, motivations and behavioural changes. This principle has its basis in the body of research that highlights the potential positive impact on various forms of learning via gamification. It is recommended that this process should be based on psychological theories. The expected benefits are increased development of individual and organisational abilities.

Achievements based on rewards consider a predictable and reasonable return of investment by the workers. Positive feedback and the implementation of either virtual or real rewards may foster stronger bonds among workers as well as a stronger commitment if these are interpreted by workers as being oriented towards self-efficacy and well-being. The expected benefits are worker satisfaction and increased ability to keep personnel.

Y generation adaptable considers that new workers, particularly the Y generation, may regard a gamified workplace as being more attractive since they find added value in work experiences they perceive as caring, fun, and engaging. It is acknowledged that they want to be rewarded repeatedly by various means. The expected benefits are recruitment and retention of workers.

Amusement Factors (Fun Elements) consider making work activities more attractive by including elements of fun and play, e.g., establishing a sense of balance between collaboration and competition focused activities. The expected benefits are improved productivity, increased satisfaction and well-being.

Transformative considers how an attractive balance between competition and collaboration may result in a transformation of current work processes within the organisation, enabling the workers to explore new perspectives, positions, and roles. In so doing, the workers may make further progress in desired skills via simulations and game-play. The expected benefits are to educate workers into new work practices, to increase productivity, and enhance individual and organisational well-being.

Wellbeing-Oriented considers the obtained results that support the view that gamification could on the one hand improve health and productivity, and on the other hand reduce health care costs, if paying attention at the workers' psychosocial experience and well-being [19]. The expected benefits are enhanced individual and organisational well-being.

Research-Generating considers the complex endeavour of designing, evaluating, and implementing gamification at work, which addresses the need to identify and formulate the potential benefits via a research-based approach. Taking a human-computer interaction (HCI) approach is recommended both in theory and practice since this way of working is beneficial in order to create the gamified workplace in the organisation. The expected benefits are a clearer view of the motives, needs, and goals of the gamified workplace and enhanced decision-making.

Knowledge-Based considers the need to have a knowledge perspective on the gamification process, either as the intended outcome or as a feedback process. A common characteristic of successful games is their focus on clearly formulated short, medium and long term key goals that are easy to monitor. Immediate and systematic feedback and rewards are a viable approach to create the desired behavioural changes via specified thresholds to reach the maximum level of achievement possible. The expected benefits are further development of individual and organisational abilities.

To summarise, these ten principles are still work in progress, although they are intended to study and cultivate first and foremost the productivity in the gamified workplace, but also psychological benefits and health promotion [5]. As pointed out by them, there are many knowledge gaps left to investigate and analyse in future work. One identified research challenge addressed by Oprescu, Jones & Katsikitis [5] is how to practically and easily assess the added value of the gamified workplace for personal and organisational wellbeing. This is exactly the kind of research that we intend to accomplish with the Imma gamification module, including learning and productivity aspects. Moreover, Oprescu, Jones & Katsikitis [5] highlight the considerable value in reshaping core ideas related to the workplaces of the future. In this particular context, Industry 4.0 is of major relevance but also the occupational healthcare providers of the future. Or as they state themselves: "Gamified workplaces can provide opportunities for a more vigorous and strategic inter-disciplinary research agenda that can stimulate further investments in the area" [5, p. 4].

2.4 Evaluating CAD/CAM

Li, Hedlind and Kjellberg [20] reviewed the state of the art of user-centred evaluation of tools for computer-aided design or computer-aided manufacturing (CAD/CAM) systems. DHM software is considered as a kind of CAD/CAM systems. The obtained result revealed that usability and UX aspects are seldom considered in the design and development of CAD/CAM systems, and there are several causes for this particular lack. Li, Hedlind and Kjellberg [20] explained that these systems' design mainly focuses on developing powerful functions for advanced engineering activities. However, a mix of functions cannot result in a credible/feasible solution without paying attention to how it works for the end-users' usability and UX. Li, Hedlind and Kjellberg [20] remark that end-users often encounter various problems to understand what to do and how to do it via the visualisations and manipulations in the usage situation. Although CAD/CAM systems are intended to facilitate engineers' work tasks, designing interaction patterns without considering the human-centred perspective often ends in poor usability, negative UX, and limited outcomes of the system's functional capacity. Neglected human-centred perspective can result in low productivity, time-consuming training, safety risks, unsatisfied and unmotivated end-users. Li et al. [20] point out that the human-centred perspective is a neglected area and much needed to increase CAD/CAM systems' performance and utility. Addressed challenges for practising a human-centred approach in the CAD/CAM domain are the limited group of end-users and the considered required amount of domain knowledge of these systems to carry out proper UX evaluation. However, more focus is needed on conducting systematic human-centred evaluations on CAD/CAM systems, both in scope and breadth [20].

2.5   IPS Gamification Modules Explained

The gamified interface consists of an HTML GUI widget connected to IPS-IMMA that displays the four gamification modules (see Fig. 1). These are the *level* module, *mission* module, *achievements* module, and *shop* module. Each module is represented by a large icon and text on the left hand side of the interface, and the user can switch between modules at any time by selecting the icon. Each module will now be explored in more detail.

Level module (Fig. 2, left): This module presents the user's Avatar, which is their representation inside the gamified interface, as well as their experience level, remaining experience points (XP) until the next level, and the rewards received upon achieving that level. Levels are a passive reward, in which the user will accumulate experience points by performing different actions in the tool, and upon reaching certain thresholds of experience points the user will advance a level; thus, the more time a user spends using the tool, the more levels that will be passively accumulated.

Mission module (Fig. 2, right): The Mission module is the main tool for improving the onboarding process. It offers a fixed path of tasks that have to be performed and that will guide the user in the process of carrying out a simulation and achieving relevant results. Completion of each task will reward the user with experience points and unlock the next task in the sequence.

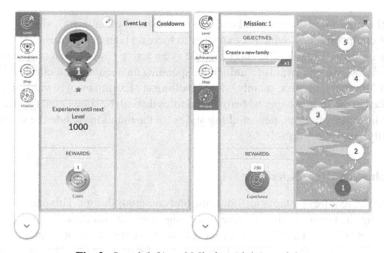

Fig. 2. Level (left) and Mission (right) modules.

Achievements module (Fig. 3): The Achievements module offers another type of passive reward system, in which the user unlocks badges and receive experience points whenever they accomplish a special action within the tool. There are two main type of achievements, the ones awarded for repetition of a task a certain number of times (for example, running 10/50/100 simulations), and the ones awarded for completing an especially complicated task (for example, running a simulation that contains more than 30 different processes). The badges awarded can then be showcased by the user to

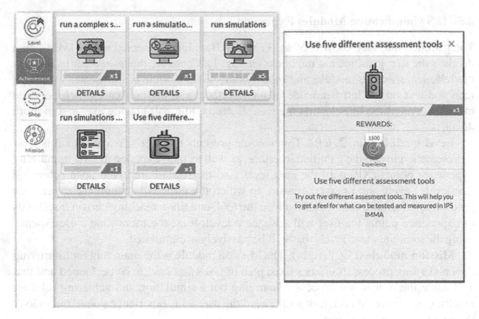

Fig. 3. The Achievements module.

indicate their accomplishments, and compared to those of other users, offering a certain degree of competitiveness which is expected to increase user engagement.

Shop module (Fig. 4): The shop module is an active reward system in which the user can choose which rewards to unlock by spending an accumulated currency (coins) rewarded for other activities, mainly when levelling up. Examples of rewards that could be unlocked in the shop are special badges and titles that can be showcased to other users; new user interface graphics, new clothing styles for the manikins inside the simulations (commonly known as "skins").

2.6 Evaluating User eXperience

A positive UX requires systematic, thorough, and conscious design. This can be achieved by following the phases in the iterative UX design lifecycle process, also referred to as the UX wheel [17; 21]. The UX design lifecycle process consists of four major interactive activities; these are: *analyse*, *design*, *implement*, and *evaluate* [17]. The purpose of the analysis phase is to understand the users' goals and needs, the activity and context in which the work is carried out, as well as the business domain. The design phase involves development of the concept, development of the interaction with the product, as well as the look and feel of the product. In the implementation phase, the focus is on realising different design alternatives, commonly using mockups and prototypes of varying detail and quality. The focus here will be on the evaluation phase, with a particular focus on evaluation of early prototypes that will be further refined.

The field of UX design (UXD) offers methods, techniques, and guidelines for creating a positive UX for all types of interactive systems for human use [17], and UXD is

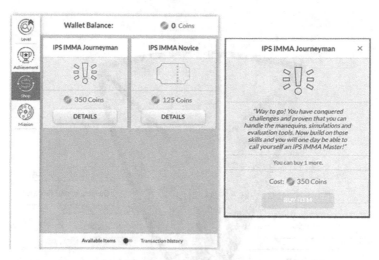

Fig. 4. The Shop module.

well-aligned with the ISO 9241-10 Standard Ergonomics of human-system interaction [18] that could be properly applied to the gamification domain. In addition to that, UXD has tools for examining many of the core elements of gamified systems, such as engagement and various feedback mechanisms [17]. This suggests a link between UX and gamification, and further suggests that gamification at work projects may benefit from taking into account the UX perspective throughout the development process.

The overarching goal of a UX evaluation, being a formative evaluation (during the development process) or a summative evaluation (on the final product), is to identify UX problems and provide answers of how to proceed to handle them. Multiple UX evaluation methods exist for examining different aspects or contexts of design, with each method typically being either analytical or empirical in nature [17]. Analytical evaluation is usually carried out without any user involvement, while empirical evaluations typically involve users [21]. Analytical methods are often used in the early stages of a product as they can provide insights and identifications of relevant UX problems fast, at minimal cost, and can be performed before using rough mockups or prototypes, as well as being used throughout a development process as "quick and dirty" evaluation methods for fast iterations [22]. Empirical evaluations are, conversely, often employed later in the process on more advanced artefacts (prototypes or early product versions) and with more user involvement [17, 22].

2.7 Evaluating Gameful Design - A Heuristic Approach

The use of heuristic analyses is well known within the fields of usability analysis [22] and UXD [17], but heuristics specifically for evaluating gamified systems are a more recent addition to researchers' toolboxes. One such set of gamification-specific heuristics have been developed by Tondello et al. [23] focus on the software's potential to afford intrinsic and extrinsic motivation for the user. This set of 28 gamification heuristics was extracted from guidelines that were written based on 12 dimensions in 3 categories of

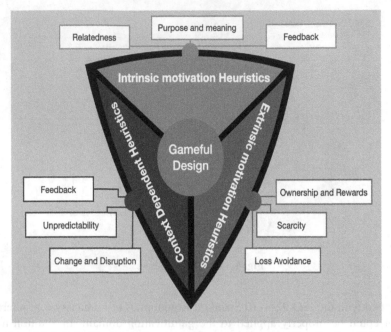

Fig. 5. Gameful design, 12 central dimensions from 3 categories of motivation (Adapted from Tondello et al. [23])

motivation (see Fig. 5) identified from existing research, with the heuristics being further modified to support a rapid evaluation of gamified systems. In addition, each heuristic is accompanied by one or more guiding questions that makes application easier and supports the analyst in providing more depth and detail for each heuristic.

The heuristics are categorised based on three types of motivations that (may) drive users to engage with the system. These categories are:

- *Intrinsic motivation* includes affordances related to the three intrinsic needs (competence, autonomy, and relatedness), as well as 'purpose' and 'meaning' as facilitators of internalisation, and 'immersion'.
- *Extrinsic motivation* includes affordances that provide an outcome or value separated from the activity itself: ownership and rewards, scarcity, and loss avoidance.
- *Context-dependent motivation* includes the feedback, unpredictability, and disruption affordances, which can afford either intrinsic or extrinsic motivation depending on contextual factors. For example, the application can provide feedback to the user regarding either intrinsically or extrinsically motivated tasks; therefore, feedback might afford intrinsic or extrinsic motivation according to the type of task with which it is associated.

All 28 heuristics will not be detailed here, but showing examples of heuristics from each category gives a useful insight into how the heuristics are formed. Following are examples of one heuristic and its accompanying guiding question from each category.

- *Intrinsic motivation*

- *Heuristic 3: Increasing Challenge:* The system offers challenges that grow with the user's skill
- *Guiding questions:*
- Does the system present challenges in a way that motivates the user to tackle them?
- Is the difficulty of the challenges adjusted to the user's ability and skill?
- Do the challenges' difficulty increase over time?

- *Extrinsic motivation*

- *Heuristic 18: Rewards:* The system offers incentive rewards for interaction and continued use, which are valuable to users and proportional to the amount of effort invested
- *Guiding questions:*
- Does the system reward the user for completing tasks or progressing in their goals?
- Does the system reward the user for continued use?
- Are rewards proportional to the amount of effort, time, and dedication that the user put into the system?
- Are the rewards meaningful and useful for the user?

- *Context-dependent motivation*

- *Heuristic 22: Clear and Immediate Feedback:* The systems always inform users immediately of any changes or accomplishments in an easy and graspable way
- *Guiding questions:*
- Does the system immediately inform the user when any change in status occur?
- Does the system immediately inform the user when any task is completed or any goal is achieved?
- Is the feedback always clear and understandable?
- Does the feedback always explain exactly what has happened and which action caused it?

Applying the heuristics involves specialists using the system, completing tasks that are seen as typical for an identified user group, Each heuristic is considered for applicability, and a rating applied on a scale of 0 (no problem) to 4 (critical problem that stops progress), and noting further detail. The specialists then compare their problem ratings and comments, and an analysis of each factor is generated. Applying heuristics to the gamification module in Imma is relatively simple as the gamification module is linear in nature, with only navigation between what to display being possible.

In many cases, including this one, not all heuristics in a list may be applicable, as cases may differ fundamentally while heuristics are commonly developed to cover a large variety of scenarios. In practice, this meant that all 28 heuristics were considered and comments added to heuristics that were deemed no to be applicable to onboarding users in Imma.

3   A Heuristic Evaluation of Imma

3.1   Procedure

Three UX and gamification specialists were planned to perform the heuristic analysis, but due to illness only two could take part. All 28 heuristics were evaluated against the Imma gamification module. Both specialists had low experience with the Imma system, one participant had some experience with CAD software, the other had no experience with CAD software.

The heuristic evaluation was performed simultaneously by both participants by going through the missions offered by the gamification module, solving those tasks in Imma, and examining the feedback provided. Notes were taken on each heuristic, and problems rated from 0 to 4. Notes and severity ratings were discussed and compared, and common themes identified.

A notebook computer with sufficient computing power to run the Imma software without noticeable issues was used, with the gamification modules and a license server system running on the same computer.

Some central issues that were identified will be presented here, along with suggestions for improvements.

3.2   Analysis and Results

The heuristic evaluation identified serious problems (rated 3–4 out of 4) in 14 heuristics out of 28. These results and the associated notes were coded for keywords to identify patterns or groupings of problems. The most common identified groupings that were seen to have a large effect on gamification were *skill progression*, *difficulty level/threshold*, *choice*, and *missions*. These are largely interconnected, with *user goals* being a common aspect between all four groupings. Other keywords were coded but were less frequent. An example of these less common, but still serious issues, is *onboarding*, which was found to be missing for onboarding into the gamification module. Another serious issue that was identified was the lack of *goals*, or a goal directed skill acquisition process. This ties into both the identified keywords of *skill progression* and *missions*.

More Details on the Four Major Keywords Identified

Skill progression was found to be an issue in at least eight of the heuristics, mostly due to a lack of clarity of what skills were to be trained next, or what skills have been acquired. Achievements were seen to be task focused rather than skill focused, negating opportunities for supporting intrinsic motivation. An over reliance on extrinsic motivators such as rewards has been shown to negatively affect learning outcomes.

Difficulty level/threshold was found to be a major hindrance, with difficulty levels of missions varying wildly and unpredictably. Even using external tutorials did not solve the second mission, as the jump in difficulty was so high. This is during a sensitive time in the onboarding when the user is getting acquainted with the basics of the program, which can lead to severe frustration and lowered intrinsic motivation, possibly leading to the user giving up due to the obstacle seeming insurmountable. As this follows a task that was achieved with relative ease it is likely that the user will assume a progressive difficulty level, and blame themselves for incompetence. Users being made to feel stupid is a well known UX issue with severe consequences [22].

An unexpected issue within the *difficulty level* category was that the functionalities of the gamification module itself were not seen as being clear without a surprising amount of clicking around; the gamification module did not guide the user towards the next thing to do, and did not highlight the missions as being central to progression.

Missions were found to be linear, and were task based rather than skill based, and not user selectable. This means that the user has no choice in what mission (or *task/activity* that supports the training of a *skill*) is next. A lack of choice can negatively affect engagement. That the missions are task based means that "tasks to be completed" were created, rather than examining what skill the user should train to progress, which is what is displayed and highlighted upon task completion. Achievements are also awarded and displayed based on tasks completed rather than skills acquired.

Choice, or the lack thereof, was seen repeatedly to be an issue. This was often linked to missions and the possibility for the user to set their own goals and tasks by e.g. selecting which mission to perform next, but also to the lack of customisability in the system, which is seen as a result of the early stage of the prototype and less critical than the aforementioned issues.

Some of these identified issues tie into other aspects that merit discussion, such as limited possibilities for *choice* in the gamification module being exacerbated by too much in the Imma software, which is always shown at full complexity and without any guidance such as that which is common in games and gamified systems. This is currently a system limitation, as the link between Imma and the gamification system is currently uni-directional, and implementing pop-over guidance in Imma may be challenging. A fully integrated (and bi-directional) solution is, however, strongly recommended if at all possible, as multiple serious issues stemmed from poor visibility of the gamification module, unclear feedback when the gamification module window ends up behind the Imma window, and the lack of path highlighting and task support in the Imma interface.

3.3 Suggestions for Improvement

The following suggestions lean heavily on the *I Play At Work* mnemonic from Oprescu, Jones and Katsikitis [5], as well as the issues lifted by Dale [2] for gamification specific improvement suggestions, but also take into account general usability and UX issues [e.g. 17, 22].

Instead of focusing on tasks completed, experience points (XP), and levels, the focus should instead be on what has been achieved, i.e. what skills have been acquired and what "I" can now achieve. This is based on the *I orientation* [5], as well as the *applying the correct motivators* aspect [2].

The *knowledge based* aspect [5] suggests that a focus should be either on the intended outcome as a more complex process, with a focus on user goals from a short term, medium term, and long term viewpoint. This suggests building the gamification modules centred around user (or UX) goals as a viable approach. Furthermore, clear, immediate, and systematic feedback also suggests that the gamification module needs an element that is always visible, either as a panel integrated into Imma or as an "always on top" display.

A mission structure based around skills and skill acquisition that also highlights previously acquired skills is suggested. The primary goal of this kind of structure is to provide the user with an overview that supports and draws from the intrinsic motivation to acquire the skills to be more competent, i.e. to get better at Imma. Missions should be clear in what is expected, even with an overview of what needs to be done, and should be mostly non-linear (i.e. selectable) after an initial introduction to the system. This kind of approach is seen as being likely to support engagement through the intrinsic motivation, but the context specific motivation that can be supported by the feedback from the system around skill acquisition is considered likely to further enhance engagement.

In addition to this, the gamification module should provide an introduction to itself, and should be set up so that the most important details are always shown. This could be suggested as being the mission structure and XP/level. Moreover, an always-on-top component is suggested, if the gamification module cannot be fully integrated into Imma. This always-on-top component should work in a similar manner to a heads up display in a game, reminding the user of the current objective (the mission) and the skill that is being explored, the current level, and progression (XP to next level, and how sub-objectives in the mission are progressing).

If rewards are used, then these should be appropriate to that skill, the task, the goal of the user, and the effort expended. Rewards should thus be context specific. Currency can be appropriate if it allows the purchase of items that link into the user's goal, or in other ways supports their engagement. This is unlikely to be useful early in the onboarding process, as the focus will be on gaining basic competence in the software.

Dale [2] suggests that *"Avoiding game mechanisms that spread out points and badges like 'sugar pellets' every time the user hits the right level"*, and *"the focus should be on visualising accomplishments, setting milestones, and communicating added value"* which both warn against focusing on points or levels, but rather highlighting users' skills as they link to the goals that the user is trying to achieve. In the case of Imma that might vary between user groups and vary based on time. An example of this is that to begin with the user may have a diffuse long term goal of being able to use Imma in general, but a shorter term goal of making a manikin move, as the user understands that they are beginning a learning process. The goals for eventually *using* Imma can thus be different to smaller and more modular goals of *learning* Imma. These learning goals, however, do eventually link to the goals for using Imma, and that is the important link to show to the user while acquiring skills. To achieve this it is possible to show a "you got 750XP and levelled up when you gained the *create a complex manikin family* skill. You now know how to create manikin families that represent the workers in your facility!" as well as showing the skills in a structure similar to a computer game "skill tree" [2].

Although the idea of a social aspect where users can compare their skill or progress to other users seems tempting this is an aspect of gamification that should be treated extremely carefully. Such an approach can lead to users feeling stressed, leading to a pressure to complete missions as fast as possible rather than to learn and explore the system. This is particularly important with complex systems that reward deep learning through testing functionalities outside of the mission structure [17, 22].

Achievements are an interesting reward system that may or may not help, depending on implementation and the user's own motivation. It is important that achievements are appropriate; in this case based on the skills acquired. However, this is a place where it is possible to be slightly more playful in the design. Although core achievements should be clearly based on skills and missions it may work to reward achievements for completing "secondary" tasks, some of which will not be explicitly requested. An example of this might be an achievement for trying out all ways of moving an object, as there exists more than one way of doing that in Imma. Or having changed all parameters in the manikin generation panel (see Fig. 1). Not all achievements must be obvious, and some may be invisible and even nearly impossible to achieve, being awarded only for playing around with the software. This can lead to small positive moments while using Imma, increasing the overall positive UX [5]. This also support the heuristics of *freedom (10)* and *self-expression (9)*, as it allows users to play around with the system and create their own path once basic skills have been acquired, yet still gain benefit from the gamification module.

A general suggestion for improving the heuristics themselves, as well as many gamification guidelines, is to remove the word "fun" from heuristic 16, *Perceived Fun*, and substitute that with "engagement". Engagement is a more useful term for gamification at work where the goal is commonly not to make the activity or software fun, but rather to support the user in increasing their skill or maintaining their skill over longer time periods. The user's skill is then a primary reward, with the gamification system often serving to increase engagement and highlight some aspects of the user's skill level, which can be achieved through highlighting goal based skill achievements. Levels and similar terms can be used, but should link with the goals and skills of the user, not just be for the sake of having levels.

4 Discussion and Conclusions

As has been mentioned, the design and implementation of gamification in complex work contexts such as that explored in this study is a relatively immature field, and as such much remains to be explored. Our goal here is to explore and combine useful gamification literature with existing research on usability and UXD to support such a complex work context, with a focus on evaluation methods and theories that can be used to inform gamified or gameful design of CAD and DHM software.

Although some issues have been raised with the object of study, the gamification module prototype developed for the Imma DHM software, it must be pointed out that the module is a work in progress and that the module as tested was created to validate that such a system could be integrated with Imma, as well as to provide a foundation for further iterative design.

Creating missions and achievements that are centred around highlighting user skills, and offering more choice as to which mission/skill is seen as a next step that would rectify many of the largest issues. This requires a deeper understanding of user goals, which is the next step. This single update is seen as likely to change the progression within the gamification module, increase the focus on intrinsic motivators (i.e. skill acquisition).

The system itself was seen by the authors as not requiring further work to meet usability goals, but when leaps in difficulty were not too large between missions then the feeling of "aha, I managed to do that" was felt to drive engagement. Conversely, completing an easy task and getting stuck on the next task was extremely demotivational.

Diving deeper, gamification can be implemented in mutually digital and analogue contexts. Implemented analogue, the use of advanced technology is unnecessary, although designing and developing analogue gamification does not require advanced technology; it is not the same as saying it is easy [24]. Practitioners and researchers alike have discussed the skillset required for designing gamification indicating a comprehensive as well as interdisciplinary knowledge regarding game design and behavioural science as well as acquaintance with the users, context and topic that will be gamified [13, 16]. Similar findings have been made within the fields of usability and UX [17]. Designing and developing gamification in a digital context has been stated as "especially challenging" [12, p. 4]. It requires skills such's as an understanding of Informatics with specialisation in computer science, human-computer interaction, and/or information systems [16]. Correspondingly, the gamifying software process comes with the challenges - prioritising development, time management, limited capacity - and risk factors - lack of team skills, ambiguous requirement, and insufficient standardisations - associated with software development [25].

Correspondingly, comprehension surrounding how to design gamification to achieve the intended operational objectives is in its infancy [12; 15; 16]. The literature on gamification design both from researchers [e.g. 15, 16] and practitioners [e.g. 26; 27] provide imperfect, limited and context-dependent rules of thumb. Consequential, both researchers and practitioners are restricted to a tentative, speculative, and costly implementation process [e.g., 12]. Even that gamification design has been an aspiring research topic during the last five years, Hassan [12] and Morschheuser [16] stress that more investigation is needed on the factors essential for a gamification project successful outcome. Consequently, in line with the present and previous research, there is a request for further systematic research into what challenges, heuristics, agents, and techniques for, not just, designing gamification, but also how to realise and evaluate it. Such research would improve the understanding of what functions and what not functions when implementing gamification and produce a fresh approach tying the gap between gamification and UX/HCI.

Most important is to make sure that the lesson that it is crucial to focus on people during the design and development of systems rather than getting lost in a focus on available technology. This lesson has been learnt and re-learnt in computer science multiple times in the last few decades, which has led to similar problems with products each time. These problems have been centred around users, or user groups that were not being taken into account in the development process, and ended up not being supported by the product. Avoiding those well-known issues should be of central importance for any gamification effort, especially as many central factors are well known by now, and methods exist to avoid many of these issues.

4.1 Next Steps

Continuing work involves mainly further iterations of the gamification model, with a first step being to formulate clear UX goals to support a skill acquisition based mission and achievement structure. Further prototyping and exploration of what integration with Imma is possible is required.

Acknowledgements. This work has been realised with support from the Knowledge Foundation and the INFINIT research environment (KKS Dnr. 20180167) who have financially supported the Synergy Virtual Ergonomics project (SVE), as well as partner organisations.

References

1. Ferreira, A.T., Araújo, A.M., Fernandes, S., Miguel, I.C.: Gamification in the workplace: a systematic literature review. In: Rocha, Á., Correia, A.M., Adeli, H., Reis, L.P., Costanzo, S. (eds.) WorldCIST. AISC, vol. 571, pp. 283–292. Springer, Cham (2017). https://doi.org/10.1007/978-3-319-56541-5_29
2. Dale, S.: Gamification: making work fun, or making fun of work? Bus. Inf. Rev. **31**(2), 82–90 (2014)
3. Deterding, S., Dixon, D., Khaled, R., Nacke, L.: From game design elements to gamefulness: defining "gamification". In: Proceedings of the 15th International Academic MindTrek Conference: Envisioning Future Media Environments, pp. 9–15 (2011)
4. Susi, T., Johannesson, M., Backlund, P.: Serious games: An overview (2007)
5. Oprescu, F., Jones, C., Katsikitis, M.: I play at work—ten principles for transforming work processes through gamification. Front. Psychol. **30**(5), 14 (2014)
6. Mitchell, R., Schuster, L., Jin, H.S.: Gamification and the impact of extrinsic motivation on needs satisfaction: making work fun? J. Bus. Res. **106**, 323–330 (2020)
7. Armstrong, M.B., Landers, R.N., Collmus, A.B.: Gamifying recruitment, selection, training, and performance management: game-thinking in human resource management. In: Emerging Research and Trends in Gamification, pp. 140–165. IGI Global (2016)
8. Armstrong, M.B., Landers, R.N.: Gamification of employee training and development. Int. J. Train. Dev. **22**, 162–169 (2018)
9. Kim, T.W., Werbach, K.: More than just a game: ethical issues in gamification. Ethics Inf. Technol. **18**(2), 157–173 (2016). https://doi.org/10.1007/s10676-016-9401-5
10. Goethe, O., Palmquist, A.: Broader understanding of gamification by addressing ethics and diversity. In: Stephanidis, C., et al. (eds.) HCII 2020. LNCS, vol. 12425, pp. 688–699. Springer, Cham (2020). https://doi.org/10.1007/978-3-030-60128-7_50
11. Burke, L.A., Hutchins, H.M.: Training transfer: an integrative literature review. Hum. Resour. Dev. Rev. **6**, 263–296 (2007)
12. Hassan, L., Morschheuser, B., Alexan, N., Hamari, J.: First-hand experience of why gamification projects fail and what could be done about it. In: CEUR Workshop Proceedings, pp. 141–150 (2018)
13. Deterding, S.: The lens of intrinsic skill atoms: a method for gameful design. Hum. Comput. Interact. **30**(3–4), 294–335 (2015)
14. Koivisto, J., Hamari, J.: The rise of motivational information systems: a review of gamification research. Int. J. Inf. Manage. **45**, 191–210 (2019)
15. Nicholson, S.: A recipe for meaningful gamification. In: Reiners, T., Wood, L.C. (eds.) Gamification in Education and Business, pp. 1–20. Springer, Cham (2015). https://doi.org/10.1007/978-3-319-10208-5_1
16. Morschheuser, B., Werder, K., Hamari, J., Abe, J.: How to gamify? A method for designing gamification. In: Proceedings of the 50th Annual Hawaii International Conference on System Sciences (HICSS), Hawaii, USA, 4–7 January 2017, pp. 1298–1307 (2017)
17. Hartson, R., Pyla, P.S.: The UX book: Agile UX design for a quality user experience. Morgan Kaufmann, San Francisco (2018)

18. ISO DIS 9241-210. Ergonomics of human system interaction - part 210: Human-centred design for interactive systems. International Organization for Standardization, Switzerland (2019)
19. Gomes, N., et al.: Steptacular: an incentive mechanism for promoting wellness. In: 2012 Fourth International Conference on Communication Systems and Networks (COMSNETS 2012), 3 January 2012, pp. 1–6. IEEE (2012)
20. Li, Y., Hedlind, M., Kjellberg, T.: Usability evaluation of CADCAM: state of the art. Procedia CIRP. **36**, 205–210 (2015)
21. Lindblom, J., Alenljung, B., Billing, E.: Evaluating the user experience of human–robot interaction. In: Jost, C., Le Pévédic, B., Belpaeme, T., Bethel, C., Chrysostomou, D., Crook, N., Grandgeorge, M., Mirnig, N. (eds.) Human-Robot Interaction. SSBN, vol. 12, pp. 231–256. Springer, Cham (2020). https://doi.org/10.1007/978-3-030-42307-0_9
22. Cooper, A., Reimann, R., Cronin, D., Noessel, C.: About Face: The Essentials of Interaction Design. Wiley, Hoboken (2014)
23. Tondello, G.F., Kappen, D.L., Ganaba, M., Nacke, L.E.: Gameful design heuristics: a gamification inspection tool. In: Kurosu, M. (ed.) HCII 2019. LNCS, vol. 11566, pp. 224–244. Springer, Cham (2019). https://doi.org/10.1007/978-3-030-22646-6_16
24. Palmquist, A.: Det spelifierade klassrummet. Studentlitteratur AB (2018)
25. Menezes, J., Gusmão, C., Moura, H.: Risk factors in software development projects: a systematic literature review. Software Qual. J. **27**(3), 1149–1174 (2018). https://doi.org/10.1007/s11219-018-9427-5
26. Chou, Y.-K.: Actionable gamification: Beyond points, badges, and leaderboards. In: Octalysis Media. Packt Publishing Ltd. (2011)
27. Zichermann, G., Cunningham, C.: Gamification by Design. In: Vasa, p. 208. O'Reilly Media, Sebastopol (2011)

Newspapers Do Work: Quick and Effective Entanglement Material for Speculation

Wan-Chen Lee[1,2]([⊠]), Hsiu-Chen Tseng[1], and Rung-Huei Liang[1]

[1] Department of Design, National Taiwan University of Science and Technology, Taipei, Taiwan
zx653612@gmail.com, liang@mail.ntust.edu.tw
[2] Department of Visual and Communication Design, Southern Taiwan University of Science and Technology, Tainan, Taiwan
chenlee@stust.edu.tw

Abstract. This research is motivated by the increasing significance of situated and sketching activities to co-speculate alternative futures. Our purpose is to present newspapers as imaginary material and how they relate to rich speculation in domestic networked-objects with regard to the emerged entanglement experience. As most studies aim at providing representation of everyday life and imaginative triggers as entanglement material for speculation, this research focuses on the relationship between news headlines and evocative objects. We then explore how collaging and sketching with everyday objects, app-icon stickers together with the present and the past newspapers help to speculate the utopian, or dystopian worlds. Findings show that newspapers become an effective catalyst to slightly defamiliarize our daily life and break the inertial thinking. Based on the collages, we design speculative products that explore the diversity of the possible IOT futures. Finally, we present illustrative cases with interpretations and heuristic implications.

Keywords: Speculative design · Newspapers · Entanglement experience · Headline · Internet of Things

1 Introduction

As the technology of Internet of Things becomes increasingly mature, our modern life has been permeated by all sorts of algorithm technology and then the traditional appearance of daily products has turned into the presentation of characters endowed with different functions such as collection, analysis, transmission, translation, etc. Relationship between people and things has become a more complicated form in which they are redefined by each other. Enlightened by agential realism of Barad [1], a scholar of New Materialism, Frauenberger [2, 3], as a scholar of design, believes that man-machine interaction field of the day will also embrace the future trend of entanglement and we are also shaping ourselves to become what we want to be through the technology we create. As a result, the encouragement of speculative method participation in development and mutual competition not only enables us to get the reconfiguration of our vision of the world but also changes the pursuit of technology to a greater focus on the exploration

© Springer Nature Switzerland AG 2021
M. M. Soares et al. (Eds.): HCII 2021, LNCS 12779, pp. 67–86, 2021.
https://doi.org/10.1007/978-3-030-78221-4_5

of how to design a meaningful relation rather than a blind pursuit of the optimization of user experience.

At present, interaction design widely adopts speculative design, future studies, culture probes and other means in the hope that it can offer more possibilities to the future and the speculative thinking can be put into practice in public life in a more concrete way through all sorts of design strategies. At present, our living environment and residential space is full of invisible, hidden or negligible data or messages. A lot of studies are committed to the exploration of how meaningful data messages are displayed via innovative process and methods in creative activities of leading design, such as situated visualization [4] and situated co-speculation [5]. The former presents data messages via all sorts of visual media or sketches including small white boards, tiles, sticky notes, photos, paper cuttings, etc. and embodies the environmental data in real life to think speculatively; the latter enables the designers and participants to conduct a dialogue with familiar household items and imagine them by means of creative collaborative co-speculation [6–8] approach via customized booklets, photos, sketches and notes to offer more diversified materials in combination with usability of schematic drawing, sticky notes and graphic annotation. The aforementioned methods generally visualize data messages to comprehend the relation between data and life and also call for more curiosity and visions towards the future via co-creative approach [5]. However, the other alternative rethinking proposals we propose raise the question from the perspective of arousing personal experience whether co-imagination could be put into practice in a faster and more effective way through abundant graphic resources in daily newspaper. We also explore in the process of collection, cutting, and collage how newspapers influence creative design process in a diversified way and how our imagination about the entanglement relation among internet-connected household items is activated.

In order to understand people's emotional sustenance [9] over household items and explore the entanglement phenomenon in the relation between things and self in the state of Internet of Things, workshop activities are conducted in the manner of research through design [10]. Based on the pluralistic property of the newspaper itself, creative space generated in the form of design workbooks [11] and collage action as same as games are used to enable the participants to unleash their imagination of ordinary household items more freely. At last, the design researchers propose eight speculative design proposals of different types of household internet-connected items through output of speculative result of the newspaper workshop and qualitative interview results.

Our contribution includes: (1) more effective generation of entanglement experience for the participants and expansion of multiple potential of speculation and imagination of household items. (2) manifold visions and creativity showed by partial perspectives [12] in the process of speculation. (3) Promotion that regards newspapers as a daily media can be regarded as the material to trigger entanglement experience to lead us to think, partake in and discuss one or multiple futures more profoundly.

2 Related Works

Situatedness has been widely applied in interaction design field. Much lived experience of feltness [13] and embodiment [14] can be obtained via in-situ investigation in most cases.

In this process, a flow of ideas must be treated as the communication and stimulation of inspiration in the form of design such as visualized sketching or photo collage. This study comprehensively discusses common situated researches on creative ideas in recent years including data-driven product design [15], situated visualization, and situated co-speculation. Inspired by the aforementioned conception activities, in order to break through the existing situation limits of items, this study draws on the workshop of theme of newspaper speculation via app-icon stickers in combination with new and old newspapers and other related materials to understand the participants' imagination about the intelligent functions of household items in the future in the state of internet-connection. We hope that the open-ended design workbook approach, as the form of presentation of speculative imagination can expand and stimulate different inspiration more freely.

2.1 Imagine Data Messages via Convenience of Stickers

In order to think about how to reflect the optimizing orientation of real time data presentation for the purpose of surpassing the product and creatively unearth many new latent possibilities of the interactive objects, Gorkovenko et al. [15] take internet-connected items as the research tool and carry out research on the users so that the experts in academic circles and within the industry can utilize sticky notes in the creative thinking process to try to find out design-related questions from the design items that have been studied and obtain the answers to the questions concerning the design of items from the data material generated by the items to explore the complicated relation between data and human behavior. Finally, the experts conceive new design practice based on the collected data and take the data-driven approach to think about possible futures. As a response to the concept of Futures Cone [16] of Voros and various definitions of future possibilities [17, 18], the experts can also, according to data speculation activities, portrait and imagine the futures of four possibilities, i.e., possible, plausible, probable, and preferable.

Equipment and data of Internet of Things, dynamic combination integrated into a whole, data for understanding our life, various possible potential conditions, and activities using sticky notes are conducive to focus on the topic of discussion to establish definite, meaningful and persistent data-collecting work. However, the activity of thinking in which sticky notes are stuck to the actual design items so that design questions are proposed and creativity is developed will inevitably be subject to some limitations due to obtainability of environmental data and the established intrinsic pattern of the objects. As a result, although the imagination of the future of data-driven products can establish connection and preliminary association between data and daily human activities, moral problems of acquisition of data still have to be solved. Besides, limited proportion of population that consents to collection of such data also affects the width of speculative imagination and special requirements. This approach must seek a breakthrough point that can support human creativity from the existing interactive patterns and relative data materials.

In order to prevent the approach of creative imagination generated by sticking sticky notes to real life items from being limited by conditions of acquiring actual environmental data, we choose app-icon stickers to replace sticky notes to enable the participants to imagine future technical functions of the household items on the basis of the present networked applications. We start from familiar applications that are inseparable from our life because the existing applications have the possibility of continuous development of functions. It enables the participants to imagine the concrete networking functions of the objects rapidly. At the same time, there is some flexible space for adding imagination freely.

2.2 Design Concept Activities of Situated Visualization

Relative data material of intelligent objects generated in the situation must be cross referenced [4:173] with physical environment related to the data and various field conditions. In order to reproduce the prototype of the situated data via creative ideas and sketching activities, Bressa and other scholars of design [4] rethink how to comprehensively apply various sketches, materials and tip text via small presentation to enhance our understanding of context relationship of the actual situation of things and concretize the experience of feeling of things. In their design concept experiment, various media that can form sketches including sticky notes, printed images and several different types of magnetic whiteboards are utilized. Bressa et al. [4:175–176] propose three objective orientations for the design concept activities, i.e. (1) Idea-centered activities in which open-ended creative ideas are encouraged in specific environment and potential design and applications that accelerate fast production are valued. (2) Task-centered activities in which visualized design in accordance with specific tasks is emphasized to actively examine and weigh the relation between actual tasks and potential visualization opportunities. (3) Hardware-centered activities in which the possibility of message visualization is discussed according to specific hardware and the participants are encouraged to pursue ideas in which technical limitation and interactive creativity are compatible with each other.

In activities of situated visualization design, the degree of familiarity of participants towards their situated space will influence the types of ideas they generate. For example, creative ideas generated at home are quite unique; while ideas generated in the office are mainly about general functions of objects. Besides, it is conducive to generation of conception related to the situated space if the ideas are drawn into sketches and placed in the space; however, in the supposition process of such creative ideas, the result of creativity development that takes idea as principal axial sometimes might depends on drawing ability and willingness of the participants. Moreover, task-orientation and hardware-orientation might, on the contrary, become an obstacle for open-ended pluralistic thinking, which will lead to the loss of possible opportunity of some potential design.

This study intends to improve the aforementioned limitations. Firstly, the situated space is transformed into various diversified field domains provided in the newspapers and multiple event contexts to try to draw forth entanglement experience of more freedom that emerges unexpectedly. Secondly, abundant graphic resources of existing newspapers are used to replace mental stress and ability limitation of the participants in the drawing process. Finally, the main objective orientation of our creative ideas is idea-centered and task-centered and the ideas are realized through subsidiary newspaper materials and app-icon stickers.

2.3   Visual Representation of Situated Co-speculation

Bespoke booklet is a speculative method that integrates household items, live-action space environment and concept sketch. Every bespoke booklet is customized for each participant. The purpose of design is to take different houses as the start of imagination of future family of Internet of Things [5]. Integrating with the open-ended form of magazine and design workbook in form, the bespoke booklet enables the designers and participants to conduct co-speculation activities and co-creative activities to obtain more space for reflection and imagination on situation fiction. In the design workshop, the designers will understand issues related to the house history, habits of family members, etc. through exploration of and visit to the living space of the participants. The research team proposes ideas regarding the imaginary family of Internet of Things according to the uniqueness of each family and draw them on the realistic photos of the houses, including comments on works, introduction page made into the booklet, several blank pages of photos with the realistic living space but without annotation so that the participants can draw their own concepts in the booklets.

In the activity of bespoke booklets, the participants are invited to draw their own concepts regarding their personal living space in relative images and photos and provide text description to propose their ideas on intelligent device in environment of Internet of Things that might exist in their own houses. The participants can not only have a dialogue with creative ideas of the designers and share ideas via the bespoke booklets but also have personal reflection on their own living space to propose their imagination. This research team finally conducts semi-structured interviews with the participants to understand their opinions on the content and form of the bespoke booklets and how they think about family relations. In the process, the bespoke booklets can acquire a lot of feedback from the participants, only they have to draw sketches on the booklets to describe their ideas and thus difficulty of creative thinking might be increased due to the capabilities of different participants. At the same time the participants have to wait for a long time to give corresponding feedback, which makes it impossible to fully realize the result of speculation quality in real time.

Situated imagination will be more concretized via the live-action photos of the living environment and objects, sketches and text description. At the same time co-speculation inspires more creative ideas. In the design practice of newspaper speculation, we integrate the aforementioned advantages with real photos and fictional sketches and enable the objects to generate defamiliarization effect [19, 20] out of their own actual context via cutting, mix-and-match and juxtaposition effects of collage so that we can re-understand the familiar things and help us imagine the new possibilities they might have to generate greater creative power.

2.4   Newspaper as Entanglement Material of Speculation

From the above small presentation such as sticky note annotation and situated visualization and concept of bespoke booklet, this research probes how to introduce speculation quality more effectively. As for preliminary design concept work on future internet-connected household items, we choose the common newspapers as the entanglement material. As a combination of a lot of text and pictures, newspaper media are closely linked to public life. Newspapers that seem to be obtained without lifting a finger might be more convenient for the participants to conduct speculative imagination work. In the newspaper layout there are a diversity of life aspects including headline news, global news, society, sports, entertainment, etc. It's easy to resonate with the participants. The digital era is filled with various information but it is difficult for people to have feelings for messages. Attention scarcity phenomenon is also prone to occur. At the present age emphasizing on efficiency, as for newspapers, more importance is attached to accuracy of headline because headlines are the eye of a piece of news. They not only point out the spirit of the messages but also directly influence the readers who will decide whether they want to further read the whole-body text.

A professionally trained journalist will apply questioning method (e.g., 5Ws) in the headline to address the title based on the fact [21:155]. As a result, the news title is somewhat storytelling and appealing. Besides, it also emphasizes precedence of title over text body [21], i.e., high-efficient words that make the readers fully informative in a short period of time must be contained in the title. The wording must be concise and have some news features. In order to master this news feature, the journalists must go through the comparative work in three aspects in the title design [21:155]: (1) Compare the things that are reviewed with other general things in life and find out the difference. (2) Compare the things that are reviewed with similar things that have been reported and find out the novelty of the former ones. (3) Make comparison among different development phases and different aspects of the things that are reviewed and find out the uniqueness of the former ones. To respond to the research on data-driven products, Gorkovenko et al. point out that not all products need data collection [15:10]. It's precisely because the journalists have thought about and compared the things they want to report before choosing them to make the events resonate with the readers and to arouse their desire to read. This research chooses newspapers as the entanglement material in hope of finding out speculation design content that could trigger the experience of the participants from the images and texts of newspapers of news value.

3   Our Study

According to the known situated speculation method, a lot of research has to resort to assistance of pluralistic methods to link the speculative imagination of the participants and thus to get the chance to achieve high-quality speculative design. In order to enable the participants to imagine the future internet-connected interactive functions of household items beyond the frame of their familiar living space and successfully generate personal experience and stories incidentally in the research process, the research combine app-icon stickers with daily newspaper material in hope of getting the most valuable speculation results. The research focuses on intelligent internet-connected functions in the development of household items. Since imagination of the public about future household items is prone to be limited by established impression of the items and they are oriented toward multi-function or function optimization, the design is not able to step out of the original frame and the imagination is easily restricted. As a result, this research replaces the current technology services with the functions of existing functions and take sixty app-icon stickers as the representative material of virtual data. Associations of the participants for interactive conditions and functions of Smart Internet of Things can be added. It's not necessary to stick to hand-drawn work to generate visualization, which is conducive to reflection of the participants on the position of specific intelligent functional services of the objects. We make the app-icon stickers into tags, which are divided into four categories: (1) Online Apps service of company entity. (2) Functional services of built-in software of computer, tablet or cellphone. (3) Life services concerning food, clothes, living, travelling and other aspects. (4) Application services related to communities. In the newspaper speculation activity, the participants can paste the app-icon sticker tags together with the copies of household items in the design workbook. If the type of application tag is not in line with requirement of the participants, they can draw on blank tags by themselves. Through the behavior of pasting, the participants can link the service functions of modern digital technology in reality. Meanwhile, there is some fuzzy imagination space of symbol interpretation. In consequence the participants will generate results of material collage experiment and the qualitative interview will provide brand-new usage context of future objects and relative thoughts. The researchers are able to understand how the participants feel about the activity. This process enables the public to take a fresh look at the household items in their life with familiar and strange experience.

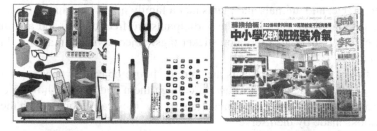

Fig. 1. Present newspaper workshop related materials.

The research process includes in total two times of experience of present newspapers and old-time newspapers for different participants. In terms of entanglement material, each participant will be given one piece of newspaper, copies of photos of household items and one package of app-icon sticker tags so that the participants can present their imagination in the manner of cutting and collage (Fig. 1). We combine newspaper speculation activity (including present newspaper speculation and old-time newspaper speculation) with method of app-icon sticker tags. This research work benefits from the combination of thematic study and design practice work. The researchers conduct qualitative interviews and collate the manuscripts word for word based on each piece of experiment material and then classify the items into different themes according to item types. Finally, the researchers make the speculation proposal to interpret the results. The process in which the participants take part in the workshop and speculation collage experiment and participate in qualitative interviews helps us find out important and effective entanglement experience from field work.

3.1 Architecture and Process of Newspaper Speculation Workshop

In the newspaper speculation workshop, household items are regarded as research objects. The participants will think about the redesign and re-development of the products. In order to guide the participants into the possible narrative context of the objects, we provide newspaper material of the day in the first newspaper speculation workshop in hope that the participants can obtain more chances of personal experience linkage from news events or stories in different pages. The participants in this workshop will get 53 reduction copies of photos of household items and different animals and plants, a complete piece of newspaper of the day (or old newspaper of the theme age), app-icon sticker tags, several sheets of blank A4 paper, clip and paste tools, drawing tools, and other relevant materials. The participants can attend the experiment in form of free cutting and pasting. If the existing tags or articles and newspaper pictures are not enough for the participants to express their ideas, they are encouraged to feel free to draw pictures and add diagrams or visual images and texts so that they can generate mutual entanglement of experience in the process of dialogue with the material and then deduce new speculation thinking:

1. Design issues are induced by the complete piece of newspaper and app-icon sticker tags we provide and household items, including sofa, refrigerator, mirror, tea pot, hair dryer, etc. and animals and plants that a family might have in the house, which are used to facilitate thinking. The participants are free to draw and add materials to the existing materials (app-icon sticker tags, objects, visual images and texts) if necessary.
2. In the first stage, the participants are free to choose objects or newspaper pictures and texts and app-icon sticker tags to collage them and explore how to establish links to household items via the materials so that they can resonate with the design workbooks made by themselves.
3. Each participant has to paste three materials including newspapers, objects and tags in the A4 design workbook and imagine speculative items that are probably to appear in the living space in the future via mutual stimulation of three materials. Household products conceived by the participants themselves can be used when necessary. The participants are free to make creative associations on the blank A4 paper to conduct imagination work of multiple products. A variety of imagination regarding the same item is allowed. Mutual relationship association among different products can also be established.
4. After all kinds of possible speculative imagination and design workbooks are finished, the participants are asked to take part in the semi-structured interview with the designer. Particularly, they will be asked to talk about new design practice of household internet-connected items, daily life vision of usage of this item in the future and their feedback to the whole process of the workshop.
5. Finally, the designers will summarize and sort out eight speculative design interpretation proposals in total from the speculation workshops of present and old-time newspapers according to the speculation experiment and interview results of the participants to describe a possible utopian future or dystopian future.

3.2 Participants

Seven participants took in the experiment in the present newspaper speculation workshop. They are named as PA1 to PA7. Four of them are ordinary office workers and three of them are students that have background in design. They are aged between 23 and 40. Average experimental time is 1 h. The workshop went individually and after each experiment, a 45-min semi-structured interview is arranged so that the participants can give feedback in real time in the experimental process and meanwhile they can discuss the generation process and results of their work with the researchers. The second workshop uses old-time newspapers to conduct speculation. Three participants took in the experiment in total and they are named as PB1 to PB3. They include a student of background in design, an office worker, and a housewife, who are aged between 27 and 31. Except that the workshop provides a complete piece of old newspaper, experiment items, experimental time and experiment content are all the same as those of the present newspaper speculation activity. Overall speaking, we have recruited ten participants in Taipei. There are four males and six females (aged between 23 and 40). In the research, we try to capture various possibilities of entanglement experience in different forms between experiences of groups of different generations and household items, network digital application functions and news events. The purpose is to find out interesting and unique vision and diversity and partial perspectives contained there, in instead of emphasis on selection of participants that represent larger groups.

4 Data Collection and Analysis: News-Headlined Story Text Stimulation

Since the journalists have specifically designed the newspaper headlines in order that the text can attract attention of the consumers and sensational title text can arouse emotional reaction of readers and bring up association of the topic, the participants are prone to indulge in much imagination. For example, PA7: *"Objects are supposed to help humans shrewdly, but seeing some anthropomorphic titles made it seem acceptable for objects to become obtuse and clumsy."* From the results of collage experiment of participants, we find that most of the participants only clip the headlines and demonstrate their entanglement experience via the news headlines together with app-icon sticker tags and household items just as PA3: *"I will read the body text of the news, only I am just interested in the headline. The body text seems to be auxiliary illustration."* Typeface and color change can be used in the news headlines to attract the readers. Therefore, the participants are attracted and their imagination is stimulated to make the speculation of household items via the headline text. Meanwhile thanks to sensational headlines and peculiar opinions, the research experiment is put forward very smoothly and the entanglement of personal experience of the participants is easily linked to create a good deal of speculation items rapidly.

Table 1. Text types of present newspaper headlines.

Types of text headlines	Content of headlines of present newspapers
Question type	Out of breath from time to time? Where did all the time go?
Emotional type	Shocked! Metabolic disorders. Cry for help
Exaggerated witness type	Strongest in the history, 10 billion of read plate for CUE, turn the side, god evolution, running so smoothly, smile resists
Naming of group and generation	Orange generation, youth 2.0
Imperative type	Do not commit suicide, synchronized statement
Urgency	Keep the job, unblock, determine ASAP, lift the ban to be open and free, salvation with sincerity
Creation of new term	Drink water of stories, touching love, from emptiness to relief, big belly takes in all, only un-softheartedness leads to success, change mood with new season
Ironic type	Disqualified time management, post-retirement world is full of difficulties, keeping each other warm, air friends, taunting, henchman, stay at home, facts of crime, make trouble on purpose, all are puzzled
Advertising sentence	Security guards, chat personnel

(*This chart is revised based on the main types of text listed by Robert W. Bly, which are sorted and classified according to the news headlines used in the present newspaper speculation experiment.)

Since all the participants will share the headlines before describing their imagination about the item content in detail in the interview process, we obtain a lot of good feedback from the participants toward the headlines. This research takes basic classification of text creation of Robert W. Bly [22] as reference and summarizes nine text categories based on the headline types used by seven participants in the present newspaper speculation workshop after modification and adjustment. The news headlines used by the participants in the present newspaper speculation experiment are summarized, classified and sorted (Table 1). We find that ironic sentences and words are used by most of people followed by exaggerated, urgent, and combined new terms. We can tell from the above that style of writing and type of the present newspaper headlines all emphasize establishment of connection with the readers in a bid to arouse curiosity and questions of readers. Also because of such features, newspapers show good speculation potential in the workshop experiment activity.

5 Results

In the following part we will introduce modern and nostalgic life themes of the newspaper speculation workshop to describe how the participants imagine the future of household internet-connected items. In the speculation activity taking newspapers as the material, the participants describe use condition of the items when they adopt newspapers in the creative development. By means of two themes of present and past, we find that events in news headlines and life of the participants are entangled. By virtue of detachment effect generated by opinions of others or atmosphere in different ages, personal memories of the participants that are triggered can be unearthed and how the household items become an indispensable part of the life of the participants is explored.

5.1   Present Life: Nowadays Newspaper Speculation

We can see the future in the present newspapers. Through the opinion and insight of journalists, newspapers have become an unusual existence in modern digital life in the era of attention scarcity. We find that compared with news photo, literal title is easier to be adopted by the participants. More than half of them is amazed by the effect created by headlines (Fig. 2, a). For example, PA1: "Diversified content of newspapers speeds up the experiment than expected. I feel more comfortable! I can link the materials freely and I do not worry that I don't have materials to talk about." It seems that the headlines have given life to the household items. For example, PA6: *"It seems that I am creating my own newspapers and journals. The language of the newspapers is so magical as if the items become alive and own many personalities."* The readers can still gain pleasure from reading of newspaper. It gives the readers more options or the reader are able to find news content they never pay attention to and then create unexpected surprises. PA2: *"Sometimes when the headline is right, I feel differently about the whole news. It's fun! Sometimes I will be amazed by my own ideas."* Newspaper materials change the participants into readers of much more initiative instead of passive receivers of fixed information. For example, news events recommended by internet explorer according to personal preference; or particular news channel subscribed by individuals via Really Simple Syndication (RSS) news reader software. PA7: *"I find it's interesting to read newspaper. I will feel something I won't have when I slide the news on cellphone. I will use characters to seek inspiration of the item and then use Apps tags. It's challenging and interesting."* News headlines resonate with personal life experience, which make people jump out of their individually specific isothermal layer. Then cutting, collage and juxtaposition skills are used to draw forth topics on the future household items rapidly. For example, PA4: *"I won't think too much when I am cutting and pasting the materials. The diversified content of newspapers is very helpful to the imaginative linkage. Thanks to Apps tags, I can be more certain of the complete functions of the items."* PA6: *"Apps tags make it easier to illustrate the items. Headlines are a feeling most of the time. But with the assistance of body text and pictures of newspaper, the overall effect makes the headline more vivid as if I am creating my own items and stories while reading newspaper."* The participants can add any type of Apps sticker tag (Fig. 2, b) that hasn't been provided freely by means of sketch drawing. Besides, possible curiosity and questions of the users are also satisfied and set free to be presented in the design workbook (Fig. 2, a-f).

Fig. 2. Experiment results of present newspaper workshop (a. PA1, b. PA3, c. PA3, d. PA4, e. PA5, f. PA7).

Most of the participants interpret some items for which they have feelings and paste them on the paper, but a few people put emphasis on the layout structure, echoing the factors in the picture and sense of wholeness, which in turn affect breadth of the observation of participants, and self-exploration and interpretation of interconnectedness of different items. PA2: "*People are always forgetful. They can't face themselves of the past and the future. As a result, taunt clock will display the possibility of doing something in the future in an ironic and humorous way. When the clock is ticking, they suddenly realize that they have lost freedom.*" Data come from human life but humans are mocked by data across time and space. PA2 interprets the picture as "*a concept of selection and reincarnation.*" "*Life is like a play that is played repeatedly.*" It makes the whole layout storytelling interesting and cautionary as well (Fig. 3).

Fig. 3. Present newspaper speculation-layout of collage case. (PA2)

5.2 Nostalgic Life: Old days Newspaper Speculation

In the part of old-time newspaper workshop, we utilize three pieces of complete old newspaper of different years. They are separately: the day of death of former president Chiang Kai-Shek (1975/04/05), the day of the return of Hong Kong to China (1997/07/01) and the day of advocacy of rotation of ruling parties (2000/3/10). Old-time newspaper speculation attempts to find out difference of perspectives in seeing things through review of newspapers with major issues of the day. When newspapers of old-time atmosphere are matched with current household items, unusual imagination of possible future tends to be stimulated. Most of the participants feel the sense of history displayed by old newspapers and they will look forward to the look of its combination with modern items (Fig. 4). PB1: "In the face of the present, it seems that today is derived from the past and I can imagine the future through time and space of the past." PB2: "Although newspapers of the past are not colorful and don't have exaggerated typefaces, they have sentiment for the old times a color left by the time."

Fig. 4. Experiment results of old newspaper workshop. (a. PB1, b. PB2, c. PB3)

When the participants get the newspaper of the day of the return of Hong Kong to China, they feel that the past is very close to the present and they would like to know how the past defines technology. At the same time, PB3 combines Messenger App tags with ovens for daily-use to respond to the headline of dialogue and declarative linguistic appeal (Fig. 4, c). PB1 conceives the inspiration for the whole set of funeral ceremony and process in the future via the report of the death of Chiang Kai-shek. The music-playing action of funeral musicians is linked to modern Spotify sticker tags. The formation of the layout is like the combination of journal or electronic book cover (Fig. 4, a). PB1: *"Looking back at the age of death of former President Chiang Kai-Shek is like reading history book. I will find materials in the newspaper and think about the possibility of application companies developing or providing new services in the future."*

6 Analysis of Speculation Interpretation Proposal

This research sorts and summarizes items liked by each participant and homogeneous item. In the present newspaper workshop and old-time newspaper workshop, particular household items are chosen and the researchers re-render eight speculation interpretation proposals in total based on the newspaper speculation workshop experiment and semi-structured qualitative interviews. In comparison with newspaper collage prototype of the participants, four of the eight speculation interpretation proposals will be deeply analyzed and discussed in the following part according to four categories of themes: (1) self-mockery-taunt clock. (2) stress relief interaction-hose of live streaming of eating. (3) ceremony communication-censer toaster. (4) spiritual sustenance-noise radio.

6.1 Self-mockery-Taunt Clock

The participant jumps out of the linear development of time expression that should be abode by through the icon of clock and utilizes speculation collage of distinct personality to integrate the concept with future clock of simple pattern. The original area for time display shrinks. More importantly, various images and texts like riddles emerge as if living in an ironic house, which presents contradictory feelings of co-existence in different time and space as a whole (Fig. 5, according to PA2). As described by PA2: "People are always forgetful. They can't face themselves of the past and the future. As a result, taunt clock will display the possibility of doing something in the future in an ironic and humorous way. When the clock is ticking, they suddenly realize that they have lost freedom." Taunt clock is able to remind us to face life again from the bottom of our heart. Life is like a movie and a dream. In face of inertia that people always follow the same old disastrous road, acceptance of sarcasm of the clock from time to time makes us remember to slow down in the hurried technological life in the future, know how to listen to various voices and take a look at every choice we make in the past.

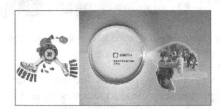

Fig. 5. Taunt clock.

6.2 Stress Relief Interaction-Plant Host of Live Streaming of Eating

As network platforms are flourishing, many animals and plants also have their own social accounts in the future and they can communicate with the public through live streaming and tweets. Meanwhile humans also look forward to exploring more ideas that are different from theirs. The green and peaceful image of the plants are displayed in the channel of YouTube. Sense of flow is created through the internal walls of the plant. Video subtitles at the bottom of the image are turned on, showing the consciousness of the plant itself or the interpretive words provided by the platform for the public and demonstrating a possible interactive mode of the occupation belonged to plant host of live streaming of eating in the future. (Fig. 6, according to PA6) as described by PA6:

"Seeing the words of synchronized statement, it reminds me of live streaming. Perhaps the plant can utilize their advantage of slowness and healing effect to earn a place in the circle of live streaming. In a speeding-up era, plants might become necessities for our soul in the future. If people can communicate in a relaxed way, there will be many different interactive modes in family life!" The speculation proposals of the researchers present many stress relief methods obtained by people from the plants via interactive expression of plant showed in live streaming. In future era when everything can be a host of live streaming, humans will learn how to live slowly from the plants and readjust the pace and frequency of life.

Fig. 6. Plant host of live streaming of eating.

6.3   Ceremony Communication-Censer Toaster

Thinking out of the frame of kitchen items that can only be used to prepare food, the time of waiting for food is transformed into an interactive process of Buddha worship. The hot smoke from the food that is baked can create pious atmosphere. People and the god can communicate with each other in rituals via vague lines on the toast and religious belief and folkways are presented in a way of both solemnity and ordinariness (Fig. 7, according to PB3). As described by PB3: *"Like the artistic conception of headline words of Changeful Situation is Emerging Rapidly, people in the future also have pious rituals to integrate spiritual sustenance with daily food. Toasters replacing censer are more aligned with practicability in the future. Pressing the button of toast baking represents lighting an incense stick. The popping toast is filled with blessings. sacrificial and praying content that people want to express more than anything else can only be conveyed through dialogue modes different from the past."* From the icon of Messenger software with which the participant endows the toaster, we will find the significance of this speculation proposal for dialogue function. In folk religious viewpoints of god worship in Taiwan, incense sticks are the media between gods and people. They are the food for the gods and also the demonstration of their power. Gods worshiped by people with incense sticks will be more capable to protect and bless people. As an indispensable item in most of the families in Taiwan culture, censer is not just a symbol in rituals. Sacrificial behaviors in the living space will also be transformed into a more life-styled communication mode to establish new relationship between gods and people.

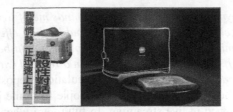

Fig. 7. Censer toaster.

6.4 Spiritual Sustenance-Noise Radio

Radios of eternal noise is a selling point? Radios are monitored by state machinery. Freedom is no longer common. People will cherish the listening of vague messages more than ever (Fig. 8, according to PB2). As described by PB2: "Future might become a controlled era when people are no longer able to listen to music freely. When we want to listen to different music channels, a lot of fuzzy voices will be mingled. Although we have radios that have the same entity as the past, it is noise no matter how we turn the button. Buttons are also like the so-called freedom. There is only decorative meaning. But it makes us to cherish them more…" Thinking about the past of the return of Hongkong in comparison with the current turbulent situation of it, the participant is particularly touched and naturally thinks about the topic of freedom. In this speculation proposal, the researchers present possible functions of radios ironically by means of technique of expression of product catalog on purpose. In the catalog headline, it seems that the radio makes people know everything. Only in actual experience of the product when people find that reality is a restricted possession. Many buttons are only nominal symbols. Finally, their only material meaning is message. Nothing more.

Fig. 8. Noise radio.

7 Discussion

Newspaper itself has many life stories so it can provide the researchers with more abundant entanglement experience data in face of much diversified experience of existing things. It contributes to the participants to conduct design activities of higher speculation quality for the everyday items. Experience of the participants is evoked by the news events and is integrated into the thinking about the specified speculation on items. On the other hand, newspapers contain a lot of news events and narrative text of judgment, which is closely linked to literary techniques to which Mark Blythe [23:5403] pays close attention, including plots (linked events), story (a sequence of events), and narrative (a broader definition including judgement). Reflection on how to make humans have feelings for items will influence our speculative imagination ability for items. Due to its own characteristics, newspaper always take news samples from events of topicality in people's life and take them as one of the materials for observation, activity trace, memory record or entanglement. No matter the newspaper is new or old, it can be a good activator that not only triggers speculation of the participants about internet-connected items but also contributes to the interaction designers to think creatively in conception activities.

7.1 Exploration of Situation Diversity from Partial Perspectives

Although it's very convenient to get information and collect inspiration via news reader software in network era, newspaper is still a tool to spark inspiration. In a context with interlaced multiple relationship, a relatively objective and dynamic subject can only be constructed through consistent mapping with partial perspectives. Since collage of news-paper speculation is extremely experimental, it is certainly unfinished and open to some degree. This design activity responds to Haraway's affirmation of partial perspective-"*There are only highly specific visual possibilities, each with a wonderfully detailed, active, partial way of organizing worlds*" [12:583]. The participants produce a lot of creative associations in the process of newspaper speculation they take part in person-ally via observation of other people's results of newspaper speculation experiment. The researchers choose items that impress the participants most from their responding mate-rials and rich diversified newspaper speculation visual cases to present the speculation design proposals they want to interpret.

News headlines add storytelling dramatic effect to life items. Collage images of newspaper speculation are like some kind of manufacturing machine of story context that can stimulate designers' or other participants' imagination ability to make the partic-ipants further produce the possibility of What If thought experiment [24] unconsciously. For example, participant PA2: "*If the clock is able to mock the user and force people to face themselves again in different time and space, how will people and things interact with each other?*" Or participant PA7: "*If censers can make things go smoothly, can we move them from the prayer table through sports without easily being limited by original functions or image of the item?*".

7.2 Diffraction of Multiple Futures from the Past Era

One can anticipate the near future by using the present newspapers. We can also use newspapers of the past to rethink history of the past as if we are having a dialogue with the past. Soro, Taylor and Brereton [25:1] believe that "*the past can be potential material for re-design.*" Old newspaper speculation attempts to find out differences of perspectives in seeing things through review of newspapers with major issues of the day. When newspapers of old-time atmosphere are matched with current household items, unusual imagination of possible future tends to be stimulated. For example, when funeral ceremony of political figure is linked to current pneumonia epidemic situation, people will associate them with the future funeral; or they will have more feelings of dependency on spiritual items. The comparison of news of the return of Hong Kong in 1997 with the present turbulent society of Hong Kong and protest for democracy and freedom also make people produce all sorts of dystopian imagination. Utilizing design, we can "*not only shape the future but also shape the past*" [25:9]. Just like what expounded in diffractive methodology [1] proposed by neo-materialism philosopher Barad based on interference phenomenon in physics. She reminds us that the interaction among all things is intra-action and entanglement within interaction among substances should be taken more seriously. That means intertwined and inseparable mutual interaction of entities instead of pre-existing different entities that interact with each other makes them exist and show themselves. Just like the future in face of different possibilities, the past is also a dynamic, multiple and subjective existence. Seeing the future through the past, relationship between them has a possibility of constant mutual negotiation and change.

8 Conclusion and Future Work

This article points out the importance of categories and quality of entanglement material as newspapers are taken as the entanglement material. Rich entanglement materials are able to inspire the participants' experience of the living situation and the categories of entanglement materials will affect the orientation of speculation results. This research puts forward that speculative thinking not only relies on linkage between items and functions but also needs entanglement material that can be linked to personal experience. Future items have multiple possibilities just as the present newspapers are able to produce utopian imagination of linear future; old-time newspapers are like archaeological work in nostalgic history of the past, which on the contrary brings about a sense of dystopian and contradictory time conflict.

Through comparison of workshop experimental process, we illustrate that newspaper has abundant daily events and rich story texts and diversified entanglement experience resources; while Apps sticker tags anchor the functions of household internet-connected items. They complement each other in the speculation process. This research finds that the generation of speculative thinking not only provides linkage between situation and co-speculation but also rearranges life context to produce a sense of alienation and then stimulate speculative imagination through news collage experiment for example in the deliberately operated process in the boundary strip of familiarity and strange feelings. This article proposes relative speculative design interpretation proposals based on the results of newspaper speculation experiment and qualitative interview data in the design practice. The article not only reflects on conception activity of speculative design but also discusses the futurity of household internet-connected items.

From the experimental process we find that newspapers have much reuse value and speculation potential. Therefore, we can regard whether there are enough entanglement experience resources as the key issue. This research recommends newspaper as a good entanglement material in the future, which can be used flexibly in preliminary conception activity before speculation design. We should also attach great importance to observation of the process in which experts in different areas transform newspaper speculation experiments into overall interpretation of speculation proposals with creativity. At the same time, the power of co-speculation should be put in good use to give enough chances to the participants or researchers to share their own speculation experience and ideas with each other and to raise questions or interpret speculation results of others. It's believed that creativity will be inspired and developed in a deeper way. We also suggest that new speculative approach experiments and relative design research be taken based on daily newspaper as the entanglement material to respond to future indispensable interaction design trend in terms of entanglement experience and multiple future.

Acknowledgement. This research was supported in part by the Ministry of Science and Technology of Taiwan (MOST 107–2410-H-011-018-MY2).

References

1. Barad, K.: Meeting the Universe Halfway: Quantum Physics and the Entanglement of Matter and Meaning, 2nd edn. Duke University Press Books, Durham (2007)
2. Frauenberger, C.: Entanglement HCI-The Next Wave? ACM Trans. Comput. Hum. Interact. (TOCHI) **27**(1), 2:1–2:27 (2019)
3. Frauenberger, C.: Entanglements. ACM Trans. Comput. Hum. Interact. **27**(1), 74–75 (2020). https://doi.org/10.1145/3364998
4. Bressa, N., Wannamaker, K., Korsgaard, H., Willett, W., Vermeulen, J.: Sketching and ideation activities for situated visualization design. In: Proceedings of the 2019 on Designing Interactive Systems Conference (DIS 2019), New York, NY, USA, pp. 173–185. ACM (2019). https://doi.org/10.1145/3322276.3322326
5. Desjardins, A., Key, C., Biggs, H. R., Aschenbeck, K.: Bespoke booklets: a method for situated co-speculation. In: Proceedings of the 2019 on Designing Interactive Systems Conference (DIS 2019), New York, NY, USA. pp. 697–709. ACM (2019). https://doi.org/10.1145/332 2276.3322311
6. DiSalvo, C., Jenkins, T., Lodato, T.: Designing speculative civics. In: Proceedings of the 2016 CHI Conference on Human Factors in Computing Systems (CHI 2016), pp. 4979–4990 (2016). https://doi.org/10.1145/2858036.2858505
7. Wakkary, R., et al.: Morse things: a design inquiry into the gap between things and us. In: Proceedings of the 2017 Conference on Designing Interactive Systems (DIS 2017), pp. 503–514 (2017). https://doi.org/10.1145/3064663.3064734
8. Wakkary, R., Oogjes, D., Lin, H. W. J., Hauser, S.: Philosophers living with the tilting bowl. In: Proceedings of the 2018 CHI Conference on Human Factors in Computing Systems (CHI 2018), pp. 94:1–94:12 (2018). https://doi.org/10.1145/3173574.3173668
9. Turkle, S., (ed.).: Evocative Objects: Things We Think With. MIT Press, Cambridge (2007)
10. Zimmerman, J., Forlizzi, J., Evenson, S.: Research through design as a method for interaction design research in HCI. In: Conference on Human Factors in Computing Systems - Proceedings, January, pp. 493–502 (2007). https://doi.org/10.1145/1240624.1240704
11. Gaver, W.: Making spaces: how design workbooks work. In: Proceedings of the 2011 CHI Conference on Human Factors in Computing Systems (CHI 2011), New York, NY, USA, pp. 1551–1560. ACM (2011). https://doi.org/10.1145/1978942.1979169
12. Haraway, D.: Situated knowledges: the science question in feminism and the privilege of partial perspective. Feminist Stud. **14**(3), 575–599 (1988). https://doi.org/10.2307/3178066
13. McCarthy, J., Wright, P.: Technology as Experience. MIT Press, Cambridge (2004)
14. Dourish, P.: Where the Action Is. MIT Press, Cambridge (2001)

15. Gorkovenko, K., Burnett, D. J., Thorp, J.K., Richards, D., Murray-Rust, D.: Exploring the future of data-driven product design. In: Proceedings of the 2020 CHI Conference on Human Factors in Computing Systems (CHI 2020), New York, NY, USA, pp. 1–14. ACM (2020). https://doi.org/10.1145/3313831.3376560

16. Voros, J.: A generic foresight process framework. Foresight 5(3), 10–21 (2003). https://doi.org/10.1108/14636680310698379

17. Amara, R.: The futures field: functions, forms, and critical issues. Futures 6(4), 289–301 (1974). https://doi.org/10.1016/0016-3287(74)90072-X

18. Amara, R.: The futures field: searching for definitions and boundaries. Futurist 15(1), 25–29 (1981)

19. Bell, G., Blythe, M., Sengers, P.: Making by making strange: defamiliarization and the design of domestic technologies. ACM Trans. Comput. Hum. Interact. (TOCHI) 12(2), 149–173 (2005). https://doi.org/10.1145/1067860.1067862

20. Bardzell, J., Bardzell, S.: Humanistic HCI. Synthesis Lectures on Human-Centered Informatics. Morgan and Claypool Publisher (2015)

21. Wang, C.-Y.: A few words on precedence of title over text body in news writing. North. Econ. Trade 9, 154–155 (2009)

22. Bly, R.W.: The Copywriter's Handbook: A Step-By-Step Guide to Writing Copy That Sells, 4th edn. St. Martin's Griffin, New York (2020)

23. Blythe, M.: Research fiction: storytelling, plot and design. In: Proceedings of the 2017 CHI Conference on Human Factors in Computing Systems (CHI 2017), New York, NY, USA, pp. 5400–5411. ACM (2017). https://doi.org/10.1145/3025453.3026023

24. Dunne, A., Raby, F.: Speculative Everything: Design, Fiction, and Social Dreaming. MIT Press, Cambridge (2013)

25. Soro, A., Taylor, J. L., Brereton, M.: Designing the past. In: Proceedings of CHI EA 2019 on Human Factors in Computing Systems. Glasgow, Scotland UK, New York, NY, USA. alt10, pp. 1–10. ACM (2019). https://doi.org/10.1145/3290607.3310424

Changes of Designers' Roles Based on Self-organizing Design Institutions

Wenjing Li[1]([✉]) [iD], Jia Liu[2,3,4] [iD], Yinan Zhang[1], and DanDan Yu[1]

[1] Art and Design, Academy, Beijing City University, Beijing, China
[2] School of Intellectual Property of Nanjing, University of Science and Technology, Nanjing, Jiangsu, China
lyuuka@aliyun.com
[3] Jiangsu Research Center for Intellectual Property Development, Nanjing, Jiangsu, China
[4] Jiangsu Copyright Research Center, Nanjing, Jiangsu, China

Abstract. The designer is the core dominating force of a design activity. In industrial society, production conditions with machining as the core have made the design activity a small part of production and established a design - manufacture mechanism in which the designer can play a role only in some links. This paper tries to build a model about distributed self-organizing design institutions in the information era, displaying how designers complete their work in this more flexible system: not only design work but also other work required by project operation, which should have been assumed by other departments or employees in a traditional enterprise organizational structure. In the new design organization, designers are no longer a role being employed and managed. Instead, they can work more freely, actively and creatively.

Keywords: Self-organizing · Design community · Maker

1 Introduction

Can design totally depend on a certain designer? The answer to this problem is no from the very beginning professional designers came into being.

In industrial society, the requirement about mass production has led to very delicate division of labor in society. With its initiative being repressed and exploited and absolute rationality becoming the dominating force, the design subject has become a "screw" in the overall social machine. During a certain period, design has broken away from its creative core and become a tool of production and manufacturing. As industrialized operation is moved from production workshops to the office of a designer, the gradually delicate division of labor has led to a complicated management situation of the enterprise organization. The completion of design achievements is not totally controlled by the designer himself. Instead, managers, salespersons, purchasers and marketing counselors will affect production selection of ultimate products.

In the era of mass-decentralized transmission based on internet and computer technology, the mode of information transmission has turned from one-to-many to many-to-many and the overall social structure is developing from perpendicularity to flattening.

M. M. Soares et al. (Eds.): HCII 2021, LNCS 12779, pp. 87–99, 2021.
https://doi.org/10.1007/978-3-030-78221-4_6

Therefore, design is no longer a privilege of professionals. Instead, computer programs, 3D printing, open source software and hardware can help ordinary people to realize their design dream. Superficially, it seems to have come back to the handicraft design stage with craftsmen as the design subject, in which, design activities, from conception, drafting, drawing to forming, are independently completed by some groups and design has come back to the overall process from thinking to practice. Designers are reconnected with each other in a new distributed self-organizing structure.

The Witkey mode and crowd-sourcing mechanism appearing after 2000 and the subsequent maker community are embryos of the new organization mode. In particular, after 2010, maker community, Fablab and community-type embedding and self-organized design tribe have become fresher forms of design organization. The decentralization of the organization system has not caused isolation. On the contrary, it has promoted the development of collaboration and design innovation, making designers able to engage in design activities more freely and actively in the new organization structure.

2   Roles of Designers in the Organization Structure

2.1   Repressed Craftsman in Agrarian Age

During the long handicraft period, China established the system of Carving names on Utensils, a rigorous management mechanism by relying on the administrative system. A whole set of systematized standard practices were established to unify all sorts of handmade utensils for the convenience of supervision and accountability. In this situation, craftsmen are only subjects to be managed. They have no ownership on their own creations, let alone intellectual property rights (Fig. 1).

Fig. 1. "Nineteenth year, Xiangbang (Chief Minister) Wan" and its inscriptions

From the pre-Qin period to Ming and Qing Dynasties, the development of Carving names on Utensils basically underwent the following three stages:

- During the pre-Qin period, inscriptions were usually carved on significant utensils like articles used for sacrificing or etiquette. Usually, the name of the owner or presenter would be carved on the utensil. During this stage, names carved on utensils were basically names of owners rather than names of craftsmen.
- In the Qin Dynasty, names, territories or positions of supervisors and producers would be carved on utensils. Just take the existing Emperor Qinshihuang's Terra-Cotta Warriors as an example. Surnames of the producers or section chief (head of a craftsmen's team, origin (central official workshop or private workshop), territories of craftsmen and counts would be carved on arms, necks, breastplates, foot boards, robe hemlines or hairpins of different terra-cotta warriors [1].
- Carving names on Utensils gradually became a stipulated system. Weapons, city-wall bricks and daily articles for aristocrats would be carved with a group of names, including names of the supervisor - chief maker - administrative officers/technical management officers - section chief - detailed craftsmen [2]. If a utensil involves different working procedures or assembled from different parts made by different workers, then craftsmen's names of different working procedures or different parts would be carved on it. For example, the eared lacquer cup from Han dynasty tombs of Pingba County were carved with names of nine people in total, including craftsmen of different working procedures such as body preparation, painting, gold plating, drawing, polishing and maintenance and the name of the section chief (Fig. 2).

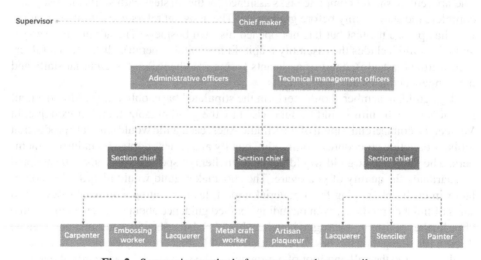

Fig. 2. Sequencing method of names carved on utensils.

2.2 Alliance of Craftsmen for Survival

The original craftsmen were linked by blood relationship. In ancient China, people were specially divided into "scholar, farmer, artisan and merchant" and the craftsmanship and social identity of artisans would be passed from generation to generation. It was also the case in ancient Europe. Though guilds existed as occupational organizations beyond family enterprises as from the ancient Greek period, their development were restricted by the state political system. It was not until the Middle Ages that they greeted their golden period, during which, the growing industrial and commercial operators would safeguard their group interest through an autonomous guild organization. "Various occupational groups would supplement original family and neighborly groups with a completely new set of relations and responsibilities." [3] Gasparo Contarini, an Italian thinker in the 16th century once commented on guilds in the Middle Ages, "For how many trades or occupations (in the Middle Ages), there would be an equal number of organizations (companies) formed by (craftsmen). Each organization had its specific laws to guide daily operation activities of craftsmen. The management organizations they chose on their own could not only meet interest appeals of the members but also settle interest disputes between them." [4].

An artisan can voluntarily join the guild as an independent individual based on his professional skills and qualification. They can be divided into three levels, i.e. master, assistant and apprentice depending on their skills and qualifications. The guild master would be responsible for attending to apprentices in skill teaching and daily life. The apprentice should complete tasks assigned by the master, learn skills modestly and complete the show ability before graduation. The assistant refers to a senior apprentice, who has passed the test but has not opened his own business. The administrative system of a guild includes the assembly (capitolium/capitol generali), chief official (aldermen/warden/gastaldo), court of assistants (committee/banca) and secretarial staffs and messengers acting as auxiliary officers.

In a guild, a member should perform the stipulated basic obligations. Moreover, all products made by him would be supervised by the guild organization. For example, in Venice, the commercial capital of the Middle Ages, each guild would stipulate production tools, production procedures, commodity quality and styles adopted by industrial members: The glass maker guild would demand smelters of specific materials to be adopted to guarantee the quality of glassware. The shoemaker guild would identify division of labor in each link ranging from material import, leather cutting, component sewing to sales of finished products, even including detailed guidance about concrete methods like "For leather polishing, the rugged leather should be burnished in water first and then be dried with sunlight or torches.", restriction about leather shoe styles like "They should be able to wrap the calf and foot of a grownup at the same time.", standards about price intervals like "The price of boots made of goat skin should be the highest." and so on [5].

Also called trade association in China, the guild organization is related to non-local business trade. The "Hang" (row) in "Hanghui" (guild), originally meaning a row of shops in a state-run concentrated market, now refers to an industry selling commodities of the same type. Stores of the same "industry" may be scattered in different places of a city, which is caused by decomposition of the system of workshops and stores. Closely related to local authorities in a feudal society, guild organizations in China needed to supply articles to governments and serve as forced labor on a regular basis and at the same time, had the nature of craftsman combo and business association.

2.3   Artists Employed in the Industrial Age

In the initial stage of industrialized development, division of labor in manufacturers was very elaborate. The space for specific workers to control product type, quality and materials were compressed to the lowest. Some workers like patternmakers in the ceramic manufacturing industry became controllers of product styles but their growing process was nothing different from that of ordinary workers and they hadn't received good artistic training. The styles of products became diversified and strange, which can be evidenced by products of Eclecticism in the Victorian era. Some enterprises began to solve this problem by employing artists beyond their own industry as patternmakers. The neoclassical style formed in the 1760–1770s by Wedgwood, a famous British ceramic brand was transmitted by bossage of classical revival spirit made by the artist John Flaxman. After Flaxman completed designs in his dwelling in London, they were posted to Etruria, where the Wedgwood factory was located. It was one of the symbols of early design occupation that design was separated from manufacturing in physical sense. In the opinion of Adrian Forty [6], there are no essential differences between the professional design activities engaged by Raymond Loewy and Henry Dreyfuss in 1820s-to combine some concept or thought with factory processing and production technologies and the work of Flaxman during his era.

However, artists in a modern enterprise have adapted to elaborate division of labor and standardized production very soon, thus successfully turning themselves into screws on the production line. As compared with artistic and social design done by William Morris in the latter half of the 19th century, those making a living by choosing design as their career become more and more powerless about "design" itself.

Designers always talk about their outstanding work in various cases. For example, they will talk about their creation steps, views about some style; attempt to create a new product, their working methods and so on and so forth. Sometimes, even a complete set of industrial design procedures (just as Norman Bel Geddes did in the early 20th century) has been formed. However, who decides whether a product can enter people's daily life is not the designer himself but the entrepreneur. Before each product is ultimately decided to be thrust into operation, there will be alternatives of several versions at least - for fabric or print, this figure may multiply by 100. However, who has the ultimate decision-making power is by no means the designer himself or the design team. Just as the following figure shows, the work of a professional designer is restricted to a very small section (Fig. 3).

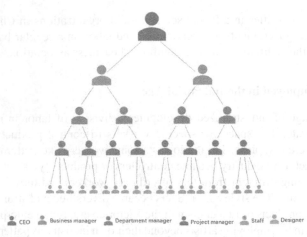

CEO   Business manager   Department manager   Project manager   Staff   Designer

Fig. 3. Organization structure generally adopted by industrial enterprises.

3 Model About Self-organizing Institutions

3.1 Knowledge Exchange Based on Internet

Knowledge exchange is the foundation of a self-organizing design institution. As early as around 2000, a new working mode called Crowdsourcing or Witkey[1] emerged in the United States, China and other countries. Innovation tasks will be released on platforms by internet. The subsequent development includes the cloud design platform, makerspace, alliance of designers and other forms, most of which come from the conception about the flat power structure in the era of mass decentralization rather than a continuation of the top-down pyramid enterprise structure. Such an organization form has reserved sufficient room for personal development and improvement of designers (Table 1).

Among the above different forms, knowledge sharing websites and reward for task websites appeared earlier (Wikipedia and InnoCentive were both set in 2001), and then the knowledge sales form. Reward for task websites could be evolution of the home-based working form for senior professionals in the late 1980s.

In comparison with crowdsourcing websites of reward for task, task release in crowdsourcing websites of knowledge sales can be completed by any user. However, the releaser can only provide task purposes and detailed requirements. The task receiver can

---

[1] These two concepts appear in China and Western countries at the same time. Feng Liu has successively published articles about the new form of online work named Witkey such as *Search Engine's Dilemma and Countermeasureson* and *The Application of Knowledge Management in the Internet——Witkey Mode in China* in his personal blog since 2005. Jeff Howe coined the word 'Crowdsourcing' in a 2006 article for Wired magazine to describe the way in which the Internet has broken down traditional employer/employee relationships to create vibrant new enterprises that are 'staffed' by informal, often large gatherings of enthusiasts. In some ways, Witkey shares same connotation with Crowdsoucing. That is, enterprises use the Internet to distribute work, find ideas or solve technical problems, while users can freely decide whether to pay time and labor costs to obtain value.

Table 1. Four types of crowdsourcing websites.

	Platform	Task releaser		Participant		Transaction contents			Case
	Charge or not	Whether some people release tasks	Whether releasers are fixed	Team or individual	Whether professional background is required	Digital contents	Entity contents	Commercial value	
Knowledge sharing	No	No	No	Individual	No	Yes	No	Small	http://wikipedia.org/ https://baike.baidu.com/
Knowledge sales	Yes	Yes	No	Individual	No	Yes	No	Relatively small	https://www.freelancer.com/ https://beijing.zbj.com/
Reward for task	Yes	Yes	Yes	Team	Yes	Yes	Maybe yes	Relatively large	https://www.innocentive.com/
Design service	Yes	No	No	Individual	Maybe yes	Yes	Yes	Relatively small	https://www.tezign.com/

submit different days and prices according to the task requirements and will not start his work until the task releaser selects him through assessment. To a large extent, it can avoid waste of intellectual resources caused by the situation that many participants are busy for one project but at last only one person gets paid.

Apart from the above forms, more and more governments or commonweal organizations adopt the crowdsourcing mode to seek solutions to public issues such as global warming, aging society and environmental pollution treatment. For example, Climate CoLab [7] is using the crowdsourcing mode to obtain proposals to deal with global climate change.

3.2 Self-organizing Design Institution

Organization Scale. With the development of creative industry, many small and medium-sized processing enterprises begin to integrate designer resources, forming workshops with a certain design and customization capacities. With professional processing technologies and advantages in specific areas, these workshops can provide customized services based on local maker communities. These workshops connected with maker communities will also hold activities similar to open days to attract people from all walks of life to know about their resources. For example, many wood processing workshops and metal processing factories on the outskirts of Beijing have established cooperative relationship with various industrial art studios in 798 Community and Caochangdi Community. Design organizations of workshop type can provide design services to small and medium-size enterprises by relying on their design skills and designers can change their working places according to their own wills. Therefore, the organization scale is relatively scattered.

Promoted by internet, personal makers or workshops gradually converge to become a community. Designers with a common goal begin to build a design team to complete a larger design project through collaboration. Therefore, design organizations of makerspace type gradually come into being. With the gradual development of their scales, some design makerspaces have maintained their positioning as a gathering place of fans or common work site, some begin to assume the function of skill training oriented to their community or city and some will support project development of creative teams and make product incubation through providing sites, tools and equipments and coordinating different resources. The scale of a makerspace is usually associated with financial support. A team with a small scale will assume project R&D, realization of prototypes and product iteration and release. A team with a larger scale can coordinate more resources or even obtain policy or financial support from the government. These design organization can usually advance projects until their products enter the market and perform long-term operation.

Under this mode, when a designer is responsible for a new design project, he can cooperate with other designers of relevant professions in the organization freely as project organizer and manager. Therefore, small design teams are formed inside the design organization. In this design team, each designer can assume several posts according to his capacity and specialty or even follow up several design projects. This situation can exactly explain the advantages of a distributed self-organizing design institution: Designers with different discipline backgrounds can produce good designs through mutual collaboration and reasonable division of labor for the same project target and with no need to waste energies on administrative affairs. The self-organizing design structure has changed the top-down hierarchical management system and terminated the leader-member relationship between designers. However, the nature of flat management makes it harder to form a greater scale. In general, a distributed self-organizing design institution has a dozen or scores of people (Fig. 4).

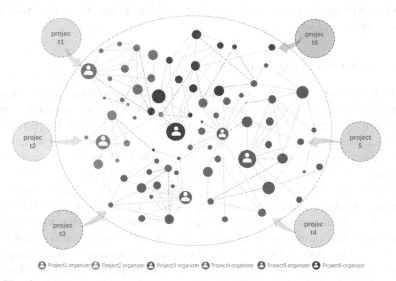

Fig. 4. Schematic diagram for composition of self-organizing design institutions

Staff Composition. Staffs in a traditional design organization are usually composed of several departments, each of which has its own managers. Such a staff composition is relatively complicated and the internal staffs will perform their own functions. Therefore, uneven distribution of design tasks, hindered communication and low working efficiency are frequently encountered. By comparison, the staff composition of a distributed self-organizing design institution is usually formed through free association of designers based on the project and there is a corresponding project organizer. The main tasks of the organizer are project undertaking, integration between sectors, coordination and communication and task assigning. The participating designers will accept tasks according to their own professional skills and specialty. In addition, administrative staffs and legal counsels can also be designers inside the organization. However, for intricate administrative and legal problems, part-time professionals can be employed to solve them. Therefore, the percentage of staff composition of a distributed self-organizing design institution is generally as follows: about 90% of designers of different professions and 10% of administrative and legal staffs (Fig. 5).

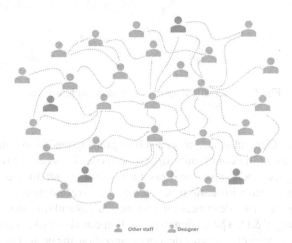

Fig. 5. Percentage of staff composition in self-organizing institutions

Procedure of Project Implementation. In the institution model, implementation of one design project requires one project principal for overall distribution. Just take design commission for a tea brand as an example. At first, the project organizer chooses 3 graphic designers, 2 interior designers and the operation secretary in the same institution to form a team. The group also invites scholars studying tea lifestyles. Based on spot investigation, it makes an intensive sorting of the material library. The graphic designers have completed the design of the brand logo, major color scheme and main graphs. The interior designers have systematically participated in designing the brand flagship store. In the stage of creative generation, the design team will help the design project to select targeted users, make creative collection and invite targeted users to participate in design decision-making. After the project is completed, the design team will draw a design commission and realize revenue transformation in the industrial chain. In this process, there is no hierarchical relationship between designers. Designers will play a role according to their specialty in different procedures and work together to complete the design project (Fig. 6).

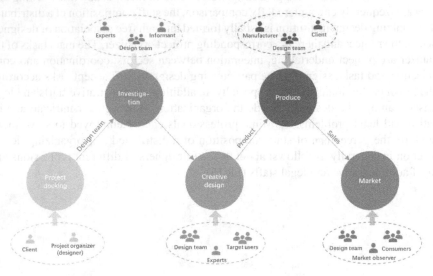

Fig. 6. Schematic diagram for project implementation

Operation Mode. Generally speaking, a self-organizing design institution will set an entity space and adopt the community operation mode. It mainly provides good work space, network space, social space and resource sharing space for free designers. The space is usually allocated with stations according to its size and shares office equipments and networks. A great many designers can rent the stations and sites in it for collaborative office or technology R&D. The design organization can also make a profit by charging rents. After a design project enters the design organization, the project principal will form a design team and tap the commercial value of the products based on actual demands of the market. After the creative of the design team is turned into products, they will be marketed eventually. The designer will consult with the enterprise about drawing design commission. In this way, he can get paid for his design. In addition, the design organization will obtain special fund subsidies from the government. The development of design organizations is vigorously supported by local governments in recent years. Many governments have formulated policies successively to support the development of creative enterprises. Apart from policy guarantee for new design organizations, they can obtain financial support.

3.3 Designer's Capacity Building in the New Mode

As the mentioned above, the position of a designer in the new model will usually change according to different project demands, therefore, the requirement about abilities of a designer will be different from the design ability system based on industrial production. In particular, the designer needn't be an expert with design background, who must have a license about some professional technology. Nor does he need to have professional knowledge and capacity like a scientist. On the contrary, he needs the capacity to deal with comprehensive problems and coordinate teams (Fig. 7).

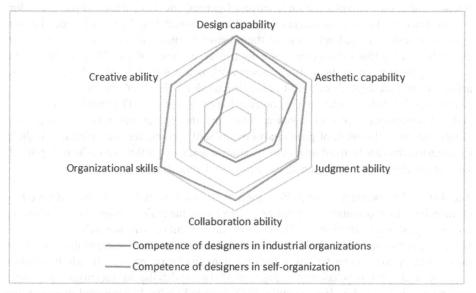

Fig. 7. Different ability constitutions of designers in an industrial organization and in the self-organizing structure.

Composition of Designers' Ability System

- Organizing ability: the ability to seek suitable members to form a team.
- Collaboration ability: the ability to communicate and cooperate with team members and make friendly interactions with affiliated parties of the project.
- Judgment ability: the ability to accurately find design problems, follow up the team's schedule and make suitable adjustment.
- Aesthetic capability: artistic pursuit.
- Design capability: be skilled in a certain professional design area and master specific skills.
- Creative ability: core of design work and energy for innovation and promotion of social development.

Problems of the New Model. Although it has been developed for about a decade, the self-organizing design institution is still new and have caused some problems while its running.

The Design Ownership Is Not Clearly Defined. Design is an artifact directly related to people's life. The power over it concerns life choices of ordinary people of an era. Ever since knowledge exchange platforms based on internet came into being, the concept of intellectual property derived from the publishing era has been blurred. Sharing and open source have become a new free choice but brought trouble to those knowledge owners unwilling to share their knowledge. Take ZBJ as an example. It is frequent that a task releaser randomly chooses the knowledge of participants but refuses to pay them for various reasons. Though the margin system has been established, the cash deposit is not enough to restrict illegal behaviors of the releaser because the price of the transaction contents is very low (The design of a logo may be worth RMB 20 Yuan only.). In a self-organizing design institution, group work is a common form and many design achievements are crystallization of collective wisdom. However, the expense must be reasonably divided according to the contribution of each person. The trust in companions and the agreement before the work are the only things they can rely on. Therefore, identification of the work of group participants will become very complicated. If their expectations cannot be lived up to, the possibility that they participate in the next project will be lowered. It will bring unstable factors to the institution.

The Anti-risk Capability of the Self-Organizing Institutions is Low. Though deemed to contain important orientations of future development, the major income source of a self-organizing design institution is still enterprise investment or government's support fund. If the commissioned project that should have become an income source of the institution fails to live up to the expectations of the organizer and the property rents, administration expenses and water and electricity charges are still a cost that the institution must pay, then bankruptcy is inevitable. For example, D9X founded in 2012 terminated its operation in 2019 and many makerspaces are tottering during the epidemic period and have an ambiguous future.

It Is Still a Niche. In general, the most important realization modes of design are still industrialized at present. Though we expect that in the near future, independent design can be realized and everyone can be a designer, the self-organizing design institution is still a niche and its profiting mode, benefit creation and social influence are still restricted to a very small range.

4   Conclusion

On the precondition that dispersion and collaborative sharing have become a tendency of social development, the previous design organization mode formed by industrial production is severely impacted and "mass entrepreneurship and innovation" have become a national policy. Self-organizing design organizations with dispersion and spirit of innovation as the core may become a new driving force for society. In the self-organizing design structure, each designer is an independent individual. They can exchange freely, work together and learn from each other in the community. They can also temporarily form a small design group in a cooperation project and complete challenges commercially through sharing of design wisdom and cooperation. However, these self-organizing design structures are slightly loose for lack of corresponding rules and systems. Our next research program will be focused on the institutional system of the self-organizing design institution, including the intellectual property protection mechanism.

Acknowledgements. This paper is the phased research result of *Research on Collaboration Innovation Modes of Design Organizations* in the funding project for cultivation of excellent talents of Beijing Municipality in 2018.

References

1. Xu, W., Liu, C., Hu, X., Liu, Q.: New pottery inscriptions in Pit 1 of Qin Terracotta Warriors and Horses and "Wu Le Gong Ming". Emperor Qinshihuang's Mausoleum Site Museum, vol. 2012, no. 7, pp. 361–371 (2012)
2. Wang, X.: Putting officials in charge, carving names on utensils: research on the handicraft management of the Chu Lacquer in Pre Qin Period. Design Research, vol. 2018, no. 02, pp. 31–36 (2018)
3. Mumford, L.: The City in History, A Powerfully Incisive and Influential Look at the Development of the Urban Form through the Ages. Trans. by Junling Song, China Building Industry Press, Beijing (2005)
4. Contarini, G.: De magistribus et republica Ventor. Trans.by Lewes Lekenor Esquire. The Common Wealth and Government of Venice, London, John Windet (1599) pp. 141–142. cited in Ning Kang: Between identity and contract -the transitional characteristics of guild in medieval Europe in the process of legal civilization. Tsinghua Forum of Rule of Law, 2017(04), P66
5. Kang, N.: Between identity and contract -the transitional characteristics of guild in medieval Europe in the process of legal civilization. Tsinghua Forum of Rule of Law **04**, P69 (2017)
6. Forty, A.: Objects of Desire: Design and Society Since 1750. Trans. By Xianxu Gou, pp. 40–41. Yilin Press, Beijing (2005)
7. Climate CoLab Homepage. https://www.climatecolab.org/. Accessed 01 Feb 2021

A Systematic Review of User-Centered Design Techniques Applied to the Design of Mobile Application User Interfaces

Percy Quezada(✉) ⓘ, Rony Cueva ⓘ, and Freddy Paz ⓘ

Pontificia Universidad Católica del Perú, San Miguel, Lima 32, Perú
{percy.quezada,cueva.r,fpaz}@pucp.pe

Abstract. Mobile Applications have become greatly important in current days, as they allow the execution of certain tasks in an efficient way. Furthermore, nowadays every person has a mobile phone which includes a huge variety of mobile applications for diverse purposes. In contrast, User-Centered Design is a framework which is used to improve or guarantee high usability and user experience in any kind of application, including mobile applications. In this paper, we present a systematic review of User-Centered Design Techniques Applied to the Design of Mobile Application User Interfaces. We performed the systematic review followed the proposed guidelines by Kitchenham and Charters, which includes 3 phases, which are the followings: Planning, Conduction and Review and analysis. 3 Research questions were developed in order to get reliable information related to User-Centered Design techniques applied to mobile applications. It is important to mention that we made an exhaustive review of each paper to determine in which phase of UCD should be classified each technique found according to the presented context. Finally, 221 studies were identified, where only 35 were finally selected for the review.

Keywords: User-centered-design · Systematic review · Mobile application · Human-computer interaction · User interfaces

1 Introduction

Nowadays, usability plays an important role in the design of any application. This is due to the fact that in the past, computers were used only by an exclusive group of people who performed highly specialized tasks [1]. However, now they are used by practically anyone since it supports day-to-day activities. Currently, people use software products as it allows specific tasks to be carried out in an optimized way. The importance of this role is because if a software product is not intuitive or it is difficult to use, users stop using the application since it significantly impairs the achievement of the user's objectives [1].

Furthermore, in recent years the number of applications has been increased by the development of mobile technology, in which usability is a factor that must be taken into account during the development of these types of applications. However, little literature is evidenced in this area since reaching the usability of mobile applications is more

© Springer Nature Switzerland AG 2021
M. M. Soares et al. (Eds.): HCII 2021, LNCS 12779, pp. 100–114, 2021.
https://doi.org/10.1007/978-3-030-78221-4_7

complicated than websites because they present unique limitations and typical features of mobile devices [2].

User-centered design is a framework that focuses on users so that the application design process involves users from start to finish [3]. Its objective is to make the systems more usable and useful by focusing on the needs and requirements of users by applying certain techniques and knowledge of usability [4].

In this paper, we present a systematic review of User-Centered Design techniques, also known by its abbreviation UCD, which have been applied to design or redesign Mobile Application User Interfaces. These have been classified according to each phase of this framework. About 221 studies were identified, of which only 35 were selected for the systematic review. Likewise, from the selected studies, we identified the reasons that prompted professionals to carry out a redesign process, as well as which software tools were used during a design or redesign of Mobile Application User Interfaces.

It is important to mention that we made an exhaustive review of each paper to determine in which phase of UCD should be classified each technique found according to the presented context, given that many of these articles did not specify in which phase they had applied them. In this way, we made a classification that can be useful for future works or research related to the application of UCD techniques in mobile applications.

2   Conceptual Framework

2.1   User-Centered Design

User-centered design, better known by its acronym UCD, is a framework that focuses on users, so that the application design process involves users from start to finish [3]. According to ISO 9241-210, this framework aims to make the systems more usable and useful by focusing on the needs and requirements of users by applying certain usability techniques and knowledge [4].

Likewise, ISO 9241-210 [4] also mentions that 4 related activities must be carried out during the design of the system, which are the following:

- Understand and specify the context of use.
- Specify user requirements.
- Produce design solutions.
- Evaluate the design.

2.2   Usability

According to Nielsen, usability cannot be defined as a property of only one dimension, since its definition is associated with five attributes, which are the following [5]:

- Ability to learn: The developed system should be easy to learn so that users can work with it as soon as possible.
- Efficiency: The system should be efficient to use so that once the user has learned the system, it is possible to generate a high level of productivity.

- Ability to memorize: The system should be easy to remember so that users who do not use the application frequently will be able to use it after a certain period of time has elapsed.
- Errors: The error rate should be low so that users make few mistakes when using the system. Also, if they do make mistakes, they should be able to recover from them.
- Satisfaction: The system should be so nice that users like to use it.

2.3 Mobile Applications

According to R. Islam, Islam and Mazumder [6], mobile applications are a set of programs that run on a mobile device and allow the execution of certain tasks for the user.

Likewise, mobile applications must be easy, friendly, and be able to run on as many mobile devices as possible [6].

In the past, only the most developed countries used mobile applications because mobile devices used to be expensive; however, currently the frequency of these has increased in developing countries [6].

2.4 Systematic Review

The systematic review of the literature consists of the identification, evaluation and selection of bibliography and materials regarding a certain research topic [7]. It is necessary to emphasize that, according to Hernández, this review must be carried out in a very selective manner, since thousands of academic publications are produced in the world year after year [8]. For example, if an initial identification of a certain topic yields 10,000 results, only a certain range of years could be chosen in order to obtain the most current trends regarding the topic of interest.

Likewise, the systematic review of the literature is divided into 3 main phases, which are the following: (1) Planning the review, (2) Conducting the review, and (3) Reporting and Analysis of the review [7].

3 Systematic Review

According to Kitchenham and Charters [7], there are many types of reviews that can be performed, including systematic mapping studies, systematic reviews, and tertiary reviews. In this paper, we have selected a systematic review.

Also, the main objective of this review is to analyze the state of the art of UCD techniques and tools applied to design or redesign mobile application user interfaces, as well as the reasons that drove the development of a redesign process.

3.1 Research Questions

The specification of the review questions is the most important part of a systematic review, since these are the ones that drive the methodology of the systematic review [7]. That is why it is necessary to define the research questions.

PICOC Criteria. This review is using the PICOC criterion (Population, Intervention, Comparison, Outcomes, Context) [9], with which general concepts were defined that allowed the development of the review questions.

It should be noted that the comparison criterion was not used, since the objective of this review is not to compare UCD techniques and tools applied to design or redesign mobile application user interfaces. Table 1 shows the general concepts defined according to the PICOC criteria.

Table 1. General concepts defined using the PICOC criterion

Criterion	Description
Population	Design or redesign of graphical interfaces of mobile applications
Intervention	User-centered design
Outcomes	Techniques and tools used in the process of redesigning graphical interfaces, as well as causes and reasons that motivated this process
Context	Academic and business context

The following questions were asked based on what is shown in Table 1:

- RQ1: What user-centered design techniques have been most frequently applied in each user-centered design phase for the design or redesign of graphical interfaces for mobile applications?
- RQ2: What software tools have been used during the application of the user-centered design framework in the design or redesign of graphical interfaces of mobile applications?
- RQ3: What were the reasons that drove the application of a redesign process in mobile applications?

3.2 Search Strategy

Selected Databases. The databases used for the development of the systematic review were selected because most of them have articles from the most relevant scientific journals in the field of Software Engineering. The chosen databases are the following:

- Scopus (www.scopus.com)
- IEEExplore (http://ieeexplore.ieee.org)

Search Terms. The search terms were defined using as a basis the general concepts in Table 1. First, the identification of the most relevant concepts was carried out. After this, a search was done for related terms for each of the concepts. Likewise, articles with more current trends are being sought, which is why only articles published between 2015 and 2020 are being considered. Table 2 shows the search terms defined according to the PICOC criterion.

Table 2. Search terms defined according to PICOC criterion

PICOC criterion	Abbreviation	Concept	Search terms
Population	C1	Mobile applications	App/Mobile App*/Mobile*/Android Based/Ios Based
Population	C2	Design/Redesign	Design*/Redesign*
Population	C3	Graphical interfaces	Interface*/User Interface/Graphical User Interface/Graphical Interface/UI/Software Interfaces
Intervention	C4	User-centered design	UCD/User centered/User-centered/User centre/User-centre/User centered design/User centered approach
Outcomes	C5	Techniques	Technique*/Method*/Proced*/
Outcomes	C6	Tools	Tool*/Instrument*
Outcomes	C7	Reasons	Reason*/Purpose*/Challenge*/Cause*

Result String. Based on Table 2, the result string is the following one:

C1 **AND** C2 **AND** C3 **AND** C4 **AND** (C5 **OR** C6 **OR** C7) **AND** PUBYEAR > 2014

3.3 Study Selection

Certain inclusion and exclusion criteria have been developed in order to get the most relevant articles for the systematic review.

Inclusion Criteria. The articles that fulfilled at least one of the following criteria were selected:

- The study shows the use of some user-centered design technique in the design or redesign of a mobile application.
- The study shows the use of some software tools during the application of the user-centered design framework in the design or redesign of a mobile application.
- The study reports reasons or causes for which a mobile application redesign process was carried out.

Exclusion Criteria. The articles that fulfilled at least one of the following criteria were excluded:

- The study is not written in English or Spanish.
- The study describes the use of techniques that do not belong to the user-centered design methodology.
- The study shows the use of algorithms for the generation of usable interfaces.

- The study presents only recommendations on the application of the user-centered design framework.
- The study presents a different theme to the area of Human-Computer Interaction

3.4   Search Results

The search was carried out on October 2, 2020, and resulted in a total of 221 articles. Table 3 shows the articles found classified for each selected database.

Table 3. Articles found classified per database.

Database	N° articles	Duplicated articles	Selected articles
Scopus	191	9	32
IEEE Xplore	30	11	3
Total	**221**	**20**	**35**

3.5   Selected Results

In this section, we present the selected articles that have been selected after applying the inclusion and exclusion criteria. Table 4 shows these results.

Table 4. Selected articles

Article ID	Authors(s)	Year	Extraction database
A1 [10]	Tobias and Spanier	2020	Scopus
A2 [11]	Almklov et al.	2020	Scopus
A3 [12]	Smaradottir et al.	2020	Scopus
A4 [13]	Soo Yun and McFadden	2020	Scopus
A5 [14]	Huilcapi-Collantes et al.	2019	Scopus
A6 [15]	García-Ruiz et al.	2019	Scopus
A7 [16]	Marcus	2016	Scopus
A8 [17]	Peischl et al.	2015	Scopus
A9 [18]	Wongta et al.	2016	Scopus
A10 [19]	Aguilar and Zapata	2016	Scopus
A11 [20]	Narvaéz et al.	2016	Scopus

(*continued*)

Table 4. (*continued*)

Article ID	Authors(s)	Year	Extraction database
A12 [21]	Calvillo-Arbizu et al.	2019	Scopus
A13 [22]	Akbar Maulana and Suzianti	2019	Scopus
A14 [23]	Priowibowo et al.	2020	Scopus
A15 [3]	Parera et al.	2019	Scopus
A16 [24]	Afrianto and Guntara	2019	Scopus
A17 [25]	Mortenson et al.	2019	Scopus
A18 [26]	Sedlmayr et al.	2019	Scopus
A19 [27]	Chan et al.	2019	Scopus
A20 [28]	Schild et al.	2019	Scopus
A21 [29]	Srinivas et al.	2019	Scopus
A22 [30]	Zhang and Shen	2019	Scopus
A23 [31]	Nguyen et al.	2019	Scopus
A24 [32]	Minda and Fuentes	2019	Scopus
A25 [33]	Bueno and Silva	2018	Scopus
A26 [34]	Giunti et al.	2018	Scopus
A27 [35]	Real and Abascal-Mena	2018	Scopus
A28 [36]	Tanaksaranond	2018	Scopus
A29 [37]	Risald et al.	2018	Scopus
A30 [38]	Wardhana et al.	2017	Scopus
A31 [39]	Karim et al.	2017	Scopus
A32 [40]	Wechsler	2015	Scopus
A33 [41]	Gutiérrez et al.	2019	IEEE Xplore
A34 [42]	Bonino et al.	2016	IEEE Xplore
A35 [43]	Lee et al.	2018	IEEE Xplore

3.6 Results

In this section we present the results for each question:

User-Centered Design Techniques Applied in Designing Mobile Applications
Table 5 shows the user-centered design techniques applied in the selected articles.

It is concluded that according to the selected articles, the most reported technique in the phase of Specify the context of use is Survey of existing users, which allows to determine user needs, current work day-to-day activities and their behavior with respect to the new system to be developed [44].

Table 5. User-Centered Design Techniques found in selected articles.

UCD phase	User centered design technique	Studies that report the use of at least one UCD technique	Quantity
Specify the context of use	Survey of existing users	A2, A15, A20, A22, A25, A27, A29, A30, A35	9
	Literature review	A18, A28, A31, A32	4
	Context of use analysis	A11, A12, A14	3
	Stakeholder analysis	A10, A29	2
	Field study	A18, A19	2
	Brainstorming	A20, A21	2
	Semi-structured interviews	A12	1
	Interviews with experts	A18	1
	Online search	A14	1
	Task analysis	A14	1
	Focus groups	A21	1
Specify user requeriments	Personas	A5, A7, A10, A12, A14, A15, A16, A18, A20, A22, A23, A26, A27, A29, A30, A32	16
	User requirements interview	A5, A6, A8, A9, A12, A14, A16, A26	8
	Scenarios of use	A5, A7, A27, A29	4
	Semi-structured interviews	A1, A10, A31	3
	Focus groups	A1, A2, A26	3
	Brainstorming	A28, A34	2
	Task analysis	A16	1
	User assessment	A10	1
	Field study	A10	1
Design	Prototyping model	A1, A3, A5, A8, A9, A10, A11, A12, A15, A16, A18, A19, A20, A21, A22, A23, A24, A25, A26, A28, A29, A30, A31, A32, A34, A35	26
	ThinkALoud	A6, A11, A31, A33, A34	5

(*continued*)

Table 5. (*continued*)

UCD phase	User centered design technique	Studies that report the use of at least one UCD technique	Quantity
	Storyboarding	A20, A27	2
	Brainstorming	A26, A35	2
	Post-experience interviews	A6, A22	2
	Affinity diagram	A35	1
	Scenarios of use	A10	1
	Satisfaction questionnaires	A2	1
	Personas	A14	1
	Wizard-of-Oz prototyping	A27	1
	Card sorting	A33	1
	Hedonic utility scale	A33	1
	Heat maps	A24	1
	Focus groups	A31	1
Evaluation	Satisfaction questionnaires	A4, A7, A9, A10, A12, A13, A14, A15, A17, A18, A21, A25, A30	13
	Assisted evaluation	A4, A7, A8, A11, A12, A13, A15, A25	8
	Post-experience interviews	A4, A9, A13, A17, A19, A31	6
	ThinkALoud	A8, A11, A13, A18, A20	5
	Usability scaling system	A13, A16, A20, A23, A30	5
	Focus groups	A17	1
	Heuristic evaluation	A26	1

On the other hand, in the requirements phase, the most used techniques were Personas and user requirements interviews.

The use of the Personas technique in most of the articles is due to the fact that it allows increasing empathy with end-users, by defining a *persona*, who represents a group of users [19]. The definition of the user groups that will use the application also serves as a source to more easily identify the stakeholders of the project to be carried out. On the other hand, the proper use of this technique allows support to the application designers in the design phase [45].

The user requirements interview technique was used mainly to obtain information about the needs or requirements of the interested parties in relation to the system to be developed [44].

Regarding the design phase, the most reported technique was the Prototyping model. Several prototype models can be presented during the development of a mobile application, which are low-fidelity prototypes and high-fidelity prototypes.

Low-fidelity prototypes are usually simple and present low-tech concepts; these are usually made with paper and pencil [46]. The main objective of this type of prototype is to present to the user the idea of the functionalities that the application would have.

On the other hand, high-fidelity prototypes are highly functional and interactive [46]. In addition, since they are the closest to the final product, they are developed in the final stages of development to evaluate usability and identify problems in the application flow [46].

Finally, the most reported techniques in the evaluation phase are satisfaction questionnaires and assisted evaluation.

The use of satisfaction questionnaires allows obtaining the subjective impressions of the end-users about the application, based on the experiences obtained when interacting with the application [44].

On the other hand, assisted evaluation allows the evaluator how the application supports users to complete tasks, in addition to providing feedback as they interact with the application [44].

Software Tools In Application of User-Centered Design Framework In Designing Mobile Applications

Table 6 shows the software tools found in the selected articles.

Table 6. Software tools found in selected articles.

Software tool	Article that reports the use of a software tool	Quantity
xCode	A9, A10	2
JustInMind	A11, A31	2
Balsamiq	A18, A20	2
WebEx	A4	1
Parse	A9	1
POP 2.0 – Prototyping on Paer	A11	1
Rehab-CYCLE	A8	1
Adobe XD	A1	1
PowerPoint	A20	1
Material UI Library	A23	1
Quant-UX	A24	1
Ninjamock	A28	1

From Table 6, it can be concluded that the software tools used during the application of the user-centered design framework are usually varied in each of the case studies found.

For the development of low-fidelity prototypes, it was found that one of the articles used the POP 2.0 tool - Prototyping on Paper, which allows the creation of wireframes through photos to graphical interfaces made on paper by the designer. In this case, the first prototype of a mobile application for the prevention of Burnout syndrome was made, which was designed with the objective of the navigation flow and the design according to the identified user requirements [20]. Likewise, for the development of the second prototype, a high-fidelity prototype was used with the JustInMind tool, which allows the creation of high-fidelity web and mobile application prototypes. The objective of this prototype was to define the graphic design and navigation flow of the application [20].

On the other hand, 2 studies reported the use of the Balsamiq tool for the development of low fidelity prototypes.

Finally, the other tools presented in Table 6 did not have as their objective the development of usability tests or user-centered design, which is why the definition of these has not been elaborated.

Reasons That Drove the Application of a Redesign Process in Mobile Applications
One of the most common reasons found in the selected studies is because the application was developed with a design that is currently considered obsolete [13].

On the other hand, it was also found that the application had very low ratings and negative comments on the digital distribution platform for mobile applications [13].

Likewise, it was reported in one of the primary studies that the development of instructions in the application was necessary because the start menus were very confusing and difficult to understand, which made the application navigation flow difficult [22].

To sum up, the reasons why a redesign process must be carried out in a mobile application are usually very varied, since the redesign arises based on the errors that may have been made when designing an application, which can be of diverse nature.

4   Conclusions

A large number of the results found are focused on the medical field. For the case of inventory management, no case was found. In summary, it can be concluded that there is very little literature related to the topic to be developed in this article, so that the project is novel.

It was observed that there are a large number of user-centered design techniques applied in the first selected studies. From these techniques, it could be concluded that a large number of the articles used the same techniques in the design or redesign of mobile applications, among which is the People technique, prototype models, and satisfaction questionnaires (See Table 5).

On the other hand, the selected primary studies, unlike the user-centered design techniques, do not present similar software tools during the application of the framework. However, it was found that a large number of the studies found used software tools for the design of graphical interfaces of mobile applications (See Table 6).

Regarding the reasons for which a process of redesigning the graphical interfaces of mobile applications had to be carried out, these tend to be of various kinds depending on the type of application. One of these reasons found was that the application had been developed with a design that was considered obsolete [13]. On the other hand, it was also found that the development of instructions was necessary to improve the navigation flow of the application [22].

Acknowledgment. This study is highly supported by the Section of Informatics Engineering of the Pontifical Catholic University of Peru (PUCP) – Peru, and the "HCI, Design, User Experience, Accessibility & Innovation Technologies" Research Group (HCI-DUXAIT). HCI-DUXAIT is a research group of PUCP.

References

1. Nielsen, J.: Usability engineering. J. Chem. Inf. Model. **53**, 1689–1699 (1993). https://doi.org/10.1017/CBO9781107415324.004
2. Kutlu Gündoğdu, F., Cotari, E., Cebi, S., Kahraman, C.: Analysis of usability test parameters affecting the mobile application designs by using spherical fuzzy sets. In: Kahraman, C., Kutlu Gündoğdu, F. (eds.) Decision Making with Spherical Fuzzy Sets. SFSC, vol. 392, pp. 431–452. Springer, Cham (2021). https://doi.org/10.1007/978-3-030-45461-6_18
3. Parera, C.H., Harlili, Satya, D.P.: Design of translator android application for sign language and indonesian using user-centered design approach. In: Proceedings - 2019 International Conference of Advanced Informatics: Concepts, Theory and Applications, ICAICTA 2019, pp. 1–6 (2019). https://doi.org/10.1109/ICAICTA.2019.8904098
4. ISO: ISO 9241-210:2019: Ergonomics of human–system interaction - Human-centred design for interactive systems (2019)
5. Nielsen, J.: What is usability? In: User Experience Re-Mastered: Your Guide to Getting the Right Design, pp. 3–22. Elsevier (2010). https://doi.org/10.1016/b978-0-12-375114-0.00004-9
6. Islam, R., Mazumder, T., Islam, R.: Mobile application and its global impact. Int. J. Eng. Technol. **10**(6), 72–78 (2010)
7. Kitchenham, B., Charters, S.: Guidelines for performing systematic literature reviews in software engineering. Technical report, Ver. 2.3 EBSE Technical Report. EBSE (2007)
8. Hernández, R., Fernández, C., Baptista, P.: Metodología de la Investigación (6ta edición). Mc Graw Hill (2014)
9. Petticrew, M., Roberts, H.: Systematic Reviews in the Social Sciences: A Practical Guide (2008). https://doi.org/10.1002/9780470754887
10. Tobias, G., Spanier, A.B.: Developing a mobile app (iGAM) to promote gingival health by professional monitoring of dental selfies: user-centered design approach. JMIR mHealth uHealth. **8**, e19433 (2020). https://doi.org/10.2196/19433
11. Almklov, E., Afari, N., Floto, E., Lindamer, L., Hurst, S., Pittman, J.O.E.: Post-9/11 veteran satisfaction with the VA eScreening program. Mil. Med. **185**, 519–529 (2020). https://doi.org/10.1093/milmed/usz324
12. Smaradottir, B.F., Fagerlund, A.J., Bellika, J.G.: User-centred design of a mobile application for chronic pain management. Stud. Health Technol. Inform. **272**, 272–275 (2020). https://doi.org/10.3233/SHTI200547

13. Kim, S.Y., McFadden, E.: Using established UX design techniques and visual enhancements to redesign an enterprise mobile app and improve employee productivity and engagement. In: Ahram, T., Falcão, C. (eds.) AHFE 2019. AISC, vol. 972, pp. 169–176. Springer, Cham (2020). https://doi.org/10.1007/978-3-030-19135-1_17

14. Huilcapi-Collantes, C., Martín, A.H., Ramos, J.P.H.: A mobile app for developing visual literacy on in-service teachers. In: ACM International Conference Proceeding Series, pp. 642–648 (2019). https://doi.org/10.1145/3362789.3362947

15. García-Ruiz, M.A., Santana-Mancilla, P.C.: Towards a usable serious game app to support children's language therapy. In: ACM International Conference Proceeding Series, pp. 1–4 (2019). https://doi.org/10.1145/3358961.3358978

16. Marcus, A.: The marriage machine: mobile persuasion/behavior change. In: Marcus, A. (ed.) DUXU 2015. LNCS, vol. 9186, pp. 513–523. Springer, Cham (2015). https://doi.org/10.1007/978-3-319-20886-2_48

17. Peischl, B., Ferk, M., Holzinger, A.: Integrating user-centred design in an early stage of mobile medical application prototyping: a case study on data acquistion in health organisations. In: ICE-B 2013 - 10th International Conference on E-Business, Part ICETE 2013 10th International Joint Conference on E-Business and Telecommunications Proceedings (2015)

18. Wongta, J., Wongwatkit, C., Boonkerd, J., Chaikajornwat, R., Maeprasart, V., Khrutthaka, C.: Enhancing course timetable management in science classrooms with user-oriented mobile application: analysis and prototype development on KMUTT-ESC case study. In: Main Conference Proceedings for the 24th International Conference on Computers in Education (ICCE) - Think Global Act Local, pp. 325–334 (2016)

19. Aguilar, M., Zapata, C.: Integrating UCD and an agile methodology in the development of a mobile catalog of plants. In: Soares, M., Falcão, C., Ahram, T. (eds.) Advances in Ergonomics Modeling, Usability & Special Populations, pp. 75–87. Springer, Cham (2017). https://doi.org/10.1007/978-3-319-41685-4_8

20. Narváez, S., Tobar, Á.M., López, D.M., Blobel, B.: Human-centered design of an mhealth app for the prevention of burnout syndrome. Stud. Health Technol. Inform. **228**, 215–219 (2016). https://doi.org/10.3233/978-1-61499-678-1-215

21. Calvillo-Arbizu, J., et al.: User-centred design for developing e-Health system for renal patients at home (AppNephro). Int. J. Med. Inform. **125**, 47–54 (2019). https://doi.org/10.1016/j.ijmedinf.2019.02.007

22. Akbar Maulana, S., Suzianti, A.: User interface redesign in a point rewards mobile application using usability testing method. In: ACM International Conference Proceeding Series, pp. 43–48 (2019). https://doi.org/10.1145/3369985.3370001

23. Priowibowo, B., Effendy, V., Junaedi, D.: Designing user interface using user-centered design method on reproductive health learning for visual impairment teenagers. In: IOP Conference Series: Materials Science and Engineering, vol. 830 (2020). https://doi.org/10.1088/1757-899X/830/2/022092

24. Afrianto, I., Guntara, R.G.: Implementation of user centered design method in designing android-based journal reminder application. In: IOP Conference Series: Materials Science and Engineering, vol. 662 (2019). https://doi.org/10.1088/1757-899X/662/2/022029

25. Mortenson, W.B., et al.: Development of a self-management app for people with spinal cord injury. J. Med. Syst. **43**(6), 1–12 (2019). https://doi.org/10.1007/s10916-019-1273-x

26. Sedlmayr, B., Schöffler, J., Prokosch, H.U., Sedlmayr, M.: User-centered design of a mobile medication management. Inform. Heal. Soc. Care. **44**, 152–163 (2019). https://doi.org/10.1080/17538157.2018.1437042

27. Chan, K.G., Deja, J.A., Tobias, J.P., Gonzales, A.V., Dancel, M.A.: Applying user-centered techniques in the design of a usable mobile musical composition tool. In: ACM International Conference Proceeding Series, pp. 152–159 (2019). https://doi.org/10.1145/3328243.3328263

28. Schild, S., Sedlmayr, B., Schumacher, A.K., Sedlmayr, M., Prokosch, H.U., St.Pierre, M.: A digital cognitive aid for anesthesia to support intraoperative crisis management: results of the user-centered design process. JMIR mHealth uHealth **7** (2019). https://doi.org/10.2196/13226

29. Srinivas, P., Bodke, K., Ofner, S., Keith, N.C.R., Tu, W., Clark, D.O.: Context-sensitive ecological momentary assessment: application of user-centered design for improving user satisfaction and engagement during self-report. J. Med. Internet Res. **21**, 1–17 (2019). https://doi.org/10.2196/10894

30. Zhang, L., Shen, P.: User experience based urban tourism app interface design. In: Proceedings - 20th International Conference on High Performance Computing and Communications. 16th International Conference on Smart City; 4th International Conference on Data Science and Systems HPCC/SmartCity/DSS 2018, pp. 1121–1124 (2019). https://doi.org/10.1109/HPCC/SmartCity/DSS.2018.00187

31. Nguyen, Q.N., Frisiello, A., Rossi, C.: The design of a mobile application for crowdsourcing in disaster risk reduction. In: Proceedings International ISCRAM Conference 2019-May, pp. 607–618 (2019)

32. Minda Gilces, D., Fuentes Díaz, R.: User-centered-design of a UI for mobile banking applications. In: Trends, T. (ed.) Botto-Tobar M, Pizarro G, Zúñiga-Prieto M, D'Armas M, Zúñiga Sánchez M, pp. 205–219. Springer, Cham (2019). https://doi.org/10.1007/978-3-030-05532-5_15

33. Bueno, J., Silva, A.: Compass: a personal organization mobile app for individuals with mental disorders. Inf. Des. J. **24**, 220–235 (2018). https://doi.org/10.1075/gest.8.3.02str

34. Giunti, G., Mylonopoulou, V., Romero, O.R.: More stamina, a gamified mhealth solution for persons with multiple sclerosis: research through design. J. Med. Internet Res. **20** (2018). https://doi.org/10.2196/mhealth.9437

35. Real Flores, G., Abascal-Mena, R.: MiGua! app for user awareness prior to adopting dogs in urban areas. In: Computing, S., Media, S. (eds.) Meiselwitz G, pp. 87–96. Springer, Cham (2018). https://doi.org/10.1007/978-3-319-91521-0_7

36. Tanaksaranond, G.: The development of a mobile map application for park and ride users. Int. J. GEOMATE **15**, 143–149 (2018). https://doi.org/10.21660/2018.49.sgi176

37. Risald, Suyoto, Santoso, A.J.: Mobile application design emergency medical call for the deaf using UCD methods. Int. J. Interact. Mob. Technol. **12**, 168 177 (2018). https://doi.org/10.3991/ijim.v12i3.8754

38. Wardhana, S., Sabariah, M.K., Effendy, V., Kusumo, D.S.: User interface design model for parental control application on mobile smartphone using user centered design method. In: 2017 5th International Conference on Information and Communication Technology. ICoICT 2017, pp. 1–6 (2017). https://doi.org/10.1109/ICoICT.2017.8074715

39. Karim, N.S.A., AlHarbi, A., AlKadhi, B., AlOthaim, N.: Mobile application on smoking cessation based on persuasive design theory. In: Proceedings of 21st Pacific Asia Conference on Information Systems "Societal Transformation Through IS/IT", PACIS 2017 (2017)

40. Wechsler, J. (Jax): HCD mobile health project. In: APCHIUX 2015: Proceedings of the Asia Pacific HCI and UX Design Symposium, pp. 16–21 (2015). https://doi.org/10.1145/2846439.2846442

41. Gutierrez Padilla, J.D.N., Alvarez Robles, T.D.J., Alvarez Rodriguez, F.J.: Interactive software system focused on basic math learning for the visually impaired. In: Proceedings - 2019 International Conference on Inclusive Technologies and Education, CONTIE 2019, pp. 72–78 (2019). https://doi.org/10.1109/CONTIE49246.2019.00023

42. Bonino, D., Alizo, M.T.D., Pastrone, C., Spirito, M.: WasteApp: smarter waste recycling for smart citizens. In: 2016 International Multidisciplinary Conference on Computer and Energy Science (SpliTech) 2016, pp. 1–6 (2016). https://doi.org/10.1109/SpliTech.2016.7555951

43. Lee, D., Frey, G., Cheng, A., Shih, P.C.: Puzzle walk: a gamified mobile app to increase physical activity in adults with autism spectrum disorder. In: 2018 10th International Conference on Virtual Worlds and Games for Serious Applications (VS-Games), Wurzburg, pp. 1–4 (2018)
44. Maguire, M.: Methods to support human-centred design. Int. J. Hum. Comput. Stud. **55**, 587–634 (2001). https://doi.org/10.1006/ijhc.2001.0503
45. Hasya Afina Sujani, P., Santoso, H.B., Yugo Kartono Isal, R.: An alternative design of dekoruma as a home and living E-commerce platform. In: 2019 International Conference on Advanced Computer Science and information Systems. ICACSIS 2019, pp. 63–68 (2019). https://doi.org/10.1109/ICACSIS47736.2019.8979707
46. Esposito, E.: Low-fidelity vs. high-fidelity prototyping. https://www.invisionapp.com/inside-design/low-fi-vs-hi-fi-prototyping/. Accessed 18 Sept 2020

Interactionist Approach to Visual Aesthetics in HCI

Johanna Silvennoinen[✉] 🆔

Faculty of Information Technology, University of Jyvaskyla, 40014 Jyväskylä, Finland
Johanna.silvennoinen@jyu.fi

Abstract. Visual Aesthetics has gathered interest among scholars in HCI research. The growing interest stems from examinations of the aesthetic-usability effect ("what is beautiful is usable"), and possibly vice versa. Thus, numerous studies focus on understanding how we make sense and experience visual entities in interacting with technology. However, theoretical, and methodological stances vary, which impact conclusions of the studies conducted, and thus, affect design implications. Visual experience research in HCI lacks detailed conceptualizations of the constituents of visual experience and understanding of how these conceptualizations affect the overall research results through implicit methodological stances taken. In this paper, an overview of methodological stances to visual aesthetics in HCI research is presented and an interactionist approach is discussed which combines objectivist and subjectivist methodological stances and enriches our understanding of current research of visual aesthetics in HCI. In addition, methodological grounds of interactionism are described and extended from cognitive processing fluency paradigm to take into account the overall complexity of visual experience. Moreover, conceptualization of visual experience from cognitive-affective perspective in line with interactionism is discussed, following with metodical considerations of interactionism, and issues related to the role of visual stimuli in examining visual aesthetics in HCI.

Keywords: Visual aesthetics · Visual experience · Methodology · Interactionism · Human-computer interaction

1 Introduction

Visual aesthetics in human-computer interaction (HCI) is a growing sub-discipline within HCI research. As a sub-discipline of HCI, visual aesthetics started to gain interest from the mid-nineties. Often referred publication by Kurosu and Kashimura [41] indicated a positive relationship between aesthetics and usability. Noam Tractinsky continued this line of research with a publication titled "What is beautiful is usable" [83]. Since then, vast amount of research has been devoted in understanding the relationship and dynamics between aesthetics and perceived usability in technology-interaction, also titled as the aesthetic-usability effect. However, differing research results have been presented of the interplay between these constituents of visual experience.

© Springer Nature Switzerland AG 2021
M. M. Soares et al. (Eds.): HCII 2021, LNCS 12779, pp. 115–127, 2021.
https://doi.org/10.1007/978-3-030-78221-4_8

Many different disciplines have concentrated on examining the dynamics of visual experience. Still, visual experience remains an intriguing research topic, despite of the multitude of research devoted to examination and explication of it. Different methodologies have been presented to disclose the contents of visual experience. However, it is not unambiguous how the contents of the visual are formed and how these are represented in different contexts. Visual experience is a complex phenomenon involving different underlying cognitive and affective processes, contributing to the formation of an overall experience. Visual representations elicit aesthetic, affective and, symbolic meanings [e.g., 9, 11, 38, 40, 63].

Visual experience as a cognitive-affective process considers visual experience as a conscious mental phenomenon involving various cognitive and affective processes, such as, attention, perception, creativity, apperception, and mental representations with information contents [69], as well as aesthetic appraisal [76]. The conceptualization of visual experience as such is in line with contemporary accounts to philosophy of aesthetics, where visual experience involves cognitive and affective processes, and the experience process is seen as an interpretative play with various stages [8]. According to traditional accounts of aesthetics, aesthetic experience is considered as an immediate response without intervening reasoning [e.g., 49, 71, 82]. This line of thought represents a different paradigm in examining visual experience than the contemporary one.

The formation of visual experience includes both top-down and bottom-up information processing [e.g., 74, 32]. In the core of visual experience are mental representations consisting of mental information contents, which can be of non-perceivable kinds, such as timeless and imaginative [66–69, 77]. Represented mental information contents are informed by the properties of the encountered technological artifacts and can be seen as the parts of experience that makes the encounters meaningful to the users [74]. To represent something as, for example timeless, requires a process of seeing something as something. This refers to the concept of apperception [27, 34, 68, 69].

Apperception integrates already existing mental information contents and new information into meaningful mental representation. Visual experience is not only formed on the basis of 'perceivable' sensory information, but also on existing mental information obtained in prior experiences [66, 68, 69]. Therefore, apperception is not mere perception, but unifies experiences. Visual experience differs from the concept of aesthetic experience in that it does not posit experience qualities (e.g., aesthetic experience as an exceptional state of mind), but indicates that visual entities are capable to elicit different experiential contents.

Several studies in HCI approach visual experience from an objectivist point of view, focusing on visual entities in technological artifacts as determinants of aesthetic experience [e.g., 4, 36, 46, 57, 84]. Another viewpoint to visual experience research approaches the phenomenon from subjectivist perspective [e.g., 43, 54], in which visual experience occurs in top-down processes of the perceiver. However, according to the definition of visual experience stated above, an interactionist approach combining objectivism and subjectivism is necessary.

Visual experience occurs in the intersection between the objectivist and subjectivist approaches. Visual experience as a process is informed by the components of visual representations with an interactionist approach that expands the traditional view of the information processing paradigm to visual experience as a cognitive-affective mental phenomenon. Theoretical and methodological research positions need to be explicated because these fundamentally affect operationalization of the studied phenomenon, metodical choices, as well as the results from which visual design implications are derived from. Thus, interactionist approach combining the objective and subjective accounts to visual experience in HCI is required to investigate the underlying dynamics of visual experiences, and to inform visual technology-design enabling understandable and experiential encounters with technology.

Structure of this paper is as follows, next objectivist, subjectivist, and interactionist approaches are presented. Then, methodological and metodical considerations are discussed following a discussion concerning the nature of stimuli on HCI research. Lastly, conclusions are presented.

2   Objectivist, Subjectivist, and Interactionist Approaches

Recent research approaches examining the relationship of visuality of technological artifacts and visual experience include two main approaches: objectivism and subjectivism [e.g., 1, 32, 73, 74]. Objectivism (also titled as screen-based design approach) is utilized in discovering bottom-up design factors affecting aesthetic experience and identifying design elements and their structural relationships in technological artifacts (e.g., web pages) that influence user experience [4, 26, 36, 57, 61]. If research is grounded on the object properties as the focus of attention, then the research approach is objectivist [e.g., 5]. Thus, objectivist, bottom-up approach to visual experience [e.g., 20] emphasize properties of visual stimuli in guiding visual attention (e.g., saliency of the stimuli) [28], and the Gestalt laws [37, 86].

Objectivist approach can be utilized in designing for usability and has been beneficial in outlining usability design guidelines [e.g., 19, 43] but is questionable of examining visual experience including aesthetic appraisals. If objectivism is utilized as an approach to detect visual design properties as determinants to create aesthetic experiences, the design would need to address a vast number of design combinations and solutions with a wide range of individual differences in preferences.

At least since Plato, critical contributors to beauty have been examined and specific visual features have been suggested to elicit aesthetic experiences, which has led to identification of some visual constructs that often contribute to perceived beauty, such as symmetry and balance [2, 21]. Plato's view to beautiful objects includes a combination of proportion, harmony, and unity. According to Aristotle universal dimensions of beauty are order, symmetry, and definiteness. Gestalt psychologists proposed, for instance, symmetry and balance as contributors to beauty [2, 21].

More recently, researchers of visual aesthetics in HCI have studied visual experiences with objectivist approach [30, 52, 53, 57, 58]. Research indicating formal, objective attributes that determine aesthetic appeal to be used for automatic composition of displays have been conducted [e.g., 57]. For example, symmetry and balance in images affect appraisals of aesthetic appeal but the positive relationship between aesthetic appeal and symmetry weakens when examined with more realistic, context-dependent stimuli [4]. Research area of computational aesthetics can be considered to follow the objectivist approach in detecting visual user interface elements and compositional structures (e.g., symmetry and visual clutter) essential to be acknowledged in designing for pleasing visual experience [30, 53, 65].

Several dimensions of aesthetic appeal have been presented. Dimensions range from visual elements [e.g., 12, 35, 55, 75], higher-level attributes [e.g., 23, 24, 26, 62, 85], multisensory experiences [48, 59] to experiential contents [e.g., 33, 74]. These dimensions include for example, overall impression, meaningfulness, and beauty [72], classical aesthetics (aesthetic, pleasant, clean, clear and symmetrical), and expressive aesthetics (creative, using special effects, original, sophisticated and fascinating) [43], and simplicity, diversity, color, and craftsmanship [54].

Objectivist approach has been criticized as universalistic due to its theoretical grounds that aesthetic laws are engrained in objects [39], and thus, would not have explanatory power in explaining visual experiences in different individual and cultural contexts [39, 50]. In addition, formal aspects of objects can be considered as secondary issues in experiences, as for example, Csikszentmihalyi [10] argues that formal features only seldomly make objects valuable to their owners, as people do not perceive formal attributes (e.g., order or disorder in composition) according to mathematical principles. Despite the evident subjective and context-dependent nature of visual and aesthetic experience, research continues examining formal features of aesthetic properties in technological artifacts.

The second approach in examining the relationship of visuality of interactive artifacts and visual experience is from top-down perspective [43, 54]. This subjectivist approach can be described with the saying 'beauty is in the eye of the be-holder'. Different to the objectivist approach, subjectivist approach is often studied with self-reports, such as questionnaires [73]. Majority of visual aesthetics in HCI research approach visual experience from subjectivist accounts. Different questionnaires have been developed in examining subjective contents of aesthetic experience [e.g., 43, 54].

The third approach, combining the objectivist bottom-up and the subjectivist top-down approaches is interactionist approach. This approach has not been utilized as much as the other two in examining the interplay of technological artifacts and visual experiences [73]. Interactionism in examining visual experience is based on cognitive processing fluency paradigm: "beauty is grounded in the processing experiences of the perceiver that emerge from the interaction of stimulus properties and perceivers' cognitive and affective processes" [64], Thus, visual experience is to be considered as a relationship between an object and a subject, rather than an essence to be grasped or determined by on object [16].

3   Methodological Considerations

What research issues are emphasized in different eras represent current values of that time. This also affects methodological decisions through which constructs, and concepts of different phenomena are examined and measured by. In addition, technological artifacts are affected by the experiential interaction goals valued and pursued in the time of their creation. Currently, visual experience research in HCI focuses on aesthetics of interaction and emotional design with emerging interest on the role of multiple senses in user experiences.

The complexity of visual experience and aesthetic appraisal research is affected by the instability of aesthetics and the difficulty of measuring it. Aesthetic experiences, appraisals, and values change in time, which also have an impact to the concepts with which visual experience is examined [e.g., 8]. Thus, value and belief systems of different eras influence the operationalizations of studied phenomena. A change in measurement unit indicates a change in belief and value systems, which further affects what is designed and how, and to whom. Changes in measurement units lead to new views on design implications and therefore has an impact on research practices. For example, in urban environment design the measurement unit has shifted from cars to humans, which has emerged a new design paradigm.

In HCI research different methodological positions can be explained with intentionality (relating to ontology) and causality (relating to epistemology), in terms whether intentionality and causal explanations are expected. This way of defining methodological positions can lead to four different positions: behaviorism, cognitivism, neuroscience, and subjectivism (Fig. 1) [31]. Intentionality is a feature of mental state that represents something and is about something [14]. Thus, intentional mental states include mental contents of what is represented [67]. Objects can be seen differently in terms of intentionality. For example, what is in the focus of a perceiver. Same technological artifact can be mentally represented with various mental contents by different people, depending for instance, on personal goals and desires. Causality explains events via cause and action. In HCI research, the concept of interaction refers to a causal relationship between a technological artifact and a human [31].

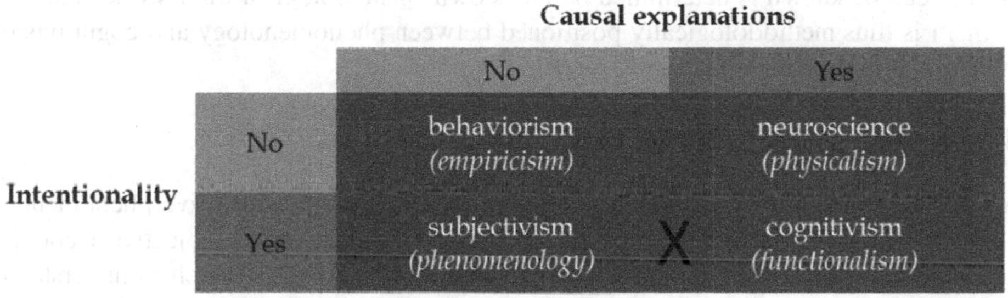

Causal explanations

		No	Yes
Intentionality	No	behaviorism *(empiricisim)*	neuroscience *(physicalism)*
	Yes	subjectivism *(phenomenology)*	cognitivism *(functionalism)*

Fig. 1. Four methodological positions in HCI [31].

These methodological positions can be utilized in HCI research to explicate underlying assumptions of studied phenomena. Without explication of methodological position phenomenon under investigation can lead to contradictory results and not to measure the phenomenon actually in question.

In behaviorism the focus is on observable and objectively measured events [78]. Explication of a studied phenomenon follows explanations from stimulus to response, not focusing on what happens in the mind of a subject. In visual experience in HCI research behavioristic stances are often conducted (also not explicitly indicated as such). Behavioral approaches can be utilized in studying mental events, such as visual experiences, if strong cognitive theory functions as the basis formulating research problems. Thus, by explicating the phenomenon under investigation, the strength of the solutions to the problem is dependent on the capacity of the utilized constructs of concepts, facts, and laws [31, 42, 69, 70].

Traditional accounts to cognitivism conceptualize human mind as a computer [e.g., 18]. Paradigms of capacity and cognitive information processing fluency have originated from the metaphor of mind as a computer. The mind processes information similarly to a production system such as a computer with sensory input and motor output responses [56]. Neuroscience takes a physicalist stance to human thinking in terms of the brains. Intentionality is considered as a physically observable function in human nervous system. A contrasting stance to neuroscience is presented by subjectivist approach based on phenomenology, which indicate that scientific ontologies depend on how we experience the world. According to Heidegger [22] and Husserl [27] the core idea in phenomenology is to examine the structure of experience. The methodological position in line with phenomenological view is referred as subjectivism because it emphasizes the importance to focus on the experience of the subject. In subjectivism intentionality means that people have mental representations, and these representations have mental information contents [68]. Human behavior and experience can be examined and explained by studying represented mental information contents.

A stance originating from phenomenology is constructivism. In the core of constructivism is an understanding that experiences are not passive observations but involves active interpretation. In HCI, and especially from the viewpoint of visual experience, both cognitivism and phenomenological positions are intertwined in experience research. It seems that the most suitable form of subjectivism in the study of visual experience is in line with Fodor's [15] notion of cognition being saturated with perception, and thus, all that can be known is determined by one's own epistemological framework. Interactionism is thus methodologically positioned between phenomenology and cognitivism (illustrated in the Fig. 1 with an X-mark).

4   Metodical Considerations

A solid investigation of visual experience in HCI as cognitive-affective phenomenon necessitates an interactionist approach, combining the objective and subjective accounts to visual experience. Interactionist approach can advance HCI research to understand experience formation in more detail, bring more predictability in connecting design decisions to experience goals [32] and to inform technology design enabling understandable and experiential encounters [74]. Examining mental information contents of visual experiences with an interactionist approach, objectivistic accounts can be utilized in detecting visual elements of object properties as a starting point in eliciting certain kinds of experiences. Explicating experiences solely from objectivistic perspective does not provide sufficient explicatory basis for visual experiences due to the deterministic and universalistic foundations of objectivism.

Visual representations constructed of perceivable elements elicit different mental information contents in people interacting with technology. However, this diversity of represented mental information contents in visual experiences does not posit that knowledge of visual experiences in HCI could not be obtained. Even though represented mental contents are highly subjective (i.e., meaningful information contents apperceived in technology interaction affected by already existing information contents [e.g.,

74], with careful operationalization of the constructs, qualitative dimensions (also non-perceivable kinds, such as timelessness and imaginativeness) attributed to the properties of technological artifacts can be examined.

Although experience is subjective (and often private) it can be approached and explicated by verbalization and obtained with interviews and protocol analysis [3], and with questionnaires [13]. To study and explain visual experiences of technological artifacts different methods can be used to obtain knowledge of visual experiences from different perspectives. In terms of interactionist stance acquiring objective and subjective data is desirable to avoid interference of metacognitive processes and to be able to connect artifact properties and experiential contents.

The need for strong theoretical underpinnings of visual experience is two-fold. In scientific research, only theoretically sound basis for operationalizing measures and discussing the results can yield useful understanding, which goes beyond single case studies. The same applies to design pursuits. Although examining how specific technological artifacts are experienced on a case-by-case basis has its benefits in informing design, this benefit is often limited to the narrow context of a certain object in investigation and on specific experience goals. Therefore, it is important in HCI design to understand the concepts of design and visual experience.

Various overlapping concepts have been used to conceptualize and operationalize measurements of visual experience. Often in HCI research the operationalization of aesthetics to be measured is conducted with a one-dimensional construct (especially in examining the aesthetic-usability effect), for example, as 'low' or 'high aesthetics' [83], pleasant or unpleasant [79], or non-appealing or appealing [80]. In these examples, the methodological grounds of visual and aesthetic experience are also un-explicated. Due to methodological lacks contradictory research results are to be reported, which also affects understanding of the phenomena and future research. It is, however, possible to posit methodological grounds from which the concepts studied are defined from and then operationalized to be measured. Thus, explicit operationalizations of utilized concepts with methodological positions are needed to advance theoretical and methodological grounds of HCI research and to produce reliable results of visual experience.

For example, dimensions of visual experience can be extracted with an Osgoodian method, where participants report their impressions of stimuli using Likert or semantic differential scales containing various adjectives. The responses are analyzed using factor analysis, which reveals latent dimensions of affective experiences [60]. Overall. different methods are needed, both objective (e.g., reaction times, eye-tracking data) and subjective data. Deductive, theory-based hypotheses can reveal certain aspects visual experience and inductive explanatory approaches can reveal other aspects. For example, a set of affects can be posited as measurement units based on results of previous research indicating elicitators of visual properties appraised as pleasurable in some specific design contexts. Through a combination of objective and subjective data visual experiences can be understood and explained in more detail.

5   Considerations of Stimuli

In addition to the theorical and methodological considerations presented, the role of visual stimuli affects visual experience research in HCI. Often in visual aesthetics in

HCI research visual stimuli are websites and mobile user interfaces. However, it is to be considered whether the stimuli can be titled as an aesthetic stimulus or should be comprehended as visual stimuli. Often the starting point is that the stimuli is titled as aesthetic, even though visual would be a more descriptive conceptualization if the formation process of visual experience is considered. If the selected stimuli would be titled as an aesthetic stimulus, it would be judged on its aesthetic qualities via some criteria or labelled as a stimulus that is considered to belong the aesthetic artifacts determined by the art world. In addition to user interfaces, visual stimuli in HCI research include maps [44] and, for example, icons [29, 51]. These visual representations are not commonly considered as "aesthetic stimuli", for instance in the research area of psychology of aesthetics [81]. However, the research approaches utilized in examining visual experience in HCI often follow similar research procedures as in empirical aesthetics (to which research in psychology of aesthetics often is based on). Therefore, classifying some visual stimuli as objects of design, art, or hybrids (between art and design, or combining these), plays an important role in selecting procedures and partly determines the research paradigm to which the research belongs to.

In models explicating the process aesthetic appraisal and aesthetic judgement [e.g., 45] the starting point of the process is the recognition of the stimuli as an object of art, for an aesthetic experience to occur. Majority of research conducted in visual aesthetics in HCI research is (whether implicitly or explicitly) in line with procedures undertaken in empirical aesthetics and psychology of art. However, the operationalizations of the studied phenomenon are not explicitly linked to the methodological foundations of empirical aesthetics [6, 7], even though the research problems and settings are similar. Thus, due to the nature of visual stimuli in HCI research, visual experience research in HCI would not be considered to belong to this research paradigm. This is partly explainable of the industry relations of HCI [47], which does not emphasize needs for basic research.

Recently, discussions of the role of aesthetic stimuli between 'art with a lower-case a' (e.g., popular culture) and 'art with upper-case A '(e.g., fine arts) have emerged. These considerations include views of examining experiences of technological (design) artifacts and representations of belonging to the research paradigm of empirical aesthetics [45, 81], or to philosophy of design aesthetics [17]. At times, design objects (not technological ones per se) have been studied as representatives of aesthetic stimuli [e.g., 25] similarly as objects of fine arts.

However, according to methodological stance of interactionism technological artifacts in HCI can be experienced as aesthetic and elicit similar appraisals as in encountering objects of art, because the experience is not in the object but occurs in the interaction between the user and the technological artifact. To put in other words, visual experience does not lie in the physical properties of an object but occurs in perceiver's mind informed by the properties of an object in attention. A stimulus is not therefore the sole determinator of the formation of visual experiences.

6 Conclusion

What visual experience is conceptualized to be determines the methodological position of the research. The explicated methodological position in examining visual experiences functions as a determinator to further research positions, operationalizations, and the chosen methods in investigating the phenomenon. Interactionism as a methodological approach to visual experience research in HCI combines objectivist and subjectivist approaches.

From an objectivist point of view (i.e., bottom-up approach), visual experience formation focuses on visual entities and their relations as determinants of aesthetic appeal [e.g., 4, 57, 84]. Visual experience from subjectivist perspective (i.e., top-down approach) posits top-down processes as the core experience occurrence [e.g., 43, 54]. Interactionist approach is based on the view that 'beauty is grounded in the processing experiences of the perceiver that emerge from the interaction of stimulus properties and perceivers' cognitive and affective processes' [64]. Thus, interactionist approach combines objective and subjective accounts to visual experience. Interactionism is extended from cognitive processing fluency paradigm with the explication of visual experience as a mental phenomenon [74]. In addition, interactionist approach to visual experience research does not differentiate between the nature of the stimuli, because aesthetics is not within the object, but occurs in the interaction between the stimuli and the perceiver.

References

1. Altaboli, A., Lin, Y.: Investigating effects of screen layout elements on interface and screen design aesthetics. In: Advances in Human-Computer Interaction, no. 5 (2011). https://doi.org/10.1155/2011/659758
2. Arnheim, R.: Art and Visual Perception: A Psychology of the Creative Eye. University of California Press, Berkeley (1974)
3. Bargas-Avila, J.A., Hornbæk, K.: Old wine in new bottles or novel challenges: a critical analysis of empirical studies of user experience. In: Proceedings of the SIGCHI Conference on Human Factors in Computing Systems, pp. 2689–2698. ACM, New York (2011). https://doi.org/10.1145/1978942.1979336
4. Bauerly, M., Liu, Y.: Computational modeling and experimental investigation of effects of compositional elements on interface and design aesthetics. Int. J. Hum. Comput. Stud. 64(8), 670–682 (2006). https://doi.org/10.1155/2011/659758
5. Bell, C.: Art. Capricorn Books, New York (1958)
6. Berlyne, D.: Aesthetics and Psychobiology. Appleton-Century-Crofts, New York (1971)
7. Berlyne, D.: Studies in the New Experimental Aesthetics: Steps Toward an Objective Psychology of Aesthetic Appreciation. Hemisphere, London (1974)
8. Carroll, N.: Beyond Aesthetics Philosophical essays. Cambridge University Press, Cambridge (2001)
9. Crilly, N., Moultrie, J., Clarkson, P.J.: Seeing things: consumer response to the visual domain in product design. Des. Stud. 25(6), 547–577 (2004). https://doi.org/10.1016/j.destud.2004.03.001
10. Csikszentmihalyi, M.: Design and order in everyday life. Des. Issues 8(1), 26–34 (1991). https://doi.org/10.2307/1511451
11. Desmet, P., Hekkert, P.: Framework of product experience. Int. J. Des. 1(1), 57–66 (2007)
12. Evans, P., Thomas, M.: Exploring the Elements of Design. Cengage Learning, Boston (2012)
13. Ericsson, A.K., Simon, H.A.: Protocol Analysis: Verbal Reports as Data. MIT Press, Cambridge (1984)
14. Fodor, J.: Fodor's guide to mental representation. Mind 94(373), 76–100 (1985)
15. Fodor, J.: Précis of the modularity of mind. Behav. Brain Sci. 8(01), 1–5 (1985)

16. Folkmann, M.N.: The Aesthetics of Imagination in Design. MIT Press, Cambridge (2013)
17. Forsey, J.: The Aesthetics of Design. Oxford University Press, Oxford (2016)
18. Frankish, K., Ramsey, W.M.: The Cambridge Handbook of Cognitive Science. Cambridge University Press, Cambridge (2012)
19. Galitz, W.: The Essential Guide to User Interface Design: An Introduction to GUI Design Principles and Techniques. Wiley, Hoboken (2007)
20. Gibson, J.: The Ecological Approach to Human Perception. Houghton Mifflin, Boston (1979)
21. Gombrich, E.: The Story of Art. Phaidon, London (1995)
22. Heidegger, M.: Being and time. English translation by J. Macquarrie and E. Robinson (1962). Basil Blackwell, Oxford (1927)
23. Hekkert, P.: Design aesthetics: principles of pleasure in design. Psychol. Sci. **48**(2), 157–172 (2006)
24. Hekkert, P., Leder, H.: Product aesthetics. In: Editor Schifferstein, H., Editor Hekkert, P. (eds.) Product Experience, pp. 259–286. Elsevier, Amsterdam (2008)
25. Hekkert, P., Snelders, D., Wieringen, P.C.W.: 'Most advanced, yet acceptable': typicality and novelty as joint predictors of aesthetic preference in industrial design. Br. J. Psychol. **94**, 111–124 (2003). https://doi.org/10.1348/000712603762842147
26. Hung, W.-K., Chen, L.-L.: Effects of novelty and its dimensions on aesthetic preference in product design. Int. J. Des. **6**(3), 81–90 (2012)
27. Husserl, E.: The Crisis of European Sciences and Transcendental Phenomenology. Northwestern University Press, Evanston (1936)
28. Itti, L., Koch, C., Niebur, E.: A model of saliency-based visual attention for rapid scene analysis. IEEE Trans. Pattern Anal. Mach. Intell. **20**(11), 1254–1259 (1998). https://doi.org/10.1109/34.730558
29. Isherwood, S.: Graphics and semantics: the relationship between what is seen and what is meant in icon design. In: Harris, D. (ed.) EPCE 2009. LNCS (LNAI), vol. 5639, pp. 197–205. Springer, Heidelberg (2009). https://doi.org/10.1007/978-3-642-02728-4_21
30. Ivory, M., Sinha, R., Hearst, M.: Empirically validated web page design metrics. In: Proceedings of the SIGCHI Conference on Human Factors in Computing Systems, pp. 53–60. ACM Press, New York (2001). https://doi.org/10.1145/365024.365035
31. Jokinen, J.P.P.: User psychology of emotional user experience. University Press, University of Jyväskylä. Doctoral Dissertation (2015)
32. Jokinen, J.P.P., Silvennoinen, J., Kujala, T.: Relating experience goals with visual user interface design. Interact. Comput. **30**(5), 378–395 (2018). https://doi.org/10.1093/iwc/iwy016
33. Jokinen, J.P.P., Silvennoinen, J., Perälä, P., Saariluoma, P.: Quick affective judgments: validation of a method for primed product comparisons. In: Proceedings of the 33rd Annual ACM Conference on Human Factors in Computing Systems, pp. 2221–2230. ACM Press, New York (2015). https://doi.org/10.1145/2702123.2702422
34. Kant, I.: Critique of pure reason. English translation by Paul Guyer and Allen Wood (1998). Cambridge University Press, Cambridge (1787)
35. Kepes, G.: Language of Vision. Paul Theobold, Chicago (1944)
36. Kim, J., Lee, J., Choi, D.: Designing emotionally evocative homepages: an empirical study of the quantitative relations between design factors and emotional dimensions. Int. J. Hum. Comput. Stud. **59**, 899–994 (2003). https://doi.org/10.1016/j.ijhcs.2003.06.002
37. Koffka, K.: Principles of Gestalt Psychology. Harcourt. Brace & World, New York (1935)
38. Krippendorff, K.: On the essential contexts of artifacts or on the proposition that "design is making sense (of things)." Des. Issues **5**(2), 9–39 (1989). https://doi.org/10.2307/1511512
39. Krippendorff, K.: Content Analysis: An Introduction to Its Methodology. Sage, Thousand Oaks (2004)

40. Krippendorff, K.: The Semantic Turn: A New Foundation for Design. Taylor & Francis CRC Press, Boca Raton, London, New York (2006)
41. Kurosu, M., Kashimura, K.: Apparent usability vs. inherent usability: experimental analysis on the determinants of the apparent usability. In: Proceedings of Conference Companion on Human Factors in Computing Systems (1995). https://doi.org/10.1145/223355.223680
42. Laudan, L.: Progress and its Problems. University of California Press, Berkeley (1977)
43. Lavie, T., Tractinsky, N.: Assessing dimensions of perceived visual aesthetics of web sites. Int. J. Hum. Comput. Stud. **60**(3), 269–298 (2004). https://doi.org/10.1016/j.ijhcs.2003.09.002
44. Lavie, T., Oron-Gilad, T., Meye, J.: Aesthetics and usability of in-vehicle navigation displays. Int. J. Hum. Comput. Stud. **69**(1), 80–99 (2011). https://doi.org/10.1016/j.ijhcs.2010.10.002
45. Leder, H., Belke, B., Oeberst, A., Augustin, D.: A model of aesthetic appreciation and aesthetic judgments. Br. J. Psychol. **95**(4), 489–508 (2004). https://doi.org/10.1348/000712604236 9811
46. Lin, Y.-C., Yeh, C.-H., Wei, C.-C.: How will the use of graphics affect visual aesthetics? A user-centered approach for web page design. Int. J. Hum. Comput. Stud. **71**(3), 217–227 (2013). https://doi.org/10.1016/j.ijhcs.2012.10.013
47. Liu, Y., Goncalves, J., Ferreira, D., Xiao, B., Hosio, S, Kostakos, V.: CHI 1994–2013: mapping two decades of intellectual progress through co-word analysis. In: Proceedings of the SIGCHI Conference on Human Factors in Computing Systems – CHI 2014, pp. 3553–3562 ACM Press, New York (2014). https://doi.org/10.1145/2556288.2556969
48. Ludden, G., Schifferstein, H., Hekkert, P.: Visual–tactual incongruities in products as sources of surprise. Empir. Stud. Arts **27**(1), 61–87 (2009). https://doi.org/10.2190/EM.27.1.d
49. Marković, S.: Components of aesthetic experience: aesthetic fascination, aesthetic appraisal, and aesthetic emotion. i-Perception **3**, 1–17 (2012). https://doi.org/10.1068/i0450aap
50. Martindale, C., Moore, K., Borkum, J.: Aesthetic preference: anomalous findings for Berlyne's psychobiological theory. Am. J. Psychol. 53–80 (1990)
51. McDougall, S., Isherwood, S.: What's in a name? The role of graphics, functions, and their interrelationships in icon identification. Behav. Res. Methods **41**(2), 325–336 (2009). https://doi.org/10.2307/1423259
52. Michailidou, E., Harper, S., Bechhofer, S.: Visual complexity and aesthetic perception of web pages. In: Proceedings of the 26th Annual ACM International Conference on Design of Communication, pp. 215–224. ACM Press, New York (2008). https://doi.org/10.1145/145 6536.1456581
53. Miniukovich, A., De Angeli, A.: Computation of interface aesthetics. In: Proceedings of the 33rd Annual ACM Conference on Human Factors in Computing Systems, pp. 1163–1172. ACM Press, New York (2015). https://doi.org/10.1145/2702123.2702575
54. Moshagen, M., Thielsch, M.: Facets of visual aesthetics. Int. J. Hum. Comput. Stud. **68**(10), 689–709 (2010). https://doi.org/10.1016/j.ijhcs.2010.05.006
55. Mullet, K., Sano, D.: Designing Visual Interfaces: Communication Oriented Techniques. Prentice Hall, New Jersey (1995)
56. Newell, A., Simon, H.A.: Human Problem Solving. Prentice-Hall, Englewood Cliffs (1972)
57. Ngo, D., Byrne, J.: Application of an aesthetic evaluation model to data entry screens. Comput. Hum. Behav. **17**, 149–185 (2001). https://doi.org/10.1016/S0747-5632(00)00042-X
58. Ngo, D., Byrne, J.: Modelling interface aesthetics. Inf. Sci. **152**, 25–46 (2003). https://doi.org/10.1016/S0020-0255(02)00404-8
59. Obrist, M., Seah, S., Subramanian, S.: Talking about tactile experiences. In: Proceedings of the SIGCHI Conference on Human Factors in Computing Systems, pp. 1659–1668. ACM Press, New York (2013). https://doi.org/10.1145/2470654.2466220
60. Osgood, C., May, W., Miron, M.: Cross-Cultural Universals of Affective Meaning. University of Illinois Press, Champaign (1975)

61. Park, S., Choi, D., Kim, J.: Visualizing e-brand personality: exploratory studies on visual attributes and e-brand personalities in Korea. Int. J. Hum.-Comput. Interact. **19**(1), 7–34 (2005). https://doi.org/10.1207/s15327590ijhc1901_3

62. Post, R., Blijlevens, J., Hekkert, P.: 'To preserve unity while almost allowing for chaos': testing the aesthetic principle of unity-in-variety in product design. Acta Psychol. (Amst.) **163**, 142–152 (2016). https://doi.org/10.1016/j.actpsy.2015.11.013

63. Postrel, V.: The Substance of Style. How Aesthetic Value is Remaking Commerce, Culture, and Consciousness. HarperCollins Publishers, New York (2003)

64. Reber, R., Schwarz, N., Winkielman, P.: Processing fluency and aesthetic pleasure: is beauty in the perceiver's processing experience? Pers. Soc. Psychol. Rev. **8**(4), 364–382 (2004). https://doi.org/10.1207/s15327957pspr0804_3

65. Reinecke, K., et al.: Predicting users' first impressions of website aesthetics with a quantification of perceived visual complexity and colorfulness. In: Proceedings of the SIGCHI Conference on Human Factors in Computing Systems, pp. 2049–2058. ACM Press, New York (2013). https://doi.org/10.1145/2470654.2481281

66. Saariluoma, P.: Chess Players' Thinking. Routledge, London (1995)

67. Saariluoma, P.: Foundational Analysis. Presuppositions in Experimental Psychology. Routledge, London, UK (1997)

68. Saariluoma, P.: Apperception, content-based psychology and design. In: Lindemann, U. (ed.) Human Behaviour in Design, pp. 72–78. Springer, Berlin (2003). https://doi.org/10.1007/978-3-662-07811-2_8

69. Saariluoma, P.: Explanatory frameworks for interaction design. In: Pirhonen, A., Isomäki, H., Roast, C., Saariluoma, P. (eds.) Future Interaction Design, pp. 67–83. Springer, London (2005). https://doi.org/10.1007/1-84628-089-3_5

70. Saariluoma, P., Oulasvirta, A.: User psychology: Re-assessing the boundaries of a discipline. Psychology **1**(5), 317–328 (2010). https://doi.org/10.4236/psych.2010.15041

71. Santayana, G.: The Sense of Beauty: Being the Outline of Aesthetic Theory. (Original work published in 1896). Dover, New York (1955)

72. Schenkman, B., Jönsson, F.: Aesthetics and preferences of web pages. Behav. Inf. Technol. **19**(5), 367–377 (2000). https://doi.org/10.1080/014492900750000063

73. Seckler, M., Opwis, K., Tuch, A.: Linking objective design factors with subjective aesthetics: an experimental study on how structure and color of websites affect the facets of users' visual aesthetic perception. Comput. Hum. Behav. **49**, 375–389 (2015). https://doi.org/10.1016/j.chb.2015.02.056

74. Silvennoinen, J.: Apperceiving Visual Elements in Human-technology Interaction Design. Jyväskylä studies in computing, 261. Jyvaskyla University Press, Jyvaskyla (2017)

75. Silvennoinen, J., Jokinen, J.P.P.: Appraisals of salient visual elements in web page design. In: Advances in Human-Computer Interaction Article ID 3676704, 14 p. (2016). https://doi.org/10.1155/2016/3676704

76. Silvennoinen, J., Jokinen, J.P.P.: Aesthetic appeal and visual usability in four icon design eras. In: Proceedings of the 2016 Conference on Human Factors in Computing Systems – CHI 2016, pp. 4390–4400. ACM Press, New York (2016). https://doi.org/10.1145/2858036.2858462

77. Silvennoinen, J., Rousi, R., Jokinen, J.P.P., Perälä, P.: Apperception as a multisensory process in material experience. In: Proceedings of the Academic Mindtrek, pp. 144–151. ACM Press, New York (2015). https://doi.org/10.1145/2818187.2818285

78. Skinner, B.F.: Contingencies of Reinforcement: A Theoretical Analysis. Appleton-Century-Crofts, New York (1969)

79. Sonderegger, A., Sauer, J.: The influence of design aesthetics in usability testing: effects on user performance and perceived usability. Appl. Ergon. **41**(3), 403–410 (2010). https://doi.org/10.1016/j.apergo.2009.09.002

80. Thielsch, M., Hirschfeld, G.: Spatial frequencies in aesthetic website evaluations – explaining how ultra-rapid evaluations are formed. Ergonomics 55(7), 731–742 (2012). https://doi.org/10.1080/00140139.2012.665496
81. Tinio, P., Smith, J. (eds.): The Cambridge Handbook of the Psychology of Aesthetics and the Arts. Cambridge University Press, United Kingdom (2014)
82. Tractinsky, N., Avivit, C., Kirschenbaum, M., Sharfi, T.: Evaluating the consistency of immediate aesthetic perceptions of web pages. Int. J. Hum. Comput. Stud. 64(11), 1071–1083 (2006). https://doi.org/10.1016/j.ijhcs.2006.06.009
83. Tractinsky, N., Katz, A., Ikar, D.: What is Beautiful is Usable. Interact. Comput. 13(2), 127–145 (2000). https://doi.org/10.1016/S0953-5438(00)00031-X
84. Tuch, A., Presslaber, E., Stöcklin, M., Opwis, K., BargasAvila, J.: The role of visual complexity and prototypicality regarding first impression of websites: working towards understanding aesthetic judgments. Int. J. Hum. Comput. Stud. 70, 794–811 (2012). https://doi.org/10.1016/j.ijhcs.2012.06.003
85. Veryzer, R., Hutchinson, W.: The influence of unity and prototypicality on aesthetic responses to new product designs. J. Consum. Res. 24(4), 374–394 (1998). https://doi.org/10.1086/209516
86. Wertheimer, M.: Laws of organization in perceptual forms. In: Ellis W.D. (ed.) A Source Book of Gestalt Psychology, pp. 71–88. Kegan Paul, Trench, Trubner & Company (1938)

Construction of a Novel Production Develop Decision Model Based on Text Mined

Tianxiong Wang, Xin Sun, Meiyu Zhou[✉], and Xian Gao

School of Art Design and Media, East China University of Science and Technology, NO. 130, Meilong Road, Xuhui District, Shanghai 200237, China

Abstract. When users choose a product, they will consider the emotional experience triggered by the product form. The Kansei engineering is considered to be the most reliable and useful method to deal with users' emotional needs. Therefore, in this study a hybrid method that combines text mining and Kansei engineering is proposed, which have integrated TF-IDF, SD, BPNN, and NSGA-II methods to extract product shape design solutions that meet user multidimensional needs. The TF-IDF is applied to analyze Kansei image factors of the product of user's review so as to realize the mining of user needs from the perspective of user real online shopping evaluation. Then, the FA is applied to analyze representative Kansei need items. Furthermore, the BPNN is used to identify the relationship between design variables and user demands, so that the prediction model is constructed. The non-dominated sorting genetic algorithm-II is used as the multi-objective evolutionary method to obtain the Pareto optimal solutions that meets the user's multidimensional needs. Taking electric bicycles as an example, the experimental results show that this proposed method can help designers to obtain the production solutions based on users' real Kansei needs.

Keywords: User need · Affective mining · Product innovation design · Decision making

1 Introduction

The increasingly competitive market and rapidly changing customer needs has forced product development companies and designers to find ways to not only save time and cost, but also meet customer needs and conform to market trends in the process of new product development [1]. Many manufacturers have to reduce cost and drastically shorten the time to market [2]. At the same time, consumers have high expectations for new products, they care about not only the functions and reliability, but also the emotional aspects, such as elegant appearance, comfortable texture and attractive elements that can meet their emotional needs [3]. Therefore, Some researchers and manufacturers conduct research on the emotional aspects of products based on a user-centric perspective. They investigate the specific needs of consumers by evaluating the psychological feedback of consumers after using the product, while manufacturers collect and analyze these feedbacks and apply the analysis results to their production development plan [4]. Kansei Engineering

© Springer Nature Switzerland AG 2021
M. M. Soares et al. (Eds.): HCII 2021, LNCS 12779, pp. 128–143, 2021.
https://doi.org/10.1007/978-3-030-78221-4_9

[5, 6] is a modern scientific method that transforms human needs into design schemes and specific design elements. "Kansei", a Japanese word which refers to the user's feelings, impressions and emotions about the product, [7] could include factors such as design, size, color, function and service. Kansei engineering is considered to be the most reliable and useful method to deal with users' emotional needs [8], which has been applied by many scholars in industrial product fields.

In the traditional research stage of Kansei Engineering, questionnaire surveys composed of Kansei attributes and product attributes lists are usually used to obtain product attributes and user experience. Questionnaire surveys are often used to obtain the relationship between emotional attributes and product design features, and among which, the most commonly used method is the Semantic Difference(SD) Method, which is a scoring standard used to measure the opinions and attitudes of respondents for a given object [9] so as to measure consumers' subjective impressions of products. In fact, apart from the high-quality results such traditional method has produced, they are small in scale and one-off, which could lead to limitations in data scale, data update, and collection efficiency [10]. In addition, under the guidance of these subjective presuppositions, customers usually express their feelings or describe their experiences passively. However, the real needs and preferences are often not unapparent and hidden in the customer's response, so it is difficult to capture the real needs of users based on these traditional user needs acquisition methods. Therefore, it is necessary to develop an automated method for effective review of consumer emotional feedback.

With the development of computer and internet technology, online shopping has become a trend that continues to impact consumption patterns, which could cause significant changes in volume and structure [11]. Millions of customers have the opportunity to compare similar products on retail platforms, such as Amazon.com or Taobao.com, to choose their favorite products and the most suitable products [12]. People can choose their favorite products in online shopping malls and browse other consumers' reviews of products, and leave their reviews of the product. Customers' expectations and future demands are also included in online customer reviews, which could help to understand consumers' experience and expectations of services and products [13]. Furthermore, this could also overcome the shortcomings of lack of authenticity caused by traditional questionnaire surveys [12]. Therefore, efficiently and accurately identifying and analyzing useful product reviews to meet the needs of current and potential customers has become the key challenge for market-driven product development. Text mining refers to the use of natural language processing, computational linguistics, and statistical analysis to systematically and automatically identify and extract useful information from the text [14]. Due to a large number of online consumer reviews, important emotional information can be extracted with the application of text mining from the consumer's perspective view in an efficient and effective way [14].

Therefore, the key objective of this research is to help designers to identify customer needs, investigate consumer preference factors, and develop product forms that meet consumer needs. To this end, we attempt to propose an integrated product development decision-making method that can analyze customer reviews and extract the real kansei needs of users. Text mining is used to mine and analyze product-related perceptual demands of users from customer reviews. Then, the experiment result of customer demands is incorporated into the product evolution process, and NN is used to construct the quantitative mapping relationship between user Kansei mage and product modeling elements, and then the NSGA-II and NN are effectively combined to develop an automatic generation Pareto product solutions that meets the multi-dimensional needs of users. Accordingly, with this proposed method, we can not only obtain the user's multi-objective demand Kansei image in a faster way, but also make full use of the multi-objective evolutionary algorithm to establish the product Kansei design model in a shorter cycle and with more efficiency. This study uses electric bicycles as a case to verify the effectiveness and applicability of this proposed method.

2 Literature Review

2.1 Text Mining

To deal with unstructured text, Feldman and Dagan [15] first used text mining as a technique for use with knowledge discovering from text (KDT), especially for the usually large, noisy and unstructured social media data. The main task of product review mining is product feature word extraction and emotional evaluation of product feature words [16], which mainly refers to extract product-related user evaluation words from the product review text through the use of natural language processing technology [17], computational linguistics, statistical analysis and other technologies to automatically identify and extract useful information from the text [18].

With the support of text mining, many scholars are committed to analyze product reviews to obtain key information related to customers' opinions and experiences about reviewed products [2]. For example, Zhu and Zhang [19] explored the consumers' dependence on online reviews and the influence of purchasing decisions. Christensen et al. [20] applied text mining and machine learning to identify and detect new product ideas from online communities which could automatically distinguish the ideal text from non-ideal text. Zheng Xiang et al. [21] used the method of text analysis to extract and analyze hotel guest experience from a large number of consumer reviews on Expedia.com, and test its relationship of satisfaction. Wang [22] proposed a perspective perception analysis framework about PRODWeakFinder, which could detect product weaknesses by considering both comparative and non-comparative evaluations from a large number of online reviews. Therefore, it can be found that many researchers have used text mining to help understand consumer behavior and experience. In fact, in KE, text mining has also been applied to the design of products and services by some scholars. Jin et al. [13] presented a method to manually convert customer requirements in online reviews into engineering features (ECs) for quality function development (QFD). Chiu [2] combined text mining method and KE to collect online product reviews, and then used the KE to identify design component factors that customers prefer. However, little of the literature is related to the application of text mining in the electric bicycles field, and the early stage of supporting product development process. Therefore, the author tried to apply web crawler tools to collect product online reviews, and then use natural language technology to rapidly constructing the user Kansei image space so as to obtain the key users' demands of electric bicycles.

2.2 Neural Networks

The neural network (NN) technology was developed by Gallant in 1993 [23]. In fact, artificial neural network (ANN) is a mathematical computational model, which could effectively imitate the structure and function of biological neural network [24]. Each neural network is composed of a group of interconnected artificial neurons to simulate the capability of NN in living creatures to automatically adjust their structure and parameters to learn data, so that the complex nonlinear data relationships can be constructed based on mapping between input variables and output variables [25]. Therefore, the main feature of artificial neural networks is that they can simulate the self-learning and organizational capabilities of the human brain, which can process incomplete data and can solve complex and ambiguous problems. The basic computing unit of a neural network is called a node, and the nodes are connected in three layers: input layer, output layer and hidden layer [24]. The most commonly used ANN model is the three-layer feedforward and backpropagation model [26]. In the actual iteration process, the output result is compared with the required value, and the resulting error signal is backpropagated through the back-propagation neural network (BPNN) layer and the weight of each network connection is gradually adjusted until the specified error standard is met. In the process of BPNN verification and subsequent operations, the network generates output variables by applying the weights established in the training process to input, which can be propagated from layer to layer. Based on the effective learning, storage and prediction capabilities, BPNN could provide a powerful means to check the complex relationship between input variables and output variables [27]. In KE, Yu et al. [24] systematically demonstrated that ANN and the Extreme Learning Machine (ELM) prediction model based on GRA are superior to other models in predicting fashion color trends. FANG et al. [28] proposed a calculation model that uses backpropagation neural network(BPNN) to simulate the psychological function of color aesthetic evaluation, and then uses genetic algorithm (GA) to effectively optimize the number of hidden layer nodes, learning rate and momentum constant of each neural network. Chen and CHANG [29] presented a research framework of incorporating linear regression model and BP neural network to determine the correlation between product form characteristics and consumer perception of product image, and finally took the knife design as an example to verify the feasibility of this proposed method. Misaka and Aoyama [30] used NN to develop and construct a system that can output crack patterns that meet the user's desired impression. Therefore, based on the relevant literature, we found that neural networks can effectively learn and imitate human non-linear thinking methods to deal with subjective and imprecise emotional activities. Therefore, we attempted to carry out BPNN to construct the mapping relationship between user Kansei images and product design factors.

2.3 Nondominated Sorting Genetic Algorithm-II

The evolutionary algorithm is a general population-based meta-heuristic optimization algorithm that imitates the principle of evolution, and it has been applied to the optimization of product design. Among them, the genetic algorithm is applied to find the optimal solution among all possible solutions. However, user needs are actually diversified, and traditional single-objective optimization could hardly meet their actual needs. Thus, in order to solve the user's multi-objective optimization problem, some efficient multi-objective evolutionary algorithms have been proposed. The novelty of the evolutionary algorithm to solve the multi-objective programming problem is that it can retain multiple different non-dominated solutions at the same time, instead of a single optimal solution [31]. Obviously, the advantage of the multi-objective evolutionary algorithm is that it does not need to assume the shape of the pareto optimal front, and it can search for a set of approximate pareto fronts, so that they are considered to be a powerful tool for solving multiobjective optimization (MOO) problem. The non-dominated sorting genetic algorithm (NSGA) proposed by Srinivas and Deb [32] is a basic type of multi-objective optimization evolutionary algorithm. Subsequently, Deb et al. [33] proposed an improved version of NSGA which is named NSGA-II. Currently, the NSGA-II is the most commonly used method of MOO algorithm, which is an elite genetic algorithm that is often used to solve multiobjective optimization problems. Specifically, it has the merits of less time complexity and it uses the elitism and crowding comparison operators to ensure diversity and uniformity for population, which is critical in obtaining the representative design solution. Besides, the NSGA-II can better maintain the dispersion and spread of solutions, and better converge in the obtained non-dominated frontier, and the diversity maintenance mechanism used in NSGA-II was found to be the best in the multiobjective evolutionary algorithm [34]. In the study of production design, Jiang et al. [35] utilized a research method that simultaneously considered emotional design and determined new product engineering specifications, which could involve the generation of customer satisfaction models, the formulation of multiobjective optimization models and the use of chaos-based NSGA-II method. Therefore, we proposed a product design method based on BPNN and NSGA-II to construct a mixed Kansei engineering system based on multi-emotional response, and generate the product shape design that meets user needs.

3 Proposed Methodologies

In order to meet the needs of users and speed up the product development process, this research proposes an automatic product form design that combines text mining and NSGA-II algorithms. Firstly, the TF-IDF feature extraction method is used to extract the key demands of product users' perceptual semantics from the internet. Then, the SD method is used to quantify the user's Kansei semantic preference, and the factor analysis (FA) is used to reduce the dimension to extract the user's key Kansei image factors. Then, the morphological analysis is used to extract the morphological elements of the electric bicycle product by the expert group, and the production model is further qualitatively segmented. Secondly, the collected product sample data and consumer evaluation demand data are used to train the neural network model, which is used to simulate the evaluation model of the product perceptual image that the user could predict adapt to the change of the product shape feature. Therefore, the map relationship between product design elements and the product's perceptual image space is constructed so as to realize the multi-dimensional prediction of the product's overall Kansei image.

Finally, we use the NSGA-II method to simulate design thinking for product iteration and innovation to generate product alternatives that meet the needs of users. Furthermore, in each iteration process, the neural network prediction model is adopted to evaluate the product solutions generated by the multiobjective evolutionary algorithm of NSGA-II so as to accurately obtain the Pareto optimal edge product design plan that meets the user's multiobjective needs.

3.1 Text Mining

Text Pre-processing. This step is going to discuss the specific elements that need to be preprocessed before text analysis. In order to make the results of text mining a representative of the majority of consumers, the number of customer comments collected by this research must be as large as possible. Firstly, once the target product is selected, we need to browse shopping websites extensively and collect representative samples of the product. As we all know, popular production can receive hundreds of comments, which reflects greater reliability. In fact, the brief comments, discussions or similar statements related to products are regarded as customer reviews. In order to make the results of text mining a reflection of the perceptual perspective of reviewers, this research only focuses on the text content, in which information about user names, dates, evaluation ratings and image information are excluded. Customer reviews from shopping websites are collected as input information, and then natural language is used for semantic analysis. However, the original comments are mixed with a lot of invalid and unclear information, only part of the information is useful for consumer or business analysis. Hence, the original comments need to be cleaned up for higher data quality. After cleaning the user comment text, we use the Jieba tool for word segmentation and part-of-speech (POS) tagging. Through word segmentation and POS tagging, each sentence in the online comment is broken down into several words for subsequent text analysis.

Text Analysis. This study uses text analysis methods to extract product-related information from preprocessed product review texts, and attempts to use natural language technology to accurately identify consumers' Kansei images of products from the collected reviews. Firstly, we apply the TF-IDF method to count the key kansei information from user reviews, and obtain preliminary Kansei word, and group them into categories according to their semantic similarity through the KJ [36] method, and divide each group into two sub-groups.

Firstly, Kansei images is the key demand to describe the user's emotional experience. By identifying the user's emotional attitude factors and their frequency of appearance, we can construct the spatial dimension of perceptual image. Therefore, we attempt to calculate the importance of each word through term frequency–inverse document frequency (TF-IDF). The TF-IDF is a commonly used weighting technique for information retrieval and text mining so as to quantify the strength of each Kansei vocabulary. Specifically, the importance of a word increases in proportion to the number of times it appears in the text, but at the same time, it decreases in inverse proportion to the frequency of its appearance in other corpus. The specific steps are as follows [37]:

For the set D containing M number of Chinese texts, we use the Jieba segmentation word tool to perform word segmentation for each text in the set $D,$ and then use the

TF-IDF algorithm to calculate its weight $TF\text{-}IDF_{i,j}$ in the text, which could represent the weight of the word t_i in the text $D_j (j = 1, 2, 3,..., M)$ and it could be calculated by Formula (1):

$$TF - IDF_{i,j} = TF_{i,j} \times IDF_i \tag{1}$$

In Eq. (2): $n_{i,j}$ is the number of occurrences of the word t_i in the text D_j, and the denominator is the sum of the number of occurrences of all words in the text D_j.

$$TF_{i,j} = \frac{n_{i,j}}{\sum_k n_{k,j}} \tag{2}$$

In formula (3), $|D|$ is the total number of texts in the corpus, $|\{j:t_i \in D_j\}|$ could refer to the text number of contained the word t_i (i.e., the number of texts with $n_{i,j} \neq 0$). If the word is not in the corpus, it will result in a denominator of zero. Thus, in general, use the $1+|\{j:t_i \in D_j\}|$ to address actual project. The high frequency of words in a specific text and the low text frequency of the words in the entire text collection can produce high-weight TF-IDF value. Therefore, the TF-IDF tends to filter common words and retain important words.

$$IDF_i = \lg \frac{|D|}{|\{j : t_i \in D_j\}|} \tag{3}$$

3.2 Developing the Predictive Models for Affective Responses

This research uses neural network models to develop non-linear predictive models that are difficult to describe with mathematical equations. Backpropagation neural network (BPNN) has the basic characteristics of neural network, and it appropriately matches the product form with the emotional response of consumers [38]. Therefore, we use BPNN to develop a predictive model of emotional response which could use a three-layer neural network and has a single hidden layer. Specifically, the input layer has 28 nodes, which is a total of 28 product shape elements corresponding to the 6 morphological variables characteristics. The input data contain 40 product design program variables, and the nodes of the output layer include multi-dimensional user demand Kansei evaluation factors.

In order to eliminate the size error, it is necessary to normalize the input and output data. Since the output parameters of the training function need to be in the interval [0, 1], the kasnei evaluation results are obviously not completely in this interval. This paper uses the fast linear transformation algorithm of Eq. (5) to normalize the data so that the experimental results are in a suitable interval. The x_i and x_i' respectively represent the values before and after normalization, x_{max} and x_{min} respectively represent the maximum and minimum values in the vector.

$$x_i' = \frac{x_i - x_{min}}{x_{max} - x_{min}}. \tag{4}$$

In this research, for the activation function of the hidden layer, use the logarithmic sigmoid transfer function [39]:

$$f(x) = \frac{1}{1 + e^{-x}} \tag{5}$$

In order to verify the performance of the neural network model, the samples in the test set are encoded as input layer parameters, and then the output layer values are further obtained. At the same time, the root mean square error(RMSE) is utilized to test the predicted and measured values, and the RMSE is selected to evaluate the accuracy of the emotional evaluation model.

$$\text{RMSE} = \sqrt{\frac{\sum_{i=1}^{n} (y_i - \hat{y}_i)^2}{n}} \tag{6}$$

Where y_i is the evaluation value given by this research participant, $\hat{y}_i$ is the predicted value from SVR, n is the specific number of data. If there is no difference between two values, the RMSE is equal to 0. Otherwise, the value of RMSE will be large.

3.3 Constructing the Multiobjective Optimisation Model

The multiobjective optimization problem in this research involves multi-dimensional emotional optimization. In this research, for the maximization problem, the multiobjective optimization model can be constructed as follows:

$$\text{Maximize } [y_1, y_2, \ldots, y_n]^T, \tag{7}$$

Where $y_i(i = 1, 2, \ldots, n)$ is the emotional response value predicted by BPNN.

3.4 Deriving the Optimal Solutions Based on the Nondominated Sorting Genetic Algorithm-II

The NSGA-II is an optimization for the traditional genetic algorithm. It has designed an elite strategy in the selection operation process, that is, after the parent population and the offspring population are merged, some inferior individuals need to be further eliminated. Thus, the remained individuals are passed through the parent population to compete with all individuals in the offspring population to obtain the best solution, which is also efficient in obtaining the optimal solution. At the same time, the NSGA-II algorithm first puts forward the definition of congestion, which means measuring the attribute factors of congestion around an individual in the same non-dominated level. The individual with a larger congestion distance could be preferentially selected, which could not only avoid the excessive concentration of individuals and fall into the local optimum, but also take more even distribution of the population in the same dominated level. Hence, the diversity of the population could be increased.

4 Case Study

4.1 Selecting Experimental Samples for Electric Bicycles

In order to determine the common shape elements of electric bicycles, select the models with more reviews through the two major e-commerce platforms of Taobao and Jing-dong, and to find the corresponding morphological data of production. The model is distinguished based on whether the shapes are the same, and then select more reviews of electric bicycles as an experimental sample, 30 products were selected on the Taobao e-commerce platform and other 30 products were selected on the JingDong e-commerce platform based on the number of reviews. Thus, a total of 60 productions are selected. We need to select representative products from most samples to improve the efficiency of subsequent emotional cognition experiments. Therefore, we formed a panel of experts to select representative products, which consisted of 10 designers with five years of product design experience (5 females and 5 males, average aged of 32.4 years). Therefore, on the basis of this quantitative statistical analysis, we could seek the reference opinions of the expert group. Thus, 40 representative electric bicycle product samples are selected from 60 products.

4.2 Construction of Kansei Images for Electric Bicycles

Kansei Vocabulary Screening and Grouping Based on TF-IDF. Firstly, the crawler is used to obtain user comment information, and then to remove words or phrases that are not related to the semantic meaning of the text, and then to perform further word segmentation processing. According to the word segmentation results, the text feature words are extracted and classified based on formula (1), so that product keywords and weight factors are extracted. Thus, a total of 184 product-related adjectives are extracted according to the weights in descending order. A focus group composed of 4 industrial designers with 3 years of work experience selected these words, and merged the same items through KJ simplification method. Hence, 24 Kansei vocabularies related to product images were selected as representative Kansei images. According to their semantics, these words are divided into 12 groups, and each group could be divided into 2 subgroups according to the positive and negative, and the positive is the A group, the negative is the B group. The result of each Kansei adjective is described in Table 1.

Determining the Key Emotional Dimensions Demands. In order to more accurately quantify the image semantic preference of users for electric bicycle products, the 7-point scale of SD method is adopted. The questionnaire consisted of 20 representative samples selected from 40 electric bicycles samples and 12 Kansei words, and 128 subjects with at least 2 years of design education background (64 women and 64 men, average age is 24.35 years old, aged 23–31 years) were recruited to participate in the experiment, which is asked to complete the questionnaire. Then, the method of sample mean statistics is used to calculate the results of the semantic preference of SD experiment.

In order to examine the factor structure of these 12 adjectives, we used factor analysis (FA) to analyze the results of questionnaires. The test result found that Kaiser-Meyer-Olkin (KMO) is 0.853, and the significance is 0.000, which could indicate that the data

Table 1. 12 group representative Kansei words

Group number	Kansei words	Kansei words
1	Dexterous	Thick
2	Cozy	Restrained
3	Dependable	Unreliable
⋮	⋮	⋮
10	Novel	Boring
11	Broad	Narrow
12	Soft	Stiff

are suitable for FA and there is a significant difference. Next, the minimum eigenvalue 1 is used as the cutoff value. Obviously, these 12 adjectives are divided into three main factors, which could account for 83.674% of the cumulative variance. Then, we adopted the adjective with the largest load factor to name this three factors, namely "Stylish-Common", "Cozy-Restrained" and "Bright-Dim". Therefore, in this study, these three factors are used as target criteria for multi-dimensional user emotional needs.

4.3   Morphological Analysis for Product Form Elements

Morphological analysis method was used to extract the shape elements of the 40 representative electric bicycle samples. In the first step, 8 subjects (product design experts) were asked to write down the key styling elements of electric bicycle products based on their knowledge and experience. The key styling features include elements that make up the contour components of the electric bicycle, such as mudguards, headlights, cushions or body lines. Then, a focus group was formed by 6 subjects, and the similar opinion of the survey results were integrated based on the KJ method. The electric bicycle can be divided into approximately six main form features, which are respectively front structure (C1), Wheel hub (C2), Waist line (C3), Cushion(C4), Headlight (C5), Fender (C6). Each styling element has its own different shape type.

4.4   Constructing the Mapping Relationship Model for Affective Responses

Constructing the Kansei Evaluation Matrix. To establish a mapping model between the user's image and the styling elements, we should obtain the experimental data of image cognition in order to establish a predictive model for the image. Therefore, a questionnaire of 7-point SD method is used to combine 40 representative samples with three emotional factors, and then 124 participants (62 women and 62 men, average age 26.75 years old, aged 21–29 years) with at least 3 years of design education background or corporate product design experience were invited to experiment research process. The average value of moment arithmetic is utilized as the evaluation result, and then based on the deconstruction process of the modeling elements, the samples are coded. Hence, the emotion evaluation matrix of electric bicycle is constructed, as shown in Table 2.

Table 2. Evaluation matrix for 40 representative production samples.

Sample no.	Design variables						Affective responses		
	C1	C2	C3	C4	C5	C6	Cozy-restrainted	Stylish-common	Bright-dim
1	5	1	6	2	1	2	4.366	4.354	5.969
2	2	3	5	2	1	2	5.497	5.865	5.821
3	4	3	4	4	5	2	4.655	5.452	5.431
4	4	4	6	4	5	2	4.741	5.541	5.519
5	4	3	1	4	5	1	4.843	4.676	5.319
6	4	4	4	4	5	2	5.425	5.589	4.428
:	:	:	:	:	:	:	:	:	:
35	4	4	5	4	5	2	4.635	5.369	5.472
36	4	3	4	4	5	2	4.966	5.759	5.932
37	1	3	2	1	1	1	6.329	5.821	6.124
38	4	4	4	4	5	2	4.337	5.583	5.528
39	4	3	3	4	5	2	4.732	4.839	5.863
40	1	3	5	2	4	3	6.325	5.748	5.918

Developing the Prediction Models Based on the BPNN. In fact, the relationship between emotional response and variables in product form design is usually highly nonlinear. In this study, the BPNN was used to establish this nonlinear relationship. This study uses the three-layer neural network with a single hidden layer. The input layer has 28 nodes, that is, 6 morphological variables of a total of 28 morphological types. The input data is 40 product design models. The three nodes of the output layer are the evaluation for Kansei image which are "Cozy-Restrainted", "Stylish-Common", "Bright-Dim". The number of neurons in the hidden layer is set as the arithmetic mean of the number of input neurons and the number of output neurons [39]. Therefore, the number of neurons for the hidden layer is determined as $(28 + 1)/2 = 14.5$, which is set to 15 neurons in this study.

Since design variables cannot be used as input parameters directly, the specific design element of electric bicycles need to be coded. The number of coded bits in each sample is the same as the total number of design levels, which is 28. The code of each design element has only one number of 1, and the rest are 0. In addition, the output parameters of the training function need to be in the interval [0,1], but the Kansei evaluation result is obviously not completely in this interval. Thus, the Kansei evaluation value needs to be normalized. In this paper, the fast linear transformation algorithm of Eq. (4) is used to normalize this data, so that the result of Kansei evaluation is scaled in an appropriate interval. Then, we imported it as an output parameter into the neural network model of electric bicycles design for further training.

In this study, the first 34 samples were set as the training set, and the last 6 samples were set as the test set. Newff is used to create NN, based on the application of ANN, the relationship between 28 design elements ($X1-X6$) and 3 high-level sensitive words ($Y1–Y3$) of the product is established. After 34 product network training, in order to verify the performance of the neural network model, the 6 samples of the test set are encoded as input layer parameters, and then the value of the output layer is obtained. At the same time, the performance of the model is evaluated based on RMSE to compare the predicted and measured values. If there is no difference or error between the output value and the expected value, the RMSE is zero. Compare the predicted value of the model with the actual value of the sample to get the RMSE. When the RMSE of the neural network is small, it means that the constructed neural network model can be used for prediction and inference in actual problems. The RMSE of Cozy-Restrainted, Stylish-Common, Bright-Dim are 0.203, 0.182 and 0.165 respectively, as shown in Table 3. According to Hsiao's research [40], the testing accuracy of both models are acceptable.

Table 3. The predictive performance of BPNN model

Kansei words	Cozy-restrainted	Stylish-common	Bright-dim
RMSE	0.203	0.182	0.165

4.5 Deriving the Design Solutions for Electric Bicycles

In order to realize the product form search based on multiobjective users' need, this research adopts the nondominated sorting genetic algorithm-II to handle this problem, which has a wide range of applications in solving multiobjective planning problems. In this study, the optimization process of nondominated sorting genetic algorithm-II starts from generating an initial chromosome population through orthogonality within the range of shape features. Each chromosome is assigned a fitness value calculated from the NN prediction model for three emotional dimensions. In each generation, the tournament selection operator could be used to select the better chromosome in the parent group, which is similar to traditional genetic algorithms, the selected chromosomes could undergo crossover and mutation operations to form offspring populations. The corresponding parameters for nondominated sorting genetic algorithm-II optimization in this study were specified as follows: 1,000 evaluations, a population size of 80, a crossover rate of 0.8, a mutation rate is set to 0.3. When the predefined generation number of 1,000 is reached, the product modeling search is terminated. A total of 80 Pareto solutions are obtained, as shown in Table 4.

Table 4. 80 production design solutions obtained.

Sample number	Design variables C_{11}–C_{63}	Affective responses		
		Cozy-restrainted	Stylish-common	Bright-dim
1	000010010010000000100100010	3.405	3.187	2.552
2	000010010010000000100100010	2.988	2.806	2.635
3	000010010010000000100100010	2.967	2.890	2.803
4	001000010010000000100100010	2.747	3.651	3.636
⋮	⋮	⋮	⋮	⋮
80	001000010100000100000100010	3.475	3.592	3.540

5 Results and Discussion

Today, whether a product can quickly become the focus of consumers' eyes has become a core factor for product success. In the previous KE researches, some scholar used the semantic difference (SD) method to construct the matching relationship between product design elements and user needs combining with statistical methods. This is an intuitive and feasible method, but the SD results may ignore the user's vague emotional recognition demand. At the same time, in the KE research, researchers only clarify user appeals based on the number of mentions during user interviews, and usually users are not aware of their true emotional appeals, and it is a qualitative method, which is imprecise. In fact, the real needs of users are usually hidden and uncertain. Therefore, in this study, we use a text mining and natural language research approach to accurately obtain customers' psychological cognitive needs for productions to dig out the real needs of users. Therefore, the web crawler is used to dig out the user's evaluation data of the product, and extract the key Kansei vocabulary through TF-IDF, and based on the expert interviews and with KJ simplification method to preliminarily determine the Kansei vocabulary.

In order to further quantify and analyze the relationship between users' multi-emotional appeals and product modeling, the BPNN was applied to construct a nonlinear quantitative mapping relationship between them. Accordingly, the RMSE was used to verify the performance of this model. Moreover, in order to maximize the user's perception of the multi-dimensional emotional image for the product, the NSGA-II is used to iterate and update the product modeling and use the mapping model trained by BPNN as the fitness function of NSGA-II, and then the Pareto solution set of product design is derived and product design solution sets that meet the multi-dimensional demands of users could further be obtained.

Therefore, the method proposed in this article uses text mining theory to accurately mine the user's implicit emotional preference factors in the product design decision process to reflect the user's actual demands. Undoubtedly, the result of this experiment not only can reflect the fuzzy cognition of users, but also meet the actual needs of customers. Therefore, this Kansei-driven method composed of TF-IDF, BPNN, and NSGA-II proposed in this study can be effectively applied to discover the mapping relationship between the multi-dimensional perceptual needs of users and the combination of product feature, and automatically generate the most optimized innovative product design plan so as to provide theoretical guidance for the designer of decision-making. Hence, the decision support model proposed by this research can not only greatly reduce the risk of new product development, but also help designers develop new products that meet customer needs. The electric bicycle was taken as an example to verify the efficiency and effectiveness of this systematic method. According to this experimental results, if the electric bicycle design scheme is developed with reference to this standard, it will meet the user's psychology need to a certain extent and improve user satisfaction. In conclusion, this research could explore product design solutions that meet user needs through the proposal research framework. It is worth mentioning that this research method is also applicable to other productions with different design elements.

6   Conclusions

Customer demand could play an important role in the realization of enterprise product innovation goals. This research takes the electric bicycle product as an example, and constructed a user demand driven product form design and development method, and also explored the development process which combines text analysis and BPNN in the product design. The main conclusions of this research are summarized as follows.

1. Based on the big data of network evaluation, Kansei adjectives of products are extracted accurately and quickly through TF-IDF, and the multi-dimensional Kansei demands of users are further clarified through FA, so that designers can quickly and efficiently obtain the Kansei needs.
2. The quantitative mapping relationship between product Kansei image and product modeling elements is constructed, and the predict value is served as the adaptability in the product evolution process.
3. The production design solutions are explored of the product modeling plan that meets the multi-dimensional emotional needs of users.

References

1. Wang, C.-H.: Combining rough set theory with fuzzy cognitive pairwise rating to construct a novel framework for developing multi-functional tablets. J. Eng. Des. 29(8–9), 430–448 (2018)
2. Chiu, M.-C., Lin, K.-Z.: Utilizing text mining and kansei engineering to support data-driven design automation at conceptual design stage. Adv. Eng. Inform. 38, 826–839 (2018)
3. Wang, W.M., Wang, J.W., Li, Z., Tian, Z.G., Tsui, E.: Multiple affective attribute classification of online customer product reviews: a heuristic deep learning method for supporting kansei engineering. Eng. Appl. Artif. Intell. 85, 33–45 (2019)

4. Vilares, D., Alonso, M.A., Gómez-Rodríguez, C.: Supervised sentiment analysis in multilingual environments. Inf. Process. Manage. **53**(3), 595–607 (2017)
5. Nagamachi, M.: Kansei engineering as a powerful consumer-oriented technology for product development. Appl. Ergon. **33**(3), 289–294 (2002)
6. Nagamachi, M.: Kansei engineering: a new ergonomic consumer-oriented technology for product development. Int. J. Ind. Ergon. **15**(1), 3–11 (1995)
7. Hsiao, Y.-H., Chen, M.-C., Liao, W.-C.: Logistics service design for cross-border e-commerce using kansei engineering with text-mining-based online content analysis. Telematics Inform. **34**(4), 284–302 (2017)
8. Lin, Y.-C., Lai, H.-H., Yeh, C.-H.: Consumer-oriented product form design based on fuzzy logic: a case study of mobile phones. Int. J. Ind. Ergon. **37**(6), 531–543 (2007)
9. Osgood, C.E.: Studies on the generality of affective meaning systems. Am. Psychol. **17**(1), 10–28 (1962)
10. Li, Z., Tian, Z.G., Wang, J.W., Wang, W.M., Huang, G.Q.: Dynamic mapping of design elements and affective responses: a machine learning based method for affective design. J. Eng. Des. **29**(7), 358–380 (2018)
11. Chin, S., Kim, K.-Y.: Facial configuration and bmi based personalized face and upper body modeling for customer-oriented wearable product design. Comput. Ind. **61**(6), 559–575 (2010)
12. Jin, J., Ji, P., Gu, R.: Identifying comparative customer requirements from product online reviews for competitor analysis. Eng. Appl. Artif. Intell. **49**, 61–73 (2016)
13. Jin, J., Ji, P., Liu, Y., Johnson Lim, S.C.: Translating online customer opinions into engineering characteristics in QFD: A probabilistic language analysis approach. Eng. Appl. Artif. Intell. **41**, 115–127 (2015)
14. Wang, W.M., Li, Z., Tian, Z.G., Wang, J.W., Cheng, M.N.: Extracting and summarizing affective features and responses from online product descriptions and reviews: a kansei text mining approach. Eng. Appl. Artif. Intell. **73**, 149–162 (2018)
15. Feldman, R., Dagan, I.: Knowledge discovery in textual databases (KDT). In: First International Conference on Knowledge Discovery and Data Mining (KDD-95), Montreal, Canada, pp. 112–117 (1995)
16. Ravi Kumar, V., Raghuveer, K.: Web user opinion analysis for product features extraction and opinion summarization. Int. J. Web Semant. Technol. **3**(4), 69–82 (2012)
17. Sagara, T., Hagiwara, M.: Natural language neural network and its application to question-answering system. Neurocomputing **142**, 201–208 (2014)
18. Liu, B.: Sentiment analysis and opinion mining. Synth. Lect. Hum. Lang. Technol. **5**(1), 1–167 (2012)
19. Zhu, F., Zhang, X.: Impact of online consumer reviews on sales: the moderating role of product and consumer characteristics. J. Mark. **74**(2), 133–148 (2010)
20. Christensen, K., Nørskov, S., Frederiksen, L., Scholderer, J.: In search of new product ideas: Identifying ideas in online communities by machine learning and text mining. Creativity Innov. Manage. **26**(1), 17–30 (2017)
21. Xiang, Z., Schwartz, Z., Gerdes, J.H., Uysal, M.: What can big data and text analytics tell us about hotel guest experience and satisfaction? Int. J. Hosp. Manage. **44**, 120–130 (2015)
22. Wang, H., Wang, W.: Product weakness finder: an opinion-aware system through sentiment analysis. Ind. Manage. Data Syst. **114**(8), 1301–1320 (2014)
23. Yeh, Y.-E.: Prediction of optimized color design for sports shoes using an artificial neural network and genetic algorithm. Appl. Sci. **10**(5), 1560 (2020)
24. Yu, Y., Hui, C.-L., Choi, T.-M.: An empirical study of intelligent expert systems on forecasting of fashion color trend. Expert Syst. Appl. **39**(4), 4383–4389 (2012)
25. Shieh, M.-D., Yeh, Y.-E.: Developing a design support system for the exterior form of running shoes using partial least squares and neural networks. Comput. Indus. Eng. **65**(4), 704–718 (2013)

26. Russell, T., Stuart, J.: Artificial intelligence: a modern approach, The People's Posts and Telecommunications Press (Posts & Telecom Press), Reference (2002)
27. Lin, Y.-C., Chen, C.-C., Yeh, C.-H.: Intelligent decision support for new product development: a consumer-oriented approach. Appl. Math. Inf. Sci. **8**(6), 2761–2768 (2014)
28. Fang, S., Muramatsu, K., Matsui, T.: A computational model simulating the mental function of multicolor aesthetic evaluation. Color Res. Appl. **42**(2), 216–235 (2017)
29. Chen, H.-Y., Chang, H.-C.: Consumers' perception-oriented product form design using multiple regression analysis and backpropagation neural network. Artif. Intell. Eng. Des. Anal. Manufact. **30**(1), 64–77 (2015)
30. Aoyama, H., Misaka, M.: Development of design system for crack patterns on cup surface based on kansei. J. Comput. Des. Eng. **5**(4), 435–441 (2018)
31. Yang, C.-C.: Constructing a hybrid kansei engineering system based on multiple affective responses: Application to product form design. Comput. Ind. Eng. **60**(4), 760–768 (2011)
32. Srinivas, N., Deb, K.: Muiltiobjective optimization using nondominated sorting in genetic algorithms. Evol. Comput. **2**(3), 221–248 (1994)
33. Deb, K., Pratap, A., Agarwal, S., Meyarivan, T.: A fast and elitist multiobjective genetic algorithm: Nsga-ii. IEEE Trans. Evol. Comput. **6**(2), 182–197 (2002)
34. Guo, F., Li, F., Nagamachi, M., Hu, M., Li, M.: Research on color optimization of tricolor product considering color harmony and users' emotion. Color Res. Appl. **45**(1), 156–171 (2019)
35. Jiang, H., Kwong, C.K., Liu, Y., Ip, W.H.: A methodology of integrating affective design with defining engineering specifications for product design. Int. J. Product. Res. **53**(8), 2472–2488 (2014)
36. Scupin, R.: The kj method: A technique for analyzing data derived from Japanese ethnology. Hum. Organ. **56**(2), 233–237 (1997)
37. Zhang, W., Yoshida, T., Tang, X.: A comparative study of tf*idf, lsi and multi-words for text classification. Expert Syst. Appl. **38**(3), 2758–2765 (2011)
38. Guo, F., Liu, W.L., Liu, F.T., Wang, H., Wang, T.B.: Emotional design method of product presented in multi-dimensional variables based on kansei engineering. J. Eng. Des. **25**(4–6), 194–212 (2014)
39. Hsiao, S.-W., Huang, H.C.: A neural network based approach for product form design. Des. Stud. **23**(1), 67–84 (2002)
40. Hsiao, S.-W., Tsai, H.-C.: Use of gray system theory in product-color planning. Color Res. Appl. **29**(3), 222–231 (2004)

Development of User-Centred Interaction Design Patterns for the International Data Space

Torsten Werkmeister[✉]

Technical University Ilmenau, Ehrenbergstraße 29, 98693 Ilmenau, Germany
torsten-werkmeister@web.de

Abstract. This paper describes a set of methods for the development of user-centred interaction design patterns (IDP) based on the International Data Space (IDS). The IDS is to be understood as a virtual market place where data and products can be bought and sold as well as related contracts concluded. Based on the existing reference model of the IDS, new types of user interfaces (UI) will be created for this purpose. It is important for the developers of the UI's that the users and the associated core tasks are known, so that the interactions can be designed in a user-friendly interface. IDP's are intended to support developers in developing applications. The patterns are design patterns and represent proven solutions for frequently occurring problems for the developers when designing the UI. They also provide design alternatives and can effectively support communication between potential end users and developers.

Keywords: Conceptual design and planning · Interaction design pattern · Human-computer interaction · User-centered interaction design · International data space

1 Introduction

The IDS is a novel concept for business to provide a global virtual marketplace based on a software architecture reference model. Software-based connectors link the company-specific systems of the participants from different industries and continents so that data and products can be exchanged globally. Against the background of human-computer interaction, this results in new and previously unknown tasks and requirements for UI's for a previously unknown user group. The user groups with their typical tasks, such as concluding contracts or monitoring the flow of products, were explored in a four-week empirical study with 15 experts. UI's are required for this, which are created by developers in the respective companies. The developers need to know the associated requirements in order to be able to convert them into UI's. To this purpose, this research paper suggests IDP. IDP's are used to document proven, recurring UI-solutions and make them reusable. In summary, the research work aims at the creation of IDP's based on an empirical study by analysing persons and core tasks of potential users. The results obtained from this research provide the basis for the design of user-centred IDP's.

© Springer Nature Switzerland AG 2021
M. M. Soares et al. (Eds.): HCII 2021, LNCS 12779, pp. 144–155, 2021.
https://doi.org/10.1007/978-3-030-78221-4_10

2   Related Work

2.1   IDS

The IDS represents a reference architecture model[1] based on a high level of abstraction [15]. Farther, the IDS is to be understood as a global virtual data room, in which the participants are enabled to exchange and link data. The human-computer interaction is technically established by the IDS-connectors which connect data of machines, processes and systems and can be controlled by the participants via UI's. This business ecosystem[2] involves different participants in specific roles who interact with each other. Figure 1 shows an abstract representation of the IDS at user level. The functions of the role enable data to be integrated and controlled, data to be made available for exchange, and data to be received from the data provider. In the exemplary scenario, the company (1) provides or exchanges data with the participant/s in other companies (n) via a connector. The associated data usage restrictions (UR) of the application case regulate the contractual framework conditions. The configuration and management of data exchange is controlled via UI. Broker and Appstore are optional factors. The establishment of contact can be made directly or via intermediaries.

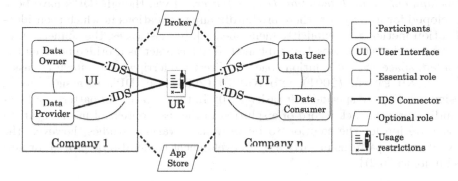

Fig. 1. Roles and interactions in the IDS according to OTTO ET AL. (2019)

In this all-encompassing scenario, the human being as a participant is essential for establishing and controlling the connections. Each participant has to take on different roles in which they have to fulfil certain tasks. These people and their tasks were identified in a preliminary study [25]. UI's have to be developed for the data owners, data providers, data users and data consumers, which are made available to the users and developers in IDP's.

---

[1] This research topic will be examined from various perspectives in further scientific papers [5,11,12].
[2] The business ecosystem is also referred to as a "value added network".

2.2 Methods to Develop IDP's

The pattern concept was developed to describe successful solutions to recurring design problems [1, 19].

The concept was taken up in computer science and transferred and further developed by a multitude of authors in the field of human-computer interaction [4, 8, 9, 13, 16–18, 20–24].

According to SEFFAH (2015), each pattern has essential elements which are: context, problem and solution [17]. In particular, the pattern collection of Alexander was analysed by JAN O. BORCHERS (2001). In this analysis he identified nine characteristics which are contained in each original pattern [4]: name of the pattern, universal applicability, example picture, context, short summary of the problem description, detailed problem description, solution approach, illustration of the solution approach, subordinate patterns.

In general, it can be noted that the context describes a recurring set of situations. The problem relates to objectives and constraints that occur in the context. In a general way, the problem describes when the pattern can be applied. The solution refers to a design form or a design rule that can be applied to solve the forces. It also includes elements that establish relationships between patterns.

Development of the Interaction Design Pattern. Even though IDP's have been developed for many years, there are hardly any publications in which their identification methods are explicitly mentioned [2]. In most cases, the connection to the user tasks is only loosely established. IDP's can act as a bridge between the problem space and the solution space by directly referring to specific user tasks. GRANLUND ET AL. (2001) AND AREND (2004) use IDP's to assign proven design solutions to specific user tasks [2, 10]. In the literature of patterns, a long-standing proven track record of a solution in the real context of use is regarded as a criterion for the solution to be proven. In various studies, however, the advantages of patterns in early use in development could also be proven for new technologies [6, 21].

3   Research Idea

3.1   Research Question

A reference architecture of the IDS model exists, but the later end users and their typical tasks are unknown. The aim of the research is to develop a set of methods with which it is possible to systematically identify IDP's. Therefore, the following research questions arise:

1. How can identified core tasks of potential IDS users be represented in IDP's?
2. How should these IDP's be structured so that developers can integrate them seamlessly into their development?

3.2   Research Method

The usability engineering process model according to SARODNICK AND BRAU (2011) was adapted as a process model. The model was chosen for the following reasons:

- Short-cycle evaluations play a major role and
- Methods can be assigned to specific problems.

For the analysis of the unknown area IDS, the following set of methods was defined as shown in Fig. 2. In the model, the steps of the procedure model are represented with continuous lines. The dashed lines represent the steps and methods to be performed in this work.

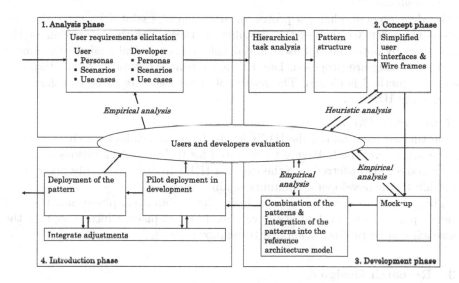

Fig. 2. Research method adapted from SARODNICK AND BRAU (2011)

1. Analysis Phase

The persona method according to COOPER (2015) was chosen for the analysis phase [7]. The approach is very well suited for the present research project because it selects the observable characteristics of people and later condenses them into personas. Personas allow an approximation of both the potential end users and the developers of the IDS in their typical workflows. Furthermore, requirements elicitation and persona development offers the possibility to derive context scenarios from which interaction design principles and patterns can be created. Knowledge about the potential end users and developers is systematically tapped and condensed from various sources via expert interviews. In addition, the developer personas are supplemented by their requirements for the way patterns are to be described.

2. Concept Phase

For the conception phase, the hierarchical task analysis (HTA) according to BENYON (2013) was chosen as a method to analyse the core tasks of the personas and to concretise and fix them as far as possible [3]. The HTA enables the identification and structuring of solution-independent tasks in an unknown area. Based on the results of the HTA and the empirical studies conducted, a pattern structure is derived. In addition, prototypical UI's in the form of Simplified User Interfaces (SUI) will be developed to provide end users and developers with an understanding of the system (mental model). The results will be analysed heuristically using the Cognitive Walkthrough method. The hypothetical users will analyse the developed courses of action in terms of utility. The results of these steps will be transferred into IDP's.

3. Development Phase

In the development phase, a prototypical design of usable UI's through wireframes is chosen to analyse the usability of these. For the evaluation of the prototypes by potential end users and developers, empirical analyses by remote usability testing are proposed. Due to the difficult accessibility of the test persons, this method is chosen. The results of these steps are to be transferred to the existing IDP's.

4. Introduction Phase

In the Introduction phase, the IDP's are to be made available to the developer community. Here, the IDP's are to be tested for their use. Adaptations are to be integrated and transferred into the existing IDP's in order to finally make them available to the developer community again.

This paper presents the results from the 1st analysis phase and the 2nd concept phase. Here, evaluations have already taken place, which show that the approach can be profitably applied to unknown areas.

3.3   Research Design

Insight into different industries is needed to develop solution-independent IDP's. In order to carry out the above process, the following was done.

Type of Data Needed

Out of 5 representative sectors that are about to introduce the IDS, 3 expert views each are needed. From these 15 experts, expert data on end users is needed (empirical analyses) to identify potential user groups and their requirements. Furthermore, expert data on developers is needed to identify the structure of the creation of the IDP's (heuristic analyses). For this, an additional 10 developers with knowledge about the IDS are needed.

Definition of Population and Sampling Procedures to be Followed

The experts were determined according to the criteria in the Table 1, which are, for example, domain specific knowledge and representativeness for different domains (these have already been described in another paper [25]).

Table 1. Selection criteria of potential end users and developers

Target group	Criterias
Potential end users	– previous knowledge of the IDS, – domain-specific knowledge, – competence of their roles, – years of experience in a domain as well as – representativeness for different domains
Developers	– previous knowledge of the IDS RAM

Time and Responsibility Specification

The study was conducted in two phases. In the first phase, the fields of business were researched. In the second phase, the requirements that the developers have for the structure of the IDP's were researched. The first study with potential users were conducted over a 14-week period from 03 April to 08 July 2020. The second study with developer were conducted over a 4-week period from 20 October to 09 November 2020. The study was conducted under the exclusive responsibility of the author of the paper.

Methods, Ways, and Procedures Used for Collection of Data

Structured telephone interviews were chosen as the method. A written document was produced which served as a guideline. In the interviews a simple form was chosen for the formulation of the questions and their suitability was tested in a pre-test. If the participant agreed to the expert discussion, he or she received a written cover letter and the document in advance. In principle, the interviews were conducted by telephone, were usually held in 30–45 min and were transcribed.

Data analysis – Tools or Methods Used to Analyze Data

The method of qualitative content analysis according to MAYRING (2010) is proposed for the analysis. The schema-based data preparation makes it possible to determine the procedural knowledge of the interview partners [14] In the analysis, categories and codes were developed and assigned.

Probable Output or Research Outcomes and Possible Actions to be Taken Based on Those Outcomes

The results of the representative research are:

– Empirical application and evaluation of the method set as well as
– Exemplary description of target groups and core tasks in the application area IDP.

3.4 Research Results

To answer research question 1: *How can identified core tasks of potential IDS users be represented in IDP's?* the following was identified.

Analysis

In the empirical studies, a number of 5 personas was identified. The description of the personas, for example, consists of elements such as name, company function, industry and motivation. These are shown in the Fig. 3.

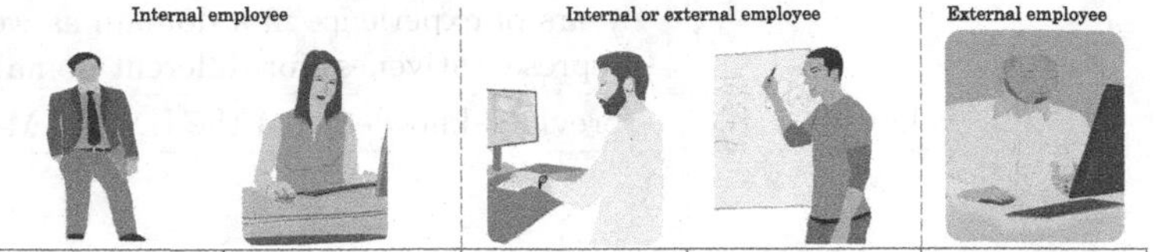

	Internal employee		Internal or external employee		External employee
Name:	David Holler	Virginia Williams	Robert Becker	Mike Chester	Dr. Paul Conner
Corporate function:	Logistics	Accounting	IT, corporate strategy	Developement	Ecosystem development
Professional function:	Logistics experts	Accountant	Consultant	Developer	Data Analyst/ Scientists
Branch:	Automotive	Agriculture	Energy	Software industry (No branch limitation)	Software industry (No branch limitation)
User Interface:	UI end user	UI end user	Mediator between UI end user, UI developer and analyst	UI developer	• UI analyst • UI designer
Aktivities:	• Sharing and communicate • Monitor, track and retriev data	• Analyze and control data & access • Monitor, track and retriev data	• Brokering, exchange and provide • Rights management	• UI development	• UI requirements analysis • Consulting
Capabilities, Knowledge of...	Domain-specific, Business processes	Domain-specific, Business processes	IT, Business processes	IT, IDS ecosystem with certifcation	IT, IDS ecosystem with certifcation
Expectations:	Trust in the ecosystem, Usability, Readiness for digitization	Trust in the ecosystem, Usability, Readiness for digitization	Data governance, Data protection/security, Promoting networking	Trust in the ecosystem	Promoting networking
Motivation:	Execute successful business processes	Execute successful business processes	Trustworthy data exchange	Meeting user needs	Linking up companies

Fig. 3. Personas overview

Figure 4 (left side) shows the persona David Holler in detail. This persona represents the end users and contrasts with the persona Mike Chester, which is shown in Fig. 4 (right side). Both personas contain further information such as a statement, IDS profile and notes of daily work.

Scenarios and Use Cases

The personas are linked to scenarios and use cases and are listed in the Table 2.

To answer research question 2: *How should these IDP's be structured so that developers can integrate them seamlessly into their development?* the following was identified.

HTA

For the personas "end user" and "developer" 32 core tasks were identified, which can be divided into 145 subtasks. The Fig. 5 shows the exemplary core task *create and manage contracts* and its subtasks.

Fig. 4. Personas: David Holler and Mike Chester

Requirements to the Pattern Design

In the further interviews the focus was on the formal design of the presentation of the IDP's for the developers, the evaluation is listed in the Table 3. The elements: *name, identification number, problem, context, application for and solution - why* were evaluated as *essential*. The elements: *example, example graphic, related pattern, similar pattern, evidence* were rated as *less important* but at least *neutral*. However, when evaluating the literature, this was considered as *essential*. In the context of the IDS, further elements were asked: *Summary/objective, Challenges, Relevant data, Main technology/IDS components, Services/Advantages and Partner/Ecosystem* proved to be *useful*, shown on the right side of the Table 3. Finally, the pattern granularity of the IDP's was asked. The evaluation of this suggests that solutions are preferred to be modular rather than holistic. This in turn suggests that developers do not prefer something specific, but rather classes or modules in order to obtain generic solutions.

Table 2. Identified use cases and scenarios

Name	Scenario ID	Scenarios	Use cases ID	Use cases
David Holler	S 8	Transport planning	UC 10	Transports
			UC 24	Communication
			UC 25	Collaboration
			UC 26	Document
	S 10	Business units, tasks, events	UC 12	Projekt Management
			UC 13	Marketing
			UC 15	Tasks
			UC 19	Research and development
			UC 22	Managing unit
			UC 29	Finance
			UC 30	Environmental Management
			UC 31	Quality assurance system
	S 11	Operating and monitoring	UC 18	IT Asset
			UC 23	Digital twins
			UC 28	Operate machines
Virginia Williams	S 1	Visit market place	UC 0	Store
			UC 20	Mediate
			UC 27	Acquiring application
	S 3	Overview and konfiguration	UC 2	Dashboard
			UC 16	Language management
	S 6	Manage data security	UC 5	Data security
Robert Becker	S 2	Managing participants	UC 1	Participants
	S 4	Create and manage contracts	UC 3	Contracts
			UC 7	Official documents
			UC 8	Legal rules
			UC 9	Business Rules
	S 5	Rights and role administration	UC 4	Rights and role administration
	S 7	Data exchange	UC 6	Data/data streams
Mike Chester	S 9	Install and setup connector	UC 21	Connector
	S 12	Development	UC 17	Development environment
Dr. Paul Conner	S 9	Install and setup connector	UC 11	Verification
			UC 21	Connector

Table 3. Requirements to the pattern design

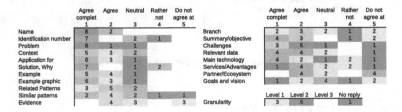

Prototyping – UI's

The core tasks passed to the HTA are mapped to UI elements. The Fig. 5 shows an example of the derived UI elements: *menu, button and dropdown*. The Fig. 6 shows an example of a developed UI-Prototype for the use case *create and manage contracts*.

Interaction Design Patterns

The Table 4 shows an IDP. The IDP is composed of the following contents: user and developer, use cases and scenarios, core tasks (HTA), UI's.

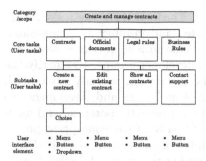

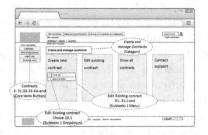

Fig. 5. HTA according to BENYON (2013) – Manage contracts

Fig. 6. SUI – create and manage contracts The bigraph B_2

Table 4. Interaction design pattern – create and manage contracts

		Solution – Why:	Optionally, new contracts or model contracts can be selected. Actors can decide which form they want to use. Both options have to be adapted in individual cases. Use consistent page layouts by defining layout templates that are used within an application and across different applications.
Name:	Create and manage contracts		
ID:	CMC		
Problem:	The central certification body, the International Data Spaces Association, has drawn up contractual framework regulations between actors. These provide model contracts for the licensing of data exchanges. These model contracts are to be adapted in individual cases and require the further processing of legal tasks. The parties can use their own contracts or use contracts from the contractual framework.	Example graphic:	
Context:	A user-centric application development process was used to analyse and specify the application's user group together with the functional and non-functional requirements of the users, including their goals and tasks. The results of the analysis then helped to define the content and functions of the application.		*Fig. 6. SUI – create and manage contracts*
Application for:	Create contracts, manage contracts	Evidence:	[Interview_2, S. 2], [Interview_3, S. 3], [Interview_13, S. 4]
		Related Patterns:	Overview and konfiguration (OK1), Business units, tasks, events (BU1)

4 Discussion and Conclusion

The process model of SARODNICK AND BRAU (2011) was flexibly adapted to the development of IDS's. The special methods such as the personas with scenarios and use cases as well as the hierarchical task analysis could be integrated well here. However, these were connected with a very high effort, such as the difficult accessibility of the specialists. Nevertheless, it was possible to condense all the experts. In this paper, the results of the 1st analysis phase and the 2nd concept phase were presented and discussed. First evaluations show that the approach can be profitably applied to unknown areas. In the further course, the SUI's are heuristically analysed according to the criterion of utility. In the development phase, these are then further developed into wireframes and analysed according to the criterion of usability. The evaluated results are included in the IDP's and made available to the developer community. In the introduction phase, the IDP's will be piloted, subjected to further adjustments and finally made available to the developer community. The application of the persona method supports the introduction of human-centred design in the domain of business ecosystems. They intensify the differentiated consideration of the widely diversified target group and the translation of user needs into concrete tasks. However, the persona method is mostly used to identify familiar people in everyday life, making it difficult to imagine in the context of the IDS. Through HTA, the task-solving process of potential end-users could be revealed and graphically represented. In addition, a systematic description can be made in a hierarchical sequence, which supports understanding in end-user and developer groups. To identify the targets and tasks, a deep understanding of the system under study is required. This poses a great challenge because potential end-users and developers are very difficult to access. The SUI's developed from this make potential end users and developers familiar with the new system already in the conception phase. Without having to repeatedly adapt the contents of the system, an initial user interface can already be provided in the conception phase, which makes it possible to obtain initial conclusions from potential end users and developers. In the presentation of SUI's, unimportant elements are not listed. The decision whether important or unimportant is seen as critical because individual needs are often in the foreground. Nevertheless, the findings can be integrated into the development process and accelerate it.

References

1. Alexander, C., Ishikawa, S., Silverstein, M.: A Pattern Language: Towns, Buildings, Construction. Center for Environmental Structure Series. Oxford University Press, Oxford (1977)
2. Arend, U.: Effiziente konstruktion von benutzungsoberflächen aus konfigurierbaren bausteinen. In: Hassenzahl, M., Peissner, M. (eds.) Tagungsband UP 2004, pp. 108–112. Fraunhofer Verlag, Stuttgart (2004)
3. Benyon, D.: Designing Interactive Systems: A Comprehensive Guide to Hci, Ux & Interaction Design, 3 edn, pp. 32–251. Pearson Education Limited, Harlow, London, New York (2013)
4. Borchers, J.O.: A Pattern Approach to Interaction Design. Wiley Series in Software Design Patterns. Wiley, New York (2001)
5. Brost, G., Huber, M., Weiß, M., Protsenko, M., Schütte, J., Wessel, S.: An ecosystem and IoT device architecture for building trust in the industrial data space. In: Cyber-Physical System Security Workshop (2018)
6. Chung, E., Hong, J., Lin, J., Prabaker, M., Landay, J., Liu, A.: Development and evaluation of emerging design patterns for ubiquitous computing, pp. 233–242 (2004). https://doi.org/10.1145/1013115.1013148
7. Cooper, A., Reimann, R., Cronin, D., Noessel, C.: About Face: The Essentials of Interaction Design, 4 edn, p. 61. Wiley, Indianapolis (2015)
8. Duyne, D., Landay, J., Hong, J.: The Design if Sites: Patterns, Principles, and Processes for Crafting a Consumer-Centered Web Experience (2002)
9. Gamma, E., Helm, R., Johnson, R., Vlissides, J.: Design Patterns - Elements of Reusable Object-Oriented Software, 1 edn. Addison-Wesley Longman, Amsterdam (1995). Reprint (2009)
10. Granlund, A., Lafrenière, D.: A pattern-supported approach to the user interface design process. In: Usability, Evaluation and Interface Design: Cognitive Engineering, Intelligent Agents and Virtual Reality, pp. 282–286 (2001). Proceeding of HCI International 2001
11. Graube, M.: Linked Enterprise Data as semantic and integrated information space for industrial data. Master's thesis, Technische Universität Dresden (2018)

12. Hupperz, M.: Entwicklung eines GUI-Papierprototyps für einen IDS-Connector unter Verwendung des Human-Centered Design Ansatzes. Master's thesis, Technische Universität Dortmund, Technische Universität Dortmund (2020)
13. Mahemoff, M.J., Johnston, L.J.: Pattern languages for usability: an investigation of alternative approaches. In: Proceedings of Australian Computer Human Interaction Conference OZCHI 1998, Adelaide, Australia, pp. 132–139 (1998)
14. Mayring, P.: Qualitative Inhaltsanalyse: Grundlagen und Techniken, 12 edn, p. 70. Beltz Pädagogik, Beltz, Weinheim and Basel (2010)
15. Otto, B., Steinbuß, S., Teuscher, A., Lohmann, S.: Reference Architecture Model, 3 edn, p. 61. International Data Spaces Association, Berlin (2019). Accessed 08 Apr 2019
16. Prinz, A.: Interaction Design Patterns für NFC-basierte Electronic Data Capture Anwendungen. Prinz Publishing (2014). http://prinz-publishing.de. ISBN 978-3-9816875-0-7
17. Seffah, A.: Patterns of HCI Design and HCI Design of Patterns: Bridging HCI Design and Model-Driven Software Engineering. HIS, p. 2. Springer, Cham (2015). https://doi.org/10.1007/978-3-319-15687-3
18. Sharp, H., Preece, J., Rogers, Y.: Interaction Design: Beyond Human-Computer Interaction, pp. 13, 501, 473. Wiley (2019)
19. Sivaloganathan, S., Shahin, T.M.M.: Design reuse: an overview. Proc. Inst. Mech. Eng. Part B: J. Eng. Manuf. 213, 641–654 (1999)
20. Spool, J.M.: Uie-the elements of a design pattern. Website: Uie (2006). Accessed 26 July 2019
21. Kunert, T., Penquitt, J., Krömker, H.: Identifizierung von Interaction Design Patterns für neue Technologien. In: Heinecke, A.M., Paul, H. (eds.) Mensch & Computer 2006: Mensch und Computer im StrukturWandel, pp. 55–64. Technische Universität Ilmenau, Institut für Medientechnik (2006)
22. Tidwell, J.: Common ground: a pattern language for human-computer interface design. Website: Common ground (1999). Accessed 26 July 2019
23. van Welie, M., van der Veer, G.C.: Pattern languages in interaction design: structure and organization. In: Human-Computer Interaction - INTERACT 2003, pp. 527–534. IOS Press, (c) IFIP (2003)
24. van Welie, M.: Interaction design patterns. Website: Welie (2001). http://www.welie.com/patterns. Accessed 09 July 2020
25. Werkmeister, T.: Personas and tasks for international data space-based ecosystems. In: Proceedings of the 4th International Conference on Computer-Human Interaction Research and Applications - Volume 1: CHIRA, pp. 202–209. INSTICC, SciTePress (2020). https://doi.org/10.5220/0010146902020209. ISBN 978-989-758-480-0

Envisioning Educational Product User eXperience Through Participatory Design Practice

Di Zhu, Sihao Cai, Chenhong Yang, Ruilin Wang, Liuyi Zhao, Siqi Feng, and Wei Liu[✉]

Beijing Normal University, Beijing 100875, People's Republic of China
{di.zhu,wei.liu}@bnu.edu.cn, {sihaocai,chenhong.yang,
ruilin.wang,zhao61,siqifeng}@mail.bnu.edu.cn

Abstract. Due to COVID-19 (Coronavirus Disease - 19), most schools have adopted remote or mixed methods to teach; therefore, students need new types of educational products to achieve a high-quality learning experience. There are many difficulties and obstacles to taking classes online. More interactions and formats need to be explored for students to absorb as much classroom knowledge as possible. The research team conducted a design workshop. Thirty-eight psychology and applied psychology students participated in this workshop using different user research methods, such as user journey maps and how-to methods. They explored educational products in five scenarios: taking physical education classes, giving online learning feedback, conducting teamwork, taking an online examination, and studying in the dormitory. Each group proposed design solutions to solve design problems in a particular context. For the 56 design problems, the participants identified 548 design solutions. The facilitator helped the group select six or seven design challenges with higher priorities. All the research data were collected, and the jobs-to-be-done (JTBD) theory was used to analyze users' needs for future educational products. The users' needs were summarized into user need clusters. This study has identified seven primary user needs and 20 sub-needs in five scenarios. The insights gained from this study may be of assistance to UX designers and UX researchers to obtain a new perspective on scenarios.

Keywords: User eXperience · Participatory design · Educational product · Design workshop

1 Introduction

The Chinese government has introduced a "suspending class, not stopping schools" policy during the COVID-19 epidemic. Therefore, there is less educational product design for studying online. Students usually use laptops, tablets, or phones with microphones and video cameras. Some of them may select the TV to watch online lectures. However, these products cannot be considered high-quality educational products. With the development of education informatization, intelligent educational hardware, as a supporting online learning service, opens a new market for the online education industry and

© Springer Nature Switzerland AG 2021
M. M. Soares et al. (Eds.): HCII 2021, LNCS 12779, pp. 156–170, 2021.
https://doi.org/10.1007/978-3-030-78221-4_11

provides new growth opportunities [1]. Online education enterprises layout intelligent hardware, change the way of education interaction, and improve the learning experience of online education, at the same time that the data collected contribute to the iterative upgrading of an online education platform. In the long run, intelligent educational hardware products are expected to be used as the entrance to online education [2], solve customer acquisition problems, and promote business value. The differentiated content of intelligent education hardware products is the key to market dominance. Online education layout smart hardware needs to be deeply integrated with online education content to build a complete ecosystem, form a closed-loop user experience, and improve user stickiness.

Furthermore, there is a trend of the online-merge-offline learning mode [3]. Students apply science, technology, engineering, and mathematics to establish connections among schools, communities, and global enterprises to develop stem literacy and improve their competitiveness in the new economy. Educational products vary from physical teaching tools to interactive intelligent tutoring systems (ITSs) [4]. The educational product, especially intelligent hardware, will be the bridge to connect online teaching and offline learning. There are many discussions on how to improve the learning experience of university students. Students have to overcome challenges such as a lack of face-to-face interaction with teachers, reaction time, and traditional classroom socialization. In underdeveloped areas, such challenges will be even more difficult [5]. Therefore, the learning activities have changed considerably, and both teachers and students should spend time getting familiarized with new learning modes. The University has used MOOCs for many years. However, none of the courses can adapt to the MOOC learning mode in a short time period.

The interaction in the learning process is significant, particularly for humanities students, so it is important to pay attention to the interaction between teachers and students and the interaction between students in the curriculum design [6]. Participatory design can guide a deeper understanding of user needs and is especially useful for designing future experiences that users never experienced before [7]. Through making sessions, participants will envision "use before actual use" [8]. In particular, the study focuses on supporting mutual learning between researchers and participants and promoting the active participation of target users as "designers" rather than consumers [9]. The cocreation process enables activating, discovering, and sharing knowledge [10]. Researchers in the participatory design process act as facilitators rather than observers. In this process, participants are encouraged to propose ideas and solutions in an open-minded environment.

2 Related Work

Several studies have found that STEM education is a transdisciplinary learning method that combines rigorous academic concepts with real-world courses. In the past, stem education research has incorporated theoretical research, design research, application research, evaluation research, and other types of research, focusing on the analysis and summary of learners, educators, and educational content in different stages of education (preschool education, higher education, vocational education, and informal education).

The analysis shows that teachers' professional background and education will lead to teachers' views on stem education. There are discussions about the differences between countries in learner types, curriculum practices, technology application, and evaluation mechanisms. In the case of the United States, for example, there is a problem in the general environment of stem education. Many students do not understand and are unwilling to engage in and research the contents of engineering and technology. Therefore, to encourage students to participate in the interactive learning of STEM concepts in practical applications and acquire professional skills online, various e-learning tools and teaching methods have been developed to adapt to modern youth habits.

Educational robots are mentioned in many studies. However, the connectivity between robot products and other devices or platforms is weak, and too many independent products of various types will create a significant cognitive burden for users. Some studies have mentioned the need to establish a set of the software and hardware and the entire process system of the course platform. The existing problem is that the initial investment is large, and it is difficult to see the results quickly. It is necessary to develop a support group for its users, and it is easier for large enterprises or the government to lead such initiatives. Therefore, it is necessary to consider building a robot education product ecology. At the same time, there is also a specific gap in teacher training. Suppose we directly teach the relevant courses or use new teaching aids to younger students. In that case, students may have some difficulties in understanding and acceptance, so we would consider first training the teachers to carry out the students' follow-up courses. Products such as Lego and the Arduino suite are currently the mainstream educational hardware products in the market. Products that can be compared by schools (education systems) will have advantages because they can be purchased and taught systematically. Schools can use products to train teachers, although this may be complex or costly. With more devices that can have a connectivity design, such products will be more popular. If it is for individual users, the unit price of single-function products should be controlled.

A relationship exists between psychological theories and education product design. Theories of this relationship include Adaptive Control of Thought model (ACT) theory, positive feedback application, game simulation teaching, meta-cognition, etc. These systems are mostly developed based on the original theory, testing the system's availability and feasibility. In the paper, cognitive modeling and intelligent tutoring, which is an improved version of ACT–PUPS theory is proposed, and the application of it is preliminarily tested [11]. One of the studies subdivided the system for different subjects and formed a perfect teaching system. The application of metacognition and feedback theory [12, 13] improves students' learning efficiency and tracks knowledge processing. The difference is that this paper on metacognition mainly combines ITS and self-regulated learning (SRL) [14] to promote students' self-learning efficiency. Game simulation teaching is intended to "teach through entertainment." The advantages of these systems are that they are based on solid theory, making them easy to test, and game simulation teaching is exciting. Some of the problems of these systems are that some applications may be considered too far-fetched, and it is difficult to combine entertainment and technicality in one system.

Part of the research will classify learners by collecting their data to recommend or evaluate learning experiences. It includes their learning style (mainly Felder Silverman model) [15], learning motivation, personality traits (mostly five prominent personalities), bloom classification [16] and emotional state [17], as well as intelligence and demographic indicators [18]. The study combines learning motivations and reinforcement, evaluates students' motivation [19, 20], and proposes different classification standards. Simultaneously, some problems need to be further explored, including the unclear effects of different types of motivation and emotions. The need to find a suitable number of specific variables is the key to personalization. The richer the personal data the greater the burden to users, such as filling in many questionnaires. The artificial intelligence model lacks accuracy in recognizing emotions and cannot trigger interventions autonomously or meaningfully.

Some studies start from special groups to study educational hardware products [21]. In the process, children and parents or designers need to participate in the use of design or help teachers assist with teaching [22]. These hardware products are used for daily communication or can promote the normal development of children's cognition. For example, online multiplayer video games and sensory channel props can help tell simple stories and encourage the normal development of children with intellectual disabilities. Another example is an app that will create a personalized learning profile for individuals [23]. The mobile phone will download the corresponding picture symbols for communication according to the location of the detection. The research advantage is that hardware products can attract children's interest [24] and effectively help children solve problems. However, this hardware is used in laboratory settings and needs to be accompanied by professionals. Some hardware products need more professional and technical personnel.

With the participatory design, designers and users are involved in creating a product, policy, or service system. In the process of participatory design, all participants hold inclusive and equal attitudes in the discussions. This process helps lead to better designs that take all stakeholders into account. However, there may be some difficulties in the specific implementation process, including user cost, user subjective attitude, the particular choice of people to participate in the design, how to ensure the smooth and efficient design process, and different participants in the conference resulting in too many views.

3   Material and Methods

3.1   The Participants

The 38 participants in the participatory design session presented in this paper are undergraduate and graduate students in the Department of Psychology. These students have vital interests in the user experience. The cohort comprised 28 female students and 10 male students. Six or seven students are assigned to a group that receives a specific educational product design topic during COVID-19.

3.2   The Process of Participatory Design

The research team conducts desk research by searching relevant papers, reports, and products to explore what kinds of needs have been studied and what opportunities exist for future educational design products. An affinity diagram is used to cluster these opportunities and conditions into contexts. By prioritizing novelty in the educational product market, the team selects five scenarios. Before conducting participatory design research, the research team designs five potential journeys of current behaviors and needs based on research findings. The teacher will provide instruction on how to use a journey map and how to brainstorm [25]. Meanwhile, five facilitators are assigned to the five teams to guide students in applying these methods and in framing design problems. Based on these problems, each team uses how-to methods to brainstorm design solutions. All research data were collected, and jobs-to-be-done (JTBD) theory [26] was used to analyze users' needs for future educational products. The needs were summarized into user needs clusters (Fig. 1).

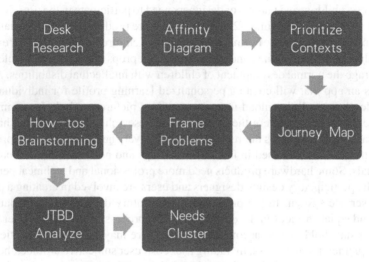

Fig. 1. The process of participatory design.

3.3 The Design Brief

During COVID-19, numerous students have to study online. Thus, there are more opportunities for online learning. Fewer products can provide high-quality service for online learning scenarios. Students have to adapt to the current learning setting. How can UX research improve the interaction between students and products, and between students and teachers? The research team proposes five scenarios: taking an exercise class, giving online learning feedback, conducting teamwork, taking the online examination, and studying in the dormitory. Each scenario entails a description and design challenges, as shown in Table 1.

Table 1. Scenario description and design challenges.

Scenario	Description	Design Challenges
Take exercise class	Students cannot attend offline physical education courses, such as Hip-pop, Yoga classes. They cannot easily follow instructions, movements, or rhythm of the teacher online	Enrich learning forms Real-time corrective actions Reduce unnecessary practice Immersive practice
Give online learning feedback	Teachers cannot see the faces of students during online teaching. Meanwhile, students are too shy to ask questions, which will interfere with the teaching process	Knowing the effect of understanding Quantitative teaching quality Answer students' questions Active classroom atmosphere
Conduct teamwork	Teamwork is a raw format of online learning. Students have to collaborate as a team to share ideas, concerns, and suggestions	Help assign tasks Real-time progress sharing Resolve team member conflicts Enhance collaboration experience
Take online examination	The examination cannot be conducted offline, so students need to use computers, tablets, and other devices to answer questions online	Reduce operation steps Answer questions more naturally Store information in time Dispel privacy concerns
Study in the dormitory	Due to the epidemic, the library and other spaces will be limited, and the dormitory has become the second choice place. However, the dormitory environment is complex, not always suitable for students to learn	Guarantee the learning environment Live and learn in isolation Make sure others rest Improve learning efficiency

Students may feel that it is difficult learning online in the exercise course scenario since there is no direct feedback from teachers as there is in a typical teaching environment. Teachers can only use words to express their intention, not by correcting the movements. Thus, students will take more time to understand the demonstration, which leads to a decrease in teaching efficiency. Furthermore, students will spend more time on after-class practice. In the in-class feedback scenarios, teachers cannot pay attention to everyone's performance as in a standard teaching environment. It is hard for them to evaluate the learning process. Considering the screen's display room, students want to see the video and presentation of the teacher. Some of the students may need reading materials. There is no room to interact with teachers even though they have encountered difficulties. This will have a negative impact on the teaching quality. In a teamwork scenario, online group interaction varies from offline group interaction. Without face-to-face communication, students usually experience a decentralization of responsibility. Most online platforms are designed for an online meeting or presentation but do not plan for collaboration. It is difficult to assign missions, present ideas, express concerns, and collaborate online. In the online examination scenario, students have to take the exam remotely. They will use tablets, smartphones, and laptops to attend the examination, and there are many preparation steps. It is a different environment than that of taking tests at home. Thus, they should apply the context of taking the test at home without watching the progress of others. In studying in a dormitory scenario, many students will learn in a dormitory instead of the library. However, the dormitory context may affect the efficiency and quality of studying. This space contains several functions, including sleeping, studying and chatting. Roommates may play computer games and eat take-out food. This will decrease the motivation of students to study.

3.4 Data Gathering and Analysis of the PD Process

The students propose stages, behavior, emotions, needs, and design problems in the journey map building process. Each group discusses these topics within the scenario's scope and write them down on Post-it notes. The facilitator helps the group select six or seven design challenges with higher priorities. Five groups brainstorm solutions together. Meanwhile, individuals only focus on the design challenges on the solution paper. The research team collects journey maps and solutions to analyze user needs and holistic design challenges. Finally, there are 56 design problems and the participants design 548 design solutions. The team analyzes data by using JTBD (jobs-to-be-done) to abstract the needs and motivations of participants. The team clusters these findings and synthesizes them into needs, which will guide the next step of the research.

4   Discussion Based on User Needs

As a result of the analysis, 20 design directions were identified, grouped into seven main clusters: avoiding disturbance, ensuring equipment, promoting learning, creating a learning atmosphere, improving learning efficiency, proper planning, and applying proper pressure. The directions were grouped according to their purpose of using the educational product. This section will describe the scenario of sub-needs.

4.1   The Framework of Future Educational Products Design

This study has identified seven primary user needs in five using scenarios, including avoiding disturbance, ensuring equipment, promoting learning, creating a learning atmosphere, improving learning efficiency, reasonable planning, and applying proper pressure. Furthermore, the study summarizes twenty sub-needs of seven primary needs (Table 2).

Table 2. The framework of future educational products design

Avoid disturbances	Ensure equipment	Promote learning	Create a learning atmosphere	Improve learning efficiency	Reasonable Planning	Apply proper pressure
Avoid being disturbed	Hardware	Independent promotion	Sense of ceremony	Stay focused	Control the progress	Educational authority
Avoid disturbing others	Software	External learning motivation	Analog offline	Keep interactions	Flexible planning	Create pressure
Prevent embarrassment		Peer support	Companionship	Cognition		
			Equality	Learning Content		

4.2 Avoid Disturbances

There are three types of avoiding disturbances: avoiding being disturbed, avoiding disturbing others, and preventing embarrassment.

Avoid being disturbed. Mengmeng learns a new dance online from the teacher at home. However, her three-year-old brother always cries, which makes her unable to hear the voice and music accompaniment explained by the teacher. How can Mengmeng be immersed in the dance class? Mengmeng does not want to be disturbed by irrelevant personnel. Therefore, the participants proposed that Mengmeng wear sports headphones to hear the teacher and the musical accompaniment. The class is not interrupted by other sounds, thereby achieving the class's purpose.

Avoid disturbing others. Jiaqi is a junior who is preparing for the IELTS test. She wants to practice her oral English online with her speaking teacher. However, the roommates are also busy with their affairs. Jiaqi is worried that practicing oral English may disturb the roommate. Therefore, how can Jiaqi reasonably inform her roommate that she is going to study? Because Jiaqi wants to know whether her roommates would be disturbed, the participants propose creating a list. All dormitory residents can fill in today's schedule list to arrange a study time in advance to avoid disturbing others.

Prevent embarrassment. Because of the epidemic, Li Lei must attend online classes at home. Nevertheless, there are many unnecessary items piled up in the bedroom. Therefore, Li Lei is worried that the teacher may suddenly call on him to turn on the camera to answer questions. At the same time, he also feels that class at home is not as strong as class at school. Therefore, how can the learning atmosphere of Li Lei alone be enhanced at home? Li Lei wants to know the camera's actual capture status in advance in case the teacher suddenly calls on him to turn on the camera. The participants suggested that they could put the extra items away to create a better learning atmosphere.

4.3 Ensure Equipment

Educational equipment has software and hardware. Before studying, students will ensure their operation.

Software. Da is a student in the dance department. The epidemic forced him to take classes at home. However, he runs into a big problem. Home is not a dance classroom, but there is teacher to guide him and he cannot see his actions in all directions every moment. Therefore, how to immerse himself in classes becomes a major problem. To support his studies, his mother buys him a set of smart mirrors with a pair of Bluetooth headphones to see all of his movements in all directions, while the teacher on the client side can see the student's actions and give guidance through the Bluetooth headphones.

Hardware. It is the end of the term, and Baibai has to take an exam online, but he does not find the phone very convenient. Because there will be mishandling when writing and reading simultaneously, the space for inputting and browsing is not suitable. Therefore, he takes out his tablet and handwrites his answers on it, which will be automatically converted into print and sent to his phone via Bluetooth to complete the exam.

4.4 Promote Learning

Students always need the motivation to maintain learning through independent promotion, external learning motivation, and peer support to encourage them to learn.

Independent promotion. The Yue is a girl with little dance training. This semester, the school offered a mandatory form class, but they could not study offline because of the new coronavirus epidemic. Their class changed to online courses. In her case, because she has no dance experience, learning from lessons online is a major challenge. How can she learn better and be more immersed in online classes? Because she needed to force herself to learn in a completely unfamiliar field, she could avoid failing the final. By doing so, the participants came up with isolating themselves from outside distractions to improve their learning efficiency.

External learning motivation. Haihai is a study committee member, and due to the epidemic, their class has changed to online courses. Many students like to listen to the course behind closed doors during their time online, which affects the communication between students compared to the offline class. As a study committee member, he was anxious about facilitating the students' opinions during the online discussion. Because he wanted to give each speaker instant encouragement and promote communication among them in this way, he proposed adding the function of flower painting on the online discussion platform to motivate the speakers.

Peer support. Wu is a student facing final revision, and the first thing she does when she wakes up every day is to pick up her important materials and study. Nevertheless, her roommate seems to be very unconcerned about her final exams and even plays comedies and laughs outside her dorm room, which affects her research. She was wondering how to remind her roommate reasonably that she needs to start studying. Because she felt that it was important for roommates to monitor each other's studies and help each other improve in this way, the participant proposed filling in today's requirements in the dormitory schedule to better understand what each other wanted.

4.5 Create a Learning Atmosphere

The main challenges of studying from home relate to the learning atmosphere. Therefore, students need to create a sense of ceremony, including analog offline learning settings, finding companionship and creating discussion space with peers.

Sense of ceremony. Duoduo is a freshman who wants to take more online courses during holidays to develop new skills. However, one problem he encountered is that there is no classroom atmosphere at home. His online class status at home is far inferior to that in the school classroom and library. Because the sun in the school library and the classroom lights are just right for studying, the atmosphere helps him stay focused. Therefore, all participants proposed using VR technology to create the same atmosphere of the library and classroom to help students study at home as efficiently as they do in school.

Analog offline. Due to the epidemic, Duoduo's final exam can only be taken online, and the teacher hands out the exam electronically. Students need to use their phones or iPads to fill out the exam. However, Duoduo still thinks it smoother to answer questions on the actual form, and writing on paper helps her feel better. The participants came up with a solution to project the electronic test paper onto the physical paper, and the writing on the paper would automatically synchronize with the electronic test paper. In this way, it is possible to answer the electronic test questions without changing the original habit of answering on paper.

Companionship. Xiaoming is in his third year of high school. He has been taking online classes at home for a month because of the epidemic. Although the teacher's content is the same as offline content, he misses the feeling of fighting for the college entrance exam together with his classmates in the classroom. He feels very lonely at home and has no motivation to review his work. It would be nice to see the class together online as well. All participants offered to watch videos of their classmates in class online but with the sound turned off. In this way, you can feel that there are people online to study with, and you are more motivated to learn.

Equality. Lily is the team leader of a winter vacation practice project. She needs to organize an online meeting and discussion among the team members during the holiday. However, she often encountered a problem: some group members could not speak actively online, and Lily could not see the other students, so she could not know the status of each group member. When offline, she can see the status of participants and make eye contact to encourage people to ask questions and make comments. Such reminders can promote positive thinking and speaking. Therefore, participants proposed the function of setting reminders to talk in the online meeting. The meeting host could automatically set the time interval of reminders to encourage each participant to speak actively, thus improving meeting efficiency.

4.6 Improve Learning Efficiency

The main feature of learning tools is to improve learning efficiency. It may help students stay focused, maintain interactions, take advantage of cognitive habits and recommend interesting learning content.

Stay focused. Xiao Wu is a sports enthusiast, so he also signs up for an online table tennis course at home. However, he encounters a problem. It is very lonely to practice table tennis alone in front of the wall during the practice time in class, and he gradually becomes resistant to the practice. How can he immerse himself in a body class? Xiao Wu is usually a person who likes to communicate with his friends. Therefore, the participants suggested that Xiao Wu and his friends could watch each other's actions and play against each other so that Xiao Wu could focus on practicing and not feel lonely.

Maintain interactions. Lily is the teaching assistant of specialized courses in the class. During the epidemic period, she needs to have courses and help the teacher pay attention to students' status. However, the usually lively classmates create a huge problem for Lily when they go online because they are reluctant to interact in class. How can the learning atmosphere of online courses be improved? Participants proposed adding buttons to improve the atmosphere, such as sending a flower or giving thumbs up, so that when the students speak it is not just an individual talking, but also the class is made more lively through the interactions between students.

Cognition. Zhou learns online during a semester and comes to the final exam time. However, he encounters a problem. The online examination requires using a mobile phone that leads to English reading with questions not on a page. If he forces himself to remember it creates a significantly increased cognitive burden. However, it is a waste of time, making him feel very agitated during the exam. How can the mobile tests be made more convenient? Participants proposed letting the question stem and questions appear on one page through a split-screen examination to reduce Zhou's cognitive burden.

Learning content. Zi Han signed up for an online body-building course to get into shape after losing her condition during the epidemic. However, after a few classes, she encounters a problem. The body shape class movements are stationary, and she begins to feel bored without the atmosphere of continually practicing offline. How can Zihan feel immersed in the body class again? The participants thought they could improve Zi Han's interest through games, such as sorting the actions in a class from simple to challenging and then passing form one level to the next after each action was in place. In this way, Zi Han is motivated by her desire to win or lose and she began to practice again.

4.7 Reasonable Planning

A good plan can ensure the quality of learning, and there are two main aspects of how to control progress and adapt the current plan to users' learning habits.

Control progress. Hao Ran has an online meeting where he and his group members have to work together on an assignment. However, during the meeting, he notices that some people do not talk while others cannot stop talking about their ideas. It becomes a problem for him to encourage group members to express their opinions during online discussions. As the group leader, he wants to balance the speaking time of each participant, so he sets up a timed prompt to force each member to participate and be able to interrupt others' lengthy speeches at any time.

Flexible planning. Hai is a street dance enthusiast who advocates freedom. Due to the epidemic, the form course she took changed to online classes. She encountered a problem of how to have an intense immersion in the exercise course that would let her have the same experience online as taking the course offline. What she needs is a high degree of freedom to learn in which she can study anytime and anywhere to improve learning efficiency. Hence, the participant proposed adding the function of offline courses so that she could learn from classes freely and at ease.

4.8 Apply Proper Pressure

Pressure can help students stay focused and improve performance, and students can introduce educational authority or create pressure to achieve this goal.

Educational authority. Lingling is a junior who takes online professional courses at home. She has been taking online lessons at home for more than a month. Her problem is now that she feels tired and slack. How can the learning atmosphere of her class be increased? She thought that she could use educational authority figures to create pressure for herself and connect learning with pressure to remind herself of her learning goal. Therefore, the participants proposed that they print an image of the teacher's human form and put it on the desk or ask her parents to supervise Lingling's learning.

Create pressure. Liuyi is a girl who loves hip-hop dance very much. She took the physical exercise course at University, but because of the new epidemic, she could not study offline in school and the class was changed to an online class. For her hip-hop experience, she is very adapted to offline class, but it is her first experience taking an exercise class online. The first problem she encountered was how to learn better and feel more immersed in an online physical education class? Because she likes to fight with her classmates when she is learning hip-hop, she can learn better in this way, so the participants want to see her friends' actions when she is in the online exercise class to compare her actions with those of her classmates and learn better.

5 Discussion

It is interesting to note that all seven needs and 20 sub-needs can be applied in educational product design. When users have experience with designers, the interaction designers create a brand-new educational product and they can verify whether the features can meet the needs of the university students. The results indicate that students would avoid disturbing others when they considered others to be studying, especially at the dormitory during the epidemic. At the same time, students try to express the importance of learning to them so that others will prevent disturbing them. A possible explanation for this might be that students think studying requires a quieter atmosphere and more personal space. One exciting finding is the need to prevent embarrassment while they are practicing, such as singing and dancing. Therefore, further study with more focus on how students can practice without feeling embarrassed from a psychological perspective is suggested. Hardware and software interactions confirm the association between users' expectations and UX design criteria.

The future design should consider the factor of users. There are three approaches to promote learning: independent promotion, external learning motivation, and peer support. When designing these products, designers should help students improve learning motivation by setting up a system of encouragement since students can experience study inertia. Further research should be undertaken to investigate motivating design in a specific context and in a particular user group. Another need students always mentioned was the atmosphere. One of the challenges of studying at home is that there is no atmosphere to concentrate on studying. The results of this study show that students are expecting the same learning atmosphere they have during normal studies. To improve the learning experience, they try to create a sense of ceremony of learning and are willing to study with friends or groups of peers with whom they can express ideas. Furthermore, attention, interaction, cognition, and content influence learning efficiency. Students propose many ways to keep them focused, such as preventing all interventions, maintaining interactions with teachers, using cognitive preferences, and selecting attractive learning content. Applying proper pressure is the other way to improve learning efficiency. Students proposed introducing educational authority and creating pressure to improve it. These results may be explained by the fact that learning efficiency has decreased since studying from home. It is difficult for students to establish a reasonable plan without teachers' direct help and planning during the epidemic. They have to control their own progress and consider many details. These results match those observed in an earlier study [26]. Therefore, students look forward to a flexible learning model that can adapt their plans.

6 Conclusion

This paper addresses an interesting challenge: what are users' needs for using educational products? The research team conducts participatory design research on envisioning future educational outcomes for university students. To analyze the participatory design workshop's findings, the team adopted JTBD theory to explore user needs behind the design solution that they proposed. This study has identified seven primary user needs and twenty sub-needs in five scenarios. The study contributes to our understanding of designing educational products in the epidemic environment. Using participatory design allows us to advance our understanding of study needs without using semi-structured interviews. The insights gained from this study may be of assistance to UX designers and UX researchers to obtain a new perspective of using scenarios. However, the small sample size did not allow the collection of data from other studies. More broadly, research is also needed to determine user needs for educational products. Further research should focus on choosing how to apply product design and evaluate performance by target user groups.

References

1. Al-Malah, D.K.A.R., Jinah, H.H.K., ALRikabi, H.T.S.: Enhancement of educational services by using the internet of things applications for talent and intelligent schools. Periodicals Eng. Nat. Sci. (PEN) 8(4), 2358–2366 (2020)
2. Verner, I., Cuperman, D., Romm, T., Reitman, M., Chong, S.K., Gong, Z.: Intelligent robotics in high school: an educational paradigm for the industry 4.0 era. In: Auer, M.E., Tsiatsos, T. (eds.) ICL 2018. AISC, vol. 916, pp. 824–832. Springer, Cham (2020). https://doi.org/10.1007/978-3-030-11932-4_76

3. Xiao, J., Sun-Lin, H.Z., Cheng, H.C.: A framework of online-merge-offline (OMO) classroom for open education. Asian Assoc. Open Univ. J. (2019)
4. Mohamed, H., Lamia, M.: Implementing flipped classroom that used an intelligent tutoring system into learning process. Comput. Educ. **124**, 62–76 (2018)
5. Adnan, M., Anwar, K.: Online Learning amid the COVID-19 pandemic: students' perspectives. Online Submission **2**(1), 45–51 (2020)
6. Larionova, V., Brown, K., Bystrova, T., Sinitsyn, E.: Russian perspectives of online learning technologies in higher education: an empirical study of a MOOC. Res. Comput. Int. Educ. **13**(1), 70–91 (2018)
7. Robert, G., Cornwell, J., Locock, L., Purushotham, A., Sturmey, G., Gager, M.: Patients and staff as codesigners of healthcare services. BMJ **350**, g7714–g7714 (2015)
8. Merkel, S., Kucharski, A.: Participatory design in gerontechnology: a systematic literature review. Gerontologist **59**(1), e16–e25 (2019)
9. Lee, H.R., et al.: Steps toward participatory design of social robots: mutual learning with older adults with depression. In: Proceedings of the 2017 ACM/IEEE International Conference on Human-Robot Interaction, pp. 244–253, March 2017
10. Langley, J., Wolstenholme, D., Cooke, J.: 'Collective making'as knowledge mobilisation: the contribution of participatory design in the co-creation of knowledge in healthcare. BMC Health Serv. Res. **18**(1), 585 (2018)
11. Sottilare, R.A., Graesser, A., Hu, X., Holden, H. (eds.): Design recommendations for intelligent tutoring systems: Volume 1-learner modeling (vol. 1). US Army Research Laboratory (2013)
12. Mitrovic, A., Ohlsson, S., Barrow, D.K.: The effect of positive feedback in a constraint-based intelligent tutoring system. Comput. Educ. **60**(1), 264–272 (2013)
13. Goldberg, B., et al.: Enhancing self-regulated learning through metacognitively-aware intelligent tutoring systems. International Society of the Learning Sciences, Boulder (2014)
14. Carro, R.M., Sanchez-Horreo, V.: The effect of personality and learning styles on individual and collaborative learning: obtaining criteria for adaptation. In: 2017 IEEE Global Engineering Education Conference (EDUCON), pp. 1585–1590. IEEE, April 2017
15. Al-Rajhi, L., Salama, R., Gamalel-Din, S.: Personalized intelligent assessment model for measuring initial students' abilities. In: Proceedings of the 2014 Workshop on Interaction Design in Educational Environments, pp. 41–48, June 2014
16. Aslan, S., et al.: Students' emotional self-labels for personalized models. In: Proceedings of the Seventh International Learning Analytics & Knowledge Conference, pp. 550–551, March 2017
17. Al-Hunaiyyan, A.A., Bimba, A.T., Alsharhan, S.: A cognitive knowledge-based model for an academic adaptive e-advising system. Interdiscip. J. Inf. Knowl. Manag. **15**, 247–263 (2020)
18. Reinerman-Jones, L., Lameier, E., Biddle, E., Boyce, M.: Motivating individual difference in an intelligent tutoring system. In: Design Recommendations for Intelligent Tutoring Systems, p. 331
19. Aslanoglou, K., Papazoglou, T., Karagiannidis, C.: Educational robotics and down syndrome: investigating student performance and motivation. In: Proceedings of the 8th International Conference on Software Development and Technologies for Enhancing Accessibility and Fighting Info-exclusion, pp. 110–116, June 2018
20. Buehler, E., Comrie, N., Hofmann, M., McDonald, S., Hurst, A.: Investigating the implications of 3D printing in special education. ACM Trans. Accessible Comput. (TACCESS) **8**(3), 1–28 (2016)
21. Robb, N., Leahy, M., Sung, C., Goodman, L.: Multisensory participatory design for children with special educational needs and disabilities. In: Proceedings of the 2017 Conference on Interaction Design and Children, pp. 490–496, June 2017

22. Chan, R.Y.Y., Bai, X., Chen, X., Jia, S., Xu, X.H.: iBeacon and HCI in special education: micro-location based augmentative and alternative communication for children with intellectual disabilities. In: Proceedings of the 2016 CHI Conference Extended Abstracts on Human Factors in Computing Systems, pp. 1533–1539 May 2016

23. Kyfonidis, C., Lennon, M.: Making diabetes education interactive: tangible educational toys for children with type-1 diabetes. In: Proceedings of the 2019 CHI Conference on Human Factors in Computing Systems, pp. 1–12, May 2019

24. Christensen, C.M., Hall, T., Dillon, K., Duncan, D.S.: Know your customers' jobs to be done. Harv. Bus. Rev. **94**(9), 54–62 (2016)

25. Zhu, D., Li, A., Wang, N., Wu, J., Liu, W.: Designed for designer: an online co-design workshop. In: Russo, D., Ahram, T., Karwowski, W., Di Bucchianico, G., Taiar, R. (eds.) IHSI 2021. AISC, vol. 1322, pp. 856–861. Springer, Cham (2021). https://doi.org/10.1007/978-3-030-68017-6_127

26. Cook, D.A., Levinson, A.J., Garside, S.: Time and learning efficiency in internet-based learning: a systematic review and meta-analysis. Adv. Health Sci. Educ. **15**(5), 755–770 (2010)

Methods and Techniques for UX Research

Operational Usability Heuristics: A Question-Based Approach for Facilitating the Detection of Usability Problems

Anas Abulfaraj[✉] ⓘ and Adam Steele ⓘ

College of Computing and Digital Media, DePaul University, 243 South Wabash Avenue,
Chicago, IL 60604, USA
Aabulfa2@mail.depaul.edu, Asteele@cs.depaul.edu

Abstract. Heuristic evaluation (HE) is a method designed to help evaluators detect usability issues in any given system. It has gained popularity since it is a discount method, meaning it does not require much time or resources. However, it has been reported that novice evaluators face difficulties when applying HE, and they produce results of poor quality when compared to the results produced by expert evaluators. For years, researchers have worked on improving HE in multiple ways by producing different heuristics, modifying and extending existing heuristics, or addressing and improving certain parts of the HE process. In this work, we provide a set of questions based on Nielsen's heuristics for evaluators to ask themselves while examining the system. This list of questions can facilitate the detection of usability problems in any given system. The list is a result of interviews we conducted with 15 usability experts from both academia and industry.

Keywords: Usability · Usability heuristics · Heuristic evaluation · Novice evaluators

1 Introduction

Heuristic evaluation (HE) is a discount usability evaluation method [1], and it is one of the most commonly used evaluation methods [2]. It is popular because it does not require many resources or much time. However, heuristic evaluation is an unstructured method, meaning that there is no clear, step-by-step way to perform it [3]. This lack of structure makes it sometimes difficult for novice evaluators to use. Therefore, the quality of the results produced by novice evaluators is poorer than the quality of the results produced by expert evaluators. This is a concern mainly because, novices are frequently being hired to perform HE, which means that without a better way for them to perform it, they will continue to produce poor results. Novices are being hired by small companies [4], as well as by researchers to perform HE in academic papers [5, 6], so it is critical that we support them in performing better HE.

Modifying HE to suit novices can be accomplished in two main ways. The first way is by developing a solid framework, or protocol, for novices to follow. This means that

© Springer Nature Switzerland AG 2021
M. M. Soares et al. (Eds.): HCII 2021, LNCS 12779, pp. 173–186, 2021.
https://doi.org/10.1007/978-3-030-78221-4_12

novices will have a clear path from the beginning of the evaluation to the submission of the results. Second, we focus on certain elements of the process, such as providing background information, increasing the understandability of the heuristics, and identifying better ways to report the results. We believe that to produce an optimal method for novices, both ways should be pursued since they are complementary. We previously published research [7] in which we developed a coherent, step-by-step protocol that thoroughly explains how HE should be performed. Additionally, [8] broke down Nielsen's heuristics to make them easier for novices to grasp. However, in this work, we are concerned with making these heuristics more operational, not merely understandable. We do this by presenting them in a way that allows novice evaluators to easily detect usability issues.

In our previous studies [7, 8], we interviewed 15 usability experts from both academia and industry. During interviews, we asked them to thoroughly describe Nielsen's heuristics, explain each heuristic, give examples, describe their significance, and discuss their applicability. We used thematic analysis [9] to categorize and organize their responses and then translated these responses into questions that evaluators could ask themselves when considering any given system. To answer these questions, they would have to examine specific parts of the system, leading them to detect usability problems more easily. The results are a list of detailed questions, with each group of questions related to a specific concept and each group of concepts related to a specific usability heuristic.

2 Related Work

Since the 1990s, HE has attracted the attention of many researchers. Nielsen and Molich first published a paper [10, 11] that coined the term heuristic evaluation. They listed 9 guidelines to help evaluators detect usability issues. A few years later, Nielsen revised the work to produce a list of 10 usability heuristics. The original claim by Nielsen was that HE is able to detect approximately 74–87% of usability issues if performed by 3–5 expert evaluators and 51% if performed by 3–5 novice evaluators [12]. However, a number of years later, a group of researchers claimed that these numbers were not accurate and claimed that 3–5 novice evaluators can detect only 23% of usability issues [13].

Since then, some researchers have started to question the reliability of HE [3]. They maintain that the results of the evaluation are a consequence of the evaluator's experience rather than the method itself. Therefore, we wondered about the role that HE as a method plays in detecting usability issues.

As a response to the criticisms and shortcomings of the method, many papers have been published to address the issues of HE. The ways in which the authors of these papers have approached the gaps differed. Some attempted to develop new heuristics, neglecting the process of HE; others chose to modify Nielsen's heuristics, and yet another group of researchers focused on addressing certain parts of the process.

To create new heuristics, there are two trends. The first is creating general usability heuristics that do not address specific systems. Nielsen's heuristics are considered to be general heuristics. In addition to Nielsen's heuristics, there are multiple other general heuristics. There is the set of heuristics created by Tognazzini [14], which is a list of

19 principles. Another general list is the one produced by Gerhardt-Powals [15], which contains 10 principles. The second trend is domain-specific heuristics. These heuristics are designed specifically to deal with certain platforms, audiences, and/or contexts. The idea behind them is to develop more specific guidelines to address specific issues that general heuristics cannot address. Examples of this trend include the Heuristic Evaluation for Child Elearning Application (HECE) [16], which is a list that is designed to address the issues of child e-learning applications. Another example is [17], which is a list of heuristics designed to address the issues of automated teller machines (ATMs).

Since Nielsen's heuristics are arguably the most popular set of heuristics, some researchers have decided to modify them, extend them, combine them and compare them to other heuristics. For example, in [18], the researchers combined Nielsen's heuristics with Tognazzini's heuristics to create a new list that contains 15 heuristics. In [19], the researchers combined Nielsen's heuristics with other heuristics to develop a modified list that consists of 11 heuristics. The researchers of [20, 21] compared Nielsen's heuristics against Gerhardt-Powals' principles.

Improving HE as a method is an area that has attracted some researchers. The first issue is improving the understandability of the heuristics. The authors of [22] examined two sets of general heuristics and identified ways in which these heuristics could be improved. The second issue is improving the use of the heuristics. The authors of [23] interviewed a number of usability experts and produced a list of tactics that can help novices use heuristics to detect usability issues. The third issue is improving the reports. The authors of [24] created a more comprehensive way of reporting usability issues that both enhances the clarity of the issues and helps in detecting usability issues.

We believe that all of the abovementioned ways of dealing with HE are important and complementary. Therefore, in our research effort, we pursued multiple directions. In [7], we developed a general protocol to be used with any set of heuristics. In [8], we detailed Nielsen's heuristics to increase its comprehension. In this work, we transformed the heuristics into a set of questions that help evaluators detect usability issues in any given system.

3 Methodology

There are multiple ways in which we can conduct such a research effort. We chose interviews because they provide the ability to dig deeply into an issue and find answers, and this method allows the participants to elaborate on their responses in detail. We specifically chose semi-structured interviews because they do not constrain the conversation like structured interviews while keeping the conversation focused, unlike unstructured interviews. The plan was to interview at least 12 participants, which is the minimum number of participants recommended to reach saturation [25].

We chose to interview usability experts from both academia and industry. We decided that including participants from academia would help us understand the underlying knowledge of the heuristics, while participants from industry would possess more hands-on experience on how to apply the heuristics in the real world. However, defining an expert proved to be difficult because there is no agreed-upon definition. Therefore, we followed the authors of [23] by defining an expert as someone who has at least 4 years of experience in the field. Furthermore, we added two screeners with two criteria: first, they should have performed HE at least 3 times; second, they should be familiar with Nielsen's heuristics, which is the one that they would be asked to discuss.

For recruitment, we used a snowball sampling technique. We started by recruiting experts we knew who met the criteria. Then, we asked them to refer us to other experts who also met the criteria. We ultimately interviewed 15 usability experts. 7 participants were from academia, and 8 were from industry; 10 participants were males, and 5 were females. Their maximum number of years of experience was 15, and their minimum number of years of experience was 4. Some interviews were conducted face-to-face (6 interviews), while others were held over a video call (9 interviews).

The participants were asked to explain Nielsen's heuristics in detail, give examples, and describe their significance, their applicability and the consequences of ignoring them. We then used thematic analysis [9] to analyze the responses. We grouped the concepts or the sub-heuristics of each heuristic, which was published in [8]. We grouped the components under each sub-heuristic and then converted these components into questions that evaluators could ask themselves while conducting the evaluation.

4 Results

Below is a table that shows the operational usability heuristics. The first column shows the original 10 heuristics of Nielsen. The second column shows the concepts under each heuristic and its definition. The third column shows the questions related to each concept.

Heuristic	Concept	Questions that should be asked
Visibility of system status	1 - **State**: Users should know what they are capable of doing in the system at any given moment	**State**: - When looking at the different elements on the system (links, buttons, etc.), do you know what you can do with them? - When any changes happen in the system, are they immediately reflected in the system? - Do changes happen immediately, or do they take time?
	2 - **Location**: Users should know what system they are in and where they are located within the system	**Location:** - Do you know in which system you are located, and can you determine this easily? - Do you know the page you are on? Can you find out easily? - Do you know where you are in relation to other parts of the system? Can you determine this easily?

(continued)

(continued)

Heuristic	Concept	Questions that should be asked
	3 - **Progress**: The user should know how far they are from accomplishing their goal	**Progress:** - When you work on an action, does the system tell you how long it will take for completion? - When you complete a multi-page task, does the system tell you how many steps are left? - When there is limited capacity in the system (storage, memory, etc.) does the system tell you how much is left? - Are progress measures accurate? If it says it takes one minute, does it really take one minute? - Are both active and passive progress measures provided?
	4 - **Closure:** Users should explicitly know that their goal was accomplished regardless of the outcome	**Closure:** - When you finish a task, does the system provide you with feedback? - Does the system give you feedback if you got either a right or a wrong result? - Does feedback appear immediately, or does it take a long time? - Can you easily interpret the feedback? - If what you did was wrong, does the system offer an explanation?
Match between system and the real world	1 - **Understandability:** The content of the system should be understandable by the users of the system	**Understandability:** - Is every piece of system content (text, icons, images, etc.) understandable, specifically, by the target audience?

(continued)

(*continued*)

Heuristic	Concept	Questions that should be asked
	2 - **Natural and logical order:** The connection and the tasks in the system should follow a natural and logical order	**Natural and logical order:** - Do the steps required to complete a task follow a natural order, i.e., do they follow the order of how the task would be done in the real world? - If not, are the steps required to complete the task logical, i.e., can you predict what the next step should be?
	3 - **Appropriateness:** The content of the system should be appropriate to the users of the system	**Appropriateness:** - Is every content element in the system (text, icons, images, etc.) appropriate? Do they match the identity of the system? - Is there an aspect of the system that might be offensive to the target audience?
User control and freedom	1 - **Reversibility:** Users should be able to undo and redo any action they take on the system	**Reversibility:** - Can you undo any action (deleted, sent, placed, etc.) you have performed on the system? - Can you redo any action (deleted, sent, placed, etc.) you have performed on the system? - Are undo and redo easy to do? - How many steps back can you undo or redo?
	2 - **Emergency exit:** The user should be able to quit any undesirable situation on the system	**Emergency exit:** - Can you escape from any situation in the system? - Is it easy to do?
	3 - **Informing users:** Users should know why the system is asking them to enter certain information, and they should know how the information will be handled	**Informing users:** - When the system asks you for personal/sensitive information, does it tell you why it is wanted? - Does the system tell you how this information is going to be stored and handled?

(*continued*)

(continued)

Heuristic	Concept	Questions that should be asked
Consistency and standards	1 - **Consistency**: Elements of meaning, function, organization, effort, and feeling should be consistent throughout the whole system	**Consistency:** - Does the system always refer to the same element by the same name across the system? - Do elements that appear identical across the system always do the same thing? - Do the interface layout and organization have a similar appearance across the system? - When you work on a multi-page task, is the same effort needed for each page, i.e., is there consistency in the effort needed for each page? - Do the multiple parts of the system have the same feel, i.e., do you perceive the different parts of the system as belonging to one unit?
	2 - **Standards:** The system should take advantage of common practices in similar systems and follow them	**Standards:** - Do you feel that your past experiences with similar systems helped you in using this system? - Does this help you in understanding content meaning? - Does it help in performing actions on the system? - Does the system organization look similar to that of other similar systems?
Error prevention	1 - **Instructions:** Sufficient instructions should be provided to the user before any given task	**Instructions:** - Does the system provide you with instructions on how to complete a certain task that requires a specific thing to be done? - Are instructions clear and easy to understand? - Are instructions clearly visible? - Are instructions too long?

(continued)

(continued)

Heuristic	Concept	Questions that should be asked
	2 - **Constraints:** The system should not allow the user to take action that will lead to obvious errors	**Constraints:** - In situations where the action/input is clearly wrong or will lead to erroneous outcome, does the system prohibit that action/input from taking place? - When you are prohibited from performing a certain action/input, do you have an idea why this has happened?
	3 - **Confirmation:** The system should ask users to confirm their actions to make sure that the action is intended	**Confirmation:** - When committing to a major action that has a long-lasting impact, does the system ask you to confirm the action?
	4 - **Notification:** The system should notify users when changes on the system are happening	**Notification:** - When an important/serious event occurs, does the system notify you? - Does the system tell you what is going to happen if you do not take a recommended action?
	5 - **Autosaving:** The system should auto-save users' input to make sure their effort will not be lost if something goes wrong	**Autosaving:** - When you are entering/writing input that takes considerable time/effort, does the system automatically save your work? - Do you know when your input is being auto-saved? - Is input retrieval easy or automatic?
	6 - **Flexible inputs:** The system should give users a choice to enter the inputs in a form with which they feel comfortable	**Flexible inputs:** - When the system asks you to enter an input that comes in different forms (date, phone number, weight, etc.), does it allow you to enter it in the form you want? - When it takes a form you like and converts it, can you see the conversion?

(continued)

(*continued*)

Heuristic	Concept	Questions that should be asked
	7 - Defaults: The system should use the most expected defaults	**Defaults:** - When you are in an empty state, are the system defaults the expected ones? - Is there any indication of exactly what the defaults are?
Recognition rather than recall	**1 - Availability:** The content that users need to accomplish certain goals should be clearly presented to them, and they should not need to rely on their memory to remember them	**Availability:** - Is everything you would need to accomplish your goal clearly presented to you? - When completing a multi-step task, is the information presented in one step also needed in other steps presented to you?
	2 - Suggestions: The system should provide users with suggestions to make the process of remembering their needs easier	**Suggestions:** - When you are in the empty state, does the system provide you with suggestions on how to proceed? - When you search for something within the system and don't exactly recall it, does the system provide you with suggestions? - When you browse the system, does it provide you with suggestions of things similar to your browsing targets? - Are these suggestions accurate?
Flexibility and efficiency of use	**1 - Flexibility:** The system should provide users with different ways to accomplish the same goal to accommodate different users and different situations	**Flexibility:** - Does the system provide you with different paths toward accomplishing the same goal? - Will users with a variety of abilities and skills be able to use the system?
	2 - Efficiency: The tasks sequence of the system should be in its simplest form	**Efficiency:** - Could the number of steps/time/effort required to accomplish a goal be reduced?

(*continued*)

(*continued*)

Heuristic	Concept	Questions that should be asked
Aesthetic and minimalist design	1 - **Aesthetic:** The system should be aesthetically pleasing to users	**Aesthetic:** - Is the system aesthetically pleasing to you? - Do the interface elements appear to be in harmony? - Are audio/video well-presented in the system?
	2 - **Organization:** The content of the system should be organized in a way that allows the user to distinguish each element	**Organization:** - When looking at the interface, are related elements organized in a way that shows their relationships? - When looking at the interface, could you easily distinguish among the different elements (menus, paragraphs, etc.)?
	3 - **Simplicity:** The system should not contain any unnecessary content that would distract the user	**Simplicity:** - Is there any extraneous content on the system (features, icons, texts, etc.) that could be omitted? - Is there anything in the interface that distracts you from properly focusing?
Help users recognize, diagnose, and recover from errors	1 - **Recognizing errors:** The user should easily recognize that an error happened	**Recognizing errors:** - When an error occurs, do you notice it? - Is the error indication the expected one, or did it take some time to notice it?
	2 - **Understanding errors:** The user should easily understand what error occurred	**Understanding errors:** - When you notice an error, do you know exactly what it is? - Can you read it easily? - Is error information written in an appropriate way? - Is it written in a way that might intimidate or try to blame you?

(*continued*)

(continued)

Heuristic	Concept	Questions that should be asked
	3 - **Recovering from errors:** The system should provide the user with a recommendation on how to resolve the error	**Recovering from errors:** - When you know of an error, do you know how to resolve it? - Is the solution presented to you in an appropriately actionable manner?
Help and documentation	1 - **Help:** The system should provide the user with means to contact the help team	**Help:** - Does the system provide you with the capability to contact the support team? - Are there multiple ways to contact the support team or only one? - Do you receive an explanation of how long it will take to receive a support team response?
	2 - **Documentation:** The system should provide the user with sufficient material to learn the system and to know how to overcome any potential obstacles	**Documentation:** - Is there documentation from which you can find solutions or learn more about the system? - Can you find all possible solutions? - Is the material easy to understand? - Can you easily find the material? - Can you easily search within the material? - Does the material prioritize the action frequency? - Is the material categorized? - If there are video/audio tutorials, are they too long? - Is contextual documentation displayed next to the major tasks?

5 Discussion

The reason for having operational usability heuristics is to facilitate the detection of usability problems and increase the quality of the results. Although this list of questions is part of a more comprehensive work that focuses on different aspects of HE, it could be used as a standalone material. The list was produced mainly to help novice evaluators.

However, we believe that even expert evaluators can benefit from it. They can use it either as a refresher to cover the bases and ensure that they did not miss anything or to only choose the things with which they are unfamiliar.

The downside of such a list is that it might be time consuming to answer every question. However, especially for novices, this lengthy process is worthwhile because the alternative would be a result of poor quality. However, we believe that after using this list a number of times, evaluators will not spend as much time on the questions because they will be more experienced and will have developed a better sense of the detection of usability issues, and answering these questions will become second nature to them.

Finally, it is necessary to validate this list of questions. Therefore, further work in comparing the performance of novice evaluators who use the list of questions against other novice evaluators who do not use them should be conducted to reveal the differences both quantitatively and qualitatively. This will explain the advantages and disadvantages of using such a method.

6 Conclusion

Heuristic evaluation (HE) is a method designed to help evaluators detect usability issues in any given system. HE is considered to be a discount usability method, which means that it does not require much time or resources. However, the method is considered unreliable by some researchers since it does not have a clear structure and depends mainly on the experience of the evaluator performing it. The goal of this work is to produce an operational list to provide the evaluator with a list of heuristics that lend themselves to detecting usability problems in any given system. Therefore, we interviewed a group of experts. Based on the interviews, the results are a list of detailed questions with each group of questions related to a specific concept and each group of concepts related to a specific usability heuristic. The questions are designed to ensure that the system adheres to a specific heuristic. In future work, we plan to do the following: first, compare two groups of evaluators, one using the list of operational heuristics and one not, and report the differences and similarities; second, adopt a similar approach to other heuristics and transform them into operational heuristics as well.

References

1. Nielsen, J.: Guerrilla HCI: using discount usability engineering to penetrate the intimidation barrier. In: Bias, R.G., Mayhew, D.J. (eds.) Cost-Justifying Usability, pp. 245–272. Academic Press, Boston (1994)
2. Rosenbaum, S., Rohn, J.A., Humburg, J.: A toolkit for strategic usability: results from workshops, panels, and surveys. In: Proceedings of the SIGCHI Conference on Human Factors in Computing Systems, pp. 337–344. Association for Computing Machinery, The Hague (2000). https://doi.org/10.1145/332040.332454
3. Cockton, G., Woolrych, A.: Sale must end: should discount methods be cleared off HCI's shelves? Interactions 9, 13–18 (2002). https://doi.org/10.1145/566981.566990
4. de Salgado, A.L., Amaral, L.A., Freire, A.P., Fortes, R.P.M.: Usability and UX practices in small enterprises: lessons from a survey of the Brazilian context. In: Proceedings of the 34th ACM International Conference on the Design of Communication, pp. Article 18. Association for Computing Machinery, Silver Spring (2016). https://doi.org/10.1145/2987592.2987616

5. Al-Razgan, M.S., Al-Khalifa, H.S., Al-Shahrani, M.D.: Heuristics for evaluating the usability of mobile launchers for elderly people. In: Marcus, A. (ed.) DUXU 2014. LNCS, vol. 8517, pp. 415–424. Springer, Cham (2014). https://doi.org/10.1007/978-3-319-07668-3_40

6. Paz, F., Paz, F.A., Pow-Sang, J.A.: Experimental case study of new usability heuristics. In: Marcus, A. (ed.) Design, User Experience, and Usability: Design Discourse, pp. 212–223. Springer, Cham (2015)

7. Abulfaraj, A., Steele, A.: Coherent heuristic evaluation (CoHE): toward increasing the effectiveness of heuristic evaluation for novice evaluators. In: Marcus, A., Rosenzweig, E. (eds.) HCII 2020. LNCS, vol. 12200, pp. 3–20. Springer, Cham (2020). https://doi.org/10.1007/978-3-030-49713-2_1

8. Abulfaraj, A., Steele, A.: Detailed usability heuristics: a breakdown of usability heuristics to enhance comprehension for novice evaluators. In: Stephanidis, C., Marcus, A., Rosenzweig, E., Rau, P.L.P., Moallem, A., Rauterberg, M. (eds.) HCI International 2020 - Late Breaking Papers: User Experience Design and Case Studies, pp. 3–18. Springer, Cham (2020)

9. Ann, B., Dominic, F., Stephann, M.: Qualitative HCI research: going behind the scenes. Synth. Lect. Hum. Centered Inform. 9, 1–115 (2016). https://doi.org/10.2200/S00706ED1V01Y201602HCI034

10. Molich, R., Nielsen, J.: Improving a human-computer dialogue. Commun. ACM 33, 338–348 (1990). https://doi.org/10.1145/77481.77486

11. Nielsen, J., Molich, R.: Heuristic evaluation of user interfaces. In: Proceedings of the SIGCHI Conference on Human Factors in Computing Systems, pp. 249–256. Association for Computing Machinery, Seattle (1990). https://doi.org/10.1145/97243.97281

12. Nielsen, J.: Finding usability problems through heuristic evaluation. In: Proceedings of the SIGCHI Conference on Human Factors in Computing Systems, pp. 373–380. Association for Computing Machinery, Monterey (1992). https://doi.org/10.1145/142750.142834

13. Slavkovic, A., Cross, K.: Novice heuristic evaluations of a complex interface. In: CHI 1999 Extended Abstracts on Human Factors in Computing Systems, pp. 304–305. Association for Computing Machinery, Pittsburgh (1999). https://doi.org/10.1145/632716.632902

14. Tognazzini, B.: First principles of interaction design (revised & expanded) (2014). https://ask tog.com/atc/principles-of-interaction-design/

15. Gerhardt-Powals, J.: Cognitive engineering principles for enhancing human-computer performance. Int. J. Hum. Comput. Interact. 8, 189–211 (1996). https://doi.org/10.1080/10447319609526147

16. Alsumait, A., Al-Osaimi, A.: Usability heuristics evaluation for child e-learning applications. In: Proceedings of the 11th International Conference on Information Integration and Web-based Applications & Services, pp. 425–430. Association for Computing Machinery, Kuala Lumpur (2009). https://doi.org/10.1145/1806338.1806417

17. Chanco, C., Moquillaza, A., Paz, F.: Development and validation of usability heuristics for evaluation of interfaces in ATMs. In: Marcus, A., Wang, W. (eds.) HCII 2019. LNCS, vol. 11586, pp. 3–18. Springer, Cham (2019). https://doi.org/10.1007/978-3-030-23535-2_1

18. Granollers, T.: Usability evaluation with heuristics. new proposal from integrating two trusted sources. In: Marcus, A., Wang, W. (eds.) DUXU 2018. LNCS, vol. 10918, pp. 396–405. Springer, Cham (2018). https://doi.org/10.1007/978-3-319-91797-9_28

19. Wheeler Atkinson, B.F., Bennett, T.O., Bahr, G.S., Walwanis Nelson, M.M.: Development of a multiple heuristics evaluation table (MHET) to support software development and usability analysis. In: Stephanidis, C. (ed.) UAHCI 2007. LNCS, vol. 4554, pp. 563–572. Springer, Heidelberg (2007). https://doi.org/10.1007/978-3-540-73279-2_63

20. Hvannberg, E.T., Law, E.L.C., Lárusdóttir, M.K.: Heuristic evaluation: comparing ways of finding and reporting usability problems. Interact. Comput. 19, 225–240 (2007). https://doi.org/10.1016/j.intcom.2006.10.001

21. Sohl, M.: Comparing Two Heuristic Evaluation Methods and Validating with Usability Test Methods: Applying Usability Evaluation on a Simple Website. Student Thesis. Linköping University, Linköping, Sweden (2018)

22. Cronholm, S.: The usability of usability guidelines: a proposal for meta-guidelines. In: Proceedings of the 21st Annual Conference of the Australian Computer-Human Interaction Special Interest Group: Design: Open 24/7, pp. 233–240. Association for Computing Machinery, Melbourne (2009). https://doi.org/10.1145/1738826.1738864

23. de Salgado, A.L., de Lara, S.M., Freire, A.P., de Fortes, R.P.M.: What is hidden in a heuristic evaluation: tactics from the experts. In: 13th International Conference on Information Systems & Technology Management - Contecsi, pp. 2931–2946. Contecsi, São Paulo (2016)

24. Cockton, G., Woolrych, A., Hall, L., Hindmarch, M.: Changing analysts' tunes: the surprising impact of a new instrument for usability inspection method assessment. In: O'Neill, E., Palanque, P., Johnson, P. (eds.) People and Computers XVII — Designing for Society, pp. 145–161. Springer, London (2004)

25. Guest, G., Bunce, A., Johnson, L.: How many interviews are enough? An experiment with data saturation and variability. Field Methods 18, 59–82 (2006). https://doi.org/10.1177/1525822X05279903

Integration of User Experience and Agile Techniques for Requirements Analysis: A Systematic Review

Silvana Almeyda$^{(\boxtimes)}$, Claudia Zapata Del Río$^{(\boxtimes)}$, and Dennis Cohn$^{(\boxtimes)}$

Pontificia Universidad Católica del Perú, Lima, Peru
{silvana.almeyda,zapata.cmp,dennis.cohn}@pucp.edu.pe

Abstract. User experience and agile techniques have grown over the last decade. However, there are not many articles that study how the integration of both proposals influences requirements engineering.

The objective of this research is to structure the available literature on the integration of agile techniques and user experience in the domain of requirements engineering.

A systematic literature review (SLR) was carried out considering duly indexed conference and journal publications. Likewise, the studies found in the four (4) selected databases followed a rigorous study selection procedure.

The systematic review recovered a total of 25 primary studies after going through a quality evaluation and revealed the different practices and strategies most used in the requirements analysis integrating agile techniques and user experience. Besides, it allowed identifying the obstacles faced by professionals in requirements engineering.

The study carried out concludes that the most used practices in requirements engineering are user stories, low-fidelity prototypes, and person. The literature provides a systematic summary and proposals for frameworks that can be incorporated into agile development projects by integrating user experience.

Keywords: Requirements engineering · Agile software development · User experience · Usability · Systematic literature review

1 Introduction

The software industry has been growing in recent years, and new techniques and best practices are being applied to improve the software lifecycle. There has also been a significant penetration of agile methodologies in the development of interactive software systems [1], causing a favorable impact on the lives of individuals and organizations. Agile methods are increasingly used to develop products and reduce development time. However, to achieve a good user experience (UX), agile methods alone are not sufficient [2]. Agility facilitates collaboration with developers but provides inadequate opportunities to work with users. Early agile formulations did not identify UX as a different

© Springer Nature Switzerland AG 2021
M. M. Soares et al. (Eds.): HCII 2021, LNCS 12779, pp. 187–203, 2021.
https://doi.org/10.1007/978-3-030-78221-4_13

aspect of software development. Besides, some popular agile methods avoided the practice of previous design with a user research phase to develop a deep understanding of users and their needs. Since then, some practices such as people have become part of the agile mainstream [3]. Integrating user experience (UX) activities into agile development is one of the main challenges for UX professionals [4], since UX and Agile have two different objectives that are product interaction with the user and code creation for a product respectively [5]. The challenge is where to merge them and how to merge them so that there is genuine interaction between the two components [5].

This research proposes to conduct Systematic Review Literature (SRL) on the integration of user experience and agile techniques for requirements analysis. It seeks to classify the studies found to obtain a compendium of strategies and case studies, as well as to detect the most relevant problems faced by professionals in requirements engineering.

This study is organized into 6 sections. Section 2 presents the background and related work, Sect. 3 presents the Protocol for Systematic Literature Review (SLR), Sect. 4 shows the results of each of the research questions, Sect. 5 presents the threats to validity of this investigation, and finally, Sect. 6 presents the conclusions and future work.

2   Background and Related Work

In this section, the concepts of agile methodologies, usability, and requirements engineering that will be used for the development of research are presented.

- *Agile methodologies*: In agile software development, work is carried out in small phases, based on collaboration, adaptive planning, early delivery, continuous improvement, regular customer feedback, frequent redesign resulting in the development of software increments delivered in successive iterations in response to constant changes in customer requirement [6].
- *Usability:* According to Nielsen [7], usability is a quality attribute that evaluates the usability of user interfaces. Also, Hassenzahl [8] indicates that the user experience (UX) is a momentary feeling, mainly evaluative (good-bad) when interacting with a product or service. The following are the most important steps in the usability engineering process:

- – Person: a person is a fictional but realistic description of a typical user or product objective; in short, it is an archetype rather than a real living human being, but people should be described as if they were real subjects [9].

- – Scenario: it seeks to close the gap in agile methodology when it comes to analyzing the working context and defining a consistent design vision [1].
- – Paper prototyping: The value of the paper prototype is that critical information can be collected quickly and inexpensively. The technique can be used over and over again with minimal resource consumption [11].
- – Heuristic Evaluation: This allows a group of usability experts to compare a site's interface with the principles of usability. The analysis allows you to identify a list of possible usability issues [12].

- *Requirements engineering:* Software requirements engineering (RE) is the process of identifying stakeholders and their needs and documenting them in a way that is capable of analysis, communication, and subsequent implementation [13].

According to Losada [14], agile integration and user-centric design (UCD) allows you to take advantage of both approaches in a hybrid method. Requirements will evolve and gradually adapt to the needs of users and customers. On the other hand, according to Schon et al. [15], Agile Software Development (ASD) is used to address the growing complexity in system development. Hybrid development models, with user-centric design (UCD) integration, are applied to deliver competitive products with an appropriate user experience (UX). Therefore, stakeholder and user engagement during Requirements Engineering (RE) is essential to establishing a collaborative environment with constant feedback loops.

3   Review Process

Systematic Literature Review (SLR) is a means of identifying, evaluating and interpreting all available research relevant to a particular research question, thematic area, or phenomenon of interest [16]. The present SLR was conducted using the guidelines proposed by Kitchenham y Charters. Figure 1 shows the review protocol proposed by [16] that was followed on this paper.

Fig. 1. Systematic literature review protocol proposed by [16]

3.1   Research Questions

The definition of research questions was carried out using the PICOC methodology (Population, Intervention, Comparison, Outcome, Context) [17] with the help of the criteria shown in Table 1. This study aims to identify best practices and application cases for integrating user experience and agile techniques into requirements analysis, seeking to answer the main question of research.

- RQ01 What are the most commonly used practices and/or strategies in the requirements analysis for the integration of user experience and agile techniques?

- Based on the main question, specific questions were asked:
- RQ02 What are the obstacles faced by requirements engineering professionals in an agile context by applying user experience?
- RQ02-1 What kind of problems were encountered based on an existing taxonomy?
- RQ03 What agile techniques are used in this research?
- RQ04 What usability techniques are presented in this research?

Table 1. PICOC

Criteria	Description
Population	Agile software development integrating user experience
Intervention	Usability metrics and requirements engineering
Comparison	This does not apply
Result	Application cases for integrating user experience and agile techniques into requirements analysis
Context	Education, learning, academic, and social

3.2 Selection of Studies

For this study, digital databases covering the largest amount of literature on the subject of research were consulted. For this reason, Scopus, IEEE Xplore, Web of Science, and ACM were chosen as they are the most important in the scientific field and because they offer a great content of high impact scientific journals. The search terms for constructing the string are shown in Table 2. The search string turned out as follows:

Table 2. Search Terms – PICOC

Criteria	Keyword
Usability	usability, user experiencie, ux, user centered, ucd
Agile	Agile, scrum, xp, kanban
Requirements analysis	requirement

(usab* OR "user experience" OR ux OR "user centered" OR ucd) AND (agile OR scrum OR xp OR kanban) AND (requirement)

Inclusion (IC) and exclusion (EC) criteria were defined to carry out the investigation: (IC.1) Publications must be written in Spanish, English, or Portuguese; (IC.2) The articles have been published since 2010; (IC.3) Publications are Conference Paper/Article/Book Chapter/Review/Book; (IC.4) Access to the content of the publication must be available; (IC.5) The paper includes the integration of agile techniques and user experience for requirements analysis considering best practices; (EC.1) Duplicate articles from the same study. The least complete version is excluded. (EC.2) The publication is not related to the user experience field. (EC.3) The publication is not related to the field of agile techniques. (EC.4) The publication does not cover the study of the integration of user experience and agile techniques for requirements analysis.

3.3 Search Strategy

The SLR has been considered 5 stages, applying the criteria according to Table 3. In the first stage, studies of the databases selected using the search strings defined in the PICOC strategy and the inclusion and exclusion criteria were considered; in the second stage, the titles and summaries of the studies found to obtain the relevant studies were reviewed; in the third stage, the introduction and conclusions of the studies resulting from the second stage were revised; in the fourth stage, a full-text reading of the resulting studies was carried out; finally, primary studies were obtained.

Table 3. Inclusion and exclusion procedures and criteria.

Process	Selection criteria
First stage	No Duplicates
Second stage	IC.1, IC.2, IC.3, IC.4, EC.2, EC.3
Third stage	EC.2, EC.3, EC.4
Fourth stage	IC.5, EC.4

3.4 Quality Assessment

A list of questions was defined to assess the quality of studies, see Table 4. The questions in the Zarour et al. [18] proposal was considered as a reference. A 3-level compliance rating scale was used to assess the quality of the studies. If the study under evaluation Yes meets the quality question is assigned 1 point if it partially meets it is assigned 0.5 points, and if It does not meet it is assigned a score of 0. Only posts with a score of more than 2.5 were accepted.

Table 4. Quality assessment

Identifier	Question
QA1	Is the objective of the investigation indicated?
QA2	Is the idea or approach presented clearly explained?
QA3	Are threats to validity taken into consideration?
QA4	Is there an adequate description of the context in which the research was carried out?
QA5	Are the findings of the research clearly stated?

3.5   Data Extraction

Searches on each database were conducted in June 2020. The studies found in the initial search were consolidated into a single.xlsx format file, where the study selection procedure was performed. Table 5 shows that the initial search had 392 results, but after applying the search strategy in Sect. 3.3, 25 primary studies were obtained.

Table 5. Search results

Database	Initial	First stage	Second stage	Third stage	Fourth stage
SCOPUS	259	257	84	42	25
IEEE Xplore	50	6	0	0	0
Web of Science	37	6	3	1	0
ACM	46	23	12	0	0
Total	392	292	99	43	25

The 25 studies selected in Table 5 were subjected to a quality assessment process and all studies were reported to exceed the minimum accepted score of 2.5. The Table 6 shows the list of the 25 selected papers (in the following link https://drive.google.com/file/d/17nDQ5eBEmSLb32FutKg6vpf3hygvEcj-/view, all the references on Table 6 are listed).

Table 6. List of accepted studies

ID	Author	Title	Year
S01	Sánchez-Hernández et al.	Integration of remote usability tests in extreme programming: A literature review	2020
S02	Losada et al.	Improving agile software development methods by means of user objectives: An end user guided acceptance test-driven development proposal	2019
S03	Sabariah et al.	Requirement elicitation framework for child learning application - A research plan	2019
S04	Kamthan and Shahmir	Beyond utility and usability: Towards affectability in agile software requirements engineering	2018
S05	Santos et al.	Study about software project management with design thinking	2018
S06	Losada	Flexible requirement development through user objectives in an Agile-UCD hybrid approach	2018
S07	Hjartnes and Begnum	Challenges in agile universal design of ICT	2018
S08	Lopes et al.	Adding human interaction aspects in the writing of User Stories: A perspective of software developers	2017

(*continued*)

Table 6. (*continued*)

ID	Author	Title	Year
S09	Schön et al.	Agile Requirements Engineering: A systematic literature review	2017
S10	Sedeño et al.	Modelling agile requirements using context-based persona stories	2017
S11	Magues et al.	HCI usability techniques in agile development	2016
S12	Kropp and Koischwitz	Experiences with user-centered design and agile requirements engineering in fixed-price projects	2016
S13	Choma et al.	UserX story: Incorporating UX aspects into user stories elaboration	2016
S14	Forbrig	Continuous requirements engineering and human-centered agile software development	2016
S15	Wanderley et al.	Evaluation of BehaviorMap: A user-centered behavior language	2015
S16	Wanderley et al.	SnapMind: A framework to support consistency and validation of model-based requirements in agile development	2014
S17	Losada et al.	A guide to agile development of interactive software with a "user Objectives"-driven methodology	2013
S18	Bourimi and Kesdogan	Experiences by using AFFINE for building collaborative applications for online communities	2013
S19	Maguire	Using human factors standards to support user experience and agile design	2013
S20	Moreno and Yagüe	Agile user stories enriched with usability	2012
S21	Gonçalves and Santos	POLVO - Software for prototyping of low-fidelity interfaces in agile development	2011
S22	Lee et al.	A usability-pattern-based requirements-analysis method to bridge the gap between user tasks and application features	2010
S23	Xiong and Wang	A new combined method for UCD and software development and case study	2010
S24	Mehrfard et al.	Investigating the capability of agile processes to support life-science regulations: The case of XP and FDA regulations with a focus on human factor requirements	2010
S25	Bourimi et al.	AFFINE for enforcing earlier consideration of NFRs and human factors when building socio-technical systems following agile methodologies	2010

4   Discussion

This section presents the general findings and results of each of the research questions.

4.1   General Findings

Relevant data were collected from the list of 25 accepted studies to extract the first results. It was reported that, in 2010, 2016, and 2018, a greater number of publications were made with 4 studies per year. Likewise, after extracting the consolidation of countries based on the authors, it was obtained that the most widespread studies are found in Spain (25%), Germany (21.43%), and Brazil (17.86%). Studies were also consolidated by publication media and it was reported that the media that found the most results were Conference Paper (88%), Article (8%), and Review (4%). Finally, the classification of studies by type of research was carried out following the proposal of Wieringa et al. [19] and it was reported that the majority of studies are proposal, evaluation, validation, and philosophical with 10 (40%), 5 (20%), 4 (16%) and 4 (16%) studies respectively.

4.2   Results of Research Questions

RQ01 What are the Most Commonly Used Practices and/or Strategies in the Requirements Analysis for the Integration of User Experience and Agile Techniques?

Figure 2 shows that the most commonly used practices are User Stories, Low Fidelity Prototypes, and Person with 15, 13, and 12 studies respectively. Similarly, there is a tendency to use scenarios, high-fidelity prototypes, and use cases in recent years.

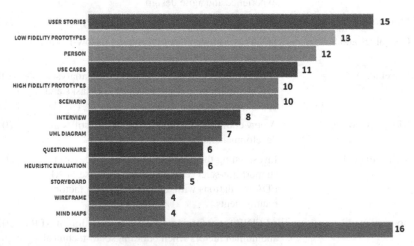

Fig. 2. Distribution of practices in requirements engineering

The results indicate that using user stories in an agile context applying user experience is the most used practice in recent years. Kamthan and Shahmir [1, 20], Sedeño et al. [21], and Choma et al. [22] in their respective studies propose a new approach to model agile requirements through user stories, integrating usability techniques. On the other hand, the study by Kropp and Koischwitz [23, 24] was found, in which they propose to introduce the role of a team called "On-site user experience consultant" (osUX consultant) that supports the integration of UCD in a Firm in agile requirements engineering under the constraints of fixed price software development projects. Also, the crucial UCD activities of the osUX consultant are grouped into four phases: initiation, conceptualization, implementation, and follow-up. Likewise, Losada [14] proposes an agile type of integration - flexible UCD and, for this, presents the User Objectives (UO) as an alternative to the usual tools to collect the requirements. Losada [14] mentions that the realization of a UO is carried out following three activities: Specification of Requirements, Presentation, and Functionality. Finally, Forbrig [25] presents a study in which he provides a process model to integrate human-centered continuous development in continuous requirements engineering, and discusses the possible applications of model-based technologies for aspects of the user interface. Forbrig's model [25] is based on SCRUM and discusses some aspects of the integration of HCD in the development process.

RQ02 What are the Obstacles Faced by Requirements Engineering Professionals in an Agile Context by Applying User Experience?

After analyzing the studies, 17 problems in requirements engineering were identified in an agile context by applying user experience. Table 7 details the problems detected based on the primary articles.

Sabariah et al. [26] mention that the lack of direct user participation in the requirements elicitation process could hurt the use of an application. A study by Hjartnes and Begnum [27] provides information on seven important challenges to solve to ensure usability in agile projects, where two of the findings are that the requirements are difficult to obtain and that user participation takes time. Likewise, Wanderley et al. [28, 29] reinforces the importance of the requirements validation and verification process but focusing on improving user collaboration in an agile process. Hjartnes and Begnum [27] indicate that collaboration between designers and developers is key since communication influences the efficiency of users' work and strengthens a common approach. On the other hand, Choma et al. [22] mention that a common vocabulary of UX concepts should be established among developers, testers, and designers. Lee et al. [30] describe that to bridge the gaps between developers and designers, various object modeling techniques and UI design patterns have been tried over the years, however, there are still difficulties in reporting the common representation of user tasks and application characteristics. Xiong and Wang [31] indicate that there is low communication efficiency between UCD specialists and developers; To do this, it proposes the Inter-Combined Model to reduce the transfer of knowledge from designers to developers. Losada [14], Choma et al. [22], and Bourimi et al. [32, 33] in their respective research they mention those non-functional requirements are often considered late in the development process

Table 7. Requirements engineering problems

ID	Problems	Study
P01	Lack of user participation (19.23%)	S02, S03, S04, S05, S07, S11, S12, S15, S16, S21
P02	Lack of common understanding of the requirements between designers and developers (11.54%)	S06, S07, S09, S13, S22, S23
P03	Lack of specification of usability requirements (9.62%)	S13, S18, S19, S20, S25
P04	Poor requirements documentation (9.62%)	S05, S10, S14, S19, S21
P05	Do not consider non-functional requirements in the early stages of the development process (7.69%)	S06, S13, S18, S25
P06	Balancing the needs of end-users with those of developers (7.69%)	S07, S17, S18, S25
P07	Lack of familiarity with tools and techniques (5.77%)	S03, S19, S23
P08	Changing requirements (5.77%)	S07, S12, S14
P09	Lack of communication from end-users and developers (5.77%)	S09, S17, S25
P10	Lack of requirements engineering training or knowledge in the development team (3.85%)	S03, S23
P11	The project with many stakeholders (1.92%)	S24
P12	Prioritization of customer requirements (1.92%)	S24
P13	Lack of usability knowledge in the development team (1.92%)	S20
P14	Lack of knowledge of usability in the client.	S12
P15	Resistance to change (1.92%)	S12
P16	The customer is aware of the needs of the system, but not of the different types of "end users" (1.92%)	S11
P17	Lack of knowledge of analysts to communicate (1.92%)	S03

or are omitted in some projects; This practice could cause tensions between project stake-holders since there would be a conceptual lack of guidance and support to efficiently meet non-functional requirements.

RQ02-1 What Kind of Problems Were Encountered Based on an Existing Taxonomy?

To classify the problems encountered, the taxonomy of critical success factors of San Feliu et al. [34]. Figure 3 shows the number of problems detected by each category. It is observed that the problem that covers a greater number of studies is the lack of user participation and belongs to the Participation category. Whereas, the category that encompasses the largest number of studies in total is Deployment.

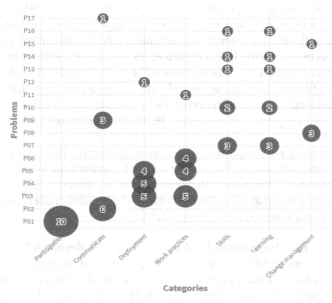

Fig. 3. Mapping of problems and categories

RQ03 What Agile Techniques are Used in This Research?

From the 25 accepted studies, information was collected to show the various agile tech-niques used in software development projects. It was evidenced that most of the research covers the study of agile development in general with a total of 13 studies. Likewise, within the techniques, SCRUM, INTERMOD, XP, AFFINE, and SNAPMIND were found with a total of 6, 2, 2, 2, and 2 studies respectively.

As part of the results, the InterMod methodology was found, proposed in 2009 by Losada et al. [35]. InterMod was born as an interactive application design methodology that proposes the use of user-centered models to define requirements, describe the human-computer dialogue, and evaluate prototypes [35]. After 2 years of the initial proposal, in 2011, the authors presented a new vision of the InterMod methodology, which proposes to integrate three philosophies: User-Centered Design (UCD), Model-Based Development (MDD), and Agile Methods (AM) [36]. This new InterMod approach proposes some model-driven development and integration activities to achieve user objectives (UO) [36]. In 2013, the authors present a guide for agile interactive software development with a methodology driven by "user objectives". Losada et al. [37] define the concept of user objectives as the operations that the user will perform in the application interface. Finally, in 2019, Losada et al. [38] present a proposal for the integration of its InterMod methodology and acceptance test-based development (ATDD) [39]. Their study aims to mitigate the shortcomings of agile development methods concerning software usability, considering the advantages of the ATDD cycle when combined with the InterMod methodology [38].

AFFINE is an agile framework for the integration of non-functional requirements engineering (NFR) initially proposed in 2010 by Bourimi et al. [32]. AFFINE is based on Scrum and aims to address three needs in the development of socio-technical systems following agile methodologies, which are: considering NFRs conceptually early in the development process, explicitly balancing the needs of end-users with those of developers, and a reference architecture that supports NFRs [32]. In 2013, Bourimi et al. [33] present collected findings from the use of AFFINE in various projects related to software development, evidencing that the first experiences promise great suitability of AFFINE for future work of a multidisciplinary nature (HCI communities and IT security/privacy in this contribution).

On the other hand, the SnapMind framework aims to make the requirements modeling process more user-centric, by defining a visual requirements language, based on mind maps, model-driven language techniques, and specific domain [28]. The SnapMind framework is mainly made up of three components: the visual domain modeling editor, the visual user scenario editor, and USE-tool [28].

RQ04 What Usability Techniques Are Presented In This Research?
In Fig. 4, the distribution of the usability techniques used in the present investigation is observed. It is observed that the greatest interest of the authors is focused on usability, User Experience (UX), and User-centered design (UCD) with 11, 8, and 8 studies respectively.

Maguire [40] extends the Human-centered design (HCD) framework in agile software development based on the ISO 9241-210 [41] standard. Lopes et al. [42] present an investigation on how developers use Human-Computer Interaction (HCI) techniques and methods to support the writing of user stories. Likewise, Moreno and Yagüe [43] explore the implications of usability both for the structure and for the process of defining user stories. Also, they present the development of an agile project (a tool for managing user stories). On the other hand, Wanderley et al. [29] focus on the cognitive evaluation of a user-centered language called BehaviorMap that aims to specify user behavior scenarios cognitively, based on the modeling of mind maps.

In the study by Santos et al. [44] the Design Thinking process is presented. Since the process is promoted for people, Santos et al. [44] indicate that it is necessary to think about how the processes that involve the end-user can work. In his study, the planning of two stages was reconsidered: Requirements Engineering and Quality Measurement. Santos et al. [44] mention that for the requirements analysis, Design Thinking allows

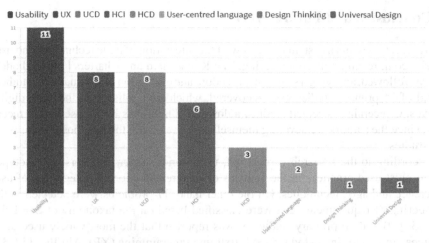

Fig. 4. Distribution of usability techniques

working on empathy to generate value for people through conversations, validations, and understanding of the user's pain.

Hjartnes and Begnum [27] present a study on Universal Design in agile ICT projects. ICT Universal Design (UD) is about creating solutions that are usable and accessible to as many end-users as possible. The study by Hjartnes and Begnum [27] presents seven Agile Universal Design (AUD) challenges.

5 Threats to Validity

According to Wohlin et al. [45], four types of validity threats are considered.

Construct Validity: Search strings were developed using the most representative words of the PICOC criteria and executed in the four selected databases. Besides, a study selection procedure was followed to ensure the integrity of the investigation. However, there may be studies that have been overlooked because they are indexed in other database repositories.

Internal Validity: To mitigate this validity, the systematic review protocol was first reviewed by the principal investigator and subsequently by two experienced researchers.

External Validity: Eight (8) relevant studies from the SCOPUS database were identified in the first instance and served as a reference for this study.

To validate that the search string did not exclude any relevant studies, it ran several times until the eight (8) selected studies were found for reference. In this way, the search string was found to work correctly for this research topic.

Conclusion Validity: To mitigate the threat of including studies that do not answer research questions or exclude relevant studies, inclusion and exclusion criteria were developed. Besides, the evaluation of the quality of studies was carried out following the checklist proposed by Zarour et al. [18].

6   Conclusion and Future Work

This research presents a systematic review of the integration of agile techniques and user experience in requirements engineering. The Kitchenham and Charters [16] methodology was followed, applying a selection procedure and evaluation of the quality of studies. A total of 25 primary studies were recovered, which are published in the main digital libraries. Concerning accepted studies, a downward trend has been observed in recent years, since the authors are devoting themselves to evaluating their proposed solution in case studies.

According to the research carried out, user stories, paper, and person prototypes are the most used practices in the analysis of requirements for the integration of user experience and agile techniques. On the other hand, 17 problems were detected in the engineering of requirements that were classified based on the taxonomy of San Feliu et al. [34]. Based on primary studies, it was reported that the most widely used agile practices are Scrum, InterMod [35–38], Extreme Programming (XP), AFFINE [32, 33] and SnapMind [28] and; Among the most used usability techniques were user-centered design, user experience, and usability. Also, the research classification was carried out based on Wieringa et al. [19] and, of the 25 accepted studies, the majority turned out to be proposals and validations with 10 and 5 studies respectively.

Based on the proposals found in the present study, as future work, an investigation could be carried out to analyze how these proposals are being carried out through case studies in the software industry, thereby validating whether the integration proposals agile techniques and user experience in requirements engineering are being put into practice or if they only remained in theory. Likewise, the research by Sedeño et al. [21] and Choma et al. [22], taking their studies to implementation through development projects, given that the user story grammar proposal that they present has not been evaluated in detail in agile projects. Finally, it is suggested to continue with the investigation of the problems faced by professionals in requirements engineering, based on the problems detected in this study. It is suggested to focus the research on how professionals are implementing software process improvement or frameworks, to solve these problems.

References

1. Kamthan, P., Shahmir, N.: Effective user stories are affective. In: Ochoa, S.F., Singh, P., Bravo, J. (eds.) UCAmI 2017. LNCS, vol. 10586, pp. 605–611. Springer, Cham (2017). https://doi.org/10.1007/978-3-319-67585-5_59
2. Hinderks, A.: A methodology for integrating user experience methods and techniques into agile software development. In: CEUR Workshop Proceedings, pp. 31–42
3. McInerney, P.: UX in agile projects: taking stock after 12 years. Interactions 24, 58–61 (2017). https://doi.org/10.1145/3029605
4. Bruun, A., Larusdottir, M.K., Nielsen, L., et al.: The role of UX professionals in agile development: a case study from industry. In: ACM International Conference Proceeding Series. pp. 352–363 (2018)
5. Mahanta, P., Kaur, B.: User experience and agile software practices – an industry perspective. In: Debruyne, C., et al. (eds.) OTM 2017. LNCS, vol. 10697, pp. 232–235. Springer, Cham (2018). https://doi.org/10.1007/978-3-319-73805-5_24

6. Matharu, G.S., Mishra, A., Singh, H., Upadhyay, P.: Empirical study of agile software development methodologies. ACM SIGSOFT Softw. Eng. **10**(1145/2693208), 2693233 (2015)
7. Nielsen, J.: Usability 101: Introduction to Usability (2012). https://www.nngroup.com/art icles/usability-101-introduction-to-usability/
8. Hassenzahl, M.: User experience (UX): towards an experiential perspective on product quality. ACM International Conference Proceeding Series, pp. 11–15 (2008)
9. Harley, A.: Personas make users memorable for product team members. In: Nielsen Norman Gr (2015). https://www.nngroup.com/articles/persona/
10. Obendor, H., Finck, M.: Scenario-based usability engineering techniques in agile development processes. In: Conference on Human Factors in Computing Systems – Proceedings (2008)
11. Rubin, J., Chisnell, D.: Handbook of Usability Testing, Second Edition: How to Plan, Design, and Conduct Effective Tests. John Wiley\& Sons, Hoboken (2008)
12. Affairs AS for P Heuristic Evaluations and Expert Reviews (2013)
13. Nuseibeh, B., Easterbrook, S.: Requirements engineering : a roadmap. In: Proceedings of the Conference on the Future of Software Engineering, pp. 1:35–46 (2000)
14. Losada, B.: Flexible requirement development through user objectives in an Agile-UCD hybrid approach. In: ACM International Conference Proceeding Series (2018)
15. Schön, E.-M., Thomaschewski, J., Escalona, M.J.: Agile requirements engineering: a systematic literature review. Comput. Stand. Interfaces **49**, 79–91 (2017). https://doi.org/10.1016/j.csi.2016.08.011
16. Kitchenham, B., Charters, S.: Guidelines for performing systematic literature reviews in software engineering. EBSE Technical Report Nr. EBSE-2007-01 (2007)
17. Petticrew, M., Roberts, H.: Systematic Reviews in the Social Sciences: A Practical Guide. John Wiley\& Sons, Hoboken (2008)
18. Zarour, M., Abran, A., Desharnais, J.M., Alarifi, A.: An investigation into the best practices for the successful design and implementation of lightweight software process assessment methods: a systematic literature review. J. Syst. Softw. **101**, 180–192 (2015). https://doi.org/10.1016/j.jss.2014.11.041
19. Wieringa, R., Maiden, N., Mead, N., Rolland, C.: Requirements engineering paper classification and evaluation criteria: a proposal and a discussion. Requir. Eng. **11**, 102–107 (2006). https://doi.org/10.1007/s00766-005-0021-6
20. Kamthan, P., Shahmir, N.: Beyond utility and usability: towards affectability in agile software requirements engineering. In: Proceedings - 2018 International Conference on Computational Science and Computational Intelligence, CSCI 2018, pp. 846–851 (2018)
21. Sedeño, J., Schön, E-M., Torrecilla-Salinas, C., et al.: Modelling agile requirements using context-based persona stories. In: WEBIST 2017 - Proceedings of the 13th International Conference on Web Information Systems and Technologies, pp. 196–203 (2017)
22. Cao, S.: Virtual reality applications in rehabilitation. In: Kurosu, M. (ed.) HCI 2016. LNCS, vol. 9731, pp. 3–10. Springer, Cham (2016). https://doi.org/10.1007/978-3-319-39510-4_1
23. Kropp, E., Koischwitz, K.: Experiences with user-centered design and agile requirements engineering in fixed-price projects. In: Ebert, A., Humayoun, S.R., Seyff, N., Perini, A., Barbosa, S. (eds.) UsARE 2012/2014. LNCS, vol. 9312, pp. 47–61. Springer, Cham (2016). https://doi.org/10.1007/978-3-319-45916-5_4
24. Kropp, E., Koischwitz, K.: User-centered-design in agile RE through an on-site user experience consultant. In: 2014 IEEE 2nd International Workshop on Usability and Accessibility Focused Requirements Engineering, UsARE 2014 - Proceedings. pp. 9–12 (2014)
25. Forbrig, P.: Continuous requirements engineering and human-centered agile software development. In: CEUR Workshop Proceedings (2016)

26. Sabariah, M.K., Santosa, P.I., Ferdiana, R.: Requirement elicitation framework for child learning application - a research plan. In: ACM International Conference Proceeding Series, pp. 129–133 (2019)
27. Hjartnes, Ø.N., Begnum, M.E.N.: Challenges in agile universal design of ICT. In: Proceedings of NordDesign: Design in the Era of Digitalization, NordDesign (2018)
28. Wanderley, F., Silva, A., Araujo, J., Silveira, D.S.: SnapMind: a framework to support consistency and validation of model-based requirements in agile development. In: 2014 IEEE 4th International Model-Driven Requirements Engineering Workshop, MoDRE 2014 – Proceedings, pp. 47–56 (2014)
29. Wanderley, F., Silva, A., Araujo, J.: Evaluation of BehaviorMap: a user-centered behavior language. In: Proceedings - International Conference on Research Challenges in Information Science, pp. 309–320 (2015)
30. Lee, S-H., Ko, I-Y., Kang, S., Lee, D-H.: A usability-pattern-based requirements-analysis method to bridge the gap between user tasks and application features. In: Proceedings - International Computer Software and Applications Conference, pp. 317–326 (2010)
31. Xiong, Y., Wang, A.: A new combined method for UCD and software development and case study. In: 2nd International Conference on Information Science and Engineering, ICISE2010 – Proceedings (2010)
32. Bourimi, M., Barth, T., Haake, J.M., Ueberschär, B., Kesdogan, D.: AFFINE for enforcing earlier consideration of NFRs and human factors when building socio-technical systems following agile methodologies. In: Bernhaupt, R., Forbrig, P., Gulliksen, J., Lárusdóttir, M. (eds.) HCSE 2010. LNCS, vol. 6409, pp. 182–189. Springer, Heidelberg (2010). https://doi.org/10.1007/978-3-642-16488-0_15
33. Bourimi, M., Kesdogan, D.: Experiences by using AFFINE for building collaborative applications for online communities. In: Ozok, A.A., Zaphiris, P. (eds.) OCSC 2013. LNCS, vol. 8029, pp. 345–354. Springer, Heidelberg (2013). https://doi.org/10.1007/978-3-642-39371-6_39
34. San Feliu, T., Garcia, S., Graettinger, C.: Critical success factors (CSF) in SPI bibliography. In: Proceedings of First International Research Workshop for Process Improvement in Small Settings, pp. 72–80 (2005)
35. Losada, B., Urretavizcaya, M., Fernández-Castro, I.: The InterMod methodology: an interface engineering process linked with software engineering stages. In: New Trends on Human-Computer Interaction: Research, Development, New Tools and Methods (2009)
36. Losada, B., Urretavizcaya, M., de Castro, I.F.: An integrated approach to develop interactive software. In: Campos, P., Graham, N., Jorge, J., Nunes, N., Palanque, P., Winckler, M. (eds.) INTERACT 2011. LNCS, vol. 6949, pp. 470–474. Springer, Heidelberg (2011). https://doi.org/10.1007/978-3-642-23768-3_60
37. Losada, B., Urretavizcaya, M., Fernández-Castro, I.: A guide to agile development of interactive software with a "user Objectives"-driven methodology. Sci. Comput. Program. **78**, 2268–2281 (2013). https://doi.org/10.1016/j.scico.2012.07.022
38. Losada, B., López-Gil, J-M., Urretavizcaya, M.: Improving agile software development methods by means of user objectives: An end user guided acceptance test-driven development proposal. In: ACM International Conference Proceeding Series (2019)
39. Koudelia, N.: Acceptance Test-Driven Development (2011)
40. Maguire, M.: Using human factors standards to support user experience and agile design. In: Stephanidis, C., Antona, M. (eds.) UAHCI 2013. LNCS, vol. 8009, pp. 185–194. Springer, Heidelberg (2013). https://doi.org/10.1007/978-3-642-39188-0_20
41. ISO (2010) Human-centred design for interactive systems. Ergonomics of human system interaction Part 210 (ISO 9241-210). Iso 9241210

42. Lopes, L.A., Pinheiro, E.G., Silva Da Silva, T., Zaina, L.A.M.: Adding human interaction aspects in the writing of user stories: a perspective of software developers. In: ACM International Conference Proceeding Series, pp 194–203 (2017)
43. Moreno, A.M., Yagüe, A.: Agile user stories enriched with usability. In: Wohlin, Claes (ed.) XP 2012. LNBIP, vol. 111, pp. 168–176. Springer, Heidelberg (2012). https://doi.org/10.1007/978-3-642-30350-0_12
44. Santos, W., Quarto, C., Fonseca, L.: Study about software project management with design thinking. In: ACM International Conference Proceeding Series (2018)
45. Wohlin, C., Runeson, P., Höst, M., et al.: Experimentation in Software Engineering (2012)

Is Your App Conducive to Behaviour Change? A Novel Heuristic Evaluation

Roxana M. Barbu[1,2(✉)]

[1] Institute of Cognitive Science, Carleton University, Ottawa, ON, Canada
[2] Macadamian, Gatineau, QC, Canada
https://www.macadamian.com

Abstract. The rise of digital health led to the accelerated emergence of health and wellness apps aimed to alter behaviours. Despite the prominence of these apps, there are no systematic approaches to evaluate their success. This paper introduces 13 heuristics, or guidelines, that facilitate the evaluation of digital solutions aimed to improve health and wellness outcomes. The present heuristic evaluation serves as a tool for teams to assess whether an app may be conducive to meaningful behaviour change.

The heuristic evaluation is rooted in a framework centered around the intricate relationship between an *app*, *user*, and *environment*. We refer to it as *the ARC framework*. The evaluation within the framework is not intended to replace existing ones such as Nielsen and Molich's usability heuristic evaluation, but to complement them. Specifically, the present evaluation does not concern itself with the user-friendliness of a product; it assesses whether an app is conducive to meaningful behaviour change. Needless to say, the app may be informed by cognitive neuroscience findings and aligned with behaviour change best practices; however, without the usability layer, users would not make it far enough to achieve their behavioural outcomes. The proposed heuristic evaluation fills a gap for evaluating whether a digital solution has the potential to lead to meaningful and long-lasting behaviour change.

Keywords: Heuristic evaluation · Behaviour change · Digital health

The paper is supported by Macadamian, a healthcare consultancy, and written in collaboration with Lorraine Chapman. The ARC framework and present heuristic evaluation were co-created by Macadamian's UX, Behaviour change and Design team led by Jennifer Fraser. The main contributors are *A*lex Soleimani, *R*oxana M. Barbu, and *C*aroline Zenns; thus, anecdotally, the *ARC* framework. My gratitude goes to Frank Spillers for our insightful discussion on the breadth of heuristic evaluations. A special thank you goes to Cathy Agyemang, for being my sounding board and for reviewing the paper more times than I can count.

© Springer Nature Switzerland AG 2021
M. M. Soares et al. (Eds.): HCII 2021, LNCS 12779, pp. 204–217, 2021.
https://doi.org/10.1007/978-3-030-78221-4_14

1   Introduction

1.1   Landscape of Digital Health

We live in a digital world, with more than 325,000 health apps having been developed [1]. The COVID-19 pandemic further accelerated this market by providing a golden opportunity for medical app developers to create a platform to feed the public the information they are seeking [2]. Another natural consequence is the shifting of the "site of care" from hospitals and clinics to home health or remote medicine.

Professionals and patients alike are wondering whether *digital healthcare is an equivalent or a better alternative to in-person care*. The ARC framework's emphasis on the environment along with the conventional user centric focus provide a means to ensure a successful transition. Digital solutions exist on a spectrum [3] assisting individuals with their health and wellness goals, such as weight and stress management, smoking cessation, and self-management of chronic conditions [4]. Users' acceptance of digital solutions [5] is on the rise. The technology is here, and users are ready to embrace it.

1.2   Acceptance is High, but Adoption?

Though health and wellness apps are increasingly popular, the adoption is low: most users stop using them after a few times [4,6]. Users may interrupt the use of an app for a myriad of reasons including health literacy or perception of one's health as poor [6]. Two dimensions that help explain continued use are *user experience* and *the users' persistence of their health goals* [4]. A systematic review reports attrition and dropout rates between 8.90% and up to 86.39% [6]. Other studies' findings are even more concerning. For example, a retroactive analysis shows that out of a cohort of 189,770 people who initiated the use of a free mobile app that promotes healthy eating, The Eatery, only 2.58% were active users. Specifically, they have taken more than one picture and used the app at least one week [7]. Needless to say, in order for the users to achieve their intended positive outcomes, they must stay on the path towards their desired behavioural outcome long enough [4].

Digital solutions are seen as a mechanism for improving outcomes by providing continuous guidance and assistance to a user. However, that is not always the case. For example, medication non-adherence has not decreased despite digital advances. In 1990, approximately a third of 315 consecutive elderly patients admitted to an acute care hospital had a history of noncompliance [8]. In 2002, medication non-adherence rates were reported at approximately 50% [9]. In 2018, a systematic review reports medication non-adherence rates of 52% to 55% among patients with gout [10]. Similar values are reported in the context of chronic conditions such as diabetes or hypertension [11]. Medication non-adherence was deemed a significant and growing public health issue in 2011 [12], and it remains a vexing challenge with non-adherence rates seemingly stagnating around 40–60% [13].

1.3   Interim Takeaways

The present landscape can be summarized as follows:

- digital health tools and apps are on the rise,
- user acceptance of health apps is high,
- user engagement and/or follow through is low.

This paper contributes by: a) introducing a new framework centered around the *app - user - environment* loop and b) providing a set of behaviour change heuristics ready to asses whether health and wellness apps have features aligned with habit formation.

2   The ARC Framework

2.1   Foundation

People rely on apps to manage their medical condition or guide them throughout the journey towards a health or wellness outcome. Companies are making such solutions more widely available and are actively promoting them. In many cases, human-centered design teams apply traditional UX methods to capture the user's needs, motivations and desires, and validate the usability of their designs. For example, heuristic evaluations assessing the *ease of use* of a solution are common. To the best of our knowledge, no assessments focus specifically on habit formation and behaviour change: *does this digital solution have the characteristics necessary to help their users change their behaviour? The ARC framework*[1], more specifically the heuristic evaluation within it, was developed with the aim to fill this gap. Behaviour change is not easy: Lally and colleagues found that individuals trying to adopt a drinking, eating, or exercising habit took between 18 to 254 days to reach a plateau of automaticity [14]. Their results suggest that the success of habit forming differs across individuals and across behaviours; individuals in the water drinking group had a higher compliance than those in the eating and exercising groups. We hypothesize that part of the variability has to do with the unique barriers, motivation(s), and circumstances of each user.

User-centric health and wellness apps should be sensitive to changing user needs, abilities, as well as changing environment. Additionally, they should be vested in helping the user form a habit that can survive barriers and continue in the absence of the app.

The core tenet of *the ARC framework* is that to be successful, a digital solution must acknowledge and account for the ever-changing intricate relationship between the digital solution, the user, and the user's environment. This *app - user - environment* loop is illustrated in Fig. 1 where the triangle shape highlights the tri-fold relationship. The *arc*-like sides represent the fluidity of this relationship.

Scenarios 1 and 2 below illustrate practical examples of the *user - environment* interaction, and the *user - app* interaction, respectively.

---

[1] The framework can inform the design of other products such as software, but, for the purpose of this paper, we are focusing on digital health and wellness apps.

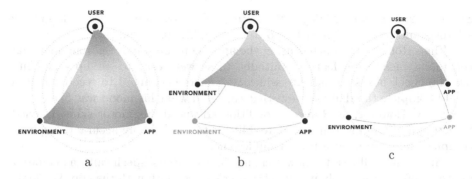

Fig. 1. The App - user - environment loop

Scenario 1: Individual Living with Diabetes During the COVID-19 Pandemic.
Sabrina is a mature woman living with diabetes. She relies on a diabetes health
app to manage her condition; specifically, her physical activity. Before COVID,
the app provided her timely reminders for her aqua fitness lessons at the community pool, and for her Tai chi class at the gym. The COVID-19 lockdown pre-
vented her from continuing to attend these classes, which prompted her to turn
off the associated reminders. Along with the reminders, the app also prompted
her with motivational quotes related to the specific physical activities she had
chosen. While she was able to turn off the reminders, the motivational quotes
kept coming, though no longer relevant. Additionally, she continued to receive
negative feedback for interrupting her streak. The app was punishing her for the
interruption. Simply put, the app did not acknowledge the lockdown, its content
was not adjusted, and Sabrina stopped receiving the guidance she needed to
continue her physical activity quest.

This scenario illustrates how an environmental change may directly impact a
user's path towards their physical health outcome. The app failed to acknowledge
this environmental change. The *arc* in Fig. 1b represented this by shortening
the *user - environment* distance; thus, highlighting the increased impact the
environmental change had on the user.

The example in Scenario 1 represents a minimum requirement. Specifically,
the app should acknowledge environmental changes that impact the users, such
as the COVID-19 pandemic, or seasonal changes, and adapt accordingly. As a
solution, the app could allow the user the flexibility to adjust their choices based
on these changes. For example, the app could allow Sabrina to change her routine
to home-workouts.

Ideally however, apps should not only respond to environmental changes, but
also proactively incorporate environmental data to improve the user's experience.
For example, a fitness app may create biking routes based on a distance inputted
by the user, time constraints, or changing traffic. A kidney dialysis app may
recommend clinic locations based on the users' means of transportation, traffic,
road closures etc.

Scenario 2: Individual Living with Multiple Sclerosis. Romeo lives with multiple sclerosis and relies on a health app to manage his condition.

When Romeo first started using the app, he made use of the reminders and the mood monitoring feature. Initially, these were easy to set up - he could use the check boxes to indicate which reminders he wanted to receive, and he would complete the daily surveys that captured what his mood was like on any given day. However, as Romeo's condition advanced, his motor skills declined. Selecting and tapping is much more difficult to do with any accuracy. Typing a complete sentence is even more troublesome.

This scenario illustrates how a change in user needs, specifically, a symptom-related change, negatively impacts the user's interaction with the app. While the tasks and features provided by the app are still consistent with the user's health outcome, the user is no longer able to complete those tasks with ease. In this scenario, the app did not account for the symptom-related journey and failed to adjust its offering to serve these emerging needs. The *arc* in Fig. 1c represented this by shortening the *user - app* distance; thus, highlighting how the app fails to assist the user towards their health outcome.

Researchers and designers are increasingly more preoccupied with capturing user needs, desires and motivations, not just in healthcare, but across industries. While that is a positive trend, it is only part of the solution. To start with, teams may conduct one or two rounds of research in the early stages of design. This captures the users' requirements at *one* point in time. User needs may be shifting, and, depending on the product or environment, they may be shifting at different rates. Digital solutions in the healthcare space should be concerned with an additional layer of complexity: needs imposed by the medical condition itself. For example, we saw in Scenario 2 how someone's motor skills may change as the person advances in their condition.

2.2   Stages

The ARC framework aligns the stages from the users' perspective, from exploring a new app, to beyond having achieved a health outcome, with the stages of the app, as illustrated in Fig. 2.

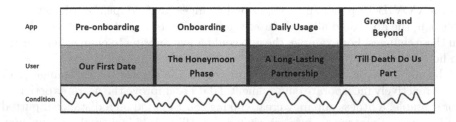

Fig. 2. Stage alignment between user and the app

The top layer illustrates the stages from the app's perspective: *pre-onboarding, onboarding, daily usage,* and *growth and beyond,* respectively. The middle layer correlates the stages of the app with a familiar analogy - the stages of forming a relationship. This highlights the user journey in relation to the app and prompts us to consider the user's needs and motivations at each stage. The third layer represents the user's medical condition. The latter does not have a static alignment with the other two layers, and it must be defined for each condition. In what follows, we review each stage with a focus on the top two layers.

Pre-onboarding refers to the time right before someone makes the decision to use an app. It is centered around the search and culminates with the user selecting an app. Given the number of health and wellness apps on the market, the user is most likely faced with the task of making a choice among a myriad of options. The app's main goal at this point is to highlight those elements that facilitate the users' job. One crucial element here is trust. It should be salient to the user *why that respective app is best suited to help them achieve their health and wellness goals.* Users often rely on reviews and ratings to evaluate an app before downloading it. However, newly released apps may not have this option. One way digital health apps may gain the users' trust is by highlighting their credibility. For example, Fabulous is a habit-building app. The first sentence on their website is "Born at Duke University, Fabulous uses behavioral science to help people make smart changes and build healthy habits." This may instill credibility by highlighting the involvement of a research team at Duke University which contributed to building a scientific approach towards habit formation.

Onboarding refers to the early interactions a user has with the app. A user's first interactions shape their future ones, and the likelikehood that there will be continued use. Thus, onboarding is a crucial aspect of user experience [15]. It is the app's opportunity to connect with the user. Oftentimes, this is where the user sets their goals and understands how this journey is going to look and feel. At this stage, there is often a trade-off between training to help the user familiarize themselves with the app, highlighting how the app brings value to the user, and collecting sufficient information to tailor and personalize their experience.

One important consideration in onboarding is to minimize time to value. As the user is signing up, they are usually asked for a ton of information, albeit, often for their benefit, to tailor their experience. Some of this information, they will know off the top of their head; some they may not know, but they can easily access; finally, some information they will have to find [16]. Let us think of Romeo again, the individual living with multiple sclerosis. The app may ask for his name and birth date, and time from diagnosis. He is likely to fill this information on the go with little to no trouble. Then the app goes on and asks details about his current medication - he may have to double check the name, but this is still easily accessible. Next, the app goes on and asks the dose of the medication when he first started taking it, five years ago - this is no longer easily accessible. Asking hard to answer questions too early in the process may cause abandonment [16]. Another element at play is trust: users may not have sufficient trust and confidence in what the app can do for them to provide such intimate details.

Daily usage is likely the stage where the user spends most of their time. Though extremely important, if the previous stages are not successful, users may abandon the app before reaching this stage. A common aim across apps is to achieve engagement; health and wellness apps have the additional requirement of facilitating habit formation as a result of this engagement. Habits are automatic behaviours, associated with a lower cognitive load. We are striving towards habit formation rather than engagement alone for several reasons including: habits are more persistent as a user may be facing barriers, and habits should not be app dependent. The *app - user - environment* loop we discussed earlier is key here. The role of the app is to help the user cultivate the habit: once the habit is formed, it can and it should be app independent.

The claim, or better yet the goal, that the app should help the user form the habit in its absence may be counter-intuitive to some. Recall we are talking about digital health solutions aiming to guide the user towards long-lasting meaningful change. In other industries, perhaps gaming, engagement alone may suffice. In the context of health, our main goal is helping the user achieve their desired health outcome. One may wonder how can an app prompt the user to become app independent. The habit-building app Fabulous found a way - they ask users to draw a certain icon on sticky notes and place those sticky notes in the environment, by their bed, on their mirror, on their desk etc. This extends the reminder outside the app.

Growth and beyond is an optional stage. Though a *Growth and beyond* stage may always be possible, it does not mean all solutions should have one. The user relies on the app to achieve a certain outcome. Once that outcome is achieved, the app has served its purpose. This stage explores the possibility that the app may be able to establish a long-term relationship allowing users to continue to grow beyond their original outcomes. How may an app continue to engage users beyond an initial endpoint, in a way that is beneficial to them? That is an interesting question that a lot of apps today might not be able to answer. In Sect. 2.3, we introduce the *Transcendence* heuristic which puts forward some ways in which the app can continue to serve the user beyond an initial endpoint.

2.3   Interim Takeaways

To maximize benefits for the user, the answers to the following questions should be "yes":

– Is the app sensitive to changing user needs?
– Is the app responding to environmental changes? Beyond that, is it incorporating the environment in its offering?
– Is the app conducive to user-independence?

   Taken together, if answered yes, these questions acknowledge that the app is sensitive to changing user needs, changing environmental needs, as well as invested in helping the user form a habit that can survive barriers and continue in the absence of the app.

3   Behaviour Change Heuristic Evaluation

3.1   Landscape of Heuristic Evaluations

Nielsen & Molich [17] defined heuristic evaluations as an informal method of analysis where evaluators assess an interface design to determine what is good and what needs to be improved. The goal of Nielsen & Molich's evaluation was to assess the user-friendliness of an interface design. Surely, heuristic evaluations with a focus on usability are foundational and should not be neglected. However, there is nothing inherent about the words "heuristic" or "evaluation" that specify it must be a "usability" evaluation per se.

   Since Nielsen & Molich, we have seen variations of the usability heuristic evaluation including revisions by the author [18]. We have also seen more niche heuristic evaluations emerging. There are guidelines to evaluate specific devices such as mobile healthcare wearables. Asimakopoulos and colleagues [19] point out that though wearable fitness trackers are gaining in popularity, there is limited understanding of which aspects of the fitness tracker contribute to user engagement and long term motivation, and they fill in that gap. Tondello and colleagues [20] put forward a novel set of guidelines, Gameful Design Heuristics, that facilitate a heuristic evaluation of gameful software.

   There are also guidelines assessing other facets of the user experience such as emotional appeal [21]. de Lera and Garreta-Domingo [21] put forward a set of ten guidelines to assess the users' affective state during an interface evaluation. The next section reviews the 13 heuristics we suggest to start assessing whether an app may lead to successful behaviour change.

3.2   Heuristics

Trust and Transparency. The app should inspire trust and be transparent. The user should not have to wonder why particular personal information is asked for. The user's information should be used solely for the intended and clearly stated purpose (e.g., not for targeted ads that may lead to additional revenue for the app). The app should be credible (e.g., done in collaboration with experts in the field, FDA approved) and be consistent with how a user would expect information to be presented or requested by a clinician or physician.

   From the users' perspective, the app should be able to answer *Should I trust you, and why?* and *Is this trust persistent throughout the app?* Furthermore, whether the user is able to assess this or not, the answer to the following question *Is the app compliant with any legal requirements that aim to protect the users and their data?* should be yes. This heuristic should be initiated in the Pre-onboarding stage; however, evidence of trust and transparency should be maintained throughout.

Motivation and Reason. Users' motivation to embark on a behaviour change journey is either intrinsic or extrinsic. Depending on the type of motivation, users may be responsive to different engagement approaches (e.g., behaviour change and/or gamification techniques). Extrinsic motivations, however, may become internalized and intrinsic over time. The app should be able to capture this transition.

Different types of motivation make it harder or easier to change one's behaviour. We often talk about intrinsic motivation facilitating the path to behaviour change. However, in the context of a medical condition, behaviour change may be required in the absence of intrinsic motivation. One may need to embark on an aggressive treatment immediately upon diagnosis. The type of motivation and changes in the users' motivation directly impact the *Engagement Mechanisms* heuristic which talks about the means by which the app ensures user adoption and retention.

The app should rely on the information shared by the user to help them answer the following question *Why am I doing this?*, along the entire journey. This heuristic should be initiated in the Onboarding stage; however, the knowledge about the users' motivation should be used to inform the Daily Usage stage.

Education. The user is kept informed about the relevance of the tasks or challenges they are presented with and has access to additional optional information to really understand the value of each task.

The app should provide sufficient guidance such that the user always has a clear answer to the question *What does this mean and how does it relate to my outcomes?* This heuristic should be initiated in the Daily Usage, though in medical conditions in particular, it is equally important that it is present in the Onboarding stage as well.

Goal Setting and Revising. Users should be able to set goals and revise them. The goals should be customizable as the user's needs or environmental circumstances change. Users should also be able to adjust the goals in light of their performance. Importantly, the goals should be aligned not just with the users' outcomes, but also informed by experts in that particular condition to ensure merit and feasibility. The goals should also be science-informed by the newest findings in psychology and design for behaviour change.

As users are advancing through the onboarding, they will ask themselves *What are the steps guiding my path to my ultimate outcome(s)?* and *Can I do this?*. The list of goals should provide a clear path to the outcome. The initial introduction to those goals should be adequate to the user's abilities or perceived abilities. In other words, the user must perceive the goals as feasible. This heuristic should be initiated in the Onboarding stage; however, it is crucial to reiterate and revise during the Daily Usage stage.

Feedback. As users are advancing in their journey, they should be receiving informative feedback on their progress. This feedback should be well-timed and actionable.

The user should be able to answer the question *How am I doing?* and *How can I do better?* at all times; thus, having a clear understanding of their performance and how to improve it. Broadly speaking, this heuristic should be present in all stages. From a behaviour change perspective, however, it is most needed in the Daily Usage stage. It is important to distinguish behaviour change related feedback from usability related feedback.[2]

Reminders and Repetition. Repetition is essential to habit formation, thus, reminders are a must. To be effective, reminders should be more than an alarm: flexible, easily personalized, allowing for user feedback, and changing over time. Reminders provide an opportunity to extend the behaviour change beyond the app. For example, Fabulous asks users to have their water bottle by the bed to facilitate water drinking first thing in the morning.

The user should be able to answer the question *How am I going to stay on track?*. This heuristic is most applicable in the Daily Usage stage.

User-Driven Customization. The user should have meaningful choices and alternatives to choose from, all of which are best tied into their type of motivation (intrinsic or extrinsic) and their environmental circumstances. The users should be allowed to adjust their choices as they advance in their journey, without affecting the outcome.

The user should be able to answer the question *Am I in charge of my own journey?*. This heuristic is best initiated in the Onboarding phase and should persist throughout the Daily Usage.

Visibility of Progress and Path to Destination. The user should be informed about their progress towards the behaviour change outcome. Ideally, this should be two-fold: tracking of the actual behaviour (e.g., glucose level, number of steps) and tracking of challenges and achievements. Challenges and tasks should be revealed gradually, in accordance with the users' progress and abilities.

The user should be able to answer the question *Where am I relative to my goal or outcome?*. This heuristic is most appropriate in the Daily Usage stage.

Engagement Mechanisms. The app should ensure user adoption and retention through a series of engagement mechanisms. These mechanisms are most effective if chosen in light of the user's motivation (see the *Motivation and Reason*

---

[2] An example of strictly usability related feedback would be how the app informs the user that they successfully submitted a piece of information. Given a button that says *Submit*, once the user clicks it, there are several ways in which the app may acknowledge that action has been successful: the button may physically change states (skeuomorphism); the button may change label to say *submitted*; or there may be a message beside the button to say, "Thank you, your application was submitted.".

heuristic). Moreover, they should be rooted into the psychology of habit formation (e.g., rewards are effective early in the process after which they should be replaced or complemented by external cues [22]) and informed by cognitive neuroscience findings (e.g., it is not rewards per se that are conducive to pleasure; it is the anticipation of a reward [23]).

The user should be able to answer the question *What keeps me coming back?*. This heuristic is most appropriate in the Daily Usage stage.

Aesthetic Experience. The overall aesthetic and theme of the app should provide the user with a sense of place, by giving them a satisfying experience that feels inviting, approachable and important. Aesthetics such as the choice of colors, imagery and tone should match the intent of the app, as well as the users' goals (for example, an app to monitor a serious health condition should not feel sterile like an operating room, but it also should not feel like a video game that is purely used for entertainment purposes).

The user should be able to answer the question *Am I immersed in my journey?*. This heuristic is best initiated in Pre-onboarding, and should persist in the Onboarding and Daily Usage stages.

Human Connection. The app should satisfy users' universal need of human connection through social interaction with other users. For example, the app should provide opportunities for social commitment. If people make a promise to others, they are more likely to follow through. If applicable, the app may provide opportunities for social competition.

The user should be able to answer no to the question *Am I in this alone?*. This heuristic is most relevant in the Daily Usage stage as the user is advancing to their outcome, but can apply in the Onboarding and Growth and Beyond stages as well.

Transcendance. The app may have clear features that serve as incentives to keep users engaged after accomplishing their primary outcome. These features should satisfy the users' universal needs such as the need to "feel good" or allow them to transcend from being learners to being mentors or contributors.

Once users have accomplished their primary goal, they may wonder *What now?*. This heuristic is most relevant in the Growth and Beyond stage, but not always applicable.

Relevance. The app or product (including features and functionalities, context, usability, appearance) should be relevant and appropriate to the immediate needs of the user at each stage of the journey. A relevant contribution is timely, sufficiently informative to ensure ease of use/understanding without leading to cognitive overload, and it supports the user towards their outcome. The details of being timely and sufficiently informative will vary across conditions and products, however, two concepts that may help with showing the right information at the right time are *progressive disclosure* and well-timed *feedback*.

The avid reader may sense some overlap between the *Education* and *Relevance* heuristics. The *Education* heuristic is particularly concerned with the user understanding how the tasks within the app relate to their condition and ultimately help them achieve their outcome. For example, an individual living with diabetes may start using an app to manage their condition. The goals provided by the app for the user to choose from include: nutrition, physical health, and sleep. A person newly diagnosed may not yet understand the intricate relationship between sleep and diabetes. The app should have a way to identify and address that knowledge gap. The *Relevance* heuristic on the other hand is a lot more inclusive where the suggested readings, recommendations, even screen functionality are context appropriate.

The user should be able to answer the question *Why and how does this apply to me?*. This heuristic applies along the entire journey.

4 Takeaways

The evaluation should be conducted by a team of multi-disciplinary experts, to maximize results. The team of evaluators should include experts in gameful design and experts with an in-depth understanding of human cognition. Expertise in gameful design can ensure the app has elements and functionalities conducive towards engagement. However, in the context of health in particular, as opposed to the gaming industry for example, it is key that this engagement is beneficial to the user. Human cognition experts look at these engagement techniques through a different lens. Additional evaluators should be experts in the product itself. For best results, evaluators should be experts in the product but also have field specific knowledge.

It is important to note that not all heuristics are relevant or equally applicable across apps. For example, an app that assists patients with an intense treatment for a three week period may not provide a sufficient time window and, more importantly, that treatment may not need to become a habit to start with. In this scenario, heuristics such as the *Transcendence* and perhaps *Human Connection* may not apply. Evaluators, product stakeholders, and experts in that medical condition should have a working session to get alignment on which heuristics are relevant. Post evaluation, it is good practice to review the findings as a group. This allows the team to prioritize the issues identified considering both behaviour change and business constraints.

In summary, this paper introduces the ARC framework, which is centered around the *app - user - environment interaction*. Within this framework, we provide a means of incorporating the behaviour change dimension in app evaluations. Specifically, we introduced 13 heuristics allowing teams to conduct a structured evaluation of behaviour change elements within a health or wellness app.

References

1. Bates, D.W., Landman, A., Levine, D.M.: Health apps and health policy: what is needed? JAMA **320**(19), 1975–1976 (2018)
2. Ming, L.C., et al.: Mobile health apps on COVID-19 launched in the early days of the pandemic: content analysis and review. JMIR Mhealth Uhealth **8**(9), e19796 (2020)
3. Gordon, W.J., Landman, A., Zhang, H., Bates, D.W.: Beyond validation: getting health apps into clinical practice. NPJ Digit. Med. **3**(1), 1–6 (2020)
4. Vaghefi, I., Tulu, B.: The continued use of mobile health apps: insights from a longitudinal study. JMIR Mhealth Uhealth **7**(8), e12983 (2019)
5. Global Market Insights. Insights to Inovation: mhealth market growth statistics 2019–2025 global projections report (2019). https://www.gminsights.com/industry-analysis/mhealth-market. Accessed 06 Feb 2021
6. Meyerowitz-Katz, G., Ravi, S., Arnolda, L., Feng, X., Maberly, G., Astell-Burt, T.: Rates of attrition and dropout in app-based interventions for chronic disease: systematic review and meta-analysis. J. Med. Internet Res. **22**(9), e20283 (2020)
7. Helander, E., Kaipainen, K., Korhonen, I., Wansink, B.: Factors related to sustained use of a free mobile app for dietary self-monitoring with photography and peer feedback: retrospective cohort study. J. Med. Internet Res. **16**(4), e109 (2014)
8. Col, N., Fanale, J.E., Kronholm, P.: The role of medication noncompliance and adverse drug reactions in hospitalizations of the elderly. Arch. Intern. Med. **150**(4), 841–845 (1990)
9. Haynes, R.B., McDonald, H.P., Garg, A.X.: Helping patients follow prescribed treatment: clinical applications. JAMA **288**(22), 2880–2883 (2002)
10. Scheepers, L.E., van Onna, M., Stehouwer, C.D., Singh, J.A., Arts, I.C., Boonen, A.: Medication adherence among patients with gout: a systematic review and meta-analysis. In: Seminars in Arthritis and Rheumatism, vol. 47, pp. 689–702. Elsevier (2018)
11. Kleinsinger, F.: The unmet challenge of medication nonadherence. Permanente J. **22** (2018)
12. Bosworth, H.B., et al.: Medication adherence: a call for action. Am. Heart J. **162**(3), 412–424 (2011)
13. Stirratt, M.J., Curtis, J.R., Danila, M.I., Hansen, R., Miller, M.J., Gakumo, C.A.: Advancing the science and practice of medication adherence. J. Gen. Intern. Med. **33**(2), 216–222 (2018)
14. Lally, P., Van Jaarsveld, C.H., Potts, H.W., Wardle, J.: How are habits formed: modelling habit formation in the real world. Eur. J. Soc. Psychol. **40**(6), 998–1009 (2010)
15. Strahm, B., Gray, C.M., Vorvoreanu, M.: Generating mobile application onboarding insights through minimalist instruction. In: Proceedings of the 2018 Designing Interactive Systems Conference, pp. 361–372 (2018)
16. Meinert, M.C.: Digital onboarding done right. ABA Bank. J. **111**(5), 30–32 (2019)
17. Nielsen, J., Molich, R.: Heuristic evaluation of user interfaces. In: Proceedings of the SIGCHI Conference on Human Factors in Computing Systems, pp. 249–256 (1990)
18. Nielsen, J.: 10 usability heuristics for user interface design (2020). https://www.nngroup.com/articles/ten-usability-heuristics/. Accessed 13 Feb 2021
19. Asimakopoulos, S., Asimakopoulos, G., Spillers, F.: Motivation and user engagement in fitness tracking: Heuristics for mobile healthcare wearables. In: Informatics, vol. 4, p. 5. Multidisciplinary Digital Publishing Institute (2017)

20. Tondello, G.F., Kappen, D.L., Ganaba, M., Nacke, L.E.: Gameful design heuristics: a gamification inspection tool. In: Kurosu, M. (ed.) HCII 2019. LNCS, vol. 11566, pp. 224–244. Springer, Cham (2019). https://doi.org/10.1007/978-3-030-22646-6_16

21. De Lera, E., Garreta-Domingo, M.: Ten emotion heuristics: guidelines for assessing the user's affective dimension easily and cost-effectively. In: Proceedings of HCI 2007 the 21st British HCI Group Annual Conference University of Lancaster, UK 21, pp. 1–4 (2007)

22. Wood, W., Rünger, D.: Psychology of habit. Annu. Rev. Psychol. **67**, 289–314 (2016)

23. Salimpoor, V.N., Benovoy, M., Larcher, K., Dagher, A., Zatorre, R.J.: Anatomically distinct dopamine release during anticipation and experience of peak emotion to music. Nat. Neurosci. **14**(2), 257 (2011)

Understanding Customer Value Propositions Through the Lens of Value Equations Method: A Systematic Approach

Jerica Drapp[1](✉) and Sasanka Prabhala[2](✉)

[1] Technology Business Development- Research, Crown Equipment Corporation, 44 S Washington St., New Bremen, OH 45869, USA
jerica.drapp@crown.com
[2] Design Research, Crown Equipment Corporation, 44 S Washington St., New Bremen, OH 45869, USA
sasanka.prabhala@crown.com

Abstract. The Value Equations method is an effective way to explain the value of a product or service to a customer using their own operational data. A Value Equation can take an abstract value and attach a dollar figure to it. Applying the Value Equations method will not only inform the customer's interest in the product, but the potential customer value created. The Value Equations method is designed to help companies find the value of the product or service offered. This paper explains the Value Equations method, how it was applied to a technology solution, and lessons learned from applying the Value Equations method. Lastly, the paper will describe a generic framework through which Value Equations can be created, by companies of any industry or size, to understand the true value of the products or services offered to the customers.

Keywords: Value equations · Customer value propositions · Ethnographic research

1 Introduction

As companies begin to invest in and create new types of innovative products or services, companies must be able to show the value of those products or services to its customers. Conversely customers should also see a value in those products and services offered. One can measure both, the value of a product or service to the customer and to the company (offering the product or service), through Value Equations. The Value Equations method is an effective tool to use to explore the value of the product or service with a customer using their own operational data. A Value Equation can take abstract value and attach a dollar figure to it.

Value is defined as "the worth in monetary terms of the technical, economic, service, and social benefits a company receives in exchange for the price it pays for a marketing offering" [1]. Traditionally when measuring value, companies typically gauge customer's potential interest in their product or service through surveys, ethnographic

© Springer Nature Switzerland AG 2021
M. M. Soares et al. (Eds.): HCII 2021, LNCS 12779, pp. 218–224, 2021.
https://doi.org/10.1007/978-3-030-78221-4_15

research, conjoint analysis, or other types of user research. Although these methods are successfully used to recognize the perceived interest of the product or service that is offered, it is difficult to understand the true value the product or service offers to the customer. The Value Equations method is designed to help companies identify the value of the product or service offered through tangible customer numbers and data. More importantly, the Value Equations highlights the true value that customers are getting out of the offerings.

At Crown Equipment Corporation, we, the research team, applied the Value Equations method to a technology solution. For the technology solution, the research team worked with the sales force data, in addition to conducting ethnographic research with customers to understand the perceived value of the product or service. The research team then conducted a Jobs to be Done (JTBD) exercise with key stakeholders to identify customer needs for the technology solution. From the JTBD exercise, the research team created the customer value propositions for the technology solution. For example, the value proposition created for the technology solution is "increasing operational safety." Lastly, the Value Equations method was utilized to validate the value propositions and to demonstrate to the customer the value the product or service can offer to them.

2 Background

Specifically, the research team used the Value Equations method at Crown Equipment Corporation to understand the true value the customer can gain, and also for Crown to validate the value propositions. The technology solution is a new feature being offered on forklift telematics system. The features of the technology solution are as follows:

1) Monitor operational safety
2) Provide customers visibility into the operational activities
3) Enable operators to take corrective action.

First, the research team conducted ethnographic research through seven customer visits. As part of the ethnographic research, the research team pitched the technology solution concept, asking the customer for feedback on perceived value through a card sort exercise (Fig. 1). In the card sort exercise, customers would rank the product or service values from most to least significant value. Each card has one value stated on it; for example, one card stated, "idle time" and another card stated, "prevent incidents." At the end of the customer visits, average ranking of each value was calculated. A few blank cards were also included for the customer to write down additional perceived values if they did not see them on the initial list.

The research team then engaged a JTBD exercise with key stakeholders. JTBD is a "framework to identify what customers would 'hire' to get a job done" [2]. JTBD is focused on the customers outcomes of completing a job, not the true value. The research team prioritized a list from most valued to least valued JTBD for the technology solution. Some of the higher ranked JTBD statements the research team gathered from the exercise was "I want to see which areas of my facility cause congestion and which are under/over utilized" for the card 'idle time.' The JTBD exercise helped the research team understand what the value propositions were for the technology solution and, in turn, what Value Equations to write to demonstrate to the customer the value the product or service can offer to them (Fig. 2).

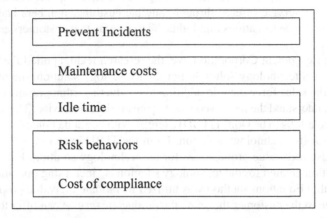

Fig. 1. Value cards for technology solution

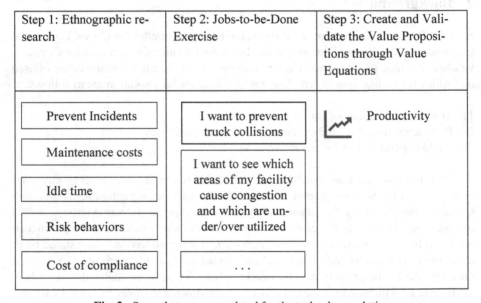

Step 1: Ethnographic research	Step 2: Jobs-to-be-Done Exercise	Step 3: Create and Validate the Value Propositions through Value Equations
Prevent Incidents Maintenance costs Idle time Risk behaviors Cost of compliance	I want to prevent truck collisions I want to see which areas of my facility cause congestion and which are under/over utilized . . .	Productivity

Fig. 2. Steps that were completed for the technology solution

The next step after JTBD exercise is creating the value propositions. "Value propositions provide a declaration of intent or a statement that introduces a company's brand to consumers by telling them what the company stands for, how it operates, and why it deserves their business" [3]. For example, one value proposition for the technology solution is "productivity." Once the value propositions are created, it is time to construct the Value Equations.

3   Value Equations Creation

The Value Equations method is to help the customer understand the true value they are getting from the technology solution. The customer can associate a true value to the technology solution with metrics from the real (operational) world.

To begin creating the Value Equations, first define the categories, measures, and magnitudes. Categories are the broad value proposition that were identified. Measures are the specific customer outcomes (via the JTBD exercise) in each category. Magnitudes are the variances for each of the measures in the categories.

Second, create a customer questionnaire. The questions in the customer questionnaire will act as the magnitude for each measure and will provide the data needed to populate the Value Equations. Questions one would want to ask within the questionnaire are the following:

- How do you measure {this category} today?
- How often does this {specific measure} happen currently?
- If you improved {specific measure}, what would that look like?
- If you improved {specific measure}, are there other related benefits that you'd achieve?
- What might prevent you from achieving this value, or might deplete the value of this offering?
- What is the frequency {magnitude} at which the {specific measure} occurs?
- How often the {magnitude} happen in the facility?

Third, it is common for customers to not have all the responses to the customer questionnaire to populate the Value Equations (e.g., data is not tracked). Hence, it is important to know the customer stance as it relates to their data maturity. The Data Accessibility Framework (Fig. 3) which is loosely based on the Data Maturity Model [3] helps identify the customer level as it relates to data maturity.

The customer questionnaire elicits information from customers that are at different levels on the Data Accessibility Framework - Data Agnostic, Data Sensitive, Data Oriented, and Data Driven. Customers who are data-agnostic have no data regarding any of the categories. Customers who are data-sensitive may have data to categories only. Data-oriented customers may have limited data to value measure(s) and magnitudes(s) for each category. Lastly, data-driven customers have most of the data to measures and magnitude for each category. For example, one category of the technology solution is productivity. Within productivity, the research team defined measures like idle time and product moved. This way, regardless of how sophisticated the customer's data is maintained, the research team could apply their data to a Value Equation. Here is an example of a generic equation that the research team used for the technology solution: Value Creation = %*{Estimated Category − [Cost of Product]}. The next section will describe more broadly the process to use to test and pilot Value Equations.

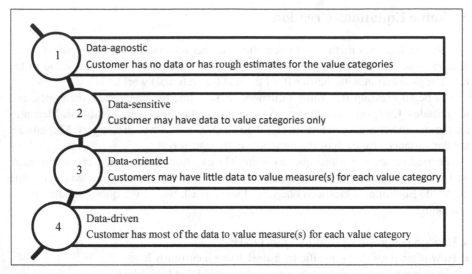

Fig. 3. Data accessibility framework

4 Test and Pilot Value Equations

Once the customer questionnaire is created and separated by the varying levels of the Data Accessibility framework, the research team tested the Value Equation with real world customer data. One option to test the Value Equation is using sample data and see if the results make sense. However, the preferred method would be to use real-world data if possible, potentially data gathered from a previous customer visit. See if there is information which is missing, or if there is a category, measure, or magnitude which may be necessary within the equation; then alter the equation if needed. This will help increase chance of success of the Value Equation during a pilot with a real customer, making sure one is capturing all necessary data to produce the most accurate Value Equation results.

The next step is to pilot the Value Equations with customers that the company has a strong, trusted relationship with for testing. The Value Equations are not ready to be tested with the entire customer base. If customers can answer the questions that have been created, then that is validation that the Value Equations are directionally accurate. If they believe something else should have also been asked, make a note. Then, revise the equation to include the additional value measure, and pilot the equation with another customer.

For example, once the research team had a general format for the Value Equation, we went out to trusted customers to validate the equation with real-world customer data. When the research team met with the customer, they gave us data points on value categories. The research team categorized this customer, based on the data given, at a Data Sensitive level. The research team plugged the data points into the Data Sensitive equation (% * [(Category 1 + Category 2 + Category 3...) − Cost of Solution] = Value Creation) and populated the value creation at three various savings percentage, respectively at 40%, 60%, and 80% savings. From there, the research team could give the customer feedback that they would save between $39,600 to $135,600 per year by investing in the technology solution (Table. 1).

Table 1. Testing of Value Equation for a Data Sensitive level with real-world customer data

Savings %	Value creation
40%	$39,600
60%	$87,600
80%	$135,600

Once the Value Equations have been piloted, it is time to interview the broader customer base. Using the questionnaire that was created, have a conversation with the customer. The first couple of questions will determine what level the customer falls within the Data Accessibility Framework. When interviewing the customer, make sure to ask follow-up questions as necessary. However, be cautious about the questions that may be asked. Customers may not always feel comfortable sharing private, confidential information.

In the example of technology solution, the research team discussed topics of safety and the number of incidents a customer may experience within a year, which can be a delicate topic. Every customer interview was handled on a case-by-case basis, figuring out where the customer fell within the Data Accessibility Framework and asking follow-up questions, when appropriate. In return of the customer sharing data, and in some cases sensitive data, it will be plugged into the appropriate equation from the Data Accessibility Framework.

Once the data has been populated, the research team can use the results to have a conservation with the customer on the value of the product or service. The research team forming the Value Equations will be able to show the customer, based upon the data given, the monetary value they can save by using the product or service, and the areas of their company that will be changed by the usage. Lastly, the research team can begin to form industry averages with customers of similar size as another way to show value, if the customer does not have data collected related to the value measures or is sensitive to sharing the data with the research team.

5   Implications of Value Equations

There are multiple benefits for creating Value Equations. One of the most important pieces Value Equations can bring to company is the ability to identify key value propositions of the product or service and the tangible, monetary value created from customer's perspective. With the technology solution, the research team found three main value propositions with safety, productivity, and facility damage. Without creating Value Equations, the research team would not have validated value propositions from a true customer perspective, only a perceived value of the product or service. In parallel, Value Equations create marketing position, like the sales message, price points, and training required. Companies understand upfront what is needed in the design and development for a Minimum Viable Product offering, as well as the creation of development roadmap. Lastly, companies learn more about the competing offers where the product or service is being benchmarked against today. Most notably, Value Equations can be universally applied across various companies, products, and services. Value Equations are fluid and flexible to change as needed and as a research team learns more from customers' data.

6 Lessons Learned of Value Equations

When creating the Value Equations method, the research team captured learnings to share. First is doing as much secondary research with publicly available information (e.g., Occupational Safety and Health Administration, Better Business Bureau) to create and show the true value of the offering that customers will care to know. By gathering readily available information, companies can measure if the Value Equations are directionally accurate prior to piloting with customer data. The next lesson learned is to not be afraid to use the Value Equations to come up with conservative estimates. This allows prioritization of initial customer interactions and findings with low risk. Ensure that the Value Equations are modified as one learns from customers and with early customer data, if needed. Lastly, build the Value Equations models that are plug and play to enable customers across the Data Accessibility Framework. Meet customers where they are at to create conversations that are beneficial to both the company and to the customer. This will also help the customer to understand concrete value of the offering.

Creating Value Equations will add time in the preliminary stages of development but will decrease time later in development. It is a generic framework that can be applied to any product or service for a company to learn about true value from the customer perspective. Value Equations are another tool to utilize when doing usability work and will not be the only tool you use. We want companies to use this tool when creating new products.

Acknowledgement. Thanks to James Euchner, founder of Outside Insights Consulting, LLC and Nick Kobernik, Design Research Intern for their contributions in the foundation of the Value Equations method.

References

1. Anderson, J.C., Narus, J.A.: Business marketing: understanding what customer's value. Harv. Bus. Rev. **76**, 53–66 (1998)
2. Christensen, C.: Clayton Christensen Institute. https://www.christenseninstitute.org/jobs-to-be-done/
3. Value Proposition: Why Consumers Should Buy a Product or Use a Service. Investopedia, 5 July 2020. https://www.investopedia.com/terms/v/valueproposition.asp
4. The Data Maturity Model – Key Concepts. http://www.anirvanbasu.com/?page_id=47

Developing and Validating a Set of Usability and Security Metrics for ATM Interfaces

Fiorella Falconi[(✉)] [iD], Arturo Moquillaza [iD], Joel Aguirre [iD], and Freddy Paz [iD]

Pontificia Universidad Católica del Perú, Lima 32, Lima, Perú
{ffalconit,aguirre.joel}@pucp.edu.pe, {amoquillaza,fpaz}@pucp.pe

Abstract. In previous works, the authors evidenced the lack of specific metrics for UX improvement in the ATM domain, and the importance of the Usability and Security of ATM interfaces, principally because it is a channel where people interact with cash. According to this, covering the lack of specific metrics for the ATM domain is very important. For that, we proposed developing and validating a set of Usability and Security Metrics for the ATM domain. To do this, first, the Security and Usability metrics that were used by other banking domains were taken as input. Second, we reviewed the metrics that the ISO 25000 standard provided. With this input, we adapted the metrics to the specific characteristics of the domain. The result was a proposal of metrics for ATMs; divided metrics focused on quantifying aspects of Usability and metrics focused on measuring aspects of security in the interfaces. It was subjected to expert judgment to establish whether the proposed metrics had what was necessary to be validated later. We consulted experts in ATM interface design and domain experts from various banks in Peru. We adapted the proposed metrics to a survey format and asked each of the experts to place a score on four aspects. Finally, we prepared and conducted User Tests containing tasks related to the withdrawal operation for the validation scenario, and we prototyped the ATM interfaces of the four most iconic banks in Peru. A SUS questionnaire followed the User Tests. The results finally obtained were compared with the results obtained from SUS in order to validate if they both gave the same trend as output. We could conclude that the Metrics proposed were validated by expert judgment and by the validation scenario previously described.

Keywords: Metrics · Automated teller machine · UX metrics · Usability · Security interfaces · Software metrics · ISO 25000 · Human-computer interaction

1 Introduction

ATMs (Automatic Teller Machine) are a type of SST (Self-Service Technologies), and the ATM domain considers ATMs that banking customers utilize for doing transactions related generally to cash. There are still many people who use ATMs to withdraw cash [1], and financial institutions need to deliver for their customers an acceptable UX (User Experience) in all its channels. It is necessary to provide methods and tools that let UX and Development teams do improvement processes, evaluations, and assessments.

© Springer Nature Switzerland AG 2021
M. M. Soares et al. (Eds.): HCII 2021, LNCS 12779, pp. 225–241, 2021.
https://doi.org/10.1007/978-3-030-78221-4_16

These methods and tools should be both qualitative and quantitative. Among quantitative methods, UX Metrics are currently very useful in this context of UX improvement.

This paper is the continuation of a previous work conducted in the past [2, 3], where we found the close relation that exists between Usability and Security when someone is using an ATM [4] and also evidenced the lack of specific metrics for these two aspects in the ATM domain. According to this, covering the lack of specific metrics for the ATM domain is very important and necessary for the industry. With a set of metrics, it will continue to contribute to the currently lacking information on the knowledge of the application of usability in ATM interface designs, which causes severe problems when users interact with this self-service [5].

In this paper, the authors explain the methodology used to search and select Security and Usability metrics used by other banking domains, such as Internet Banking. Another input was the metrics that the ISO 25000 standard provided. With that input, we developed a proposal of a set of Usability and Security Metrics for the ATM domain, having an expert judgment for each of the 35 metrics. To end this work, the set of metrics was validated by conducting user tests and then comparing the results obtained using questionnaires SUS (System Usability Scale) [6] and the results obtained by applying the proposed metrics.

In the second part, this paper contents an explanation of the methodology that we used to collect the guidelines and select the input metrics. In the third part, we present the proposal for the usability and the security interface metrics. In addition, we explain the results from the judgment expert. In the fourth part, we explain each part of the process to validate the proposal metrics: Selecting Interfaces, Template development, user test, and Interface evaluation. At the end of the fourth part, we present the results of the validation process. To finish, in the fifth part, we discuss the conclusions and the possible future work related to this paper.

2 Methodology

In this part of the paper, we explain the input of this work, the ATM guidelines, and the metrics that we used to build the new metrics.

2.1 Research

As mentioned, we already have a list of usability and security metrics for Internet Banking channel [2]. This list of metrics has 13 metric categories divided into two parts: 6 of them are metrics to evaluate the security of that channel, and 7 of them are metrics to evaluate the usability of that channel's interfaces.

In ISO 25000 [7], we found six groups of usability metrics that have for evaluating the degree to which a user can use a product or system to achieve specific objectives with effectiveness, efficiency, and satisfaction in a specific context of use. For security metrics, five groups are mentioned to assess the degree to which a product or system protects information and data; so that people or systems have the degree of access to the data appropriate to their types and levels of authorization. Each of the metrics in the ISO25000 has a metric ID. In Table 1, we informed which Metrics ID were considered for this work, specifying which group and type of metric they correspond. As a result of searching for usability and security metrics in the literature and ISO25000, we obtained 193 metrics.

Table 1. Groups of metrics from ISO 25000

Type of metrics	Group	Metrics ID
Usability metrics	Appropriateness recognizability	UAp-1-G UAp-2-S UAp-3-S
Usability metrics	Learnability	ULe-1-G ULe-2-S ULe-3-S ULe-4-S
Usability metrics	Operability	UOp-1-G UOp-2-G UOp-3-S UOp-4-S UOp-5-S UOp-6-S UOp-7-S UOp-8-S UOp-9-S
Usability metrics	User error protection	UEp-1-G UEp-2-S UEp-3-S
Usability metrics	User interface aesthetics	ULn-1-S
Usability metrics	Accessibility	UAc-1-G UAc-2-S
Security metrics	Confidentiality	SCo-1-G SCo-2-G SCo-13-S
Security metrics	Integrity	SIn-1-G SIn-2-G SIn-3-S
Security metrics	Non-repudiation	SNo-1-G
Security metrics	Accountability	SAc-1-G SAc-1-S
Security metrics	Authenticity	SAu-1-G SAu-2-S

2.2 Selection

In order to identify which metrics, of the 193 metrics found, make sense and can be adapted to the ATM channel, we worked by reviewing each of the metrics and looking

Table 2. Association between usability guidelines and metrics

Guideline	Metric	From
1: Visibility of system status	UOp-5-S	ISO 25000 [7]
2: Visibility of transaction status	ULe-4-S	ISO 25000 [7]
3: Visibility and clarity of the relevant elements of the system	Category: Interface 2. Graphics and multimedia	SLR [2]
4: Match between system and the real world	Category: Interface 1. Design principles	SLR [2]
5: User control and freedom	UOp-6-S Category: Navigation 2. Ease use of the site	SLR [2]
6: Consistency between the elements of the system	UOp-1-G UOp-8-S	ISO 25000 [7]
7: Errors prevention 8: Prevention of forgetting the bank card	UEp-1-G	ISO 25000 [7]
9: Recognition rather than recall	Category: Navigation 1. Logical structure	SLR [2]
10: Appropriate flexibility of features	UAc-2-S	ISO 25000 [7]
11: Aesthetic and minimalist design	ULn-1-S	ISO 25000 [7]
12: Help users recognize, diagnose, and recover from errors	ULe-3-S UEp-3-S	ISO 25000 [7]
13: Proper distribution of the content display time	Category: Internet banking application security features 1. Automatic timeout feature for inactivity	SLR [2]
14: Correct and expected functionality	UEp-1-G UOp-7-S	ISO 25000 [7]
15: Recoverability of information against failures	ULe-3-S	ISO 25000 [7]
16: Previous vision of restrictions in the interaction	UOp-2-G	ISO 25000 [7]
17: Customization in the interface design	UOp-3-S UOp-4-S	ISO 25000 [7]
18: Efficiency and agility of transactions	ULe-2-S Category: Technical aspects 1. Loading speed	ISO 25000 [7] SLR [2]

for if it was possible to associate it with one of the guidelines proposed for the ATM domain [3, 8]. It is necessary to specify that the compiled guidelines are based on the need to convey confidence and clarity to users when interacting with ATMs [9]. Table 2 and Table 3 show which metrics were associated with each guideline, and we informed which was the input if that metric was taken from the ISO 25000 or from the metrics found in the Systematic Literature Review (SLR).

Table 3. Association between security guidelines and metrics

Guideline	Metric	From
1: Protection of sensitive data	*Category: General online security and privacy information to the Internet banking customers* *1. Account aggregation or privacy and confidentiality*	SLR [2]
2: Show information clearly	*Category: Content* *1. Online banking information*	SLR [2]
3: Log for time-out	*Category: Internet banking application security features* *1. Automatic timeout feature for inactivity*	SLR [2]
4: Visible security	*Category: General online security and privacy information to the Internet banking customers* *Online/Internet banking security information that the banks provide* *Category: Content* *2. Bank information and communications*	SLR [2]
5: Build trust	*Category: Internet banking application security features* *1. Automatic timeout feature for inactivity* *Category: Reliability* *2. Transaction procedure* *Category: Reliability* *1. Registration* *Category: Interface* *3. Style and text*	SLR [2]
6: Notifications and alerts	*Category: User site authentication technology* *1. Two-factor authentication for login and/or for transaction verification available*	SLR [2]
7: Security depending on the risk	*Category: User site authentication technology* *2. Login requirements*	SLR [2]

3 Proposal of Metrics for ATM Interfaces

Following the definition of metrics as a measurement scale and method used for the measurement of attributes that influence one or more quality characteristics [10] and after making the association between the 25 ATM guidelines and the metrics found, we proceeded to adapt these metrics to the ATM domain, adapting the language used or the terms that were specific to Internet Banking. Besides, new formulas were generated for the metrics without a formula, and the existing formulas in ISO 25000 were refined.

The result was a proposal of 35 metrics for ATMs, divided into two groups, the first one, with 23 metrics focused on quantifying aspects of Usability, and the second one, with 12 metrics focused on measuring aspects of security in the interfaces. Each proposed metric includes a metric identification code, the metric's name, a description of the information that the metric provides, and the formula to calculate.

It is essential to highlight that in all the proposed formulas, the recommended value is the closest to number 1.

3.1 Proposal of Usability Metrics for ATM Interfaces

Table 4 shows the 23 metrics that correspond to the Usability Metrics for ATM interfaces.

Table 4. Proposal of usability metrics

ID	Metric	Information provided	Formula
U1	Status monitoring capability	What proportion of system states can be monitored?	$X = A/B$ $A = N°$ of states that can be monitored $B = N°$ of states
U2	Self-explanatory user interface	What proportion of the steps allow users to complete the task without prior study, training or seeking outside assistance?	$X = A/B$ $A = N°$ of steps correctly identified $B = N°$ of steps present
U3	Graphics and multimedia	What proportion of the graphics correctly explain some relevant aspects in ATM navigation?	$X = A/B$ $A = N°$ of easy to understand graphics $B = N°$ of graphics
U4	Principles of design	What proportion of the graphs are correctly interpreted?	$X = A/B$ $A = N°$ of graphs are correctly interpreted $B = N°$ of graphics
U5	Ability to undo	What proportion of the possible user actions provides an option for commit or the ability to undo?	$X = A/B$ $A = N°$ of possible user actions with confirmation or undo option $B = N°$ of possible user actions

(*continued*)

Table 4. (*continued*)

ID	Metric	Information provided	Formula
U6	Easy to use	Easy to use What proportion of ATM screens gives the option to return to the main page or go back?	X = A/B A = N° of screens where you can go back to the main page or go back B = N° of screens
U7	Operational consistency	How many possible user actions are consistent in behavior and appearance with similar interactions?	X = A/B A = N° of possible consistent user actions B = N° of possible user actions
U8	Consistent appearance	What proportion of screens looks similar to other interfaces in the same banking operation?	X = A/B A = N° of screens with a similar appearance to other interfaces of the same banking operation B = N° of screens
U9	Avoid user operation error	What proportion of the possible actions of the user has mechanisms to avoid the error?	X = A/B A = N° of the possible actions of the user have mechanisms to avoid the error B = N° of possible user actions
U10	Logical structure	In what proportion of possible user actions help was requested?	X = 1−A/B A = N° of possible user actions where help was requested B = N° of possible user actions
U11	Supported languages	What proportion of languages are implemented in the ATM?	X = A/B A = N° of languages implemented B = N° of languages are considered necessary
U12	Aesthetic appearance of the interfaces	What percentage of screens are considered pleasant in appearance?	X = A/B A = N° of screens that are considered pleasant in appearance B = N° of screens
U13	Error message	In what proportion is an error message displayed when entering a data wrong?	X = A/B A = N° of error messages implemented B = N° of data entry options
U14	Recovery error	What proportion of errors can be corrected?	X = A/B A = N° of errors that the user can correct B = N° of errors
U15	Automatic timeout due to inactivity	What proportion of screens has insufficient time at the ATM?	X = 1−A/B A = N° of screens that were closed before finishing interacting with them B = N° of screens

(*continued*)

Table 4. (*continued*)

ID	Metric	Information provided	Formula
U16	Data entry error	To what extent does the system provide a suggested value to avoid data entry errors?	X = A/B A = Number of suggested values to avoid data entry errors B = N° of data entry options
U17	Category of understandable information	To what extent does the system organize the information into categories familiar to users at the ATM?	X = A/B A = N° of functionalities found correctly B = N° of functionalities
U18	Compressibility error messages	What proportions of the ATM error messages indicate the reason why the error occurred and how to resolve it?	X = A/B A = N° of error messages indicating the reason why it occurred and suggesting ways to solve it B = N° of error messages
U19	Clarity in the messages	What proportion of the ATM messages that transmit a restriction are clear?	X = A/B A = N° of clear messages that convey a restriction B = N° of messages that transmit a restriction
U20	Functional customization	What proportion of ATM functionalities can be customized?	X = A/B A = N° of functionalities can be customized B = N° of functionalities
U21	Customizable user screen	What proportion of elements on the screen can be customized in appearance?	X = A/B A = N° of screen elements can be customized B = N° of elements
U22	Default input fields	What proportions of the data entry fields are populated with the default values?	X = A/B A = N° of data entry fields are filled with default values B = N° of data entry fields
U23	Loading speed	What proportion of waiting screens are shown, where the customer has not interacted?	X = 1−A/B A = N° of waiting screens are displayed B = N° of screens

3.2 Proposal of Security Metrics for ATM Interfaces

Table 5 shows the 12 metrics that correspond to the Security Metrics for ATM interfaces.

Table 5. Proposal of Security Metrics

ID	Metric	Information provided	Formula
S1	Privacy and confidentiality	What proportion of the information displayed on the screen complies with privacy principles and the privacy law?	$X = A/B$ $A = N°$ of information displayed that complies with privacy principles and privacy law $B = N°$ of information displayed on the screen
S2	Information	What proportion of information on the purpose of the functionality, charges, terms, conditions, and technical requirements is complete?	$X = A/B$ $A = N°$ of functionalities that show complete information $B = N°$ of functionalities
S3	Automatic time-out function for inactivity	What proportion of screens has a time limit (maximum minutes)?	$X = A/B$ $A = N°$ of screens have a time limit $B = N°$ of screens
S4	Security provided by banks	What proportion of screens shows threat information, general security guidelines, security alerts, and security used in the ATM on the appropriate screens?	$X = A/B$ $A = N°$ of screens showing information on threats, general security guidelines, security alerts, and security used $B = N°$ of screens
S5	Banking information and communications	What proportion of screens has the telephone numbers or addresses of the bank available?	$X = A / B$ $A = N°$ of screens have the telephone numbers or addresses of the bank available $B = N°$ of screens
S6	PIN error limit at login	Does the login to the ATM have a limit of authentication errors?	$X = A$ or B $A = $ There is no authentication error limit $B = $ Has a limit of authentication errors
S7	Registry	What proportion of interactions caused it to be difficult to log in?	$X = 1 - A/B$ $A = N°$ of interactions that cause difficulty in logging in $B = N°$ of interactions to start the session

(continued)

Table 5. (*continued*)

ID	Metric	Information provided	Formula
S8	Disconnection process	What proportion of screens has 1 or more ATM session disconnect modes?	X = A/B A = N° of screens have 1 or more session disconnection modes B = N° of screens
S9	Record	What proportion of functionalities does the history of actions show to the user?	X = A/B A = N° of functionalities show the history of actions to the user B = N° of functionalities
S10	Style and text	What proportion of security notifications and alerts are clear to users?	X = A/B A = N° of notifications and security alerts are clear to users B = N° of notifications and alerts
S11	Requirements	Is extra information requested (number of bank credit cards, customer ID, email address, password, personal code, security number, etc.) to increase the risk of the transaction?	X = A or B A = No extra information is requested as risk increases B = If extra information is requested when risk increases
S12	Double factor	What proportion of functionalities requires two-factor authentication at the ATM?	X = A/B A = N° of functionalities request two-factor authentication B = N° of functionalities

3.3   Expert Judgment on Proposed Metrics

The 35 proposed metrics were adapted to a survey format, in which each participant was asked to rate, on a Likert scale [11], the following aspects:

- Clarity of the metric
- Identification of characteristic being measured
- Applicability of the metric
- Appropriate formula

Confirming that the proposed metrics comply with these four aspects will help to decide if it is a valid metric according to the above, referring to what was developed by Kitchenham [12]. It was established that those with a score greater than three would be taken as accepted metrics, while the metrics that obtained a value equal to or less than three would be discarded from the list of proposed metrics.

Four domain experts from two of the major national banks and two ATM interface design experts were contacted to respond to the survey provided. Table 6 and Table 7 show the average result obtained in each aspect for each of the metrics.

The results of the surveys showed that the 35 metrics obtained an average score greater than three in the four aspects mentioned. As mentioned, the score would be the deciding factor to exclude any of the proposed metrics. Since none of the metrics obtained a score equal to three or less, we concluded that the 35 metrics developed are valid to carry out an evaluation of usability and security of interfaces for ATM.

Table 6. The average score for Usability metrics

ID	Clarity	Identification	Applicability	Appropriate formula	Final score
U1	3.67	4.00	3.83	4.33	3.96
U2	4.00	4.00	4.17	3.83	4.00
U3	3.83	3.83	2.83	3.67	3.54
U4	3.67	3.67	3.33	3.50	3.54
U5	4.17	3.83	4.00	4.00	4.00
U6	4.50	4.17	4.17	4.33	4.29
U7	4.17	4.00	3.83	4.00	4.00
U8	3.83	4.00	3.50	4.00	3.83
U9	4.17	4.33	4.17	3.67	4.08
U10	3.67	3.83	3.67	3.50	3.67
U11	4.17	3.83	3.50	4.00	3.88
U12	4.00	3.33	3.00	3.33	3.42
U13	3.83	3.50	3.83	3.33	3.63
U14	3.33	3.83	3.50	3.50	3.54
U15	3.67	4.00	3.83	3.33	3.71
U16	4.00	4.33	4.17	3.83	4.08
U17	3.83	4.00	3.67	3.67	3.79
U18	4.83	4.33	4.17	4.17	4.38
U19	3.67	4.00	3.83	3.83	3.83
U20	3.67	3.33	3.17	3.50	3.42
U21	3.17	3.50	3.00	3.33	3.25
U22	3.83	4.17	3.83	4.17	4.00
U23	3.83	4.00	3.33	3.50	3.67

Table 7. The average score for Security metrics

ID	Clarity	Identification	Applicability	Appropriate formula	Final score
S1	3.83	3.83	3.67	3.67	3.75
S2	3.67	4.00	3.83	3.83	3.83
S3	4.17	4.00	3.83	4.00	4.00
S4	4.17	4.00	4.33	3.50	4.00
S5	4.00	3.83	4.00	4.00	3.96
S6	3.67	4.17	4.00	3.67	3.88
S7	3.67	4.00	3.83	3.50	3.75
S8	3.67	4.17	4.00	4.17	4.00
S9	3.50	3.67	3.17	3.67	3.50
S10	4.50	4.33	4.00	4.33	4.29
S11	3.17	3.50	3.83	3.33	3.46
S12	4.17	4.17	4.00	3.83	4.04

4   Validation of the Metrics

In order to validate the proposed metrics, two evaluations were carried out for each transaction flow that exists in the ATMs of banks that operate in Peru. The first evaluation was carried out with the proposed metrics, and the second evaluation was carried out using the SUS questionnaire. For these evaluations, it was necessary to perform a user test [13] to complete the SUS questionnaire and collect the information necessary to complete all proposed metrics' evaluation fields.

4.1   Validation Process

Selecting Interfaces. For this validation, the four most important banks in Peru were selected [14], which we will call A, B, C, and D. Subsequently, it was selected to evaluate the transaction to withdraw money in local currency from a savings account with a debit card since this transaction is the most used in ATMs.

Template Development. An Excel template was prepared to facilitate the calculation for the evaluators. This template had the following sections:

- Instructions: This section mentioned the way in which the fields in the Usability Metrics and Security Metrics sections should be filled.
- Definitions: This section gave some definitions of terms used in metrics to clarify any doubts.
- Usability metrics: The 23 metrics were presented with the spaces to fill in the answers to the questions posed in each of them. This sheet indicated with an asterisk which were the questions that needed information from the user test.

- Security metrics: The 12 metrics were presented with the spaces to fill in the answers to the questions posed in each of them. This sheet indicated with an asterisk, which were the questions that needed information from the user test.
- Results: By having formulas related to the previous tabs, this section showed the results of each of the metrics and the result obtained by taking an average of all the metrics.

User Test. A user test was carried out to collect that information to complete the fields marked with an asterisk. The metrics for which it is necessary to perform a user test are:

- U4
- U10
- U12
- U15
- U17
- U19
- S7
- S10

The user test was conducted with 20 users aged between 22 to 71 years, all with experience making ATM withdrawals. This information was obtained from the pre-test that was carried out. Furthermore, all participants were informed of the objective of the test.

For the test, a prototype of the withdrawal flow of an account in Soles of the 4 main banks in Peru was made. These prototypes were made with the Invision tool [15] and placed in real ATMs located in a development laboratory (see Fig. 1).

Users performed the following tasks in random order:

- Bank A: Withdraw S/20 from a savings account and request to see the balance on the screen.
- Bank B: Withdraw S/20 from a savings account and do not request a voucher.
- Bank C: Withdraw S/50 from a savings account and do not request a voucher.
- Bank D: Withdraw S/20 from a savings account and request to see the balance on the screen.

In the end, the participants completed a SUS questionnaire for each flow performed.

In addition, we asked some questions related to the mentioned metrics, taking as support the screens of the printed prototypes.

Interface Evaluation. To perform the evaluation with the metrics and obtain the data that serves to answer the questions of each metric, multiple withdrawals were carried out in the four banks selected to have the necessary data. This activity and the analysis of each screen of the withdrawal flow allowed completing all the necessary fields for the 35 metrics.

Each of the evaluations was carried out in a different template to avoid confusion and handle the data separately.

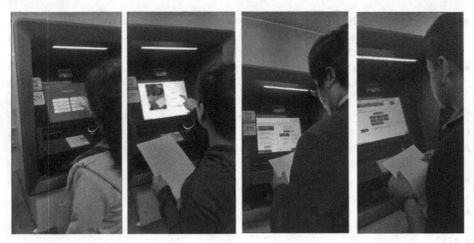

Fig. 1. Users performing the test

4.2 Results

As a first step, we collected the results of the SUS questionnaires. To obtain the final score, which ranges from 0 to 100, we add the results with the following formula [16]:

$$S = [(PP1 - 1) + (PP3 - 1) + (PP5 - 1) + (PP7 - 1) + (PP9 - 1)]$$
$$+ [(5 - PP2) + (5 - PP4) + (5 - PP6) + (5 - PP8) + (5 - PP10)]$$

S = Sum

PP = Question score

Then, we multiplied 2.5, and the result obtained (S). The average of the results obtained was calculated, and the results are shown in Table 8.

Table 8. SUS finale score

Bank	Score
A	81.13
B	87.75
C	73.25
D	84.38

As a second step, the results obtained with the metrics proposed in each bank were reviewed. The result obtained by each of the banks, according to the calculations of the metric templates, is shown in Table 9.

The evaluation carried out using the metrics proposed in this work given as a final score, a result directly related to that obtained in the evaluation with the SUS questionnaire. Figure 2, shows how the four banks obtained the same position compared to their competitors.

Table 9. ATM metrics finale score

Bank	Score
A	54.16
B	62.98
C	53.85
D	62.24

With this result, the validation of the proposed metrics was approved.

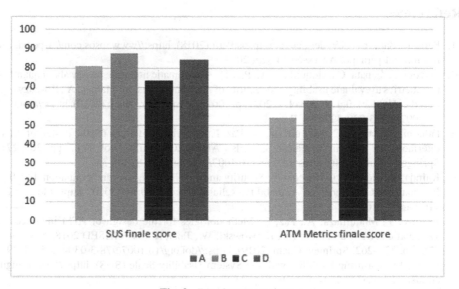

Fig. 2. Results comparison

5   Conclusion and Future Works

This work responds to the problem of having subjective evaluations of ATM interfaces since a tool is proposed to carry out quantitative evaluations.

The contribution of the guidelines raised above and ISO standards was considered essential since the metrics have been raised in correlation to the established guidelines for the usability and security of ATM interfaces.

It was validated that the 35 metrics satisfy the needs expressed by the people who work related to the design and development of ATM interfaces.

In addition, it was determined that, in the face of an improvement in issues of usability or security in the interfaces, no matter how minimal, it will be evidenced in the score of the result.

As future work, it is considered necessary to continue carrying out evaluations with the elaborated metrics, carrying out user tests with other or new operations, and confirming the results obtained and strengthening the tool.

It is also proposed to automate or facilitate data entry to the templates to help the evaluator obtain results more quickly.

Acknowledgment. We want to thank the ATM lab in BBVA Perú for its support along with the research. In addition, we thank the "HCI, Design, User Experience, Accessibility & Innovation Technologies (HCI DUXAIT)". HCI DUXAIT is a research group from the Pontificia Universidad Católica del Perú (PUCP).

References

1. Perú, I.: Bancarización del peruano. Ipsos Perú (2018). https://www.ipsos.com/es-pe/bancar izacion-del-peruano. Accessed 14 Sept 2019
2. Falconi, F., Zapata, C., Moquillaza, A., Paz, F.: A systematic literature review about quantitative metrics to evaluate usability and security of ATM interfaces. In: Marcus, A., Rosenzweig, E. (eds.) HCII 2020. LNCS, vol. 12202, pp. 100–113. Springer, Cham (2020). https://doi.org/10.1007/978-3-030-49757-6_7
3. Falconi, F., Zapata, C., Moquillaza, A., Paz, F.: Security guidelines for the design of ATM interfaces. In: Ahram, T., Falcão, C. (eds.) AHFE 2020. AISC, vol. 1217, pp. 265–271. Springer, Cham (2020). https://doi.org/10.1007/978-3-030-51828-8_35
4. Kainda, R., Fléchais, I., Roscoe, A.: Security and usability: analysis and evaluation. In: 2010 International Conference on Availability, Reliability and Security (2010). https://doi.org/10.1109/ares.2010.77
5. Aguirre, J., Moquillaza, A., Paz, F.: Methodologies for the design of ATM interfaces: a systematic review. In: Ahram, T., Karwowski, W., Taiar, R. (eds.) IHSED 2018. AISC, vol. 876, pp. 256–262. Springer, Cham (2019). https://doi.org/10.1007/978-3-030-02053-8_39
6. Sauro, J.: Measuring Usability with the System Usability Scale (SUS), https://measuringu.com/sus/. Accessed 24 Nov 2019
7. International Standard. ISO 25000:2014. Systems and software engineering — Systems and software Quality Requirements and Evaluation (SQuaRE) Last reviewed and confirmed in 2020. International Organization for Standardization (2014). https://www.iso.org/standard/64764.html
8. Chanco, C., Moquillaza, A., Paz, F.: Development and validation of usability heuristics for evaluation of interfaces in ATMs. In: Marcus, A., Wang, W. (eds.) HCII 2019. LNCS, vol. 11586, pp. 3–18. Springer, Cham (2019). https://doi.org/10.1007/978-3-030-23535-2_1
9. Subsorn, P., Limwiriyakul, S.: A comparative analysis of internet banking security in Thailand: a customer perspective. Procedia Eng. **32**, 260–272 (2012). https://doi.org/10.1016/j.proeng.2012.01.1266
10. International Standard. ISO 9126:2000. Software engineering — Product quality — Part 1: Quality model. International Organization for Standardization (2001). https://www.iso.org/standard/22749.html
11. Trochim, W.M.K.: Likert Scaling. Research Methods Knowledge Base. https://conjointly.com/kb/likert-scaling/. Accessed 05 Aug 2020
12. Cueva, J.M.: Métricas de usabilidad en la Web, 2–24. (2014). http://di002.edv.uniovi.es/~cueva/asignaturas/masters/2005/MetricasUsabilidad.pdf

13. Moran, K.: Usability Testing 101. Nielsen Norman Group (2019). https://www.nngroup.com/articles/usability-testing-101/
14. Marcés, E.: Los cuatro bancos más grandes crecieron en utilidades y créditos en el 2018. Semana Económica (2019). https://semanaeconomica.com/economia-finanzas/banca/329588-los-cuatro-bancos-mas-grandes-crecieron-en-utilidades-y-creditos-en-el-2018
15. Hebert, K., Yoo, F.: Enterprise. InVision (2021). https://www.invisionapp.com/enterprise
16. TW. Measuring and Interpreting System Usability Scale (SUS). UIUX Trend. (2020) https://uiuxtrend.com/measuring-system-usability-scale-sus/

Challenges and Opportunities
on the Application of Heuristic Evaluations:
A Systematic Literature Review

Adrian Lecaros$^{(\boxtimes)}$ (iD), Freddy Paz(iD), and Arturo Moquillaza(iD)

Pontificia Universidad Católica del Perú, Av. Universitaria 1801, San Miguel,
Lima 32, Lima, Peru
adrian.lecaros@pucp.edu.pe, {fpaz,amoquillaza}@pucp.pe

Abstract. Heuristic evaluation belongs to the usability inspection methods and is considered one of the most popular methods since it allows to discover over 75% of the total usability problems involving only 3 to 5 usability experts, in comparison with user tests. However, certain problems and challenges have been identified at the time of their execution. In this study we present the results of conducting a Systematic Literature Review (SLR) to identify case studies, challenges, problems, and opportunities on the execution of heuristic evaluations in the context of a research for the automation and formalization of the process. For this SLR, we have employed the protocol proposed by Kitchenham and Charters. The research was carried out on September 7 of 2020 and retrieved a total of 167 studies of which 37 were selected for this review. The results show that the main challenges are related to the low suitability of the chosen set of heuristics and the low expertise of usability evaluators. Additionally, we have identified that exist very few software solutions that support and automate the process. Finally, we have found that there were many protocols to follow when applying a heuristic evaluation, like the definition of new usability heuristics for a given case of study. According to the results obtained, we can conclude that it is necessary to develop and validate a tool based on a formal protocol that supports and automate the heuristic evaluation process, that gives solutions to the challenges and opportunities identified in this research.

Keywords: Human-computer interaction · Usability · Heuristic evaluation · Systematic literature review · Challenges · Opportunities

1 Introduction

Nowadays, usability is a very important aspect of User Experience in the context of the interaction between users and software products, since it establishes a fundamental role in the use, acceptance and interaction of users with those software products and is a quality aspect that allows the increasing of satisfaction and the use of information and functionalities that systems provide [1]. Moreover, heuristic evaluation belongs to usability inspection methods [2]. Although it is considered one of the most popular

© Springer Nature Switzerland AG 2021
M. M. Soares et al. (Eds.): HCII 2021, LNCS 12779, pp. 242–261, 2021.
https://doi.org/10.1007/978-3-030-78221-4_17

methods, because it will allow the discovery of over 75% of the total usability problems involving only 3 to 5 usability experts, compared to those with user tests that require a high number of end users [3], certain problems and challenges have been identified at the time of execution. In this study, we present the results of conducting a Systematic Literature Review (SLR) to identify case studies and papers about challenges, problems, and opportunities on the execution of heuristic evaluations, in the context of a research that looks for the automation and formalization of the whole process. For this SLR, we have employed the protocol proposed by Kitchenham and Charters [4] to give answer to research questions identified, related to detect challenges of conducting heuristic evaluations on software products, and details about how those evaluations were executed, and evaluation objectives were reached. Besides, we also looked forward to identifying the characteristics of software solutions that currently exist that allow the automation of the heuristic evaluation process on software products and what protocols or formal processes are being used to improve the performance of those heuristic evaluations.

This paper is structured in the following way. In Sect. 2, we describe the main concepts belonging to the Human-Computer Interaction area that were used in the study. In Sect. 3, we present the conduction of the systematic literature review. In Sect. 4, we discuss the results of our research. Finally, in Sect. 5 we present the conclusions of the research and the future works to be done.

2 Background

2.1 Usability

Usability, according to ISO 9241-210-2019 [5], is the "extend to which a system, product or service can be used by specified users to achieve specified goals with effectiveness, efficiency and satisfaction in a specified context of use".

Additionally, Jacob Nielsen [3] defines it as the evaluation of five attributes the user interface of a system must have, which are the following:

- Learnability: The system should be easy to learn so that the user can perform some tasks with the system as quickly as possible.
- Efficiency: The system should be efficient during its use to provide the highest level of productivity possible.
- Memorability: The system should be easy to remember so that the casual user is able to use it again after a period of leaving it, without the need to relearn how it works.
- Errors: The system should provide a low error rate so that users make as few errors as possible and can quickly recover from them. Errors considered catastrophic must not occur.
- Satisfaction: The system should be pleasant to use, so that users are subjectively satisfied while using it.

2.2 Heuristic Evaluation

According to Andreas Holzinger [2], Heuristic Evaluation (HE) belongs to usability inspection methods and is the most common informal method. For its execution, it requires usability experts who can identify if the dialogue elements or other interactive software elements follow the established principles of usability.

According to Jacob Nielsen [3], the heuristic evaluation allows the inspection of what is good and bad in the interface of a system, which could be done through one's own opinion or, ideally, through the use of well-defined guidelines. The author also maintains that the main goal of the evaluation is to find usability problems in the design of an interface that is carried out through a group of evaluators who will inspect and judge it through usability principles called heuristics. Additionally, a single evaluator can find only 35% of the usability problems in an interface; however, each evaluator usually encounters different types of problems; for this reason, he recommends the participation of 3 to 5 evaluators to obtain the best cost-benefit ratio. These evaluations are performed singularly, and then, upon completion, the results are compared for overall usability analysis.

3   Systematic Literature Review

According to Barbara Kitchenham and Stuart Charters [4], Systematic Literature Review (SLR) consists of identifying, evaluating, and interpreting the most relevant available studies and allows to answer review questions about an area or phenomenon of interest. Additionally, for this study, we will use the formal protocol proposed by Kitchenham that consists of the review being carried out in three phases: (1) planning, (2) conducting and (3) reporting.

Planning consists of defining stages to identify the need for the review, as well as the specification of research questions, developing and evaluating review protocols. Additionally, the conduction will allow the identification of the review, selection of primary studies, as well as the extraction, monitoring and synthesis of data. Finally, the reporting phase will facilitate the specification of propagation mechanisms, as well as providing formatting and review of the main report generated.

For the execution of the process, we used a web tool called Parsifal [6], and the phases of this methodology are presented in the subsequent sections.

3.1   Review Goal

The main goal of this review, as the starting point to be addressed within the planning phase of the SLR protocol, is to perform an empirical review of the heuristic evaluation process in software products, which represents the main studies that show the application of a software solution that allows the automation of its execution, as well as the reasons, causes, challenges, problems, opportunities, and motivations that lead researchers to its development.

3.2   Review Questions

According to the Kitchenham protocol, the development of review questions of the area or phenomenon of interest, as part of the planning phase, will allow the identification of primary studies in the search processes related to them, as well as extracting and synthesizing the information needed to answer them. To carry out these reviews, the PICOC criteria was used, defined by Mark Petticrew and Helen Roberts [7], which will allow defining points of view such as (1) Population, (2) Intervention, (3) Comparison, (4) Outcome and (5) Context of the questions that will be answered as a result of the systematic review. Likewise, it should be mentioned that the Comparison criterion will not be used as, for the scope of the research, it will not be necessary to make comparisons as there is only one intervention. Table 1 shows the results of the application of the PICOC criteria.

Table 1. Criterion results by using PICOC

Criterion	Description
Population	Sofware products
Intervention	Heuristic evaluation
Outcome	Software solutions, web sites, support tools, challenges at excecution, protocols
Context	Academic, industry

According to the review objectives and criteria defined in the PICOC table, the following review questions were developed:

- RQ1. What are the challenges that occur when conducting heuristic evaluations on software products?
- RQ2. What are the characteristics of current software solutions that allow the automation of the heuristic evaluation process in software products?
- RQ3. What are the characteristics of the formal protocols or processes that are being used to improve the performance of heuristic evaluations in software products?

3.3 Search Strategy

Search Engine. Four search engines have been considered to carry out the research: Scopus, ISI Web of Science and IEEE Digital Library, for their relevance in Software Engineering, and Alicia Concytec, for having information sources from Perú, where thesis, articles, reports and books can be found from various institutions in the country.

Search String. To form the search strings to be used in the selected search engines we defined the keywords from the criteria established in the PICOC table. Once the most important concepts for the review process had been identified, we proceeded to search for synonyms for each one. Table 2 shows the result of grouping each concept with its synonyms and the PICOC criterion to which they belong.

Then, it was necessary to define a main search string that includes each keyword joined with its synonyms through the **OR** connector, as well as the union of each group obtained with the **AND** connector. Additionally, an asterisk was considered at the end of words that have more than one conjugation, since this allowed us to consider its

Table 2. Keywords and synonyms

Keyword	Synonyms	PICOC Criterion
Software solution	Software product, software system, web application, website	Population
Heuristic evaluation	Heuristic assessment, heuristic inspection	Intervention
Challenge	Conflict, difficulty, problem, trouble	Outcome
Protocol	Approach, procedure, process	Outcome
Tool	Automation, automatization, support system	Outcome

conjugations and plurals. Finally, a range of search years was set for the studies obtained, which, in this case, were the last five. The result of the aforementioned was the following search string:

- ("software solution*" **OR** "software product*" **OR** "software system*" **OR** "web application*" **OR** "website*") **AND** ("heuristic evaluat*" **OR** "heuristic assessment*" **OR** "heuristic inspection*") **AND** ("challenge*" **OR** "conflict*" **OR** "difficult*" **OR** "problem*" **OR** "trouble*" **OR** "protocol*" **OR** "approach*" **OR** "procedure*" **OR** "process*" **OR** "tool*" **OR** "automation*" **OR** "automatization*" OR "support system*") AND PUBYEAR > 2014

Inclusion and Exclusion Criteria. As not all the studies found will be helpful in answering the questions of the systematic review to be carried out, inclusion and exclusion criteria were defined to allow each of the studies to be selected or discarded.

For this reason, the study inclusion criteria were:

- IC1. The study provides a software solution that automates the heuristic evaluation process in software products.
- IC2. The study shows challenges, problems or difficulties that do not allow the adequate execution of the heuristic evaluation process in software products.
- IC3. The study presents protocols or formal processes used in heuristic evaluation processes of software products.
- IC4. The study reports a case study of heuristic evaluation in a software product.

Likewise, the exclusion criteria for discarding studies were:

- EC1. The study is written in a language other than English or Spanish.
- EC2. The study was published before 2015.
- EC3. The study does not provide information related to the area of Computer Engineering or related matters.
- EC4. The study is related to hardware usability problems.
- EC5. The study shows a different type of usability evaluation from heuristic evaluation.

- EC6. The study focuses on usability but does not mention the heuristic evaluation process.
- EC7. The study deals with an area of Human-Computer Interaction other than usability.

3.4 Search Results

After executing the defined string in each search engine, on September 7th, 2020 a total of 167 studies were extracted, of which 43 were duplicates, and 37 were selected as from the application of the defined inclusion and exclusion criteria. Table 3 shows the detail of the number of studies found in each search engine, as well as the number of duplicate and selected studies.

Table 3. Number of extracted, duplicated and selected studies

Search Engine	# Extracted Studies	# Duplicated Studies	# Selected Studies
Scopus	116	0	35
ISI Web of Science	29	23	1
IEEE Digital Library	20	19	0
Alicia Concytec	2	1	1
Total	**167**	**43**	**37**

Additionally, Table 4 shows the selected primary studies in order to answer the review questions:

Table 4. Selected primary studies

ID	Study	Quote	Search Engine
S01	Usability Problem Areas on Key International and Key Arab E-commerce Websites	[8]	Scopus
S02	Usability evaluation of web-based interfaces for Type2 Diabetes Mellitus	[9]	Scopus
S03	Heuristic Evaluations of Cultural Heritage Websites	[10]	Scopus
S04	PROMETHEUS: Procedural Methodology for Developing Heuristics of Usability	[11]	Scopus
S05	A formal protocol to conduct usability heuristic evaluations in the context of the software development process	[12]	Scopus
S06	WebSite Canvas Model: Propuesta de un modelo visual para la ideación estratégica de sitios web	[13]	Scopus

(continued)

Table 4. (*continued*)

ID	Study	Quote	Search Engine
S07	Visual Clarity Checker (VC2) to support heuristic evaluation: To what extent does VC2 help evaluators?	[14]	Scopus
S08	Observation and heuristics evaluation of student web-based application of SIPADU-STIS	[15]	Scopus
S09	Usabilidad en sitios web oficiales de las universidades del ecuador	[16]	Scopus
S10	The E-health Literacy Demands of Australia's My Health Record: A Heuristic Evaluation of Usability	[17]	Scopus
S11	Experimental validation of a set of cultural-oriented usability heuristics: e-Commerce websites evaluation	[18]	Scopus
S12	A heuristic evaluation on the usability of health information websites	[19]	Scopus
S13	Websites with multimedia content: A heuristic evaluation of the medical/anatomical museums	[20]	Scopus
S14	A Heuristic Evaluation for Deaf Web User Experience (HE4DWUX)	[21]	Scopus
S15	A comparative study of video content user interfaces based on heuristic evaluation	[22]	Scopus
S16	Heuristic evaluation for Virtual Museum on smartphone	[23]	Scopus
S17	A User-Centered Design for Redesigning E-Government Website in Public Health Sector	[24]	Scopus
S18	Developing Usability Heuristics: A Formal or Informal Process?	[25]	Scopus
S19	Automated Heuristic Evaluator	[26]	ISI Web of Science
S20	Método para la evaluación de usabilidad de sitios web transaccionales basado en el proceso de inspección heurística	[27]	Alicia Concytec
S21	Usability testing of conferences websites: A case study of practical teaching	[28]	Scopus
S22	Evaluating the usability of the information architecture of academic library websites	[29]	Scopus
S23	A perception study of a new set of usability heuristics for transactional web sites	[30]	Scopus
S24	Comparing the effectiveness and accuracy of new usability heuristics	[31]	Scopus
S25	Automation of usability inspections for websites	[32]	Scopus

(*continued*)

Table 4. (*continued*)

ID	Study	Quote	Search Engine
S26	Quantifying the usability through a variant of the traditional heuristic evaluation process	[33]	Scopus
S27	University students' heuristic usability inspection of the national library of Turkey website	[34]	Scopus
S28	Usability heuristics evaluation in search engine	[35]	Scopus
S29	A collaborative RESTful cloud-based tool for management of chromatic pupillometry in a clinical trial	[36]	Scopus
S30	Heuristic Evaluation of eGLU-Box: A Semi-automatic Usability Evaluation Tool for Public Administrations	[37]	Scopus
S31	The Relationship of the Studies of Ergonomic and Human Computer Interfaces – A Case Study of Graphical Interfaces in E-Commerce Websites	[38]	Scopus
S32	Evaluation of usability heuristics for transactionalweb sites: A comparative study	[39]	Scopus
S33	Heuristics for grid and typography evaluation of art magazines websites	[40]	Scopus
S34	Usability of tourism websites: a case study of heuristic evaluation	[1]	Scopus
S35	Programmer experience: a set of heuristics for programming environments	[41]	Scopus
S36	Exploring the usability of the central library websites of medical sciences universities	[42]	Scopus
S37	Heuristic Usability Evaluation of University of Hong Kong Libraries' Mobile Website	[43]	Scopus

Finally, Fig. 1 shows a map with the geographical distribution of the origin countries of the selected studies.

3.5 Data Extraction

Once the list of relevant studies had been selected to answer the review questions, it was necessary for each study to be represented within a data extraction form, which allows distributing and specifying the most relevant information from each scientific article to answer the research questions. Table 5 shows the data extraction form that includes the fields, the description for each one and which research question will be answered with its completion.

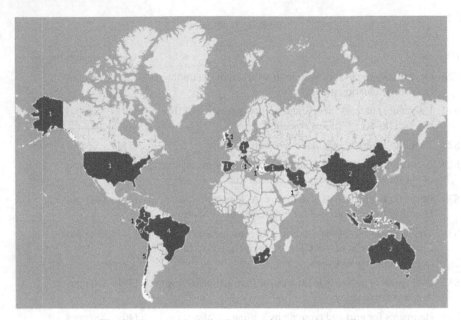

Fig. 1. Geographical distribution of the selected studies

Table 5. Data extraction form

Field	Description	Answers the RQ
ID	ID assigned to the study that will begin with the letter "S" followed by a number. Example: S05	All RQs
Title	Study title	All RQs
Publication year	Year of publication in which the study was conducted	All RQs
Authors	Authors who have participated in the study	All RQs
Language	Language in which the study is published	All RQs
Country	Origin country of the study	All RQs
Context	Shows if it is an academic or industrial context	All RQs
Types of challenges	Classification of the problems in the execution of the heuristic evaluation process to transactional websites through keywords that allow their grouping	RQ1

(continued)

Table 5. (*continued*)

Field	Description	Answers the RQ
Challenges description	Detailed description of the types of challenges encountered	RQ1
Proposed solutions to challenges	Description of the proposed solutions to the challenges encountered respectively	RQ1
Support tools used	Description of the support tools used to support the execution of the heuristic evaluation process	RQ2
Automated process description	Detailed description of the automated process within the execution of the heuristic evaluation	RQ2
Type of software solution used	Specify whether it is a web solution, a mobile app, or a desktop app	RQ2
Methodologies applied to build the solution	Description of the methodologies that have been used to build the solution that allows automation	RQ2
Benefits of automation	Specification of what are the benefits obtained after automation through the software solution	RQ2
Types of protocols or formal processes	Classification of protocols or formal processes through keywords that allow their grouping	RQ3
Formal protocols or processes description	Detailed description of the protocols or formal processes found	RQ3
Benefits of using formal protocols or processes	Description of the benefits as a result of the application of the established formal protocols or processes	RQ3

4   Data Analysis and Results

After reviewing the 37 primary studies found, the largest number of studies come from Peru, Chile, Brazil, with 6, 5 and 4 selected studies, respectively. The foregoing shows that Latin America is a primary source in the investigation of heuristic evaluation process.

Likewise, the number of studies obtained per year of publication show that the investigations of the heuristic evaluation process are increasing, and that great interest has been aroused in the subject, mainly in 2017 and 2018 with 9 studies in each year. However, it is important to consider that the review was carried out at the beginning of September 2020, so studies that will be published from that date to the end of that year had not been taken into consideration, showing indications that more studies could be considered than in 2019, since to that date we considered 6 studies in each of those years.

Finally, the most relevant information was extracted from each study in the extraction form and, in this way, the research questions posed for the systematic review were answered. The answer to each research question will be presented in the following sections.

4.1 Answer to Review Question RQ1

The answer to the research question of "what are the challenges that occur when conducting heuristic evaluations on software products?" is divided by grouping the information obtained by 15 studies into 9 main challenges. Table 6 shows the challenges and the studies in which they were found.

Table 6. Studies that include challenges conducting heuristic evaluations

Challenge	Research Studies	# Studies
Low adequacy of Nielsen heuristics	S05, S18, S19, S23, S24, S26, S32	7
Low experience and number of evaluators	S01, S10, S21, S27	4
Lack of formalization in the heuristic evaluation process	S05, S20, S21	3
Manual processing of large amounts of information	S01, S19	2
Lack of formalization creating new heuristics	S03, S04	2
Insufficient comparison between results of groups of heuristics	S10	1
Use of expensive support tools	S19	1
Insufficiency in identifying problems	S21	1
Lack of quantitative analysis	S26	1

Descriptions of the challenges and solutions proposed in the literature are presented below.

1. Low adequacy of Nielsen heuristics: Nielsen heuristics are often unable to cover new categories of software applications that have emerged in recent years [S05, S23 & S26], because they were designed towards the usability measurement in traditional web applications [S18, S24], which could cause important aspects or usability problems not to be considered in recent web pages due to their evolution compared to traditional ones [S18, S19 & S32]. The literature review has provided a solution, which is the development of new heuristics to obtain more specific and accurate results [S05, S23, S24, S26 & S32] that capture usability problems that could have been avoided [S19], thus how to formalize the design process through a methodology [S18].

2. Low experience and number of evaluators: Evaluators, as they are not end users of the websites to be inspected through heuristic evaluation, could not consider usability problems that are later perceived by the user [S01]. This situation is related to the lack of experience of evaluators, since, if they don't have enough experience, it is very likely that the evaluation will not be carried out properly, especially if it is the case of evaluators who execute the test for the first time. [S01 & S10] or if they are undergraduate university students [S27]. The literature review has provided two solutions that can be applied to treat the problem: consider evaluators who have vast experience in usability, on web pages or in the topic of interest [S01 & S10], as well as increasing the amount of evaluators [S10]. On the other hand, a study considers that, if more than 5 evaluators participate, it is very likely that more than one evaluator has identified several usability problems, generating redundant results; For this reason, it is argued that 5 evaluators are sufficient as proposed by Nielsen [S21].

3. Lack of formalization in the heuristic evaluation process: Authors of different usability studies do not agree on how heuristic evaluations should be carried out, which gives rise to different interpretations by specialists [S05] as there are only general guidelines on how to run the evaluation [S20]. Likewise, the dialogue elements to be considered in the evaluation are not specified, which could cause subjectivity in considering which ones to evaluate [S22]. The literature review has provided two solutions, which are the use of a protocol that allows the formalization of the heuristic evaluation process [S05 & S20] and the definition of a framework that allows defining the dialogue elements to be evaluated [S22].

4. Manual processing of large amounts of information: Heuristic evaluation is usually carried out manually, which generates delays in evaluations and in the effectiveness of their planning [S19]. Likewise, the result of the execution is a large number of reports obtained by evaluators that then must be manually synthesized into a single report to perform the analysis [S01]. The literature review has provided a solution, which would be the use of an automatic heuristic evaluation tool that supports the performance of the evaluations [S19].

5. Lack of formalization creating new heuristics: The generation of new heuristics that support the heuristic evaluation process could pose a problem, since the added heuristics could be redundant, inconsistent and even very specific to a particular context, impairing the heuristic evaluation process [S03]. Likewise, there may be deficiencies in its validation, as well as a lack of rigor, robustness and standardization in the effectiveness of its analysis [S04]. The literature review has provided a solution, which would be the formalization of the process of generating new heuristics that have previous studies in the area of interest to validate its relevance [S03 & S04].

6. Insufficient comparison between results of groups of heuristics: If more than one group of heuristics is used to perform the evaluations, it may not be possible to obtain an adequate comparison on which was more effective if they are used by the same evaluator, since the found problems by using one heuristic allow him to have knowledge about the same problems prior to using the next one [S10]. The literature review has provided a solution, which is the application of a single heuristic for a group of evaluators, thus distributing heuristics by groups to obtain unbiased results [S10].

7. Use of expensive support tools: Evaluators must invest considerable amounts of money if they want assistance from support tools that provide some automation of the usability evaluation [S19]. The literature review has provided a solution, which would be the use of a low-cost automatic heuristic evaluation tool to support the performance of the evaluations [S19].

8. Insufficiency in identifying problems: Although heuristic evaluation allows finding a large number of usability problems, its only use could cause certain problems to be overlooked that could later be found by users [S22]. The literature review has provided a solution, which would be the use of heuristic evaluation in conjunction with user tests [S22].

9. Lack of quantitative analysis: Techniques used to carry out usability evaluations do not usually result in a numerical value about the usability of the system and the studies that show measurement proposals require a large amount of time and human resources to complete [S26]. The literature review has provided a solution, which is a method to obtain quantitative results carried out by specialists without the need for user participation [S26].

4.2 Answer to Review Question RQ2

The answer to the research question of "what are the characteristics of current software solutions that allow the automation of the heuristic evaluation process in software products?" is divided by grouping the information obtained by 4 studies into 4 software solutions. Table 7 shows the software solutions and the studies in which they were found.

Table 7. Studies that include software solutions

Software Solution	Research Studies	# Studies
WebSite Canvas Model (WSCM)	S06	1
Visual Clarity Checker (VC2)	S07	1
Automated Heuristic Evaluator (AHE)	S19	1
Automation of usability inspections for websites	S25	1

Software solutions descriptions, automated processes, methodologies that have been employed, and the benefits of their application are presented below.

1. WebSite Canvas Model (WSCM): Consists of a visual support tool for the conception and ideation of websites that, although its main function is not the execution of heuristic evaluations, could be used as a support through its sections applied to the inspection [S06]. As it is only considered as a support possibility, there is no mention of an automated process, methodologies employed, or benefits of automation.

2. Visual Clarity Checker (VC2): Consists of a heuristic evaluation support tool in two aspects: (1) acceleration of the evaluation by improving clarity in images and (2) contribution in recommendations and descriptions of problems with greater reasoning and technical relevance [S07]. The automated process consists of providing

support in problem detection with images when evaluating visual clarity through heuristic evaluation. Likewise, the solution type is a web page developed in PHP, whose automation benefit is the automatic detection of usability problems related to visual clarity of images [S07].

3. Automated Heuristic Evaluator (AHE): Consists of a tool that will serve as support for the validation of the evaluation of websites applying principles of usability heuristics [S19]. The automated process consists of automating the verification process of the existence of links on the page to be evaluated to show if they are valid or invalid, as well as the redirection and total quantity. In addition, it will allow an automatic increase of image sizes to the maximum available so that they become more visible. Additionally, it will allow assigning a score between 0 to 100 according to the ease of reading of the page. Also, the type of solution is a web page developed by using the Rapid Application Development (RAD) methodology, due to the short duration of the project, using programming languages like PHP, JScripts and HTML. Finally, the automation benefit will allow to serve as support to evaluators by facilitating link searching within the page, image visibility in the highest available quality and the automatic execution of an ease of reading test. In this way, the amount of manual work that evaluators must carry out when executing a heuristic evaluation is reduced [S19].

4. Automation of usability inspections for websites: Consists of an automation system for website usability inspections, which uses the usability test proposed by Torres-Burriel as a basis, with the objective of filling in general data, inspection and qualification of each heuristic, and graphical and numerical analysis of the obtained results [S25]. The automated process consists of performing a heuristic evaluation in the system and obtaining an automatic report with the percentage of compliance and average obtained by each heuristic. Likewise, the solution type is a desktop application developed in Java programming language with the use of tabs and tables developed through JTabbedPane class and JTable components respectively, as well as the use of JFreeChart library for graphics and analysis of results. Finally, the benefit of automation will be to be a great support in conducting usability inspections in website portals, to identify different elements to improve their usability [S25].

4.3 Answer to Review Question RQ3

The answer to the research question of "what are the characteristics of the formal protocols or processes that are being used to improve the performance of heuristic evaluations in software products?" is divided by grouping the information obtained by 33 studies into 6 main protocols. Table 8 shows protocols or formal processes and the studies in which they were found.

Descriptions of formal protocols or processes and their benefits are presented below.

1. Definition of new heuristics: Definition of new heuristics is a fundamental protocol applied in the execution of heuristic evaluations, since, despite having the Nielsen heuristics, these will not always be able to cover what is required for the usability evaluation of a particular software [S01 & S03], as well as relate to the object of study [S04]. For this reason, the benefits obtained with the definition of new heuristics are

Table 8. Studies that include protocols or formal processes used in the excecution of heuristic evaluations

Challenge	Research Studies	# Studies
Definition of new heuristics	S01, S03, S04, S11, S14, S18, S22, S23, S24, S29, S31, S32, S33, S35	14
Nielsen derived evaluation items	S12, S13, S15, S21, S27, S28, S30, S34, S36, S37	10
Comparison and grouping between evaluations	S01, S08, S10, S17, S18, S23, S24, S32	8
Qualification methods	S02, S16, S34	3
Methodologies applied to heuristic evaluation	S09, S22, S26	3
Formal processes with properly defined steps	S05, S20	2

the best representation of the case study [S01] that could not be performed using only Nielsen heuristics [S03] and obtaining usability problems that are desired to be found in a particular system [S04, S11, S14, S22, S23, S24, S29, S31, S32, S33 & S35]. Additionally, methodologies applied to the generation of new heuristics [S18] such as PROMETHEUS are presented, which will allow dividing the process into stages that validate that the heuristics are being properly constructed, iterating through a refinement step if necessary [S04].

2. Nielsen derived evaluation items: One of the protocols used for the evaluation that is derived from Nielsen is the use of its ten heuristics in conjunction with the eight Schneiderman golden rules for grouping them into evaluation elements [S12]. Additionally, in another protocol, phases are used for the application of the evaluation, which consist of the initial navigation on the website to judge the flow, perception and dynamics of the interaction, and then, in the second phase, use the metrics of Nielsen usability heuristics [S13]. Other studies show that Nielsen heuristics could be used in conjunction with metrics to enrich the collected data [S27], with attributes defined in ISO / IEC 25023 [S28] and in conjunction with case study-specific heuristics [S34]. Finally, the ten Nielsen heuristics could also be applied by themselves to perform usability evaluations [S15, S21, S30, S36 & S37].

3. Comparison and grouping between evaluations: Comparison of results of the execution of heuristic evaluations between the country to be evaluated versus key international pages allows to provide improvement indicators and recommendations of good practices [S01]. Likewise, evaluation questions grouping allows comparisons between the generated groups to be made, in order to obtain more precise answers [S08]. Additionally, dividing heuristic evaluations into groups by used heuristics allows comparisons to be made of how many usability problems have been found with each one [S10]. Complementarily, if a heuristic evaluation is made to a website and then an additional one is made to the improved site as a result of the first evaluation, it will be possible to quantitatively compare how much the score has improved

[S17]. Finally, the comparison of test execution with Nielsen heuristics in contrast to newly designed heuristics allows the measurement of their effectiveness [S18, S23, S24 & S32].

4. Qualification methods: The use of Nielsen severity rating and Olson's ease of fix will allow to provide a quantitative assessment according to the severity of the usability problem encountered and how easy or difficult it will be to fix it [S02]. Likewise, another form of rating is the use of a heuristic evaluation questionnaire that consists of assigning a score of five points on the Likert scale for the evaluation of prototypes [S16], as well as adding structured sub-elements to the defined heuristics whose questions can be used by evaluators [S34].

5. Methodologies applied to heuristic evaluation: The protocols oriented to heuristic evaluation methodologies show the proposal for the use of a heuristic method based on ISO-9241–151 standard that consists of the execution of a heuristic evaluation by applying indicators divided into criteria that allow each indicator to be assessed, which facilitates the evaluation of results by criterion as well as in general [S09]. In addition, a framework is defined for the evaluation of dialogue elements in web pages so that the evaluators consider the same previously defined elements to be evaluated, as well as a definition of a workflow that allows its applicability in other types of software [S22]. Finally, the definition of a quantitative evaluation procedure of the results of a heuristic evaluation is proposed to obtain consistent and quantifiable results without the need for user participation [S26].

6. Formal processes with properly defined steps: The heuristic inspection process can be fully formalized through five duly defined steps: (1) planning, (2) training, (3) evaluation, (4) discussion and (5) report [S05 & S20]. In this way, this formalization consolidates the different ways in which evaluations are carried out into a single one, allowing interpretations on how to carry them out to be reduced [S05 & S20].

5 Conclusion and Future Works

During the application of the protocol to carry out systematic reviews by Kitchenham, three research questions were defined to carry out an empirical review of the heuristic evaluation processes in software products using search engines as a source that allowed to obtain studies relevant to the posed questions.

The first question sought to answer what are the challenges that occur when conducting heuristic evaluations on software products, for which, the literature provided 19 studies that allowed to identify 9 main challenges, of which the (1) low adequacy of the Nielsen heuristics, (2) low experience of the evaluators and (3) lack of formalization in the heuristic evaluation process are the most noticeable. Literature allows us to conclude that the sole use of Nielsen heuristics can pose a great challenge for heuristic evaluation by not considering characteristic aspects of emerging software products that do not fit into general heuristics. Also, the low experience of the evaluators represents a significant problem since the evaluation is likely not carried out correctly as important usability problems could not be considered. Finally, the lack of a formal process prevents the inspection from being carried out in a single way, resulting in various interpretations that could outcome imprecise and incorrect executions of heuristic evaluations.

The second question sought to answer what are the characteristics of current software solutions that allow the automation of the heuristic evaluation process in software products, for which the literature provided 4 studies that allowed to identify 4 software solutions: (1) WebSite Canvas Model, (2) Visual Clarity Checker, (3) Automated Heuristic Evaluator, and (4) Automation of usability inspections for websites. The first one showed a possible visual support tool for the heuristic evaluation; however, it has not been tested yet. The second and third studies show tools on websites that allow support for heuristic evaluation, from a support for clarity evaluation, to the automation of link detection, image quality increase and reading ease testing, respectively. Finally, the fourth study shows a desktop application that allows the heuristic evaluation to be carried out digitally in its entirety, giving the possibility of generating automatic reports after processing the input information for the qualification of each heuristic. In conclusion, although there are tools and software solutions that support the heuristic evaluation process, the literature shows a limited number of studies that have focused on its automation, which allows us to identify an area of study that has not yet been explored in depth.

Finally, the third question sought to answer what are the characteristics of the formal protocols or processes that are being used to improve the performance of heuristic evaluations in software products, for which the literature provided 33 studies that allowed the identification of 6 main protocols, of which highlight the formal processes with duly defined steps, having the highest level of coverage to the heuristic evaluation process compared to the others by allowing the definition of steps that cover the inspection in its entirety, from planning to reports. In addition, these processes contribute to the reduction of the interpretations of the usability evaluators on how to carry out a heuristic inspection.

For future projects, the support of the given challenges in the execution of heuristic evaluations could be provided through the development of a software solution, based on the 4 solutions found in the literature, taking into greater consideration the problems that were mentioned the most: low adequacy of the Nielsen heuristics, low experience of the evaluators and lack of formalization in the heuristic evaluation process. Likewise, protocols used for its implementation will be taken into consideration as a basis for the automation of the process by the proposed solution, focusing mainly on the formal process of heuristic evaluation as part of the formal process protocol with duly defined steps.

Acknowledgments. This study was highly supported by the Section of Informatics Engineering and the research group "HCI, Design, User Experience, Accessibility & Innovation Technologies" (HCI-DUXAIT) of the Pontificia Universidad Católica del Perú (PUCP).

References

1. Huang, Z.: Usability of tourism websites: a case study of heuristic evaluation. New Rev. Hypermedia Multimed. **26**, 55–91 (2020). https://doi.org/10.1080/13614568.2020.1771436
2. Holzinger, A.: Usability engineering methods for software developers. Commun. ACM. **48**, 71–74 (2005). https://doi.org/10.1145/1039539.1039541
3. Nielsen, J.: Usability Engineering. Morgan Kaufmann Publishers Inc., San Francisco (1993)

4. Kitchenham, B., Charters, S.: Guidelines for performing Systematic Literature Reviews in Software Engineering (2007)
5. International Organization for Standardization: ISO 9241–210–2019 (2019)
6. Muhammed, M.T., Waeal J, O., Bijan, R.: Applying deep learning techniques for big data analytics: a systematic literature review. Arch. Inf. Sci. Technol. 1 (2018). https://doi.org/10. 36959/863/756.
7. Petticrew, M., Roberts, H.: Systematic reviews in the social sciences: a practical guide. Blackwell Publishing, Malden (2006). https://doi.org/10.1002/9780470754887
8. Hasan, L., Morris, A.: Usability problem areas on key international and key arab e-commerce websites. J. Internet Commer. **16**, 80–103 (2017). https://doi.org/10.1080/15332861.2017. 1281706
9. Davis, D., Jiang, S.: Usability evaluation of web-based interfaces for Type2 Diabetes Mellitus. In: IEOM 2015 - 5th International Industrial Engineering and Operations Management Proceeding (2015). https://doi.org/10.1109/IEOM.2015.7093713
10. Lam, D., Sajjanhar, A.: Heuristic evaluations of cultural heritage websites. In: 2018 Int. Conf. Digit. Image Comput. Tech. Appl. DICTA 2018. (2019). https://doi.org/10.1109/DICTA. 2018.8615847.
11. Jiménez, C., Cid, H.A., Figueroa, I.: PROMETHEUS: procedural methodology for developing heuristics of usability. IEEE Lat. Am. Trans. **15**, 541–549 (2017). https://doi.org/10.1109/ TLA.2017.7867606
12. Paz, F., Paz, F.A., Pow-Sang, J.A., Collazos, C.: A formal protocol to conduct usability heuristic evaluations in the context of the software development process. Int. J. Eng. Technol. **7**, 10–19 (2018). https://doi.org/10.14419/ijet.v7i2.28.12874
13. Sanabre, C., Pedraza-Jiménez, R., Codina, L.: WebSite Canvas Model: propuesta de un modelo visual para la ideación estratégica de sitios web. Rev. española Doc. Científica. **41**, 221 (2018). https://doi.org/10.3989/redc.2018.4.1542
14. Ghazali, M., Sivaji, A., Abdollah, N., Khean, C.N.: Visual Clarity Checker (VC2) to support heuristic evaluation: to what extent does VC2 help evaluators? In: Proceedings - 2016 4th International Conference on User Science and Engineering i-USEr 2016, pp. 182–187 (2017). https://doi.org/10.1109/IUSER.2016.7857957
15. Maghfiroh, L.R.: Observation and heuristics evaluation of student web-based application of SIPADU-STIS. J. Phys. Conf. Ser. **1511**, 0–10 (2020). https://doi.org/10.1088/1742-6596/ 1511/1/012019
16. Pincay-Ponce, J., Caicedo-Ávila, V., Herrera-Tapia, J., Delgado-Muentes, W., Delgado-Franco, P.: Usabilidad en sitios web oficiales de las universidades del Ecuador. Rev. Ibérica Sist. e Tecnol. Informação, pp. 106–120 (2020)
17. Walsh, L., et al.: The e-health literacy demands of Australia's my health record: a heuristic evaluation of Usability. Perspect. Heal. Inf. Manag. **14** (2017)
18. Díaz, J., Rusu, C., Collazos, C.A.: Experimental validation of a set of cultural-oriented usability heuristics: e-Commerce websites evaluation. Comput. Stand. Interfaces. **50**, 160–178 (2017). https://doi.org/10.1016/j.csi.2016.09.013
19. Chen, Y.N., Hwang, S.L.: A heuristic evaluation on the usability of health information websites. In: Bridging Research and Good Practices towards Patient Welfare - Proceedings of the 4th International Conference on HealthCare Systems Ergonomics and Patient Safety, HEPS 2014, pp. 109–116 (2015)
20. Kiourexidou, M., Antonopoulos, N., Kiourexidou, E., Piagkou, M., Kotsakis, R., Natsis, K.: Websites with multimedia content: a heuristic evaluation of the medical/anatomical museums. Multimodal Technol. Interact. **3** (2019). https://doi.org/10.3390/mti3020042
21. Yeratziotis, A., Zaphiris, P.: A heuristic evaluation for deaf web user experience (HE4DWUX). Int. J. Hum. Comput. Interact. **34**, 195–217 (2018). https://doi.org/10.1080/10447318.2017. 1339940

260   A. Lecaros et al.

22. Eliseo, M.A., Casac, B.S., Gentil, G.R.: A comparative study of video content user interfaces based on heuristic evaluation. In: Iberian Conference on Information Systems and Technologies Cist. (2017). https://doi.org/10.23919/CISTI.2017.7975820

23. Motlagh Tehrani, S.E., Zainuddin, N.M.M., Takavar, T.: Heuristic evaluation for Virtual Museum on smartphone. In: Proceedings - 2014 3rd International Conference on User Science and Engineering: Experience. Engineer Engage, i-USEr 2014. 227–231 (2015). https://doi.org/10.1109/IUSER.2014.7002707

24. Puspitasari, I., Indah Cahyani, D.: Taufik: a user-centered design for redesigning e-government website in public health sector. In: Proceedings - 2018 International Seminar on Application for Technology of Information and Communication, Creation Technology Human Life, iSemantic 2018, pp. 219–224 (2018). https://doi.org/10.1109/ISEMANTIC.2018.8549726

25. Quinones, D., Rusu, C., Roncagliolo, S., Rusu, V., Collazos, C.A.: Developing usability heuristics: a formal or informal process? IEEE Lat. Am. Trans. **14**, 3400–3409 (2016). https://doi.org/10.1109/TLA.2016.7587648

26. Ahmad, W.F.W., Sarlan, A., Ezekiel, A., Juanis, L.: Automated heuristic evaluator. J. Informatics Math. Sci. **8**, 301–306 (2016)

27. Paz Espinoza, F.A.: Método para la evaluación de usabilidad de sitios web transaccionales basado en el proceso de inspección heurística. Pontif. Univ. Católica del Perú. 275 (2018). file:///C:/Users/UTM-BIBLIOTECA/Downloads/PAZ_FREDDY_USABILIDAD _SITIOS_WEB_%20INSPECCI%C3%93N_HEUR%C3%8DSTICA.pdf

28. Halaweh, M.: Usability testing of conferences websites: a case study of practical teaching. In: Uden, L., Hadzima, B., Ting, I.-H. (eds.) KMO 2018. CCIS, vol. 877, pp. 380–389. Springer, Cham (2018). https://doi.org/10.1007/978-3-319-95204-8_32

29. Silvis, I.M., Bothma, T.J.D., de Beer, K.J.W.: Evaluating the usability of the information architecture of academic library websites. Libr. Hi Tech. **37**, 566–590 (2019). https://doi.org/10.1108/LHT-07-2017-0151

30. Paz, F., Paz, F.A., Arenas, J.J., Rosas, C.: A Perception study of a new set of usability heuristics for transactional web sites. In: Karwowski, W., Ahram, T. (eds.) IHSI 2018. AISC, vol. 722, pp. 620–625. Springer, Cham (2018). https://doi.org/10.1007/978-3-319-73888-8_96

31. Paz, F., Paz, F.A., Pow-Sang, J.A.: Comparing the effectiveness and accuracy of new usability heuristics. Adv. Intell. Syst. Comput. **497**, 163–175 (2017). https://doi.org/10.1007/978-3-319-41956-5_16

32. Chanchí Golondrino, G.E., Pérez Oliveros, D., Campo Muñoz, W.Y.: Automation of usability inspections for websites. In: Ruiz, P.H., Agredo-Delgado, V. (eds.) HCI-COLLAB 2019. CCIS, vol. 1114, pp. 124–137. Springer, Cham (2019). https://doi.org/10.1007/978-3-030-37386-3_10

33. Paz, F., Paz, F.A., Sánchez, M., Moquillaza, A., Collantes, L.: Quantifying the usability through a variant of the traditional heuristic evaluation process. In: Marcus, A., Wang, W. (eds.) DUXU 2018. LNCS, vol. 10918, pp. 496–508. Springer, Cham (2018). https://doi.org/10.1007/978-3-319-91797-9_36

34. Inal, Y.: University students' heuristic usability inspection of the national library of Turkey website. Aslib J. Inf. Manag. **70**, 66–77 (2018). https://doi.org/10.1108/AJIM-09-2017-0216

35. dos Santos Pergentino, A.C., Canedo, E.D., Lima, F., de Mendonça, F.L.L.: Usability heuristics evaluation in search engine. In: Marcus, A., Rosenzweig, E. (eds.) HCII 2020. LNCS, vol. 12200, pp. 351–369. Springer, Cham (2020). https://doi.org/10.1007/978-3-030-49713-2_25

36. Iadanza, E., Fabbri, R., Luschi, A., Melillo, P., Simonelli, F.: A collaborative RESTful cloud-based tool for management of chromatic pupillometry in a clinical trial. Health Technol. **10**(1), 25–38 (2019). https://doi.org/10.1007/s12553-019-00362-z

37. Federici, S., et al.: Heuristic evaluation of eGLU-box: a semi-automatic usability evaluation tool for public administrations. In: Kurosu, M. (ed.) HCII 2019. LNCS, vol. 11566, pp. 75–86. Springer, Cham (2019). https://doi.org/10.1007/978-3-030-22646-6_6

38. de Menezes, M., Falco, M.: The relationship of the studies of ergonomic and human computer interfaces – a case study of graphical interfaces in e-commerce websites. In: Marcus, A., Wang, W. (eds.) HCII 2019. LNCS, vol. 11586, pp. 474–484. Springer, Cham (2019). https://doi.org/10.1007/978-3-030-23535-2_35

39. Paz, F., Paz, F.A., Pow-Sang, J.A.: Evaluation of usability heuristics for transactionalweb sites: a comparative study. Adv. Intell. Syst. Comput. 448, 1063–1073 (2016). DOI: https://doi.org/10.1007/978-3-319-32467-8_92

40. Retore, A.P., Guimarães, C., Leite, M.K.: Heuristics for grid and typography evaluation of art magazines websites. In: Kurosu, M. (ed.) HCI 2016. LNCS, vol. 9731, pp. 408–416. Springer, Cham (2016). https://doi.org/10.1007/978-3-319-39510-4_38

41. Morales, J., Rusu, C., Botella, F., Quiñones, D.: Programmer eXperience: a set of heuristics for programming environments. In: Meiselwitz, G. (ed.) HCII 2020. LNCS, vol. 12195, pp. 205–216. Springer, Cham (2020). https://doi.org/10.1007/978-3-030-49576-3_15

42. Okhovati, M., Karami, F., Khajouei, R.: Exploring the usability of the central library websites of medical sciences universities. J. Librariansh. Inf. Sci. 49, 246–255 (2017). https://doi.org/10.1177/0961000616650932

43. Fung, R.H.Y., Chiu, D.K.W., Ko, E.H.T., Ho, K.K.W., Lo, P.: Heuristic usability evaluation of university of hong kong libraries' mobile website. J. Acad. Librariansh. 42, 581–594 (2016). https://doi.org/10.1016/j.acalib.2016.06.004

Consumer Experience Research Based on the Background of Experience Economy and Digital Economy

Jing Liu and Zhen Liu[(✉)] [iD]

School of Design, South China University of Technology, Guangzhou 510006,
People's Republic of China
liuzjames@scut.edu.cn

Abstract. Experience economy and digital economy have special significance and importance under new market conditions. Although the experience economy and the digital economy have played an important role in influencing the consumer experience, and researchers have done extensive research, there are few reviews on consumer experience in the context of the experience economy and the digital economy. Therefore, based on the literature review, this article aims to explore the research progress of consumer experience related fields in the context of experience economy and digital economy. Through the Web of Science database, the bibliometric research method is adopted, and the VOSviewer visualization software is used for keyword co-occurrence analysis. The main contributions of this research include: (1) showing the year of all publications, visualize keywords, analyze the co-occurrence of keywords, discuss high-frequency keywords, research hotspots and trend discussions; (2) overview of the current experience of consumers in physical retailers, online shopping, travel, food, and space environments under the current experience economy and digital economy; (3) revealing the bad experience of the shared service platform to consumers Negative impact; and (4) exploreing the ways in which cities, websites, brands and service industries create consumer experience. It provides trends for researchers, policy makers, organizations, and enterprises who discuss the experience economy, digital economy, and consumer experience in the future.

Keywords: Experience economy · Digital economy · Consumer experience ·
Keyword co-occurrence · VOSviewer

1 Introduction

The world is in a new stage of evolutionary development. The forthcoming revolution is dramatically changing the fields of human activities, such as education, culture, and economy. At the same time, they are also creating new concepts and methods, such as behavioral economy, digital economy, and experience economy [1].

Pine and Gilmore [2] first put forward the view of "experience economy", indicating that the experience economy has higher value than goods, goods and services. In the

© Springer Nature Switzerland AG 2021
M. M. Soares et al. (Eds.): HCII 2021, LNCS 12779, pp. 262–277, 2021.
https://doi.org/10.1007/978-3-030-78221-4_18

experience economy, consumers can become passive participants or active participants in the experience, and the physical and psychological connectivity determines the intensity and value of the experience, and is based on the customer's absorption and immersion in the experience [3]. Pine and Gilmore [4] believe that experience is emotional, and the emotions felt by buyers will have value because they are memorable. From a corporate perspective, the term experience means using service as a stage and commodities as props to create unforgettable events that consumers want to remember in the future. The person who has experienced this emotion will cherish it, and when the activity is over, the value it creates will remain in his or her memory. The experience economy focuses on creating touching, surprising, and unforgettable feelings for consumers. Therefore, experience has become the most basic element of this economic model [5].

The term "digital economy" [6] spreads from science news to mass media. In 2017, as the profitability of cryptocurrency increased, people paid more attention to it. The development of new trade and property rights relations such as the economy based on digital platforms has become one of the impacts of global technological changes and consumer experience digitalization [7]. The digital economy has significantly changed the shopping experience of consumers, and digital environment provides conditions for the design of consumer experience, and consumer experience is a prerequisite for accepting innovation [8]. Digital technology helps to transfer many business processes into the digital environment [8]. Experience is understood as economic advice that can provide effective and expected results for a product or brand in the target market in a digital environment [9].

Although the experience economy and the digital economy have played an important role in influencing the consumer experience, and researchers have done extensive research, there are few reviews on consumer experience in the context of the experience economy and the digital economy. Based on the literature review, this research explores the research progress of consumer experience in the context of experience economy and digital economy, and hopes to provide assistance to researchers, policymakers, organizations, and enterprises in related fields.

2 Research Methods

This paper uses the bibliometric method, and use the VOSviewer visualization software to analyze the keyword co-occurrence to start the research. The bibliometric map is a quantitative method used to visualize the bibliometric factors of various scientific publications in different network forms [10], and to study scientific knowledge, which belongs to the category of scientometrics [11]. The data used in this article comes from the core collection of Web of Science (WoS), with the "experience economy", "digital economy", and "consumers" as the search topics, and the VOSviewer bibliometric software for keyword co-occurrence research. The keyword co-occurrence method has been applied to various fields and has been fully recognized, such as medical treatment [12, 13], disaster response [14], and social participation of the elderly [15] and other fields. Chen et al. [16] and Huane et al. [17] showed that keywords help to concentrate and refine the core views and topicality of the literature in this field, and can reflect the research hotspots and trends in this field [18].

3   Results

3.1   Literature Retrieval

The database used in this article comes from the core collection of Web of Science (WoS), and the publications are indexed under the theme of "Experience Economy * Digital Economy * Consumers". The time span is all years, including 2000 to November 2020.

According to Fig. 1, the experience economy, digital economy, and consumer-related publications in the past 20 years shows that 2016 was an obvious turning point. From 2000 to 2016, the number of articles published fluctuated, with a maximum of 3 articles and a minimum of 0 articles per year. However, since 2016, the number of articles published each year has been on the rise, and currently (2020) has reached the peak of the number of annual publications. It can be predicted that this field will have greater development potential in the future.

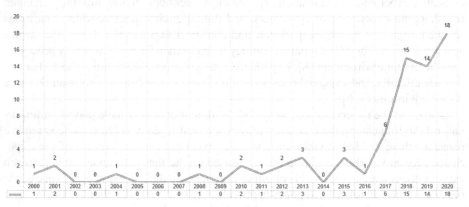

Fig. 1. "Experience Economy*Digital Economy*Consumers" related publications in Web of Science (WoS).

3.2   VOSviewer Keyword Co-occurrence Analysis

Import all articles into the software VOSviewer (version 1.6.15) to generate a term map of co-occurrence clustering, and perform keyword co-occurrence analysis. The keywords reflect the research hotspots and trends in this field [18]. In the "experience economy * digital economy * consumer" related literature, a total of 469 keywords that appeared once and 78 keywords with a frequency of two were collected. The following will show two aspects, namely network visualization, and overlay visualization.

Keywords Network Visualization. In the keyword co-occurrence cluster map, can see text labels, circles, lines, and color areas. By default, items are represented by labels and circles. The size of the item label and the circle determines the weight of the item, and the distance between the two items or (and) the strength of the connection represents the strength of their affinity [19]. Different color areas represent different types of clusters. In Fig. 2, all terms are divided into eight clusters, with keywords with different weights in each cluster. Table 1 lists the 8 clusters with the highest weight keywords based on the keyword co-occurrence frequency and the total keyword link strength. The link strength represents the co-occurrence frequency [20].

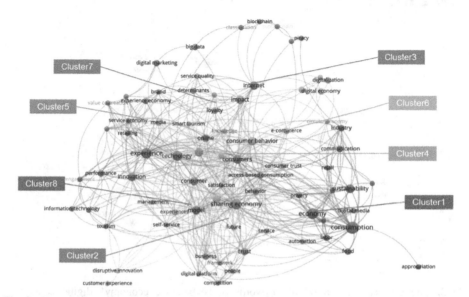

Fig. 2. Keyword co-occurrence clustering of "experience economy* digital economy* consumers" via VOSviewer.

Table 1. Weight keywords of "experience economy* digital economy* consumer" via keywords network visualization of VOSviewer.

Colors	Clusters	Weight keyword	Occurrences	Total link strength
	Cluster1	Consumption	10	47
	Cluster2	Sharing economy	8	44
	Cluster3	Technology	7	41
	Cluster4	Information	5	24
	Cluster5	Consumers	5	30
	Cluster6	Consumer behavior	5	30
	Cluster7	Social media	5	26
	Cluster8	Experience	8	44

Keywords Overlay Visualization. From the overlay visualization, it is clear that the changes in research hotspots and trends in related literature in recent years. Figure 3 shows the research situation in the past five years. From the past to the present, the color has gradually changed from purple and blue to green and yellow. And sort out the research hotspot keywords in the past five years into Table 2.

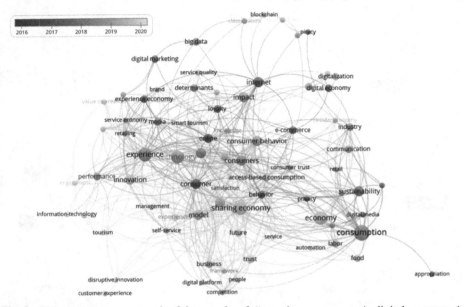

Fig. 3. The co-occurrence trend of keywords of "experience economy* digital economy* consumer" via VOSviewer.

Table 2. Hot keywords in the field of "experience economy* digital economy* consumer" in the past five years via keywords overlay visualization of VOSviewer.

Years	Color range	Keywords
2016		Internet, e-commerce, digital economy, experience economy, loyalty, online, privacy, behavior, digital media, piracy
2017		Digital marketing, big data, sustainability, experience, technology, media, performance, social media
2018		Supply chain, information, retailing, communication, consumer behavior, digital technologies, labor
2019		Sharing economy, digitalization, value co-creation, trust, customer experience, digital platform, disruptive innovation, food
2020		Tourism, information-technology, engagement, management, satisfaction, automation, service

3.3 Consumer Experience

The consumer experience is derived from a set of interactions between the consumer and a product, a company or a part of its organization, which triggers a reaction. This experience is strictly personal, meaning that consumers participate in different levels including rational, emotional, sensorial, physical, and spiritua [21, 22]. Schmitt [23] from the basic concept of "different levels of participation", the modular concept of the consumer experience concept was proposed. Including: sensory experience (sensory); emotional experience (feeling); creative cognitive experience (thinking); physical experience, behavior, and lifestyle (behavior); social identity experience related to the reference group or culture (relevant) [21]. In the context of experience economy and digital economy, researchers have explored offline physical retail stores, maintaining competitiveness by capturing consumer experience, and expanding consumer experience from physical stores to online shopping. Digitalization promotes the upgrading of consumer experience, such as consumer travel experience, food experience, and space experience.

Physical Store Experience. Digital technology is democratizing production tools, creating new promotion and distribution channels, and people increasingly believe that shopping in physical stores is more expensive and time-consuming than shopping online [24]. However, some retailers still have a strong attractive consumption space by improving the consumer experience. Physical stores attract more consumers by providing entertainment and novel in-store experiences, thereby creating a superior retail experience [25–28], Cultivating in-store consumer experience is a value creation strategy that supports these physical retailers in the digital age [24]. Some researchers believe that the store experience is created by the interaction between consumers and store elements, such as atmosphere and store design, including colors, music, lighting, etc. [29, 30]. And through consumer social interaction in the store, including the relationship developed with store personnel and other consumers [31–34]. Therefore, the store experience consists of the place (scene) where the experience occurs, the services provided, and (eventually) the co-produced place [35]. Companies in many industries strive to "stage" the environment, artifacts, and environment to promote interaction and allow consumers to co-create their own experiences. Crucially, space is not only a place of production or a container for economic activities, but also an important place of consumption, shaping the interaction and communication between producers, intermediaries and consumers [36]. Studies have shown that some bars and independent record stores remain competitive in the digital age. Young people go to bars to drink and influence their drinking experience by creating an atmosphere [37]. They stated that drinking in a dark atmosphere is a relief, allowing them to escape the visual judgment of others [37]. Darkness provides a way for young people to temporarily escape from spatial, social, and sensory norms [38]. Similarly, in an era where music can be played at the push of a button, visiting a record store is a valuable cultural experience for many consumers [39]. The ritualization and tactile experience of visiting record stores and consuming vinyl records are still attractive. Some stores create distinction, value and loyalty by organizing events and creating opportunities for interaction and socialization [24].

Online Shopping Experience. With the popularity of smart phones, users can communicate, locate, notify, educate, and shop at almost any place at any time [40]. Consumers can now easily access other consumers' reviews to evaluate suppliers and compare products [41]. In the new retail environment, the shopping experience of consumers is closely related to the new communication technology (ie social media), from a store-based experience to a "network experience", which stems from the widespread use of new communication technologies by consumers collecting information, they are willing to share some information with others, and at the same time establish a new digital intermediary relationship with retailers [35]. For example, social interaction related to the store experience is no longer limited to social activities in the store, nor does it require the company of other consumers (including friends, partners, relatives, etc.) or the actual presence of the seller [35]. Because social networks like Facebook provide consumers with a larger social network that can interfere with the shopping experience on all levels [35].

Consumers are becoming more and more digital and gradually adopting digital services [42]. Digitalization has been injected into daily life and transferred power from marketers to consumers [43]. The issue of online transactions taking precedence over offline transactions is under discussion, and most experts tend to cooperate and complement each other with online and offline businesses. The main reason is to provide consumers with the best shopping experience. The focus of creating a digital ecosystem is to integrate various services to provide consumers with simpler, faster and more convenient choices, remuneration and product delivery [8].

Travel Experience. In the "Era of Tourism 4.0", the digital revolution is changing the behavior of tourists, companies and destinations, projecting them into an intelligent perspective, enabling tourists to obtain useful information faster, thereby improving their travel experience [44]. In recent years, a leisure society eager for "real" experience has emerged. The technological revolution based on the sharing economy has blurred the travel boundaries of tourist destinations. Independent tourists are no longer limited to traditional tourist institutionalized spaces, but seek experiences that can be integrated into local culture [45]. For example, for Airbnb guests, the way of experience is the most important, and consumers are more interested in the unique and local real travel experience that Airbnb can provide [46]. Therefore, marketers should pay attention to the diversity of each potential experience, city and characteristics, so that tourists "live like a local." The influence of digital technology on tourists' behavior before, during and after travel has become more and more important, so that traditional tourists are transformed into digital tourists and smart tourists [44]. Every tourist is different, with unique experiences, motivations and desires [47]. New, experienced, mature and demanding travelers need to interact with suppliers to meet their own specific needs and desires" [47].

With the help of new technology, the overall travel experience can be improved. The best travel experience is a comprehensive combination of functions related to traditional service management processes and product experience projects that involve all experience fields [48, 49] and also use technology to promote value co-creation [44]. Now technology and data analysis allow for customized services and visitor experiences, but it must be ensured that automation does not lead to a disconnect between online and in-person communication [47]. At the same time, it is necessary to emphasize the importance of maintaining consumer privacy and data throughout the process to win the trust of consumers [47].

Food Experience. The development of the Internet has changed the way people shop. Online shopping, apps, and delivery services are changing the way consumers access retail services, including full meals [50]. Food is gradually moving in the direction of choice and self-determination, not only in terms of its practical benefits (savings, convenience, and customized attention), but also as a broader concept that enriches the real experience and the real relationship between people Contact [51]. Although consumers have been "eat with their eyes" for some time, in the end, it is the taste and texture of the food that leads to a good experience, which creates the desire to buy again [52]. Consumers are attracted by product sources, ingredients, and inspiring stories, such as "locally sourced" meat, "homemade", "authentic" and "farm" descriptors [53]. At the same time, consumers have increased their desire to create and provide restaurant-quality gourmet experiences [53].

Space Experience. "Atmosphere" refers to the "emotional" emotions that the spatial arrangement evokes in the sensory bodies of its users [54]. In the experience economy, aesthetic perception can be manipulated by actively creating atmosphere [55]. With the rapid development of digital visualization technology in architecture studios, architecture is also paying more and more attention to issues of atmosphere and sensory effects [56–58]. Since the 1970s, architects have steadily evolved from hand-drawn images to computer-generated visualizations [55]. Computer-generated images are far from "mere" glamorous performances, but a new form of urban visualization, capturing and marketing the feeling of specific manifestations [55]. Digital images can evoke and manipulate the atmosphere of a specific place, emphasizing the experience quality of new buildings and urban environments [55]. In order to describe and present specific sensory, specific systems and emotional experiences to attract customers and consumers, this demonstrates the importance of digital technology in building the "performance infrastructure" of the experience economy [55].

3.4 Negative Consumer Experience

Poor experience will have a negative impact on consumers. Researchers mainly discussed some of the existing sharing platforms, including research on access-based product service systems, car sharing, and clothing rental.

The development of the digital economy has given birth to new business models, one of which is the sharing economy. In essence, the sharing economy, also known as collaborative consumption or access-based consumption, is a consumption trend that uses products instead of acquiring ownership. This consumption trend is promoted through shared services [59].

Sharing economy transactions represent a type of "liquid consumption" [60]. In the sharing economy, user experience usually requires access to a product owned by another consumer who rents out its excess capacity. Therefore, the behavior of previous users may change the conditions or performance of shared resources and affect the experience of the next consumer [61]. The access-based product service system (AB-PSS) can influence the consumer experience in many ways. For example, if the consumer's smartphone battery runs out, the supplier's application fails, and the product's built-in sensor fails, the service delivery of AB-PSS may be affected, and the consumer's negative experience will be triggered negative emotions [42]. Schaefers et al. also provides evidence that user misbehavior will damage the experience of subsequent users, for example, leaving garbage and spills in shared cars [62]. The researchers also revealed the obstacles to the development of clothing rental agencies and found that when another person or object interacts with an item, the item may be considered contaminated. Pollution is an obstacle to the success of leasing, because most of the impact of pollution incidents on customer experience is recorded as a negative impact, and the worst result is to completely reject the entire leasing concept [63]. When investigating the overall experience of point to point (P2P) consumers who stay and vacation, the researchers also found three structures that can influence the overall experience, including (i) price-quality relationship; (ii) risk perspective; (iii) society Interaction [64]. Poor consumer experience will lead to customer churn to a certain extent. Customer churn refers to the loss of customers from one operator to another [65]. Researchers explored the driving factors of the loss of digital natives and loyalty in Turkey, and found that improving customer satisfaction can significantly increase customer loyalty and help minimize customer churn [66]. More importantly, a key factor in determining consumer satisfaction is the consumer's service quality experience. Consumer service factors such as telephone quality, billing, and brand image will affect consumer loyalty and willingness to churn [67].

The sharing platform has limited control over the quality of user experience. Therefore, future research should record the impact of consumers on subsequent consumer behaviors, and how these behaviors affect consumer experience and consumer lifetime value [61]. For example, in addition to providing insights into user decisions, machine learning and artificial intelligence technologies may also help sharing platforms identify problems in matching mechanisms to optimize customer experience [68]. Digital technology is still developing rapidly, and the implementation of 5G mobile networks in the future can improve the reliability of these services, and may realize new and large data applications and services that require real-time data exchange [42].

3.5 Creation of Consumer Experience

City Experience. Recent urban and economic development policies place great emphasis on promoting experiences [69]. For cities, making and promoting festivals is a way to implement experience planning. The introduction of festivals into urban planning has become a prominent planning tool to promote local urban and economic development, consumer experience and urban image [69]. At the same time, Häusserman and Siebel stated that the "festivalization of urban politics" is no longer limited to the organization of sporadic large-scale events, such as world exhibitions, Olympics or international film festivals. It can penetrate cities and economic development on a smaller scale [70]. In the end, eventization not only includes the acceleration logic of more and more experience plans, but also embodies the process of transforming urban space itself into the staged experience of event consumption [69].

Website Experience. Websites with better experience may affect users' frequent and continuous return visits to the website, keep e-commerce consumers loyal [71], and encourage consumers' purchase intentions [72]. Researchers explored the user experience of the website from several factors such as practical quality, hedonic quality and user value, and found that directness, attractiveness, and happiness account for the greatest weight. This means that the usefulness and convenience of the website make users more confident in using the website. The clarity and conciseness of website information, that is, the convenience of use, is an important factor that affects the perceived user experience. A website must have an attractive appearance, a sense of refinement, and bring happiness, which means that the website needs to work accurately and meet user expectations, providing users with time and information satisfaction and self-satisfaction [73]. Therefore, a website with a good user experience will become an advantage and good commercial value. By avoiding the possibility of loss of sales level, it will provide significant benefits for all participants in e-commerce, thereby increasing the sales value of products or services [74].

Brand Experience. Brand is a marketing tool that creates consumer experience [75]. Brand experience is defined as "subjective, internal consumer reactions (sensations, feelings, and cognitions), as well as the behavioral response evoked by the brand-related experience attributes in consumer interaction with the brand, purchase and consumption of the brand [76]". The intensity of brand experience affects consumers' ability to infer brand personality, and affect brand satisfaction and loyalty [76]. Once a brand disappoints consumers, the breakdown of the consumer-brand relationship may resemble a relationship breakdown or divorce [77–79].

Brands can promote consumer well-being by evoking certain types of experiences [80]. For example, for hotel guests, the main concern of tourists is not the brand's experiential service itself, but whether the experience provided by the brand meets its brand promise [46]. Therefore, hoteliers and marketers should concentrate their marketing resources to build a coherent, recognizable, and differentiated brand, realize their brand promises, and enhance consumers' travel experience [46]. Enable consumers to establish a deep and meaningful relationship with the brand [81].

Service Experience. In the consumer service industry, service personnel are the center for various target consumers to enhance the online shopping experience [82]. High-quality employee behavior is reflected in fast delivery and effective resolution of consumer dissatisfaction [83]. These human factors create a good buying atmosphere for consumers, portray a good image and loyal and satisfied consumers [84]. The education level and empathy of employees will affect the way customers complain, and the way they handle delivery. Companies should consider employee behavior when formulating strategies [85]. In addition to the consumer industry, customer experience is still one of the key competitiveness of enterprises in manufacturing [86]. Researchers explored consumers' attitudes towards recycled clothing and found that the correct communication timing between employees and consumers and paying attention to consumers' shopping experience can promote consumers' purchase of remanufactured products [87].

4 Discussion

The experience economy and digital economy have special significance and importance in the new market conditions. Experiential marketing and digital marketing help with establishing long-term relationships with consumers and form stable connections in the market [1]. Experiential marketing has its own particularities, which emphasizes the emotional experience and feelings of consumers, while digital marketing using digital tools provides address links and mobile communications for the brand's target audience [1].

For current consumers, the key word is experience [88]. Physical retailers maintain their competitiveness in the digital age by cultivating in-store consumer experience by creating an in-store atmosphere, holding events, and creating interaction. Consumers' shopping, travel, eating, space and other experiences have been greatly improved in the digital context, and the experience dimension of consumption has also become an era of online and offline sharing and social relationships [89]. The development of new types of trade and property relations, such as the economy based on digital platforms, has become one of the effects of global technological changes and the digitalization of consumer experience, shifting consumer behavior from acquisition to sharing [7]. However, the development of many digital sharing platforms is currently hindered by consumers' bad experience, such as clothing rental [63], accommodation and vacation [64]. Consumer experience is also a key factor in determining customer satisfaction and customer loyalty, and severe cases can also lead to customer loss. Therefore, many researchers are actively exploring how to improve the consumer experience, such as creating and promoting festivals to create consumer experience for the city, and also making a great contribution to improving the website experience, brand experience and service experience.

5 Conclusion

This paper uses bibliometric research method to explore the research progress of consumer experience in the context of experience economy and digital economy. The research results show that VOSviewer is a good data visualization software, which can objectively display the weight of keywords in the literature, research hotspots and the affinity between keywords, and keyword co-occurrence is also a reliable analysis method. In addition to pursuing the benefits of tangible product functions, consumers also pursue a sense of extraordinary, joy and enjoyment. The experience economy focuses on providing consumers with great, unique and profound experiences. At the same time, the digital economy provides conditions for the design of consumer experience, enabling companies to carry out large-scale differentiation and market segmentation to change consumer experience. The main contributions of this research include: (1) showing the year of all publications, visualize keywords, analyze the co-occurrence of keywords, discuss high-frequency keywords, research hotspots and trend discussions; (2) overview of the current experience of consumers in physical retailers, online shopping, travel, food, and space environments under the current experience economy and digital economy; (3) revealing the poor experience of the shared service platform to consumers negative impact; and (4) exploreing the ways in which cities, websites, brands and service industries create (enhance) consumer experience. The main limitation of the current study is that only data from one database WoS is used. Some related publications may be indexed by other databases, but not in WoS. However, because each database has different publication indexes and citation counts, article retrieval cannot combine and present data across multiple databases. Future follow-up studies can consider using data from different databases to compare with the results reported in this study.

Acknowledgements. This research is supported by "South China University of Technology Central University Basic Scientific Research Operating Expenses Subsidy, project approval no. XYZD201928, (x2sjC2191370)".

References

1. Fejling, T., Torosyan, E., Tsukanova, O., Kalinina, O.: Special aspects of digital technology-based brand promotion. In: IOP Conference Series-Materials Science and Engineering, vol. 497. IOP Publishing Ltd, Bristol (2019)
2. Pine, B.J.N., Gilmore, J.H.: Welcome to the experience economy. Harvard Bus. Rev. **76**, 97–105 (1998)
3. Montaudon-Tomas, C.M., Pinto-Lopez, I.N., Yanez-Moneda, A.L.: Virtual reality in hospitality and tourism educational programs: preparing students for the experience economy. In: Chova, L.G., Martinez, A.L., Torres, I.C., (eds.), INTED Proceedings. pp. 7090–7098. Iated-Int Assoc Technology Education & Development, Valenica (2020)
4. Pine, B.J., Gilmore, J.H.: The Experience Economy: Work is Theatre and Every Business a Stage. Harvard Business School Press, Cambridge (1999)
5. Tu, J., Yang, C.: Consumer needs for hand-touch product designs based on the experience economy. Sustainability **11**(20647) (2019)
6. Pimenova, E.M.: Specificity of sustainability assessment for industrial enterprise functioning in the digital economy. In: Ashmarina, S.I., Mantulenko, V.V., Vochozka, M. (eds.) ENGINEERING ECONOMICS WEEK 2020. LNNS, vol. 139, pp. 3–10. Springer, Cham (2021). https://doi.org/10.1007/978-3-030-53277-2_1
7. Polyanin, A., Golovina, T., Avdeeva, I., Vertakova, Y., Kharlamov, A.: Standardization of business processes based on the use of digital platforms. In: Soliman, K.S., (ed.). pp. 3904–3912. Int Business Information Management Assoc-Ibima, Norristown (2019)
8. Bozhuk, S., Krasnostavskaia, N., Maslova, T., Pletneva, N.: The problems of innovative merchandise trade in the context of digital environment, In: IOP Conference Series-Materials Science and Engineering, vol. 497. IOP Publishing ltd, Bristol (2019)
9. Schmitt, B.: There's No Business that's Not Show Marketing in an Experience Culture (2005)
10. Damar, H.T., Bilik, O., Ozdagoglu, G., Ozdagoglu, A., Damar, M.: Scientometric overview of nursing research on pain management. Revista Latino-Americana De Enfermagem 26(e3051) (2018)
11. Powell, T.H., Kouropalatis, Y., Morgan, R.E., Karhu, P.: Mapping knowledge and innovation research themes: using bibliometrics for classification, evolution, proliferation and determinism. Int. J. Entrepreneurs. Innovation Manage. **20**(3–4), 174–199 (2016)
12. Devos, P., Menard, J.: Trends in worldwide research in hypertension over the period 1999–2018 a bibliometric study. Hypertension **76**(5), 1649–1655 (2020)
13. Yeung, A.W.K., et al.: Natural products in diabetes research: quantitative literature analysis. NAT PROD RES (2020)
14. Feng, Y., Cui, S.: A review of emergency response in disasters: present and future perspectives. Nat. Hazards **105**(1), 1109–1138 (2020). https://doi.org/10.1007/s11069-020-04297-x

15. Fu, J., et al.: Global scientific research on social participation of older people from 2000 to 2019: a bibliometric analysis. Int. J. Older People Nurs. (e12349), (2020).
16. Chen, C., Dubin, R., Kim, M.C.: Emerging trends and new developments in regenerative medicine: a scientometric update (2000–2014). Expert Opin. Biol. Therapy **14**(9), 1295–1317 (2014)
17. Huang, L., Chen, K., Zhou, M.: Climate change and carbon sink: a bibliometric analysis. Environ. Sci. Pollut. Res. **27**(8), 8740–8758 (2020). https://doi.org/10.1007/s11356-019-074 89-6
18. Li, H., An, H., Wang, Y., Huang, J., Gao, X.: Evolutionary features of academic articles co-keyword network and keywords co-occurrence network: Based on two-mode affiliation network. Physica A-Stat. Mech. Appl. **450**, 657–669 (2016)
19. CWTS Homepage. https://www.cwts.nl/. Accessed 17 Nov 2020
20. Pinto, M., Pulgarín, A., Escalona, M.I.: Viewing information literacy concepts: a comparison of two branches of knowledge. Scientometrics **98**(3), 2311–2329 (2013). https://doi.org/10.1007/s11192-013-1166-6
21. Gentile, C., Spiller, N., Noci, G.: How to sustain the customer experience: an overview of experience components that co-create value with the customer. Eur. Manage. J. **25**(5), 395–410 (2007)
22. Lemke, F., Clark, M., Wilson, H.: Customer experience quality: an exploration in business and consumer contexts using repertory grid technique. J. Acad. Mark. Sci. **39**(6), 846–869 (2011)
23. Schmitt, B.H.: Experiential Marketing. The Free Press, New York (1999)
24. Hracs, B.J., Jansson, J.: Death by streaming or vinyl revival? Exploring the spatial dynamics and value-creating strategies of independent record shops in Stockholm. J. Consum. Cult. **20**(4), 478–497 (2020)
25. Bäckström, K., Johansson, U.: Creating and consuming experiences in retail store environments: Comparing retailer and consumer perspectives. J. Retail. Consum. ServicesRetail Consum. Behav. **13**(6), 417–430 (2006)
26. Verhoef, P.C., Lemon, K.N., Parasuraman, A., Roggeveen, A., Tsiros, M., Schlesinger, L.A.: Customer experience creation: determinants, dynamics and management strategies. J. Retail. Enhancing Retail Custom. Experience **85**(1), 31–41 (2009)
27. Pantano, E.: Benefits and risks associated with time choice of innovating in retail settings. Int. J. Retail Distrib. Manage. **44**(1), 58–70 (2016)
28. Willems, K., Smolders, A., Bregman, M., Luyten, K., Schoning, J.: The path-to-purchase is paved with digital opportunities: an inventory of shopper oriented retail technologies. Technol. Forecast. Soc. Chang. **124**, 228–242 (2017)
29. Yoon, S.: Antecedents and consequences of in-store experiences based on an experiential typology. Eur. J. Mark. **47**(5–6), 693–714 (2013)
30. Campo, K., Breugelmans, E.: Buying groceries in brick and click stores: category allocation decisions and moderating effect of online buying experience. J. Interact. Mark. **31**, 63–78 (2015)
31. Verhoef, P.C., Lemon, K.N., Parasuraman, A., Roggeveen, A., Tsiros, M., Schlesinger, L.A.: Customer experience creation: determinants, dynamics and management strategies. J. Retail. **85**(1SI), 31–41 (2009)
32. Mohan, G., Sivakumaran, B., Sharma, P.: Store environment's impact on variety seeking behaviour. J. Retail. Consum. Serv. **19**, 419–428 (2012)
33. Pantano, E., Migliarese, P.: Exploiting consumer-employee interactions in technologyen-riched retail environments through a relational lens. J. Retail. Consum. Serv. **21**(6), 958–965 (2014)

34. Rapp, A., Agnihotri, R., Baker, T.L., Andzulis, J.M.: Competitive intelligence collection and use by sales and service representatives: how managers' recognition and autonomy moderate individual performance. J. Acad. Mark. Sci. **43**(3), 357–374 (2015)
35. Pantano, E., Gandini, A.: Shopping as a "networked experience": an emerging framework in the retail industry. Int. J. Retail Distrib. Manage. **46**(7), 690–704 (2018)
36. Hracs, B.J., Jakob, D.: Selling the stage: exploring the spatial and temporal dimensions of interactive cultural experiences. In: Lorentzen, A., Schröder, L., Larsen, K.T. (eds.) Spatial Dynamics in the Experience Economy, pp. 71–87. Routledge, New York (2015)
37. Wilkinson, S.: Drinking in the dark: shedding light on young people's alcohol consumption experiences. Soc. Cult. Geography **18**(6), 739–757 (2017)
38. Edensor, T., Falconer, E.: Dans Le Noir? Eating in the dark: Sensation and conviviality in a lightless place. Cult. Geographies **22**, 601–618 (2014)
39. Hayes, D.: Take those old records off the shelf: youth and music consumption in the postmodern age. Popular Music Soc. **29**(1), 51–68 (2006)
40. Probst, W.N.: How emerging data technologies can increase trust and transparency in fisheries. ICES J. Mar. Sci. **77**(4), 1286–1294 (2020)
41. Sparks, B.A., Perkins, H.E., Buckley, R.: Online travel reviews as persuasive communication: the effects of content type, source, and certification logos on consumer behavior. Tourism Manage. **39**, 1–9 (2013)
42. Tunn, V.S.C., van den Hende, E.A., Bocken, N.M.P., Schoormans, J.P.L.: Digitalised product-service systems: Effects on consumers' attitudes and experiences. Resour. Conserv. Recycl. **162**(105045) (2020)
43. Labrecque, L.I., Vor Dem Esche, J., Mathwick, C., Novak, T.P., Hofacker, C.F.: Consumer power: evolution in the digital age. J. Interact. Mark. **27**(4SI), 257–269 (2013)
44. Pencarelli, T.: The digital revolution in the travel and tourism industry. Inf. Technol. Tourism **22**(3), 455–476 (2019). https://doi.org/10.1007/s40558-019-00160-3
45. Lim, S.E.Y., Bouchon, F.: Blending in for a life less ordinary? Off the beaten track tourism experiences in the global city. Geoforum **86**(July), 13–15 (2017)
46. Mody, M., Hanks, L., Dogru, T.: Parallel pathways to brand loyalty: Mapping the consequences of authentic consumption experiences for hotels and Airbnb. Tourism Manage. **74**, 65–80 (2019)
47. Navio-Marco, J., Manuel Ruiz-Gomez, L., Sevilla-Sevilla, C.: Progress in information technology and tourism management: 30 years on and 20 years after the internet - Revisiting Buhalis & Law's landmark study about eTourism. Tourism Manage. **69**, 460–470 (2018)
48. Pencarelli, T., Forlani, F. (eds.): The experience logic as a new perspective for marketing management. ISAMS, Springer, Cham (2018). https://doi.org/10.1007/978-3-319-77550-0
49. Shobri, N.D.M., Putit, L., Fikry, A.: Blending functional and emotional experience with the experience economy model to understand resort experience. Int. J. Innov. Bus. Strategy **9**(1), 55–63 (2018)
50. Mintel: Global food and drink trends 2016 (2016). http://www.mintel.com/global-food-and-drink-trends-2016
51. Morcellini, M.: "La comunicazione fa bene. La dieta mediterranea nelle reti della cultura e dei media" in Azienda Speciale della Camera di Commercio di Imperia PromImperia, Dieta Mediterranea. Atti del Forum Imperia 13–16 novembre 2014, FrancoAngeli, Roma (2014)
52. Batt, P.J.: Consumer sovereignty: exploring consumer needs. Agri-Product Supply Chain Management in Developing Countries. ACIAR Proc. **119**, 77–87 (2004)
53. Batt, P.J.: Responding to the challenges presented by global megatrends. In: Drew, R., (ed.), Acta Horticulturae, vol. 1205, pp. 1–12, Int Soc Horticultural Science, Leuven 1 (2018)
54. Reckwitz, A.: Affective spaces: A praxeological outlook. Rethinking History: J. Theory Pract. **16**, 241–258 (2012)

55. Degen, M., Melhuish, C., Rose, G.: Producing place atmospheres digitally: architecture, digital visualisation practices and the experience economy. J. Consum. Cult. **17**(1), 3–24 (2017)
56. Pallasmaa, J.: The Eyes of the Skin: Architecture and the Senses. Academy, London (1996)
57. Zumthor, P.: Atmospheres: Architectural Environments-Surrounding Objects. Birkhauser, Basel (2006)
58. Zumthor, P.: Padgett, L.; Oberli, M.; Schelbert, C.: Thinking architecture. Walter de Gruiter Gmb H Publisher (2006)
59. Fitranda, A.R., Balqiah, T.E., Astuti, R.D.: Sharing Services amongst Emerging Adulthood: Is ours better than mine? Evidence from Indonesia. In: Soliman, K.S., (ed.), pp. 8245–8257. Int Business Information Management Assoc-Ibima, Norristown (2019)
60. Bardhi, F., Eckhardt, G.M.: Liquid Consumption. J. Consum. Res. **44**(3), 582–597 (2017)
61. Eckhardt, G.M., Houston, M.B., Jiang, B., Lamberton, C., Rindfleisch, A., Zervas, G.: Marketing in the sharing economy. J. Mark. **83**(5), 5–27 (2019)
62. Schaefers, T., Wittkowski, K., Benoit, S., Ferraro, R.: Contagious effects of customer misbehavior in access-based services. J. Serv. Res. **19**(1), 3–21 (2016)
63. Clube, R.K.M., Tennant, M.: Exploring garment rental as a sustainable business model in the fashion industry: Does contamination impact the consumption experience? J. Consum. Behav. **19**(4), 359–370 (2020)
64. Pappas, N.: The complexity of consumer experience formulation in the sharing economy. Int. J. Hospit. Manage. **77**, 415–424 (2019)
65. Glady, N., Baesens, B., Croux, C.: Modeling churn using customer lifetime value. Eur. J. Oper. Res. **197**(1), 402–411 (2009)
66. Gerpott, T.J., Rams, W., Schindler, A.: Customer retention, loyalty, and satisfaction in the German mobile cellular telecommunications market. Telecommun. Policy **25**(4), 249–269 (2001)
67. Uner, M.M., Guven, F., Cavusgil, S.T.: Churn and loyalty behavior of Turkish digital natives: empirical insights and managerial implications. Telecommun. Policy **44**(1019014) (2020)
68. Huang, D.L., Luo, L.: Consumer preference elicitation of complex products using fuzzy support vector machine active learning. Mark. Sci. **35**(3), 445–464 (2016)
69. Jakob, D.: The eventification of place: Urban development and experience consumption in Berlin and New York City. Eur. Urban Regional Stud. **20**(4SI), 447–459 (2013)
70. Hausserman, H., Siebel, W.: Festivalisierung der Stadtpolitik: Stadtentwicklung durch grosse Projekte. Westdeutscher Verlag, Opladen (1993)
71. Zufwari, F.: Next Digital. Next Digital Indonesia, Jakarta (2017)
72. Aidil: Faktor-faktor yang Mempengaruhi Kemampuan Penyusunan Laporan Keuangan Pemerintah Daerah. Universitas Sumatera Utara, Medan (2010)
73. Hellianto, G.R., Suzianti, A., Komarudin.: User experience modeling on consumer-to-consumer (c2c) e-commerce website. In: Ali, A.Y., (Ed.), IOP Conference Series-Materials Science and Engineering, vol. 505, IOP Publishing Ltd, Bristol (2019)
74. Webarq: Website dan Manfaatnya untuk Pelaku E-commerce. Webarq Digital, Jakarta (2011)
75. Holt, D.B.: Why do brands cause trouble? A dialectical theory of consumer culture and branding. J. Consum. Res. **29**(1), 70–90 (2002)
76. Brakus, J.J., Schmitt, B.H., Zarantonello, L.: Brand experience: what is it? How Is It Measured?. Does It Affect Loyalty? J. Mark. **73**(3), 52–68 (2009)
77. Aaker, J., Fournier, S., Brasel, S.A.: When good brands do bad. J. Consum. Res. **31**(1), 1–16 (2004)
78. Gregoire, Y., Tripp, T.M., Legoux, R.: When customer love turns into lasting hate: the effects of relationship strength and time on customer revenge and avoidance. J. Mark. **73**(6), 18–32 (2009)

79. Johnson, A.R., Matear, M., Thomson, M.: A coal in the heart: self-relevance as a post-exit predictor of consumer anti-brand actions. J. Consum. Res. **38**(1), 108–125 (2011)
80. Schmitt, B., Brakus, J.J., Zarantonello, L.: From experiential psychology to consumer experience. J. Consum. Psychol. **25**(1), 166–171 (2015)
81. Fournier, S.: Consumers and their brands: developing relationship theory in consumer research. J. Consum. Res. **24**(4), 343–373 (1998)
82. Dunne, P., Lusch, R., Carver, J.: Retailing. Cengage Learning, Boston (2010)
83. Maruyama, M., Trung, L.V.: Supermarkets in Vietnam: opportunities and obstacles. Asian Econ. J. **21**(1), 19–46 (2007)
84. Turley, L.W., Chebat, J.C.: Linking retail strategy, atmospheric design and shopping behaviour. J. Mark. Manage. **18**(1–2), 125–144 (2002)
85. Singh, S., Mondal, S., Singh, L.B., Sahoo, K.K., Das, S.: An empirical evidence study of consumer perception and socioeconomic profiles for digital stores in Vietnam. Sustainability **12**(17165) (2020)
86. Riemensperger, F., Falk, S.: How to capture the B2B platform opportunity. Electron. Mark. **30**(1), 61–63 (2020). https://doi.org/10.1007/s12525-019-00390-7
87. Vehmas, K., Raudaskoski, A., Heikkilae, P., Harlin, A., Mensonen, A.: Consumer attitudes and communication in circular fashion. J. Fashion Mark. Manage. **22**(3), 286–300 (2018)
88. EY.: The upside of disruption. Megatrends shaping 2016 and beyond (2016). http://www.ey.com/gl/en/issues/business-environment/ey-megatrends
89. Bakardjieva, M.: Internet Society: The Internet in Everyday Life. Sage Publications, London (2005)

A Study on Scale Construction of Adjective Pairs for Evaluating Audiovisual Effects in Video Games

Takashi Nakamura[1]($\boxtimes$), Kazunori Miyata[2] ⓘ, Haruki Yamamoto[1], and Hisashi Sato[1]

[1] Kanagawa Institute of Technology, Atsugi Kanagawa 2430292, Japan
tnakamura@ic.kanagawa-it.ac.jp
[2] Japan Advanced Institute of Science and Technology, Nomi Kanazawa 9231211, Japan

Abstract. The semantic differential (SD) method is widely used to quantify and measure the impressions given by stimuli such as words or images. To evaluate impressions using the SD method, it is necessary to construct scales with adjective pairs according to the target concept and purpose. The aim of this study is to examine a scale construction consisting of adjective pairs for the SD method to evaluate the impressions given by effects composed of visuals and sounds in video games. Using 37 adjective pairs selected from three sources (free writing, comments from judges of competitions, and past research), we conducted a questionnaire using the SD method with video game movies as stimuli. Factor analysis was conducted on the results of the questionnaire, and eight different factors were extracted. This result will enable us to easily construct adjective pair scales to measure the impressions of users to audiovisual feedback from video games using the SD method.

Keywords: SD method · Video games · Audiovisual feedback · Sensitivity assessment · Factor analysis

1 Introduction

The semantic differential (SD) method, devised by the American psychologist C. E. Osgood and colleagues [1], has been widely used in various fields as a method of quantifying and measuring the impressions given by evaluation targets such as words and images. In the SD method, words, images, sounds, or a combination of these elements that are to be evaluated are called concepts. In studies using the SD method, it is common to perform factor analysis on the results, as Osgood did. Factor analysis of the results of verbal impressions using the SD method has shown that the three factors of value, activity, and competence are often extracted in common. However, various other factors may be extracted when the concept is different [2, 3]. When using the SD method, the scales of adjective pairs should be constructed according to the target concept and the purpose of the study. On one hand, if there are existing studies using the SD method for the target concept, it is best to select adjective pair scales based on the results of that study's factor analysis. On the other hand, if there are no existing studies using the SD method for the concept, it is necessary to construct new scales of adjective pairs.

© Springer Nature Switzerland AG 2021
M. M. Soares et al. (Eds.): HCII 2021, LNCS 12779, pp. 278–291, 2021.
https://doi.org/10.1007/978-3-030-78221-4_19

1.1 Previous Work that Used the SD Method to Identify Psychological Factors

Because the purpose of this study is to examine Japanese adjective pairs using the SD method, we mainly surveyed Japanese literature. In this section, we describe previous studies that have used the SD method to identify psychological factors.

In a study by Okada et al. [4] aimed at extracting emotional factors associated with the appreciation of paintings, four factors, including an activity factor, were extracted. In addition, the differences in impressions between figurative and abstract paintings were analyzed based on these factors [4]. While paintings are a kind of still image, some studies have used the SD method to extract psychological factors from motion pictures. Narita et al. [5, 6] also extracted psychological factors from high-definition television (HDTV) and three-dimensional (3D) HDTV videos, respectively. In both cases, eight factors were extracted. Despite the similar source, some of the extracted factors were different between HDTV and 3D HDTV.

In addition to research about psychological factors related to visual stimuli, there have also been some studies about the psychological factors related to auditory stimuli. For instance, Sugihara et al. [7] conducted a factor analysis related to listening to music. They found that the impressions can be composed of as many as 10 factors, such as comfort and elation factors.

In this research, a combination of video (movies) and audio (music and sound effects) were presented to subjects as stimuli for the visual effects in video games. In a study by Suzuki et al. [8] on the subjective impressions of auditory stimuli, visual stimuli, and their combinations, it was suggested that the effect of either auditory or visual stimuli is stronger regardless of the subject and that the effect of either stimulus is stronger depending on the type of stimulus.

The images in video games are basically computer graphics (CG). In Hayashi et al.'s research [9] on impressions of landscape images, they used the SD method to evaluate 3D CG stills and movies of landscape images created using virtual reality modeling language (VRML), and then they conducted a factor analysis. As a result, three factors were extracted for photographs, two factors for still images with VRML, and three factors for videos with VRML.

Some SD studies related to video games have investigated the factors that influence the image of characters in video games. For example, Kao et al. [10] performed factor analysis after an SD survey and identified three factors in the perceptual space of hero characters: brave factor, visionary factor, and moral factor.

1.2 Other Related Research Evaluating Video Games

Although not directly using the SD method, there have been several studies that evaluated the impressions given by video games. Shirai et al. [11] successfully applied the factor analysis method without using the SD method to classify game genres in a study aiming to classify game genres using subjective evaluation. In the study by Yoshida et al. [12], which aimed at selecting terms to evaluate game content, six terms—"innovative," "realistic," "fantastic," "fun for many," "lots of waiting time," and "comical"—were selected to evaluate game content as the result of processing using techniques such as analysis of variance and cluster analysis.

1.3 Related Work About Audiovisual Effects in Video Games

The purpose of this paper is to select adjective pair scales for the SD method that will measure the impression given by audiovisual effects in video games. In this article, the term "video game effects" refers to the combination of visuals, such as character animations and particle animations, and audio, such as sound effects and short music, that provide feedback to the player on the outcome of the game, such as success or failure, and the reaction to the player's actions.

Swink calls these "polish" elements [13]. Polish elements do not affect the game mechanics directly, and if they were removed, the essential functions of the game would not be changed. However, Swink describes polish elements as factors that have a substantial impact on the player experience.

A concept related to visual embellishments in video games is "juiciness," which refers to excessive positive feedback in video games [14]. There are several related studies on the impact of juiciness on players. An empirical study by Hicks et al. [15] confirmed that visual embellishment in video games can improve the player experience and make the game more attractive. Although early studies [16] had not clarified whether juiciness influences player behavior and experience, several recent studies have shown that juiciness can affect player behavior and performance. For example, in a large-scale empirical study by Kao [17] using an action role-playing game, it was found that player performance decreased when juiciness was either absent or excessive. In other words, it can be interpreted that moderate juicy feedback increases player performance. Kao's research revealed that the degree of juiciness also affects other player behaviors, such as playing time.

The audiovisual effects in video games are important not only in terms of the psychological impact on player experience but also in terms of their impact on player behavior and performance. However, there are few studies detailing how to evaluate these factors. Therefore, in this study, the SD method is applied to evaluate the impressions given by the audiovisual effects in video games. The purpose of this study is to clarify the psychological factors related to video game effects by analyzing the results of factor analysis and to construct adjective pair scales for measuring and evaluating the impression of audiovisual effects in video games using the SD method.

2 Methods

2.1 Overview of Experimental Methods

In this study, adjective pairs were collected to construct a scale from the SD survey using the following three steps: (1) "Presenting video game effects as stimuli to the subjects and collecting their impressions by free description and selecting adjective pairs"; (2) "Extracting words that describe video game effects from the comments of the contest judges and selecting adjective pairs"; and (3) "Selecting adjective pairs suitable for evaluating video game effects from the representative adjectives used in past studies on the SD method." A commercially available dictionary of Japanese antonyms [18] was used to decide the antonyms used to make the adjective pairs.

After the adjective pairs were selected by the three aforementioned collection methods, the adjective pairs were integrated. The integrated adjective pairs were then used to conduct an SD questionnaire survey using the audiovisual effects in video games as stimuli.

Finally, the results of the questionnaire survey using the SD method were examined by factor analysis using SPSS software (IBM Corp., Armonk, NY, USA).

2.2 Collecting Adjective Pairs Using the Definition Method

Nine kinds of video game effects were presented to eight students as stimuli in the form of movies up to 30 s in length, and they were asked to provide their impressions of each video game effect in a questionnaire. The format of the questionnaire was the definition method [19], in which a sentence is completed by putting words in the format "It feels like (), it feels like ()." We selected five game titles from three platforms (iPad, Nintendo Entertainment System, and PlayStation 4), and presented them as the stimuli, such as for success or failure, in audiovisual effects in the scenes. All the videos presented to the subjects were recorded from the actual game play using a video capture device. The audio output from the game consoles or iPad was recorded simultaneously with the video. When the video was presented to the subject, headphones were used so that the subject could hear the audio as well as the video. The video was played in a loop, so that subjects could easily think of words while watching the video. The list of movies presented to the subject is shown in Table 1. Figure 1 shows the thumbnails of the symbolic scenes used from the movies.

As a result of collecting words using the definition method, a total of 206 words describing the video game effects were collected, after correcting for spelling errors and integrating synonyms. Next, a histogram was drawn from the results, and a count of the frequency of occurrence of each word showed 66 words with a frequency of occurrence of two or more times. Adjective pairs were constructed using the extracted 66 words. The adjectives that were already in an oppositional relationship and could be used to make adjective pairs were merged to form three adjective pairs of six words. In the end, 32 adjective pairs were selected, excluding 28 words for which there were no antonyms and 28 words for which the resulting adjective pairs were considered to be synonymous with other adjective pairs.

2.3 Collecting Adjective Pairs from Evaluation of Contests

As a second collection method, we extracted and selected adjectives and adjectival verbs that described video game effects from the comments of judges who evaluated the winning works of a competition for video game effects. We selected the video presentations of the results from the fourth [20] and fifth [21] BISHAMON Effect Contest [22], which is a competition sponsored by Matchlock Corporation. Matchlock Corporation is the developer of BISHAMON, a creation tool for 3D visual effects used in video games. The words describing the effects were extracted from the judges' comments in the videos.

Table 1. List of videos presented during the questionnaire on the definition method.

Video	Title of the game (platform)	Content of audiovisual effects
Video A	Candy Crush (iPad)	The candies disappear as a result of the chain reaction
Video B	Candy Crush (iPad)	The scene of stage clear
Video C	Crossy Road (iPad)	Player gets hit by a car and crushed
Video D	Crossy Road (iPad)	The player falls into the water and splashes up
Video E	Super Mario Bros. (FC)	Mario tramples Goomba
Video F	Super Mario Bros. (FC)	Mario is hit by a Goomba and falls off the screen
Video G	Super Mario Bros. (FC)	The scene of stage clear (1–1)
Video H	Dynasty Warriors 8 (PS4)	A special move is activated
Video I	Burnout Paradise (PS4)	The player's car crashes

(FC = Family Computer/Nintendo Entertainment System; PS4 = PlayStation 4)

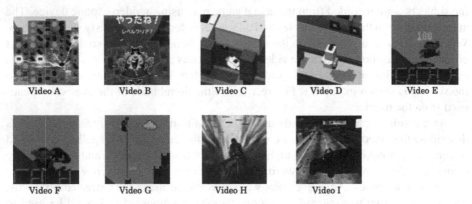

Fig. 1. Thumbnail of videos presented during the questionnaire on the definition method.

A total of 96 words were extracted from the comments, from which 13 adjectives with a frequency of two or more times were extracted. Then, after integrating three words with overlapping meanings, we created and examined adjective pairs for the extracted 10 words. Finally, we selected five adjective pairs. Table 2 shows the five adjective pairs from evaluation of contests.

2.4 Collecting Adjective Pairs from Past Research

As a final collection method, we selected 68 sets of adjective pairs from the representative adjective pair scales used in a past study applying the SD method described in Inoue et al.'s [2] study on SD adjective pairs. In their study, they cross-sectionally summarized the adjective scales used in the SD method for various stimuli other than video games, and thus, it was deemed appropriate to find candidates for adjective pairs that could also be used in the evaluation of video game effects. From the 68 sets of adjective pair

Table 2. Adjective pairs from evaluation of contests.

No.	Adjective	Antonym
1	clean	messy
2	assembled	disassembled
3	stable	unstable
4	pleasant	disgusting
5	polite	rude

scales, 47 pairs of adjectives were selected, excluding 21 pairs that had already been selected by the comments of the judges of the competition. The adjective pairs that were considered appropriate for evaluating the impression of the video game effects using the SD method were scored based on the subjective evaluation of three researchers, including the authors. The evaluation procedure was as follows: The scorers rated the adjective pairs on a five-point scale from zero to four in terms of appropriateness, and the total score was calculated. Then, the adjective pairs with higher total scores were considered for adoption. A total score of eight points or more, which indicated that two or more of the scorers agreed with the adoption, was the criterion for adoption.

As a result of the scoring, seven adjective pair scales that received eight or more points were extracted from the 47 adjective pair scales. Of these seven adjective pairs, two pairs that were considered synonymous with already selected adjective pairs were eliminated, and finally, five adjective pair scales were newly added. Table 3 shows the five adjective pairs from past research.

Table 3. Adjective pairs from past research.

No.	Adjective	Antonym
1	noisy	quiet
2	dynamic	static
3	masculine	feminine
4	cheerful	gloomy
5	complex	simple

2.5   Selecting Adjective Pairs for SD Survey

Next, we integrated the adjective pair scales extracted from the three collection methods. Then we made a final determination of the adjective pairs to be used for the evaluation by the SD survey.

The adjective pairs extracted from the representative adjective pairs used in past studies had already been subjectively evaluated by several researchers to determine whether they were appropriate for evaluating video game effects. Therefore, the validity of the 34 adjective pairs extracted from the two methods, the definition method and the judges' comments, which had not been evaluated for validity, were examined by subjective evaluation. Six scorers, including the author, scored the adjective pairs from the viewpoint of validity in the same way as the scoring evaluation conducted for the adjective pairs in past studies.

As a result, two sets of adjective pairs were excluded, and 32 pairs were selected. Table 4 shows the 37 adjective pair scales that were finally selected by integrating the 32 pairs with five pairs extracted from previous studies.

Table 4. The final 37 adjective pairs selected for the questionnaire using the SD method.

No.	Adjective	Antonym	No.	Adjective	Antonym
1	pleasant	disgusting	20	high	low
2	fun	painful	21	interesting	boring
3	cubic	planar	22	real	fictional
4	likable	obnoxious	23	sharp	dull
5	fast	slow	24	gentle	severe
6	bright	dark	25	realistic	ideal
7	clean	messy	26	successful	failed
8	good-looking	bad-looking	27	started	finished
9	light	heavy	28	delightful	disagreeable
10	new	old	29	calm	restless
11	flamboyant	modest	30	warm	cold
12	happy	sad	31	stable	unstable
13	safe	dangerous	32	polite	rude
14	strong	weak	33	noisy	quiet
15	fierce	tame	34	dynamic	static
16	assembled	disassembled	35	cheerful	gloomy
17	looks difficult	looks easy	36	masculine	feminine
18	looks delicious	looks bad	37	complex	simple
19	good	bad			

2.6 Questionnaire Survey Using the SD Method

Using the 37 sets of adjective pair scales finally selected, we conducted a questionnaire survey using the SD method to evaluate the impressions received from video game effects. To recruit a wide range of subjects, we conducted the SD method online questionnaire survey using the web-based online questionnaire service QuestionPro [23]. The bipolar rating scale questionnaire required for the SD method could be implemented online by using this service. Seven video game movies were presented as stimuli, and seven scales of the SD method of evaluation were conducted using 37 selected adjective pair scales. In past studies, seven-point or five-point scale has often been used when conducting SD surveys, but we used the seven-point scale because it was thought to be more common, based on past studies. Table 5 shows a list of the seven videos presented as stimuli. The symbolic thumbnails of the presented videos are shown in Fig. 2. The order in which the adjective scales were presented was randomized when the survey was conducted.

The participants were 49 males and females in their teens to 50s.

Table 5. List of videos presented as stimuli during the survey using the SD method.

Video	Title of the game (platform)	Content of audiovisual effects
Video A	Candy Crush (iPad)	The candies disappear as a result of the chain reaction
Video D	Crossy Road (iPad)	The player falls into the water and splashes up
Video F	Super Mario Bros. (FC)	Mario is hit by a Goomba and falls off the screen
Video H	Dynasty Warriors 8 (PS4)	A special move is activated
Video I	Burnout Paradise (PS4)	The player's car crashes
Video J	Backflip Madness (iPad)	The player character fails to land
Video K	Super Monkey Ball 2 (GameCube)	The player character goes off course and falls

(FC = Family Computer/ Nintendo Entertainment System; PS4 = PlayStation 4).

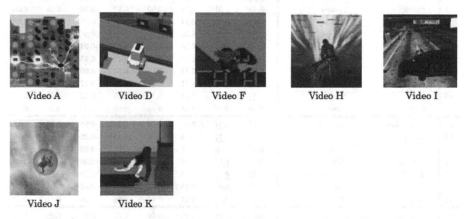

Video A   Video D   Video F   Video H   Video I

Video J   Video K

Fig. 2. List of thumbnails presented during the survey using the SD method.

2.7 Factor Analysis

Factor analysis was conducted using SPSS 25.0 on the data obtained from the SD questionnaire survey.

The maximum likelihood method was used for factor extraction, and the Kaiser–Guttman rule was applied to determine the number of factors. Because the total number of factors with eigenvalues greater than 1.0 was eight, we interpreted that there were eight factors in the impressions received from the video game effects. Based on the set number of factors, factor rotation operations using the Promax method (k = 3) were performed. From the obtained factor loadings for each adjective pair, if there was an adjective pair for which the absolute value of the factor loadings of all eight factors for each adjective pair did not have a value of 0.40 or higher, referring to the Fukuda guide book [19], the corresponding adjective pair was removed, and the factor rotation operation was repeated.

3 Results

As a result of the factor analysis, we obtained the factor loadings shown in Table 6. In addition, Table 7 shows the factor scoring table, which indicates the strength of each factor's involvement in the seven types of movies presented to the subjects in the SD questionnaire survey. In addition, Table 8 shows the correlation matrix between the factors.

Table 6. The adjective pairs scale and the factor loadings.

No.	Adjective Pairs		Factors							
			1	2	3	4	5	6	7	8
1	fierce	*tame	**0.80**	-0.13	0.00	-0.12	-0.13	0.00	-0.07	0.10
2	noisy	*quiet	**0.79**	0.07	0.13	-0.13	-0.02	-0.26	-0.03	0.03
3	*calm	restless	**-0.75**	0.01	0.15	0.02	0.12	0.24	-0.08	0.06
4	flamboyant	*modest	**0.72**	0.08	0.17	0.13	0.04	0.05	0.06	-0.08
5	fast	*slow	**0.72**	0.00	-0.20	0.00	-0.08	0.06	0.00	0.05
6	dynamic	*static	**0.67**	-0.02	-0.14	0.10	-0.06	-0.03	-0.03	0.01
7	cubic	*planar	**0.57**	0.02	-0.07	0.02	0.27	0.13	-0.04	0.11
8	strong	*weak	**0.55**	-0.16	0.34	-0.10	0.04	0.09	0.12	0.03
9	complex	*simple	**0.54**	-0.06	0.11	-0.10	0.11	0.12	0.02	-0.20
10	sharp	*dull	**0.52**	-0.09	0.13	0.19	0.13	0.12	-0.02	-0.07
11	high	*low	**0.49**	0.35	-0.08	-0.06	0.09	0.08	-0.16	-0.03
12	*masculine	feminine	0.22	**-0.71**	-0.06	0.09	-0.06	-0.05	0.00	0.11
13	warm	*cold	-0.05	**0.71**	0.16	-0.08	-0.03	-0.05	-0.01	0.09
14	bright	*dark	0.11	**0.68**	0.07	0.18	-0.05	0.08	-0.06	-0.04
15	cheerful	*gloomy	0.22	**0.61**	-0.07	0.27	-0.06	-0.04	0.01	-0.03
16	likable	*obnoxious	-0.10	**0.50**	-0.09	0.01	-0.09	0.27	0.08	0.16
17	light	*heavy	-0.05	**0.47**	-0.15	0.06	-0.17	0.02	0.05	-0.05
18	looks delicious	*looks bad	0.03	**0.47**	0.12	-0.07	0.26	0.04	0.08	0.11
19	successful	*failed	-0.03	0.08	**0.95**	-0.06	-0.03	-0.06	-0.06	0.03
20	started	*finished	-0.09	0.02	**0.71**	-0.01	-0.08	0.03	-0.05	-0.08
21	happy	*sad	-0.03	0.19	**0.68**	0.06	-0.06	-0.09	0.13	0.07
22	good looking	*bad looking	0.10	-0.22	**0.48**	0.29	-0.10	0.26	-0.07	0.04
23	interesting	*boring	-0.11	-0.10	0.00	**0.81**	0.03	0.03	-0.02	0.06
24	fun	*painful	0.04	0.14	0.03	**0.78**	0.04	-0.12	0.12	-0.02
25	delightful	*disagreeable	0.00	0.32	0.00	**0.61**	-0.01	-0.05	-0.09	0.06
26	real	*fictional	0.07	-0.18	-0.06	0.01	**0.71**	-0.08	0.07	0.05
27	realistic	*ideal	-0.05	0.05	-0.17	0.06	**0.63**	-0.06	-0.08	-0.05
28	clean	*messy	0.13	0.23	-0.08	-0.11	-0.09	**0.65**	0.03	0.05
29	polite	*rude	-0.09	0.04	0.09	-0.01	-0.03	**0.50**	0.03	-0.12
30	gentle	*severe	-0.08	0.08	-0.03	0.01	-0.02	0.05	**0.94**	-0.01
31	pleasant	*disgusting	0.00	0.06	0.02	0.17	0.00	-0.05	-0.01	**0.90**
	Square sum of loadings after rotation		5.44	4.49	3.17	3.57	2.04	1.87	2.39	2.45

Table 7. Factor scoring table for each movie.

Video (Title of game)	Factor 1	Factor 2	Factor 3	Factor 4	Factor 5	Factor 6	Factor 7	Factor 8
Video_A (CandyCrush)	0.12	-0.78	-0.77	-0.06	0.45	-0.12	-0.57	-0.17
Video_D (CrossyRoad)	0.61	-0.36	0.22	-0.07	0.03	-0.23	-0.22	-0.04
Video_F (SuperMarioBros)	0.81	-0.40	0.45	-0.18	0.55	0.33	-0.28	-0.03
Video_H (DynastyWarriors)	-0.86	0.92	-0.94	-0.10	-0.23	-0.34	0.23	-0.29
Video_I (BurnoutParadise)	-0.84	0.86	0.05	-0.06	-0.80	0.03	0.37	-0.08
Video_J (BackflipMadness)	0.67	0.37	0.56	0.51	-0.19	0.36	0.34	0.60
Video_K (SuperMonkeyBall)	-0.51	-0.61	0.44	-0.03	0.19	-0.03	0.14	0.02

Table 8. Matrix showing correlations between factors.

Factor	1	2	3	4	5	6	7	8
1	1.00	-0.25	0.15	0.22	0.11	0.07	-0.26	0.12
2	-0.25	1.00	-0.06	0.31	-0.40	0.08	0.35	0.26
3	0.15	-0.06	1.00	0.24	0.06	0.41	0.30	0.29
4	0.22	0.31	0.24	1.00	-0.21	0.29	0.10	0.47
5	0.11	-0.40	0.06	-0.21	1.00	0.24	-0.21	-0.10
6	0.07	0.08	0.41	0.29	0.24	1.00	0.13	0.27
7	-0.26	0.35	0.30	0.10	-0.21	0.13	1.00	0.18
8	0.12	0.26	0.29	0.47	-0.10	0.27	0.18	1.00

4   Discussion

Based on the results of the factor analysis, we will discuss the psychological factors related to audiovisual effects in video games.

4.1   Psychological Factors Related to Video Game Effects

The factors were interpreted based on the adjective pairs scale that constituted each factor, and each factor was named as shown in Table 9. Factor 1 (static–dynamic factor) is considered to be similar to the activity factor in prior studies [2, 3]. Factor 3, Factor 4, and Factor 8 may correspond to the evaluation factors in prior studies, but because the factors were extracted separately, they may be the factors when video game movies are used as the target concept.

Factor 3 (failing–succeeding factor) has not been extracted in the factor analysis of the SD method using video, audio, or a combination of the two as stimuli in prior studies [4–8], so it is assumed to be a psychological factor unique to video games. Factor 4 (boring–interesting factor) is not necessarily unique to video games but might be a factor unique to entertainment content, such as games and films. We hope that future research will reveal whether similar factors can be extracted from psychological factors in the evaluation of entertainment content other than video games.

Table 9. Named factors and adjective pairs with high factor scores.

	Factor name	Adjective pairs with high scores	
Factor 1	static–dynamic	fierce	tame
Factor 2	cold–warm	masculine	feminine
Factor 3	failing–succeeding	successful	failed
Factor 4	boring–interesting	interesting	boring
Factor 5	fictional–real	real	fictional
Factor 6	messy–clean	clean	messy
Factor 7	difficult–easy	gentle	severe
Factor 8	feel bad–feel good	pleasant	disgusting

4.2 Discussion of the Relationships Between the Extracted Factors

We also found that there was a seemingly paradoxical evaluation of the audiovisual effects of video games, with a high sense of failure and a high sense of fun at the same time. Looking at the Video_F (SuperMarioBros) item in the factor score table (Table 7), the score for Factor 3 (failing–succeeding factor) was 0.45, indicating a high sense of failure, while Factor 4 (boring–interesting factor) was -0.18, indicating a high sense of interestingness. The same factor scoring table shows that both Video_F (SuperMarioBros) and Video_J (BackflipMadness) were rated as having a high sense of failure in Factor 3 (failing–succeeding factor), but when we look at the rating in Factor 8 (feel bad–feel good factor), Video_F (SuperMarioBros) is almost neutral (-0.03), while Video_J (BackflipMadness) is 0.60, biased toward the impression of disgusting.

The results of Factor 3 (failing–succeeding factor) and Factor 8 (feel bad–feel good factor) were extracted separately, suggesting a direction in which there is not much discomfort even when failure occurs. In this respect, Video_K (SuperMonkeyBall) shows the same tendency as Video_F (SuperMarioBros). A previous study using biometric responses suggested that players of Super Monkey Ball 2 felt positive emotions when they failed (went off course) [24]. In Super Monkey Ball 2, the feedback of failure (the player-controlled ball goes off course and falls to the back of the screen) gives the impression of high failure but almost no discomfort, which may support the positive emotions of failure in the previous study. However, it is easy to assume that the expression of player emotions is a complicated mechanism, and this aspect cannot be ruled out. Further research is needed to analyze the factors that contribute to positive emotions during failure in video games.

In the factor correlation matrix (Table 8), the correlation coefficients with absolute values of 0.40 or higher are the combination of Factor 3 (failing–succeeding factor) and Factor 6 (messy–clean factor) with Factor 2 (cold–warm factor) and Factor 5 (fictional–real factor). The positive correlation between Factor 3 (failing–succeeding factor) and Factor 6 (messy–clean factor) suggest that when the sense of failure is high, the sense of neatness tends to also be high. The negative correlation between Factor 2 (cold–warm factor) and Factor 5 (fictional–real factor) indicates that there is a relationship between higher feminine impressions and higher fictional (unrealistic) impressions, and vice versa, between higher masculine impressions and higher realistic impressions. In the factor score table, the casual game Candy Crush presented in Video_A has a high feminine impression and a high unrealistic impression. On the other hand, games such as Burnout Paradise, presented in Video_I, have a high masculine impression and can be interpreted as giving a realistic impression.

4.3 Discussion About Application of the Results of This Study

The results of this study will contribute to making it easier to measure the impressions of video game effects using the SD method and may be applied to the game industry for uses in addition to research purposes.

By applying the method of searching for still images from the numerical data of impressions applying the SD method to the audiovisual effects of video games, as discussed by Agui et al. [25], it is expected that it would be possible to search for video game effects based on their impressions. However, the number of adjective pairs to be used for the query is expected to be too large, which would have a negative impact on the usability of the query. Therefore, using the results of this study, it will be possible to reduce the number of adjective pairs. For instance, Unity, a game engine that is widely used for game development, has an AssetStore [26] selling a large number of 3D models, visual effects, background music, sound effects, and other materials for games. Currently, the only way for users to find the best visual effects for their game is to search by popularity or keywords. In the case of assets with animations such as visual effects, it is necessary to check the preview video on the AssetStore to verify them, which requires a lot of time and effort to find the desired effect. By applying the results of this study, it would be possible to narrow down the list of visual effects in the AssetStore by specifying the degree of impression, such as "realistic" or "fictional," and also the degree of impression, such as "succeeding" or "failing."

4.4 Limitations and Recommendations for Future Research

Because the purpose of this study is to select Japanese adjective pairs for studying the impressions of video game effects using the SD method, there may be cases where the method cannot be used as is for other languages or where different factors might be extracted in a factor analysis. It is important to note that the adjective "omoshiroi" in Japanese has multiple meanings other than the meaning of "interesting" in English. For the actual Japanese adjective pairs used, please refer to our previous paper [27]. However, the list of adjective pairs used in this paper will be useful when researching audiovisual feedback of video games in multiple languages. The difference of psychological factors depending on language is a topic for future research.

In this study, we evaluated only the combination of video and audio. According to a past study [8], different factors might be extracted in the conditions for video only, audio only, and their combinations.

This study is about the audiovisual effects of video games in general; however, the genre of video game videos prepared as stimuli did not cover all genre of video games. If the video game genre or platform were limited, the adjective pairs and the extracted factors might lead to different results. The selection of adjective pairs and the extraction of factors when limiting the genre and platform are future tasks.

In addition, while we played pre-recorded videos to stimulate the subjects with the audiovisual effects of the video game in this study, the effects are not given interactively in real time in response to the player's actions as the player actually plays the video game. Therefore, there is a possibility that the stimuli from the recorded video and the stimuli while the player is actually playing the game are different. This is a future topic of research to verify whether there is such a difference.

5   Conclusion

In our current study, we examined the scale construction of adjective pairs to be used in the SD method for measuring the impression of video game effects. The results of this study are expected to be applied to the evaluation using the SD method, which measures not only the audiovisual effects of video games but also movies of scenes in video games. In future research, we are considering narrowing down the number of adjective pairs to be used in questionnaire surveys using the SD method so as not to increase the burden on the questionnaire participants. By applying the results of this study, we would like to continue our research on the effects of audiovisual feedback in video games on players and their associated factors.

References

1. Osgood, C.E., Suci, G.J., Tannenbaum, P.H.: The Measurement of Meaning. University of Illinois Press, Urbana (1957)
2. Inoue, M., Kobayashi, T.: The research domain and scale construction of adjective-pairs in a semantic differential method in Japan. Japan. J. Educ. Psychol. **33**(3), 253–260 (1985). https://doi.org/10.5926/jjep1953.33.3_253
3. Ichihara, S.: The perspective of the research for the semantic differential and the problems to be solved. Japan. J. Ergon. **45**(5), 263–269 (2009). https://doi.org/10.5100/jje.45.263
4. Okada, M., Inoue, J.: A psychological analysis about the elements of artistic evaluation on viewing paintings. J. Yokohama Natl. Univ. **31**, 45–66 (1991)
5. Narita, N., Kanazawa, M.: Psychological factors of 2-D/3-D HDTV sequences and evaluation method of their overall impressions. J. Inst. Image Inf. Telev. Eng. **57**(4), 501–506 (2003). https://doi.org/10.3169/itej.57.501
6. Narita, N., Kanazawa, M., Yuyama, I.: Analysis of psychological factors of hi-vision and 3-D hi-vision sequences. ITE Tech. Rep. **23**(9), 63–68 (1999). https://doi.org/10.11485/itetr.23.9.0_63
7. Sugihara, T., Mormoto, K., Kurokawa, T.: Fundamental characteristics of kansei for music through the SD Method. ITE Tech. Rep. **25**(48), 57–63 (2001). https://doi.org/10.11485/itetr.25.48.0_57
8. Suzuki, J., Sagawa, Y., Sugie, N.: Dependency of subjective impressions on the combinations of musics and images. J. Inst. Image Inf. Telev. Eng. **55**(7), 1053–1057 (2001). https://doi.org/10.3169/itej.55.1053
9. Lim, E., Honjo, T.: Validity of VRML images in landscape evaluation. Journal of Japanese Institute of Landscape Architecture **65**(5), 693–696 (2001). https://doi.org/10.5632/jila.65.693

10. Kao, C., Fan, I.: A study of image for heroic characters in video games. Asian J. Soc. Sci. Humanit. **4**(1), 118–125 (2015)
11. Shirai, A., Koike, Y., Sato, M.: The quantify of the human excitement while playing computer game. In: Part 1: Categorizing the game genres using the subjective evaluation. Proceedings of Game Programming Workshop 2001, no. 14, pp. 33–40 (2001)
12. Yoshida, J., Hasegawa, H., Kasuga, M.: Selection of evaluation terms for video game contents using cluster analysis. ITE Tech. Rep. **32**(21), 9–12 (2008). https://doi.org/10.11485/itetr.32.21.0_9
13. Swink, S.: Game Feel: A Game Designer's Guide to Virtual Sensation. Taylor & Francis, Abingdon (2009)
14. Juul, J.: A Casual Revolution: Reinventing Video Games and Their Players. MIT Press, Cambridge (2009)
15. Hicks, K., Gerling, K., Dickinson, P. Abeele, V.: Juicy game design: understanding the impact of visual embellishments on player experience. In: Proceedings of the Annual Symposium on Computer–Human Interaction in Play (CHI PLAY 2019), pp. 185–197. ACM, New York (2019). https://doi.org/10.1145/3311350.3347171
16. Juul, J., Jason, B.: Good feedback for bad players? A preliminary study of "juicy" interface feedback. In: Poster session presented at first joint FDG/DiGRA conference, Dundee, United Kingdom (2016)
17. Kao, D.: The effects of juiciness in an action RPG. Entertain. Comput. **34**, 100359 (2020). https://doi.org/10.1016/j.entcom.2020.100359
18. Henshusho, S.: Sanseido hantaigo tairitsu jiten. [Sanseido Dictionary of Antonym]. Sanseido, Tokyo (2017). (in Japanese)
19. Tadahiko Fukuda Laboratory, Human Performance Laboratory, Fukuda, T., Fukuda, R.: Ningen kogaku gaido: kansei wo kagakusuru houhou. [Ergonomics Guide: The Science of Sensitivity]. Scientist Press, Tokyo (2009). (in Japanese)
20. Results Presentation of 4th Game Effect Contest. https://youtu.be/uiax-Cp4csY. Accessed 20 June 2018
21. Results Presentation of 5th Game Effect Contest. https://youtu.be/uTiu-XhpuBIm. Accessed 20 June 2018
22. Game Effect Contest Official, https://www.gameeffectcontest.com/. Accessed 20 June 2018
23. QuestionPro. https://www.questionpro.com/ja/. Accessed 24 Aug 2018
24. Ravaja, N., Saari, T., Salminen, M., Laarni, J., Kallinen, K.: Phasic emotional reactions to video game events: a psychophysiological investigation. Media Psychol. **8**(4), 343–367 (2006). https://doi.org/10.1207/s1532785xmep0804_2
25. Agui, T., Nagao, T., Nakajima, M.: A study for image retrieval using semantic differential technique. J. Inst. Telev. Eng. Jpn. **44**(6), 788–790 (1990). https://doi.org/10.3169/itej1978.44.788
26. Unity AssetStore. https://assetstore.unity.com/. Accessed 30 Dec 2020
27. Yamamoto, H., Nakamura, T., Miyata, K., Sato, H.: Selecting pairs of adjectives for semantic differential method for evaluating impression given by video game effects. ITE Tech. Rep. **43**(9), 109–112 (2019)

A Review of Automated Website Usability Evaluation Tools: Research Issues and Challenges

Abdallah Namoun$^{(\boxtimes)}$ [iD], Ahmed Alrehaili [iD], and Ali Tufail [iD]

Faculty of Computer and Information Systems, Islamic University in Madinah, Madinah, Saudi Arabia
{a.namoun,alrehailiium,ali.tufail}@iu.edu.sa

Abstract. Web usability is a critical factor for visitors' acceptance and satisfaction. The prevalence of various free and proprietary website testing tools enabled the fast evaluation of the usability of websites. However, their effectiveness in providing meaningful, consistent, and valid results remains questionable. In this study, we initially devised a usability framework that incorporates 19 usability dimensions and investigated the compliance of 10 popular web usability testing tools to this framework. Next, we applied the automated evaluation to nine websites spanning three major categories, namely e-commerce, vacation rentals, and education. On a positive note, the tools inspected a wide range of aspects, including performance, SEO, page size, accessibility, and security. However, our in-depth analysis revealed numerous critical issues. First, usability seems to be ignored or distorted by most of the tools. Second, the automated tools exhibited variable and contradictory scores concerning the analysis of the same websites. Third, the analysis reports were vague and complicated for non-technical users. Fourth, the tools identified and explained issues affecting the technical implementation of the websites, overlooking web usability flaws. Fifth, only four tools (i.e., SEOptimiser, Dareboost, Website Grader, and Sure Oak) gave recommendations to remedy performance bottlenecks and improve the quality of the websites. Lastly, the inner working of the tools does not seem to incorporate the theoretical foundations of usability, which calls for urgent collaboration between industry experts and HCI practitioners and researchers.

Keywords: Automatic web usability evaluation · Perceived usability · Automated web evaluation tools · Usability testing · Website design · Web usability issues

1 Introduction

The recent statistics indicate that there are approximately 1.82 billion websites worldwide, used by more than 4.66 billion active users [28]. Positively perceived usability is a vital ingredient to websites acceptance and continued success [10]. Al-Debei et al. [21] consider usability as a key web quality metric, which in turn affects the perceived

© Springer Nature Switzerland AG 2021
M. M. Soares et al. (Eds.): HCII 2021, LNCS 12779, pp. 292–311, 2021.
https://doi.org/10.1007/978-3-030-78221-4_20

benefits and trust towards online shopping. Moreover, the first few seconds of the user interaction with websites are proclaimed to have a lasting impact on the user impression and potential future re-visits [25, 26]. Indeed, the Internet is buzzing with both off-the-shelf commercial and research website analysis tools to assist web designers and site owners in forming an initial understanding of their websites' perceived usability (e.g., [3]). However, it remains unclear how these testing tools contribute towards (1) identifying the real usability problems users face and (2) improving web designs through practical recommendations. Moreover, these tools provide contradictory results raising questions about the validity and consistency of their suggestions [3].

Website evaluation may take varying forms, including heuristic evaluation, cognitive walkthrough, user testing, analytical modeling, and automated evaluation [22, 23]. Understanding the usability of a website without involving human subjects offers several benefits, such as reducing the testing costs, detecting errors and issues early, and quickly evaluating the design aspects of the site [24]. These benefits can be realized using automated website evaluation tools. However, the first step towards verifying whether the website evaluation tools are providing meaningful and useful results is to identify the appropriate dimensions of usability to be measured. In other words, what are the boundaries within which one has to evaluate the websites' perceived usability?

This paper provides an up-to-date and in-depth analysis of the recent website usability evaluation tools, focusing on their key features, strengths, and weaknesses. Website usability testing tools are continually evolving and adjusting to the technological changes taking place. We systematically chose and analyzed ten testing tools. We applied the evaluation on selected popular websites spanning different domains to understand their effectiveness and consistency. The research presented herein is motivated by three key research questions:

- **RQ1.** What usability dimensions are evaluated by the current web usability testing tools?
  This question aims to explore the conformance of the testing tools to the well-defined dimensions of usability. This will empower us to identify the gaps between the theoretical recommendations in academia and real practices in the industry.
- **RQ2.** What aspects and features do these testing tools assess that could help designers understand the quality of their websites?
  This question aims to understand the features that are considered relevant to assessing the quality of websites. Moreover, attempting to answer this question will inform us about the tools' consistency concerning the analysis results. This question aims to understand the features that are considered relevant to assessing the quality of websites. Moreover, attempting to answer this question will inform us about the tools' consistency concerning the analysis results.
- **RQ3.** What issues prevail during the use of automated web usability testing tools?
  This question aims to pinpoint the shortcomings and challenges of operating the selected tools and interpret the results of the analysis. We hope that answers to this question will motivate the developers of these tools to elevate any challenges.

The remainder of this paper is divided into five sections. Section two reviews the concept of usability and works undertaken in this area. Section three details the materials and testing procedures that were followed to analyze the results of the selected tools. Section four presents the results of the web usability testing of nine different websites. Section five highlights the current issues of automated web evaluation. Section six summarizes some key recommendations for future research.

2 Background Works

2.1 Web Usability and Its Dimension

Indeed, usability is a complex construct that incorporates several dimensions. The traditional definition stipulates usability from three perspectives, namely effectiveness, efficiency, and satisfaction [14]. However, recent usability models extend this definition to include further constructs, such as learnability, flexibility, performance, among others [1, 2, 6]. There is an overarching need to understand the user interface elements and factors that influence website design and usability [11, 13]. As such, we conducted a survey of the standard dimensions of usability for inclusion as a criterion of analysis. Subsequently, we benchmarked the most popular web evaluation tools against the usability definitions and dimensions reported in the literature (see Table 1).

Table 1. Common usability dimensions extracted from relevant works.

Usability Dimension	Jokela et al. [14]	Quesenbery [6]	Chen et al. [12]	Green and Pearson [11]	Nielsen [15]	Verkijika and De Wet [30]
Effectiveness	✓	✓	✓			
Efficiency	✓	✓	✓		✓	
Satisfaction	✓		✓		✓	
Engagement		✓				
Error tolerance		✓			✓	
Learnability		✓	✓		✓	
User-related attributes			✓			
Memorability					✓	
Online services						✓
Accessibility						✓
Information Architecture						✓
User help						✓
Navigation			✓			✓
Legitimacy						✓
Content			✓			
Credibility			✓			
Interactivity			✓			
Responsiveness			✓			
Download Delay			✓			

Automating the evaluation of websites usability brings about various tangible benefits such as reducing the costs of analysis (i.e., with respect to time and resources), eliminating the need for usability experts and user testing, and providing objective evaluation results [10]. The usability evaluation of websites has to be linked to measurable and realistic metrics to make any real impact [13]. Below we briefly describe the most notable attempts to automate the measurement of usability evaluation of websites.

Data envelopment analysis was performed on 23 Jordanian universities [7] by utilizing four tools, namely GSiteCrawler, Site24x7, Web page size lookup, and Maximine. The study focused on extracting essential features of the websites to improve the usability, design, and performance. The authors claim that only four websites could be classified as efficient. Similarly, Benaida and Namoun [8] used Web Page Analyser and GTmetrix to evaluate seven key usability components for three Arabic websites. The study concluded that modern websites still suffer from various performance issues, including slow loading speed.

Website Grader and PageRank Checker were utilized by Mittal and Sridaran [9] to rank 10 Indian university websites. The authors proposed a set of guidelines to improve the performance of the websites. However, they did not make use of elaborative parameters to measure the usability, design, and performance of the websites. Kwangsawad et al. [4] used SEOptimer, Website Grader, and Qualidator to measure several factors of website quality. Nevertheless, this study focused on a single website and did not cover other websites for comparison.

Amilbahar and Cordero [5] evaluated the performance of the Department of Education website in the Philippines. They employed various tools, such as Site Analyzer, SEO Site Checkup, Website Grader, and Lipperhey. The analysis revealed many weaknesses concerning several usability parameters. In another study, Kaur et al. [3] assessed the usability of several Indian websites using four tools with respect to performance, number of requests, speed, among others. The selected tools included Pingdom, GTmetrix, Website Grader, and Site Speed Checker.

2.2 Automated Software Testing

Normally the development of software (e.g., websites, applications, and interactive systems) is a daunting and time-consuming activity [34]. The software industry and academic communities perform different types of testing to ensure the quality of the produced software artifacts [32]. Efforts to automate testing have emerged to cut costs and expedite the development process [31]. This process is usually referred to as test automation. Alas, industry-academia collaboration to provide adequate testing was highlighted as a significant issue [33]. Garousi et al. [32, 34] recommend providing additional ways for software engineers to improve the reliability of their testing. The literature instructs carrying out several automated tests, including load, stress, performance, and user interface tests [34]. Our research helps bridge the gap between industry and academia to ameliorate the evaluation of the quality of websites.

2.3 Web Usability Testing Landscape

Kronbauer et al. [16] proposed a hybrid usability evaluation of smartphone applications. With the help of experimental studies, they concluded that evaluating smartphone applications by combining metrics, contextual, and user feelings' data could benefit both the developers and users of web applications. Similarly, Bader and Pagano [18] propose a lightweight and automated method to capture mobile applications' usability issues. Their proposed heuristic can help to find out low discoverability issues. Gonzalez-Calleros et al. [19] propose yet another automated user interface evaluation method. The study is based on the UsiXML to measure the performance of users using various parameters, including user errors, total execution time, and workload.

Website usability and user experience are considered very important. However, it is costly to measure them both [17]. The authors propose a mechanism to collect precise requirements to test the user experience thoroughly. Later, they propose an open-source tool that can be used to perform usability testing. The post-deployment usability bugs report contributes to most of the cost required for software maintenance [20]. The communication gap between the developer and end-users is thought to be the main contributor to these usability bugs. The authors suggest a usability evaluation framework that can precisely measure the usability metrics. They tested their framework on two real industrial software systems.

3 Materials and Methodology

Usability evaluation techniques may take various shapes, including surveys, interviews, cognitive walkthrough, and user testing [35]. Surveys and user testing were the most used evaluation techniques making up 40% of the techniques. However, given our study's context and motivations, we opted to apply automated evaluation using software [35]. In this type of evaluation, a software tool is used to simulate user activities and record performance results. The software tool often generates reports and logs to identify any potential issues and suggest actionable recommendations for designers.

We selected and investigated ten state-of-the-art web testing tools comprehensively. To reduce bias, our selection of the tools was performed systematically. Effectively, we have (1) conducted a free search on Google search engine and checked online tool reviews and (2) reviewed related studies over the past ten years (2010–2021). Next, we have calculated the occurrence (i.e., popularity) of each tool. The leading search words and phrases that were used to retrieve the selected tools included: ("usability testing tools", "web usability testing tools", "automated web evaluation tools").

However, since our searches returned testing tools covering different areas, we applied some exclusion criteria to finalize our list. Table 2 summarizes the critical exclusion criteria that were applied. Out of the returned pool, the top 10 reported website analysis tools were chosen for inclusion in our automated web evaluation. Table 3 highlights the key features of the selected automated web usability evaluation tools.

The procedure of our automated usability evaluation comprised the following activities:

Table 2. Inclusion criteria for web usability analysis tools.

Inclusion Criteria	Criterion
Focus of testing	Web usability
Year	[2010 - February 2021]
Pricing	Free
Type of testing	Automated
Availability	Available (Not discontinued)
Evaluation score	Scores in 100% or A-F range

- Selecting nine websites from three genres, specifically e-commerce, vacation rental, and education (i.e., university) due to their increased importance (see Table 4).
- Running a full usability analysis on each website using each of the ten web usability evaluation tools (listed in Table 3).

Table 3. Our selected web usability testing tools.

Web evaluation tool	Focus of the tool	Free/Licensed	Key features	Metrics measured
Website Grader [38]	Grade a given website and highlight the weaknesses	Licensed	Checks a specific site for page titles, meta descriptions, and headings	Performance, SEO, Mobile-friendliness, Security
Site Analyzer [37]	Perform a 360° analysis for any website	Licensed	Performs crawling, rank tracking, backlinks, and page analysis	SEO, Performance
SEOptimiser [36]	Identify problems and suggest actionable recommendations	Licensed	Offers white label reports, SEO crawler, and auditing	SEO, Usability, Performance, Social, Security
GTmetrix [39]	Performs the analysis and suggests features and options to optimize the website	Free/ Licensed	Analyzes the webpage with Google Lighthouse, suggests performance improvements related to Largest Contentful Paint, Total Blocking Time, and Cumulative Layout Shift	Performance, speed, number of issues, page size, structure

(continued)

Table 3. (*continued*)

Web evaluation tool	Focus of the tool	Free/Licensed	Key features	Metrics measured
Web Dev [40]	Suggests steps to improve the user experience	Free	Provides tools for web development, audit and performance measurement. Provides guidance to enhance performance	SEO, best practices, performance, accessibility, speed Index, number of issues
Dareboost [41]	Performs an in-depth audit and suggests features to optimize the website	Free	Performance test, web page analysis, competitive analysis	Latency, weight, speed, number of issues
Page Locity [42]	Analyzes the web page and recommends steps for optimization	Free	Performs analysis to check the web content, gives recommendations to improve the performance and improve the code structure	SEO, Code Insights, performance, number of issues
Nibbler [43]	Provides a report with detailed scores of 10 key performance parameters	Free	The given website is analyzed on the pre-set parameters, and a scoring report is generated for the website	Experience, technology, accessibility, marketing, mobile optimization
Sure Oak [44]	Checks the websites against various parameters and provides the scores and recommendation report	Free	Sure Oak uses website SEO checker to measure several factors, including SEO, usability, security, etc. The report also provides the recommendation for performance optimization	SEO, usability, performance, security, number of issues, page size, social
Geek Flare [45]	Performs the audit of the given website with more than 50 parameters and recommends improvements	Free	Geek Flare audits the website on various parameters like performance, time etc. using different tools. The report includes recommendations for improvement	Performance, score, best practice score, SEO score, loaded time, page size

- Inspecting and contrasting the scores and reports generated by the tools.
- Evaluating the usability of the tools and benchmarking them against the dimensions specified in Table 1.

Table 4. Our selected websites for the automated evaluation.

	Genre One: E-commerce	Genre Two: Vacation Rentals	Genre Three: Education
The selected websites	1. Amazon (www. amazon.com)	1. Airbnb (www.air bnb.com)	1. Cambridge university (www. cam.ac.uk)
	2. Ebay (www.ebay. com)	2. Baitok (www.bai tok.com)	2. MIT university (www.mit.edu)
	3. Alibaba.com (www.alibaba. com)	3. Booking (www. booking.com)	3. Harvard university (www.harvard.edu)

Figure 1 shows examples of analysis results of two tools, e.g., Dareboost and Web Dev, applied to Amazon and Baitok websites, respectively.

Fig. 1. Sample results: Amazon website analyzed by Dareboost (left) and Baitok website analyzed by Web Dev (right).

4   Results and Discussion

In our comparison quest, we discovered that the usability testing tools provide a myriad of results focusing on various unexpected aspects. This section is organized in a way to answer the questions posited in the Introduction section.

RQ1. What usability dimensions are evaluated by the current web usability testing tools?

One of the essential aspects that we investigated is the number of usability dimensions assessed by the ten tools. Our literature review revealed approximately 19 dimensions that make up the concept of usability (refer to Table 1). However, our in-depth inspection showed that only nine dimensions are evaluated by the analysis tools, as shown in Table 5. These dimensions include content (9/10), download delay (9/10), efficiency (8/10), accessibility (7/10), information architecture (4/10), navigation (2/10), interactivity (2/10), and responsiveness (1/10). SEOptimiser came out as the most comprehensive analysis tool covering up to 6 usability dimensions, followed by Site Analyzer, Website Grader, Web Dev, and Sure Oak (5 dimensions each).

Notably, 11 key usability dimensions, such as effectiveness, engagement, error tolerance, learnability, user-related attributes, memorability, online services, user help, legitimacy, and credibility were not evaluated by the tools. On the other hand, the testing tools measured other aspects (e.g., code insights, technology, SEO, and security) that are not captured in the previous works listed in Table 1. This is discussed in detail in the next research question (RQ2).

Table 5. Usability dimensions assessed by web analysis tools; the most common in bold.

Usability Dimension	#/10	SEOptimiser	Site Analyzer	Website Grader	GTmetrix	Web Dev	Dareboost	Page Locity	Nibbler	Sure Oak	Geek Flare
Effectiveness	0										
Efficiency	**8**	✓	✓	✓	✓	✓		✓		✓	✓
Satisfaction	1								✓		
Engagement	0										
Error Tolerance	0										
Learnability	0										
User-related attributes	0										
Memorability	0										
Online services	0										
Accessibility	**7**	✓	✓	✓		✓	✓		✓	✓	
Information											
Architecture	4		✓		✓			✓	✓		
User help	0										
Navigation	2	✓				✓					
Legitimacy	0										
Content	**9**	✓	✓	✓		✓	✓	✓	✓	✓	✓
Credibility	0										
Interactivity	2	✓								✓	
Responsiveness	1			✓							
Download delay	**9**	✓	✓	✓	✓	✓	✓	✓		✓	✓
Total	-	6	5	5	3	5	3	4	4	5	3

RQ2. What aspects and features do these testing tools assess that could help designers understand the quality of their websites?

A total of 23 aspects were evaluated by ten usability testing tools (Table 6). The most occurring aspects were overall score (8 times), performance (8 times), search engine optimization (SEO) (7 times), page size (6 times), number of issues (5 times), and number of recommendations (4 times). The remaining aspects (i.e., 17) appeared in no more than 3 tools. This signifies discrepancies in the aspects deemed as essential for website quality by each tool. Interesting, only two tools referred to usability, namely SEOptimiser and Sure Oak. The design aspect was measured by Site Analyser. Website accessibility was measured by three tools only (i.e., Site Analyser, Web Dev, and Nibbler).

Table 6. Web quality aspects measured by our usability testing tools, most common in bold.

Criterion	#/10	SEOptimiser	Site Analyzer	Website Grader	GTmetrix	Web Dev	Dareboost	Page Locity	Nibbler	Sure Oak	Geek Flare
Overall Score	8	✓	✓	✓	✓	χ	✓	✓	✓	✓	χ
Performance	**8**	✓	✓	✓	✓	✓	χ	✓	χ	✓	✓
SEO	**7**	✓	✓	✓	χ	✓	χ	✓	χ	✓	✓
Page Size	**6**	✓	χ	✓	✓	χ	✓	χ	χ	✓	✓
# of Issues	**5**	χ	✓	χ	✓	✓	✓	✓	χ	χ	χ
# of Recommendations	**4**	✓	χ	✓	χ	χ	✓	χ	χ	✓	χ
Security	3	✓	χ	✓	χ	χ	χ	χ	χ	✓	χ
Accessibility	3	χ	✓	χ	χ	✓	χ	χ	✓	χ	χ
Social	2	✓	χ	χ	χ	χ	χ	χ	χ	✓	χ
Best Practices	2	χ	χ	χ	χ	✓	χ	χ	χ	χ	✓
Loading time	2	χ	χ	χ	✓	χ	χ	χ	χ	χ	✓
Usability	2	✓	χ	χ	χ	χ	χ	χ	χ	✓	χ
Speed	2	χ	χ	✓	χ	χ	✓	χ	χ	χ	χ
Speed Index	1	χ	χ	χ	χ	✓	χ	χ	χ	χ	χ
Mobile Optimization	1	χ	χ	χ	χ	χ	χ	χ	✓	χ	χ
Latency	1	χ	χ	χ	χ	χ	✓	χ	χ	χ	χ
Marketing	1	χ	χ	χ	χ	χ	χ	χ	✓	χ	χ
Design	1	χ	✓	χ	χ	χ	χ	χ	χ	χ	χ
Content	1	χ	✓	χ	χ	χ	χ	χ	χ	χ	χ
Structure	1	χ	χ	χ	✓	χ	χ	χ	χ	χ	χ
Code Insights	1	χ	χ	χ	χ	χ	χ	✓	χ	χ	χ
Technology	1	χ	χ	χ	χ	χ	χ	χ	✓	χ	χ
Experience	1	χ	χ	χ	χ	χ	χ	χ	✓	χ	χ
Total ✓	-	8	7	7	6	7	6	5	6	8	5
Total χ	-	15	16	16	17	16	17	18	17	18	18

Figure 2. shows that the page size (measured in megabytes) calculated by the tools differed considerably even for the same websites. SEOptimiser and Sure Oak gave similar results. E-commerce websites were reported to have the lagest size in comparison to holiday rentals and education websites. This is anticipated since e-commerce websites host many products that are usually exhibited in the form of images. It is well known that page size impacts the performance and loading time of websites.

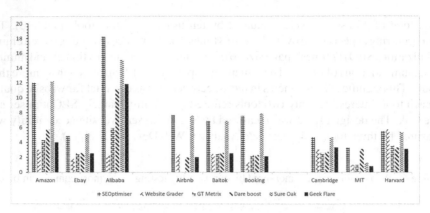

Fig. 2. Page size (in MB) of all websites as calculated by the analysis tools.

A close look at the performance analysis shows fluctuating scores for the same website using different testing tools (see Fig. 3). The scores are assigned out of 100, ranging between 47 and 75/100. Generally, the education websites received the highest performance scores (mean score = 69.75) in comparison to the e-commerce (mean score = 56.45) and holiday rentals (mean score = 50.20) websites.

The Harvard website and Ebay website showed the highest deviation from the average performance score. Despite their low average scores, the holiday rental websites showed the least fluctuation in their performance scores.

Search engine optimization (aka SEO) focuses on increasing user traffic to the website by optimizing its content and adding catchy keywords to the metadata of the site. Moreover, SEO helps websites become more discoverable by web crawlers of major search engines such as Google, Bing, and Yahoo. The nine websites' SEO median scores ranged from 68 to 92/100, as depicted in Fig. 4. The score variability was significant for three websites, namely Alibaba, Airbnb, and Amazon. The educational websites exhibited the least discrepancies and best SEO scores.

Figure 5 depicts the number of issues identified by five analysis tools on our selected websites. Site Analyzer reports, on average, the maximum number of issues (i.e., 18) across all categories. Whereas GTmetrix reports the least number of issues (i.e., 5) across all categories. In the education category, all tools reported the highest number of issues on the MIT website, while in vacation rentals, most issues were linked to the Baitok website. Lastly, for the e-commerce category, Alibaba suffered from the highest number of issues.

Only five analysis tools (i.e., Dareboost, Site Analyzer, Web Dev, Page Locity, and GTmetrix) were powered to extract and report issues, focusing mainly on security, best practices, SEO, and performance. Table 7 highlights various security issues, which are identified by just three tools, i.e., Dareboost, Site Analyzer, and Web Dev. The tools consider at least one of the security issues in their testing process. Site Analyzer assesses the maximum number of security aspects (6/11), while Dareboost assesses five security aspects and Web Dev assesses only one security aspect (e.g., JavaScript vulnerabilities). Boosting the security of websites may enhance user trust and credibility of the site.

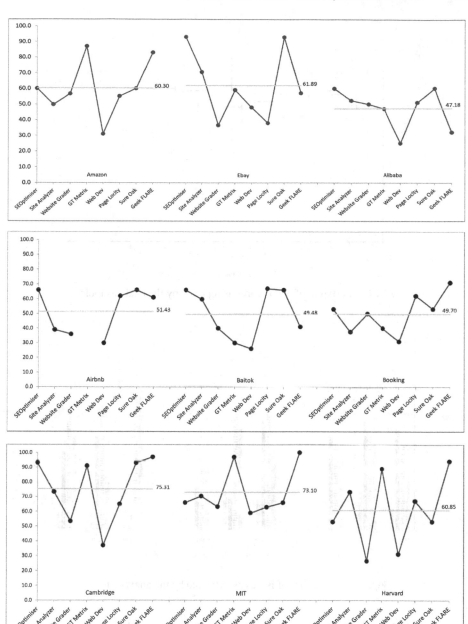

Fig. 3. Performance analysis of e-commerce (top), vacation rentals (middle), and education (bottom) websites; scores are assigned out of 100.

Table 8 refers to the non-conformance in implementing the best practices by the selected websites. Four analysis tools assessed nine best practices, mainly image resizing,

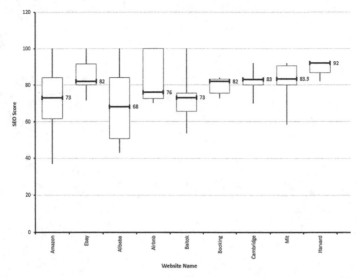

Fig. 4. A boxplot of SEO scores as reported by the analysis tools.

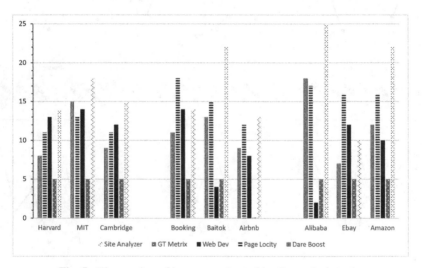

Fig. 5. The number of issues as extracted by the analysis tools.

number of links, color contrast, among others. Site Analyzer and Web Dev measure four best practices, while Dareboost measures three best practices, and Page Locity measures only one best practice.

Table 9 highlights the major SEO issues detected within the websites. 11 SEO criteria were evaluated by the tools, focusing on alternative text for images and text title, heading issues, robots.txt file, among others. Site Analyzer measures six SEO aspects, followed by Dareboost (five aspects), Page Locity (four aspects), and Web Dev (three aspects).

Table 7. Security-related issues as identified by the analysis tools.

Security Themes	Occurrences	Analysis Tools
Issues related to content security policy/header	2	Dareboost, Site Analyzer
Includes JavaScript libraries with known security vulnerabilities	1	Web Dev
Page is exposed to "clickjacking" type attacks	1	Dareboost
SSL certificate	1	Dareboost
X-XSS- Protection	1	Site Analyzer
2 cookies are not secure	1	Dareboost
Disable the auto detection of resource type	1	Dareboost
www redirection 301	1	Site Analyzer
Reliable links	1	Site Analyzer
Page shows technologies installed on your web server	1	Site Analyzer
Deploy IPv6 protocol	1	Site Analyzer

Table 8. Best practices-related issues as identified by the analysis tools.

Best Practices Themes	Occurrences	Analysis Tools
Images are resized on browser side	2	Dareboost, Web Dev
Links related Issues such as discernible name link canonical, huge number of links	2	Web Dev, Site Analyzer
Labels related issues	2	Dareboost, Site Analyzer
Background and foreground colors do not have a sufficient contrast ratio	1	Web Dev
A HTML tag has 7 classes	1	Page Locity
Buttons do not have an accessible name,	1	Web Dev
642 CSS selectors are too complex	1	Dareboost
Language has to be defined, Microdata, No script tag	1	Site Analyzer
Social Media linking: Twitter card	1	Site Analyzer

Table 10 summarizes the key issues impacting the performance of websites. Overall, the tools measure 19 diverse performance criteria. These criteria focus on web implementation malpractices, server delays, use of unnecessary resources, and disuse of content delivery networks. These issues increase the loading time of the sites, which eventually influences user satisfaction. A total of five tools measure at least one of the performance parameters. Dareboost measures 10 parameters, followed by Web Dev (9/19), GTmetrix (5/19), Page Locity (4/19), and Site Analyzer (4/19).

Table 9. SEO-related issues as extracted by the analysis tools.

SEO Themes	Occurrences	Analysis Tools
Alternative text missing	3	Page Locity, Site Analyzer, Dareboost
Titles related issues	2	Site Analyzer, Page Locity
Text/html ratio is too low	2	Page Locity, Site Analyzer
Site doesn't use Open Graph properties	2	Dareboost, Site Analyzer
Heading related issues	2	Page Locity, Web Dev
Robots.txt is not defined	2	Web Dev, Dareboost
Keywords density	1	Site Analyzer
Sitemap	1	Site Analyzer
Links crawlability	1	Web Dev
Explain the purpose of each from field	1	Dareboost
Some resources do not define their content type	1	Dareboost

Table 10. Performance-related issues as extracted by the evaluation tools.

Performance Themes	Occurrences	Analysis Tools
Alternative text missing	4	Page Locity, Site Analyzer, Dareboost, Web Dev
Avoid the inline CSS	3	Page Locity, Site Analyzer, Dareboost
Server response time has to be faster	3	Web Dev, Page Locity, Dareboost
Remove unused JavaScript/Resources	3	Web Dev, Dareboost, Page Locity
Avoid integrating your styles directly into HTML file	2	Site Analyzer, Dareboost
Eliminate render blocking resources	2	GTmetrix, Web Dev
Removed duplicated or unused CSS	2	Web Dev, Dareboost
Separate/Group JavaScript file to optimize loading time	2	Site Analyzer, Dareboost
Deploying CDN	1	GTmetrix
Long main thread tasks	1	GTmetrix

(*continued*)

Table 10. (*continued*)

Performance Themes	Occurrences	Analysis Tools
Avoid chaining critical requests	1	GTmetrix
Use HTTP/2	1	GTmetrix
Browser errors were logged to the console	1	Web Dev
Images are loaded too early	1	Dareboost
Preload key requests	1	Web Dev
Avoid http-equiv <meta> tags	1	Dareboost
Missing children of elements with an ARIA '[role]'	1	Web Dev
Missing source maps for large first-party JavaScript	1	Web Dev
One resource is unreachable	1	Dareboost

Figure 6 depicts the number of recommendations suggested by four testing tools, namely Dareboost, Sure Oak, Website Grader, and SEOptimiser. Overall, the number of recommendations produced to improve the quality of e-commerce websites exceeded the recommendations suggested for educational and vacation rental websites. The analysis was inconsistent, showing varied results for the same site (e.g., Alibaba, Booking, and Amazon), yielding between 2 and 20 recommendations per site. SEOptimiser and Sure Oak gave considerably more recommendations in comparison to Website Grader and Dareboost. In all websites, Website Grader gave the least number of suggestions.

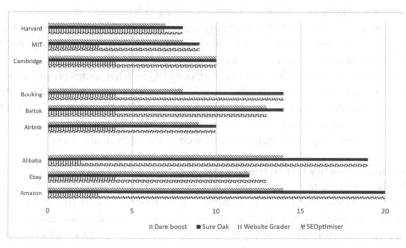

Fig. 6. The number of recommendations provided by the web analysis tools.

4.1   Final Verdict on the Web Usability Evaluation Tools

To rank the analysis of candidate tools, we judged them on three metrics, specifically (1) consistency of analysis, (2) depth of analysis reports, and (3) clarity of issues and recommendations. Overall, there was no clear, holistic winner for all evaluation criteria since each tool outperformed its rivals in different aspects. However, the tools that seem to provide broad, consistent, and thorough analysis include Web Dev, Dareboost, and SEOptimiser (see Table 11).

Table 11. The final verdict on current website evaluation tools.

Judgement Criterion	1st Rank	2nd Rank	3rd Rank
Performance	Web Dev	Page Locity	Site Analyzer
SEO	Page Locity	Geek Flare	Site Analyzer
Number of issues	Dareboost	Site Analyzer	Web Dev
Number of recommendations	SEOptimiser	Sure Oak	Dareboost
Page size	Dareboost	Geek Flare	GTmetrix
Accessibility	Web Dev	Nibbler	Site Analyzer
Security	Website Grader	SEOptimiser	Sure Oak

5   Major Research Issues and Challenges

The results show that automated web analysis tools measure a bench of various quality constructs, such as performance, SEO, and security, which might be considered more critical than usability. Moreover, no single testing tool covers all usability dimensions suggested in the literature (Table 1). Usability seems to be viewed as a holistic concept, and it is unclear which attributes are being considered by the tools to assess website usability. When we applied the tools on the nine popular websites, the analysis reports revealed discrepancies in the quality and usability scores for the same site.

In attempting to answer the third question (i.e., RQ3- What issues prevail during the use of automated web usability testing tools?), the findings demonstrate that, although the automated evaluation tools are generally easy to operate, the results might not be so obvious to read and interpret. Below we conclude with a set of issues that ought to be addressed to ameliorate the effectiveness of web usability evaluation tools.

- **Issue One: Usability lost in translation**
  All but two tools did not measure the construct of usability directly despite its increased importance. Moreover, it was observed that, at best, only 6 out of 19 usability dimensions were assessed by the evaluation tools. The tools focused on assessing other features, such as performance, SEO, and page size. Undeniably these aspects do impact the perceived usability; however, the analysis did not link the results to clear-cut explanations of the usability dimensions, such as efficiency, learnability, memorability, and satisfaction.

- **Issue Two: Inconsistency and invalidity of analysis scores**
  One of the major shortcomings emerging in the analysis is the inconsistency and discrepancy of the overall and feature scores for the same websites. Such variance raises serious concerns about the meaning, validity, and confidence in the results. While this could be associated with the way scores are calculated by each testing tool, it is unclear how the calculations are carried out.
- **Issue Three: Difficult interpretation of testing results**
  Although the scores are assigned by each tool as a percentage out of 100 or A-F rank, it was challenging to understand the produced reports and their explanations. The meaning and rationale for the given scores or ranks were missing. No references or benchmarks were given to enhance our understanding of the actual quality of websites. Moreover, the use of technical jargon by some tools complicated the analysis reports, especially for a non-technical audience.
- **Issue Four: True usability issues are on the run**
  Only five tools extracted issues, but these were related to security, best practices, SEO, and performance. Notably, no single tool extracts and reports web usability issues, which is a major cause of concern about the effectiveness of the current tools for web designers.
- **Issue Five: Lack of actionable recommendations**
  Only four tools offered recommendations, but these were mainly implementation-related suggestions to overcome some of the highlighted issues. These recommendations are generic, vague, and less related to usability, and therefore less useful for the design.
- **Issue Six: Evident gap in industry-academia cooperation**
  The obtained results emphasize the need for software testers and HCI researchers to work closely together to tailor the tools for web designers and practitioners. Such tools would need to incorporate various dimensions of usability and design in their analysis.

6   Conclusion

This paper performed an in-depth inspection of ten well-known web usability testing tools. The tools were applied to nine prominent websites spanning three main categories, specifically e-commerce, vacation rentals, and education. Overall, the education websites fared better in most of the tools than e-commerce and holiday rentals websites. Despite the need for automated web testing, the findings demonstrated numerous overarching challenges, including the inconsistency and ambiguity of the evaluation reports. We call upon the research community to conduct user testing and benchmark the results against the usability scores of web testing tools. This will pinpoint any gaps between the tools' analysis and real user experiences. Moreover, industry practitioners and HCI researchers should work hand in hand to facilitate knowledge transfer and incorporate the prominent usability dimensions and theories. In the future, we plan to extend our analysis to other automated tools, especially those assessing mobile web interfaces.

References

1. Hamzah, A., Wahid, F.: Reexamining usability dimensions: the case of social media. In: 3rd International Conference on Information and Communication Technology (ICoICT) , Bali Indonesia, pp. 332–335. IEEE (2015)
2. Bader, F., Schön, E.M., Thomaschewski, J.: Heuristics considering UX and quality criteria for heuristics. Int. J. Interact. Multimedia Artif. Intell. **4**(6) (2017)
3. Kaur, S., Kaur, K., Kaur, P.: An empirical performance evaluation of universities website. Int. J. Comput. Appl. **146**(15), 10–16 (2016)
4. Kwangsawad, A., Jattamart, A., Nusawat, P.: The performance evaluation of a website using automated evaluation tools. In: 4th Technology Innovation Management and Engineering Science International Conference (TIMES-iCON) , Thailand, pp. 1–5. IEEE (2019)
5. Amilbahar, S.J., Cordero Jr, M.A.: Website performance analysis of the learner information system (LIS)-department of education. In: 12th CEBU Int'l Conference on Advances in Science, Engineering and Technology (ICASET). Cebu Philippines (2018)
6. Quesenbery, W.: The five dimensions of usability. Content and complexity: Information design in technical communication, 1st edn. Routledge, New York (2003)
7. Najadat, H., Al-Badarneh, A., Al-Huthaifi, R., Abo-Zaitoon, A., Al-Omary, Y.: Evaluating Jordanian universities' websites based on data envelopment analysis. In: 8th International Conference on Information and Communication Systems (ICICS) , Irbid Jordan, pp. 159–164. IEEE (2017)
8. Benaida, M., Namoun, A.: Technical and perceived usability issues in arabic educational websites. Int. J. Adv. Comput. Sci. Appl. **9**(5), 391–400 (2018)
9. Mittal, A., Sridaran, R.: Evaluation of websites' performance and search engine optimization: a case study of 10 Indian University Websites. In: 6th International Conference on Computing for Sustainable Global Development (INDIACom), New Delhi India, pp. 1227–1231. IEEE, March 2019
10. Dingli, A., Cassar, S.: An intelligent framework for website usability. In: Advances in Human-Computer Interaction, pp. 1687–5893 (2014)
11. Pearson, J.M., Pearson, A., Green, D.: Determining the importance of key criteria in web usability. Management Research News (2007)
12. Chen, Y.H., Germain, C.A., Rorissa, A.: An analysis of formally published usability and Web usability definitions. Proc. Am. Soc. Inf. Sci. Technol. **46**(1), 1–18 (2009)
13. Esmeria, G.J., Seva, R.R.: Web usability: a literature review. In: DLSU Research Congress (2017)
14. Jokela, T., Iivari, N., Matero, J., Karukka, M.: The standard of user-centered design and the standard definition of usability: analyzing ISO 13407 against ISO 9241–11. In: Proceedings of the Latin American Conference on Human-Computer Interaction, Rio de Janeiro Brazil, pp. 53–60. Association for Computing Machinery (2003)
15. Nielsen, J.: Usability 101: Introduction to usability (2012). https://www.nngroup.com/articles/usability-101-introduction-to-usability/. Accessed 29 Oct 2020
16. Kronbauer, A.H., Santos, C.A.S., Vieira, V.: Smartphone applications usability evaluation: a hybrid model and its implementation. In: Winckler, M., Forbrig, P., Bernhaupt, R. (eds.) HCSE 2012. LNCS, vol. 7623, pp. 146–163. Springer, Heidelberg (2012). https://doi.org/10.1007/978-3-642-34347-6_9
17. Sivaji, A., Tzuaan, S.S.: Website user experience (UX) testing tool development using Open Source Software (OSS). In: Southeast Asian Network of Ergonomics Societies Conference (SEANES), Langkawi Malaysia, pp. 1–6. IEEE (2012)
18. Bader, D., Pagano, D.: Towards automated detection of mobile usability issues. In: Software Engineering 2013-Workshopband. Society for Computer Science, Aachen Germany (2013)

19. Gonzalez-Calleros, J., Osterloh, J.P., Feil, R., Lüdtke, A.: Automated UI evaluation based on a cognitive architecture and UsiXML. Sci. Comput. Program. **86**, 43–57 (2014)
20. Muhi, K., et al.: A semi-automatic usability evaluation framework. In: Murgante, B., Misra, S., Carlini, M., Torre, C.M., Nguyen, H.-Q., Taniar, D., Apduhan, B.O., Gervasi, O. (eds.) ICCSA 2013. LNCS, vol. 7972, pp. 529–542. Springer, Heidelberg (2013). https://doi.org/10.1007/978-3-642-39643-4_38
21. Al-Debei, M.M., Akroush, M.N., Ashouri, M.I.: Consumer attitudes towards online shopping. Internet Research (2015)
22. Fernandez, A., Insfran, E., Abrahão, S.: Usability evaluation methods for the web: a systematic mapping study. Inf. Softw. Technol. **53**(8), 789–817 (2011)
23. Nagpal, R., Mehrotra, D., Bhatia, P.K.: The state of art in website usability evaluation methods. Design Solutions for User-Centric Information Systems, pp. 275–296 (2017)
24. Bakaev, M., Mamysheva, T., Gaedke, M.: Current trends in automating usability evaluation of websites: can you manage what you can't measure?. In: 11th International Forum on Strategic Technology (IFOST), Novosibirsk Russia, pp. 510–514. IEEE (2016)
25. Reinecke, K., et al.: Predicting users' first impressions of website aesthetics with a quantification of perceived visual complexity and colorfulness. In: Proceedings of the SIGCHI conference on human factors in computing systems, pp. 2049–2058. Association for Computing Machinery, Paris France (2013)
26. Pengnate, S., Sarathy, R., Lee, J.: The engagement of website initial aesthetic impressions: an experimental investigation. Int. J. Hum.-Comput. Interact. **35**(16), 1517–1531 (2019)
27. Kaur, S., Kaur, K., Kaur, P.: Analysis of website usability evaluation methods. In: 3rd International Conference on Computing for Sustainable Global Development (INDIACom) 2016, New Delhi India, pp. 1043–1046. IEEE (2016)
28. Internet Stats & Facts: List of Internet, eCommerce, Hosting, Mobile & Social Media Statistics for 2021. https://websitesetup.org/news/internet-facts-stats/. Accessed 08 Feb 2021
29. Green, D.T., Pearson, J.M.: Integrating website usability with the electronic commerce acceptance model. Behav. Inf. Technol. **30**(2), 181–199 (2011)
30. Verkijika, S.F., De Wet, L.: A usability assessment of e-government websites in Sub-Saharan Africa. Int. J. Inf. Manage. **39**, 20–29 (2018)
31. Ahmad, J., ul Hassan, A., Naqv, T., Mubeen, T.: A Review on Software Testing and Its Methodology. i-Manager's J. Software Eng. **13**(3), 32 (2019)
32. Garousi, V., Felderer, M., Kuhrmann, M., Herkiloğlu, K.: What industry wants from academia in software testing? Hearing practitioners' opinions. In: 21st International Conference on Evaluation and Assessment in Software Engineering, pp. 65–69. Association for Computing Machinery, Karlskrona Sweden (2017)
33. Garousi, V., Felderer, M.: Worlds apart: industrial and academic focus areas in software testing. IEEE Softw. **34**(5), 38–45 (2017)
34. Devi, J., Bhatia, K., Sharma, R.: A relative analysis of programmed web testing tools. Int. Res. J. Eng. Technol. (IRJET) **4**, 386–389 (2017)
35. Paz, F., Pow-Sang, J.A.: A systematic mapping review of usability evaluation methods for software development process. Int. J. Software Eng. Appl. **10**(1), 165–178 (2016)
36. SEOptimer. https://www.seoptimer.com/. Accessed 01 Feb 2021
37. Site Analyzer. https://www.site-analyzer.com/. Accessed 01 Feb 2021
38. Website Grader. https://website.grader.com/. Accessed 01 Feb 2021
39. GTmetrix. https://GTmetrix.com/analyze.html. Accessed 01 Feb 2021
40. Web.Dev. https://web.dev/. Accessed 01 Feb 2021
41. Dareboost. https://www.dareboost.com/. Accessed 01 Feb 2021
42. Page Locity. https://pagelocity.com/. Accessed 01 Feb 2021
43. Nibbler. https://nibbler.silktide.com/. Accessed 01 Feb 2021
44. Sure Oak. https://www.sureoak.com/. Accessed 01 Feb 2021
45. GeekFlare. https://gf.dev/website-audit. Accessed 01 Feb 2021

Web Analytics for User Experience: A Systematic Literature Review

Fryda Palomino$^{(\boxtimes)}$, Freddy Paz , and Arturo Moquillaza

Pontificia Universidad Católica del Perú, Av. Universitaria 1801, San Miguel, Lima 32, Peru
fpalominod@pucp.edu.pe, {fpaz,amoquillaza}@pucp.pe

Abstract. User experience is an essential software quality concept for companies nowadays. Development teams attempt to guarantee that their digital products provide a satisfying experience. Likewise, several evaluation methods have emerged to determine if the software product's interfaces are understandable, intuitive, and attractive to users. However, few of these methods suggest the use of data analytics for user experience evaluation. Many companies use tools that allow them to obtain multiple data about using their leading websites but do not use this information to generate relevant results that can be used to improve the design of their graphical interfaces. In this study, we present the results of conducting a systematic literature review to identify case studies that report web analytics usage to evaluate websites' user experience. The search retrieved a total of 315 papers. The databases used for this review were: Scopus, Web of Science, IEEExplore, and ACM Digital Library. After applying the inclusion and exclusion criteria, 18 relevant articles were obtained, which have allowed answering the research questions. The results show a tendency to incorporate data analysis to explain specific design problems or usability issues. Additionally, we have identified some methodological proposals that have been established on how to use data analytics for the user experience evaluation process and some metrics that could offer relevant information about the degree of ease of use of a website.

Keywords: User experience · Web analytics · Systematic review · Human-computer interaction

1 Introduction

Today, web-based applications have marked their presence in almost every field of our daily lives, from educational websites to e-government portals, online shopping, and many more [1]. All of these applications have a common goal, which is to provide the user with an efficient, effective, secure, and aesthetic tool to help them meet their needs and achieve a goal with effectiveness and satisfaction [2].

In this context, User Experience is a relevant factor to stand out from the business competition. That is, if the user does not perceive a good User Experience as a result when interacting with a website, he will opt for other options available on the Internet [3]. This will generate in the company, losses of potential customers and consumers and

© Springer Nature Switzerland AG 2021
M. M. Soares et al. (Eds.): HCII 2021, LNCS 12779, pp. 312–326, 2021.
https://doi.org/10.1007/978-3-030-78221-4_21

prevent it from achieving its objectives. For this reason, many researchers have developed different methods to evaluate the User Experience. Web Analytics is one method that is beginning to be used to evaluate user behavior on the website.

This is because Web Analytics collects information about how users interact on a website and then transforms it into quantitative data that can be analyzed, offering a variety of information that, depending on the Web Analytics tool used in the evaluation, can provide information from how users arrived at the website to the technical details about the device with which the user accessed the website [4]. Therefore, it is important to know how to identify the metrics and tools to be used in the evaluation to obtain favorable results in the User Experience evaluations.

Besides, one of the advantages present in Web Analytics is that the information obtained by this method belongs to a considerable statistical sample of users. Since, the various tools of Web Analytics capture information from almost all users entering the website [5]. In this way, Web Analytics can help detect potential problems that users experience when interacting with the website.

For this reason, this research work aims to identify studies in the literature where the application of Web Analytics in the evaluation of the User Experience of websites is reported. In this way, to identify the existing metrics and methodologies and how they are used for the evaluation of the User Experience. Also, this review aims to identify the tools used by Web Analytics and determine if the data collected about the use of websites is being used efficiently for decision making in improving the User Experience.

2 Background

For this research, it is important to understand the concepts that will be explained below.

2.1 Web Analytics

Since the first browser and the World Wide Web emerged in 1993, log files have been used to track web requests. Subsequently, the analysis of these log files helped the emergence of Web Analytics to understand the interaction between a user and a website [6].

Web Analytics allows analyzing the behavior of a user when interacting with a website or a mobile application [5] through the collection and subsequent analysis of this collected data. Generally classified in on-site and off-site analysis [7]. On-site analysis refers to the data collected within the website such as, for example, the number of visits to a website, the percentage of people who entered and left without doing anything on the site, the average duration of the session of users, among others. Instead, off-site analysis refers to information that includes data from other sources, generally external sources, such as surveys, market reports, comparison of competitors, etc.

However, a limitation present in Web Analytics is the lack of qualitative understanding of the data collected in the user's interaction with the website [8]. Despite presenting this limitation, it is currently used mostly in traffic monitoring, e-commerce optimization, digital marketing, information architecture, among other uses [6].

2.2 User Experience

With the technology revolution and the emergence of the Internet, the paradigm of empowering a user to use a system shifted to expecting a system to meet user expectations. With this change, concepts such as User Experience, usability, and Human-Computer Interaction began to emerge and gain importance [9].

User Experience, according to ISO 9241–210, is the set of perceptions and responses of a user before, after, or during the use of a product, system or service [10]. This interaction can be direct, operating the website from a device, or indirect, feeling the effect of seeing and thinking about the website [9].

3 Systematic Review

For this research, a systematic review of the state of the art literature was conducted to identify studies related to the objective of this research. For this systematic review, the characteristic methodology in the area of Software Engineering proposed by B. Kitchenham [11] has been used, which proposes the identification, evaluation, and interpretation of all primary studies related to the topic of interest.

3.1 Researched Questions

To meet the objective of the systematic review, the following questions have been proposed:

RQ1: In which application domains is the use of Web Analytics reported for the evaluation of the User Experience and what are its objectives?
RQ2: What metrics are reported to evaluate the User Experience through Web Analytics?
RQ3: What tools are reported to evaluate the user experience through web analytics and what are they used for?
RQ4: What methodologies are reported to evaluate the User Experience through Web Analytics and what advantages/disadvantages do they possess?

To identify the relevant concepts covered in this systematic review, Kitchenham methodology [11] sets out the PICOC criteria (Population, Intervention, Comparison, Outcomes, and Context). In this case, the comparison criterion will not be applied since we are not looking to compare two types of intervention, but rather to establish studies of Web Analytics applied to the domain of sites for the evaluation of User Experience. Table 1 shows the PICOC criterion applied to the project.

3.2 Search Strategy

For the formulation of the search chain, concepts were established to allow greater precision in the results of the relevant information. These concepts were formed from the combination of the terms previously defined in the Population, Intervention, and Outcomes criteria established in Table 1 and their synonyms corresponding to each term.

Table 1. Definition of PICOC criteria

Criterion	Description
Population	Websites
Intervention	Web Analytics
Outcomes	Case studies where Web Analytics methods are applied for the evaluation of User Experience
Context	Academic and Industrial

C1: "stud*" / "research*" / "case*" / "case study"
C2: "method*" / "process" / "technique*"
C3: "analytic*" / "data analytics" / "data-driven
C4: "web"
C5: "user experience" / "UX" / "usability" / "user centered" / "user centered" / "user-centered"

For the construction of the search chain, the OR connectors joined similar terms and the AND connectors joined different concepts. As a result, the final format was obtained ((C1 OR C2) AND C3 AND C4 AND C5), which was adapted to each previously defined search engine. The final search chain was:

(("stud*" OR "research*" OR "case*" OR "case study") OR ("method*" OR "process*" OR "technique*")) AND ("analytic*" OR "data analytics" OR "data-driven") AND ("web") AND ("user experience" OR "UX" OR "usability" OR "user centered" OR "user-centered" OR "user centered") AND PUBYEAR > 2015.

3.3 Search Process

The search process has been considered the most recognized databases in the area of Software Engineering. These databases were Scopus, IEEE Xplorer, ACM Digital Library, and Web of Science.

In addition to the primary search, a secondary search was conducted according to the process established by B. Kitchenham [11]. For this, all the references of the papers considered as relevant studies were reviewed. Based on this review, it was determined that it was necessary to include some of these additional studies. This second review process consisted of selecting those articles from the bibliographic reference that meet the inclusion criteria and whose case study reported is similar to the initial one.

3.4 Selection of Primary Studies

In the total of articles obtained from the primary and second search, relevant articles that meet the following criteria were included in the research: (1) *Studies that report an evaluation of the User Experience of software products through Web Analytics*, (2) *Studies that report web analytics metrics to evaluate the User Experience of software products through Web Analytics*, (3) *Studies that report methodologies for evaluating the*

User Experience of software products through Web Analytics, and (4) *Studies that report tools to evaluate the User Experience of software products through Web Analytics.*

Likewise, papers that meet the following criteria were excluded from the research: (1) *Studies where the User Experience is related to hardware,* and (2) *Studies written in a language other than English or Spanish.*

3.5 Data Extraction

Applying the previously defined search chain, a total of 315 articles were obtained in all the databases, from which, applying the inclusion and exclusion criteria defined later, the relevant articles were obtained. Table 2 shows the detail of the search results obtained.

Table 2. Search results for each database

Databases	Search Results	Duplicate Papers	Relevant Papers
Scopus	246	–	12
ACM	25	7	1
IEEE Xplore	19	6	0
Web of Science	95	42	5
Total	**315**	**55**	**18**

The data extraction form contains both general information for identifying the source of information and information that will help answer the previously defined review questions. The format defined for the data extraction form is shown in Table 3.

Table 3. Data extraction form format

Field	Description	Type Information
ID	Unique code to identify the scientific article	General
Author	Author(s)	General
Title	Title of the scientific article	General
Font type	Magazine, congress, book chapter	General
Source	Name of the magazine, congress, or book	General
Year of publication	Year in which the study was published	General
Link	URL of the article found	General
Country	Country of affiliation of the authors	General

(continued)

Table 3. (*continued*)

Field	Description	Type Information
Database	Name of the search engine where the article was found	General
Case Study	Object of study	Related to question 1
Mastering the case study	Type of study	Related to question 1
The objective of the case study	What is intended to be evaluated or analyzed in the study case?	Related to question 1
Reported Metrics	If metrics were reported in the User Experience (Y/N) evaluation	Related to question 2
Metrics used	What metrics are used in the study	Related to question 2
Reported methodologies	If metrics were reported in the User Experience (Y/N) evaluation	Related to question 3
Methodology used	What methodology is used in the study	Related to question 3
Advantages of the reported methodology	Reported advantages of the methodology used in the case study	Related to question 3
Disadvantages of the reported methodology	Reported disadvantages of the methodology used in the case study	Related to question 3
Reported tools	If metrics were reported in the User Experience (Y/N) evaluation	Related to question 4
Tool used	Which tool is used in the study	Related to question 4
Use of the tool	What the tool specializes in	Related to question 4

3.6 Data Analysis and Results

Finally, we proceeded to analyze the twenty articles identified above to seek to answer the research questions posed at the beginning of chapter two and to determine, subsequently, whether the data collected about website usage is being efficiently leveraged for decision making in improving the User Experience. These papers are described in Table 4.

Table 4. Papers determined as relevant

ID	Paper Title
A01 [8]	Museum Collections and Online Users: Development of a Segmentation Model for the Metropolitan Museum of Art
A02 [12]	Optimizing new user experience in online services
A03 [13]	Analyzing Wikipedia Users 2019; Perceived Quality Of Experience: A Large-Scale Study
A04 [14]	Evaluation of ementalHealth.ca, a Canadian mental health website portal: Mixed methods assessment
A05 [1]	Evaluating usability of a web application: A comparative analysis of open-source tools

(continued)

Table 4. (*continued*)

ID	Paper Title
A06 [15]	Designing the information architecture of a complex website: A strategy based on news content and faceted classification
A07 [16]	UX metrics: Deriving country-specific usage patterns of a website plug-in from web analytics
A08 [17]	U-index: An eye-tracking-tested checklist on webpage aesthetics for university web spaces in Russia and the USA
A09 [18]	Usability and accessibility analysis of selected government websites in Sri Lanka
A10 [19]	Click analytics: What clicks on webpage indicates?
A11 [20]	Validation of the three web quality dimensions of a minimally invasive surgery e-learning platform
A12 [21]	Teaching Intuitive Eating and Acceptance and Commitment Therapy Skills Via a Web-Based Intervention: A Pilot Single-Arm Intervention Study
A13 [22]	Measuring the User Experience on a Large Scale: User-Centered Metrics for Web Applications
A14 [23]	All that glitters isn't gold: The complexities of use statistics as an assessment tool for digital libraries
A15 [24]	Website Redesign: A Case Study
A16 [25]	Evaluating the usability of COMSATS Institute of Information Technology library website A case study
A17 [26]	Mobile Clinical Decision Tools Among Emergency Department Clinicians: Web-Based Survey and Analytic Data for Evaluation of The Ottawa Rules App
A18 [27]	The Formative Design of Epilepsy Journey: a Web-Based Executive Functioning Intervention for Adolescents with Epilepsy
A19 [28]	Comparing Efficacy of Web Design of University Websites: Mixed Methodology and First Results for Russia and the USA
A20 [29]	Analysis of Website using Click Analytics

RQ1: In which application domains is the use of Web Analytics reported for the evaluation of the User Experience and what are its objectives?

For this question, we were able to identify a variety of domains in the case studies reported that evaluate the User Experience through Web Analytics. These study domains are detailed in Table 5.

Table 5. Reported domains where web analytics is applied in the User Experience evaluation

Domain	Papers	Quantity
Informative	[1, 8, 13, 15, 17, 23–25, 28]	10
Health care	[14, 20, 21, 26, 27]	5
E-commerce	[16, 19, 29]	3
Social network	[12, 22]	2

Based on the results (see Fig. 1), it is observed that most of the case studies in which the User Experience is evaluated through Web Analytics are focused on informative websites, of which a variety of different study objectives have been reported. For example, understanding user behavior, analyzing the usability of websites to identify potential problems, evaluating the aesthetic design of the website, among others.

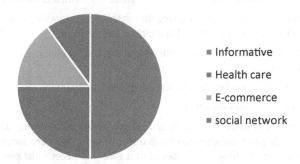

Fig. 1. Proportion of the reported domains where Web Analytics is applied

In addition to the information domain, in the other reported domains, a pattern of common objectives has been found in each domain. For example, the health care domains have the common objective of evaluating user perception, utility, and satisfaction. On the other hand, the e-commerce domains have a common objective of evaluating user behavior in their interaction with the website or application with a specific goal. Finally, social network domains have the common objective of evaluating the user's interaction with the website to predict their behavior.

In conclusion, it can be observed that depending on the domain of the website to be evaluated, the approach of Web Analytics changes to adapt to the needs and objectives of each domain. Another important point to emphasize is the interaction of the domain with the users, since depending on the domain to be evaluated, the user's behavior can vary concerning the objective of the website. So, the usefulness of the metrics, tools, and methodologies to be used in the different websites to be evaluated depends on the domain of the website and its evaluation objectives.

RQ2: What metrics are reported to evaluate the User Experience through Web Analytics?

For this question, we were able to identify a variety of metrics used in the evaluation of User Experience through Web Analytics in each case study. These metrics are detailed in Table 6.

Table 6. Reported metrics for user experience evaluation

Papers	Reported Metrics
A01	Percentage of new sessions, average session length, the average number of pages on a website that the user makes during a visit by user profile, and device type
A02	The number of visits, time spent on the registration form, and duration of the session
A03	The number of visits, users accessing the system depending on the system browser and the operating system used, characteristics of the page
A04	Number of users, number of sessions, frequency and timeliness of sessions, user demographics
A05	Number of visits, number of sessions, bounce rate, maximum session time
A06	Number of visits links searched
A07	Number of clicks to the plug-in, time used to analyze the incoming data, the total number of plug-in recommendations, number of steps that were successfully performed from the plug-in, number of times the user accepts the plug-in recommendations, number of orders performed without the plug-in
A08	No metrics were reported
A09	Website loading time, website latency
A10	The element that receives the most clicks, the rate of interaction of visitors with the other elements, a link that receives more clicks between the redundant links present
A11	The average number of clicks per task, percentage of users who completed the task, average total task time, task efficiency
A12	The average number of modules completed, average session time, user ID, number of modules completed per person
A13	Number of visits, session length, the latency of seven days of active use, earnings
A14	Number of sessions, number of visits, percentage of bounce
A15	Percentage of clicks on each page, most visited pages of a website
A16	Number of users in other countries
A17	Number of sessions of the application, frequency of use
A18	Session duration, the number of pages visited on a website
A19	Number of sessions, length of visit, statistics of revisits
A20	Element that receives the most clicks, the rate of interaction of visitors with the other elements, a link that receives more clicks between the redundant links present

Where, after analyzing this set of reported metrics, it can be seen that this list of metrics can be divided into three categories. These categories are the ones mentioned below:

- *Generic metrics*, which are the basic metrics found in most Web Analytics tools.
- *Click-based metrics*, which are the metrics found mostly in Web Analytics tools that specialize in analyzing user clicks.

- *Event-based metrics*, which are metrics customized to the needs of the research target. Therefore, these metrics are not found in basic Web Analytics tools.

Where the most used metrics in the evaluation of the User Experience are the generic metrics since they offer basic information about the interaction between the user and the website. However, if you want specific information about user behavior you can choose other types of metrics such as click-based or event-based. Likewise, Table 7 synthesizes the information showing the 10 most used metrics in each of these studies.

Table 7. Most reported metrics in the case studies

Metrics	Papers	Quantity
Number of visits	A01, A02, A03, A05, A06, A13, A14, A18, A20	9
Number of sessions	A14, A17, A19, A20	4
Duration of the session	A01, A02, A12, A18	4
Rebound percentage	A05, A14	2
Number of clicks	A07, A11	2
Number of clicks per link	A06, A10	2
Revisit Statistics	A19	1
Profits	A13	1
Number of users per country	A16	1
New sessions or users	A01	1

Based on the results of Table 7, it can be determined that the most reported metrics are those related to user sessions and visits to a website. For example, in the case study "All that glitters isn't gold: The complexities of use statistics as an assessment tool for digital libraries" [23], the reported metrics help identify the frequency of website visits and the most visited pages of the website. In this way, these metrics allowed the analysis of the relationship in the growth of the website with the increase of information that was uploaded by the organizers. The five main metrics reported in Table 6 will be described below:

- *The number of visits* indicates the number of pages of a website where a user interacted, it is equivalent to counting the number of pages read from a book [23].
- *The number of sessions* identifies the number of times a user interacted with the website [23].
- *The duration of the session* identifies the time a user interacted with the website.
- *Bounce rate* identifies the number of visits in which users leave the site from the landing page without further navigation [1].
- *The number of clicks* identifies the areas of a website that receive the most clicks [19].

RQ3: What tools are reported to evaluate the User Experience through Web Analytics and what are they used for?

For this question, we were able to identify a variety of tools used in the evaluation of User Experience through Web Analytics. These tools are detailed in Table 8.

Table 8. Reported tools for user experience evaluation

Tool	Papers	Quantity
Google Analytics	A01, A04, A05, A06, A12, A13, A14, A15, A16, A17, A18	11
CrazyEgg	A10, A20	2
Client-based tracking	A07	1
WAVE	A09	1
GooglePageSpeed	A09	1
Insight, google Mobile-Friendly Test	A09	1
Pingdom tool	A09	1
PowerMapper	A09	1

According to the results obtained, Google Analytics is the most used tool for the evaluation of the User Experience through Web Analytics, since it is useful for tracking and reporting information about the characteristics of web traffic and user behavior with the content of the website [8, 14, 22]. One of the advantages of this tool is the free access available online [1] In addition to having different functionalities and being easy to use [23, 30]. However, there are other more specialized tools such as those listed below:

- *CrazyEgg*, which specializes in analyzing website design and user behavior based on click-through analysis [19].
- *WAVE, google page speed insight, google Mobile-Friendly Test, Pingdom tool, and PowerMapper*, specialized in measuring the loading speed of websites to analyze, identify and solve low loading speed problems [18].
- *Client-based tracking*, a tool specially created to guarantee the proper implementation of the plug-in that takes care of obtaining web traffic [16].

Where, depending on the objectives of each evaluation, the right tool should be chosen to be used in each case study. Because each tool has different characteristics that can favor the evaluation of the User Experience.

RQ4: What methodologies are reported to evaluate the User Experience through Web Analytics and what advantages/disadvantages do they possess?

For this question, we were able to identify a variety of methodologies used in the evaluation of User Experience through Web Analytics. These methodologies are detailed in Table 9.

Table 9. Reported methodologies for user experience evaluation

Methodology	Papers	Quantity
Survey + Analytic	A01, A04, A17, A18	4
Mixed methodology	A08, A16, A18, A19	4
A/B testing	A02, A03, A05	3
Click analytics	A10, A15, A20	3
UX metrics	A07	1

According to the results, it can be determined that the most commonly used methodology is the combination of the survey and Web Analytics, since the latter states that the limitation of the lack of understanding of quantitative data can be resolved with the qualitative data that is extracted by surveys [8]. In addition to this methodology, other methods have been reported to evaluate the User Experience through Web Analytics such as those detailed below:

A/B testing, which consists of using two versions of the same application in a comparative analysis to determine the final result [1, 12]. However, this methodology is not suitable when it is required to know the user's browsing history or more precise information on problems a user faces that affect the website's User Experience [13].

UX metrics, which consists of evaluating the User Experience based on six principles detailed below [16]:

- *Adoption*, associated with the number of link clicks.
- *Complexity*, associated with the time used to analyze the incoming data.
- *Task Success*, associated with the total number of recommendations of the plug-in.
- *Continuity*, associated with the number of steps that were completed by the plug-in.
- *Trust*, associated with the number of times the user accepts the recommendations of the plug-in.
- *Mastery*, associated with the number of orders without the plug-in.

The advantage of this methodology is that unlike other methods based on data related to the feelings and emotions of the user, this method is based on the real activities of users. However, if an adequate approach is not defined for the metrics defined by this methodology, an adequate result will not be achieved [16].

E-mis validity, a methodology specially developed for any clinical area involving the MIS (minimally invasive surgery) technique, in which subjective metrics are analyzed based on questionnaires and checklists for the evaluation of content and usability. In addition to objective metrics based on Web Analytics for the evaluation of User Experience [20].

Mixed methodology, in which two evaluation methods have been identified. The first combines web crawling, web analytics, and heat map analysis based on eye-tracking and qualitative usability analysis of the composite graphic model of a website [31] to evaluate how the usability of a website, the navigation that occurs between pages of a website, and the graphic model of the website relate to each other [28].

The second method combines the methodology of qualitative data extraction through surveys, Web analytics to obtain quantitative data, and heuristic evaluation that involves hiring a professional usability expert to determine if the website is aligned with usability principles [32]. This methodology gives researchers the advantage of being able to infer usability and accessibility problems present on the website [27].

Click analytics, which evaluates the relationship between user clicks and website elements by determining which areas received the most clicks or which areas were avoided through heatmaps, scroll maps, confetti maps, lists, or overlay maps [29]. These visual representations give an advantage to this methodology since the data obtained is easily interpreted. Besides, it identifies the data associated with each click, such as new or recurring users, operating system, browser, search engine, and more [19]. However, if you wanted to know more precise data, such as users who only entered and left the website without taking any action, you could no longer employ this methodology. Another disadvantage of this methodology is the need for expert guidance when interpreting the clicks, as this task can be difficult [29].

4 Conclusions

From the systematic review carried out, it can be determined that Web Analytics is a concept that has recently taken interest in the application of the User Experience evaluation, where the studies that have mostly reported the use of this method are the cases of the informative area. Also, it should be noted that depending on the domain of the case study, user behavior when interacting with the website varies. Therefore, depending on the domain of the website and its objectives, the appropriate metrics, tools, and methodologies must be chosen to obtain favorable results in the evaluation of the User Experience.

Besides, several metrics used in the evaluation of User Experience through this method were identified, being those related to visits and sessions in a website the most used in the different methodologies reported. These metrics are part of a group of metrics that can be classified as generic metrics since most Web Analytics tools offer this type of metrics. However, if you want specific information about user behavior, you should opt for another set of more specialized metrics. Among these sets of metrics, you can classify them into click-based and event-based to obtain relevant information concerning the objective of the User Experience evaluation.

Another point to highlight is the existence of several tools, which are responsible for extracting the quantitative data for the evaluation of the defined metrics, so the choice of the tool to be used will depend on how the tool is adapted to these metrics. One of the most reported free tools is Google Analytics because it has many features and is easy to use. However, there are more specialized tools in other areas of Web Analytics that can be used if you want to achieve optimal results in the evaluation of User Experience.

However, it can be observed that Web Analytics has a limitation and that is the lack of understanding of the quantitative data generated to improve the User Experience, so it is often used traditional methods such as surveys for the extraction of qualitative data that can complement the quantitative information and thus obtain better results. This can be seen in the different reported methodologies where Web Analytics is used to evaluate the User Experience, in these methodologies Web Analytics is usually used with other types of qualitative and quantitative methods, to complement each other and obtain optimal results in the evaluation of the User Experience.

Acknowledgement. This study is highly supported by the Section of Informatics Engineering of the Pontifical Catholic University of Peru (PUCP) – Peru, and the "HCI, Design, User Experience, Accessibility & Innovation Technologies" Research Group (HCI-DUXAIT). HCI-DUXAIT is a research group of PUCP.

References

1. Kumar, R., Hasteer, N.: Evaluating usability of a web application: a comparative analysis of open-source tools. In: 2017 2nd International Conference on Communication and Electronics Systems (ICCES), pp. 350–354. IEEE (2017). https://doi.org/10.1109/CESYS.2017.8321296
2. Hartson, R., Pyla, P.: Chapter 1 - What Are UX and UX Design? In: Hartson, R., Pyla, P. (eds.) The UX Book 2nd edn., pp. 3–25. Morgan Kaufmann, Boston (2019). https://doi.org/10.1016/B978-0-12-805342-3.00001-1
3. Jokela, T.: When good things happen to bad products: where are the benefits of usability in the consumer appliance market? Interactions. **11**, 28–35 (2004)
4. Beasley, M.: Chapter 1 - Introduction. In: Beasley, M. (ed.) Practical Web Analytics for User Experience, pp. 1–7. Morgan Kaufmann, Boston (2013). https://doi.org/10.1016/B978-0-12-404619-1.00001-0
5. Beasley, M.: Chapter 3 - How web analytics works. Presented at the (2013). https://doi.org/10.1016/B978-0-12-404619-1.00003-4
6. Zheng, J., Peltsverger, S.: Web analytics overview. Presented at the January 1 (2015)
7. Kaushik, A.: Web analytics 2.0: The art of Online Accountability and Science of Customer Centricity. Wiley, New York (2009)
8. Villaespesa, E.: Museum collections and online users: development of a segmentation model for the metropolitan museum of art. Visit. Stud. **22**, 233–252 (2019). https://doi.org/10.1080/10645578.2019.1668679
9. Hartson, R., Pyla, P.: Chapter 28 - Background: UX Evaluation. Presented at the (2019). https://doi.org/10.1016/B978-0-12-805342-3.00028-X
10. ISO 9241–210 (2010)
11. Kitchenham, B., Charters, S.: Guidelines for performing systematic literature reviews in software engineering (2007)
12. Soong, K., Fu, X., Zhou, Y.: Optimizing new user experience in online services. In: Proceedings - 2018 IEEE 5th International Conference on Data Science and Advanced Analytics, DSAA 2018, pp. 442–449 (2019). https://doi.org/10.1109/DSAA.2018.00057
13. Salutari, F., Da Hora, D., Dubuc, G., Rossi, D.: Analyzing Wikipedia users 2019; perceived quality of experience: a large-scale study. IEEE Trans. Netw. Serv. Manag. (2020). https://doi.org/10.1109/TNSM.2020.2978685
14. Jeong, D., Cheng, M., St-Jean, M., Jalali, A.: Evaluation of ementalHealth.ca, a Canadian mental health website portal: Mixed methods assessment. J. Med. Internet Res. 21 (2019). https://doi.org/10.2196/13639
15. Ruzza, M., Tiozzo, B., Mantovani, C., D'Este, F., Ravarotto, L.: Designing the information architecture of a complex website: a strategy based on news content and faceted classification. Int. J. Inf. Manage. **37**, 166–176 (2017). https://doi.org/10.1016/j.ijinfomgt.2017.02.001

16. Lachner, F., Fincke, F., Butz, A.: UX metrics: deriving country-specific usage patterns of a website plug-in from web analytics. In: Bernhaupt, R., Dalvi, G., Joshi, A., K. Balkrishan, D., O'Neill, J., Winckler, M. (eds.) INTERACT 2017. LNCS, vol. 10515, pp. 142–159. Springer, Cham (2017). https://doi.org/10.1007/978-3-319-67687-6_11

17. Bodrunova, S.S., Yakunin, A.V.: U-index: an eye-tracking-tested checklist on webpage aesthetics for university web spaces in Russia and the USA. In: Marcus, A., Wang, W. (eds.) DUXU 2017. LNCS, vol. 10288, pp. 219–233. Springer, Cham (2017). https://doi.org/10.1007/978-3-319-58634-2_17

18. Gopinath, S., Senthooran, V., Lojenaa, N., Kartheeswaran, T.: Usability and accessibility analysis of selected government websites in Sri Lanka. In: Proceedings - 2016 IEEE Region 10 Symposium, TENSYMP 2016, pp. 394–398 (2016). https://doi.org/10.1109/TENCONSpring.2016.7519439

19. Kaur, K., Singh, H.: Click analytics: what clicks on webpage indicates? In: Proceedings on 2016 2nd International Conference on Next Generation Computing Technologies, NGCT 2016, pp. 608–614 (2017). https://doi.org/10.1109/NGCT.2016.7877485

20. Ortega-Morán, J.F., et al.: Validation of the three web quality dimensions of a minimally invasive surgery e-learning platform. Int. J. Med. Inform. **107**, 1–10 (2017). https://doi.org/10.1016/j.ijmedinf.2017.07.001

21. Boucher, S., et al.: Teaching intuitive eating and acceptance and commitment therapy skills via a web-based intervention: a pilot single-arm intervention study. JMIR Res. Protoc. **5**, e180 (2016). https://doi.org/10.2196/resprot.5861

22. Rodden, K., Hutchinson, H., Fu, X.: Measuring the user experience on a large scale: user-centered metrics for web applications (2010). https://doi-org.ezproxybib.pucp.edu.pe/10.1145/1753326.1753687, https://doi.org/10.1145/1753326.1753687

23. Perrin, J.M., Yang, L., Barba, S., Winkler, H.: All that glitters isn't gold: The complexities of use statistics as an assessment tool for digital libraries. Electron. Libr. **35**, 185–197 (2017). https://doi.org/10.1108/EL-09-2015-0179

24. Wu, J., Brown, J.F.: Website redesign: a case study. Med. Ref. Serv. Q. **35**, 158–174 (2016). https://doi.org/10.1080/02763869.2016.1152142

25. Sheikh, A.: Evaluating the usability of COMSATS institute of information technology library website a case study. Electron. Libr. **35**, 121–136 (2017). https://doi.org/10.1108/EL-08-2015-0149

26. Quan, A.M.L., et al.: Mobile clinical decision tools among emergency department clinicians: web-based survey and analytic data for evaluation of the ottawa rules app. JMIR Mhealth Uhealth. **8**, e15503 (2020). https://doi.org/10.2196/15503

27. Glaser, N.J., Schmidt, M., Wade, S.L., Smith, A., Turnier, L., Modi, A.C.: The formative design of epilepsy journey: a web-based executive functioning intervention for adolescents with epilepsy. J. Formative Des. Learn. **1**(2), 126–135 (2017). https://doi.org/10.1007/s41686-017-0011-3

28. Bodrunova, S.S., Yakunin, A.V, Smolin, A.A.: Comparing efficacy of web design of university websites: mixed methodology and first results for Russia and the USA. In: Proceedings of the International Conference on Electronic Governance and Open Society: Challenges in Eurasia, New York, NY, USA, pp. 237–241. Association for Computing Machinery (2016). https://doi.org/10.1145/3014087.3014113

29. Kaur, K., Singh, H.: Analysis of website using click analytics. Int. J. Comput. Sci. Eng. Technol. **5** (2015)

30. Hasan, L., Morris, A., Probets, S.: Using google analytics to evaluate the usability of e-commerce sites. In: Kurosu, M. (ed.) HCD 2009. LNCS, vol. 5619, pp. 697–706. Springer, Heidelberg (2009). https://doi.org/10.1007/978-3-642-02806-9_81

31. Guzdial, M., Santos, P.J., Badre, A., Hudson, S.E., Gray, M.H.: Analyzing and visualizing log files: a computational science of usability. Georgia Institute of Technology (1994)

32. Nielsen, J.: Usability Engineering. Morgan Kaufmann, San Francisco (1994)

Validation of a Questionnaire to Evaluate the Usability in the Peruvian Context

Freddy Paz[1]([✉]) [ID], Freddy Asrael Paz[2] [ID], Arturo Moquillaza[1] [ID], Joel Aguirre[1] [ID],
Fiorella Falconi[1] [ID], Jaime Diaz[3] [ID], and Hilmar Hinojosa[1]

[1] Pontificia Universidad Católica del Perú, San Miguel, Lima 32, Peru
{fpaz,amoquillaza}@pucp.pe, {aguirre.joel,ffalconit,
hhinojo}@pucp.edu.pe
[2] Universidad Nacional Pedro Ruiz Gallo, Lambayeque, Peru
fpaz@unprg.edu.pe
[3] Depto. Cs. de La Computación e Informática, Universidad de La Frontera, Temuco, Chile
jaimeignacio.diaz@ufrontera.cl

Abstract. Usability is considered one of the most significant aspects to contemplate during the software development process. For this reason, it is necessary to have tools that allow development teams and specialists to evaluate whether the interface design proposals are usable, understandable, and easy to use. One of the widely used instruments to determine if an interface design is usable are questionnaires. There are some proposals aimed at capturing the perception of end-users. Still, very few approaches are focused on covering all aspects of E-Commerce applications and are aimed at specialists in Human-Computer Interaction. In this study, we have used a proposal of a new questionnaire that was developed considering an in-depth analysis of the literature and the information collected from two consulting firms. This new assessment tool intended to provide specialists a way to perform more accurate usability evaluations that cover all aspects of a software in the E-Commerce domain and at the same time allows to quantify the level of user experience. The questionnaire was used to evaluate the usability of the three main E-Commerce websites in Peru. The results show that, despite being the most relevant platforms in the country, they must improve many aspects of usability. There is little concern on the part of companies in offering websites that are intuitive and that generate satisfaction to end users.

Keywords: Human-computer interaction · User experience · Assessment tool · Quantifying method · Usability questionnaire

1 Introduction

Usability represents an essential quality attribute in the construction of software products [1]. Several evaluation methods have emerged as a consequence to ensure the design of interfaces that are usable, easy to use, understandable and attractive [2]. In the same way, there are also a number of methodological procedures that allow specialists to verify if the user interfaces meet the minimum standards of usability [3]. In this wide range of

© Springer Nature Switzerland AG 2021
M. M. Soares et al. (Eds.): HCII 2021, LNCS 12779, pp. 327–336, 2021.
https://doi.org/10.1007/978-3-030-78221-4_22

available tools to measure usability, the questionnaires stand out for being a straightforward method that does not demand the consumption of multiple resources. However, few are the proposals of questionnaires cover all the aspects that are relevant in a particular software category. Most of these questionnaires that exist in the literature to evaluate the usability of a software product, are focused on generic and global aspects. When developing applications of very specific categories such as the medical, mathematical or even electronic commerce domain, new features appear that must be considered to ensure the ease of use of the final product [4]. It is not the same for a specialist to analyze the usability of an app designed for mobile devices than a touchscreen-based system or an interface embedded in a technological device. Attention should be paid to new features since each type of system has its own peculiarities.

In e-commerce web applications, there are aspects related to the financial transaction, the purchase process, the feedback from users on products and services, the security of the sensible information (credits cards and personal information), etc., that affect the end-user experience [5]. These aspects, despite being important in the analysis of the user experience, are not covered by the current evaluation proposals, especially by the questionnaires. However, Bonastre and Granollers [6], through an exhaustive study of Nielsen's heuristics and a literature review in conjunction with collected information from two consulting firms, developed a new proposal that has proven to be effective in this area. This new set of guidelines has been validated in the assessment of twenty-one E-Commerce websites, demonstrating that it is possible to identify a greater number of problems when this new proposal is used compared to the current evaluation questionnaires [7]. In this study, we have tested the approach proposed by Bonastre and Granollers in the evaluation of the three leading E-Commerce websites in Peru. The intention of this research was to provide more experimental evidence on this evaluation instrument and determine if it is applicable to websites from a different cultural context. Likewise, it has been possible to determine whether the most important local companies in the country take this quality aspect into consideration, such as usability for the design and development of their websites.

This document is structured as follows. In Sect. 2, we detail the new assessment questionnaire that has been used to measure the level of usability of the Peruvian e-commerce websites. In Sect. 3, the design of the case study is described. In Sect. 4, we present the obtained results and a brief analysis of them. Finally, in Sect. 5, conclusions and future works are established.

2   A New Usability Evaluation Proposal

Within the wide range of usability evaluation methods that exist [8], questionnaires represent a more feasible instrument to use than procedures that require, for instance, preparation of material, training, and recruitment of participants, such as user tests. In the same way, questionnaires solve the problem of the qualitative approaches. Using a questionnaire, it is possible to quantify the level of usability of a software product [9]. Obtaining a numerical value on the level of usability offers the possibility of making comparisons. Many times, when the engineers employ *parallel design*, and there are multiple proposals, quantifying the usability can be a decisive factor in selecting the best option. Similarly, when a company intends to know how far it is from its main competitors, this value can be helpful for decision making [10]. Another advantage of questionnaires is that there is not much complexity to use them. The evaluators must interact previously with the software product and after that, they must answer about the degree of compliance with each of the items established in the questionnaire. One difference that has implications in the calculation of the final value is that some proposals establish YES/NO questions for the evaluation, while other approaches set up a Likert scale for the items.

In the usability questionnaires such as SUS [10], SUMI [11], CSUQ [12], ASQ [13], etc. that are widely recognized by the academia and industry, the items have the purpose of evaluating a specific usability construct or sub-attribute. Many specialists have made an effort to define the concept of usability and have concluded that this feature is composed of others. One of the most accepted approaches by the scientific community is Nielsen's proposal [14] that defines usability in five components: (1) learnability, (2) efficiency, (3) memorability, (4) errors, and (5) satisfaction. Similarly, another highly employed approach is the definition specified by the the ISO/IEC 9126 standard [15] that establishes that usability is composed of five sub-attributes: (1) understandability, (2) learnability, (3) operability, (4) attractiveness, and (5) usability compliance. The items included in the questionnaire are intended to evaluate the different aspects that comprise usability. However, the known and conventional proposals have been developed with an exclusive focus on usability and its sub-attributes, leaving aside aspects of the software product. Through previous studies, it has been demonstrated that to ensure a good user experience, it is necessary to focus on specific attributes of the software product category. For example, it is not possible to evaluate the user experience that a videogame provides, if aspects of gameplay and playability are not taken into consideration [16]. In the same way, it is not possible to carry out a proper inspection of the user experience that a banking system generates, if the perception of security conveyed by the system is not taken into account and analyzed [17]. Electronic commerce web applications are not exempt from this scenario, and in this specific area it is necessary to consider aspects such as: (1) the security of personal information and financial transactions, (2) the degree of available information that can be visualized about the products and services offered on the website, (3) user help and support functionalities, (4) the possibility of obtaining references and feedback from other users about the products and services, (5) the capacity of the system to be customized according to user preferences, among others [6].

Given the gap of the traditional proposals present, Granollers and Bonastre [6] developed a new questionnaire that addresses all aspects that are relevant and essential in a usability evaluation to an E-Commerce website. After an exhaustive review of the literature and an in-depth analysis of the most important aspects reported about e-commerce applications on the web, the authors formulated a questionnaire with 64 items grouped into 6 categories: (1) Need recognition and problem awareness, (2) information search, (3) purchase decision making, (4) transaction, (5) post-sales behavior, and (6) factors that affect the UX during the whole purchase process. Most of the questions have been designed to be answered on an agree-disagree Likert scale from 1 to 5, where: 1 represents "strongly disagree", 2 "disagree", 3 "neither agree nor disagree", 4 "agree" and 5 "strongly agree". Nevertheless, a smaller percentage has been formulated as YES/NO questions. In Table 1 details an example of the some of the questions formulated as part of the proposal.

Table 1. Example of a selection of questions formulated in the new usability evaluation proposal for E-Commerce websites [6].

Item	Description	Answer
Does the website provide a search box to locate products and information?	It must be visible at the top right of the page and it must continue throughout the whole site	(1 2 3 4 5)
Does the search have advanced features that allow for a limit to great variety of criteria (features, categories, etc.)?	The advanced features must correspond customer's needs. This helps to retrieve the most relevant results	(1 2 3 4 5)
Does the search engine provide the customer's expected results?	An analysis of customer searches must be made to optimize search results	(1 2 3 4 5)
Are there appropriate mechanisms, such as filters or facets to refine the search results?	After doing a simple or advanced search, the results can be refined by applying these mechanisms. They must correspond customers' needs and be easy to undo	(1 2 3 4 5)
Do the pages and sub-pages provide orientation elements?	To orientate it is necessary to use breadcrumbs titles and subtitles	(1 2 3 4 5)
Does the checkout process include a progress indicator at the top of the checkout pages?	Usually, it is a progress bar which indicates the steps that are missing to complete the purchase and the steps that have already been completed	(Yes / No)

Unlike the current assessment instruments, the new Granollers and Bonastre proposal [6], is directed to be answered by specialists who have an extensive knowledge about the concept of usability and have experience in the area of Human-Computer Interaction. On the contrary, most of the proposals mentioned above as SUS [10], SUMI [11], CSUQ [12], ASQ [13], etc., aim to analyze the perception of end-users. The traditional proposals have an approach to collect the opinion of the participants regarding a software product. In the case of the new proposal, the questions are aimed at determining whether the system meets certain characteristics that would significantly improve the degree of user experience. Likewise, the proposal includes technical questions that would be hard to answer for people who are unfamiliar with the topic. The purpose of this novel contribution is for the technology specialist to be able to answer based on their technical knowledge and expertise, and thus determine both the degree of usability and the aspects of improvement.

To calculate the final numerical usability value of the system, the authors have established that a sum of all the values is necessary. However, those questions that are YES/NO would receive a value of 5 if the answer is affirmative and a value of 1 if the answer is negative. Considering that there are 64 items, the maximum value obtainable is 320 and the minimum value is 64. However, in an update of the proposal, Granollers establishes that when those answers that 64 points would represent a null level of usability of the system (because it is induced that all the answers are of type "Strongly disagree" or in their defect negative for the case of questions YES/NO) and 320 points would represent that the system fully covers all the aspects that are necessary to guarantee an appropriate and satisfactory level of user experience [7].

3   Design of the Case Study

In this study, we have used the usability evaluation proposal established by Granollers and Bonastre [6] for e-commerce websites. The research was intended to test this new approach in the assessment of the three main e-commerce websites in Peru. In this way, what is intended is to place more evidence that can be used afterward to generalize the use of this instrument in different contexts and settings. Likewise, it has been possible to determine the degree of importance that both usability and user experience have for local companies.

The websites to be evaluated were selected according to a previous research [18] in which an accessibility evaluation was carried out to determine the Peruvian companies that meet the guidelines indicated in the international WCAG 2.0 standard. From this study, three websites were selected:

- Saga Falabella (www.falabella.com.pe)
- Ripley (www.ripley.com.pe)
- Linio (www.linio.com.pe)

Regarding the process, Granollers and Bonastre [6] determine that in each evaluation of a specific website, 3 to 5 evaluators must participate. In this experimental case study, three specialists in the field of Human-Computer Interaction were requested to participate. It can be established that all specialists that agreed to contribute with this study, have the same degree of expertise because they all have multiple projects carried out in this area as well as published research papers. In addition, all they have technological formation in careers related to Computer Science.

Once the evaluators kindly and voluntarily agreed to participate in our study, they received an Excel template that was previously prepared. This template detailed an informed consent protocol that the evaluators had to sign to be part of this case study. Likewise, instructions for the evaluation process were provided. The evaluators were requested to spend 30 to 45 min browsing each website. After the interaction, the specialists were asked to answer each of the items in the questionnaire. This process was repeated at different time intervals for the evaluation of each of the websites. However, it was the same evaluators who participated in the three evaluations of the three websites. Likewise, the template was configured with both the questions and the possible answers to each of the items, to avoid possible errors in the evaluation.

Once the evaluators finished conducting the evaluation, the templates were collected to be analyzed and processed by the authors of this research. The results were interpreted taking into consideration the percentage of compliance with all the aspects indicated in the proposal. Figure 1 summarizes the evaluation process.

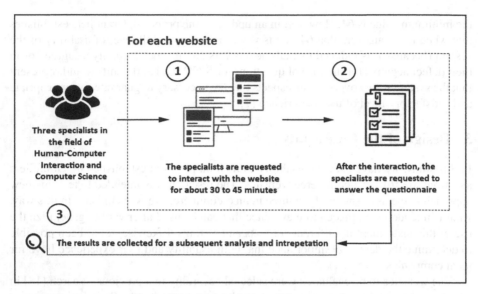

Fig. 1. Experimental design of the case study

4 Analysis of the Results

The usability evaluation was performed during the month of January 2021. Due to local restrictions on holding face-to-face meetings because of the Covid-19 scenario, the evaluation was carried out virtually. The templates were sent to the specialists via email and subsequently the information was collected in the same way. Since there is no automated system, the results have been analyzed and interpreted manually.

Table 2, 3 and 4 detail the usability scores obtained for each of the evaluated websites. We observe that the scores obtained are uniform, which is an indicatory that the three specialists have evaluated with the same orientation, and that the questionnaire could be reliable. It is possible to determine some rating are different in some categories, however this does not mean that one evaluator is more accurate than the others, simply indicates that to increase the reliability of this evaluation would need to introduce more specialists into the experiment. We can also appreciate that although usability levels are not are high, they are almost remarkably similar values.

In Table 5, the final score of usability for each website is presented. From these obtained results, it is possible to highlight that apparently there is a correlation between the relevance of the website and the level of usability it presents, given that this selected sample corresponds to the three most relevant Peruvian local websites chosen in order of importance. Likewise, it is possible to determine that despite being the most representative websites on the E-Commerce domain in Peru, the level of usability identified is quite low, evidencing that there is indeed little concern currently by companies about this quality attribute.

Through an analysis of the total scores obtained by all the evaluators: 181, 176, 208 for *SagaFalabella*, 171, 178, 172 for *Ripley* and 165, 149, 156 for *Linio*, it is possible to conclude that the level of usability of E-Commerce websites in Peru is low. Despite being

Table 2. Average of the scores obtained for each category in the usability evaluation conducted to the E-Commerce website of www.sagafalabella.com.pe.

Evaluated category	Average of the scores		
	E1	E2	E3
(1) Need recognition and problem awareness (14 items)	3.29	3.14	3.64
(2) Information search (6 items)	2.83	2.83	3.17
(3) Purchase decision making (13 items)	2.38	2.54	3.08
(4) Transaction (10 items)	3.60	3.30	3.90
(5) Post-sales behavior (4 items)	3.50	4.24	4.50
(6) Factors that affect the UX during the process (17 items)	2.18	1.88	2.41

Table 3. Average of the scores obtained for each category in the usability evaluation conducted to the E-Commerce website of www.ripley.com.pe.

Evaluated category	Average of the scores		
	E1	E2	E3
(1) Need recognition and problem awareness (14 items)	2.89	3.14	3.21
(2) Information search (6 items)	2.50	2.67	2.83
(3) Purchase decision making (13 items)	2.54	2.69	2.38
(4) Transaction (10 items)	3.20	3.30	3.10
(5) Post-sales behavior (4 items)	3.50	3.75	3.00
(6) Factors that affect the UX during the process (17 items)	2.18	2.06	2.12

Table 4. Average of the scores obtained for each category in the usability evaluation conducted to the E-Commerce website of www.linio.com.pe.

Evaluated category	Average of the scores		
	E1	E2	E3
(1) Need recognition and problem awareness (14 items)	3.21	2.43	2.79
(2) Information search (6 items)	1.17	1.33	1.67
(3) Purchase decision making (13 items)	2.38	2.31	2.08
(4) Transaction (10 items)	3.30	3.30	3.20
(5) Post-sales behavior (4 items)	3.00	2.75	2.50
(6) Factors that affect the UX during the process (17 items)	2.18	1.94	2.24

frequently visited, widely promoted websites, these do not consider all the necessary aspects to guarantee a satisfying interaction experience.

Table 5. Final scores on the usability level of the evaluated websites.

Website	Final score	Score remaining	Percentage covered
www.sagafalabella.com.pe	188.33	131.67	48.57%
www.ripley.com.pe	173.67	146.33	42.84%
www.linio.com.pe	156.67	163.33	36.20%

5 Conclusions and Future Works

Usability is a quality attribute that must be considered in the development of software products to guarantee success in the market. This becomes much more important for companies dedicated to the field of electronic commerce since there are multiple options on the web and the competition is high. Given the relevance of usability and the need for development teams to ensure that products are easy to use, intuitive, understandable and attractive, methods have been developed that evaluate whether a software product meets the features and aspects that allow guaranteeing a satisfying interaction experience.

Questionnaires have emerged as one of the most used and widely accepted methods. In addition, they are easy to use and apply, as they do not require many resources like other existing methods. However, one of the problems with the current proposals is that they do not cover all the aspects that affect the experience of the end-users. To face with this problem, Granollers and Bonastre carried out a systematic review of the literature in search of identifying all the most important aspects that should be present in E-Commerce websites. Based on an analysis of several studies and the information obtained from two consulting companies, they developed a new questionnaire composed of 64 items that covers, in addition to usability aspects, the characteristics that every e-commerce website must have in order to be usable. Most of the items in the questionnaire have been constructed under a 5-point Likert scale, where the specialist must verify the degree of compliance of the item by answering from 1 to 5, where 1 is referred to "strongly disagree" and 5 is referred to "strongly agree". However, some items have been established as YES/NO questions. Likewise, the proposal is accompanied by a mode of interpreting the results, whose score can range between 64 and 320, depending on the degree of compliance with the aspects.

The objective of this study was to use the new usability evaluation proposal in order to generate more evidence for a future generalization of this evaluation instrument, and also, to determine if the main companies in Peru dedicated to the electronic commerce sector are concerned that their websites are usable and allow the achievement of the user's goals. In this sense, the voluntary participation of three specialists from the Human-Computer Interaction area was requested, who kindly agreed to determine, based on the new evaluation questionnaire, the level of compliance of the three most important websites in Peru.

With reference to a previous study, the three most relevant websites were selected for evaluation. A virtual process was established because of the current scenario that makes it not possible to carry out the experimental case study in a laboratory. The results show that, despite being the most relevant platforms in the country, they must improve many aspects of usability. There is little concern on the part of companies in offering websites that are intuitive and that generate satisfaction to end-users. This coincides in a certain way with the previous results of an accessibility evaluation carried out to these same sites, in which it was evidenced that despite being the most visited sites, they were not complying with the minimum international accessibility standards, restricting the use of these technologies and undermining the right that all people with different abilities and capacities have to technological advances. Regarding the evaluation instrument, it was possible to determine that the results obtained by the different specialists, despite being low, are similar. It is possible to mention that the instrument is reliable. However, it is necessary to carry out more experiments and apply statistics to confirm this statement.

Finally, in relation to future works, it is expected to use this new proposal in other scenarios, possibly for the evaluation of E-Commerce websites from other countries and even to incorporate a greater number of specialists to analyze whether the degree of correlation varies. With a greater amount of data from future experiments, it would be possible to apply statistics that allow corroborating the internal and external validity of the instrument in order to generalize its use to any scenario. The intention of future research that arises from this work is to provide an instrument that can be used by academia and industry for the development of high-quality software products that are usable and that generate satisfaction to end-users.

Acknowledgment. The authors would like to thank all the participants involved in the experiments. Also, all the members of the *"Centro de Estudios de Ingeniería de Software, CEIS"*, *"User Experience & Game Design – Research Group, UXGD"* and *"HCI, Design, User Experience, Accessibility & Innovation Technologies Group, HCI-DUXAIT"*. UXGD is a member of the HCI-Collab network, and HCI-DUXAIT is a research group of the Pontifical Catholic University of Peru (PUCP) – Peru.

References

1. Paz, F., Paz, F.A., Villanueva, D., Pow-Sang, J.A.: Heuristic evaluation as a complement to usability testing: a case study in web domain. In: 2015 12th International Conference on Information Technology - New Generations, pp. 546–551 (2015). https://doi.org/10.1109/ITNG.2015.92
2. Salinas, E., Cueva, R., Paz, F.: A systematic review of user-centered design techniques. In: Marcus, A., Rosenzweig, E. (eds.) HCII 2020. LNCS, vol. 12200, pp. 253–267. Springer, Cham (2020). https://doi.org/10.1007/978-3-030-49713-2_18
3. Paz, F., Pow-Sang, J.A.: A systematic mapping review of usability evaluation methods for software development process. Int. J. Software Eng. Appl. **10**(1), 165–178 (2016). https://doi.org/10.14257/ijseia.2016.10.1.16
4. Paz, F., Paz, F.A., Pow-Sang, J.A.: Experimental case study of new usability heuristics. In: Marcus, A. (ed.) DUXU 2015. LNCS, vol. 9186, pp. 212–223. Springer, Cham (2015). https://doi.org/10.1007/978-3-319-20886-2_21
5. Diaz, E., Flores, S., Paz, F.: Proposal of usability metrics to evaluate e-commerce websites. In: Marcus, A., Wang, W. (eds.) HCII 2019. LNCS, vol. 11586, pp. 85–95. Springer, Cham (2019). https://doi.org/10.1007/978-3-030-23535-2_6

6. Bonastre, L., Granollers, T.: A Set of Heuristics for user experience evaluation in E-commerce websites. In: 7th International Conference on Advances in Computer-Human Interactions (ACHI 2014), pp. 27–34, Barcelona, Spain (2014)

7. Granollers, T.: Validación experimental de un conjunto heurístico para evaluaciones de UX de sitios web de comercio-e. In: 2016 IEEE 11th Colombian Computing Conference (CCC), pp. 1–8. (2016). https://doi.org/10.1109/ColumbianCC.2016.7750783

8. Fernandez, A., Insfran, E., Abrahão, S.: Usability evaluation methods for the web: a systematic mapping study. Inf. Softw. Technol. **53**(8), 789–817 (2011). https://doi.org/10.1016/j.infsof.2011.02.007

9. Paz, F.: Application of a new questionnaire to measure the usability: a case study in the e-commerce domain. Int. J. Adv. Trends Comput. Sci. Eng. **8**(1.4), 395–297 (2019). https://doi.org/10.30534/ijatcse/2019/6081.42019

10. Brooke, J.: SUS: a "quick and dirty" usability scale. In: Jordan, P.W., Thomas, B., McClelland, I.L., Weerdmeester, B. (eds.) Usability Evaluation in Industry, pp. 189–193. Taylor & Francis, Bristol (1996)

11. Kirakowski, J., Corbett, M.: SUMI: the software usability measurement inventory. Br. J. Edu. Technol. **24**(3), 210–212 (1993). https://doi.org/10.1111/j.1467-8535.1993.tb00076.x

12. Lewis, J.R.: IBM computer usability satisfaction questionnaires: psychometric evaluation and instructions for use. Int. J. Hum.-Comput. Interact. **7**(1), 57–78 (1995). https://doi.org/10.1080/10447319509526110

13. Bangor, A., Kortum, P.T., Miller, J.T.: An empirical evaluation of the system usability scale. Int. J. Hum.-Comput. Interact. **24**(6), 574–594 (2008). https://doi.org/10.1080/10447310802205776

14. Nielsen, J.: Usability 101: Introduction to Usability (2012). https://www.nngroup.com/articles/usability-101-introduction-to-usability/. Accessed 02 Feb 2021

15. International Organization for Standardization: ISO/IEC 9126-1:2001, Software engineering — Product quality — Part 1: Quality model. Geneva, Switzerland (2001)

16. Desurvire, H., Caplan, M., Toth, J.A.: Using heuristics to evaluate the playability of games. In: CHI 2004 Extended Abstracts on Human Factors in Computing Systems, pp. 1509–1512. Association for Computing Machinery, Vienna, Austria (2004). https://doi.org/10.1145/985921.986102

17. Falconi, F., Zapata, C., Moquillaza, A., Paz, F.: Security guidelines for the design of ATM interfaces. In: Ahram, T., Falcão, C. (eds.) AHFE 2020. AISC, vol. 1217, pp. 265–271. Springer, Cham (2020). https://doi.org/10.1007/978-3-030-51828-8_35

18. Paz, F., Paz, F.A., Villanueva, D., Moquillaza, A., Arenas, J.: Accessibility evaluation of peruvian e-commerce websites. Int. J. Adv. Trends Comput. Sci. Eng. **9**(1), 558–561 (2020). https://doi.org/10.30534/ijatcse/2020/76912020

Visual Languages and Information Visualization

Design Research on Visualization of Life Behavior and Rhythm

Wa An[1](⊠), Manhai Li[2], and Ye Chen[3]

[1] Guangzhou Academy of Fine Arts, Guangzhou 510000, China
[2] Chongqing University of Posts and Telecommunications, Chongqing 400065, China
[3] Denali Technology Co., LTD., Guangzhou 510000, China

Abstract. Traditional scientific research on visualization has gradually changed from emphasizing order and stability to disorder and changes of new science. The visual expression of lifestyle helps designers to understand people's real life and create more ideal design works to meet people's life demands. This essay discusses how to understand life behavior and rhythm by integrating philosophy, sociology and other interdisciplinary knowledge. It focuses on how to visually present people's life behavior and rhythm through visual graphics, so as to understand the living habits and characteristics of a person and a group of people.

Keywords: Lifestyle · Behavior · Rhythm · Visualization

1 Introduction

We live in a world of life-behavior data. However, the data itself cannot 'convey information', and it needs to be organized through some logic before the formation of meaningful information. Visualization, an organized branch of science, was originated from the National Science Foundation (NSF) report *Visualization in Scientific Computing* [1]. Data visualization is a way to present the value of data which includes data processing, analysis and presentation, and the process of showing the knowledge in the data by presenting the data as a chart and combined with human-computer interaction. Designer Nathan Shedroff divided the process of human's knowledge and understanding about the world into four stages: data, information, knowledge and wisdom [2]. In recent years, traditional scientific research on visualization has gradually changed from emphasizing order, simplicity and stability to the disorder, complexity and change of the new science. Life is complex, and so are the data it produces.

The author began to explore how to record and visualize people's life behaviors in 2015, and proposed four dimensions of understanding lifestyle: behavior, rhythm, relationship and meaning by combining the knowledge of sociology, behavioral science, design science, psychology and other interdisciplinary subjects. This paper focuses on how to visually present people's life behavior and rhythm through visual graphics, so as to understand the living habits and characteristics of a person and a group of people.

M. M. Soares et al. (Eds.): HCII 2021, LNCS 12779, pp. 339–350, 2021.
https://doi.org/10.1007/978-3-030-78221-4_23

2 Understand Life Behavior and Rhythm

2.1 Elements of Lifestyle

Philosophy, sociology, economics, psychology and other disciplines have always taken 'lifestyle' as an important research object or context. Many scholars have understood the elements of lifestyle from their own perspectives. For example, Mead, a western scholar believes that human life is a meaning system constructed by four elements, namely human consciousness, social interaction, environment and behavior [3]. David Popno (1999, p. 620) pointed out in *Sociology* that social life is composed of non-personal factors and personalized factors [4]. Non-personal factors consist of physical environment, culture, society, economy, technology, population and other factors. Physical environment includes natural environment and artificial environment of life. Personalized factors formed by individual's physiology, psychology, education background and so on. In the *Encyclopedia of China, Sociological Volume* [5], lifestyle is defined as "a system of all activity forms and behavioral characteristics formed by different individuals, groups or members of the society to meet their own life needs under certain social conditions and values". Chinese scholar Lu Yuanzhen (2001, p. 19) et al. divided the lifestyle into behavioral habits, life time, life rhythm, life consumption and life space [6]. Dong Hongyang believes that lifestyle includes living conditions, living subjects and living forms.

In recent years, design has begun to focus on how to affect and change people's lifestyle through design. It is obviously unreasonable to understand lifestyle through traditional graphic design, product design, space design and other design majors, so we need to find new dimensions of understanding. Professor Richard Buchanan proposed the "Four Orders of Design" for the design of symbols, objects, behaviors and meanings [7], and pointed out that design could be used as an in-depth and essential method to guide the lifestyle and values. From the perspective of taking lifestyle as a design object, the author proposed that lifestyle elements are behavior, rhythm, relationship and meaning [8] through 4-year doctoral research. These four elements can be used as both design objects and lifestyle influence factors (as shown in Fig. 1). Meaning is the core of each element. The behavior, relationship and rhythm are driven and guided by the meaning of life. Behavior is the direct embodiment of life, such as eating, sleeping, working, shopping and others are daily behaviors. Rhythm includes the intensity, continuity and repetition of what happens in life; Relationship includes strong and weak relationship as well as symbolic one. The visualization method that introduced in this paper is to present the state of life through the visual expression of life behavior and rhythm.

2.2 Life Behavior

Behavior is the direct response of people to various things in the environment. The exploration of behavior is often combined with people's cognition, attitude, intention, ability and other factors. Behaviors can be divided into short-term behaviors and long-term behaviors through lifestyle. A lifestyle is a cycle from a short-term, unstable state, to a relatively long-term and stable state, and then to an unstable state. When a short-term behavior develops into a long-term one, it is the formation of habits. The Transtheoretical Model of Change (TTM) [9] integrated 18 major interdisciplinary theories such

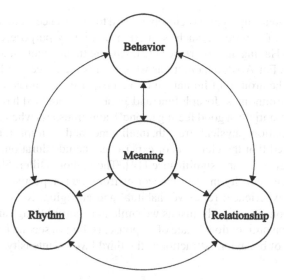

Fig. 1. Four elements of lifestyle and their relationship

as psychological therapy and behavioral change, believing that human behavior needs to go through five stages: pre-intention stage, intention stage, preparation stage, action stage and maintenance stage [10]. It is also pointed out that different behavior transformation strategies should be adopted at each stage to help people make the transition from short-term actions to long-term maintenance.

2.3 Life Rhythm

Everyone has their own life rhythm. Some things happen infrequently, but are quite influential (for example, a trip to Disney can be unforgettable); some things happen every day (eating, sleeping, etc.) but you don't feel it anymore. The study of rhythm is often considered in conjunction with "emotion" and "experience". For example, time seems to pass fast when you are happy and pass slowly when you feel painful. The author refers to the elements of time rhythm proposed by Michelle Berryman, the experience design director of THINK Interactive in the United States, in his speech at UX Australia conference in 2014 [11]. With the consideration of the interviews and insights of real users, he summarized the sub-elements of life rhythm as intensity, continuity and repetition. The intensity, repeatability and continuity of rhythm are not isolated, but interrelated and reinforcing each other. Intensity refers to the degree to which an event affects people, including the influence on emotions, abilities, values, etc. People in different environments have different experiences, and the intensity will also change with the development of the behavior. Continuity refers to how long an activity lasts or how long it exists. Repetition is the repetition of an activity. If intensity and continuity can occur within a single period, repeatability needs to be considered in a broader time dimension. From the perspective of motivation, repeatability can be divided into autonomous repetition and intrusive repetition.

It can be seen that life rhythm is closely related to experience. John Dewey described the characteristics of experience, such as emotion, continuity, purpose, completeness and thoughtfulness in Having an Experience [12]. Among them, emotion and continuity are related to rhythm. For Aristotle, emotions were interesting aspects of human existence. He realized that the arousal of human emotional experience comes from our own perception of our surroundings. Joseph Pine and James Gilmore [13] have mentioned that "experience" is essentially a good feeling in one's consciousness when one has reached a certain level of emotion, physical strength, intelligence and even spirit. In Making Meaning, it is mentioned that the elements of experience include duration, intensity, width, interaction, trigger point and significance [14]. The authors Diller, Shedroff and Rhea divided experience intensity in three categories from the perspective of creating meaningful customer experience: reflexive, habitual and engaging. Reflexes are an almost unconscious response to stimuli, just as we smile at beautiful things and frown at difficulties. They are an unintentional state of response. Habit is a second level of intensity, a repetitive pattern of behavior. Attraction is the third level of intensity, such as pleasure, surprise, etc.

3 Visualization of Life Behavior and Rhythm

3.1 Visual Presentation

How are lifestyles recorded, described and presented? People's life or experience will leave traces, which can reflect the state, process and result of people's activities. Cristiano Castlefranchi, an Italian cognitive scientist referred the unconscious behavior of human life as "implicit communication", for example, a variety of books piled up on the desk indicted that the owner of the desk may be busy in studying or did not develop a good habit of clearing up; the dense footprints left on the sand suggest that many people have walked on this beach.

The life data recorded and analyzed in this paper are not massive big data, but mainly small data generated by personal daily life behaviors, such as daily life habits, process and experience of completing things, so as to discover the characteristics behind life behaviors and reflect the pattern of life rhythm. Instead of relying on computers to visualize large amounts of data, this paper explores qualitative visualization methods. The visualization cases of life behavior and rhythm introduced in this paper mainly use time series and narrative visualization methods, including the comprehensive use of Gantt chart, bubble timeline, radial bar chart, flow chart, linear process diagram, stacked area chart, Euler chart, alluvial diagram and pin map. Table 1 summarizes the various visualization methods and features described in this paper to express lifestyle.

Table 1. Symbols to visualize life behavior and rhythm

Visualization methods	symbols	Behavioral rhythm of life			
		Behaviors	continuity	repetition	intensity
甘特图 Gantt Chart		✓	✓	✓	✓
气泡时间图 Bubble timeline		✓	✓	✓	✓
流程图 flow chart		✓	✓	✓	
线性流程图linear process diagram		✓		✓	✓
堆叠面积图Stacked Area Chart		✓	✓	✓	✓
欧拉图 Euler Diagram		✓			
冲击图Alluvial diagrams		✓		✓	✓
地图 Pin maps		✓		✓	✓

3.2 Time Series Present Behavior Habits

From the above explanation of life behavior and life rhythm, it can be seen that behavior and rhythm are closely related to the concept of "time". The visualization of time dimension has always been an important part in data visualization research. The visualization method of time series data is commonly used to express the time sequence, flow, classification, event and other information. Time series can be divided into different levels of time scale, such as year, month, day, hour, minute, second, etc. The key of visualization of time series data is to show the trend and regularity of data changing over time. Time series also has two states: instant and continuity, which is consistent with the formation of life behavior habits, as well as the repetition and continuity of life rhythm mentioned above. The time scale of the same level can reflect the internal periodic characteristics of human behavior. Time series of different levels have the relation of including and being included.

Bubble Timeline is a way of displaying a series of events or items on a timeline, with variables displayed as the size of the bubble. Essentially speaking, the bubble timeline is the visualization of composite data that includes a scaled timeline and proportional area chart. The use of mobile phone is the most frequent thing in daily life. Based on the bubble time chart, Fig. 2 shows a student's behavior pattern by recording his use of mobile phone for three consecutive days, including the time and function of using mobile phone. The size of the bubble shows how long this function has been used. The student's daily preferences and habits can thus be concluded from this figure.

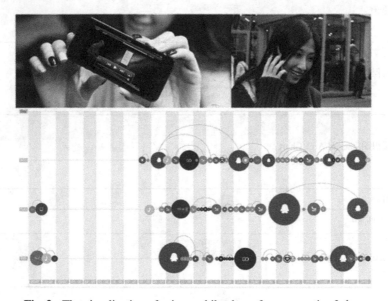

Fig. 2. The visualization of using mobile phone for consecutive 3 days

Gantt chart is a kind of chart showing the progress and proportion of events. It is a good way to show the content of the life behavior, the start and end time as well as the duration of the behavior, and to clearly see the differences among various behaviors. The common Gantt chart tools are LifeLines [15] TipoVis [16] LiveGantt [17]. Game is a common behavior in life. Figure 3 shows a student recording his life of playing games for 3 consecutive years. This figure uses Gantt chart as the basic logic and presents in a circular way, showing the type of game, the start and end time (i.e., duration) of each game, and how much you like different games.

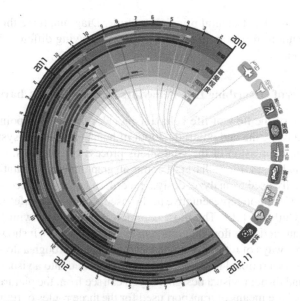

Fig. 3. The visualization of life for playing games in three consecutive years

3.3 Euler Diagram Shows the Hierarchical Relationship of Life Behavior Habits

Euler Diagram is a graphical way of expressing set relations based on a hierarchical description. The key of this diagram is to show how they overlap. Nodes with lower hierarchy are nested within their parent nodes, and the size of the nested nodes is smaller than that of their parent nodes. The hierarchical relationships expressed include spatial relationships (including overlap, inclusion, or neither) and set relationships (intersection, subset, and non-intersection). The sequence of hierarchy and inclusion relationship are determined by the scale of the data. The use of folders on the computer can reflect the situation of a person's daily work, as well as their own file management habits. Figure 4 is a document made by two students majoring in interaction design from the Hong Kong Polytechnic University in 2009 (the left is made by the author) to record their daily use

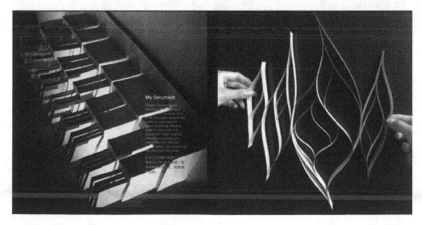

Fig. 4. The behavioral relationship diagram of using folders on the computer daily

of computers. Using the structural principle of Euler Diagram, three three-dimensional visual models without forms are made out of paper, showing different behavior habits of using computers.

3.4 The Process of Describing Life Behaviors Through Flow Chart

The visualization of the flow of life behavior includes the starting point of the behavior, the nodes midway, the end point; the input of human action and system output; the record and visual expression of the continuous process of emotions, setbacks, repetitions, mistakes and so on. Flow chart is a common graphical representation of a process or workflow, usually used to analyze, design, record, and manage processes or programs in various fields. Common representative tools based on flows are LifeFlow [18], Event-Flow [19], and OutFlow [20]. The most common flow chart is swim lane flow chart, workflow diagram, and data flow diagram. On the right of Fig. 6, it shows that a student has recorded three ways of returning home every weekend through a flow chart. The left side of Fig. 5 shows a rational flow chart that is transformed into a visual graph which is easy to understand through visual design. As you can see from the picture on the left, the length of time and the means of transport used for the three routes of returning home are different. The student mentioned that she would choose different routes under different circumstances. The first route in red is the one with the shortest time which she chooses in most situations. The subway is the main means of transportation on this route, and she needs to sit nearly 20 stations. On the second route, bus is the main transportation. She can sleep on the bus, so she chooses this route when she is tired. The third route has the longest walk, so the time consumed is the longest. However, when it is not very urgent, she will choose this route as she could do some exercises. It can be seen that

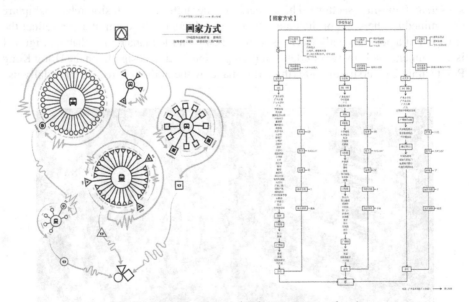

Fig. 5. The route of returning home every weekend

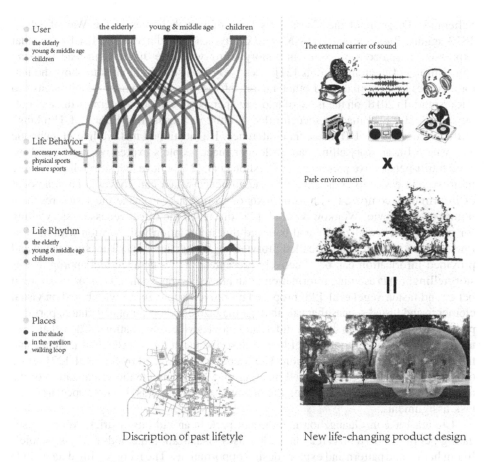

Fig. 6. Visualization and design plan of lifestyle in Liuhua Lake area

there is more than one behavioral path for people to complete a certain thing in their life, and users will choose different paths with different requirements. Through the visual research of such life behavior, we can dig out users' specific life habits and patterns, as well as the reasons behind that.

4 Comprehensive Applications of Visualization Methods to Tell Life Stories

Life story is quite complex which integrates time, behavior, process, and emotion. Many data of life activities cannot be calculated by rational mathematical formulas, thus making designers start to consider the integration of visualization technology and "storytelling" in pursuit of a visualization method that expresses a more easy-to-understand lifestyle. Storytelling has always been an effective way to convey information and knowledge. It has been applied in visualization for a long time. As early as the 19th century, the

Schematic Diagram of the Continuous Loss of French Forces in the War of 1812–1813 against Russia produced by Minard is a typical case diagram of visualization that expresses the process of events in a storytelling way. The diagram, instead of using any complex data analysis tools [21], uses two-dimensional graphics to show the history, route, time, climate and other factors of the war development which is easy to understand. In 2018, on the issue of audience perspective under modern media technology, Thalhofer [22] made a speech titled "Future of Storytelling-Future of Thinking" in the Vertice Festival/Transmedia conference. He mentioned that we live in a chaotic era, where linear storytelling can no longer meet people's expressive needs, and we need multi-perspective presentation. Gershon et al. [23] believe that storytelling is more intuitive and easier to be accepted by the audience which can convey a large amount of information compared with using texts or words and can make the visual result as intuitive as a movie. Wojtkowski et al. [24] discussed the effectiveness of storytelling for information visualization, and believed that information visualization with the following three attributes can be called Storytelling Visualization: (1) The constructed and provided information can be effectively presented; (2) As detailed and appropriate as storytelling; (3) Presenting information in an attractive way so that it can be understood better and faster. Segel et al. [25] proposed narrative visualization styles based on visual elements and visual scenes that can analyze magazine styles, annotated charts, partition posters, flow charts, comic strips, slides, and movies/videos/animations. Chen et al. [26] used the visualization tool GameFlow to describe the state of basketball matches and the process of intense confrontation. The MeetingVis designed by Shi et al. [27] uses a timeline method to form an overall meeting plan and complete the visualization of the meeting content review combining the behavior of participants, keynote speeches, and task assignments.

Liuhua Lake in Guangzhou is an urban park in an old city district. After investigating people's life in this area, the author uses visualization methods to show people's living habits and pattern and explore design opportunities. The recorded life data include various types of behavior activities carried out by different user groups (retired elderly, middle-aged and young people, and children) in the venue, as well as the frequency and flow of behavior activities. Combined with the geographic location where the behavior occurred, a visualization diagram of people's living conditions in the area (shown on the left in Fig. 6) can be developed. This visualization diagram combines three visualization methods: alluvial diagrams, stacked area chart and map. Designers use alluvial diagrams to show the relationship between crowds and behavioral activities. Alluvial diagram is a flow chart originally used to represent changes of network structure over time. The first line is the crowd, the three colors represent the three types of crowds, and the horizontal width represents the number of such crowds. Corresponding to the behavioral activities of the second line below, it can be seen that "listening to books" is a unique activity of the elderly, while exercises, rest, and eating are activities shared by the three groups of people. The third line is the visualization of crowd density over time (24 h a day). Stacked area graphs are used to show the frequency of activities of different groups of people at different time nodes. The higher the curve is, the more active the crowd becomes over time. The fourth line shows the specific geographic location and quantity of the behavior with the combination of map. This lifestyle visualization diagram helps the designer to propose a design scheme with the elderly as the main design object (as shown on the right in Fig. 6): through a listening-to-book space product design, it provides a place for listening to books which the elderly likes, gathers the elderly who love to listen to stories to listen to and share stories together, and encourages interaction between different groups of people.

5 Conclusion

Design needs to give meaning to technology in modern society, and then guide reasonable lifestyles and values. Different from the visualization that relies on large amounts of data and calculations, the visualization of lifestyle requires a full understanding of the nature of life and the choice of multiple visualization methods. This paper combines data thinking with design thinking and interactive behavior research. It tries to use various visualization methods to show people's life behavior and rhythm by recording small data in people's daily lives. Through the recording, analysis and visual display of this kind of behavior, it can help designers find the pattern of the user's lifestyle, identify unreasonable points and unsatisfied needs, so as to find better design opportunities.

Acknowledgements. This research is supported by the National Social Science Fund of China (18CG201), and a special project in the key areas of artificial intelligence and rural revitalization for colleges and universities in Guangdong province (2019KZDZX2033).

References

1. McCormick, B.H., DeFanti, T.A., Brown, M.D.: Visualization in scientific computing. In: Computer Graphics, vol. 21, no. 6 (1987)
2. Shedroff, N.: An overview of understanding. In: Wurman, R.S. (ed.) Information Anxiety, 2edn., p. 27. Doubleday Books, New York (2000)
3. Mead, G.H.: Mind Self and Society, pp. 68–80. University of Chicago, Chicago (1992)
4. Popno, D.: Sociology, 10th edn., p. 620. Renmin University of China Press, Beijing (1999)
5. Encyclopedia of China. Sociology, p. 369. Encyclopedia of China Press, Beijing (1991)
6. Lu, Y.: National Fitness and Lifestyle, p. 19. Beijing Sport University Press, Beijing (2001)
7. Buchanan, R.: Branzi's dilemma: design in contemporary culture. Des. Issues **14**(1), 3–20 (1998)
8. Wa, A.: Lifestyle design based on experience perspective. Faculty of Humanities and Art. Macau University of Science and Technology, Macau (2019)
9. Prochaska, J.O., Velicer, W.F.: The transtheoretical model of health behavior change. Am. J. Health Promote **12**, 38–48 (1997)
10. Prochaska, J.O., DiClemente, C.C.: Stages and processes of self-change of smoking: toward an integrative model of change. J. Consult Clin. Psychol. **51**, 390–395 (1983)
11. Berryman, M.: Exploring the Cadence of great Experiences. UX Australia 2014. https://dius.com.au/2014/11/27/user-experience-cadence/
12. Dewey, J.: Having an Experience. Art as Experience, pp. 35–57. Capricorn Books, New York (1939)
13. Pine, B.J., Gilmore, J.H.: The Experience Economy, p. 191. China Machine Press, Beijing (2008)

14. Diller, S., Shedroff, N., Rhea, D.: Making meaning: how successful businesses deliver meaningful customer experience. New Riders (2005)
15. Plaisant, C., Milash, B., Rose, A., et al.: LifeLines: visualizing personal histories. In: Proceedings of the SIGCHI Conference on Human Factors in Computing Systems, pp. 221–227. ACM Press, New York (1996)
16. Han, Y., Rozga, A., Dimitrova, N., et al.: Visual analysis of proximal temporal relationships of social and communicative behaviors. Comput. Graph. Forum **34**(3), 51–60 (2015)
17. Jo, J., Huh, J., Park, J., et al.: Live Gantt: interactively visualizing a large manufacturing schedule. IEEE Trans. Visual Comput. Graphics **20**(12), 2329–2338 (2014)
18. Wongsuphasawat, K., Gomez, J.A.G., Plaisant, C., et al.: LifeFlow: visualizing an overview of event sequences. In: Proceedings of the SIGCHI Conference on Human Factors in Computing Systems, pp. 1747–1756. ACM Press, New York (2011)
19. Monroe, M., Lan, R.J., Lee, H., et al.: Temporal event sequence simplification. IEEE Trans. Visual Comput. Graphics **19**(12), 2227–2236 (2013)
20. Wongsuphasawat, K., Gotz, D.: Exploring flow, factors, and out-comes of temporal event sequences with the outflow visualization. IEEE Trans. Visual Comput. Graphics **18**(12), 2659–2668 (2012)
21. Kosara, R., Mackinlay, J.: Storytelling: the next step for visualization. Computer **46**(5), 44–50 (2013)
22. Thalhofer, F.: Future of storytelling - future of thinking. https://www.researchgate.net/public ation/329427770_Future_of_Storytelling_-_Future_of_Thinking. Accessed 14 July 2019
23. Gershon, N., Page, W.: What storytelling can do for information visualization. Commun. ACM **44**(8), 31–37 (2001)
24. Wojtkowski, W., Wojtkowski, W.G.: Storytelling: its role in in- formation visualization. http://citeseerx.ist.psu.edu/viewdoc/download?doi=10.1.1.99.4771&rep=rep1&type= pdf last accessed 2019. 07.14.
25. Segel, E., Heer, J.: Narrative visualization: telling stories with data. IEEE Trans. Visual Comput. Graphics **16**(6), 1139–1148 (2010)
26. Chen, W., Lao, T.Y., Xia, J., et al.: Game flow: narrative visualization of NBA basketball games. IEEE Trans. Multimedia **18**(11), 2247–2256 (2016)
27. Shi, Y., Bryan, C., Bhamidipati, S., et al.: Meeting Vis: visual narratives to assist in recalling meeting context and content. IEEE Trans. Visual Comput. Graphics **24**(6), 1918–1929 (2018)

YERKISH

A Visual Language for Computer-Mediated Communication by an Ape

Marco Cesare Bettoni[(✉)]

Steinbeis Center Knowledge Management and Collaboration, 4059 Basel, Switzerland
marco.bettoni@weknow.ch

Abstract. Yerkish is a visual language designed for exploring the extent to which great apes could be taught to acquire linguistic skills. This instrumental aspect of Yerkish as part of an experimental communication study had a strong influence on its design and must be kept in mind all times. For this reason, the *first* part of this paper briefly outlines the context in which the Yerkish language originated: the LANA research project (1970–1976). In the *second* part, the language itself is presented in more detail: first the main distinction between an ordinary and a "correlational" grammar like that of Yerkish, then its lexicon composed of graphic word symbols, so-called "lexigrams" and finally its grammar with examples of Yerkish sentences. We propose that the LANA project was successful because Yerkish grammar is fundamentally different from ordinary grammars; for this reason, the *third* part gives a brief introduction to the foundation of Yerkish in Silvio Ceccato's Operational Methodology, particularly his idea of the correlational structure of thought from which the term "correlational" was derived for distinguishing the grammar of Yerkish from other ordinary grammars.

Keywords: Correlational grammar · Operational methodology · Notional sphere

1 Introduction

Yerkish is a visual language developed and used from 1970 to 1976 in the context of the LANA project at the Yerkes Primate Research Center in Atlanta for investigating the abilities of great apes to communicate with humans by means of a language [1, 16–18]. Yerkish is named after Robert Yerkes, an American primatologist who, in 1930, had established the first National Primate Research Center in the USA. The basic ideas of the project were: a) to introduce a *computer* for monitoring, recording and reacting to all sentences formulated by the experimental animal, an infant female chimpanzee called Lana; b) to use a *visual* language, in view of the success of the Gardners with their chimpanzee Washoe, who had learned to communicate visually in American Sign Language [10]. The project was successful; Lana acquired linguistic competence (see the Appendix, Table 4) and the team *"felt that her identity was well worth preserving"* [23] so that the whole project was renamed after her - the "Lana Project".

© Springer Nature Switzerland AG 2021
M. M. Soares et al. (Eds.): HCII 2021, LNCS 12779, pp. 351–371, 2021.
https://doi.org/10.1007/978-3-030-78221-4_24

2   The Experimental Environment

A Plexiglas cubicle the size of a small room was built on to an existing wall that had a window to the outside of the Yerkes Center. One of the Plexiglas walls was dedicated to the *interaction board* used by Lana (keyboard, visual displays, dispensers, etc. see Fig. 1) whereas the computer itself and all its external components were placed just outside the cubicle [25].

Input to the computer was achieved by means of two keyboards (one for Lana and one for the experimenters), each arranged in panels of 25 keys. Four such panels were in use at the end of the project in 1976, corresponding to a total of 100 keys that Lana had learned to use.

Each key was labelled by means of abstract, geometrical designs: visual elements that von Glasersfeld called "lexigrams" [19] and developed as abstract graphic symbols to be used as words in the Yerkish language (Fig. 2). The lexigrams were obtained by combining 2, 3 or 4 simple graphic elements and one color selected from a set of only 9 basic design elements (Fig. 3) and 7 background colors.

Fig. 1. The chimpanzee Lana working at her keyboard

Above the keyboard, in the experimental chamber, was a sturdy horizontal bar that Lana had to hang on to in order to switch on the system (Fig. 1). Directly above the keyboard there was also a row of visual displays, seven small projectors in which the lexigrams appeared one by one from left to right, as their keys were being pressed on the keyboard. This provided Lana with feedback concerning the part of the message she had already typed in, and also with a linear representation of the sentence she was composing. A signal light on the right of the projectors lit up when the "period" key was pressed and terminated the message (the "end-of-message" signal for the computer).

Thus, when several keys were pressed in succession, ending with the period key, the corresponding string was sent to the computer, which contained the vocabulary,

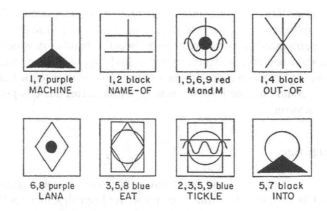

Fig. 2. Examples of lexigrams

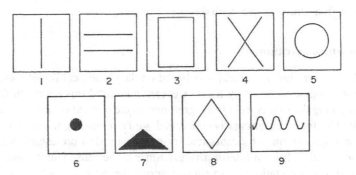

Fig. 3. Set of 9 basic design elements

the grammar of Yerkish, the automatic parser and the rules for activating a dispenser and other devices in response to the string Lana had produced. The parser took this string as a "sentence" and analyzed it to establish whether or not Lana had produced a grammatically correct sentence in terms of Yerkish grammar [16].

Below Lana's keyboard was the row of food and drink dispensers (vending devices), activated by the computer (Fig. 1); they provided all sorts of food and drink (like apple, bread, chow, banana, water, milk, juice etc.) and Lana learned to feed herself using Yerkish sentences typed on the keyboard. Besides providing food and drink, the computer could respond to requests correctly formulated in Yerkish by playing taped music or sounds, projecting movies and slides as well as opening and shutting a window.

Regardless of the outcome of the grammatical analysis, the system printed out the English word corresponding to each lexigram activated and recorded - at the end of the string - whether or not it was found to be correct. Messages originating from the researcher's keyboard were also recorded by the computer.

The computer itself (a PDP-8/E minicomputer from Digital Equipment Corporation), the terminal with a keyboard for the researchers, the printer and an auxiliary instrumentation rack were all placed just outside the experimental chamber in which Lana lived: from here, the experimenters could interact with Lana by typing sentences that were displayed above her keyboard, on a second row of projectors (similar to the first mentioned before) and they could also see how she was behaving during the computer-mediated communication session.

3 The Language

The grammar of Yerkish is a direct derivative of the "correlational" grammar implemented by von Glasersfeld in the Multistore parser for English sentences [1, 11–15].

A correlational grammar of this type is fundamentally different from an ordinary grammar. Due to misunderstandings that have haunted the development of correlational grammar since the beginning, I will dwell for a moment on the essential aspects that distinguish it from ordinary grammars.

3.1 Correlational Grammar

The correlational grammar of Yerkish is based on the theoretical framework of Operational Methodology conceived by Silvio Ceccato who used this approach for defining and implementing the first correlational grammar in the context of Mechanical Translation [4, 20]. This type of grammar is concerned with *interpreting* the content of a given piece of language in terms of a canonical form, composed of pre-established semantic elements or modules. It is an *interpretive* grammar in the sense that it consists of rules that govern this interpretation; these rules describe the language only indirectly, since what they actually describe is a *cognitive* model of the language user in the receiving role. Thus, while the term "grammar" is predominantly used to indicate the formalized description of a language, e.g. Chomsky [9], a "correlational grammar" is, instead, the description of an *interpretive system*.

The main difference from ordinary grammars consists of shifting of focus from characteristics of words and sentences, qua *linguistic* items, to the characteristics of concepts and conceptual structures, qua *cognitive* items. A parser that is intended to extract the conceptual content from pieces of language must be able to identify not only the conceptual items involved, but also the relational concepts by means of which they are connected with one another. The linguistic expressions for those relational concepts (connectives) that link items on the conceptual level were called "correlators" by Ceccato, and he therefore spoke of a "correlational grammar" for his approach.

3.2 Constraints

Because Yerkish had to be an instrument of an experimental animal communication study, its design was subject to research and budget constraints that were specific to the Lana project (see Sects. 1 and 2).

There were essentially three *animal research* constraints:

1. Drawing on the experience with the chimpanzee Washoe, who had learned to communicate visually in ASL (see Sect. 1), Yerkish had to be a *visual* language with a lexicon of unitary word-symbols that could be represented singly on the keys of a keyboard.
2. In order to make the acquisition of the language easier for Lana, both lexical items and sentence structure were to be as *univocal* as possible.
3. In order to make participation in communication events, as well as their evaluation, as accessible as possible to researchers and observers, the structure of Yerkish was to be close enough to English to allow word-by-word translation.

Budget restrictions due to limited project funding caused additional constraints:

- The lexigrams of Yerkish had to be such that the feedback projectors above the keyboard could be all of one single type, able to display all the lexigrams. This is why the lexigrams were designed from a set of only 9 basic design elements (Fig. 3) and 7 background colors.
- The size of the PDP-8/E computer limited the universe of discourse of Yerkish to a maximum of 250 lexigrams, 46 lexigram classes and 46 lexigram connectives (correlators, see next, Sect. 3.5).
- The size of the computer's workspace also limited the real-time processing of a given sentence during computer-mediated communication. The computer resources needed for this processing depend on the number of the lexigrams from which the string is composed; thus, in order to be on the safe side (use less computer workspace than available), the sentence length was initially limited to 7 lexigrams. Later experience showed that the PDP-8/E could handle up to 10 lexigrams and plans were made to increase the sentence length accordingly.

3.3 Essential Characteristics of Language

Language as a communicatory system has three indispensable characteristics [17]: a) it has a set, or *lexicon*, of artificial signs; b) it has a set of rules, or *grammar*, that governs the creation of sentences as sequences of lexical entries; c) its signs are used as *symbols*. Due to the above-mentioned shift in Yerkish from the linguistic to the cognitive perspective, the following description of its lexicon and grammar will be more intertwined (in particularly with semantics) than in an ordinary grammar.

3.4 Lexicon

The lexicon of Yerkish was developed by von Glasersfeld, starting from a list of things that would presumably interest a young chimpanzee (and the experimenters) and could be available during the project. There were about 150 words in this preliminary vocabulary. After compiling the lexicon of Yerkish, the lexical items were divided into classes (see Table 1). This classification is determined by the relational characteristics of the conceptual items and specifies the potential of each item for entering into structural relations with the members of the other classes (for situational representations); during the process of interpretation, the *linguistic* structures of the input (like phrases and sentences) will then be connected with the *conceptual* structures that the lexigram classification makes possible (semantic connection).

In fact, since Yerkish was designed based on a "correlational" approach to language [15], the lexigram-classes were defined in terms of cognition (functional, conceptual characteristics of the associated concepts) and not, like in an ordinary descriptive grammar, in terms of language form (morphology and the formal roles that words play in sentences, like noun, verb, adjective, etc.). Thus, the lexigram classes contained in the lexicon specify the *semantic* connections between elements at the linguistic level and elements at the conceptual level.

In the case of "things" this is, for instance, the kinds of activity which they can perform as *actors* and the kinds of activity in which they can play the role of *patient*; and in the case of "activities" it is, for instance, the kinds of *change* they bring about. Thus, items associated with concepts like being able to eat, drink, groom, tickle, give things or make things happen were collected in the lexigram class "Autonomous Actor" and divided into four sub-classes: "familiar primates" (lexigram Lana and lexigrams for the first names of technicians and experimenters, like Tim or Shelley), "unfamiliar primates" (lexigram visitor), "non primates" (lexigram roach) and "inanimate actor" (lexigram machine).

In the case of items that can be eaten and items that can be drunk, the lexigrams designating them were divided into "Edibles", i.e. suitable patient/objects like bread or raisin for the activity designated by EAT and "Drinkables", i.e. suitable patient/objects like water and milk for the activity designated by DRINK. Together they constituted the lexigram *general type* of "Ingestibles" which was marked on the keyboard by a red background of the corresponding lexigrams (see Table 2).

Several lexigrams were assigned to classes designating relational concepts like the class "partitive proposition" (lexigram of), the class "semantic indicator" (lexigram name-of) and the class "attributive marker" (lexigram which-is).

3.5 Grammar

Like the lexicon, the grammar of Yerkish is also "correlational" and hence interpretive in the sense previously explained. Any lexigram sequence that the parser can *interpret* by means of the rules of its primitive syntax is to be considered correct whereas any input that it cannot is to be considered mistaken.

Yerkish has three classes of sentences: statements, requests, and questions. Requests are differentiated from the others by first pressing a key called "please"; questions have to begin with a question mark.

The correlational approach to language is based on the assumption that sentences express, at the language level, sequences of mental operations (attentional operations) performed at the cognitive level [5]. The most important of the mental operations are obviously those that establish connections among conceptual items (operands) and in doing so, build up complex structures. These relational concepts, that Ceccato called *correlators* [4], are connective functions used at the mental level during the process of correlating. In natural languages, correlators are indicated using a variety of means, either implicitly or explicitly.

A correlator is always a binary function in that it links two mental operands, two concepts - the left-hand correlatum LH and the right-hand correlatum RH - and thus forms a new unit (a triad) called a "correlation". Implicit correlators are indicated in phrases or sentences merely by the juxtaposition of the two lexical items they link, and "explicit" correlators are indicated by specific words (like propositions, conjunctions, etc.). In the following, we will use "correlator" both for the relational concepts and for the linguistic devices that express them (Fig. 4).

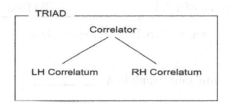

Fig. 4. A correlator (triad) as a binary function

In 1975, the Yerkish grammar used by Lana operated with the correlators listed in Table 3 "Operational Correlators" (see the Appendix). In this table, each correlator is specified by 3 attributes: 1) an ID number for the correlators, 2) lexigram classes or sub-classes for the LH correlatum, 3) lexigram classes or sub-classes for the RH correlatum.

First-Level Correlations – Example A
To give an example, consider correlator No. 11:

- at the *cognitive* level, this correlator can be paraphrased as: "stationary activity (ingestion of solids) involving edibles (solid food stuff)"; it connects a concept of the lexigram class VE with a concept of the lexigram sub-classes EU or EM (Fig. 5);
- at the *linguistic* level, in the lexigram class VE there is only one lexigram, EAT (Table 1), hence: *LH correlatum = EAT*; instead, in the lexigram class Edibles, we can choose from 2 sub-classes with a total of 7 lexigrams, for instance: *RH correlatum = RAISIN*; finally, for the correlator itself, there is no explicit lexigram, it is an *implicit correlator*, expressed merely by the juxtaposition of the two lexigrams (Fig. 6).

Since the order of succession of the two items in the linear linguistic expression is obligatory (cannot be reversed), it is not enough for the grammar merely to supply the information that correlator No. 11 can link the lexigrams EAT and RAISIN; the grammar must also specify that, in this correlation, EAT has to be the left-hand piece (LH) and RAISIN the right-hand piece (RH). This information is part of the permanent lexicon of the system. It is recorded here by means of "correlation indices" (Ic's), which consist of

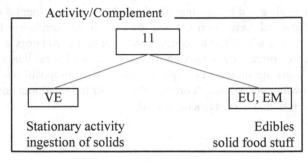

Fig. 5. Correlator 11, *cognitive* level

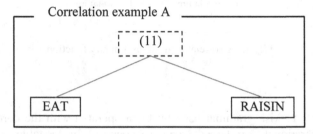

Fig. 6. Correlator 11, *linguistic* level: "EAT RAISIN"

the ID number of the potential correlator plus the indication as to whether the items to which this Ic is assigned can function as a LH-piece or as RH-piece.

First-Level Correlations: Example B
To expand on the example above, let us consider a correlation with correlator No. 01:

- at the cognitive level, this correlator can be paraphrased as: "autonomous animate actor performing stationary activity", where "stationary activity" means activities that do not involve a change of place on the part of the actor, nor a change of hands on the part of a patient. This correlator can connect a concept of the sub-classes AP ("familiar primates", i.e., the researchers), AV ("visiting primates", i.e., unnamed human or non-human visitors) or AO ("non-primates") with a concept of the sub-classes VE ("ingestion of solids"), VD ("ingestion of liquids") or VA ("relational motor act").
- at the *linguistic* level, in the three lexigram sub-classes AP, AV and AO, we can choose among 7 lexigrams, for instance: *LH correlatum = LANA*; and also, in the three sub-classes VE, VD and VA, we can choose from 7 lexigrams, for instance: *RH correlatum = EAT*. Finally, like in the previous example, for the correlator itself there is no explicit lexigram (Figs. 7 and 8).

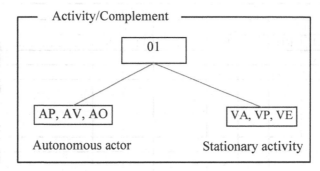

Fig. 7. Correlator 01, *cognitive* level

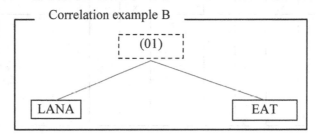

Fig. 8. Correlator 01, *linguistic* level: LANA EAT

Correlational Products and Matrix

Given the lexigram sequence LANA EAT of example B, the interpretive grammar finds that lexigram LANA, belonging to class AP, bears the Ic [01, LH], while lexigram EAT, belonging to class VE, bears the Ic [01, RH]. On the strength of this, the grammar will allow the correlation "LANA EAT" with correlator No. 01.

For the parser, "allowing a correlation" means recording it as a possible part-interpretation of the input string. As such, it is recorded as a *product* P in order to be tested for its potential correlability with other parts of the input.

The information on the basis of which first-level correlations are formed (connecting single lexigrams as in correlation example A and B) constitutes a *matrix of correlational indices* which, in the computer, is stored as part of the permanent lexicon (see Fig. 9). In this matrix, the correlational data required to form the examples A and B are represented by markers (x) at the *intersection* of a column with a row; thus, the Ic's are obtained by combining the LH or RH correlatum found at the head of the marked *column* with the lexigram class found at the beginning of the marked *row*. In 1975, the implementation of Yerkish grammar had $n = 34$ correlators and $m = 35$ lexigram classes, corresponding to a matrix of 2380 correlation indices [16].

Higher-Level Correlations: Example C

If the input string contains a higher-level structure, for instance a phrase obtained by adding a lexigram to already correlated lexigrams, like in "LANA EAT RAISIN" (example A + example B), then the parser of Yerkish, in order to be able to handle this in

Lexigram Class	Correlators									
	01		02		....	11		....	n	
	LH	RH	LH	RH		LH	RH		LH	RH
AP	x									
AO	x									
.										
.										
.										
EU							x			
.										
.										
VE		x				x				
.										
.										
.										
m										

Fig. 9. Matrix of correlation indices

exactly the same way as single lexical items, assigns a set of Ic's to each product P that represents its particular potential for functioning as a component (LH-piece or RH-piece) of a new and larger correlation that links it with other lexical items or phrases.

The procedure that assigns these Ic's to a given product is what might be called the dynamic part of the grammar.

In case of "LANA EAT RAISIN", the parser assigns the Ic [01 RH] to the phrase "EAT RAISIN" (Fig. 10). In order to do this, there has to be an operational assignation rule that makes sure that a *first-level correlation* produced by correlator No. 11 (we call this product P11) is assigned the Ic [01, RH] so that it can be linked in a *second-level correlation* with the preceding lexigram LANA, which bears the Ic [01, LH].

But this assignation must be made contingent upon the condition that the product P11 does, in fact, contain a lexical item of sub-class VE, VD or VA as a LH-piece; because only if P11 contains a member of the class "Stationary Activities" can it function as an activity of the actor designated by the LH lexigram LANA.

Higher-Level Correlations: Example D

Yerkish structures can, of course, have more than two levels. Here is an example of a Yerkish sentence with 5 correlational levels which, in English, would read: "Is there no piece of apple here?" [16] (Fig. 11):

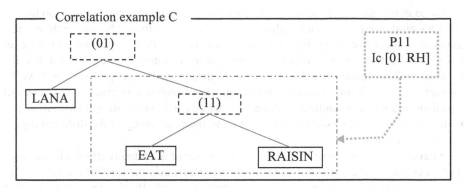

Fig. 10. Higher-level correlation 01 + 11: LANA EAT RAISIN

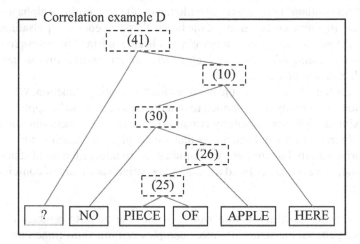

Fig. 11. Correlational network (binary tree) with 5 levels and 5 correlators

4   The Correlational Structure of Thought

The correlational approach to language that von Glasersfeld applied in developing Yerkish was based on investigations of mental activities that Silvio Ceccato had begun in 1939 [6]. Together with a group of scholars living in Italy, he proposed from the beginning to study thought and its contents in terms of operations [2, 3]. Because of this "operational approach" or "operational methodology," Ceccato's group was called the "Italian Operational School" (in Italian: *Scuola Operativa Italiana*).

His research activity was devoted to understanding the basic structure and dynamics of thought production, the development of an operational solution to the problem of semantics (connection of thought and language) and applications of operational methodology in machine translation experiments.

The basic assumption of operational methodology is that the essential function (or activity) for the constitution of any mental content is the function of *attention*. In fact, it is easy to notice that, without attention, we do not have mental content, i.e., no mental life. Our clothes are in contact with our body: do we feel them? Not if we do not pay attention to them. We are typing on the computer keyboard: are we aware of our finger touching a key? Not if we do not pay attention to it. Similarly, we do not notice the noise of traffic outside or understand what someone in the group is saying if we do not pay attention. In other words, the dynamism of physical interaction between our organism and our surroundings proceeds on its own account without constituting any mental content unless we direct our attention to the functioning of the different organs of hearing, touch, etc.

Attention, however, is not limited to this function of making present the functioning of other organs; in fact, attention is not applied continuously but for *discrete intervals* of time, ranging from a tenth of a second to a second and a half: after this time, attention detaches itself and after a short pause, can be applied again. In this way, as it is applied and detached repeatedly, it fragments the functioning of other organs into discrete pieces (so-called "praesentiata" or recepts) and builds an oscillation similar to alpha waves in the brain or to the rhythmic contractions of the heart. This conception of pulsating attention and of *discrete microunits of mental activity* has been confirmed by neurophysiological experiments suggesting that "*the seemingly continuous stream of consciousness consists of separable building blocks*" [21, 22].

A third function of attention could be called the "generating" function. Why? Because it allows attention not only to be applied to other organs but also to be applied to nothing (a state of simple vigilance, an empty attention) or to its own functioning instead, thus generating discrete attentional fragments that are not pieces of hearing, touch, vision or other sensorial activity but are purely attentional microunits (attentional states).

We would, however, never build a seemingly continuous stream of consciousness, if there were not:

1. "Categorization" as the function which enables the mind to produce concepts by combining attentional states into more complex combinations (macrounits).
2. "Perception" as the function which enables the mind to produce percepts by applying some results of categorization to recepts.
3. "Correlation" as the function which enables the mind to assemble concepts and percepts into thoughts.

The operation of *categorization* was allocated this name because it produces mental constructs that Ceccato, in honor of Kant, has called "mental categories." Thus, mental categories comprise those mental constructs which are composed only of combinations of discrete attentional fragments and do not contain anything originating from observation.

Examples of mental categories are the more or less complex combinations (concepts) of attentional microunits designated by words like "thing," "object," "beginning," "end," "part," "whole," "element," "group," "set," "point," "line," "and," "or," "singular," "plural," "space," "time," "number," "1," "2," "3," etc. Each category is differentiated from the others by the number of discrete attentional states (fragments) which it comprises and by the way in which they are combined.

The operation of *correlation* is what constitutes thinking. It assembles the attentional units in a binary tree. The basic structure of thought, according to Silvio Ceccato, is always a triad, called a "correlation," composed of two correlates assembled together by a correlator [4, 7]. This triad has a characteristic dynamism, an order of operational precedence in that the first correlate, or first mental construct, is the first in time to be constituted (or activated) and is then held present (active) during the constitution of the correlator, which in its turn is held present during the constitution of the second correlate, or second mental construct. The correlates can be concepts, percepts or entire thoughts but the correlator is always a purely attentional microunit, a mental category.

Correlation constitutes the dynamism of thought, of which the triad is the smallest unit. The larger units of thought are obtained by using a *correlation as a correlate* in another correlation, which in its turn can become a piece of a third correlation, and so on, until a greater or smaller *correlational network* is assembled. Pronouns and other words with recall functions then make it possible for complete correlational networks to be reused as elements in other correlations.

5   Language and Thought

A fundamental function of language consists of ensuring that thoughts can be reified. One way of reifying thoughts is by designating them, i.e., by establishing a viable correspondence between the polyphonic structure of thought and a linear sequence of perceivable items. Given a background of operational methodology, with its attentional model of mental contents and its correlational model of thinking, we are now in a position to explain language in a completely different way: an operational way!

Ordinary grammars explain, for instance, vocabulary items (the lexicon) by assigning them as elements to classes such as "noun," verb," "adjective," etc. by virtue of some feature that is identified as common to all the members of a class. Since many members do not display all the required characteristics of their class, grammars usually proceed by subdividing a class according to the specific or "exceptional" features of certain items.

One might call this the botanist's, zoologist's or retailer's approach: as with trees, flowers, birds, reptiles, dishwashers or chairs, this kind of explanation is useful with word items of a natural language only for the purpose of *describing a catalogue*. However, for users and developers of a language – for instance children acquiring it from their interactions or machine translation researchers using it in experiments – the main purpose is not description but the interpretation and production of sentences, i.e., combinations of items. For this reason, the usefulness of the explanation depends on its ability to accurately specify in operational (functional) terms the items involved. This characterization in functional terms is exactly what the correlational approach provides by means of a minute and rigorous discrimination of a word-item's eligibility as a correlatum or correlator within a correlation [13].

To reify a simple correlation into a linguistic form, each single element must be designated by means of at least two indications: one to say what it is (referential function) and the other to say what function it performs in the correlation (correlational function), whether that of correlator or that of the first (left hand) or second (right hand) correlatum. In order to supply these indications, languages can basically offer two means: on the one hand, they use a particular phonic or graphic material (spoken or written words), and on the other hand, they use the order of succession into which this material is put (word sequence). Only by providing these six indications (3 for the items and 3 for their place in the correlation) can we identify two expressions such as "green bottle" and "bottle green" as two different correlations or units of thought.

Mostly a correlation will be designated by employing two or three words (or whole sentences in a correlational net), which means that the required indications are distributed among two or three words, but usually the correlations that occur more frequently are indicated by only two words, one for the first and one for the second correlatum, whereas the correlator remains tacit. How can we understand a correlation of this kind in which there is no explicit word for the correlator? In some cases, the correlator is indicated by changes in the form of designation of one of the correlates but in all other cases, indication of the appropriate correlator has to be deduced from a widespread knowledge and a common cultural heritage behind any language, for which Ceccato has coined the terms "Notional Sphere" and "Constellation" [4], which were precursors to methods of knowledge representation such as frames and scripts in early Artificial Intelligence research [24].

Knowing how certain things are related allows the designation to be made more efficiently by reducing the number of explicit indications, thus making communication more rapid, flexible and adjustable [8]. For example, consider the expressions "to eat an apple" and "to eat an hour" (for instance in: "*You may also need to eat an hour before training...*"): without a general culture which allows us to distinguish between food items and time intervals, the correlation expressed in the previous sentences could not be correctly produced or interpreted.

As a consequence of this close connection to knowledge and experience, language cannot merely be considered as a strictly organized and classified system of words and phrases: it must also be approached as an extremely intuitive arrangement of things, intuitive in its production and intuitive in its interpretation [12].

This is not to say that language does not include logical functions and logical implications, but it embraces very much more: for instance, interpretations that are "correct" merely because they are much more probable than others, given our experience of the world in which we live and our knowledge of how certain things are related (notional sphere).

6 Conclusion

Lana learned to communicate successfully in Yerkish. She was the first ape to work with a computer keyboard and the first to show that chimpanzees could form syntactically correct sentences, recognize abstract written symbols, read and complete incomplete sentences appropriately. On many occasions, using appropriate Yerkish sentences, Lana made it quite clear that she was not only capable of forming concepts and of using lexigrams but also able to participate in a manner of living that we call language, i.e., that she could experience a recursive coordination of behavioral coordinations, through which she could recursively influence what she was experiencing (see Table 4). How did Lana correctly concatenate the lexigrams? How did she learn to do that? Was it merely due to good training practice on the part of the primatologists? My hypothesis is that the success of Lana is primarily down to the fact that Yerkish enabled her to learn the grammar rules in a suitable way. In which sense suitable? In the sense that the correlational structure of Yerkish matched her conceptual abilities. As a consequence, I see the success of Yerkish in the Lana project as a demonstration of the viability of Silvio Ceccato's Operational Methodology that forms its theoretical foundation.

Appendix

- Table 1. Operational Lexigram Classes

Table 1. Operational Lexigram Classes [16]

Lexigram class	Abb.	English translation of lexigrams	Comments
Autonomous Actors	AP	BEVERLY, SHELLEY, TIM, LANA	Familiar primate (human and non-human)
	AV	VISITOR	Unfamiliar primate
	AO	ROACH	Non-primates
	AM	MACHINE	Inanimate actor
Absolute Fixtures	FA	FLOOR, KEYBOARD, ROOM	Items that cannot move or be moved
Relative Fixtures	FF	DOOR, PUSH-KEY (push-button), WINDOW	Items that can move but not change place
Transferables	TF	BALL, BLANKET, BOWL, BOX, BUCKET, DOLL, PLATE, STICK	Items that can change place and/or hands
Edibles	EU	M&M (candy), RAISIN	Dispensed as unit
	EM	APPLE, BANANA, BREAD, CHEW, COOKIE	Dispensed in pieces
Drinkables	ED	COKE, JUICE, MILK, WATER	
Parts of Body	PB	BACK, EAR, EYE, FINGER, FOOT, HAND, HEAD, MOUTH, TUMMY	Can change place but not hands
States, conditions and categories			
Colors, touch, etc.	ST	BLACK, BLUE, GREEN, ORANGE, PURPLE, RED, WHITE, YELLOW, DRY, WET, HARD, SOFT, COLD, HOT, OPEN, SHUT, CLEAN, DIRTY	As attributed to items
Locational	LS	AWAY, DOWN, HERE, UP	As attributed to items
Ambiental Conditions	CD	COLD n., DARKNESS, HEAT, LIGHT n., MOVIE, MUSIC, SLIDE n., VOICE	Sights, sounds, smells, etc. are treated as states of the environment that can be caused (MAKE) by an agent

(continued)

Table 1. (*continued*)

Lexigram class	Abb.	English translation of lexigrams	Comments
Conceptual Categories	CT	BEGINNING, BOTTOM, COLOR, CORNER, END, PIECE, SIDE, TOP	As applied to spatio-temporal items
Activities			
Stationary	VE	EAT	Ingestion of solids
	VD	DRINK	Ingestion of liquids
	VA	BITE, GROOM, HIT, HOLD, TICKLE	Relational motor act
Locomotive	VB	CARRY	Transferring (place change)
	VC	PULL, PUSH	Requiring contact and force
	VG	BRING, GIVE	Causing change of hands
	VL	MOVE, SWING, TURN	Change of place
Stative	VS	LIE, SLEEP, STAND	Maintaining position in place
Conceptual	VM	MAKE	Causative, creating change
	VP	SEE	Perceptual activity
	VW	WANT	Conative activity
Prepositions			
Locational	LP	IN, ON, OUTSIDE, UNDER	
Directional	DP	BEHIND, FROM, INTO, OUT-OF, THROUGH, TO, TO-UNDER	
Partitive	PP	OF	
Determiners & Markers			
Determiners	DD	THIS, THAT	Demonstrative
	DQ	ALL, MANY, NO (not one), ONE	Quantitative
	DC	LESS, MORE	Comparative
Semantic	NF	NAME-OF	Indicating semantic nexus
Identity-Difference	ID	SAME-AS, OTHER-THAN	
Attributive	WR	WHICH-IS	Also relative clause marker
Sentential		PLEASE	Request (imperative)
		"?"	Query (Interrogative)
		NOT	Negation
		YES	Affirmation
		"." (period)	End-of-message marker

- Table 2. Semantic Color-Coding of Lexigrams

Table 2. Semantic Color-Coding of Lexigrams [16]

Color	General Type	Lexigram classes (abb.)
Violet	Autonomous Actor	AP, AV, AO, AM
Orange	Spatial Objects, Spatial Concepts	FA, FP, TF, CT, WP
Red	Ingestibles	EU, EM, ED
Green	Parts of Body	PB
Blue-Grey	States and Conditions	ST, LS, CD
Blue	Activities	VA, VB, VC, VD, VE, VG, VL, VM, VP, VS, VW
Black	Prepositions, Determiners, Particles	DC, DD, DO, DP, LP, ID, NF, PP
White (+)	Affirmation	"YES"
Yellow (+)	Sentential Modifiers	Query, Please, Negation, Period

- Table 3. Operational Correlators connecting lexigram classes and sub-classes

Table 3. Operational Correlators connecting lexigram classes and sub-classes [16].

LH Correlatum lexigram class & sub-classes	Correlator ID	RH Correlatum lexigram class & sub-classes
Actor/Activity		
Autonomous actor AP, AV, AO	01	stationary activity VA, VP, VE
Autonomous actor AP, AV, AO	02	transferring activity VB
Autonomous actor AP, AV, AO	03	act. requiring contact and force VC
Autonomous actor AP, AV, AO	04	perceptual activity VP
Autonomous actor AP, AV, AN	05	causing change of hands VG
Causative agent AP, AV, AM	06	causing change of state VM
Actor AP, AV, A0, FP, TF, EU, PB	07	change of place VL
Item capable of changing location AP, AV, AO, FP, TF, EU, EM, ED, PB	08	stative activity VS
Conative agent AP, AO, AV	09	conative activity VW

(continued)

Table 3. (*continued*)

LH Correlatum lexigram class & sub-classes	Correlator ID	RH Correlatum lexigram class & sub-classes
Predicative Copula		
Item with perceptual characteristics AP, AV, AO, FA, FP, TF, EU, EM, ED, PB, CD, WR	10	predicated state ST, LS
Activity/Complement		
Ingestion of solids VE	11	solid food stuff (as patient) EU, EM
Ingestion of liquids VD	12	ED liquid (as patient)
Stationary motor activity VA	13	any spatial item (as patient) AP, AV, AO, FA, FP, TF, EU, ED, PB
Transferring VB	14	item capable of change of place AP, AV, AO, TF, EU, ED, PB
Contact and force VC	15	any spatial item (as patient) (same as for 13!)
Perceptual activity VP	16	any perceptual item (as result) AP, AV, AO, FA, FP, TF, EU, EM, ED, PB, CD
Change of hands VG	17	handable item (as patient) AO, TF, EU, ED
Causing change VM	18	CD, CS condition or state
Conative activity VW	19	desired item (as result) AO, TF, EU, ED, CD, VE, VD, VS
Activity/Spatial Adjunct		
Change of place VC, VL (and P's: 14,15,17)	21	target location LS (and P's: 22)
Directional preposition DP	22	specification of target AP, AV, AO, FA, FP, TF, EU, EM, ED, PB
Stative activity localization VS, (and P's 11, 12, 13)	23	specification of location LS (and P's 24)
Locational preposition LP	24	specification of location (same as for 22!)
Relation Whole/Part		
Item considered "part" PB, CT	25	PP partitive preposition
Item considered "part" P's: 25	26	item considered "whole" AP, AV, AO, FP, TF, EU, EM, ED, PB, DD
Naming Function		
Semantic indication NF	27	AV, DD item to be named
New lexigram or WHAT	28	item designated

(*continued*)

Table 3. (*continued*)

LH Correlatum lexigram class & sub-classes	Correlator ID	RH Correlatum lexigram class & sub-classes
Conceptual Categorization		
Determiner DO, DC, DD	30	any item singled out AP, AV, AO, FA, FP, TF, ED, EU, EM, PB, CD, CT
Relative Clause		
Item to be qualified AP, AV, AO, FA, FP, TF, EU, EM, ED, PB, CD	31	restrictive marker WHICH-IS (WR)
Comparative State		
Quantitative determiner DQ	32	ST, LS, LP, DP state
Identity Function		
Identify-difference marker ID	33	term of comparison AF, AV, AO, FA, FP, TF, EU, EM, EU, PB, CD, DD
Sentence Modifiers		
Request marker PLEASE	40	expression turned into request
Question marker QUERY	41	expression turned into question
Negation marker NOT	46	expression negated

- Table 4. Yerkish conversation with Lana recorded on May 6th, 1974

Table 4. Yerkish conversation with Lana recorded on May 6th, 1974 [16]

On the preceding days, Lana had learned the lexigrams for a bowl and a metal can, BOWL and CAN. This had been accomplished by first using objects whose names were already known to her, putting an M&M candy inside them, and asking her:
? WHAT NAME-OF THIS
On May 5th she reliably replied with the correct lexigram when the reward was placed in the bowl or in the can. The next morning Tim (Timothy V. Gill, a primatologist, member of the project team) came in with the bowl, the can, and a cardboard box. While Lana was watching, he put an M&M candy in the box, and the following exchange took place in Yerkish:

Lana	? TIM GIVE LANA THIS CAN
Tim	YES
-	*Tim gives her the empty can, which she at once discards*
Lana	? TIM GIVE LANA THIS CAN
Tim	NO CAN
Lana	? TIM GIVE LANA THIS BOWL

(*continued*)

Table 4. (*continued*)

Tim	YES
	Tim gives her the empty bowl
Lana	? SHELLEY - (*Sentence unfinished*)
Tim	NO SHELLEY
-	*Shelley, another team member who worked with Lana, is not present*
Lana	? TIM GIVE LANA THIS BOWL
	Before Tim can answer, Lana goes on
Lana	? TIM GIVE LANA NAME-OF THIS
	A spontaneous generalization of GIVE, not foreseen by the grammar of Yerkish, since NAME-OF had not been classified as a possible object of GIVE!
Tim	BOX NAME-OF THIS
Lana	YES (*Short pause, and then*) ? TIM GIVE LANA THIS BOX
	Tim gives it to her, she rips it open and eats the M&M

References

1. Bettoni, M.: The Yerkish language - from operational methodology to Chimpanzee communication. Constr. Found. **2**(2), 32–38 (2007). Festschrift in honor of Ernst von Glasersfeld
2. Ceccato, S.: Language and the table of Ceccatieff. Hermann & Cie, Paris (1951)
3. Ceccato, S.: Consapevolizzazione dell'Osservare, mod. 3", Atti del Congresso di Metodologia. Ramella, Torino (1953)
4. Ceccato, S., et al.: Linguistic Analysis and Programming for Mechanical Translation. Feltrinelli: Milan/Gordon & Breach, New York (1960/1961)
5. Ceccato, S.: A model of the mind. Methodos **16**, 3–78 (1964)
6. Ceccato, S.: Un tecnico fra i filosofi, vol. 1 & 2. Marsilio, Padova (1964/1966)
7. Ceccato, S.: Correlational analysis and mechanical translation (1967). Reprinted in: Nirenburg, S., Somers, H., Wilks Y. (eds.): Readings in Machine Translation. MIT Press, Cambridge (2003)
8. Ceccato, S., Zonta, B.: Linguaggio, Consapevolezza, Pensiero. Feltrinelli, Milan (1980)
9. Chomsky, N.: Aspects of the Theory of Syntax. M.I.T. Press, Cambridge (1965)
10. Gardner, R.A., Gardner, B.T.: Teaching sign language to a chimpanzee. Science **165**, 664–672 (1969)
11. von Glasersfeld, E.: Multistore - a procedure for correlational analysis. Automazione, e Automatismi **9**, 2 (1964)
12. von Glasersfeld, E.: An approach to the semantics of propositions. In: Proceedings of the Conference on Computer-Related Semantic Analysis, Las Vegas, USA, 3–5 December 1965, pp. XIII 1–24. National Science Foundation & Office of Naval Research, U.S. Air Force (1965)

13. von Glasersfeld, E., Pisani, P.P.: The Multistore System MP-2, Scientific Progress Report. Georgia Institute for Research, Athens, Georgia (1968)
14. von Glasersfeld, E., Pisani, P.P.: The Multistore parser for hierarchical syntactic structures. Commun. Assoc. Comput. Mach. **13**(2), 74–82 (1970)
15. von Glasersfeld, E.: The correlational approach to language. Thought Lang. Oper. **1**(4), 391–398 (1970)
16. von Glasersfeld, E.: The Yerkish language for non-human primates. Am. J. Comput. Linguist. **1**(3), 1–55 (1974)
17. von Glasersfeld, E.: Linguistic communication: theory and definition. In: Rumbaugh, D.M. (ed.) Language Learning by a Chimpanzee: The LANA Project, pp. 55–71. Academic Press, New York (1977a)
18. von Glasersfeld, E.: The Yerkish language and its automatic parser. In: Rumbaugh, D.M. (ed.) Language Learning by a Chimpanzee: The LANA Project, pp. 91–129. Academic Press, New York (1977b)
19. von Glasersfeld, E.: Radical Constructivism: A Way of Knowing and Learning. Falmer Press, London (1995)
20. Hutchins, J. (ed.): Early Years in Machine Translation. John Benjamins, Amsterdam (2000)
21. Lehmann, D., Strik, W.K., Henggeler, B., Koenig, T., Koukkou, M.: Brain electric microstates and momentary conscious mind states as building blocks of spontaneous thinking: I. Visual Imagery and abstract thoughts. Int. J. Psychophysiol. **29**, 1–11 (1998)
22. Lehmann, D., Koenig, T., Pascual-Marqui, R.D., Koukkou, M., Strik, W.K.: Functional tomography of EEG microstates of visual imagery and abstract thought: building blocks of conscious experience. Brain Topogr. **12**, 298 (2000)
23. Rumbaugh, D.M. (ed.): Language Learning by a Chimpanzee: The LANA Project. Academic Press, New York (1977)
24. Sowa, J.: Conceptual Structures. Information Processing in Mind and Machine. Addison-Wesley, Reading (1984)
25. Warner, H., Bell, C.L.: The system: design and operation. In: Rumbaugh, D.M. (ed.) Language Learning by a Chimpanzee: The LANA Project, pp. 143–155. Academic Press, New York (1977)

The Canadian Cultural Diversity Dashboard: Data Storytelling and Visualization for the Cultural Sector

Sara Diamond$^{(\boxtimes)}$, Rittika Basu, Shunrong Cao, and Ajaz Hussain

Visual Analytics Lab, OCAD University, 100 McCaul Street, Toronto, ON M5T 1W1, Canada
sdiamond@ocadu.ca

Abstract. The Canadian Cultural Diversity Dashboard (CCDD) is an interactive online data visualization dashboard designed to elicit insights regarding diversity in the consumption and creation of cultural expressions in Canada. While designed for a particular context it is broadly applicable. Urgency for this type of analytics has amplified given the negative impacts of COVID-19 on the cultural sector and mounting concerns around racial justice and inclusion in society, reflected in considerations regarding cultural funding and creation. The complex, scalable, heterogenous, and multivariate data sets that underlie the CCDD are sourced from demographic data and include factors such as age, geographic location, education level, literacy levels, immigration status, linguistic background and languages spoken, race, Indigenous identity, disability, and gender. Each demographic segment is analyzed according to cultural consumption and creative expression across a breadth of disciplines from literary, visual, to performing arts. We discuss the challenges of collecting, analyzing, and representing diverse demographic data, including biases in data collection. We implemented a dashboard interface to enhance user experience (UX), because similarly to visualizations acting as a repository for data, the dashboard interface is a repository for the visualizations. We considered the level of interaction and user engagement needed to explore this data which led us to the use of an interactive dashboard. A narrative visualization and infographics strategies are combined in order to support editorial layering and interaction design in a co-design project, allowing us to increase research in the application of these two fields.

Keywords: Visual analytics · Diversity · Inclusive design · Demographic survey data · Visual metaphors · Data storytelling · Infographics · Narrative visualization · User centered design · Interaction design

1 Introduction

The Canadian Cultural Diversity Dashboard (CCDD) is an interactive online data visualization dashboard meant to elicit insights regarding the diversity of publics consuming and creating culture in Canada. CCDD supports policy, planning and decision-making within Canada's Department of Canadian Heritage (DCH) and is equally a communications tool for use with DCH stakeholders. Understanding the needs and interests of

© Springer Nature Switzerland AG 2021
M. M. Soares et al. (Eds.): HCII 2021, LNCS 12779, pp. 372–384, 2021.
https://doi.org/10.1007/978-3-030-78221-4_25

diverse populations is required to design effective services and programs; to address inequity; celebrate and support cultural practices and identities; and understand links between demographic diversity, health, well-being, and culture. Urgency for this type of analytics has amplified given the negative impacts of COVID-19 on the cultural sector and mounting concerns around racial justice and inclusion in cultural funding and creation.

The complex, scalable, heterogenous, and multivariate data sets that underlie the CCDD are sourced from survey and census data available through Statistics Canada [1, 2]. Demographic data includes factors such as age, geographic location, education level, literacy levels, immigration status, linguistic background and languages spoken, race, Indigenous identity, disability, and gender. Each demographic segment is analyzed according to cultural consumption and creative expression across a breadth of disciplines from literary, visual, to performing arts. The advantage of interactive visualization in interpreting such a large multivariant data set is that it helps decision makers focus their full cognitive and perceptual capabilities on the analytical process in managing complex diversity data [3] and supports exploration of context and the discovery of patterns [4]. A requirement of diversity analysis is the inclusion of small data sets, or edge cases, in order to represent marginalized groups who are not always consulted in data collection, or to see emerging trends. Prototype design was informed by prior research in narrative visualization, infographics and multi-variant data visualization and inclusive design. We used a co-design approach with diversity and culture domain experts from the Department of Canadian Heritage. The outcome is the Canadian Cultural Diversity Dashboard (CCDD) which allows two points of entry to the data analysis, from the perspective of creative disciplines or from the perspective of demographic segments.

2 Related Work

2.1 Diversity Data

Demographic data at minimum includes the following aspects of human populations: size, distribution, composition, components, determinants, and consequences of population change. Statistics Canada [1, 2] collects "Canadians at Work and Home", a survey of approximately 20,000 respondents that explores respondents' views about work, home, leisure and well-being, and the relationships between these. As well as work and family life the survey collects opinion and factual data on culture and leisure, use of communications technology, labour, society and community. These data can allow policy analysts, governments, cultural institutions, the creative sector at large, and diverse and equity seeking groups to better understand the behaviours of cultural consumers and producers. There is a boomerang effect as these behaviours are in part the result of existing policies and practices by governments and the cultural sector. BIPOC (Black, Indigenous, People of Colour) artists have offered concerns that their cultural practices, unless popular culture, are not recognized by funding agencies. Gaps in data between self-reported identities and grants or opportunities provided can indicate unmet need or bias in jury processes. For example, recent studies of public art in Toronto have shown that women, racialized and Indigenous artists are poorly represented in commissions, yet self-report as artists interested om public art [5, 6]. For these reasons ArtWorxTO, a year of public art in Toronto will favour Indigenous and racialized artists and curators in order to rebalance opportunities and better served massive populations in the city who fit these categories.

Diversity data requires sensitivity in collection processes, and awareness of the dynamic nature of categories, "In addition to revising typical measures of demography, our developing understanding of multiple and overlapping social identities (e.g., race, ethnicity, gender expression, sexual orientation, etc.) has led to the inclusion of not just more dimensions, but of more refined dimensions" [7, pg. 5]. They underscore the importance of intersectionality, that is the ways that identities are multi-factored. and combinatory approaches to analysis. They recommend constant revisions of definitions such as gender identity or racial identities. Challenges exist when categories in data sources have not yet been updated to contemporary understandings. The government of Canada has changed its gender categories to include non-binary definitions, but after the data we were working with was collected. This was a specific challenge for our team in choosing icons.

Pitoura [8] underscores the importance of "social-minded measures" in gathering, analyzing, and representing data. She states, "In a technical context, diversity ensures that all different kinds of entities are considered and represented in the output of an algorithmic process. It has been extensively studied in information retrieval, search, and recommendations for a variety of reasons. Diversity-enhanced results address ambiguity and cover different information intents, avoid redundancy and enhance information content, and increase user engagement". Disability studies emphasize the need to be inclusive not only of major trends but groups and practices on the margins [9]. Bias emerges through rounding errors that remove populations that appear small but may simply be underrepresented through data collection methods As Walny et al. [10] emphasize, visual analytics research continues to seek approaches to represent edge cases. For some data sets we needed to design for extremely small numbers in the diverse and inclusive data that represented sub-populations and their relationship to cultural practices, aiming to make these visible, readable, and comparable to the large numbers. We needed to represent multiple factors from the data to represent intersectional qualities of Canadians' choices of culture, both for fairness and to engage the intended users of the CCDD. Representing diversity also required consideration of infographic icons that are used for the visualizations, as well as strict adherence to inclusive design standards.

2.2 Data Storytelling: Narrative Visualization and Infographics

Narrative visualization structures data in order tell a story, or multiple stories from its representation. Narrative visualizations can bridge explanatory visualizations and explorative visualizations [11]. Ghidini et al. [12, pg. 2] explain, "Narrative elements in data visualization are able to provide explanation about the subject, and often support a structured interpretation." Hullman and Diakopoulos [13] argue that narrative strategies provide a means to communicate data, prioritize interpretations directly or indirectly through visual hierarchies, explore multifaceted connotations, and address audience knowledge and socio-cultural differences. They develop a series of rhetorical techniques to structure visualizations based on their observations of visualization practices. Designers direct interpretation by creating visual hierarchies. Hullman and Diakopoulos [13] define, "four editorial layers that can be used to convey meaning, including the data, visual representation, textual annotations, and interactivity" [13, pg. 2233]. Designers choose the data that they will represent or omit using filtering techniques; their representations then carry these choices into the visual domain using metonymy or metaphor to suggest meanings that are not evident in the data or categorize data in different ways to emphasize values. Annotations direct the viewer's attention and interaction design leads the viewer to specific subsets of data. Beyond these layers, provenance is a means to identify data sources. Other linguistic tools that build meaning are contrast and classification. "Procedural rhetoric" are editorial choices such as spatial ordering, partial animations, menus, or search bars that drive the viewer's experience. Their framework serves as a constructive feedback mechanism for the designer in understanding how different individuals interpret designs and visuals.

Segal and Heer [14] differentiate interaction strategies for narrative visualizations according to the degree to which users are directed through the visualization or supported to explore freely. These are a "Martini Glass", Interactive Slideshow" or "Drill-Down Story". Our approach was closest to the latter, "the user can interact with particular points of the visualization to reveal additional details and background information relevant to the main theme" [11, pg. 9] Our research challenges arguments that explicit metaphors are no more effective in engaging visualization viewers than simple graphs [15]. Diamond [16] demonstrates that graphs are culturally bound as are all representations. Bateman et al. [17] suggest that it is not the use of metaphors in visualization that is the problem but the appropriate choice of metaphor.

Smiciklas [18] contradicts Boy's findings that narrativity has no impact on visualization legibility or interpretation, by illustrating the ways that infographics which are narrative by definition, have impacted significant societal decisions. Infographics can mobilize cognitively entrenched spatial patterns known as image schemas which are a recurring structure within our cognitive processes to establish patterns of understanding and reasoning [19]. Harrison et al. [20] studied image schemas and determined that engagement occurred rapidly, within 500 ms of seeing a graphic. They catalogue users' aesthetic preferences by demographics, specifically age, education level and gender and propose, "When optimizing the design of an infographic to make a good first impression, therefore, designers should aim for a low to medium complexity (e.g., by choosing a limited number of image and text areas), and a medium to high colorfulness" [20, pg. 1190] if they wish to reach their largest audience. As an alternative, designers can design for specific sub-groups, knowing their preferences and build a dashboard that allows personalization. Storytelling strategies combined with succinct graphics appear to enhance data analysis.

3 Methodology

Our co-design approach drew from Sedlmair et al. [21] who propose four steps for visualization design: analyze a specific real-world problem faced by domain experts; design many possibilities to address the problem; validate the proposed design with the domain experts (users); reflect the lessons learned during the design development. We gained an understanding of the communications strategies and internal culture of our

Heritage Canada partners. They were new to visual analytics but had a strong background in data analytics, infographics, and text-based narrative. We held workshops to share visualization techniques and approaches to infographics, joined by iterative sketching, prototyping and critiques. Other stakeholders, including cultural communities celebrate effective storytelling and powerful visual imagery. For all of these reasons we decided on a data storytelling approach that combined narrative visualization and infographics.

4 Visualization Approach

We chose a mix of narrative visualization and infographics techniques, responding to the needs of our collaborators and the larger cultural community in order, "to provide models of actual and theoretical worlds and provide manipulation of data" [4, pg. 3]. To apply narrative techniques, we needed to identify suitable visualization typologies to summarize the multidimensional data and present it in context using infographics techniques without influencing or biasing analysis. We researched The Data Visualization Catalogue, a library of different information visualization types [22] matching data visualization typologies, their functions, and their applications to the data narratives they intend to reflect. The Data Viz Project [23], includes interactive data models [D3.js [24] as does Bostock et al.'s D3 data-driven documents [25]. As does Bostock et al.'s D^3 data-driven documents [25]. The diversity demographic data was structured in spreadsheets; we translated it using *Flourish Studio* [26] *Tableau* [27], a charting tool, *Datawrapper* [28, 29] and *D3.js* [25] into visualizations.

We chose a series of visualization typologies for this project. An Alluvial diagram reviews distribution, elicits comparisons, indicates correlations, and displays trends over time. A Sunburst Diagram serves to visualize hierarchical data, with parts to a whole, depicted by concentric circles with sliced outer rings. Best practices in visualization offer different ways of analyzing the same data in order to encourage users' critical engagement with the data [4]. Both the Alluvial Diagram and Sunburst Diagram provide comparisons and distributions, which means, there could be a few choices of visualization types for the same data set. A Chord Diagram visualizes the interrelationships between entities. A Violin Plot visualizes the distribution of data and its probability density. A Pictorial Chart uses relative sizes or repetitions of the same icon, picture, or symbol to show comparison between volumes. A Radial Column Chart uses a grid of concentric circles where bar charts are plotted. A Choropleth Map displays divided geographical areas or regions that are in relation to a data variable. A Donut Chart functions identically to a pie chart, except for the blank space inside that we use to display information. A Treemap displays hierarchical data as a set of nested rectangles with subcategory rectangles inside. At times we combined two different visualization types such as a Choropleth map of Canada for overview and pie charts for detail. We tried various approaches to edge case analytics (including semantic zooms) to represent small data, making these visible, readable, and comparable to the large numbers.

Pictograms, symbols, and icons can be more easily read and understood by individuals without demanding a particular language. Drawing from infographics principles, of blending data with design to support the rapid understanding of data, we implemented graphical cues and pictographs in our data visualization and in explanatory sections. For example, to represent disability status, we illustrated the 'Key Findings' section of the dashboard with icons of Braille, the writing system for visually impaired; sign language communication tool for deaf individuals; and we included an icon of the active wheelchair. Disability status and cultural consumption is presented in Fig. 1. These strategies were carried into prototype design.

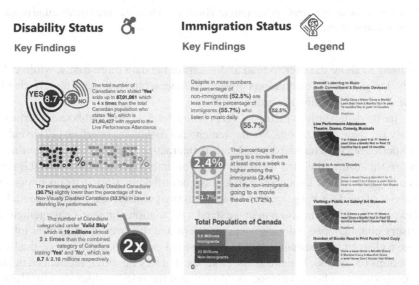

Fig. 1. Example of the implementation of Pictograms, Semiotics, and Iconography

5 Prototype

5.1 Design Strategy

The chosen visualization typologies act as infrastructures where we embedded the metaphors which function as the bridge to interpret the data or data context. Metaphors are a catalyst to propel audiences' insights into the data story. At times we used info-graphics to frame visualizations, situating these within a creative medium (Music for example). In other instances, we used pictograms or symbols within graphs in order to correlate numbers with their context. In Fig. 2 (a and e) the radio image frames analytics regarding radio listening in Canada. A Donut Chart not only functions for comparisons, proportions, parts-to-a-whole, but also fits in the "radio", giving interactors a quick idea of proportional distribution of the data. When hovering on different colors which represent different frequencies, the users can see the corresponding numbers and legends in the graph. We used text annotations with highlighted keywords in order to focus the viewer's attention and provide interpretation of the data. These processes speak to the editorial layer of choosing data and expressing the data through appropriate representations that suggest meanings not immediately imminent within the data [13].

In Fig. 3 the data indicates the proportion of the population going to movie theatres, hence we used the metaphor of "cinema seat" as an icon to represent numerical data. The

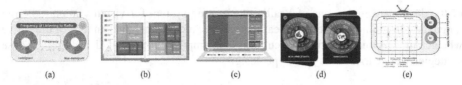

Fig. 2. These show several implementations of visual metaphors that use visualization typologies to analyze creative medium

icon is used to allow the user to read and interpret the data more easily, while colours add a level of gender differentiation between attendees; blue representing self-identified males and red self-identified females.

Similar to visualizations acting as a repository for data, the dashboard interface is a repository for the visualizations. We implemented a dashboard interface [17] to enhance User Experience. We considered the level of interaction and user engagement needed to explore this data which led us to the use of an interactive dashboard which nestles between Segal and Heer's concept of slide show or drill down story in its openness. From our analysis of the data, we gained the insight that two points of entry were needed. Users could explore a creative medium to understand a population segment's engagement with it, or users could choose a demographic segment and discover their cultural interests. To make a clear and consistent structure, we divided the dashboard space vertically into three sections (columns): Visualization, Legends, and Key Findings, referenced in Fig. 3. These constructs can be understood as "procedural rhetoric" as discussed by Hullman, and Diakopoulos [13]. We divided the dashboard space into three columns. Navigation buttons such as backward, forward, back to the homepage, are represented by an icon button next to the title "gender" which shows the infographic when hovering on it, as well as the "source" button at the bottom which shows our data source. We aimed to keep the dashboard functions concise with sufficient information and context for the visual analytics.

We considered the user navigation while designing the interface prototype. For example, in Fig. 3 there is an icon button next to the title "gender" which shows the infographic when hovering on it, as well as the "source" button in the bottom which shows our data source, ensuring that we provide the user with provenance. By applying these interactive buttons, along with the hovering effect on the graph which presents the percentage above the pictorial chart, we aim to keep the dashboard concise while containing sufficient information and context for the visual analytics. The interaction creates an enhanced user experience to allow users to immerse in the visualization that tells the data story. This strategy adopts Segal and Heer's "transition guidance" approach [14, pg. 7].

In Fig. 4 visualizations present two demographic factors, gender, and year of immigration in relation to movie watching practices on digital devices. A Treemap Visualization provides a hierarchical representation of proportional data in the form of nested rectangles, visualizing the proportion of individuals who reported watching a movie or film on any device in the past 12 months by year of immigration and gender. The data is framed by a laptop metaphor.

The colour scheme plays a significant role in branding the research, corresponding with the Heritage Canada's use of colours to depict specific artistic disciplines. We

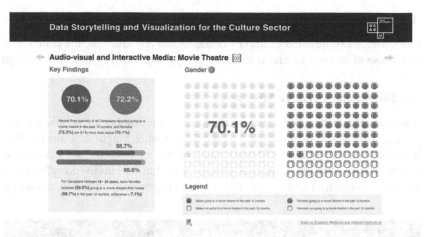

Fig. 3. These visualizations provide an analysis of attendance at movie theatres organized by gender.

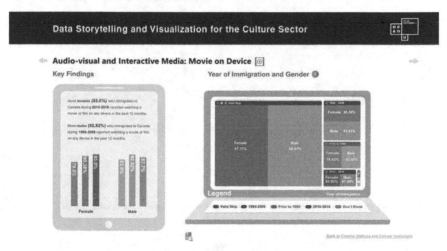

Fig. 4. Gender and immigration status in relation to digital media consumption on a device. Data labels are used as a semiotic tool to provide interpretation for users.

intentionally kept the format minimal to avoid stealing the attraction of the data visualizations which represented the subject matter. We applied a similar colour scheme to all the visualization and kept the contrast of color design for accessibility strictly complied with the WCAG principle which stands for Web Content Accessibility Guideline, with regard to the wide diversity of our audiences.

5.2   Data Storytelling - Two Examples from the Dashboard

We now provide two detailed examples of dashboard construction, the choice of visualizations, use of metaphors and interaction design and analysis indicated through the
strategy.

Mother Tongue and Creative Mediums

Description: Figure 5 depicts the distribution of the number of people engaged in
various Creative Mediums segregated as per their mother tongue in Canada. The data
labels on bars display only the lowest values of the set from the six main linguistic
categories. The creative mediums are presented by further subdivisions/linked nodes
which include listening/making to music (digital or conventional radio), attending live

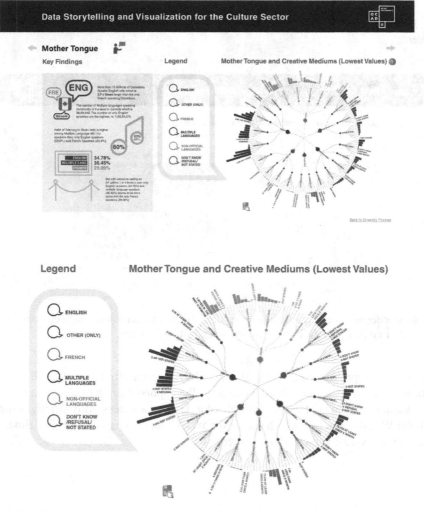

Fig. 5. Mother Tongue and Creative Mediums along with the DataViz Close-up

performances (dance, theatre, etc.), written works (frequency of reading habit), Cultural institutions (art galleries, libraries, museums, nature parks, historical sites) are included in addition to audio-visual and interactive media (TV, Online, movie theatre etc.)

Color Coding: Six vibrant colours are used to represent the official, non-official and other multiple languages spoken by the Canadian population. Speech bubbles, musical notes, national symbols, and gallery icons are used for accurate, and more rapid readability.

– *Key Findings:*

• More than 15 Million of Canadians Speak English only which is 2.7 times larger than the only French-speaking Canadians.
• The number of multiple language speaking communities is the least in Canada which is 36,69,640. The number of only English speakers is the highest, 1,52,54,676.
• The habit of listening to Music daily is higher among Multiple Language (60.1%) speakers than only English speakers (53.6%) and French Speakers (43.4%).
• With respect to visiting an Art gallery 1 to 4 times a year, English speakers (34.78%) and multiple language speakers (35.45%) seem to be more active than the only French speakers (29.09%).

Live Performance Attendance

Description: Figure 6 represents the Sunburst data visualization made up of concentric circles, visualizing the hierarchical distribution of Canadian population by their gender (self-identified males and females) and their live performance attendance (including Theatre, Drama, Comedy and Musicals). The further subdivisions or leaf nodes represent the number of times (frequency) of the visits by the audience separately over a period of a year.

Color Coding: The warmer colours like red, orange, and pink hues represent the female ratio while the cooler colours such as green, blue, and purple depict the male ratio. The gender icon has been constructed within the layout of the Sunburst diagram. Visual textures/patterns are used for making minimal values legible.

– *Key Findings:*

• Women (36.4%) attend live performances more than men (31.9%) by 4.5%, 1–4 times in a year.
• Women consist of 50.6% of Canada's population, 15.23 million.
• Men consist of 49.3% of Canada's population, 14.84 million.
• The difference between the Men's and women's numbers are high in all the demographics except for in the 'At least once a month' category where the same percentage (2%) of Men & Women have attended live performances equally with respect to their population.

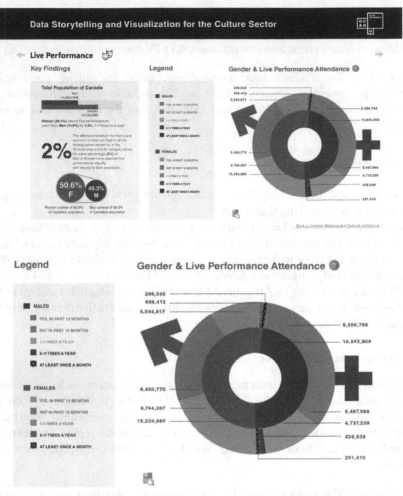

Fig. 6. This set of visualization analyzes attendance at live performances on the basis of gender.

6 Conclusion and Future Work

6.1 Conclusions

The application of narrative devices and rhetorical strategies [13] allowed effective use of layers of meaning and interpretation of this complex multidimensional data set and the design of improved user interaction. The concept of Provenance Rhetoric [13, 2011, pg. 4] was of value to the analysis of our inclusive data set, where it was important to cite data sources, designated by a source button. It allows stakeholders to understand the qualities and limits of the data used for analysis and visualization. We also revealed methodological choices, through a question mark "how to read" button, providing a level of transparency which Fernandez et al. [7] emphasize when dealing with diversity data. We were rigorous in matching metaphor to subject. The concept of Mapping Rhetoric [13, pg. 4–5] inspired our application of visual metaphors and metonymy, including colour mappings, in which different colors represent different groups. We used typographic emphases, an element of Linguistic-based Rhetoric [13, pg. 5–6] such as sizing and bolding texts to direct users.

Our prototype bridges infographics and narrative visualization. Design choices considered the users' familiarity of data visualizations. The pictograms and infographics provided clear data information by using on unintrusive and objective visual style. These extracted key insights which helped the users, included those without visualization knowledge. to capture and understand the data.

By developing an interactive visualization strategy, we discovered correlations in the data and allowed discovery over well sequenced navigation which would not have been possible through static infographics and lengthy text descriptions [20]. Our research methods and argue that designers must effectively represent diversity and inclusion data analysis in ways that can address diverse stakeholders, from equity seeking groups, to policy analysts, to agencies and companies implementing diversity strategies.

6.2 Future Work

Interest in representing demographic data in relation to cultural creation and consumption continues to grow in Canada and elsewhere, allowing for the ongoing development of our prototypes. The representation of diversity data requires constant review and revision. Having worked with existing data sets we will explore expanded methods of accessing diversity data and structuring this data (including survey data from Statistics Canada, Heritage Canada, and cultural funding agencies), we will experiment with narrative strategies that frame data without directing users' conclusions [30]. We will consistently update our design of demographic icons for a range of gender identities, Indigenous and racialized identities, and vetting these with our partners and their stakeholders.

References

1. Statistics Canada: Surveys and Statistical Programs - General Social Survey: Canadians at Work and Home (GSS) (2017). https://www23.statcan.gc.ca/imdb/p2SV.pl?Function=getSurvey&SDDS=5221
2. Statistics Canada: Surveys and Statistical Programs - General Social Survey: Canadians at Work and Home (GSS), Statistics Canada, 201 (2016). https://www23.statcan.gc.ca/imdb/p2SV.pl?Function=getSurvey&SDDS=5221
3. Pham, T., Hess, R., Ju, C., Zhang, E., Metoyer, R.: Visualization of diversity in large multivariant datasets. IEEE Trans. Vis. Comput. Graph. 16(6) (2016)
4. Meirelles, I.: Design for Information: An Introduction to the Histories, Theories, and Best Practices Behind Effective Information Visualizations. Rockport Publishers, Beverly (2013)
5. Diamond, S., Silver, D.: Redefining Public Art in Toronto. OCAD University, Toronto (2017)
6. City of Toronto (2020). https://www.toronto.ca/explore-enjoy/history-art-culture/public-art/public-art-strategy/
7. Fernandez, T., et al.: More comprehensive and inclusive approaches to demographic data collection. School of Engineering Education Graduate Student Series. Paper 60 (2016). http://docs.lib.purdue.edu/enegs/60

8. Pitoura, E.: Social-minded measures of data quality: fairness, diversity, and lack of bias. J. Data Inf. Qual. **12**(3), 8 (2020). Article 12
9. Trewin, S., et al.: Considerations for AI fairness for people with disabilities. AI Matters **5**(3), 40–63 (2019)
10. Walny, J., et al.: Data changes everything: challenges and opportunities in data visualization design handoff. IEEE Trans. Vis. Comput. Graph. In: VIS 2019 Conference, 1 August 2019 (2019
11. Rodríguez, M.T., Nunes, S., Devezas, T.: Telling stories with data visualization. In: NHT 2015: Proceedings of the 2015 Workshop on Narrative & Hypertext, 2015 September, pp. 7–11 (2015)
12. Ghidini, E., Santost Caroline, Q., Manssourt, I., Silveira Milene, S.: Analyzing design strategies for narrative visualization. In: IHC 2017, Joinville, Brazil. 23–27 October 2017, © 2017 ACM (2017)
13. Hullman, J., Diakopoulos, N.: Visualization rhetoric: framing effects in narrative visualization. IEEE Trans. Visual. Comput. Graphics **17**(12), 2231–2240 (2011)
14. Segel, E., Heer, J.: Narrative visualization: telling stories with data. IEEE Trans. Visual. Comput. Graph. **16**(March), 1139–1148 (2010)
15. Boy, J., Detienne, F., Fekete, J.-D.: Storytelling in information visualizations: does it engage users to explore data? In: CHI 2015, Seoul, Republic of Korea, 18–23 April 2015 (2015)
16. Diamond, S.: Lenticular galaxies: the polyvalent aesthetics of data visualization. In: Kroker, A., Kroker, M. (eds.) C Theory, Reprinted 2012 Critical Digital Studies Reader. UT Press, Toronto (2010)
17. Bateman, S., Mandryk, R.L., Gutwin, C., Genest, A., McDine, D., Brooks, C.: Useful junk? The effects of visual embellishment on comprehension and memorability of charts. In: Proceedings of the SIGCHI Conference on Human Factors in Computing Systems, pp. 2573–2582 (2010)
18. Smiciklas, M.: The Power of Infographics. Que Publishing, Indianapolis (2012)
19. Lengler, R., Moere, A.V.: Guiding the viewer's imagination: how visual rhetorical figures create meaning in animated infographics. In: 2009 13th International Conference Information Visualisation, Barcelona, pp. 585–591 (2009)
20. Harrison, L., Reinecke, K., Chang, R.: Infographic aesthetics: designing for the first impression. In: CHI 2015, Seoul, Republic of Korea, 18–23 April 2015 (2015)
21. Sedlmair, M., Meyer, M., Munzner, T.: Design study methodology: reflections from the trenches and the stacks. IEEE Trans. Visual. Comput. Graph. **18**(12), 2431–2440 (2012)
22. Ribecca, S.: The Data Visualization Catalogue (2019). https://datavizcatalogue.com/
23. Data Viz Project—Collection of Data Visualizations to Get Inspired and Finding the Right Type. Data Viz Project. https://datavizproject.com/. Accessed 11 Mar 2020
24. D3 Data Driven Documents (2020). https://d3js.org/
25. Bostock, M., Ogievetsky, V., Heer, J.: D^3 data-driven documents. IEEE Trans. Visual. Comput. Graphics **17**(12), 2301–2309 (2011)
26. Duncan, C., Houston, R.: Flourish Studio – Data visualization and Storytelling (2012). https://flourish.studio/
27. Murray, D.G.: Tableau Your Data! Fast and Easy Visual Analysis with Tableau Software. Wiley, Hoboken (2013)
28. Datawrapper. Create Charts and Maps with Datawrapper (2020). https://www.datawrapper.de/
29. Munzner, T.: Visualization Analysis and Design. A K Peters Visualization Series, CRC Press, Boca Raton (2014)
30. We thank Heritage Canada for the funding that supported this research and our collaborators there, Marke Ambard, Allyson Green, Julia Collier and other members of their team

Visual Writing at the State-of-the-Art?

Jochen Gros[✉]

Hochschule Für Gestaltung, University of Art and Design
Offenbach Am Main, Offenbach, Germany
`mail@emoji-language.com`

Abstract. On the digital road to visual writing, pictograms, icons and signs are becoming available for everyone, following the example of emojis. They can be installed in digital fonts and written by keyboard in a line with letters, to illustrate or replace words. Emojis are close to achieving this state-of-the-art. Pictograms first require modified typography. This allows them to be reduced to letter-size and to embed in digital fonts like emojis. While, considering the advantages and disadvantages of pictograms and emojis, an experimental design will demonstrate how both types of visual characters can be combined in a hybrid writing system. A further step in visualizing language is based on an almost self-evident grammar that can apply equally to emojis, pictograms, and signs. In theory, the project refers to the fact that digital technology is creating a new economy of image processing, and to the realization that the *Pictorial Turn*, the rehabilitation of visual thinking, is now also being expressed in everyday language, in emails, chats and tweets. The feasibility of this project will currently benefit in particular from an input method that is already used for Chinese words and was implemented by Apple in 2020 with iOS 14. With this method, emojis (and possibly pictograms, icons, and signs) appear in a menu bar when words are entered, and a single tap can replace the letters. Future perspectives are concerned with the emotional and semantic possibilities of animated emojis and pictograms.

Keywords: Pictograms · Emojis · Information graphics · GUI · Visual grammar

1 Introduction

As a designer, the author was involved in the development of the theory of "product language" (Gros 2021) as well as in research projects on "design language" in the transition period from mass production to computer-controlled manufacturing (Gros 2003b). His interest in visual language developed in parallel, but it was just the other side of the same coin: As the theory of design language "translates" signs into words, visual writing "translates" words into signs. Further background is provided by the history of design, in which the development of the modern pictogram by Otto Neurath still holds a very prominent place (Neurath 1991). However, the history of the pictogram also tells us how the project of a pictographic writing system with grammar and vocabulary failed, not least for technical and economic reasons. So, only the rise of digital technology promised a new beginning. The philosopher Vilém Flusser, for instance, examined the "logic of digital technology" and recognized an unprecedented potential for new means and tools

© Springer Nature Switzerland AG 2021
M. M. Soares et al. (Eds.): HCII 2021, LNCS 12779, pp. 385–400, 2021.
https://doi.org/10.1007/978-3-030-78221-4_26

of visualizing language. In his book "Does Writing Have a Future?" he described digital image processing as a serious challenge to the alphabet due to the rise of, more complex, faster, and cheaper forms of visual communication (Flusser 1987). Back in the 1980s, this was all theory, but since then, the practice has passed some fundamental milestones: Pictograms reduced to letter-size could be embedded in digital fonts like Times and Helvetica; new input methods replaced words with visual characters; emojis expanded the visual vocabulary, demonstrating the state-of-the-art in technology, availability, and usability. All of this, together with an increasingly intuitive grammar, is now leading to the experimental design of hybrid visual writing, which includes pictograms and emojis along with letters. Furthermore, there lies the question of how animated pictograms and emojis can not only emotionally enrich a pictorial script, but also can make it semantically more detailed and self-evident.

Finally, the iPad, with its touch screen and stylus, not only offers cursive writing a gateway into the digital age, but also enables new pictorial handwriting, even visual calligraphy. This might be a distant vision, but it helps to remember that pictorial scripts have always been much closer to art and culture than the alphabet, and along with computerized tools that engrave letters and pictorial characters in wood, stone, or metal, visual writing could also enrich the language of architecture and design beyond information graphics, if not as a "new ornament".

2   On the Digital Road to Visual Writing

2.1   Language or Writing?

Visual sign systems are often referred to as visual languages, but as soon as we perceive a sign system as visual writing, not only the point of view changes but also the concept of design. This includes the intention to associate all signs with one (or more) corresponding terms of a spoken language—similar to the Chinese script, which can be written and read in different languages.

2.2   Pictograms in Letter Size

Since the rise of computers, visual writing has come to rely on digital technology. In the 1980s, however, pictorial characters, such as pictograms, could use only a few pixels to fit clearly into a line along with letters and numbers. Some of the first examples were made with a Macintosh computer and MacPaint, a bitmap-oriented program provided by Apple since 1984 (see Fig. 1).

Fig. 1. Pictograms in letter-size made in 1988 with a Macintosh computer

Emojis today, can certainly use many more pixels and still fit in a line. On the road to visual writing, however, these early pictograms were already some steps ahead. Their body language enabled, for instance, the representation of personal pronouns such as "I" and "you" and auxiliary verbs like "have" and "want" (see Fig. 2). In the following years, these pictograms were used to illustrate a comprehensive visual grammar (Gros 2003a), which has remained essentially the same in its subsequent versions, although this grammar was then also represented with different pictograms and published as "Pictoperanto" (Gros 2011).

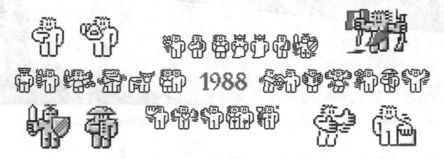

Fig. 2. Vocabulary of pictograms

2.3 Digital Fictional

Progress in computer graphics enabled a higher pixel density and thus a linear representation of pictograms. In the exhibition "Digital Fictional", which was shown in 1993 at the Carmelite Monastery in Frankfort, pictograms in this linear style were already used to "translate" a fresco painted by Jörg Ratgeb in the 16th century (see Fig. 4). This "translation" was lost, but the underlying grammar with 30 "rules" is still available in the catalog (Gros 1993). It contains, for example, epitomes, such as that for "art" and multiple epitomes, such as those for "traffic" and "clothing" (see Fig. 3), which resemble the Chinese character for "bright" that combines the pictograms for "sun" and "moon" (明).

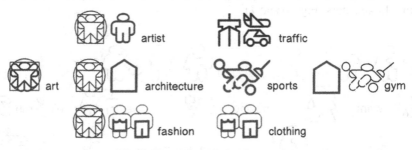

Fig. 3. Examples of visual grammar

Fig. 4. "Translation" of a fresco in the exhibition of digital fictional 1993

3   Visual Characters in Digital Fonts

The international design congress "Typo Berlin" took place in 2004 using the motto "Typo Talks". The authors contribution now could be designed in vector graphics and installed with a digital font like Aral, Times or any Chinese typeface (Fig. 5).

Fig. 5. A pictorial font like Arial and Times

This approach was further elaborated in the book "Pictograms Icons & Signs. A Guide to Information Graphics" (Gros 2006a, 2005b), along with a German, a Japanese, and a Chinese edition. Since these pictograms are embedded in a digital font, they could be printed like letters (Figs. 6 and 7).

Fig. 6. Visual grammar in vector graphics

I will love my father's cats.

Fig. 7. Experimental sentences

Basic research on visual writing systems can hardly predict who will use them, in what context, and for what purpose. This will be the subject of applied research and experimental design, in which digital fonts must be tested in a wide range of applications, far beyond informing illiterates. These applications could be, for instance, eye-catching headlines, slogans, user interfaces, presentations, cookbooks, children's books, emails, and chats—or perhaps, haiku. The following experiment is a very free "translation" referring to Issa: *The proud knight. High upon his steed. Steps down to see a flower* (Fig. 8).

Fig. 8. Visual "Translation", based on a Haiku by Issa

Another demonstration with this pictorial font was selected in the competition "Welche Sprache spricht Europa?" ("Which Language does Europe speak?"), which was announced by the Young Academy at the Berlin-Brandenburg Academy of Sciences and Humanities. On this occasion, the concept of visual writing could at least illustrate how much Europe would benefit from such a writing system (Gros 2005a) (Fig. 9).

Quelle langue parle l'Europe
Quale lingua parla Europa
Welche Sprache spricht Europa

Fig. 9. Word Literally: "Which Language speaks Europe?"

4 Sign-Typing. The Decisive Step to Usability

Two technological advances are shaping the future of visual writing: digital fonts and input methods for writing signs via the keyboard (or voice input). This *sign-typing* is already possible either with the programming of Open-Type fonts, initially called *icon-typing* (Gros 2006b, 2008, 2009), or with *emoji-typing*.

4.1 Icon-Typing

Programming OpenType fonts can enable users to automatically replace (or illustrate) certain words with pictograms. To demonstrate this "magic" function, several hundred pictograms in a classic black and white style have been modified to fit in a line. The following visualization of terms and sentences is based on the same grammar as in earlier fonts and is written by typing words on a keyboard (Fig. 10).

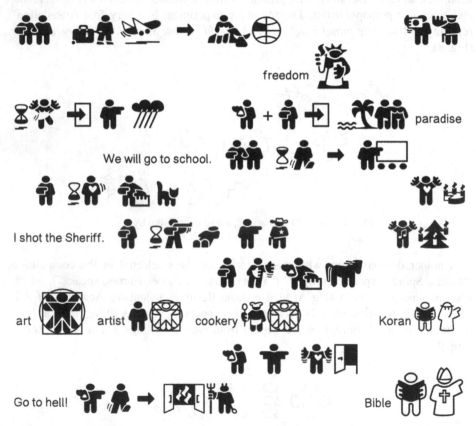

Fig. 10. A "Magic" Font that Replaces Words with Pictograms

4.2 Emoji-Typing

Emojis are preinstalled with digital fonts in cell phones and computers for a decade now, but it's only in recent years that they can be written by typing words on a keyboard. The forerunner of this method was the input system of Chinese writing. Here, if you type "che" (car) you can write the word either with a classic character or with an emoji. In principle, however, this input method can also display pictograms or other signs (Fig. 11).

Fig. 11. Emoji-typing, as introduced, and as possible

Apple introduced essentially the same method with iOS 14, and now we can expect this method to catch on because of its ease of usability and because in an ever-growing vocabulary certain emojis really can't be found any other way (Fig. 12).

Fig. 12. Apple emoji-typing since iOS 14, as introduced, and as possible

Using this input method, we get used to the literal meaning of emojis (or pictograms) without explicit learning. In other words: We are already on the home stretch to new visual writing, even if any hurdles remain, that has less to do with technology than with typography and grammar.

5   Visual Grammar

More than 1300 emojis represent the current state-of-the-art in visual writing, but why can't we still use them to write a simple sentence like "I love you"? This is due to the general difficulty of using photorealistic images as characters. In principle, little can be done about this. Only through the formation of compound terms, the current vocabulary of emojis can be expanded by some abstract terms. Thus, the following examples may be just a small step to visual writing, but the very attempt to form compound terms with emojis implies nothing less than a paradigm shift from viewing emojis as emoticons to viewing emojis as pictorial characters (Fig. 13).

Fig. 13. Compound terms with emojis

Before taking the next steps, it seems useful to consider the advantages and disadvantages of emojis and pictograms. The advantages of emojis do not only include their technological edge. Emojis have evolved in a communicative process like a spoken language, and whereas the vocabulary of pictograms has split into Babylonian variants, the international Unicode Consortium is warily eyeing the introduction of new emojis in a manner, not unlike the Oxford English Dictionary's scrutiny of developments in the English language. Another advantage of emojis is that they are freely available to everyone, whereas the use of pictograms is usually restricted by copyright laws and license fees. Pictograms are therefore mainly used by professional designers in commercial applications. In contrast, the emergence of emojis is almost comparable to the transition from professional scribes to general literacy. Moreover, emojis have also become popular because of their cute and colorful design, but this is not always an advantage, as the photorealistic style of emojis is associated with a rather childish image, which excludes emojis from certain applications and almost the entire field of information graphics. However, the most serious problem with emojis is their inability to visualize abstract concepts. Thus, there is still no emojis for personal pronouns like "I" and "you". We all know gestures with this meaning, but the problem with emojis is: which person should represent these gestures, with which gender, color, age, haircut, clothes? This kind of problem becomes even more apparent when it comes to notions like "human", "friendship" or "community", where the meaning implies an abstraction from all variable characteristics (Fig. 14).

Fig. 14. Abstract Terms with Pictograms

Also missing in the vocabulary of emojis are terms referring to sex and crime. Photorealistic emojis would trigger too much emotion in these areas. So, for example, the emoji term "gun" is only shown as a toy and nude emojis are considered too explicit. Pictograms, on the other hand, are less suspected of being pornographic. Nevertheless, any self-evident representation of visual concepts for sex and crime will always remain delicate (Fig. 15).

Fig. 15. Delicate terms in any visual vocabulary

After weighing pros and cons, a comprehensive sign vocabulary that allows for complete sentences is probably most easily achieved through a combination of emojis and pictograms, where both can make use of their respective advantages. See (Gros 2020). The following design is meant to give the first impression of such a hybrid visual writing system (Fig. 16).

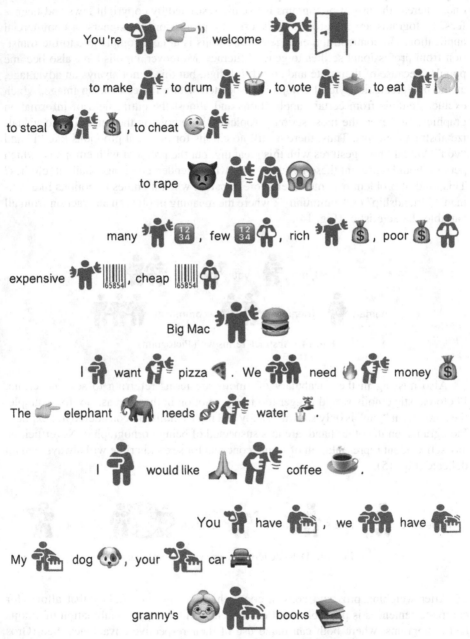

Fig. 16. Respective benefits of emojis and pictograms

Who knows, if we will ever use a pictorial script with all tenses of the verb? Yet, this possibility seems of theoretical interest and might prove useful someday (Fig. 17).

Fig. 17. Tenses of the verb

Last but not least, the implementation of a visual writing system also poses an organizational problem. This concerns the integration of pictograms, icons and signs into the Unicode system, as is already the case with alphabets and emojis.

6 Tickets to Unicode?

Actually, there are already a few pictograms in the Unicode system, but they are just a pitiful remnant from the early days of computers (Fig. 18).

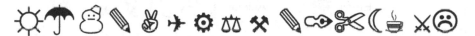

Fig. 18. Pictograms in the unicode system

The Unicode Consortium was established to set a global standard for all alphabetical characters and visual signs, but "The Annex of Universal Languages" alone refers to 15 different sign systems (Walthert 2020). Applications for universal code numbers must therefore be reviewed, as is already the case with emojis. Now, one can certainly criticize the way this review process is conducted, as well as the membership and legitimacy of the Unicode Consortium itself. Without Unicode, however, the worldwide success of emojis would not have happened, and various considerations by developers of sign systems to hack or circumvent Unicode could easily cause a new Babylon. In this conflict between standard and diversity, a synthesis seems possible if the Unicode numbers are assigned to terms rather than signs. Thus, the standard refers, for instance, to adjectives such as "cheap" and "expensive", or to verbs such as "go" and "went", but corresponding signs can be created in any style and offered in various fonts, so that they can be used by different people in different contexts, basically like the ABC, which is offered not only as Times and Helvetica. Then, it is not the Unicode Consortium that decides whether a sign set is acceptable, but the user, just by choosing a sign font, as we choose between alphabetic fonts. In this way, even a complete text could be converted from one sign system to another, as we can display a text in Times or Helvetica. Thus, a direct comparison between different character fonts becomes possible, which can be very instructive, especially in the early days of visual writing.

7   Beyond the Model of Hieroglyphics

The implementation of visual writing within the next decades seems to be a very ambitious project, if not a vision. According to the logic of "digital technology", however, this is just another milestone on the digital road to visual writing, because there are also new possibilities that go far beyond the ancient model of hieroglyphics. Most important are animated signs.

7.1   Signs in Motion and Hot Emotion

Animated letters are possible but make little sense, as compared to animated emojis and pictograms. They express stronger emotions and allow more detailed and self-explanatory formulations. This is especially true with the verb. Take, for example, "to speak". In the vocabulary of emojis, this verb is visualized like a pictogram since it apparently cannot be represented in the style of emojis. With an animation, on the other hand, just two figures taking turns like in a flipbook can represent the verb in a more natural and self-evident way. Animations can also include determinatives to express, for instance, the past tense or to turn "speak" into "sing", "curse" or "lie" (Fig. 19).

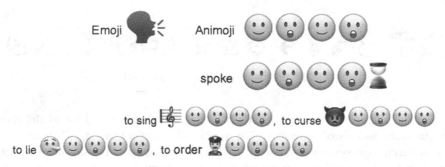

Fig. 19. Animation Sequences

Pictograms with detailed body language can make even more use of animation than emojis that focus on facial expressions. See, http://www.emoji-language.com and (Gros 2020). Following are three sequences with animated pictograms. Theoretically, however, it is now also possible to display complete sentences not in a line, but on a single spot, quasi as visual writing in the z-axis (Fig. 20).

Fig. 20. Animation Sequences

7.2 Pictorial-Handwriting

Although handwriting has lost its former importance, the iPad with touch screen and digital pen opens up at least a small path to the digital future of cursive writing and, why not, of pictorial handwriting. This means more than scribbling smileys and stick-figures in a text or on a PDF. Pictograms, too, can be scribbled as characters representing terms, and with simple apps, they can even be animated by anyone as in a flipbook (Fig. 21).

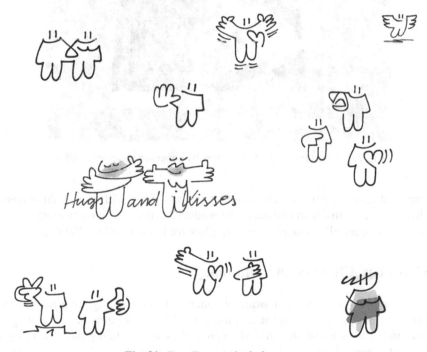

Fig. 21. Doodlgrams depicting terms

Certainly, it seems very doubtful that visual handwriting can ever be written as fluently as a cursive script (Gros 2013, 2017, 2018). In terms of technology, however, it seems quite possible that even clumsy scribbles can be automatically converted into typographic or calligraphic pictograms. Input systems for Chinese handwriting already make use of this technology.

7.3 From the Digital to the Material World

With computer-controlled milling, laser engraving and 3D printing any kind of digital writing can be easily transferred to the material world, and we can do it right from the computer or tablet. Thus, the engraving of alphabetic letters in wood, metal, or stone with CNC (Computer Numeric Controlled) tools is already common practice, but what does this technology mean for new visual writing? This is hard to predict, but throughout the history of visual writing, handwriting and calligraphy this mixture of information, emotion and art has also shaped the contemporary styles of architecture and consumer goods. This all ended only when manual labor became prohibitively expensive and the assembly line symbolized progress and modernity (Fig. 22).

Fig. 22. Transfer of digital characters by computer-controlled milling

Today, it may seem rather unlikely that visual writing will ever again become a significant narrative in our architectural and product language, but custom manufacturing with computer-controlled machines would allow for just that. (Gros 2003b).

8   Concerns, Chances and Summary

For many decades we have been aware of concerns that the pictogram poses an attack on rational thinking and the spirit of modernity. These concerns are not easily dismissed, and with progress in pictorial writing, they will certainly increase in significance and weight. Emojis, which are still perceived in the tradition of emoticons, seem to be largely excluded from these concerns. In reality, however, emojis are more than just fun, they are actually what the word emoji literally means, e-picture moji-characters, albeit in an early stage of visual writing. All in all, the increasing use of emojis and pictograms do indeed give further cause for concern and criticism, but now this discussion has a fundamentally new point of reference. Writing no longer has to decide between word and image. Both can be used and cultivated under the same technological and economic conditions. A mere revival of the historical iconographic controversy would therefore be an atavism. Yet, the question of how to evaluate the increasing interaction between word and image, socially and culturally, linguistically and morally, still seems largely open. With this in mind, the present paper could only illustrate and reinforce Vilém Flusser's assumption that the "logic of digital technology" will lead to something like new visual writing — however the zeitgeist may design, use and judge it.

References

http://emoji-language.com is becoming an information hub for further illustrations, animations, and YouTube videos

Flusser, V.: Die Schrift – Hat Schreiben Zukunft? Immatrix Publications, Göttingen (1987). In English: Does Writing Have a Future? Roth, N.A. (trans.), p. 208. University of Minnesota Press (2011)

Neurath, O.: Gesammelte bildpädagogische Schriften. Hölder-Pichler-Tempsky Verlag, Wien (1991)

Gros, J.: Neue Bilderschrift (New Pictorial Script, a visual Grammar in German and English). In: Digital Fiktional, Katalog zur Ausstellung im Frankfurter Karmeliter Kloster. Hermann Schmidt Verlag, Mainz (1993)

Gros, J.: Icon-Language.com – Piktogramm, Pictogram All Yours. Books on Demand, Norderstedt (2003a)

Gros, J.: Art customization – individualization and personalization are characteristics of art. In: Tseng, M.M., Piller, F.T. (eds.) The Customer Centric Enterprise, Advances in Mass Customization and Personalization. Springer, Heidelberg (2003b). https://doi.org/10.1007/978-3-642-554 60-5_7

Gros, J.: Icon-word. In: Welche Sprache spricht Europa? BWV, Berliner Wissenschafts-Verlag, Berlin (2005a)

Gros, J.: Entwicklung einer icon-sprache. In: Abdullah, R., Hübner, R. (eds.) Piktogramme und Icons, Pflicht oder Kür?. Hermann Schmidt Verlag, Mainz (2005b)

Gros, J.: A language of icons. In: Abdullah, R., Hübner, R. (eds.) Pictograms Icons & Signs – A Guide to Information Graphics. Thames & Hudson, New York (2006a)

Gros, J.: Icon Typing. Pictograms and Icons in OpenType. Books on Demand, Norderstedt (2006b)

Gros, J.: Icon-language. From vision to icon-typing. In: Proceedings of the OpenOffice Conference, Beijing (2008)

Gros, J.: Picoglyphs – Typography, Technology and Semantics of a New Pictorial Script. In: Prepare for Pictopia. Pictoplasma Publishing, Berlin (2009)

Gros, J.: Pictoperanto – Pictograms, Icons, Pictorial Fonts, Books on Demand, Norderstedt (2011)

Gros, J.: The Graphic Turn to Digital Handwriting and Drawing, Apple iBook (2013)

Gros, J.: Piktogramme als Emojis, Apple iBook (2017).

Gros, J.: Piktogramm trifft Emoji – Zum Stand digitaler Bilderschrift, Apple iBook (2018)

Walthert, E.: The Annex of Universal Languages. Printed and distributed by the Palace of Typographic Masonry. http://www.palaceoftypographicmasonry.nl

Gros, J.: Digital Picture-Fonts Get the Rosetta Stone Rolling. Apple iBook (2020)

Gros, J.: Stilwandel unter MitSprache des Designs. Rückblick auf die Entwicklung und den Gebrauch der Theorie der Produktsprache. In: Schwer, T., Vöckler, K. (eds.). Der Offenbacher Ansatz. Zur Theorie der Produktsprache. Transcript Verlag, Bielefeld (2021)

http://www.jochen-gros.de. Accessed 01 Dec 2020

http://www.icon-language.com, Accessed 01 Dec 2020/12/01.

Expressions of Data: Natural State, Specific Application, and General Pattern

Manhai Li[1]([✉]), Wa An[2], and Xi Wang[3]

[1] Chongqing University of Posts and Telecommunications, Chongqing 400065, China
limh@cqupt.edu.cn
[2] Guangzhou Academy of Fine Arts Guangzhou, Guangzhou 510006, China
[3] University of Minnesota, Minneapolis, MN 55455, USA

Abstract. With the explosive growth of data volume, more and more data are processed into various kinds of valuable products, which is the trend of the development of the times and the broad demand of the society. The work aims to analyze the different expressions of data and explore the research paradigm of data artifacts. When data becomes the object of design, there are also ethical problems. Creating meaningful data artifacts is the goal of making these data valuable, which is an important thing. Based on the cases of various products driven by data and those artifacts made by data, a classification study is conducted through induction and summary, three expressions of data are illustrated: natural state, specific application, and general pattern. The classification concerns mainly on the meaning rather than the depth or difficulty of data processing, also having nothing to do with these management dimensions of data, such as volume, variety, and velocity.

Keywords: Big data · Data artifacts · Expressions · Data commercialization

1 Introduction

Data have become a torrent flowing into every area of our lives. Things have been changed by network science. In the digitized world, data is presented anywhere and anytime—in every sector of organizations, day and night. Millions of networked sensors are being embedded in the physical world in devices such as automobiles, mobile phones, and other consumer devices including iPads and laptops that create, store and communicate massive data in the age of the Internet of Things.

Like the language, data is a kind of tool or medium for the human being to communicate, which is the inevitable outcome of the development of human society. With the increase in data volume, the ability of human is constantly improving. User behavior data collected through various sensors and websites embedding sites can more accurately and reliably reflect the real intention of individual users, because most of the data are recorded by unconscious triggers of consumers, so it can effectively reflect the personality, preferences, and willingness of consumers, and avoid researchers' cognitive bias and understanding ambiguity [1].

© Springer Nature Switzerland AG 2021
M. M. Soares et al. (Eds.): HCII 2021, LNCS 12779, pp. 401–412, 2021.
https://doi.org/10.1007/978-3-030-78221-4_27

There is strong evidence that data can play a significant economic role to the benefit not only of private commerce but also of national economies and their citizens, like creating momentous value for the economy of the world, enhancing the competitiveness and efficiency of companies or organizations and creating a substantial economic surplus for consumers. If US health care could use data to drive efficiency and quality, the potential value from data in the sector could be more than $300 billion in value every year, two-thirds of which would be in the form of reducing national health care expenditures by about 8 percent in operational efficiency improvements alone by using data. Another example, in the private sector, a retailer using data creatively and effectively has the potential to increase its operating margin by more than 60% [2].

In order to better explore how to make data produce greater value, let's review the relevant knowledge of data.

1.1 Data

As an English word, "data" comes from Latin, to mean known or confirmed facts. It was first used around 1640. Since 1897, it has been used to express the meaning of quantifiable facts collected for future reference. In the period of the establishment of modern science, data was applied to scientific research, and data collection became the basis of induction, deduction, and verification of scientific theory, and the basis of quantitative research in the field of natural science. For example, the weight, volume, landing time and other data of the object can be accurately recorded and analyzed, and the motion law of the free-falling body deduced from the formula can be reproduced by experiments. These data that can be verified are the basis for Galileo to discover the natural law, thus establishing Galileo's historical position in the scientific community. After the first computer came out in 1946, "data" began to have the meaning of computer information that can be recorded and stored, and then data has a large number of applications in the field of computer applications.

Fig. 1. The trajectory of a firefly is a kind of data.

In the global knowledge network era, Virginia M. Rometty, the CEO of IBM, points out, "Data is becoming a new natural resource...[3]". As a class of assets, data refers to symbols that can be recorded to describe the characteristics of things [4]. Because the historical span of data existence time is very large, data forms are also diverse. Data sources can be divided into social media, sensor data, system data, and data formats that can be divided into text, picture, audio, video, etc. As a resource, "data" includes not only unstructured data in today's big data category, including pictures, sounds, videos, etc., as well as data derived from the calculation, but also ancient digital abstract symbols and records. As the "data" of resources, the granularity can be large or small. For example, the scanned image of the ID card can be data, and the number and head picture on the ID card can also be data.

Specifically, the data mentioned here has three basic elements: 1. Be able to describe the characteristics of things, such as static attributes such as height and weight, and dynamic attributes such as speed and trajectory. 2. Be able to use measurement methods, such as weight of five pounds, length of six meters, etc. 3. It can be recorded in some way, such as writing with pen and paper, shooting with a camera, recording with a recorder, etc. The way of recording relies on technical means, the technical means of different times are different, so the scope of data in different periods is not the same. The trajectory of a firefly only becomes data when it is recorded by a camera (see Fig. 1). The sound did not seem as data in ancient times because ancients were unable to record sound. Nowadays, modern audio equipment can not only collect and record sound but also convert it into an audio digital signal, which makes people can develop interesting applications such as voice input methods. Like images and text, the sound has become an important type of data.

1.2 Big Data

If we say that the importance of data rises to a new era, we have to mention "big data". The concept of big data is proposed and promoted from the field of computer science, especially through the business operation and promotion of Oracle, Microsoft, and Cisco, big data has not only become a popular buzzword in the field of Internet technology and application but also, in fact, it has been integrated into the work, learning, and life of the general public from all aspects.

Recent developments in network science and social computing illustrate the fundamental shifts in communication, computing, collaboration, and commerce brought about by this trend, which generate amounts of data. Companies generate a fast-growing volume of information, transferring trillions of bytes of business data between their customers, suppliers, and operations. Meanwhile, as organizations go about their business and interact with individuals, they are producing an enormous amount of transactional data that is generated as a by-product of other activities. Consciously or unconsciously billions of individuals around the world contribute to amounts of big data by using social media sites, smartphones, and industrial machines. In a word, any activity of consumers in the digital environment, such as searching, communicating, browsing, sharing, buying and so on, would create its enormous trails of data.

Amounts of new applications and services that facilitate collective action and social interaction online with a rich exchange of multimedia information and evolution of aggregate knowledge have come to dominate the Internet. Like Twitter, Facebook, YouTube, LinkedIn, and Flickr are some of the brand names that dominate their respective social computing segments. These online sites generate amounts of data, containing social information and social knowledge. Specifically, in the year of 2012, Google alone processed about 24 petabytes (or 24,000 terabytes) of data every day [5]. While Twitter had more than 400 million Tweets per day and more than 140 million active users who log in at least once per month [6].

Data is experiencing the development process from "offline" to "online", from "static" to "flowing", from "closed" to "open". With the continuous progress of artificial intelligence, virtual reality, the Internet of things and other technologies, the development and evolution speed will be accelerated, and the impact will be expanded. Nowadays, data is accompanied by people anytime and anywhere, bringing lifestyle changes to all fields and society as a whole. In 2007, humankind was able to store 2.9×10^{20} optimally compressed bytes, communicate almost 2×10^{21} bytes, and carry out 6.4×10^{18} instructions per second on general-purpose computers [7].

2 Data as Products

2.1 Data Artifacts

Data was no longer regarded as static or stale, whose usefulness was finished once the purpose for which it was collected was achieved. Rather, data became a raw material of business, a vital economic input, used to create a new form of economic value. In fact, with the right mindset, data can be cleverly reused to become a fountain of innovation and new services. The data can reveal secrets to those with humility, willingness, and the tools to listen [8].

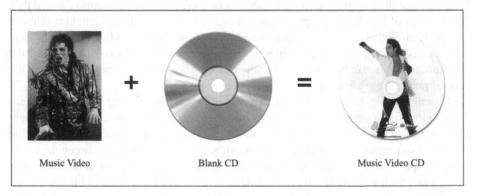

Music Video   Blank CD   Music Video CD

Fig. 2. The data artifact and the carrier

The data artifacts refer to the products made by data as raw material. It should be emphasized that the raw materials processed must be data. These data artifacts are immaterial, just like data themselves, without any physical characteristics. For example, Music Television is exactly a kind of data artifact, which comprehensively processing with various types of data such as sound, text, image, and video. People are willing to buy such immaterial products to meet their sophisticated emotional or identity needs.

These data artifacts need carriers to transfer, transact and show. Some of these carriers are material, like blank CDs or tapes. Some of them are immaterial, such as the iTunes platform or the Tencent music platform. The Music Video CD people buy contains two parts of content: The Music Video as data artifacts and The Blank CD as carriers (see Fig. 2).

The recognition of data can be traced back to primitive society. Especially in the practice of food collection and distribution, primitive humans gradually realized that they need something to record and describe the changes in the world, for instance, keeping records by tying ropes was one of the ways. When the amount of data accumulates to a certain extent, the data provide the possibility to restore and express the development trend of things. For example, people can build the same house quickly based on structural data. In extreme terms, if complete data can be collected and analyzed, the data can reflect the real world vividly.

People in different regions of the world use different technologies to produce different applications in different periods, resulting in different expressions of data. Limited by the lack of recording tools in ancient times, the data generated by human society was small, and the transaction of data was also small, so there was no clear concept of data artifacts. In the process of social evolution and development from industrialization to informatization, the data volume shows explosive growth, which affects all aspects of social life, the concept of data artifacts becomes more and more popular. In the era of big data, it is necessary to inquire about the logical relationship among these data artifacts.

2.2 Meaningful Data Commercialization

From the agricultural society to the industrial society, data was generated in every manufacturing process. While in the information age, as the amount of data has exploded, data is becoming more and more popular to discuss. At different times, people had different views on data. In the beginning, the data was irrelevant and ignored, while now the identity and emotion play momentous roles in the ultimate success of data commercialization, at the same time, the custome's experience of interacting with data is a positive one.

A meaningful experience is any process we're conscious of and involved in as it happens. As an individual, all of those things happen in the course of daily life express parts of your identity and define you in significant ways, including the tasks you do, the responsibilities you hold, the relationships and decisions you make, etc. The meaning of what you do is reflected in the process of experience. Data-driven companies need to evoke meaning through user experiences. As we've suggested, the experience people have with products, services, and events are only partly due to what a company might envision and endeavor to provide. The bulk of the experience is created by the consumers; that's how it becomes highly relevant for the individual.

Meaning helps us understand the world and ourselves, learn, and make sense of what's around us. It provides a framework for assessing what we value, believe, condone, and desire. Anything that supports a sense of meaning supports the basis for understanding and action, making it extremely valuable to us [9]. For example, millions of downloadable songs are not just because of fickle consumers, but because each of these items is a building block in the reality which we increasingly prefer they fit our concept of self. As we selectively purchase or reject these items, they become inextricably part of how we construct meaning in our lives.

The demand for meaning may be the defining characteristic of what makes us human [10]. It is common in advanced consumer markets that products and services have been already designed to meet sophisticated emotional or identity needs. The new generation of consumers who have grown up with smartphones and instant messaging are talking more frequently and passionately about meaning in their lives, expressing a desire for—even expecting—meaningful experiences from daily necessities. The emotions of young people are easy to light up when they learn about something capable of making their friends develop a stronger sense of community. Take iPod as an instance, what makes the iPod an overwhelming success is the union of invention, design, and marketing into a seamless whole that evokes meaning in the enjoyment of music by concentrating on the customer's experience. It goes beyond simply selling digital music to selling the sensation of freedom, wonder, and control. This wildly popular product integrated and reinforced a desirable musical experience, meeting the customer's demand for meaning.

3 Expressions of Data

The expressions of data can be divided into three types: natural state, specific application, and general pattern. The classification concerns mainly on the meaning rather than the depth or difficulty of data processing, also having nothing to do with these management dimensions of data, such as volume, variety, and velocity [11]. This classification has boundaries to shape and constrain the meaning of data artifacts but is not rigidly fixed and determinate. This classification is a placement, which is the classic feature of design thinking [12]. The boundary gives a context or orientation to thinking if design thinking is to be regarded as more than a series of creative accidents.

3.1 Natural State

After data processing, even in a complex way, the objective attributes of data have not been changed, still original, just like crude oil processing without chemical reaction. The objective attributes of the data are about validity, accuracy, integrity, and precision, aiming at describing the objective world. Most of the data visualization just makes the data presentation more intuitive and exquisite, keeping data in the original natural state. For example, the lunar calendar is a set of objective and stable data, which can be commercialized in many forms, such as bound sheets of paper hanging on the wall, in a watch, on the desktop, as a JavaScript object and many more instances. No matter in which form, the data is fixed and clear to everyone, without any ambiguity.

The original expression of data is the natural state. Figuratively speaking, the data artifacts in the natural state are like crude oil, the original product of oil (see Fig. 3).

An example is the Human scale manual, which is easy for designers to get the best advice visually. The human scales, like the length and size of human limbs, are important data for designers to improve the experience of the objects, such as a wheelchair. Some

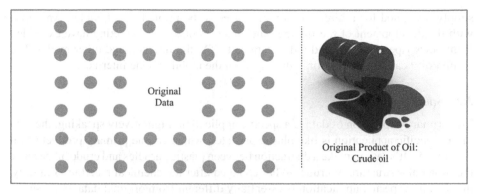

Fig. 3. The natural state of data.

Fig. 4. Human scale manual as a data artifact.

companies correlate the data and elaborate on the Human Scale Manual. Though these data are made to practical cards (see Fig. 4). They are still in the natural state.

Another example. The historical data of social stability, economic achievement, scientific and technological levels, and territorial area are publicly recorded in the original natural state. Different scholars use this data in different ways. Some scholars combine these data with the global economic data of the same period in history to get the proportion of each dynasty in the total world economic force at that time, which is used to support their academic views. Professor Xin Xiangyang comprehensively used these data to draw out the rise and fall of Chinese dynasties, intuitively restoring and expressing changes in Dynasties for more than 4,000 years [13].

Data artifacts are in a natural state not because of limited technical capabilities. While the carriers of data artifacts may change with the development of technology. For example, the commodity catalog is made by pictures, materials, prices, effects of commodities, which are all different kinds of data, expressing the characteristics of the commodity. The commodity catalog is always a kind of data artifacts in the natural state, with the development of direct marketing. Direct marketing is a form of communicating an offer, where organizations communicate directly to a pre-selected customer and supply a method for a direct response. It used to be printed as a booklet. And now, with the development of the Internet, the channels of direct marketing have expanded from newspapers, posters and radio stations to TV, the Internet, and other media. The commodity catalog is commonly displayed on the mobile phone interface.

3.2 Specific Application

The primary expression of data is a specific application. Figuratively speaking, the data in the specific application is like plastic particles, which are the primary product of oil (see Fig. 5). It's easy to make a distinction between plastic particles and crude oil because the molecular structure of crude oil has changed after the chemical reaction. Similarly, the data in a specific application is essentially different from original data, because the function and form go beyond the data itself after complex processing.

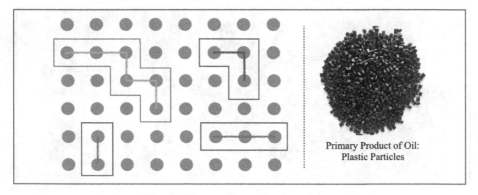

Primary Product of Oil:
Plastic Particles

Fig. 5. The specific application of data.

In the process of exploring and considering the world, people often encounter various specific problems. Data is the link between the objectivity of things and the subjectivity of human beings, helping people to understand the world. For hundreds of years, scientific researchers have been testing theoretical hypotheses and experimental schemes by monitoring and analyzing data synthetically until the truth of the problem is discovered. The value of data lies in the influence of people's decision-making methods because data can be used as a reference for people to discover the implicit relations they don't realize and then solve specific problems. For example, we have seen such strong correlations with Google Flu Trends: the more people in a particular geographic place search for particular terms through Google, the more people in that location have the flu [14]. In 2004 Wal-Mart peered into its mammoth databases of past transactions: what item each customer bought and the total cost, what else was in the shopping basket, the time of day, even the weather. By doing so, Wal-Mart noticed that before a hurricane, not only did sales of flashlights increase but so did sales of Pop-Tarts. Based on the data, Wal-Mart knows flashlights should stock at the front of stores next to the hurricane supplies to boost its sales [15].

For example, the MAPS.ME is an essential offline application for traveling, which is based on OpenStreetMap data. The digital map is a kind of data artifacts, which keep the data in natural state Users can find the location. While the navigation function driven by data is a specific application. Through the processing of these data, users can intuitively find their driving distance from one place to another, as well as the specific driving path, which can solve the user's travel problem (see Fig. 6).

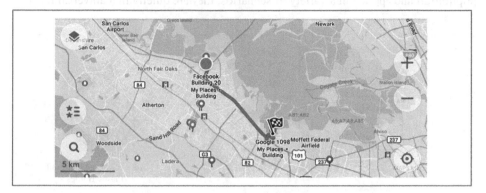

Fig. 6. Routing to a specific location by MAPS.ME

Another example, based on data gathered by Kansei Engineering [16], an ergonomic chair can be designed to make the user feel comfortable: the height of the chair naturally fits with user's cervical vertebra, the curve of the chair is consistent with user's physiological feeling. This concrete and effective result is generated by the correlation between different kinds of data. The data have been processed into improving the user experience of the chair.

In daily life and work, people mostly tend to focus on whether data can solve their problems instead of inquiring what data is working and how it works. Data can be processed into some kinds of products or services, through which people can feel that data is working behind them, but they cannot accurately know which data is playing a role. The ergonomic data or the map data has changed qualitatively after being processed. Instead of caring about the accuracy of specific data in Kansei Engineering, people only care about whether these data applications can solve their problems. People are willing to pay more for ergonomic chairs, due to the invisible data artifacts.

With the development of network science and social computing, big data has been acting as an important role in social research. For example, the data science team in Facebook has carried out a lot of researches to find widely applicable patterns from the massive data of human social behavior, to promote the process of human understanding of their behavior [17]. Four features of big data, like volume, correlation, flowability, and diversity, are conducive to solve wicked problems [18]. Here is a case. Albert-Laszlo Barabasi, one of the world's foremost authorities on the science of network theory, examined all logs of millions of people's mobile phone calls for four months, using a large scale of a dataset on a societal level. He unexpectedly discovered that people with lots of close friends are far less important to the stability of the network structure than the ones who have ties to more distant people. It suggests that there is a premium on diversity within a group and in society at large [19].

3.3   General Pattern

The advanced expression of data is the general pattern. Figuratively speaking, the data artifacts in general pattern is like the plastic bottles, which are the advanced product of oil (see Fig. 7). Just like plastic bottles are daily necessities, being used by a wider population and applied in a variety of scenarios, they are quietly in a universal form.

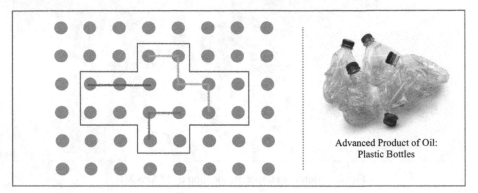

Advanced Product of Oil:
Plastic Bottles

Fig. 7. The general pattern of data

Based on all manner of specific data applications including data services, people can deeply find profound logic behind them. The profound logics are not common features of these applications, but the general patterns which can be used to explain the questions in these applications. For example, Zhima Credit, also known as Sesame Credit, is a private credit scoring and loyalty program system developed by Ant Financial Services Group, an affiliate of the Chinese Alibaba Group. Zhima Credit is a data artifact, using data from Alibaba's different services to compile its score. It integrates the needs of different data-driven applications, which usually help users to solve concrete problems. Customers receive a score based on a variety of factors based on social media interactions and purchases. Those with high rankings can rent bikes or cars without leaving a deposit and skip lines at hospitals by paying after they leave. The Zhima Credit as a data artifact is made by data as raw material, which are consumption data, credit card repayment data, transfer data and so on. It can be widely used in the field of public services, which has a wide range of social significance and has a macro impact on the choice of today's social credit system. It is worth noting that the Zhima Credit is refined and processed based on various wind control schemes of multiple banks. Before that, banks and other financial institutions have assessed and calculated the default risk of users and formed a restraint mechanism for specific services such as loan quotas.

It is worth mentioning that the popularity of usage is just one of the characteristics, not the only one. For example, the lunar calendar is widely used, but it is in a natural state, while not in general pattern.

4 Conclusion

In the era of big data, data is not just about extra output or subsidiary force or core competency, but raw materials in the process of data commercialization, which is an inevitable trend. With the explosive growth of data volume, more and more data are processed into various kinds of valuable products. We find that the value of data and meanings of data artifacts are related to the expressions of data.

There are three types of expressions of data: natural state, specific application, and general pattern. The original expression of data is the natural state, mostly used to restore and express things. The primary expression of data is in a specific application, focus on finding and solving problems. The advanced expression of data is the general pattern, used by a wider population and applied in a variety of scenarios.

This classification has boundaries to shape and constrain the meaning of data artifacts but is not rigidly fixed and determinate. The process from the natural state to the general pattern is for the greater value of data artifacts, by achieving more meanings of data. This classification is a placement, which is the classic feature of design thinking. The boundary gives a context or orientation to thinking if design thinking is to be regarded as more than a series of creative accidents.

Acknowledgement. "This   work   was   supported   by 重庆邮电大学博士启动基金/引进人才项目 (K2020-201)".

References

1. Watts, D.J.: A twenty-first century science. Nature **445**, 489 (2007)
2. McKinsey Global Institute: Big data: The next frontier for innovation, competition, and productivity. McKinsey Co. 156 (2011). https://doi.org/10.1080/01443610903114527
3. Rometty, V.M.: 2013 IBM annual report (2013)
4. Li, M.: Research on Data Commercialization Design Based on Valued-Dimension (2019)
5. Davenport, T.H., Barth, P., Bean, R.: How big data is different. MIT Sloan Manag. Rev. **54**, 43–46 (2012)
6. Geron, T.: Twitter' s Dick Costolo: Twitter Mobile Ad Revenue Beats Desktop On Some Days. Forbes. 10–13 (2012)
7. Hilbert, M., López, P.: The world's technological capacity to store, communicate, and compute information. Science (80−). 332, 60–65 (2011). https://doi.org/10.1126/science.1200970
8. Mayer-Schonberger, V., Cukier, K.: Big Data: A Revolution That Will Transform How We Live. Work and Think. Houghton Mifflin Harcourt, Boston (2013)
9. Geertz, C.: The Interpretation of Cultures (1973)
10. Diller, S., Shedroff, N., Rhea, D.: Making meaning: How successful businesses deliver meaningful customer experiences (2008)
11. Laney, D.: 3D Data Management: Controlling Data Volume, Velocity and Variety. Meta Gr. Inc. Applicatio, 4 (2001)
12. Buchanan, R.: Wicked problems in design thinking. Des. Issues **8**, 3–20 (1992). https://doi.org/10.2307/1511637
13. Xin, X.: Product Innovation In A Cultural Context. Carnegie Mellon Univ. 100 (2007)

14. Ginsberg, J., Mohebbi, M.H., Patel, R.S., Brammer, L., Smolinski, M.S., Brilliant, L.: Detecting influenza epidemics using search engine query data. Nature **457**, 1012–1014 (2009). https://doi.org/10.1038/nature07634
15. Hays, C.L.: What Wal-Mart Knows About Customers' Habits (2004)
16. Kalantary, S., Seraji, J.N.: The concept of hedonomics and Kansei engineering method in ergonomics: a narrative overview. Int. J. Occup. Hyg. **9**, 1–8 (2017)
17. Boyarski, D., Butter, R., Krippendorff, K., Solomon, R., Tomlinson, J.: Design in the Age of Information: A Report to the National Science Foundation. Raleigh, NC Des. Res. Lab. North Carolina State Univ. 184 (1997)
18. Li, M., Xin, X.: An approach to the wicked problems in design: case studies on data-driven companies. In: ISIDC 2018 Conference, pp. 563–569 (2018)
19. Barabasi, A.-L.: Bursts: The Hidden Patterns Behind Everything We Do, from Your E-mail to Bloody Crusades (2011)

Pasigraphy: Universal Visible Languages

Aaron Marcus[✉]

Aaron Marcus and Associates, 1196 Euclid Avenue, Berkeley, CA 94708, USA
Aaron.Marcus@bAMandA.com

Abstract. The author explains universal visible languages and discusses several examples from history. He focuses in particular on LoCoS, invented by Yukio Ota in 1964.

Keywords: Design · Mobile · Pasigraphy · Semiotics · Signs · Visible language

1 Introduction

Throughout history, linguists, designers, engineers, and scientists have sought to develop universal visible languages, in which signs communicate their meaning easily, and are consistent and logical, allowing for extension and change. In this paper, we explore these topics: Definition, history, and examples of pasigraphy; Ex. 1: Blissymbolics; Ex. 2: LoCoS; and LoCoS for Mobile Devices (LMD).

2 What is Pasigraphy?

Pasigraphy is universal writing. Each sign represents a concept, not necessarily word(s), or sound/s of spoken languages. The term comes from Greek πᾶσι (pasi) "to all" + γράφω (grapho) "to write". The objective of a universal visible language is to be intelligible to all persons, even those with no verbal language skills (*e.g.,* children, brain-damaged individuals, *etc.*), *i.e.,* as easy to use as ordinary numerals. The study of pasigraphy is a subset of linguistics, and/or semiotics, the science of signs as explained by Eco [1].

3 History of Pasigraphy

Early "Examples" of Pasigraphy: Examples of widespread, if not truly universal visible language systems occur in human history. Early Egyptian hieroglyphics (Fig. 1) and Chinese writing (Fig. 2) used ideograms, but also phonograms and pictograms.

Many pasigraphic schemes originated in Europe in the 17th and 18th centuries. Leopold Einstein reviews 60 attempts, especially languages, *e.g.,* Gottfried, Leibnitz, Alexander von Humboldt. Related to these are philosophical, constructed languages [2–6] by Lodwick, Urquhart, Dalgarno, and Wilkins. Leibniz [7] created *Lingua Generalis* (or *Lingua Universalis*) in 1678, a lexicon of characters upon which one might perform calculations yielding true propositions automatically.

© Springer Nature Switzerland AG 2021
M. M. Soares et al. (Eds.): HCII 2021, LNCS 12779, pp. 413–425, 2021.
https://doi.org/10.1007/978-3-030-78221-4_28

Fig. 1. Egyptian hieroglyphics.

Fig. 2. Ancient Chinese writing.

Modern Extensible Sign Systems: In the last century, several groups have created innovations, but not complete languages; they are large, systematic, extensible sign collections. Examples include: Neurath Isotype, 1925–34; International Sports Events Sign Systems (*e.g.*, Munich Olympics, 1972); Visualizing Global Energy Interdependence sign system, East-West Center, 1978. (See examples in Figs. 3, 4, 5.)

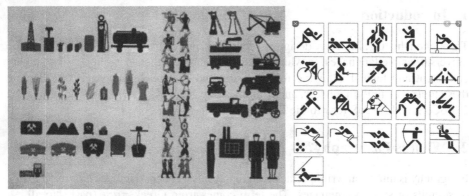

Fig. 3. Neurath Isotype: Pictographic Signs in Statistical Displays, Vienna, 1925–34, as shown in Gerd Arntz, Otto Neurath, Ausstellungstafel Mundaneum Den Haag, From Weirich, "Society of Signs: From Pictogram to Emoji", 2020.

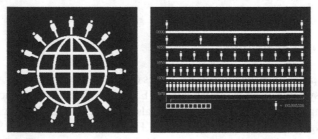

Fig. 4. International Event Sign System for the Munich Olympics, a very rational, gridded set designed by Otl Aicher's studio.

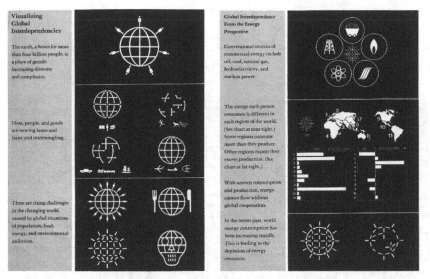

Fig. 5. East-West Center (EWC), Honolulu: 1000 signs (together with charts, maps, and diagrams, to explain global energy interdependence and other EWC analyses. Designed by the author with six other Research Fellows at the EWC, 1978.

4 Example 1: Modern Pasigraphic Visible Languages, Blissymbolics

Charles K. Bliss (CKB) (1897–1985) created (1942–49) an ideographic writing system inspired by Chinese. Born Karl Kasiel Blitz in Austro-Hungarian Czernowitz now Ukrainian Chernivtsi, he was a prisoner of the Nazi death camps of Dachau and Buchenwald and later was a refugee in the Shanghai Ghetto and in Sydney, Australia.

His Bliss Symbols (or Semantography) (Fig. 6) [8] consist of several hundred basic symbols, each representing a single concept and were easy to learn, read, and write. Bliss Symbols have seen use for people with speaking disorders, esp. by Shirley McNaughton, Ontario, since 1971, with cerebral palsy children. CKB failed to get the United Nations to establish Blissymbolics as an official language. He had similar objectives to the proponents of Esperanto, Gestuno, Isotype, *etc.* Blissymbolics is different from the world's major writing systems: the signs do not correspond to sounds of any spoken language. Note that Basic Chinese consists of about 3000 signs, and software developers of the US computer-aided design company Computervision asserted in 1985 that the company had created about 10,000 icons in about 10 years.

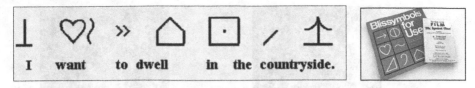

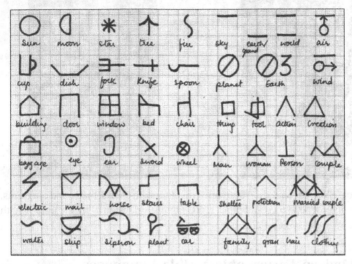

Fig. 6. Sample Blissymbolics. Source: http://www.alysion.org/handy/a lthandwriting.htm. Books: Blissymbols for Use (Ed., Barbara Hehner) and a film about Mr. Symbol Man, National Film Board of Canada. Sample signs: Source http://www.decodingculture.in/2010/02/no-bliss-without-leaf.html.

5   Example 2: Modern Pasigraphy, LoCoS (Lovers Communication System)

In *1964,* Yukio Ota, an internationally known Japanese graphic designer, invented LoCoS. He published a Japanese guide in 1973 and an English guide in 2017 (Fig. 7 [9]. Mr. Ota taught LoCoS internationally since 1964; he claims people can learn basic grammar and key signs in one day. LoCoS societies and organizations have arisen in Japan and elsewhere. In 2007, the author worked with Mr. Ota (Fig. 7) on a prototype mobile version [10], which is summarized here. See also [11].

Sentences in LoCoS: LoCoS can show complete expressions, equivalent to sentences, formed by three rows of squares read from left to right (Fig. 8). The main contents appear in the center row (Fig. 9). Signs in the top and bottom rows act as adverbs and adjectives respectively. At the time of its development, because of space constraints in mobile devices, LMD LoCoS used only one row and followed English grammar (subject-verb-object).

Comparison of LoCoS with Other Languages: LoCoS is different from alphabet languages. Meaning and form (appearance) in LoCoS are more closely tied. LoCoS is also

Fig. 7. Cover of English-language explanation of LoCoS and photograph of Mr. Ota (left) and author (Center), working on the mobile version of LoCoS, 2007.

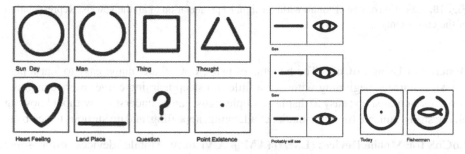

Fig. 8. Individual and combined LoCoS signs.

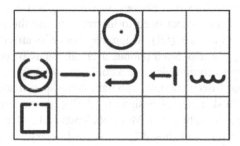

Fig. 9. Example sentence, "That fisherman will come back from the seat today."

different from other universal visible languages. Bliss Symbols uses more abstract signs (symbols); LoCoS uses more concrete (visually self-revealing or more iconic) signs. LoCoS is similar to, but different from Chinese ideograms in the Japanese language (Kanji). LoCoS is less abstract: signs are of concrete objects much as "road signs" show pictures of those objects such as hills or bridges. Like Kanji, one sign stands for one concept, although there are compound concepts. According to Mr. Ota, LoCoS re-uses signs more efficiently than traditional Chinese.

LoCoS Pronunciation: Mr. Ota has suggested rules for LoCoS pronunciation (Fig. 10), but he did not analyze conventions across major world languages for phonetic efficiency or viability. LMD does not currently use audio input/output. Pronunciations are necessary for denoting names of people and places.

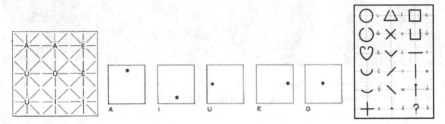

Fig. 10. Location of vowel sound within a sign. Representation of all the vowels. Representation of the consonants.

Benefits of Using LoCoS: The benefits of using LoCoS are many: easy to learn, progressive learning beginning with just a little; no steep learning curve; users can guess correctly at new signs; easy to display; simple signs; can be understood without knowing all the signs; suitable for mass media; challenging, appealing, and mysterious to newbies.

LoCoS for Mobile Devices (LMD) (AM + A Vision): Mobile devices offer some special advantages for LoCoS and other universal visible languages. Universal visible-language messaging can take advantage of mobile phones, which connect people world-wide and which can show, on smart phones, visual images. For example, people who don't speak the same language but need to interact can use the phones to do so, and will use a graphical user interface (UI), which may not be localized to their language or which can be daunting to grasp. Such phones users also may be people who speak the same language but want to communicate in a cool new way, *e.g.*, teenagers, children, or young adults. Users may also be people who have some speech/accessibility issues.

Then current (2007) sketches of designs by AM + A concerned prototypes for a LoCoS Mobile Device (LMD) based on Motorola V505 and Nokia 7610 phones. AM + A also considered a LoCoS-English and future needs like expanding the sign system of LoCoS and exploring other visual attributes of the signs (such as color, thickness, and stroke ends).

LMD Assumptions and Objectives: Developing World: There is continually growing mobile phone use in developing countries. In November 2020, China is reported to have 1.6 billion phone subscriptions, with about 448 million Internet phones in India in 2020, per statistia.com. People seem willing to spend up to 10% of their income for phones and services, often their only link to civilization. For many, mobile phones may be the first phone ever seen/used. Literacy is still poor, especially user-interface literacy. Numeracy may be better. Mobile voice communication still may be expensive and unreliable. Mobile messaging may be slow but cheaper, and more reliable. Texting may be preferred to voice communication in some social settings. Consequently, LMF may make it easier for people to communicate, especially with a universal visible language that can be learned in one day.

LMD Assumptions and Objectives: Industrialized World: In the developed world, young people (15–25) have a high aptitude for picking up new visible languages and UI paradigms. For example, *Gyaru-moji* is a "secret" written language improvised by Japanese girls, a mixture of Japanese syllables, numbers, mathematical symbols and Greek characters. *Gyaru-moji* takes twice as long for input as standard Japanese. 15–25 Year-olds frequently text message, in addition to talking on their phones. It seems likely that young people would enjoy messaging in LoCoS: it would be unlike anything they have used before, aesthetic and expressive, easy to learn, offering a fresh new way to message.

LMD User/Use Context: Many users in developing countries have never used a mobile phone before. The phone's entire UI could also be in LoCoS, including the UI for voice conversations. Younger users in the industrialized world might interested in a new "cool" or "secret" communication system. The success of *gyaru-moji* in Japan seems to prove this. Veteran mobile phone users could use a LoCoS mode as an add-on application to their existing phones. Travelers in countries that do not speak the travelers' languages would find LMD useful. The device need not even be a phone.

LMD User Profiles and Use Scenarios: AM + A proposed three use scenarios for its LMD concept prototype: Micro-Office, with Srini, a man in a small town in India; Young Lovers, with Jack and Jill, boyfriend and girlfriend, in the US; and Tourist in a Restaurant, Jaako, a Finnish tourist in France. Use-scenario details are as follows:

Micro-Office: Srini in India lives in a remote village that does not have running water, but just started getting access to a fledgling wireless network, which is not reliable or affordable enough for long voice- conversations, but adequate for text messaging. Srini's mobile phone is his only means of non-face-to-face communication with his business partners. Srini's typical communication topic: should he go to the next village to sell, or wait for prices to rise?

Lovers: Jack and Jill text-message each other frequently, with 5–10 words per message and 2–3 messages per conversation thread. They think text-messaging is "cool" and would be even cooler sending text messages in a private, personal, or secret language not familiar to most people looking over their shoulders.

Tourist in a Restaurant: Jaako, a Finnish tourist in a restaurant in Paris, communicates with a waiter; they do not speak common language. A typical sequence of speech would be: "May I sit here?", "Would you like to start with an appetizer?", "I'm sorry; we ran out of that.", "Do you have lamb?". All communication could take place via a single LoCoS device; Jaako and the waiter would take turns reading/replying.

Design Implications: Any universal visible language must be simple and unambiguous, input must occur quickly and reliably, several dozen LoCoS signs must fit on one mobile device screen.

6 LMD Challenges

Extending LoCos: Future challenges include extending the LoCoS vocabulary for everyday use. The then current 1000 + signs (mostly as shown in Mr. Ota's book) are not sufficient for common use scenarios. A more complete language may require 3000 + signs, similar to Basic Chinese. New signs cannot not be arbitrary; they must follow current patterns.

LoCoS UI: There should be a mobile phone UI that utilizes (only) LoCoS signs for the developing-country user (see Fig. 11), for those whose native language no other UI has been localized well, and for the occasional LoCoS fanatic.

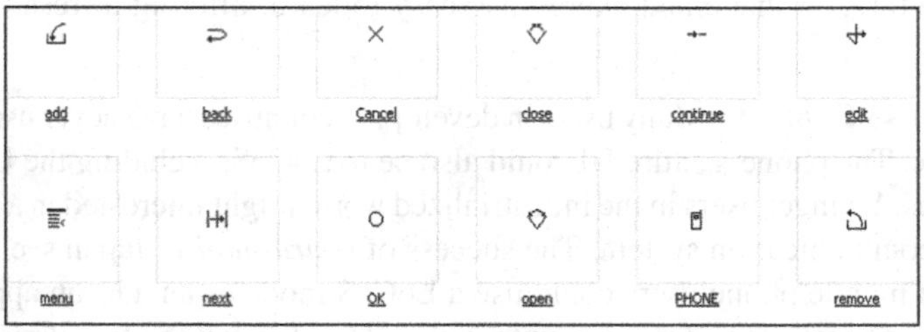

⌞	⊐	✕	◇	––	╋
add	back	Cancel	close	continue	edit
☰	↦	○	◇	▯	◠
menu	next	OK	open	PHONE	remove

Fig. 11. Examples of typical UI functions and example signs for which LoCoS equivalents must be designed.

Revising LoCoS Signs: Some are religiously/culturally biased. It is difficult to please everyone, but there is a need to compromise among the major cultures of the target users. Examples include Ota's sign for "priest", which would not do well in Buddhist countries, or for "restaurant" which might be mistaken for "bar" (see Fig. 12).

Fig. 12. LoCoS signs for Priest and Restaurant.

Convincing Target Users to Try to Learn LoCoS: Non-English speakers need to get used to the English subject-verb-object structure; for example, in Japanese, the verb comes last. LoCoS expressions can be ambiguous. There needs to be dictionary support, preferably on the MD itself. Examples include: "What is the LoCoS sign for the word X, if any?" or "What does this LoCoS sign mean?".

Displaying Small LoCoS Signs: There are trade-offs among legibility, readability, and density of signs per screen. What should the pixel dimensions of sign be? Older Japanese phones and websites with smaller signs often seem to use 13 × 13. AM + A/Ota decided in 2007 on 15 × 15 for LMD use, the same density as smaller, more numerous English signs. (See Fig. 13) The design team at the time considered: should some signs be anti-aliased? We wondered if there were enough phones to support display of grayscale pixels? Is a sign easier to recognize/understand if anti-aliased? With higher-resolution modern smart phones this issue may be moot.

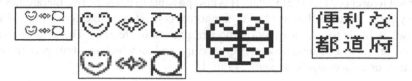

Fig. 13. Examples of small LoCoS signs and Japanese small characters.

How to Input Correct LoCoS Signs Quickly, Reliably: Users may not know what signs looks like, or what users have in mind might not be in the vocabulary yet. The solution seemed to be to select signs from menu lists (Fig. 14).

Fig. 14. Menu of signs as shown in a prototype design.

Such menus were used in Japanese phones in 2007. A primary issue is: How to find 1/3000 signs via 128 × 128 pixel screens with 36 signs? The then current HTML prototype pursued a 2-level hierarchy: Each sign is in one of 18 domains. Each domain's list of signs is accessible with 2–3 keystrokes. 3000 Signs/18 domains means about 170 signs per domain. 170 signs/36 signs per screen means about 5 screens. Remaining to be considered: a 3-level hierarchy.

Input Navigation Challenges: These included: Navigating a screen-full of signs to desired one. Using numerical keys 1–9 for 8-direction movement/navigation from central Key-5 position, which also acts as a Select key. For cases in which signs do not fit onto one screen (*i.e.*, more than 36 signs), Key 0 should be used to scroll downward. There were problems with strict hierarchical navigation.

We found it very difficult to make an intuitive taxonomy of all concepts in language. Users would have to learn which concept is in which category. Shortcuts are needed to frequently used signs. There might be different (complementary) taxonomies. Examples are: Form, grouping signs that look similar (*e.g.*, containing a circle); Properties (concrete *vs.* abstract, man-made *vs.* natural, micro *vs.* macro); Schemas (domains of HTML prototype), *e.g.*, Apple and Frying Pan in the same domain, because both are in a "food/eating" schema.

Most objects/concepts belong to several independent (orthogonal) hierarchies, so why not select from several? This would be similar to multi-faceted navigation, similar to the "20 questions" game, but would require much fewer questions because users can choose from up to a dozen answers to each, not just two. Software should sort hierarchies presented to users by most "granular" It is also possible to navigate two hierarchies with one key press. A real solution would incorporate context-sensitive "guessing" of what sign user is likely to use next, as on modern phones for texting. The solution would be based on context of sentences user are writing and on which symbols/patterns users frequently use. An example appears in Fig. 15.

	Concrete	Abstract	Don't know
Man-Made	1	2	3
Naturally -Occurring	4	5	6
Both	7	8	9
Don't Know	*	0	#

Fig. 15. Example of two-dimensional categories of concept selection.

Other LMD Input Challenges: If the phone has a camera, users could write signs on paper and send a picture of that paper. An alternative to navigate-and-select is to draw signs: like Palm® Graffiti™ that requires a device with a touch screen or to construct each sign by combining, rotating, and re-sizing 16 + basic shapes. Mr. Ota suggested an external keyboard approach, which he developed for LoCoS (Fig. 16); AM + A has not yet pursued this idea.

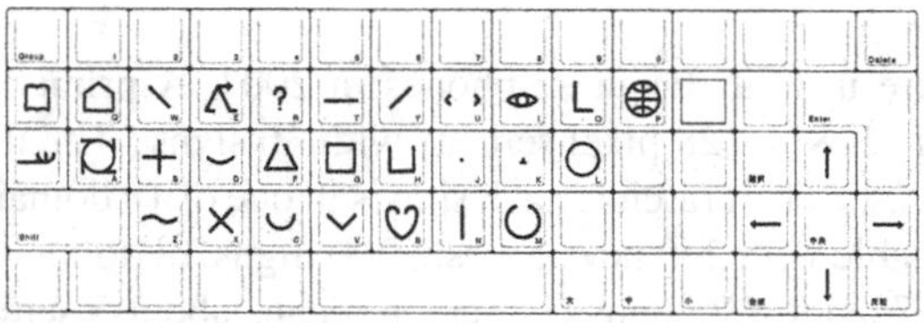

Fig. 16. Mr. Ota's keyboard to select LoCoS sign parts to create complete signs.

Alternative LMD Input Techniques: These include: Motorola iTAP ®m which uses stroke-order sequential selection and was used for 320 million Chinese phones and 90 million text messaging (2003), inputting via either Pinyin or iTAP. (Fig. 17). LoCoS could use sequential selection, or mixed stroke/semantic selection.

LMD Infrastructure: Wireless-networks encoding/transmission protocols must be established. Securing interest/support of telecom hardware and services is necessary.

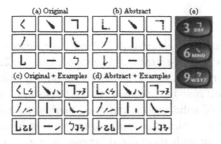

Fig. 17. Chinese input techniques.

7 LMD Then-Current Situation in 2007

Language: There were about 1000 published signs, not quite sufficient to converse for modern, urban, technical situations. There was a need for larger community of users, contributors of new signs.

Implementation on Mobile Devices: The then current prototype shows example screens (Fig. 18).

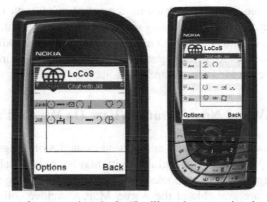

Fig. 18. Two sentences of conversation: Jack: "I will send you music, please listen". Jill: "I am going to bed now, will listen tomorrow". Literal translation of a chat: Joe: where? You, Bill: Restaurant. Joe: I will go there. Bill: happy new year.

LMD Next Steps: The team recognized the need to develop an online community for interested students, teachers, and users; to select moderators; to suggest new design ideas; to determine ideal taxonomies of language (*e.g.*, to break up language into about 18 domains); to make mobile phone UI decisions; to consider technical issues and business implementation, and to conduct detailed user-experience tests.

8   LoCoS 2.0

The team also considered next-generation LoCoS 2.0 research, which was currently underway, to explore new possible attributes to enhance LoCoS: 2D alternate layouts, 3D possibilities; enhanced graphics, add-on illustrational/photographic components; colors of strokes: solid, gradient; font-like characteristics: thick-thins, serifs, cursives, italics, bold, *etc.*; backgrounds of solid colors, patterns, photos; animation; additional signs from international sets, *e.g.,* vehicle transportation, operating systems, *etc.*; combinations with emoji development, or with specialized languages, e.g., "girl signs" in Japan; and characteristics of LoCoS poetry, literature, ambiguous semantics.

9   Current Status of LoCoS in 2007 and Future R + D Issues

LoCoS was ready for a large deployment experiment; it was suitable for typical work/play environments. Research regarding enhancements for LoCoS 2.0 seemed worthwhile. We considered possible funders of next-generation development across several hardware and service platforms/environments. AM + A prepared an intranet site about LoCoS: http://bamanda.com/locos/.

AM + A/Ota considered these future issues: explore cross-cultural issues in use scenarios; explore combination signs to reduce ambiguity of primary signs, similar to hieroglyphics usage; develop metrics to compare LoCoS with other systems like Blissymbolics; study density of signs (*e.g.,* shrinkability for use with watches); ease of composing, editing; benefits of color to reveal grammar or other coding; and degree of ambiguity and techniques for disambiguation; degree of cross-cultural validity, clarity, and value. Much user-experience research remains to be done.

10   What, So What? Now What? Where Do We Go From Here?

This paper has introduced the history and several examples of pasigraphic visible languages. Yukio Ota (yukioota@mug.biglobe.ne.jp) may be contacted about further development. Many pasigraphy-related books and documents, including specific Bliss and LoCoS documents, are available at the Aaron Marcus archive collection, Letterform Archive, San Francisco, www.letterformarchive.org.

References

1. Eco, A.: Theory of Semiotics. University of Illinois Press, Chicago (1976)
2. Lodwick, F.: A Common Writing (1647)
3. Lodwick, F.: The Groundwork or Foundation laid (or So Intended) for the Framing of a New Perfect Language and a Universal Common Writing (1652)
4. Urquhart, S.T.: Logopandecteision (1652)
5. Dalgarno, G.: Ars signorum (1661)
6. Wilkins, J.: An Essay towards a Real Character, and a Philosophical Language (1668)
7. Von Leibniz, G.W.: Lingua Generalis (or Lingua Universalis) (1678)
8. Bliss, C.K.: Semantography (Blissymbolics). Semantography Publications, Sydney (1965)

9. Ota, Y.: LoCoS: Visual Sign Language for Global Communication, in English, Amazon Books (2019). https://www.amazon.com
10. Marcus, A.: m-LoCoS UI: a universal visible language for global mobile communication. In: Jacko, J.A. (ed.) HCI 2007. LNCS, vol. 4552, pp. 144–153. Springer, Heidelberg (2007). https://doi.org/10.1007/978-3-540-73110-8_16
11. Marcus, A.: Icons/symbols and more: visible languages to facilitate communication. In: Marcus, A. (ed.) HCI and User-Experience Design . Human–Computer Interaction Series, pp. 53–61. Springer, London (2015). https://doi.org/10.1007/978-1-4471-6744-0_8
12. Lin, S.: Graphics matters: a case study of mobile phone keypad design for Chinese input. In: Proceedings of the CHI Conference (CHI 2005), Extended Abstracts for Late-Breaking Results, Short Papers, Portland, OR, USA, pp. 1593–1596 (2005)

Emojitaliano: A Social and Crowdsourcing Experiment of the Creation of a Visual International Language

Johanna Monti[1]([⊠]), Francesca Chiusaroli[2], and Federico Sangati[1,3]

[1] UniOR NLP Research Group, University of Naples L'Orientale, Naples, Italy
jmonti@unior.it
[2] University of Macerata, Macerata, Italy
f.chiusaroli@unimc.it
[3] OIST Graduate University, Onna, Japan

Abstract. Inspired by the historical models of artificial and auxiliary languages, Emojitaliano is the result of a social and crowdsourcing experiment which was conducted by a group of seventeen translators, followers of the "Scritture brevi" blog, and led to the creation of an international language based on emojis. The experiment was carried out during 2016 on Twitter in the framework of the translation into emoji of *Pinocchio*, the famous Italian tale. Emojitaliano consists of 1) a repertoire of stable and coherent lexical correspondences between the emoji UNICODE set and the Italian language and 2) a set of predefined simplified rules agreed on during the translation process. Emojitaliano is stored in @Emojitalianobot, an online tool and digital environment for translation into emoji, running on Telegram, the popular instant messaging platform. It is the first open and free Emoji-Italian translation bot based on UNICODE descriptions, which contains a glossary with all the senses assigned by the translators to emojis during the translation process of the famous Italian novel. This paper presents the translation projects of Emojitaliano, the background and its lexicon and grammar and finally Emojitalianobot.

Keywords: Emoji · Emojitaliano · Emojitalianobot · Pinocchio

1 Introduction

Emojitaliano is the result of a social and crowdsourcing experiment which led to the creation of a visual international language based on emojis: it is the output of an intersemiotic translation process from a linguistic code, Italian, to a non-linguistic one (emojis). The experiment gave rise to a number of interpretation and translation problems which were solved by the definition of a set of word-pictograms correspondences and rules. The emojis are the famous pictograms used in Instant Messaging systems and in social networks, iconic and symbolic representations of referents in the real world available on all mobile devices. Emojis are the evolution of emoticons, the famous combination of

© Springer Nature Switzerland AG 2021
M. M. Soares et al. (Eds.): HCII 2021, LNCS 12779, pp. 426–441, 2021.
https://doi.org/10.1007/978-3-030-78221-4_29

punctuation and diacritic marks used to represent the expressions of the human face in Computer-Mediated Communication (CMC) in the Eighties.

The emojis created in Japan first as the well-known yellow faces have rapidly gained worldwide popularity in digital communication, and the complete standard set was adopted by UNICODE in 2010 and made available in iPhones in 2011. Their popularity culminated in the choice by Oxford Dictionaries of the 'Face with Tears of Joy' emoji, as the 'word' that best reflected the ethos, mood, and preoccupations of 2015. In October 2016, the Museum of Modern Art acquired the original collection of emoji distributed by NTT Docomo in 1995. To date, the UNICODE emoji set, last updated in September 2020 counts 3,521 emojis characters and sequences, including Smileys & Emotion, People & BodyComponent, Animals & Nature, Food & Drink, Travel & Places, Activities, Objects, Symbols and finally Flags[1].

The uses and values of pictograms may vary from culture to culture and from language to language, and in addition, the images of emojis can change on the basis of the different vendors and operative systems used, as shown in the Full Emoji List[2]. The general aim of the UNICODE emoji set is therefore to provide an inclusive and international system understandable worldwide, given the potentially universal essence of the nature of pictograms linked to their iconic symbolism.

Despite the cultural differences, the availability of this common standardized repertoire provides an interesting opportunity to a linguistic enquiry with the aim to ascertain if emojis represent, indeed, concepts and ideas universally and independently from the various national languages or if there is the need to resort to a network of shared meanings through a shared set of correspondences between natural languages and the emoji set. With this purpose in mind, the translation into emojis of *Pinocchio*, the famous Italian tale by Collodi, was launched on Twitter in 2016: the experiment based on the linguistic declination of emoji, allowed us to retrace phases in the history of scriptures that concern the pre-alphabetic epochs, especially relating to the ideographic and logographic stages. In this way, it was possible to observe how, beyond the ideal potentialities as a universal language, theoretically capable of overcoming language barriers, emojis give rise to various interpretations with immediate consequences on the unique transmission/understanding of messages.

2 Related Work

Emojis were conceived as a playful way to communicate and are widely used on social media, as can be seen by the real time tracking of all emoji used on Twitter in Emojitracker[3], and in Instant Messaging applications.

In the wake of their worldwide notoriety, a series of translation experiments into emojis of famous literary texts, both poems and novels, as well as everyday language texts have been carried out. The most famous experiment is *Emoji Dick* by Fred Benenson (2010), a crowdsourced translation into emojis of the masterpiece by Melville on Amazon

---

[1] https://unicode.org/emoji/charts/emoji-counts.html.

[2] https://unicode.org/emoji/charts/full-emoji-list.html.

[3] https://emojitracker.com/.

Mechanical Turk: the plan involved 800 people, divided into a group of translators paid five cents per translation, and a group in charge of choosing the best translations, paid two cents per vote (About Emoji Dick, 2009)[4]. Printed in 2010, it became the first emoji novel accepted into the Library of Congress. Benenson's main goal was to understand the influence and impact of digital media on language and literacy:

"I'm interested in the phenomenon of how our language, communications, and culture are influenced by digital technology. Emoji are either a low point or a high point in that story, so I felt I could confront a lot of our shared anxieties about the future of human expression (see: Twitter or text messages) by forcing a great work of literature through such a strange new filter"[5].

Besides, a series of posters in emoji titled *Wonderland, Neverland, Pleasureland* was designed by Joe Hale[6].

Although methodologically different, both projects, even if integral translations into emojis, are characterized by the absence of a linguistic and grammatical approach needed for the reconstruction of meaning.

Besides, other experiments are characterised by the intertwining of emojis and text such as *Emoji Dickinson* and the translation in emoji of the *Address to the State of the Union* by Obama, famous as the Twitter account *@Emojibama*[7].

Further translations into emojis of the same kind, specifically addressed to Millennials, are the *OMG Shakespeare* series and *Bible Emoji: Scripture 4 Millennials*, both billed on iTunes. The latter translation is also available as an online translator of Bible verses[8] and a Twitter feed[9] that has been active since August 2015.

There are a number of academic projects, related to the translation of text into emojis: at the University of Oregon, inspired by Henry Jenkins' (e.g., 2010, 2006) notion of "participatory culture," two "Emoji Literature Translation Contests", took place in two courses by Alisa Freedman: "Digital Age Stories: Literature and New Media in Japan and the United States" (mixed college and graduate seminar, fall 2015) and "Japanese Popular Culture in the World" (lower-division undergraduate seminar, winter 2017)[10].

---

[4] "About Emoji Dick," 2009, at http://www.emojidick.com, accessed 17 November 2017.

[5] Sally Law, 2009. "The revolution will be crowdsourced (and cute)," New Yorker (22 September), at https://www.newyorker.com/books/page-turner/the-revolution-will-be-crowdsourced-and-cute, accessed 5 December 2020.

[6] http://www.joehale.info/visual-poetry/one-hundred-thousand-emojis.html.

[7] https://twitter.com/emojibama.https://www.theguardian.com/us-news/ng-interactive/2015/jan/20/-sp-state-of-the-union-2015-address-obama-emoji.

[8] http://www.bibleemoji.com/.

[9] https://twitter.com/BibleEmoji.

[10] https://firstmonday.org/article/view/9395/7567.

3 The Emojitaliano Projects

3.1 *The Pinocchio in Emojitaliano* Project

The first Emojitaliano translation project is *Pinocchio in Emojitaliano* launched on Twitter in February 2016 by F. Chiusaroli, J. Monti and F. Sangati [1] and published as a volume by the editor Apice libri in 2017[11] (Fig. 1):

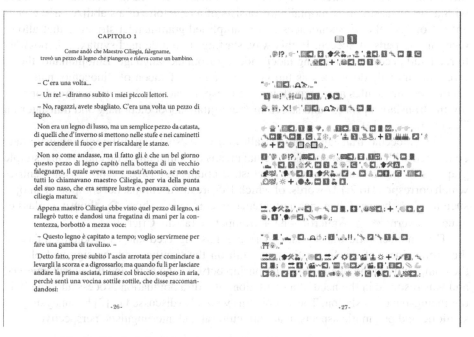

Fig. 1. The incipit of the printed version of *Pinocchio in Emojitaliano*

    The translation of the famous children's novel was carried out by the followers of the *Scritture brevi* blog (by F. Chiusaroli and F.M. Zanzotto) and the first fifteen chapters have been translated, which correspond to the original novel published by Collodi in 1881. Every day tweets with sentences taken from the novel were posted on Twitter and the followers suggested their translations in emoji; at the end of each day, the official version of the translations was validated and published. In 2017 a facing-page version of the translation was published: this modality was chosen to establish a direct and immediate visual relationship between the text in emoji and the source text so as to limit the inevitable difficulties and interpretative drifts.

---

[11] http://www.apicelibri.it/catalogo/pinocchio-in-emojitaliano/351?path=catalogo; the book is available on Amazon; https://www.amazon.it/Pinocchio-emojitaliano-Francesca-Chiusaroli/dp/8899176442/ref=sr_1_1?dchild=1&qid=1608387789&refinements=p_27%3AFrancesca+Chiusaroli&s=books&sr=1-1.

The project was backed up by the Emojitalia discussion group on Telegram, where translators met to discuss problems, solutions, suggest improvements of the bot, debate the translation choices and communicate in emoji.

Unlike previous literary translation projects in emojis, such as the translations of *Moby Dick* or *Alice in Wonderland*, this is the first translation of an Italian novel into emoji, broadening in this way the horizon with respect to the exclusive "anglocentric" perspective. A further novelty of this experiment is the creation of a standardized code, titled Emojitaliano. Inspired by the historical models of artificial and auxiliary languages with a universal statute, Emojitaliano consists of a repertoire of a stabilized and coherent set of lexical correspondences and a simplified grammatical structure that allows recognizing parts of speech. In this way, starting from a defined syntax, it is possible to read and decode the meaning independently from the language. Emojitaliano, therefore, was initially developed as the grammar and the lexicon of Pinocchio, namely a set of predefined rules and a repertoire of correspondences Italian-emoji agreed on during the translation process and stored in @emojitalianobot dictionary and translator on Telegram.

The Pinocchio translation project allowed crowdsourcing different linguistic data connected with the use of emojis as actual means of communication and not just simple graphics to express amusement or interest. It counts 611 tweets, 980 glossary entries which correspond to 2,127 words, of which 185 are multi-emojis, i.e. compound emojis, such as 🏠🔨house + hammer and wrench = carpenter's shop, 🏠🍷house + glass of wine = tavern; 🎤🎺microphone + trumpet = Talking Cricket.

This intersemiotic translation experiment has triggered known problems linked to the arbitrariness of the linguistic sign, both on the signifier and the signified planes: the complexity of the one-to-one relationship between the noun and the object emerged and was resolved in the need of a regulation, of a disambiguation process and finally in the facing-page translation. These problems were also discussed in [2] by analysing the semiotic and pragmatic aspects in an intercultural and interlinguistic perspective.

3.2 Other Translation Projects

Starting from *Pinocchio in Emojitaliano*, the set method has been applied in a series of subsequent translation experiments carried out in social media again, and both by university students and individual translators [as in 3].

The first experiment consisted of the translation of the first twelve fundamental principles of the Italian Constitution. The translation was realized by an individual author (Marina Pierani, aka @ineziessenziali on Twitter) with the supervision of the Emojitaliano research group (Chiusaroli, Monti, Sangati) (Fig. 2).

The author worked to the definition of a specialized lexicon, completely different from that of *Pinocchio* which is literary and Tuscan-based. Moreover, the translation had a renewed repertoire at disposal, because of the new emoji acquisitions which regularly improve the UNICODE set about every six months[12]. The result was a technical translation of a legal text both on a lexical and syntactic level and through which a relevant amount of international legal entries were added to the Emojitaliano vocabulary,

---

[12] https://emojipedia.org/faq/#how-many.

Fig. 2. The translation of the Italian Constitution into emoji

such as ★ *Repubblica* (republic), 👊 *diritto* (right), 👯 *democratico* (democratic), 🧍🧍 *cittadini* (citizens), 👥👥 *sociale* (social), 🏠⚖️ *Stato* (state).

During the Italian national day of the Republic (April 25th), in collaboration with the national newspaper *Repubblica*, a game was organized on Twitter which consisted in the challenge to read the text in Emojitaliano and to recognize the correspondent principle of the Constitution (Fig. 3):

Fig. 3. The Twitter game concerning the identification of the articles of the Italian Constitution from the translation into emoji.

The game moved from the assumption of basic knowledge of the constitutional text by the Italian readers who could look-up the Emojitalianobot for consultation. The main goal of the challenge was to verify the degree of comprehensibility of the text based on the semantic evocation capacity of the emojis.

Besides, it is worth mentioning the translation of Giacomo Leopardi's poem *L'infinito* (The infinite), in 2019, that is the first attempt to translate a poetic text, grammar and lexicon into emoji (Fig. 4):

Fig. 4. The translation in emoji of *L'infinito* poem by Leopardi.

As already happened with Collodi's story, once again the translation and matching work between emoji and words was a collective task and took place on Twitter with the help of the #scritturebrevi community. On a semantic level the first difficulty was, as usual, to find pictograms for all the concepts expressed in the original version of the poem, with the further challenging aim of reproducing the poetry of the text. We wanted to build the poetic Emojitaliano, without distorting the structure of our language: this involves the decision to keep the basic order of the elements of the sentence, as Emojitaliano requires (SVO) to respect the primary requirement of legibility for non-native readers. The poetical expression was therefore searched in terms of aesthetics, specifically by eliminating all those functional elements that in Emojitaliano are traditionally rendered by emoji 'button' and 'arrow symbols'[13]. Among these symbols, the emoji for the personal pronoun 'I' as adopted in *Pinocchio* was for the same purpose substituted with the 🧍'person standing emoji'[14], clearly as a more striking image of the 'I' symbol[15]. This adoption was inspired by the just acquired emoji, of the person represented in a

---

[13] https://emojipedia.org/symbols/.

[14] https://emojipedia.org/search/?q=standing.

[15] https://emojipedia.org/information/.

standing position in UNICODE 13.0 in 2019[16], that is a neutral image with respect to the previous 'walking' and 'running person' ones used in Pinocchio.

In the choice of the correspondences between emoji and words, we worked, as always, on the meaning, on the level of metaphor and similar figures for the transposition of both abstract and concrete meanings. Thus the figure of the planet 🪐 translates the word 'superhuman', while the ⏳ hourglass and the ∞ infinity symbol respectively translate 'always' and 'infinite'. The search for the poetic effect has sometimes consisted in the choice of aesthetically rich emojis over emojis for basic meanings. So if the verb 'io sento' ('I hear') is translated with the 👂 "ear" symbol, 'io odo' ('I hear') is translated with the 🎧 headphone emoji[17]; likewise the 🔒 padlock, first used to indicate the verb 'close' or 'exclude', is here instead replaced by the 🗝 'old key' emoji[18].

4 Emojitaliano

4.1 The Emojitaliano Lexicon

Emojitaliano is the result of a creative rewriting experiment that consists in the creation of a repertoire semantically motivated, with correspondences between the emoji UNICODE set and meanings in the Italian language. When one-to-one correspondences were absent or impossible, new correspondences were created through the combination or resemantization of existing signs, exploiting the iconic but also symbolic potentialities of this visual language.

The Emojitaliano code, in this way, takes advantage of the pictographic quality of emojis (as a sign of referents), but also of their abstract values (a sign of concepts) for the assignment of meanings. Besides, their logographic dimension allows to "read" the signs in a specific language.

On this basis, correspondences between pictograms and realia were immediate, such as for instance between the emoji 🏠 and the corresponding concept of *house*, while a further step was necessary when correspondences between concepts and emojis were not so immediate such as for instance for the word *bottega* (workshop) so important for the novel by Collodi, being related to the joiner's workshop of Geppetto, the father of Pinocchio.

The solution in these cases has been the introduction of a combination of two or more emojis: for the word *bottega* the solution was to combine two emojis ⌊🏠⚒⌋, one for *house* and one for *tools*, identified graphically in the text by being inserted between frames.

Other combinations show the recourse to evocative values belonging to the collective consciousness and/or to shared traditions such as for the word *colpa* (fault), expressed through ⌊👨👩🍎⌋ that represents the meaning sequence of "man-woman-apple", referring to the well-known, but culture-specific, bible image. A further interesting aspect concerns the translation of proper names of the characters of the novel: in Emojitaliano we aim at the linguistic representation by linking the connotations taken from the

---

[16] https://emojipedia.org/person-standing/.

[17] https://emojipedia.org/headphone/.

[18] https://emojipedia.org/old-key/.

conventional iconography with the instances. Names semantically transparent allowed literal translations, such as *Ma(e)stro Ciliegia*, defined by the compound *mastro (carpentiere)* (master-carpenter) e *ciliegia (frutto)* (cherry). The recourse to some qualities and characteristics of the character is necessary with opaque names: it is a procedure based on the ethnolinguistic principle of the "sema lessicogeno" (lexicogenic sema) by Cardona, that can involve the metaphorical and symbological level: Pinocchio is always the *runner* 🏃, also when he does not run, even if the counterpart *pedestrian* 🚶 is available; *Geppetto* is the *good father* 👨 ❤️. The same applies to the *cricket*, for which no emoji was available at the time of translation: the characteristics of the character as the crackly voice representing the traditional moral were summarized in 🎙️ 🎺 (the master + the trumpet).

4.2 The Emojitaliano Grammar

In the framework of the project also a grammar was developed, to assign to the translated text into emoji a specific syntax, inspired by the idea of language universals, combinatorial logic, and artificial and philosophical languages. The idea to recur to a specific grammar is due to the observation [4, 5] that invented languages, completely arbitrary, are destined to fail and therefore it is necessary to start from an actual language, i.e. in our case the Italian language. The norm structure foresees, among the simplification rules, the prevalence of parataxis instead of hypotaxis, the fixed SVO word order, the absence of inflection in favour of the analytic expression of nouns and verbs. Deixis prevails on abstract notations as in *questo* 👆(this) and *quello* 👉(that), and the concrete relationship represents the reference to assign the meanings keeping in mind as much as possible the UNICODE sense: *picchiare* (to beat) 👊, *salutare* 👋(to say hello). The original punctuation has been kept, but some emotional faces have been used to represent some specific state of mind. The marked syntactic structures have been eliminated to ease the identification of the functions through the position in the sentences.

The grammar contemplates 1) general rules; rules concerning 2) the articles, 3) personal pronouns, 4) verbs, 5) adjectives and nouns, 6) adverbs, 7) connectives, 8) idiomatic expressions.

General Rules

- The reading direction is from left to right.
- The syntactic order is Subject Verb Object (SVO).
- Passive sentences are transformed into active sentences to comply with the SVO word order.
- The subject is always expressed.
- The two symbols ⌊ and ⌋ mark the beginning and the end of compound signs: ⌊🏠🛠️⌋ = *bottega* (workshop).

Rules Concerning the Articles

- The definite article is omitted: *la casa* (the house) = 🏠.
- the indefinite article is marked as before the noun: *una casa* (a house) = 1️⃣🏠.

Rules Concerning the Personal Pronouns

- The singular personal pronouns are **i** = *io* (I), 👆 = *tu* (you), 🧍 = *egli* (he), 🧍‍♀️ = *ella* (she), ⌊👆🎩⌋ = *Voi, Ella* (You) (as courtesy pronouns).
- The plural form of the personal pronouns are obtained by reduplicating the singular form ⌊**ii**⌋ = *noi* (we), ⌊👆👆⌋ = *voi* (you), ⌊🧍🧍⌋ = *essi* (they - masculine), ⌊🧍‍♀️🧍‍♀️⌋ = *esse* (they feminine), ⌊👆🎩👆🎩⌋ = *Voi, Elle* (You) (as courtesy pronouns).
- These pronouns are used both as subject and object pronouns.
- The possessive pronouns are obtained by adding ⏩ before the personal pronouns: ⌊⏩ ⌋ = *my* (of me). The possessive pronouns are placed after the noun and are invariable.

Rules Concerning the Verbs. The rules of the verb foresee the compulsory subject and for the representation of the verb tenses, the distinction between past and future has been introduced and obtained by means of affixes such as in: ⌊👟◀⌋*andare* (go) *past tenses*, ⌊👟▶⌋*andare* (go) *future tenses*, while the present tense has no specific mark. Compound verb tenses have been simplified and assimilated to the few categories identified.

More specifically:

- The verb is invariable but the subject should be expressed: **i** '有 = *io sono* (I am), 👆'有 = *tu sei* (you are), ⌊👆👆⌋'有 = *voi siete* (you are).
- Verb marker: ' (on the left of the emoji), for example: 👟 = *scarpa* (shoe), '👟 = *andare* (to go).
- The verb only with the marker ' is used for the infinitive, indicative simple, and/or present tenses.
- Past tense marker: ◀ Example: **i** '⌊👟◀⌋ = *io sono andato* (I have gone), *io andavo* (I was going), *io andai* (I went), *io ero andato* (I had gone), and so on.
- Future tense marker: ▶ Example: **i** '⌊👟▶⌋ = *io andrò* (I will go), *io sarò andato* (I will have gone), and so on.
- Gerundive and Present participle marker: ⬅ Example: '⌊👟⬅⌋ = *andando* (going), *andante* (going).
- Causative marker: ➡ Example: '⌊➡👟⌋ = *far andare* (to make go).
- Reflexive marker: 🔙 postponed to the verb. Example: '⌊🗣🔙⌋= *rispondersi* (to answer to him/herself).
- Reciprocal marker: 👥 postponed to the verb. Example: '⌊👊👥⌋ = *picchiarsi* (to beat each other).
- Conditional marker: 🤔 Example: **i** '⌊🤔👟⌋ = *io andrei* (I would go).
- Imperative and Exhortative marker: ❗ Example: 👆 '⌊❗👟⌋ = *vai!* (go!).

- Interrogative marker: 👍 Example: 👍 'L **?** 👞 ⌋ = *vai?* (do you do?).
- Impersonal marker: 👉 Example: 👉'🌧 = *piove* (it rains).

Rules Concerning Adjectives and Nouns

- The adjective is placed on the right of the noun: 🏠☀ = (la) bella casa (the nice house), (la) casa bella (the nice house).
- The natural gender is assigned to nouns, while the morphological annotation is absent.
- The plural of nouns is obtained by reduplicating the sign or by adding the numeral: 🍎 *la mela* (apple), 🍎 *una mela* (one apple), 🍎🍎 *le mele* (the apples), 🍎 *tre mele* (three apples).
- The plural of adjectives follows the same rule as the nouns and is obtained by reduplicating the sign: ⌊🏠🔨⌋ 👀 = *bottega sporca* (dirty workshop), ⌊🏠🔨🏠🔨⌋⌊👀👀⌋ = *botteghe sporche* (dirty workshops).
- The marker ◄is inserted on the right of the verb but without diacritic sign ' to indicate the past participle (used as adjective or noun). Example: ⌊👞 ◄⌋ *andato* (gone).
- The possessive adjective is obtained by adding ⏩ before the personal pronoun: ⌊⏩ i⌋ = *mio* (my).
- The diminutive form is obtained by adding 👶 after the adjective. Example: ⌊🐮 👶⌋ = *vitellino* (small calf).
- The pejorative form is obtained by adding 👹 after the adjective. Example: ⌊👁 👹⌋ = *occhiacci* (stink eyes).
- Comparative of majority: 📊 🕸 ➡ *più sottile di* (thinner than)
- Relative superlative: ⌊🕸 💯 ⌋ *il più sottile* (the thinnest)
- Absolute superlative: ⌊🕸 🔝 ⌋*sottilissimo* (very thin)

Rules Concerning Adverbs

- The symbol ⬅ is added on the right of the adjective to transform it in adverb. Example: 🐌 = *lento* (slow), ⌊🐌 ⬅⌋ = *lentamente* (slowly).

Rules Concerning Connectors

- *E* (and) (conjunction) ➕ Example: 🚶 ➕ ⌊😀💙⌋ '👞 🔙◄⌋ ►🏠 = *Pinocchio e Geppetto tornarono a casa* (Pinocchio and Geppetto went home).
- *O, invece di* (or, instead of) (adversative) 🔁 Example : ⌊🚶🚶⌋ '有⌊😵😵⌋ 🔁 ⌊🚶🚶⌋ '有 ⌊😈😈⌋! = *Sono matti o imbroglioni!* (They are mad or cheaters!)
- *Che* (That) (objective conjunction) ⬇ Example: 🚶 'L👀◄⌋ ⬇ 🤖 'L🔙◄⌋ = *egli vide che il burattino si muoveva* (he saw that the puppet was moving).

- *Che* (Who, that) (relative pronoun) ⤵ Example: 🚶, ⤷ 'L 😊◀⌋, 'L ◀⌋ = *Pinocchio, che aveva fame, mangiò* (Pinocchio, who was hungry, ate).
- *Di* (of) ▶▶ Example: 👃 ▶▶ 🚶 = *il naso di Pinocchio* (the nose of Pinocchio); 🪵 ▶▶ ▮ = *pezzo di legno* (piece of wood).
- *A* (to) (direction) ▶ Example: 🧍👣 ▶🏠 = *io vado a casa* (I go home).
- *Da* (from) (origin, derivation) ◀ Example: 🧍 'L 👣 🤚⌋ ◀🏠 = *io vengo da casa* (I come from home).
- *In* (in, at) (inside) ◻ Example: 🧍' ◻🏠 = *io mangio in/a casa* (I eat at home).
- *Su* (on) 🔺 Example: ' 🔺 = *salire su* (to get on).
- *Giù* (down) 🔻 Example: 👅 🔻 = *con la lingua giù* (with the tongue down).
- *Sopra qualcosa (on something)* ⤵ Example: 🧍 L🔨◀⌋ ↖⤴🎋 = *egli mise il martello sul tavolo* (he put the hammer on the table).
- *Sotto qualcosa* (under something) ⤴ Example: 🧍 L🔨 ◀ JL 👟👟⌋ ⎽ = *egli mise le scarpe sotto il letto* (he put his shoes under the bed).
- *Al centro di* (at the center of, between, in the middle of) ◎ Example: ◎ L◻🏠 J = *al centro della stanza* (in the center of the room).
- *Con* (with) (company) ⫽ Example: 🚶 'L 👣 🔙 ◀ J ▶ 🏠⫽ L 👨 💙J = *Pinocchio tornò a casa con Geppetto* (Pinocchio went home with Geppetto).
- *Per, a causa di* (for, due to) ✓ Example: 🚶'L😱 ◀ J ✓👤 L👂 ◀ J L👿 ✗👿 ✗ J 'L👣 🤚 J = *Pinocchio era spaventato perché (per il fatto che) sentiva gli assassini arrivare* (Pinocchio was scared because (due to the fact that) he heard the killers coming).
- *Per, allo scopo di* (for, for the purpose of) ↗Example: ↗ 🚶'L👄 ◀ JL🌼⌋ = *affinché/perché Pinocchio consegnasse le monete* (for/for the purpose of Pinocchio to deliver the coins).
- *Verso, contro, di fronte a, nei confronti di* (towards, against, in front of, regarding) VS Example: L👨 💙J L'😲 ◀ J VS 🚶 = *Geppetto si voltò verso Pinocchio* (Geppetto turned to Pinocchio).
- *Così che* (so that) (consecutive) 🔝➡(even distant in the sentence). Example: 🚶 'L 😱 ◀ J L🔝➡J 🧍' L 😖 ◀ J = *Pinocchio era tanto spaventato che tremava* (Pinocchio was so scared that he was trembling).
- Benché   (although)   (concessive)   L➕🔔 😖 JExample : L➕🔔 😖 J 🚶 🙍 'L🤚‼ ◀ J, 🚶 'L 👣 ◀ J ▶ 🏠 = *benché non volesse (anche se non voleva), Pinocchio andò a casa* (although he didn't want to (even if he didn't want to), Pinocchio went home).

Rules Concerning Idioms. Idiomatic or figurative expressions were translated without using word-for-word translations and expressive resources on a semantic basis were adopted to express the general meaning of the idiom. The glossary contains the original idioms used in the source text and the equivalent translations into Italian. Example: 'L👊🔝 J = *darne un sacco e una sporta* (lit. give a sack and a shopping bag) with the meaning of *picchiare forte* (to beat wildly).

5 Emojitaliano Bot

Emojitalianobot [6] is the first open and free Emoji-Italian translation bot on Telegram. It was developed to support the translation project of *Pinocchio in Emojitaliano*. Emojitalianobot contains (i) the Emoji-Italian dictionary which amounts to 3,165 translation into Italian of 1,186 emojis, (ii) the Emoji-English descriptions based on UNICODE and (iii) a glossary with all the uses of emoji in the translation of *Pinocchio*. The bot also offers an asynchronous multiplayer game to guess the meanings of emojis in Italian.

Emojitalianobot is an ideal test bench to experiment with new approaches like crowdsourcing and gamification in the field of Natural Language Processing (NLP) since it collects new meanings associated with emojis through the translation projects and the game. The Pinocchio project, games and features available in the bot to learn or guess the meaning of emoji are devised to enjoy the bot while using it and at the same time to give users the opportunity to develop linguistic descriptions of emoji tailored to their actual perceptions.

The most important reward for playing with the bot is the awareness of helping develop a linguistic resource for one's mother tongue, and the pride in contributing to it. Since its release on Telegram, the project was an instant success, becoming a viral web phenomenon thanks to the Scritture brevi community, the *Pinocchio* translation in emojis and subsequent translation projects. Currently, the bot has more than 2,500 users.

5.1 Bot Design and Interactions

When users add Emojitalianobot to their contacts on Telegram, the bot greets them and displays the main menu, which foresees seven buttons (Fig. 5).

Each button introduces a different functionality which is shortly explained at the beginning of each session (Fig. 6).

The button " « ▌ ▌ 🆎 ↔ 😊 »" allows users to translate from Italian into emoji and vice-versa (Fig. 6). Users can use this function 1) to know the Italian CLDR short name for the UNICODE emoji characters and sequences or 2) to know the emoji characters and sequences associated with an Italian word.

"🏴󠁧󠁢󠁥󠁮󠁧󠁿 🆎 ↔ 😊"allows users to translate from English into emoji and vice-versa. Users can use this function 1) to know the English CLDR short name for the UNICODE emoji characters and sequences or 2) to know the emoji characters and sequences associated with an English word.

"🔤 📐 GRAMMATICA" allows users to browse the grammar (Fig. 7) developed for the Emojitaliano project. It contains 8 rules, namely 1) general rules; rules concerning 2) the articles, 3) personal pronouns, 4) verbs, 5) adjectives and nouns, 6) adverbs, 7) connectives, 8) idiomatic expressions (see Sect. 4.2).

" 📜 COSTITUZIONE" presents the parallel text translation into emoji of the Italian constitution. Users can read the translation article by article.

" 🎭 INVITA UN AMICO" allows users to invite friends to join the bot.

" 🎰 GIOCA!" activates a game modality. Two different games are available: 1) it is possible to guess a possible translation into emoji of an Italian word (Fig. 8) or 2) a possible translation into Italian of an emoji. The bot shows players an instance of emoji (game 1) or of a word (game 2) one at a time. The bot acknowledges the correct answer

Fig. 5. Emojitaliano bot main menu.

Fig. 6. Translation from Italian into emoji and vice-versa.

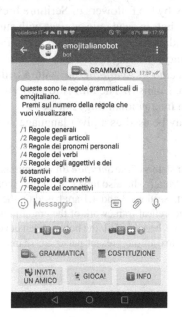

Fig. 7. The Grammar menu.

Fig. 8. Game.

by the player with the message: "Hai indovinato!" (You guessed it!). If the player does not guess the correct answer, the bot provides the correct translation(s). During both game modalities, players may ask for some help from the system if they do not know the answer: in this case, pressing the UN AIUTO? (A help?) button, users are given four possible emojis (game 1) or four possible words (game 2) among which to select the right solution. At the end of each game it is possible to play again or to leave the game. Figure 8 shows an interaction between the bot and the player during Game 1: the bot asks the player to guess a possible translation of the emoji.

"i INFO" provides information about the bot and a link to the Emojitalia community.

6 Conclusions

The main contribution of this paper is the description of an innovative social and crowd-sourcing experiment of the creation of a visual international language. The paper provides thorough information concerning the creation of Emojitaliano, Emojitalianobot, a Telegram application specifically devoted to the intersemiotic translation experiment for Italian into emojis and the various translation experiments carried out on Twitter since 2016.

Emojitaliano was used in several translation processes of different types of texts, ranging from *Pinocchio*, the famous Italian tale by Collodi, to the Italian Constitution. This is the first attempt of a visual language based on emojis with a specific lexicon and a proper grammar created in a collaborative way by the followers of Scripture brevi.

The Emojitaliano research group is using the bots in academic courses with students and in the same contexts is also testing the readability of Emojitaliano texts. Further Italian literary texts and the basic Italian vocabulary are going to be translated. The group is also working on an English version of *Pinocchio in Emojitaliano*, with a trilingual parallel text and glossary (Italian, Emojitaliano, English). The aim is to prove that the only way to assert that the emoji repertoire is an international linguistic code is through the path of translation [7], and Emojitaliano may be used as a pivot language and as a lingua franca to that purpose (Emojilingua) [8].

Acknowledgements. Our thanks go to the Italian translators of the *Scritture Brevi* community for their contributions. The paper has been written by J. Monti, who also took care of the theoretical framework of the automatic translation of the project. Sections 3 and 4.1 are based on the Introduction to [1] by Chiusaroli, who took care of the theoretical framework of the emojilingua and coordinated the translations on social media. Section 5 is based on [6]; the bot has been developed by F. Sangati. The Emojitaliano project and the full text of the present paper are shared by all authors.

References

1. Chiusaroli, F., Monti, J., Sangati, F.: Pinocchio in Emojitaliano, Sesto Fiorentino, Apice libri (2017)
2. Monti, J., Chiusaroli, F.: Il codice emoji da Oriente a Occidente: standard Unicode e dinamiche di internazionalizzazione in RASSEGNA ITALIANA DI LINGUISTICA APPLICATA; XLIX 2-3/2017, Roma, Bulzoni, pp. 83–102 (2017)

3. Chiusaroli, F.: Emojitaliano (Genesi 1.1.), in Genesi 1.1. Alcuni percorsi traduttivi; Parma, Edizioni Bottega del Libro, pp. 73–79 (2017)
4. Eco, U.: La ricerca delle lingue perfette. Roma-Bari: Laterza, éd. fr. Éditions du Seuil, Paris (1993)
5. De Saussure, F.: Course in general linguistics. In: Bally, C., Sechehaye, A. (eds.). Baskin, W. Trans. The Philosophical Society, New York 1959. (reprint NY: McGraw-Hill, 1966)
6. Monti, J., Sangati, F., Chiusaroli, F., Benjamin, M., Mansour, S.: Emojitalianobot and Emoji-WorldBot: new online tools and digital environments for translation into emoji. In: Proceedings of the Third Italian Conference on Computational Linguistics CLiC-it 2016, pp. 211–215. Accademia University Press, Torino (2016)
7. Chiusaroli, F.: La scrittura in emoji tra dizionario e traduzione. In: Proceedings of the Second Italian Conference on Computational Linguistics, CLiC-it 2015, Trento, 3–4 December 2015; pp. 88–93. Accademia University Press, Torino (2015)
8. Chiusaroli, F.: Da Emojipedia a Pinocchio in Emojitaliano: l'"emojilingua" tra scritture e riscritture, in Homo Scribens 2.0. Scritture ibride della modernità, pp. 45–87. Franco Cesati, Firenze (2019)

Research on Information Visualization Design Based on Information Weight- a Case Study of Information-Based Scene Design of the Airport

Yiyu Ouyang[1] and Yi Liu[2(⊠)]

[1] Guangzhou Academy of Fine Arts, No. 257 Changgang Road,
Guangzhou, People's Republic of China
[2] Province Key Lab of Innovation and Applied Research on Industry Design,
No. 257 Changgang Road, Guangzhou, People's Republic of China

Abstract. Objective-Information visualization can enhance the effectiveness and efficiency of information communication by decreasing people's cognitive load. Thus, the effectiveness of human cognitive information will affect the accuracy and efficiency of information communication. To speed up the individual decision-making process, this thesis attempts to work out a new design method and improve the information visualization design from the cognitive characteristics and information weight. Methods-Firstly, the relationship between information weight and cognitive capability is explored through literature analysis. From this part the researcher know that the course of information communication will be affected by information sources and presentation modes and information receivers. To learn about the impact degree of the three factors on information visualization, the researcher made four types of visualized information boards based on the weight distribution of various flight information, and launched visual cognition experiments on passengers of different ages. During the experiment, the reaction time of each passenger to find information on different boards was recorded. Finally, the average response differences of four types of flight information boards facing two groups of travelers of different ages are analyzed through correlation analysis and variance analysis and significant difference method. Outcome-Both groups present the same rule, that is, the higher the information weight, the smaller the average response difference. Beside, the main effects of age group and information weight level are highly significant. Conclusion-Information weight can accelerate the cognitive speed of receiver by affecting the structure of information presentation; age influence the way the information receiver collects information; the dependence of information receiver on his or her established experience will affect the efficiency of information communication.

Keywords: Information visualization · Information weight · Cognitive speed

1 Research Background and Significance

Information visualization is a new pattern of manifestation of design, which can turn abstract data into a form of visual presentation, so as to enhance people's understanding

M. M. Soares et al. (Eds.): HCII 2021, LNCS 12779, pp. 442–456, 2021.
https://doi.org/10.1007/978-3-030-78221-4_30

of data. It is intended to boost the effectiveness and efficiency of information communication, decrease people's cognitive load, and enlarge people's capacity of information processing per unit time. Traditional computer graphics and scientific visualization study the visualization of spatial data field, while information visualization refers to the visualization of non-spatial data. The focus of research is to present the hidden information and laws in data through visual graphics. The innovation is to deepen users' understanding of data meanings while conforming to human cognitive laws, and then guide the retrieval process and speed up the retrieval via visual images [1]. Larkin and Simon [2] revealed that one of the principal advantages of visualization is that it can help to classify and divide common information into groups, thus avoiding a large volume of searches. Munzner holds that visual design should give consideration to the limitations of computers and monitors as well as the limitations of human beings [3]. Since the users of information visualization technology are human being, human's preference for information and human's limitations in reasoning should be taken into account.

Visualization is a technology, which represents a large amount of information and the complex relationship between information [4] by means of visual representation, and the key step to achieve visualization effect is to acquire information sources and distinguish information types in a correct way. Before being organized, information sources are in a chaotic state. If visual modification is adopted directly, it will result in that the visual information displayed does not match the actual content. The weight of information can measure the importance of individual information elements in the whole information. Screening and integrating the acquired information sources by weight can realize the order of information at the organizational level and lay a foundation for boosting the transmission efficiency of visual contents. The research on information weight in visual design chiefly proceeds from the expression effect of the algorithm result of increasing information weight. Li Wei [5] proposed to combine automatic clustering with visualization method by means of low-dimensional spatial clustering, and visualize the results of analytic hierarchy process (AHP), which can determine the index weight, so as to boost the accuracy and efficiency of AHP. Mohammad Ghoniem [6] et al. worked out a spatial-aware tree map algorithm - weighted map, which can provide better aspect ratio and make the area of each rectangle in visual cartography entirely proportional to the weight it represents. Raghuveer Devulapalli [7] et al. came up with a simple and fast calculation algorithm of Voronoi diagram weight, which divides the space of information visualization into multiple partitions and controls the shapes of these partitions. Lu Xiaomin [8] et al. put forward a method to calculate and visualize the target weight of point groups, which overcomes the disadvantage that the weight of point groups is tremendously affected by local density in traditional algorithms, and makes the map image intuitive.

Despite that the expression of information weight in visual design has aroused the concern of scholars, the research on the cognitive characteristics and impact of information weight in information visualization has not yet been launched. Cognition is a course in which people acquire and apply knowledge, which is also known as the course of information processing [9]. Individual ways of organizing and processing information will present individual differences [10]. With reference to cognitive theory, cognitive demand is the tendency of individuals to deal with tasks that require cognitive efforts, laying emphasis on course orientation, while people's behavior of collecting information belongs to the cognitive course that requires efforts. They will choose to acquire information based on the importance dimension of their own perception of information, which will enhance their sensitivity to important information and make it easier to acquire such information, that is, the weight distribution of individual information will affect the individual's cognitive speed. Thus, the research on the relationship between information weight and cognitive efficiency needs to be further deepened.

In view of people's cognitive characteristics of information and based on the information scenes of the airport, this thesis explores the average response differences of different age groups to drawing boards of flight information with different information weights, and gains the core elements that affect the cognitive efficiency of users and the relationship between the core elements in information visualization design, offering effective design guidance for information visualization design based on information weights, in a bid to enhance the readability of information visualization and boost the effectiveness and efficiency of information communication.

2 Information Weight and Cognitive Capability

2.1 Information Weight and Relationship of Information Presentation

When people get information, they generally need to know clearly which part of the whole content they are getting as well as the relationship between local contents. However, during information processing, people can only concentrate on one event and object as confined to their limited attention resources. In view of the characteristics of individual attention information, Furnas came up with the focus and scene display technology [11] in 1981, highlighting that in the course of displaying a large amount of information, the local details that people take an interest in and the related global information must be balanced to a certain degree, so as to increase people's rapid understanding of large-scale information. Throughout the decision-making course, individuals tend to choose information that is consistent with their own decisions, beliefs and attitudes, while ignoring those inconsistent information; this course is called selective information presentation [12]. During and after the decision-making, individuals will search and evaluate information based on the importance and reliability of information, while in the subsequent stage of information processing, the understanding of information will be interfered by factors such as personal preferences, values and attitudes, resulting in deviations [13]. The order of information presentation will also affect the effect of information processing, and the information processing methods of search and sequential search will result in different psychological mechanisms. If the information is presented one by one in sequence, the individual's response to the preference information will be stronger than that gained by presenting it simultaneously [14]. Thus, the accuracy of people's cognition of information is determined by the matching degree between the primary and secondary relationship of presenting information and the individual's own weight of information.

2.2   Cognitive Capability of Human Factors in Information Design

Cognitive capability refers to the capability to process, store and extract information through the human brain, stimulate human senses through external things, identify, analyze and judge them by the human brain, and finally make corresponding responses to the outside world. With reference to the theory of reducing uncertainty, people will receive information with familiar and sure structure quickly, that is, the organizational structure of information will affect the cognitive speed. Richard Saul Wurman considers that the main obstacle for human to use information is the information anxiety resulting from the explosive growth of information; to address this issue, it is essential to furnish users with an information access path to present and convey information in a simple and easy-to-understand way, so that information can be cognitively understood [15], that is, it is necessary to consider the structure of information presentation from the perspective of human cognitive capability. Information cognition refers to people's understanding of information and its environment, as well as their mastery and views on information [16]. Human beings depend on a large number of psychological processes when visualizing information, including information reading, integration and reasoning [17]. In other words, what kind of information to choose for processing and utilization is closely associated with people's internal cognitive structure. Hence, human cognitive structure plays a decisive role in the way and nature of receiving information [18]. This also suggests that the essence of information acquisition and utilization is a cognitive action, and the human brain transforms the relationship between information through the time and space capability in cognitive capability, and integrates information into a cognitive model. When the information design mode built artificially by guiding visual perception is consistent with the information cognitive mode integrated by the brain, it can boost people's cognitive efficiency. Throughout this course, information forms a mapping relationship between explicit coding and implicit cognition via spatial and organizational structure. Thus, the matching degree between the spatial representation structure formed by information design and the cognitive structure of human information determines the accuracy and efficiency of information communication.

Moreover, the entire information processing course chiefly includes information input, information processing, information output and information feedback. In this course, selective attention is paid to deciding and controlling which information will be further highlighted and processed, and enhancing the individual's sensitivity to this information. Selective attention is essentially a sort of ordering of things by individuals in light of the existing rules, and tends to choose those contents characterized by strong stimulation intensity and meeting their own needs [19]. Attention is the course of selective processing of objective stimulation signals [20]. The basic function of attention is selection, and its core is the selection and analysis of information. When individuals point to and concentrate on certain objects in psychological activities, they will selectively input, course, utilize and feed back information in limited time and energy, which is a prominent feature of human cognitive behaviors. The stronger the directionality of specific information, the irrelevant information will be excluded from the information processing system of the brain, and the faster the information will be recognized. Thus, the sensitivity of individuals to guiding information determines the speed of information communication.

Nevertheless, anyone's memory capability and information processing capability are rather limited. As learned from the classification of memory in the structure of human memory [21], the capacity of sensory memory can store any data in a rather short time, but working memory can only process limited information simultaneously, while long-term memory can store unlimited information theoretically. Working memory and speed of information processing will decrease with age [22]. Based on this phenomenon, Hasher, Stoltzfus, Zacks and Rypma came up with the inhibition theory of cognitive aging [23], that is, with the increase of age, irrelevant information in working memory takes up the space of target information, so it is hard for individuals to pay attention to the target information while suppressing the attention to irrelevant information. Human aging will affect a number of cognitive capabilities, including thinking, learning, memory and decision-making [24]. People's cognitive capability takes on an inverted U-shaped growth, and gradually presents a nonlinear decline after the age of 30 [25]. Due to the different characteristics of working memory and long-term memory in human aging, the elderly tend to rely on their established experience rather than learn new concepts for performing a new task [26]. This suggests that aging will affect the capability of information processing; to make up for the loss of cognitive efficiency, individuals tend to transform information relations by simpler and single processing methods.

Information structure is closely associated with people's internal cognitive structure; besides, the speed of gaining information is associated with the individual's cognitive sensitivity to information; and apart from that, aging affects cognitive capability and weakens the capability to process information. Thus, cognitive capability will affect people's perception of efficiency, accuracy and readability of information communication in information design.

2.3   Transformation Model of Information Visualization

In the view of Card [27], information visualization is composed of a series of transformation course from original data to visual form and then to human perception and cognition system. By transforming the original data into data table form, the data table is mapped to visual structure by visual mapping, and the visual structure is composed of visual representations such as spatial position, marks and graphic attributes of marks. Finally, the visual structure is transformed and output to the display carrier based on the parameters such as position, scale and size. The following figure shows the reference model of information visualization. (see Fig. 1).

The key to the transformation of this model is visual mapping, which renders it easy to perceive and understand the data via visual representation or metaphor while keeping the original appearance of the data. Information visualization can be understood as two mapping processes: encoding and decoding [28]. Encoding refers to mapping data into visual elements of visual graphics, such as words, colors, symbols, etc., while decoding refers to people's interpretation of visual elements. Cognitive psychological process is a course in which people operate the information received from the outside and the information stored inside themselves; this process proceeds from the time of individual recognition to visual graphics, that is, the individual's decoding of information, which chiefly depends on the individual's cognitive capabilities such as visual experience, association and knowledge. To meet their own needs, individuals will selectively process

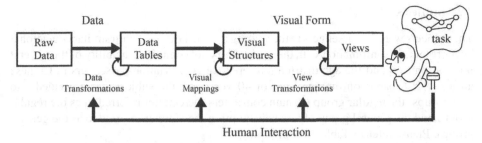

Fig. 1. Reference model of information visualization [27]

the presented complex information flow, and only accept the main information with enormous demand significance, and then start to search, discover, select and judge in the information flow cyclically. Thus, when the visual structure is effectively treated as graphic attributes based on human cognitive characteristics, people can instantly perceive a large amount of information and acquire original real information.

3   Research Objects and Methods

The course of information communication will be affected by information sources, information presentation modes and information receivers. To learn about the impact degree and relationship of the three factors on information visualization, we set up an experiment to test the individual's reaction speed differences based on different information weight visualization design, wishing to receive the factors that affect the information receiver's access to effective information and the presentation mode of effective information communication.

3.1   Experimental Design

Proceeding from the search speed and accuracy of information weights, the experiment explores the change of cognitive efficiency in information visualization design with different weights. In view of the characteristics of users' preferences for information, it is a vital factor to judge the cognitive efficiency of information visualization whether the visualization design with different information weights accords with users' habits and whether it is convenient for users to acquire information in an accurate and quick way. Thus, hypotheses H1-H3 is put forward based on the cognitive characteristics and cognitive development theory of individual information processing:

H1: the smaller the information weight, the more reaction time is needed, and the worse the cognitive efficiency of information visualization is; otherwise, the better.

H2: the older the individual is, the more reaction time is needed, and the worse the cognitive efficiency of information visualization is; otherwise, the better.

H3: there exist differences in cognitive capability among individuals of different ages: the older the individual is, the worse the learning capability is, and the smaller the difference in cognitive efficiency of information visualization with different weights is.

3.2 Subjects

The subjects were 28 passengers in the waiting area of the airport with similar educational background. In combination with the growth curve of cognitive capability of the general population [25] and the age distribution report of civil aviation passengers in Chinese airports [29], based on the age limit of 40 years old, the subjects were divided into two groups: the regular group of main consumers (hereinafter referred to as the regular group) and the general group of less consumption (hereinafter referred to as the general group). Please refer to Table 1 for grouping.

Table 1. Basic information of subjects.

Group	Number	Age
The general group	9	59 ± 9.5
The regular group	19	25.6 ± 5.5

3.3 Experimental Equipment

The experimental materials are three information drawing boards with the same content (190 mm * 680 mm in length and width), and several boarding passes with different content (60 mm * 130 mm printed with flight number, planned time, destination name and seat number). HONOR V30 with OXF-AN00 model is used to record the oral report.

3.4 Experiment Implementation

This experiment is designed by 2 (age) × 4 (information weight) in a mixed way. Therein, information weight is the internal variable of the subject. The 2 levels of independent variables of age are: general group and regular group. The information weight is divided into four levels by means of questionnaire interview to acquire the viewing order of dynamic display screen of flight information for users of different ages and experience in flying.

No weight - not classify flight information
High weight - classify flight information based on flight number
Medium weight - classify information based on destination name
Low weight - classify information based on planned flight time
Dependent variable is an index indicating passengers' cognitive speed, which is the average response difference needed by passengers to find the position of designated flight on the dynamic display screen of flight information. The smaller the response difference, the faster the cognitive speed.

3.5 Data Analysis and Summary

Average response difference is an index indicating cognitive speed, and the test results of travelers of different ages are exhibited in Table 2. Under the four information weight levels, the average reaction difference and standard deviation of reaction time in the general group are the largest; both groups present the same rule, that is, the higher the information weight, the smaller the average response difference; when the average response difference with high information weight is small, it suggests that the increase of information weight contributes to the increase of cognitive speed.

Table 2. Average response difference MS of passengers under different information weight levels

Age	N	Information Weight											
		No weight			Low weight			Medium weight			High weight		
		M	SD	SE	M	SD	SE	M	SD	SE	M	SD	SE
The general group	9	15.074	6.8996	2.2999	13.852	6.7518	2.2506	10.926	6.5908	2.1969	9.963	4.8917	1.6306
The regular group	19	11.554	4.9173	1.1281	10.272	3.9705	.9109	6.896	2.1416	.4913	6.644	1.7694	.4059
All	28	12.686	5.7470	1.0861	11.423	5.1880	.9804	8.192	4.4273	.8367	7.711	3.4160	.6456

Among the factors affecting passengers' cognitive speed, the main effects of age group and information weight level are highly significant ($P < 0.01$). This reveals that information weight level and age are vital factors affecting cognitive speed, as displayed in Table 3. Thus, H2 holds. The interaction between age and information weight level is not significant, and there is no correlation between the two. Furthermore, we can infer that H3 is not established. Figure 2 displays the estimated edge mean of the average response difference of each group.

Table 3. Variance analysis of passengers' cognitive speed

SOV	df	MS	F	Sig.
Age	1	318.715	15.472	.000
Information weight	3	143.489	6.965	.000
Age × Information weight	3	.549	.027	.994

Visual clustering based on the weight of information can affect the decision-making speed. The higher the weight of information, the stronger the guidance of visual clustering, the greater the capability to affect the time spent on decision-making, and the faster the cognitive speed. As can be learned from Fig. 2, on the whole, the response difference takes on a distinct downward trend along with the increase of information weight. The

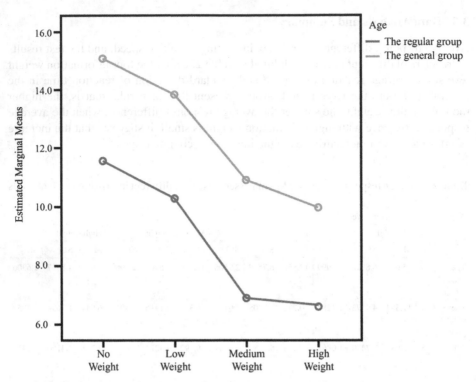

Fig. 2. Estimated marginal means of average difference under different information weight levels

results of variance analysis also present that different information weight levels affect passengers' cognitive speed significantly. The results of multiple comparisons among groups show that the difference is all highly significant between no weight and medium weight ($P < 0.01$), between no weight and high weight ($P < 0.01$), between low weight and high weight ($P < 0.01$), and between low weight and medium weight ($P < 0.05$). (see Table 4).Thus, H1 holds.

Table 4. LSD multiple comparison of average difference at different information weight levels

(I) Groups	(J) Groups	Mean difference (I-J)	Std. error	Sig.
No weight	Low weight	1.2631	1.2762	.325
	Medium weight	4.4940[*]	1.2762	.001
	High weight	4.9750[*]	1.2762	.000
Low weight	No weight	−1.2631	1.2762	.325
	Medium weight	3.2310[*]	1.2762	.013
	High weight	3.7119[*]	1.2762	.004
Medium weight	High weight	.4810	1.2762	.707

4 Factors Affecting Information Visualization

4.1 Information Volume and Presentation Structure

The rationality of information volume affects the disorder degree of individual information processing system, and the presentation structure of information representation with the same information volume will affect the cognitive effect of different groups of people. Moreover, information volume serves as the basis of structure of information presentation, and the irrationality of information will decrease or offset the guidance of structure of information presentation. Thus, whether the information volume increases or decreases without weight, or whether the structure of information presentation does not match the cognitive structure of information collectors, it will slow down the individual's cognitive speed of information and decrease the transmission efficiency of information visualization. This view has been verified in experiments, and there is a significant difference in the speed of finding designated flight columns when passengers are confronted with information drawing boards with different information weights, that is, the speed of finding information drawing boards with high and medium information weights is faster than that without information weights. In the information visualization design without weight, the two age groups present the deficiency of information processing capability, and the cognitive speed is slower than that in the information visualization design with high and medium weight. In comparison with the information drawing boards without weight, the information drawing boards with high weight and medium weight integrate the repeated information, that is, decrease the volume of invalid information. In the viewpoint of information theory, as the information amount increases, the information entropy increases, and the disorder degree of human information processing system increases as well, thus making the information processing more complicated and objectively increasing the difficulty of decision-making. However, there is no significant difference in the searching speed between the unweighted information drawing board and the low-weighted information drawing board, which suggests that simply clustering repeated information to decrease the information volume can not distinctly speed up the individual's cognition of information. Thus, it is required to rationalize the information volume. The reasonable information volume should be effective, which can not merely eliminate the cognitive uncertainty and satisfy the individual's demand for information, but avoid the information volume that affects the individual's cognitive speed due to the cognitive load arising from too much information. The information volume is reasonable when the individual can address the demand through the relevance of the information provided. Therefore, before visually mapping the information, it is necessary to know the key information that the individual needs to understand the content, sort the importance of the information, and filter it based on the value of the information itself. In the face of the same information volume, if an information factor can't be replaced by other information factors, its information value will be greater, and individuals will be guided by this information factor further. At this time, the factors are clustered as information features, and the formed hierarchical structure integrates repeated irrelevant information, which enhances the order of individual information processing system and improves the information communication effect of information visualization from the cognitive aspect. To increase the cognitive speed of individuals in information visualization, proceeding from the information content needed by individuals to address their needs, the information presented is rationally screened, and the effective information is selected for transmission; the effective information is visually represented in cluster structure, and the information associated with solving their needs is centrally guided by the explicit hierarchical structure.

To verify the above viewpoint, the subjects were interviewed prior to the experiment, and the information sorting on the dynamic information screen of flights was recorded. Besides, during the experiment, the reaction attitude and reaction time of the subjects to the information drawing boards with different information weights were observed and recorded. It turned out that the response speed of the subjects to the information drawing boards classified based on the information at the top of the sorting was faster than that of the information drawing boards without weights. The experimental results clearly indicate that the rationalization of information needs to address their needs and the weight distribution of these factors in combination with the key information factors needed by individuals; the lower the uniqueness of information factors pointing to the content, the lower the capability as information features, and the more insensitive individuals are to this information. Furthermore, the information clustering structure can guide the information receiver to select the right information volume and process it effectively, decrease the entropy of the receiver's information processing system, enhance the order degree of the system, accelerate the individual's cognitive speed, and boost the accuracy and efficiency of information communication.

4.2 Differences of Information Receiver

Individual differences of different types of information receivers will exert an impact on the effectiveness of information visualization, which is chiefly manifested in the cognitive characteristics of information processing and the way of collecting information, while the information weight level produces no significant impact on the cognitive speed of information receivers of different ages. In light of the experimental results, the interaction between age group and information weight level is not significant in cognitive speed, and the response speed trend and amplitude of different information weight levels to different age groups are consistent, but there is no correlation between the two. The change of individual age is the principal factor that produces different types of information receivers, which affects the speed of information communication from the cognitive speed of the information receiver. Aging will weaken the individual's capability of selective attention, but simultaneously, it provides relatively sufficient time for subjective selection and processing of information to ensure the accuracy of information acquisition. Thus, in the experiment, the group of older age on average needs more reaction time than the group of younger age on average, but the accuracy of the two groups is the same. The style change of individuals in learning things is affected by age, which gradually changes from the way of defining information based on stimulating communication given by external environment reference to the way of defining information relying more on own internal reference, which is not easily affected and interfered by external factors. From the perspective of information processing, it is further analyzed that the receivers who rely on internal reference will conduct overall scanning or sequential scanning when acquiring information, while the receivers using external reference will adopt local focusing. The presentation mode of flight information in information drawing boards is chiefly visual, and the information of different flights is listed simultaneously. Older receivers will tend to their own original information classification methods, and they will search for information based on the order of information in information drawing boards, while younger receivers will quickly adapt to the information structure of information drawing boards, and they will make jumping search in consideration of information classification characteristics. Based on the way individuals choose information and their learning capability to adapt to external stimuli, information receivers can be classified into adaptive and insensitive types. Adaptive information receivers can achieve a good balance between the speed and accuracy of processing information, and the way of collecting information is a dynamic and continuous course. In the course, information is defined by combining established experience and external reference stimulation. Facing the new information structure, information distribution rules can be quickly found, and key information can be accurately gained to meet individual needs. On the other hand, insensitive information receivers will decrease the use of working memory, and address individual needs on the strength of more established experience. When they meet enormous differences between the structural form of information and the cognitive structure, it is hard for them to adapt to the new information structure by learning capability to achieve the expected goal. Besides, in the course of information screening, the search process is repeated many times until the target information is successfully found. The differences of information receivers will affect the effectiveness of information communication in the course of information visualization. It is suggested to address the problem of information communication efficiency by understanding the information cognitive needs of different types of information receivers and improving the information structure. The design of information visualization for insensitive information receivers should follow the conventional cognition, learn about the degree and order of their attention to different information, split the complex information by taking the information with high attention as the information feature, and gradually present the information in combination with specific scenes, so as to help them increase their selective attention to key information and decrease the pressure of information receivers when facing a large amount of disordered information. When oriented to adaptive information receivers, the information structure should be provided with obvious and regular classification methods, and the information as classification features must be the information elements needed by individuals in the operation course of resolving their needs. By clustering effective information, the complexity and redundancy of information expression can be reduced, and the length of the receiver's search path can be shortened.

5 Summary

By analyzing the cognitive characteristics and reaction speed of users confronted with different information weights, this thesis is intended to offer scientific design guidance for enhancing the readability of information and boosting the effectiveness of information communication in information visualization design. The research reveals the following:

1. Information weight can decrease the entropy of the receiver's information processing system, enhance the order of the cognitive system, and guide the information visualization cognitively by influencing the presentation structure of information.
2. The cognitive speed of users with younger age on average is significantly faster than that of users with older age on average; the former will learn quickly in consideration of the actual situation, while the latter tend to rely on their established experience, that is, the dependence of information receivers on established experience will affect the efficiency of information communication. This suggests that the key to enhance the efficiency of information communication is the matching degree between the presentation structure of information and the way users search for information.
3. When collecting information, younger information receivers will concentrate more locally, and can screen information quickly in the course of information processing. This demonstrates that redundant information should be avoided as much as possible in information visualization design, and the identifiability of information can be increased by way of clustering.
4. By analyzing the importance of the key information needed by individuals to address their needs, the rational screening of the information volume can eliminate the cognitive uncertainty of individuals in the course of information processing, and enhance the effectiveness of information communication at the level of boosting cognitive efficiency in combination with the clustering structure of information.
5. Since there exist differences in cognitive characteristics of information processing and ways of collecting information, information receivers can be classified into adaptive type and insensitive type. Adaptive information receivers can quickly learn the information classification rules by virtue of their strong learning capability, and clustering should be used in the information visualization design for this type. However, insensitive information receivers tend to address the demand by relying on established experience; thus, when improving the information structure, it is essential to know the weight distribution of this type of information receivers to the key information, split the information while maintaining the basic consistency, and guide the individuals to address the demand by means of one-way layered presentation of information.

References

1. Liu, W.: From cognition to perception: on information visualization technology. China Comput. Users **48**, 52–53 (2003)
2. Larkin, J.H., Simon, H.A.: Why a diagram is (sometimes) worth ten thousand words. Cogn. Sci. **11**(1), 65–100 (1987)
3. Munzner, T.: Visualization Analysis and Design, 1st edn. CRC Press, Boca Raton (2014)
4. Zhou, N., Yan, P., Liu, W.: On the methods of information resources visualization. In: The Proceedings of Digital Library: IT Opportunities and Challenges in the New Millennium. Research Center for Information Resources, Wuhan University, Beijing (2002)
5. Li, W.: The application of visualization method in building index weights. J. Xinyang Normal Univ. (Natl. Sci. Ed.) (3), 338–340 + 343 (2005)

6. Ghoniem, M., Cornil, M., et al.: Weighted maps: treemap visualization of geolocated quantitative data. In: Kao, D.L., Hao, M.C., Livingston, M.A., Wischgoll, T. (eds.) Conference on Visualization and Data Analysis 2015, vol. 9397. SPIE-IS&T Electronic Imaging, San Feancisco (2015)

7. Chen, C.M.: Spatial partitioning algorithms for data visualization. Proc. SPIE – Int. Soc. Opt. Eng. **9017**, 164–167 (2013)

8. Lu, X.M., Yang, Z.H., Yan, H.W.: Visualization of the target weight of point group. J. Lanzhou Jiaotong Univ. **4**, 133–137 (2018)

9. Peng, R.L., Zhang, B.Y.: Cognitive Psychology, 1st edn. Education Press, Hangzhou (2004)

10. Qiu, F.D., Wu, M.Z.: An experimental research on the influence of cognitive styles and negative emotions on tourism decision-making. Psychol. Sci. **28**(5),1112–1114 (2005)

11. Furnas, G.W.: The FISHEYE view: a new look at structured files. In: Card, S.K., Mackinlay, J., Shneiderman, B. Readings in information visualization: using vision to think, pp. 312–330. Morgan Kaufmann Publishers Inc., San Francisco, CA, USA (1999)

12. Fischer, P., Schulz-Hardt, S., Frey, D.: Selective exposure and information quantity: how different information quantities moderate decision makers' preference for consistent and inconsistent information. J. Pers. Soc. Psychol. **94**(2), 231 (2008)

13. Frey, D.: Recent research on selective exposure to information. Adv. Exper. Soc. Psychol. **19**(1), 41–80 (1986)

14. Jonas, E., Schulz-Hardt, S., Frey, D., et al.: Confirmation bias in sequential information search after preliminary decisions: an expansion of dissonance theoretical research on selective exposure to information. J. Personal. Soc. Psychol. **80**(4), 557 (2001)

15. Rosenfeld, L.: Information architecture: looking ahead. J. Assoc. Inf. Sci. Technol. **53**(10), 874–876 (2014)

16. Xing, W.H., Yuan, J.M.: Cognitive psychology analysis of users information service. Inf. Sci. **11**, 1404–1408 (2004)

17. Trafton, J.G., Kirschenbaum, S.S., Tsui, T.L., et al.: Turning pictures into numbers: extracting and generating information from complex visualizations. Int. J. Human-Comput. Stud. **53**(5), 827–850 (2000)

18. Zhang, Y.: The psychoanalysis on users in network information service. Lib. Inf. Serv. (3),36–38 + 47 (2004)

19. Zhou, P.S.: On emerging of cognitive bias and its relationship with need for cognitive closure. Psychol. Res. **10**(5), 11–18 (2017)

20. Lavie, N., Driver, J.: On the spatial extent of attention in object-based visual selection. Percept. Psychophys. **58**(8), 1238–1251 (1996)

21. Young, J.Q., Van Merrienboer, J.J.G., Durning, S.J., et al.: Cognitive load theory: implications for medical education: AMEE guide No. 86. Med. Teach. **36**(5), 371–384 (2014)

22. Schulz, M., Roßnagel, C.S.: Informal workplace learning: an exploration of age differences in learning competence. Learn. Instruct. **20**(5), 383–399 (2010)

23. Hasher, L., Stoltzfus, E.R., et al.: Age and inhibition. J. Exper. Psychol. Learn. Mem. Cogn. **17**(1), 163–169(1991)

24. Park, D.C.: The basic mechanisms accounting for age-related decline in cognitive function. In: Park, D.C., Schwarz, N. Cognitive Aging: A Primer, pp. 3–21. Psychology Press, London (2000)

25. Yang, B.X., Wang, Z.Q., Cao, L.M., et al.: The relationship between the growth of cognitive ability and age. J. Clin. Psychiatry **25**(5), 316–318 (2015)

26. Umanath, S., Marsh, E.J.: Understanding how prior knowledge influences memory in older adults. Perspect. Psychol. Sci. **9**(4) (2014)

27. Card, S.K., Mackinlay, J.D., Shneiderman, B.: Readings in Information Visualization: Using Vision to Think. 1st edn.Morgan Kaufmann Publishers Inc., San Francisco, CA, USA (1999)

28. Wünsche, B.: A Survey, classification and analysis of perceptual concepts and their application for the effective visualisation of complex information. In: Proceedings of the 2004 Australasian Symposium on Information Visualisation, pp. 17–24. Australian Computer Society, Inc., AUS (2004)
29. CADA Report: China Air Passenger Trends in 2018. http://www.cadas.com.cn/news/-201901 1608215500001.html. Accessed 16 Jan 2019

From Hieroglyphs to Emoji, to IKON: The Search of the (Perfect?) Visual Language

Cesco Reale[1]([✉]) [iD], Marwan Kilani[2] [iD], Araceli Giménez[3] [iD], Nadu Barbashova[1] [iD], and Roman Oechslin[1] [iD]

[1] KomunIKON, Neuchâtel, Switzerland
{cesco.reale,nadu.barbashova,roman.oechslin}@komunikon.com
[2] Freie Universität Berlin Germany– Swiss National Science Foundation, Bern, Switzerland
[3] Department Interactive Graphics, Higher Education School of Art and Design, Castellón de la Plana, Spain
agimenez@easdcastello.org

Abstract. Writing evolved from the expression of the meanings to the expression of the sounds. In modern times new projects like Emoji came back to semantic writings. We show some main characteristics of these ancient and modern systems, analyzing aspects that can be improved, and describing IKON, a new iconic language conceived as a new step in the evolution of visual languages. We discuss a case study about hair and gender, how these theoretical results were applied in some IKON icons, and a test to evaluate the comprehensibility of these icons through a tool called iconometer. Finally, we discuss WIKON, a crowdsourced extension of IKON.

Keywords: Visual semiotics · Iconic languages · Logographies · Semasiographies · Icons · Emoji · Iconometer · Vidsemiotiko · Ikonaj lingvoj · Logografioj · Semasiografioj · Ikonoj · Emoĝioj · Ikonmezurilo · Sémiotique visuelle · Langues iconiques · Sémasiographies · Icônes · Iconomètre · Semiótica visual · Lenguas icónicas · Logografías · Semasiografías · Íconos · Iconómetro · Visuelle Semiotik · Ikonische sprachen · Logographien · Semasiographien · Ikonometer

1 Introduction

Most human languages emerged as spoken languages, while writing was later developed as a tool to record them. Logograms and semagrams were important elements in most of the earliest writing systems, but they became less and less common over time, losing ground to phonograms. This trend started to be somehow reversed in modern times, with the invention of semasiographies, i.e. languages conceived to write and to express only (or mainly) meanings rather than sounds. Emoji are a contemporary, very widespread and somehow popular development stemming from this trend. However, although they are used by a large part of human population, Emoji are far from being a coherent language. In general, the contemporary iconic world is lacking a consistent linguistic

© Springer Nature Switzerland AG 2021
M. M. Soares et al. (Eds.): HCII 2021, LNCS 12779, pp. 457–476, 2021.
https://doi.org/10.1007/978-3-030-78221-4_31

framework to turn the current reality of stuttered visual words into one of complex iconic sentences. We believe that many iconic languages will appear in the coming years and this field of research will become increasingly important. The aim of this article is to present our solution to this state of affairs: ikon, a new iconic language that aims at improving the existing offer for visual communication. So far we have defined the grammar, the compositional and graphic guidelines, and we have designed an initial set of icons. Although they are not yet publicly available, beta versions of web and mobile apps implementing it already exist, thus making it possible to use the language and practically test its potential.

The present article is structured as follow: Sect. 2.1 analyzes the use of logograms and semagrams in the earliest writing systems. Section 2.2 presents some characteristics of modern semasiographies. Section 3 introduces IKON's guidelines. Section 4 shows a practical case study about hair and gender: how gender is codified through hair, how we applied this theoretical background in some of our icons, how we performed a test to check how these icons are understood, through a tool called Iconometer. Finally, Sect. 5 presents the technical requirements of WIKON, a crowdsourced extension of IKON.

2   Writing Meanings in Ancient and Modern Times

2.1   Pre-modern Non-phonographic Systems

No language has probably ever been fully recorded with a purely non-phonographic (non-PH) system. Rather, non-PH systems usually manifest themselves in two more restricted forms. First, we find purely non-PH systems that are limited in their scope and can only transcribe concepts belonging to specific semantic subsets. Such systems were and still are used to encode information about very specific domains, and may have played crucial roles in the emergence of true, fully fledged writing systems. The second common manifestation of non-PH systems is as partially non-PH strategies to encode selected lexical or morphological elements within mixed non-phonographic/phonographic writing systems.

Accounting Tokens, Early Bureaucracy and Clan Marks. The origins of the Mesopotamian cuneiform writing system are believed to lie in a series of clay tokens of different shape and decoration used to count and record commodities collected or exchanged [1, 2]. Some tokens corresponded to numerals or specific measures, while others represented goods or commodities (such as "sheep", "metal", "wool"). Tokens worked as a non-PH system limited to a specific domain: trade and accounting. Some tokens had abstract geometrical forms, while others imitated the shape of their corresponding items. At the beginning, the tokens themselves were probably understood as units of the item they symbolized. Later on, it was the impression of a specific token onto a clay tablet that was used as a representation of a specific item or quantity. Finally, drawings in the shape of the impressions replaced the tokens altogether. Once items started to be drawn, the range of concepts that could be translated into written signs expanded very quickly, resulting in a whole set of logograms representing commodities, quantities, names, places, and basic concepts. This non-PH system was limited to accounting

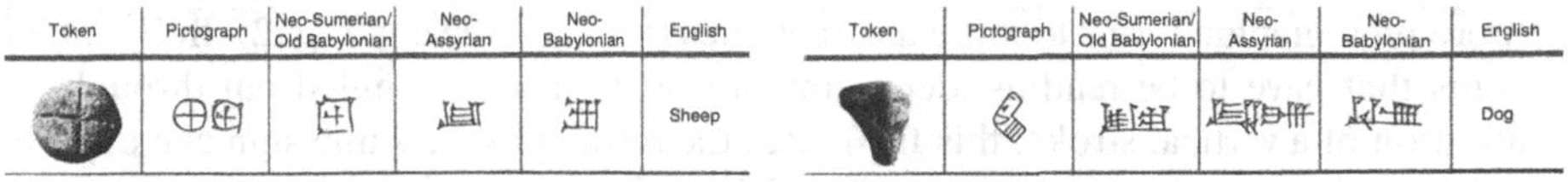

Token	Pictograph	Neo-Sumerian/ Old Babylonian	Neo-Assyrian	Neo-Babylonian	English	Token	Pictograph	Neo-Sumerian/ Old Babylonian	Neo-Assyrian	Neo-Babylonian	English
	⊕⊞	囙	屵	州	Sheep		✎	阯⫼	⫼⫻	𒇽⫼	Dog

Fig. 1. From tokens to pictographs (from [3], p 135)

purposes and was not suited to represent a language. Yet, the system was rather efficient for its purpose, and spread widely inside and outside Mesopotamia (Fig. 1).

The emergence of writing in Egypt is less well attested and presented phonograms since its earliest attestations [1, 4]. Other systems preexisted them: seals and marks on vessels were used in trade and administration. These systems were non-PH as they used conventional signs to identify and represent items and names.

Finally clans' emblems have been attested in China and Eurasia at least since the Bronze Age, and can be interpreted as very specialized non-PH. They might have played a role in the emergence of writing in China [1, 5, 6].

Non-phonographic Although complex writing systems extensively employing phonographic and non-PH strategies do exist today (Chinese and derived script being the obvious example [6], the most significant examples are represented by ancient scripts. Besides classical Chinese, which survives today, the most illustrative examples are provided by Cuneiform [2], Egyptian [4], and Mayan hieroglyphs [7]. The emergence of the Maya script is difficult to analyze due to the dearth of evidence. By contrast, it is likely that the pure non-PH systems described above played a role in the emergence of the Cuneiform, Egyptian and Chinese writing systems. Their evolution appears to have followed similar trajectories: while the original non-PH systems were suited for very specific uses, the need of the emerging pre- or proto-states to record more complex information must have quickly proved to be limited to effectively transcribe any natural language. In all three cases, this problem was solved in analogous ways: by adding phonograms to the systems. The way phonograms and non-phonograms interact is complex and follows different strategies. Here we discuss the two main subcategories of non-PH signs that are attested in these systems: ideograms and classifiers.

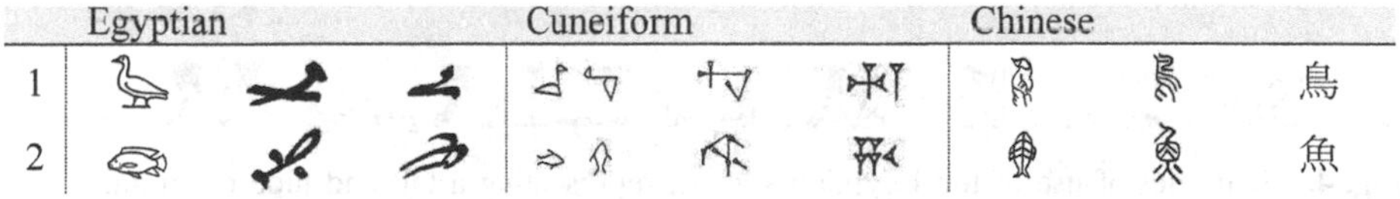

	Egyptian			Cuneiform			Chinese		
1	🦆	⟵	⟵	⊲ᷟ	⊤⩔	⊁⫓	𩾌	𩾌	鳥
2	🐟	🔺	🔺	⇨⩘	𝍖	𝍖	𩵋	𩵋	魚

Fig. 2. Evolution of the characters for "bird" (1) and "fish" (2) to more abstract forms.

- IDEOGRAMS: ideograms can be described as single signs that represent one concept, word, or morpheme without encoding any phonetic information. These signs often transcribe words referring to concrete items and less frequently verbs, abstract concepts or morphemes. They can be highly pictographic (as in the case of most Egyptian or Mayan hieroglyphs) or abstract (as in the case of numerals), or they can evolve from more pictographic forms to more abstract ones (See [8] - see e.g. Fig. 2). In Egyptian, signs that have to be read as ideograms are often visually singled out through the addition of a vertical stroke: this facilitates the reading as the same sign can often be used as ideogram, phonogram, or classifier. In fact, these strokes work as semantic classifiers conveying the information [+ideogram]. Ideograms can combine with phonetic complements in various ways and for various purposes, such as to disambiguate the pronunciation or to provide information about additional morphological elements [2, 6, 9, 10] (Fig. 3).

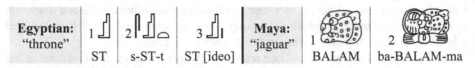

Fig. 3. Examples of Egyptian and Mayan non-phonographic signs in their simple form (1), with phonetic complements (2), and with a stroke indicating a logographic (3 – only Egyptian).

- CLASSIFIERS: classifiers are signs added to words to provide additional information about their nature or semantic domains. Classifiers are attested in various forms and degrees of frequency, in all these ancient writing systems [2, 6, 9–11]. Their functioning and conceptualization can be quite complex, often changed over time and in several ways. It is still a subject of an open and lively academic debate that cannot be discussed here in detail – Fig. 4 provides a basic example from Egyptian [11–13]. As for Chinese, most of the characters in use today can be analysed as being composed of a phonetic element and a semantic radical. The phonetic element is built according to a rebus principle, namely it is taken from a character that has (or had) a similar pronunciation to the word that is being written. The radical, instead provides a general indication of the semantic domain of the word being transcribed. For instance, the following words are all somehow related with "water", and their corresponding characters all contain the radical 氵 = [water/liquid/humidity]: 海= hǎi = "sea", 河= hé = "river", 汤= tāng = "soup". Radicals thus work like classifiers in other scripts, but they are integral parts of the characters themselves, rather than being additional, distinct signs [5].

Fig. 4. Examples of use of the Egyptian sign ₹, representing a tail and hide of an animal, as classifier for the semantic domain [animal] (from [12], 102).

Non-Phonographic Characters – Forms. Non-phonographic characters can be built and used in various ways. Here are the most common ones [1, 2, 5, 6, 9–11, 13]:

- PICTOGRAMS: the signs represent what they mean – by far the most common case.

- PICTOGRAPHIC SCENES: two or more ideographic elements are combined together in "scenes" meant to describe a different concept or word. See e.g. the Chinese character 泪 = lèi = "tear(s)", composed of ⺡= [water/liquid/humidity] and 目= [eye], or the character 武= wǔ = "military", "armed forces", composed of 止 = [foot/marching person] and 戈= [halbard/weapon(s)]
- METAPHORICAL/SYMBOLIC SIGNS: concepts can be expressed ideographically through signs built on metaphors or conventional symbols. Although metaphors and conventional symbols are often culturally specific, parallel developments can be recognized in different, unrelated scripts. For instance, both the Chinese character 日and the Egyptian hieroglyph ☉are (or derive from) pictographic representations of the "sun" and can be used to write the word "sun". Yet, in both systems they can also be used (usually as classifiers/radicals) in the spelling of words related with the concept of [time]; see e.g. Chinese 時= shí = "time" or Egyptian ⌐⌐☉ = nw = "time".
- ABSTRACT SIGNS: some concepts can be represented through abstract, often geometrical signs that have no explicit relation with the underlying word or concept, although some of these forms may have, or may originate from, specific cultural associations that justify their use; see e.g. Egyptian ∩ = 10.
- HYPERONYMIC COMBINATIONS: occasionally, multiple pictographic representations of related items can be combined to represent the general category those items belong to. This solution is occasionally found in Egyptian hieroglyphs; see e.g. the case of different kinds of bread being combined to write ⌒θ = t = "bread (in general)" or that of different types of cattle used as a hyperonimic determinative in the word ⌐⌐⌐ 𓃿𓃿𓃿 = mnmn.t = "cattle (in general)".

2.2 Modern Semasiographies

Modern semasiographies have their roots in the works of 17th century philosophers. John Wilkins, for instance, conceived the Real Character, a pasigraphy in which every symbol represents a meaning. It is based on an ontological classification of the reality in form of a tree, where a letter is associated to each node of the tree. Each concept in the tree is represented by the sequence of letters from the tree root to the node.

Modern semasiographies can be grouped into several categories. Here we present some most known examples, the lists are not exhaustive and can have intersections.

- SECTORIAL VISUAL LANGUAGES: these languages were conceived for specific purposes. The International Code of Signals (ship flags) is completely abstract and arbitrary, its aim was clear readability for a small set of messages. Road signs instead join abstract pictograms (interdictions, danger, etc.) with iconic ones (people, natural elements, etc.). Begriffsschrift was conceived to write logic and mathematics, so it is abstract for the nature of its domain. VCM is a recent project (2006) developed at the Univ. of Paris 13, and has a very precise grammar of categories and classifiers for medical sentences.
- PASIGRAPHIES: these languages were all conceived to be handwritten. Transcendent Algebra applies concepts of mathematics to grammar and everyday language. Bliss, the most famous in this group, was applied since 1971 in AAC (see following group). LoCoS has a 2D syntax and can also be pronounced. Emoticons, Picto, Safo, aUI,

Nobel, Earth language, Letters to Jill, Sitelen Sitelen, Sitelen Pona are also in this group.

- AAC ICONIC LANGUAGES: languages for Augmentative and Alternative Communication, created for disabled people, such as PCS, Widget, Minspeak, Sclera, Beta, Pixon, ArasAAC, FreeSpeech and many others. All these languages were generally conceived only for basic communication and are often based on the spoken languages of their environment.
- ART AND GRAPHIC PROJECTS. Isotype was mainly meant to represent statistic information, it has almost no grammar. Elephant's memory has the almost unique characteristic to be readable starting from different points of the sentence (FreeSpeech has also this feature). Piktoperanto has a well-developed grammar with also hyperonyms and semantic compositionality. Although Dì Shū is not a language –it is a book only in icons–, it has a surprising comprehensibility, due also to the simplicity of the content being narrated. Letters to Jill and Genesis are also part of this group.
- RESEARCH PROJECTS: Yerkish was created to investigate the communicative potential of apes, VCM (for medicine) has already been mentioned.
- WEB BASED AND APPS: White-o-glyphics, Zlango (language for SMS, with high language dependency), iConji, Lookji.
- EMOJI FAMILY: Emoji, Emojitaliano (partially crowdsourced, it defines a grammar for Emoji conceived for italophones), Openmoji, Sitelen Emoji, Emojese (it defines a grammar for Emoji, with the addition of some non Emoji symbols).
- MODERN LOGOGRAPHIES: Sitelen Sitelen, Sitelen Pona, Sitelen Emoji, and Yingzi are probably the only modern semasiographies born to represent an oral language in a purely logographic way. The first three are different systems to write semantically the minimalist language Toki Pona; the last one is a proposal to write English through logograms, like Chinese.

A presentation of several of these semasiographies was given by some representatives of the KomunIKON team [14]. Here we present a Table 1 to compare some main characteristics of these modern semasiographies. We will analyze four categories.

- COMPOSITIONALITY: several iconemes[1] (or icons) can be compound in a more complex icon whose meaning is the semantic composition of the original meanings.
- ICONICITY: relation between the visual signifier and the signified; high iconicity means that for most signs there is a good possibility to guess their meanings; absent iconicity means that in every sign there are no clues to guess its meaning.
- UNIVERSALITY: capacity to express meanings whose semantic fields are not bound to a specific area; absent universality means that the semasiography was conceived only for a specific domain; very high universality means that the semasiography was conceived to potentially become expressive like natural languages.
- LANGUAGE INDEPENDENCE: a logography has no language independence, because it was created to write a specific language; a low language independency means that there are several phrases based on an idiomatic use of a language and that might not

---

[1] Iconeme: the smallest meaningful visual unit in an image or in an icon; it represents a certain concept that would not be represented by taking away a part of the iconeme.

be easily understood by people that do not speak that language. For example: "I am going to do" generally expresses future, not movement, so if "going" in this case is expressed showing movement, there is language dependence.

Table 1. Comparison of modern semasiographies.

Semasiography	Composit.	Iconicity	Universality	Lang. Indep.
Int. code of signals	Absent	Absent	Absent	Total
Begriffsschrift	Total	Absent	Absent	Total
Road signs	High	Medium	Absent	High
Transcendent algebra	High	High	High	Total
Isotype	High	High	Medium	High
Bliss	High	Low	Very high	Total
LoCoS	High	Low	Very high	Total
Yerkish	Absent	Absent	Low	Total
Nobel	Medium	Low	Total	Total
AAC iconic languages	High	High	Medium	Medium
Earth language	Medium	Low	High	Total
Piktoperanto	High	High	High	Total
Emoticons	Absent	Medium	Absent	Total
Emoji	Absent	High	Absent	High
Emojitaliano	High	Medium	High	Medium
Elephant's memory	High	Medium	High	Total
White-o-glyphics	High	Medium	High	Total
Zlango	Medium	High	Medium	Medium
VCM	Total	High	Low	Total
iConji	Medium	High	High	High
地书(Dì shū)	Low	Very high	High	Total
Sitelen Sitelen	High	Very low	Very high	Absent
Sitelen Pona	High	Very low	Very high	Absent
Sitelen Emoji	High	High	Very high	Absent
Emojese	High	High	High	Medium
IKON	Very high	Very high	Very high	Total

As it appears from the comparison illustrated in the table, no semasiography is compositional, iconic, universal, and language independent. For this reason, we have conceived IKON (pron. "eekon"/'i:kon/), in order to create a powerful and easy-to-use semasiography that can satisfy these characteristics. In this perspective, IKON has several characteristics that can be found in other semasiographies.

IKON allows semantic compositionality by joining icons (as in Bliss, LoCoS and Piktoperanto), the use of grammar categories (Bliss), the consistent use of iconemes (as in VCM), the possibility of a 2D syntax (as in Begriffsschrift, LoCoS and Elephant's memory), high iconicity (as in AAC languages and Emoji). IKON definitely avoids the abstractness of Yerkish, that had the specific function to test the abstraction skills of apes. It also avoids the language dependency existing in several semasiographies such as Zlango (that borrowed several constructions from English, such as the interrogative "do", expressed with the icon for "do/make") and present also in several AAC languages, that follow some expressions of national languages because they are aimed at small groups of disabled people, who often live in a monolingual context.

3   IKON Guidelines

3.1   Theoretical and "Philosophical" Framework

IKON is defined not only by objective factors, but also by a selection of theoretical principles and values that define the "soul" of the project. The main ones are:

- LANGUAGE-INDEPENDENT: icons are built to be as language-independent as possible. Semantically different concepts are always represented by different icons, even when they correspond to homonyms in a given language (e.g. "play" can have at least three different meanings (games, theatre and music) so in IKON we have one icon for each meaning). Similarly, no icon is designed on idiomatic constructions, as these are both language- and culture-specific.
- INTERNATIONAL: IKON aims to be easily understood, and therefore efficiently used, across different countries and societies, without being specific to any.
- ICONIC AND INTELLIGIBLE: IKON aims to be easily understandable by people of different backgrounds. Pictographic, highly iconic representations are favoured, while abstract symbols are used only when no better alternative is identified, or when it is already widely used (e.g. road signs).
- CROSS-CONTAMINATED, I.E. LEARNING FROM THE PAST: IKON is not conceived to reinvent the wheel, rather the opposite: the thorough study of logographic and semasiographic strategies found in ancient and modern scripts, planned languages, pasigraphies, and iconic languages is fundamental for us, and IKON conceptually or practically integrates many features derived from this (often millenary) experience.
- HUMAN-CENTRED: IKON is conceived as human-centred, at least at the beginning. This means that whenever an icon may refer to an undetermined subject, actor or patient, humans are used as generic "placeholders". For instance, personal pronouns are illustrated with people, but one can easily imagine contexts where the pronouns do not refer to humans. Obviously, one can hope and expect that in the future the language will evolve including non-human-centred icons, but these will be secondary developments stemming from a human-centred default.

- INCLUSIVE: IKON respects and promotes diversity in every form (gender, sexual orientation, ethnic groups, phenotypes, etc.). It does so in two ways: either a) through identity-specific icons for each distinct subgroup characterizing specific identities (e.g. specific icons and symbols commonly used by the LGBT + communities are available to represent various genders and sexual orientations), or b) by using unspecified and identity-neutral icons (e.g. unspecified human silhouettes are coloured in grey, so that no actual skin tone is privileged or discriminated). If neither of these solutions is possible, or applying some generalizations/assumptions about identities leads to significant improvements in an icon readability, then the most inclusive solution will be adopted (see below for a practical example).
- TRANSCULTURAL: IKON will include culturally and geographically specific icons that can better reflect the actual realities of the users. For instance, there will be several icons for "seasons" corresponding to the different seasonal cycles around the world.
- UNCENSORED: IKON is conceived to be a complete language, therefore it must include icons representing things or concepts that may be perceived by some as disturbing or offensive, such as sexual, racist or vulgar meanings.
- PRECISE: in principle, icons are not conceived to be "subject to interpretation", rather each of them is conceived to represent a specific concept, idea, action or item and are defined as in a dictionary.

3.2 Linguistic Guidelines

IKON has guidelines concerning three linguistic dimensions: semantics, grammar/morphology, and syntax. For reasons of space, we discuss here only the semantic guidelines. Regarding the other two dimensions, suffice to say that IKON has dedicated strategies to represent verbal (e.g. tenses, moods, diathesis, etc.) and non-verbal (e.g. number, logical relationships, etc.) morphology, and syntactic relations. Moreover, the very visual nature of the IKON language makes it possible to use very flexible syntactic approaches which can even go beyond the mono-dimensional limit intrinsic in the spoken languages and their written forms.

Semantic Dimension. The following principles underlie the design of IKON:

- CONSISTENCY: in order to increase consistency, IKON icons are built according to a finite number of patterns (see Sect. 3.3). Moreover, wherever it is possible, iconemes present in a given icon maintain the same meanings in other icons across the system. Finally, selected iconemes and graphic elements have standardised functions across the system, thus resulting in high coherence and internal referentiality (e.g. red geometrical forms are used, in various icons, as neutral placeholders for generic "items").
- COMPLETENESS: the iconic lexicon of IKON is continuously growing through the inclusion of new icons conceived both by us developers and by the users. However, this growth is not random: in order to be usable from the very beginning, the iconic lexicon of IKON is built in a reasoned way, starting from a core set of around 500 icons covering basic concepts, that can be used both directly to communicate complex ideas, and indirectly as "building blocks" to create new "compound words". This set is

the synthesis of: 65 semantic primes (Wierzbicka); 100 Leipzig Jakarta list words; 120 Toki Pona roots (Lang); 215 Swadesh list words (Swadesh); 500 Minilex words (Gunnemark); 850 BASIC English words (Ogden).

3.3 Compositional Rules

IKON icons can be classified into a finite number of categories characterized by specific forms, patterns and strategies that allow a high degree of flexibility in visually representing complex or abstract concepts and reinforce the coherence and understandability of the whole system. We present here a selection of such categories:

Simple Icons. Simple icons are the most basic icons available in IKON. They are:

- PICTOGRAPHIC ICONS: these are the simplest and most common icons, their functioning is: what is represented is what is meant. In these icons, items are often represented in prototypical and conventional ways, rather than (hyper-)realistically – the stress is on the type of item in general, rather than on a specific kind of it.
- SYMBOLIC ICONS: although IKON aims at avoiding abstract elements, at times the most efficient way to express a concept is through an (often already widely known) abstract sign (e.g. road signs).
- CONTEXTUAL ICONS: some items and concepts are easier to understand when they are visualized together, within a given context. Contextual icons exploit this property: they are built as visual scenes with several elements, use graphic markers (such as arrows, circles, colour oppositions, etc.) to point to one specific sub-element of the whole picture. In this case what is highlighted, given the context, is what is meant.

Compound Icons. Compound icons are formed by combining together different sub-elements according to a restricted number of patterns. Their main types are (Fig. 5):

- JUXTAPOSED ICONS: few specific icons are composed by the simple juxtaposition of two or more elements that could work as independent icons (e.g. icons for "what" = "which-thing", "when" = "which-time", "where" = "which-place").
- CONTRASTIVE ICONS: some concepts are better understood (and often are meaningful only) when expressed through oppositions. Contrastive icons are thus built by juxtaposing images of contrasting items or situations, and by highlighting the one corresponding to the specific meaning of the icon. E.g. the concept "calm" can be represented by highlighting the calmer sea in an icon with calm and turbulent sea.
- HYPERONYMIC ICONS: as already realized by ancient users of complex scripts (see §2.1), as well as modern ones (e.g. Piktoperanto), there are concepts that can be understood as ensembles of different but related elements. In IKON, by default hyperonymic icons are usually built by combining a selection of four different but related items, four being a good average both for graphic and conceptual reasons. E.g.: "flower" + "sun" + "dead leaf" + "snowflake" = "season(s)". However, hyperonymic icons with more or less than four elements are also possible, when needed.
- HYPONYMIC ICONS: in addition, if one of the elements of a hyperonymic icon is highlighted, it becomes a contextual icon representing the hyponymic concept. E.g.:

to express the concept of "autumn", one can highlight the "dead leaf" in the "season" icon – the dead leaf alone would be understood as "dead leaf", and not as "autumn".

- PROCESS ICONS: Process Icons represent concepts involving some form of change, evolution, development, or cycle. They are built by picturing, within the same icon, several stages of a given phenomenon, and by connecting such stages with arrows that indicate the development of the phenomenon itself. E.g. if arrows are added to the "season" icon, we obtain a process icon meaning "year/ seasonal cycle".
- ICONS WITH CLASSIFIERS: as the complex scripts discussed above, IKON can also use classifiers. Icons with classifiers contain two distinct pictures: a main one in the centre representing the primary meaning of the icon, and a smaller secondary one, usually in the upper right corner, indicating its general conceptual or semantic domain.

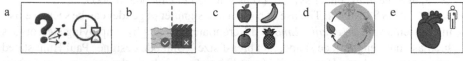

Fig. 5. Selection of IKON's icons: a) Juxtaposed icons meaning "when", from "which" + "time" = "when"; b) Contrastive icon meaning "calm", from "calm"/"turbulent"; c) Hyperonimic icon meaning "fruit" d) Hyponimic icon meaning "autumn", from the basic process icon "year"; e) Icon with classifier meaning "heart", with a picture of the heart as main element, and a classifier indicating that it is a body part.

3.4   Graphic Guidelines

- VECTORIAL: readable at 30 px and at 4000 + px (vectorial)
- TEXT-FREE: in general, text is avoided as much as possible, in order to keep language independence. There can be exceptions: letters, brands, proper names, sentences/words about phonetics or linguistics.
- BACKGROUND INDEPENDENT: no background is applied to the icons, unless it is meaningful.
- COLOURED AND BLACK-AND-WHITE: a palette of 24 colours was chosen; each icon exists also in black and white.
- PIXEL PERFECT: all icons are aimed to be pixel-perfect on 48 by 48 pixels; diagonal lines are at slopes 1:1, 1:2, 1:3 or 1:6.
- ARROWS: arrows are normally used to show one object inside one scene.
- CONTRASTIVE ICONS: contrast between 2 scenes is expressed by default through small symbols "yes-no" (green V or red X); contrast between more than 2 scenes is expressed by default by graying out (or crossing out) the contrastive scenes and circling the signified scene.

4   Case Study: Hair and Gender

4.1   Introduction - the Semiotics of Gender in Digital Communication

As visual communication becomes more widespread, questions arise as to how to create signs that are both recognizable and useful. As digital media becomes more ubiquitous, the field of digital semiotics is emerging. Lacković defines digital semiotics as "studying, analysing, conceptualizing, theorizing, producing and using digital signs across domains of educational and everyday life" [15]. In visual communication there are potentially multiple ways to signify gender. The use of haircut and the use of gender symbols are two gender signifiers already in use.

4.2 Haircuts, Gender Symbols and Their Meanings

- GENDER SYMBOL AS SIGNIFIER: Gender symbols ♀(female), and ♂(male) are commonly used to signify gender. Originally functioning as planetary symbols to denote planets Venus and Mars respectively, these symbols first signified biological sex in 1767 [16]. The *female sign* emoji and *male sign* emoji were approved by Unicode in 1993, and the transgender symbol (⚧)was added to Unicode in 2005.
- HAIRCUT AS SIGNIFIER: The use of haircut as a signifier of gender can be seen in existing systems such as *emojis*. *Emojis* differentiates genders by employing stereotypes such as "hair length, face shape, and breast size." Unicode designer Paul Hunt stated "the main visual cue [for emoji] is just hairstyle […] that's the main salient feature between the gendered depictions" [17]. In 2019 Google released 53 gender-neutral icons which also relied on different haircuts to signify a spectrum of gender identity.
- HAIRCUTS IN DIFFERENT SOCIETIES: Various scholars have observed how hair can be a symbol for different kinds of identity, including gender and sexual identity, both at the individual and group level [18, 19]. Moreover, Kurt Stenn notices that, across human societies, there is an almost universal tendency for women to have longer hair than men [20]. These studies thus suggest that the long/short hair can be seen as legitimate gender signifiers.

There are however cases in which this trend does not apply. In the Maasai culture women and children shave their heads, and only warrior men have long hair [21]. Similarly, ancient Celtic warriors and Viking warriors had long hair [22]. The queue, or topknot, was a popular style of long hair worn by men in Manchuria and China in the Qing dynasty [23]. Sikh men traditionally do not cut their hair, letting it grow their whole lives; this tradition continues in contemporary society [24]. Despite the general tendency for women to have long hair, there are exceptions that show haircut is not a universal gender signifier.

Preliminary Conclusions. There must be some level of agreement on the meaning of gender signifiers in order for them to be useful. Lacković suggests that both abstract and concrete concepts require widespread agreement to be functional [15]. However, several factors can cause differing interpretations of signifiers. Herring and Dainas found that both age and gender influence how people interpret the function of emojis [25]. Guntuku found both normative and culture specific patterns in how emojis represent concepts in different countries [26].

In light of this analysis we have conceived some icons that represent family relationships and show gender with different gender signifiers: only gender symbols, only haircuts, or both gender signifiers. We aimed to be clear while avoiding gender stereotypes or discrimination. In the following paragraph we will show a test conceived to validate the comprehension of these family icons.

4.3   Icon Cladogram: An Analysis on the Synthesis of the Image

According to the definition of Galaburda [27], the style of the icons of this study is called *Glyph Icons* (also called solid icons): a single flat ink icon, without an outline. The minimal drawing, the minimal form, basic shapes from simple geometric figures, when combined create more complex images. Human proportions are taken into account both to differentiate male and female figures, differentiate adult and child figures, and to depict neutral bodies.

Family icons present the same aesthetic coherence and the same style, although there is an evolution in the drawing from different degrees of synthesis of human forms. The program used to draw is Adobe Illustrator, a very powerful vector drawing software. The *pen* and *curvature tool* was used to draw, drawing without an outline and filling polygons with colour.

In the classification by Villafañe [28] there are $11°$ of iconicity. The degree 4 is the pictogram; in that same degree the term icon is included, which is the minimum expression of form, like the shape of the silhouettes; the function of the icon is to give information. We are based on the scale of iconicity of Villafañes (1985), although we know there is a previous scale (A.A. Moles 1971), but the latter is not our reference because it is not updated. Another classification is needed to analyze the sample icons, according to their level of complexity. There are three degrees of synthesis of the image, where the first degree is the most complex and the last the most synthetic.

Degree of Synthesis 1. This classification is the synthesis of the most complex image, subclassified as *Gender Signifier*, nomenclature made in the gender study in the previous paragraphs; these icons have a female or male body and a hairstyle according to them, is subclassified as "haircuts"; in the second version the bodies are neutral but a gender symbol appears to identify the protagonist figure, called "symbol"; the third variation is the union of the first two, a hairstyle and a body according to a concept of masculinity or femininity in addition to a gender symbol which we will call "haircut plus symbol".

Degree of Synthesis 2. It is a less complex classification than synthesis degree 1, because it contains an associated element such as rings or a heart. These elements, easier to understand than gender symbols, are called "Gender neutral." This classification is given by a context or by a relation to something.

Degree of Synthesis 3. This is the classification with a higher degree of synthesis, and it is subdivided into two categories, "association by group" and "association by context." In the first subclassification the icon images serve a uniform group, which represents a single word that defines the group. In the second subclassification you are no longer asked to define a group, but to define an individual of a group, which is identified by association in a hierarchy or order within the group, (see Fig. 6).

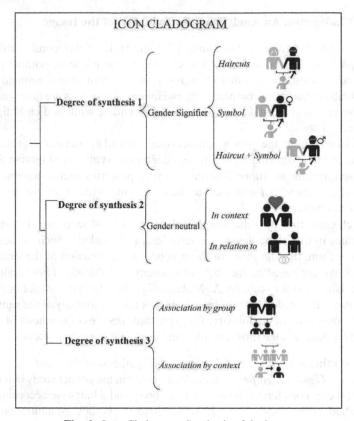

Fig. 6. Icon Cladogram. Synthesis of the image

4.4 Colour Palette of Icons

The colour palette in the icons of the family is reduced to four colours, but only two are significant, the colour black (PANTONE Black 6 C) and grey (PANTONE 420 C), two other colours appear as details, yellow for the rings for the married and husband or wife icons (PANTONE 137 C), and red for the icon of the couple in the romantic couple (PANTONE Bright Red C). This colour palette strikes a balance between functionality and aesthetics, taking into account the small 48 × 48 ppp format.

The black colour marks the main figure or figures, sometimes aided by an arrow and in some cases by a scheme, and the grey colour is for the secondary figures, creating a context to understand the main figure filled in black, it is important that the tonal difference of this chromatic binomial is significant, since the icons are very small and require large colour differences.

4.5 Iconometer Test

Our objective was to compare the level of certainty that participants had on interpretations of family icons using hair as a gender signifier, gender symbols as a gender signifier, and icons that have no gender signifiers.

Iconometer. The iconometer is a software developed by the Univ. of Geneva (Peraya, Strasser; 2002) [29] in order to implement the theoretical approach proposed by Leclercq (1992) [30] to assess the degree of polysemy of a visual representation (icon, diagram, figurative image, photograph, etc.) and measure its adequacy to its prescribed meaning.

Preparation and Test Design. This Iconometer Family Test focuses on a group of visual images to represent family relationships. All visual images were designed by Araceli Gimenez Lorente following the linguistic proposals of the KomunIKON linguistic team. The family relationships included gender-specific as well as gender-neutral visual images. The family relationships represented include: mother, father, parents, aunt, uncle, aunt or uncle (gender neutral), daughter, son, child (gender neutral), brother, sister, female cousin, male cousin, cousin, spouse (gender neutral), family, married couple, romantic couple, grandmother, grandfather, grandparent (gender neutral), grandson, granddaughter, grandchild (gender neutral).

Some icons signified gender through hair, some through symbols (♀ and ♂), some through both hair and symbols, and some did not include any gender signifiers.

The Iconometer Family test presents the participant with a visual image with no other text. Below the image are 7 possible meanings, the final options being always "I do not know/ no meaning." The participant must distribute a total of 100 points among the different meanings according to certainty. The participant must give the most points to the meaning that seems most certain, and has the option to give 100 points to a single meaning. Participants rated the 32 visual images (icons) using this system and had no prior exposure to the visual images before participating.

Participants. 78 participants from various gender and age demographics (15–70) took the test. They came from 15 different countries as their country of birth, and spoke 24 languages in total.

Results. On average there was no significant difference in accuracy or certainty when comparing gender symbols, hair cut, or the combined gender signifiers. Participants gave on average 65 points to the "Father" option when viewing the father icon (hair cut) and 71 points to the father icon (symbol). Participants gave on average 77 points to the option "Mother" when viewing the mother icon (hair cut) and 74 points when viewing the mother icon (symbol). These similarities were consistent with other family icons, showing that both haircuts and symbols are useful to signify gender both in terms of accuracy and certainty.

The test showed that some icons had lower levels of certainty and accuracy. Participants responded to the "Spouse" icon by choosing the "Couple" option slightly more frequently than "Spouse" giving "Couple" on average 40 points, and "Spouse" only 37 points. The test also showed low accuracy and low certainty for icons signifying grandparent-grandchild relationships, such as "Grandfather" and "Grandmother." Participants frequently chose "Step father" and "Step mother" for these icons respectively, rating the intended meaning with equal or lower certainty, when compared to the alternate meaning, as seen in the Table 2 below.

This suggests that the chosen design for representing grandparent-grandchild relationships is not generally recognizable.

Table 2. Icons whose intended meaning was not well understood.

Icon	Intended meaning	Alternate meaning
Grandfather	Grandfather - 23 points	Step father - 45 points
Grandmother	Grandmother - 32 points	Step mother - 36 points
Granddaughter	Granddaughter - 24 points	Step daughter - 39 points
Grandson	Grandson - 38 points	Step son - 37 points
Grandparent	Grandparent - 22 points	I do not know - 42 points
Grandchild	Grandchild - 25 points	Step son or daughter - 48 points

5 Four Phases Towards a Collaborative Language: WIKON

5.1 What Is WIKON?

Mobile users make use of emojis as a shorthand communication or to express their feelings. However, there are several drawbacks with off-the-shelf libraries of smileys and emojis. First of all, standard built-in sets from keyboards and social media platforms are usually predefined and non-modifiable. Furthermore, less common emojis can be ambiguous or imprecise. In addition to that, these emojis can only replace certain words in a phrase, but often fail to represent more complex ideas and concepts. On the other hand, even a full set of standard emojis is still too limited to express simple grammatical sentences.

To overcome these hurdles, we suggest a collaborative platform. Not only can users see a predefined set of graphic elements, but they can also create their own. This is where WIKON comes into play. Through a simple process this user-submitted content shall also be made available to the community for reuse and modification. The graphical elements live with the community. Some may be recycled and re-adapted while others may be discarded and forgotten. In short WIKON is a platform that enables the community to collaborate on the iconic language.

The advantages of such a system are that a diverse crowd of collaborators fosters inclusion and reduces the risk of biases (be it cultural, gender-based or educational). It also allows for an easy means of extension and the set of available ikons (IKON icons) can grow immensely in a controlled manner. Lastly, it enables the users to customize their own language or select a certain style.

This system shall be self-organized and self-sustaining. It shall be made more and more complete in an automated fashion and allow for addressing current issues and societal topics without intervention and control.

5.2 How to Get to WIKON in 4 Steps?

All the phases and their respective enabling of collaboration are namely:

- PHASE 0: Access to a predefined set only
- PHASE 1: Submissions not allowed, elements can be added for personal use only

- PHASE 2: Allow submissions, reviewed and approved by internal experts
- PHASE 3: Allow submissions, reviewed by collaborators, approved by experts
- PHASE 4: Allow submissions, reviewed and approved by community

These phases imply several technical requirements. PHASE 0 describes the current state of the art. Every member of the linguists' team can create, read, update and delete all ikon entries through a graphical user interface (GUI). This GUI accesses the database where the graphical elements and metadata is stored. Then the data is loaded to the local mobile storage by installing the app. The app and the database are currently decoupled. Within the app the user can select ikons to create and modify a sentence. Finally, the user can export it as an image to any other app.

In PHASE 1 every user shall be enabled to add individual graphical elements for further use. From a technical perspective this can be achieved by letting the user upload images directly within the app. During the same step the user also needs to provide the minimum required information. This allows for correct data handling, search optimization and makes sharing them easier. The information that needs to be provided is not limited to but includes an image, an identifier, a translation into a language and a description as well as technical metadata.

PHASE 2 adds up on the previous phase by allowing the users to submit their propositions for a review process. This review process serves several purposes. It is a Go/NoGo waypoint that can be used to filter out content. It can also increase the quality and reduce redundancy by letting linguists modify or amend the provided data. Lastly, this process will also be particularly helpful in determining the users' needs and drawing statistics based on user-provided input. From this data we can identify topic trends, language gaps and pain points of the app users.

At the end of the reviewing process, the expert can decide if this user-submitted ikon shall be taken up into the database and thus be made available to the rest of the community. In technical terms this means that the application end-point is synchronized with the database, either by a GET or API call or using cloud provided options such as direct sync methods (e.g. firebase). The database has two separate storage tables; one for currently available ikons and the other for suggestions to be reviewed. The GUI shall implement a tool that facilitates reviewing, amending and approving a bulk of suggestions.

In PHASE 3 we want to give more power to the users. Not only can they make suggestions, but a small pool of selected collaborators can now also review these suggestions. They can alter the ikons and add information, before it finally has to be approved by an internal expert. This step shall increase the level of inclusion of the language and its users. It also reduces the workload of the team for reviewing the suggestions. In order for the user to receive the status of reviewer, one has to either have made significant contributions in the previous phases or be part of a trusted network (known language experts and direct correspondents with the team). In this phase, the GUI that allows to review and approve the ikons needs to be made available to a much bigger circle. This requires an extended login and user authentication process, as well as additional contributions.

In PHASE 4 the motto is: The community shapes the language. New ikon submissions come from the users, are reviewed and are approved by the users. This gives the full level of flexibility to the language. This allows a faster process of making an ikon available to the public and users can also benefit from a much broader vocabulary and ikon repository.

This final step towards massive collaboration has bigger technical implications than the previous ones. For one, the solution needs to be scalable, which can only be guaranteed if data that can appear, can also disappear. There are several solutions to this problem, such as automatic removal based on days since last being used, a down-vote system of least favorite ikons or an individual check of relevance. Furthermore, additional checks will have to be set up that enhance the reviewing process, to detect duplicates, redundant information or to suggest similar content. Note that at this point, filtering and censoring will no longer take place. Finally, the users shall also be able to choose specific language packages, icon styles and vocabulary topics for download locally to improve offline experience.

5.3 Evaluation of the Proposed Solutions

In order to evaluate the quality of our solution, we oriented ourselves by looking at the guidelines provided by the National Information Standards Organization [31]. We namely commented on the 9 principles to assess solutions for building good digital collections. Picking up on every single principle is out of scope for this work. Thus, we refer to them by keywords and encourage the interested reader to consult the original report (Table 3).

Table 3. Evaluation of building a good digital collection.

Nr.	Principle	Phase 1	Phase 2	Phase 3
1	Explicit development policy	Clear	Medium	Medium
2	Metadata (scope, format, ownership, integrity)	Medium	Easy	Medium
3	Curated (actively managed) resources	Easy	High	Medium
4	Broadly available and accessible	Low	High	High
5	Respect intellectual property rights	Preserved		
6	Record and feedback data usage	Difficult	Medium	Medium
7	Interoperable (make data shareable)	Difficult	Easy	Easy
8	Integrated into user workflow	Little extra effort	Extra effort	Extra effort
9	Sustainable over time	Easy	Medium	Medium

5.4 Conclusion of Evaluation

In the case of Wikon, the two principles about the metadata (principle 2) and the resource curation (principle 3) are inversely correlated, since active curation leads to an organized and harmonized metadata management, while a fully self-organized system tends to be more divergent. These two principles vary strongly over the 4 phases. This stems from the fact that a uniform and concise metadata management cannot be guaranteed, unless providing crucially detailed information is enforced. Especially towards the last phase when full self-organization takes over, it will be difficult to impose adherence of metadata management to a certain standard. It was an intentional design to keep the integrability (principle 8) high and therefore the extra effort of contribution low.

Considering the above analysis we can deduce that our suggested solution and the 4-phase plan is particularly well-performing when it comes to data availability and accessibility (principle 4), interoperability (principle 7) and sustainability (princ. 9).

Acknowledgments. The authors address special thanks to Alejandro Sanchez Medina (KomunIKON) for his technical support, Edgar Walthert (KomunIKON) for the graphic guidelines, Leila Cachot and Sylvestre Thiaw (ICAN) for the production of the shown icons, Daniel Peraya and Stéphane Morand (Univ. Geneva) for their support about the iconometer.

References

1. Rogers, H.: Writing Systems: A Linguistic Approach. Blackwell Pub, Blackwell Pub, Malden (2005)
2. Schmandt-Besserat, D.: How Writing Came About. University of Texas Press, Austin (1996)
3. Davies, W., Dubinsky, S.: Language Conflict and Language Rights: Ethnolinguistic Perspectives on Human Conflict. Cambridge University Press, Cambridge (2018)
4. Regulski, I.: A Palaeographic Study of Early Writing in Egypt. Peeters, Leuven (2010)
5. Boltz, W.G.: The Origin and Early Development of the Chinese Writing System. American Oriental Soc, New Haven (2003)
6. Qiu, X.: Chinese Writing. Society for the Study of Early China, Berkeley (2000)
7. Coe, M.D., Van Stone, M.: Reading the Maya Glyphs, 2nd edn. Thames and Hudson, London (2005)
8. Salomon, R.: Some principles and patterns of script change. In: Houston, S.D. (ed.) The Shape of Script: How and Why Writing Systems Change, pp. 119–133. School for Advanced Research Press, Santa Fe (2012)
9. Mora-Marín, D.F.: Full phonetic complementation, semantic classifiers, and semantic determinatives in ancient mayan hieroglyphic writing. Ancient Mesoamerica **19**(2), 195–213 (2008)
10. Stauder, A.: On system-internal and differential iconicity in Egyptian hieroglyphic writing. Signata **9**, 365–390 (2018)
11. Goldwasser, O.: Prophets, Lovers and Giraffes: Wor(l)d Classification in Ancient Egypt. Harrassowitz, Wiesbaden (2002)
12. Goldwasser, O.: Where is metaphor?: conceptual metaphor and alternative classification in the hieroglyphic script. Metaphor Symbol **20**(2), 95–113 (2005)
13. Chantrain, G., di Biase-Dyson, C.: Making a Case for multidimensionality in ramesside figurative language. In: Werning, D. (ed.) Proceedings of the Fifth International Conference on Egyptian-Coptic Linguistics (Crossroads V), Berlin, 17–20 February 2016, pp. 41–66. Widmaier Verlag, Hamburg (2018)
14. Reale, C., Müller, A.: From Hieroglyphs to Emoji: breve historio des langues visuelles. Polyglot Gathering (2019). https://www.youtube.com/watch?v=eiiHciieVWF8&list=PLzUsi_uF2QwbYTR67iGEKFANQ9ZQO-btQ. Accessed 20 Dec 2020

15. Lacković, N.: Thinking with digital images in the post-truth era: a method in critical media literacy. Postdigital Sci. Educ. 442–462. (2020)
16. Stearn, W.T.: The origin of the male and female symbols of biology. Taxon, **11**(4), 109–113 (1962)
17. Piñon, N.: (2020). https://mashable.com/article/gender-inclusive-emoji-designer/?europe=true
18. Synnott, A.: Shame and glory: a sociology of hair. Br. J. Sociol. **38**(3), 381–413 (1987). https://doi.org/10.2307/590695
19. Bromberger, C.: Pour une ethno-trichologie tibétaine. Ateliers d'anthropologie (2018)
20. Fabry, M.: (2016). https://time.com/4348252/history-long-hair/
21. Gilbert, E.: Broken Spears - a Maasai Journey, pp. 136. Atlantic Monthly Press (2003)
22. Sherrow, V.: Encyclopedia of Hair: A Cultural History. Greenwood Publishing Group, Santa_Barbara (2006)
23. Ebrey, P., Walthall, A., Palais, J.: Pre-modern East Asia: To 1800: A Cultural, Social, and Political History (2006)
24. Singh, J.: Head first: young British sikhs, hair, and the Turban. J. Contemporary Relig. **25**(2), 203–220 (2010). https://doi.org/10.1080/13537901003750894
25. Herring.S., Dainas. A.: Gender and Age Influences on Interpretation of Emoji Functions. ACM Transactions on Social Computing (2020). https://doi.org/10.1145/3375629
26. Chandra Guntuku, S., Li, M., Tay, L., Ungar, L.H.: Studying cultural differences in emoji usage across the East and the West. In: Proceedings of the International AAAI Conference on Web and Social Media (2019)
27. Galaburda, J.: Icon design guide. Everything you need to know about icon design to get started! Available at: http://iconutopia.com/files/Icon-Design-Guide-by-IconUtopia.pdf
28. Villafañe, J.: Escala de iconicidad de Justo Villafañe. http://catarina.udlap.mx/u_dl_a/tales/documentos/mdi/davila_c_me/apendiceC.pdf
29. Peraya, D., Strasser, D.: L'iconomètre: un outil de formation et de recherche pour mesurer le degré de polysémie des représentations visuelles. In: Le Meur, G. (Ed.). Université ouverte, formation virtuelle et apprentissage. Communications francophones du Cinquième Colloque Européen sur l'Autoformation. Barcelone, pp. 225–236. Paris: L'Harmattan (2002
30. Leclercq, D.: Audio-visuel et apprentissage, Liège. Université de Liège, Service de Technologie de l'Education (1992)
31. NISO, A.: Framework of guidance for building good digital collections, pp. 61–62 (2007)

An Interface for User-Centred Process and Correlation Between Large Datasets

Dimitris Spiliotopoulos[1]([✉]) [iD], Theodoros Giannakopoulos[2], Costas Vassilakis[2] [iD],
Manolis Wallace[2] [iD], Marina Lantzouni[3] [iD], Vassilis Poulopoulos[3] [iD],
and Dionisis Margaris[3] [iD]

[1] Department of Management Science and Technology, University of the Peloponnese,
Tripoli, Greece
dspiliot@uop.gr
[2] Department of Informatics and Telecommunications, University of the Peloponnese,
Tripoli, Greece
th.giannakopoulos@soda.dit.uop.gr, {costas,wallace}@uop.gr
[3] Department of Digital Systems, University of the Peloponnese, Sparta, Greece
m.lantzouni@go.uop.gr, {vacilos,margaris}@uop.gr

Abstract. Standard database query systems are designed to process data on a single installation only, and do not provide optimal solutions for cases that data from multiple sources need to be queried. In these cases, the sources may have different data schemata, data representations etc., necessitating extensive coding and data transformations to retrieve partial results and combine them to reach the desired outcome. Differences in schemata and representations may be subtle and remain unnoticed, leading to the production of erroneous results. The goal of this paper is to present an easy-to-use solution for the end users, enabling them to query data from a given set of databases through a single user interface. This user interface allows users to visualize database contents and query results, while facilities for uploading and validating the data are also accommodated. To demonstrate the applicability of our approach, a use case is presented where data from two different sources are uploaded into the system and thereafter the data from the two databases can be utilized in tandem. The usability evaluation involved software developers in free evaluation scenarios.

Keywords: User interface · Usability · Query · Multiple data sources ·
Visualisation · Big data

1 Introduction

Nowadays, services and data are offered by multiple providers and when a result must be produced based on a combination of information found in different providers/DBs, a substantial amount of work is required, either to develop custom solutions or appropriately configure and tune software [1–4]. Examples of this phenomenon include shopping (where a supermarket further away may have an offer on some merchandise we want to buy, however this purchase incurs higher fuel consumption), everyday news or finding a

© Springer Nature Switzerland AG 2021
M. M. Soares et al. (Eds.): HCII 2021, LNCS 12779, pp. 477–494, 2021.
https://doi.org/10.1007/978-3-030-78221-4_32

vacation destination. To better demonstrate the motivation of this work, let us consider a scenario where a newly married couple have a strict budget of 3,000 Euros to go on vacation in a European capital. The information required to plan this vacation is dispersed across at least 4 different databases (living expenses, air travel, accommodation service and car rental service) and therefore, the interested couple (or a mediating programmer) would have to write a significant amount of code (multiple queries for a single result or ranked results, followed by more code to combine the partial results). In the latter case, the interested party must manually search for available rooms in the location(s) of interest, mode of travel (e.g., plane, boat), possibly car rental, food costs/expenses, etc. Even if it is done using software (e.g., programmatically invoking appropriate web services), the overall task will be computationally expensive, since the solution space that should be searched equals the Cartesian product *accommodation* × *travel* × *car rental*, and the identification of the global minimum is a difficult task [5, 6]. If, however, all the necessary information were on a single database, the overall task would be greatly simplified, because a single query (e.g., SQL) would suffice to retrieve the desired result, and the DBMS would appropriately optimize the query execution plan, exploiting the physical organization of the data, index structures, histograms and other structures to compute the results in an efficient fashion. However, as noted above, in real life scenarios the information is dispersed across multiple sources/databases, each employing its own data representation, and henceforth it is not possible to use a single query to gather the results.

The goal of this work is to present the implementation of an easy-to-use solution, through which the end user can query data from a given set of databases through a user interface (UI) [7]. The UI would also provide a graphical representation of the given databases and the ability to upload data and validate the data via a GUI. To this end, the solution was implemented as a web-based application, on top of the Laravel framework [8, 9]. Before the implementation commenced, a survey was conducted to identify tools providing the desired set of functionalities, however no such tools were identified.

In order to be able to query an information repository (e.g. a database, data warehouse, Google Cloud/S3 buckets, Google Big Query tables, etc.) specific access rights should be given to the corresponding parties beforehand. Process-wise, this can be really time-consuming and impractical, since it involves communication between parties entailing access requests, examination of the relevant justifications to reach decisions whether the requests will be honoured or denied, communicating the decisions to the requesting parties and applying the decisions to the database authorization subsystem, and finally querying the corresponding datasets. Furthermore, users should familiarize themselves with diverse UIs, which raises usability considerations [10–13].

Taking all the above into account, the tool presented in this paper provides a manageable solution to facilitate users' access to multiple resources under a unified process and from within a single UI, allowing the end-user to query multiple given datasets. To demonstrate our approach, a use case entailing data from two different sources is presented. More specifically, both our data sources originate from art museums, namely the Tate Gallery (https://www.penn.museum/collections/objects/data.php) and the Penn Museum (https://github.com/tategallery/collection). In the presented use case, only the CSV format files were used. The different data structures from our sources were mapped to corresponding structures in the unified database, in order to store the data; additionally, associations were established between data elements as appropriate, e.g., for the data that originate from the *tategallery* collection, associations between artists and the corresponding artwork were established based on the artist identifier; similarly, for the data that originates from the penn.museum collection, associations between the origin of the artworks and the artworks were established.

The remainder of the paper is presented as follows: Sect. 2 overviews related work. Section 3 presents the proposed application. In Sect. 4 we present the system administration functionalities, and, finally, Sect. 5 concludes the paper and outlines the future work.

2 Related Work

Although database query optimization and personalization are fields that have been the subject of significant research efforts in the recent past [14–19], research in cross-database query optimization and personalization is extremely less developed. Li et al. [20] proposed a data querying integrated heterogeneous processing model containing four components: data set, data source, data model, and analysis tool and introduced a unified data model, and proposed the SimbaQL query language, for the description of the data processing steps against the unified data model.

Hu et al. [21] proposed three kinds of distributed storage and query of multi-source heterogeneous data optimizations. These were based on secondary index, secondary index based on hotscore, and cache strategy based on the Redis hot data. The aforementioned schemes were analysed and evaluated. The query optimization of HBase hot data, which was based on the Redis hot data caching strategy, was proven to yield the best results. Wu et al. [22] focused on heterogeneous data management strategy of multi-source culture and a data service method. They also proposed and established a strategy for storing multi-source heterogeneous culture databases on MongoDB. Then, they explored the sharing, indexing and query mechanisms for the culture database. Finally, they constructed the prototype system for culture data management prototype system.

Liu et al. [23] proposed a versatile event-driven data model in HBase for multi-source power grid, which was used to solve the multi-source data hereditary compatibility issues. For query performance improvement, a Virtual Column Family mechanism was designed and implemented. Chen et al. [24] proposed an intelligent search method that was multi-database oriented. The aim of that approach was to mitigate the deficiencies of big data storage, search and usage of power dispatching and control systems. Their work divided the data into three tiers: model, runtime and real time analysis data. Then a unified intelligent search, management, and storage method was constructed for multitudinous control and dispatch of big data, in order to achieve performance improvement on diverse analytics using big data search, application, display and storage.

Miyamoto et al. [25] implemented a system of multiple databases. It was based on MySQL and utilised the SPIDER storage engine, in order to overcome the data migration problem between single storage units (databases) in the multi-database system. That system was used to evaluate the incremental data migration technique. Daniel et al. [26]

presented a scalable model persistence framework based on a modular architecture that enabled the modelling of storage into multiple data stores, termed as NEOEMF. The framework provided three new model-to-database mappings. They were designed to complement existing persistence methods and enable the storing of models in graph, column, and key-value databases. NEOEMF provides two APIs. The first is a standard API that ensures compatibility with the Eclipse Modelling Framework API and supports the NEOEMF integration with existing modelling tools, requiring minimal code base change. The second is an advanced API that ensures improved scalability for specific modelling scenarios through support of special features that complement the standard EMF API.

Rachman and Saptawati [27] proposed an approach for intervolving linguistic-based and constraint-based schema matching techniques into matched, hybrid combination schemas. Hybrid combination matching results are used in the matching of individual schemas to complement each other. The hybrid schemas can be applied in query rewriting as multi-database query processing. Phungtua and Chittayasothorn [28] developed a multi-database instance matching system that is used to retrieve data from separate sources. The data may be references to different attribute details and unique identifiers. The database instances are matched using entity resolution [29–31]. An ontology is used to store the semantic relations between the identified entity instances that are matched. The users may use queries to the ontology, which are then rewritten by the system to create appropriate references to the original instances of the multiple databases.

Naik [32] described a method for data retrieval from multiple heterogeneous distributed relational database management systems such as MS Access, MySQL, and PostgreSQL into the Oracle RDBMS using the Heterogeneous Gateway Services by Oracle. The method requires the developer to download and install the software, use open database connectivity to create the data source names, modify the system parameters, check the connections, create synonyms for remote database tables into Oracle, create database links and access data from non-Oracle databases. The approach necessitates the manipulation of data from Oracle in remote databases via PL/SQL command execution. Finally, troubleshooting is required to address the generated common errors.

While some of the works listed above aim to provide access to users to multiple resources under a unified process and within a single and comprehensive UI, some of them require substantial IT staff contribution (e.g. [32]), while others target different needs (e.g. [25] addresses the issue of data migration) or focus on a specific domain only (e.g. [23]). This paper aims to fill this gap, providing a solution that enables the end-user to query multiple datasets under a single UI, with no requirements for technical expertise.

3   The Application

The following subsections elaborate on the functionality of the proposed system that is available to the end-user, and more specifically (a) query formulation, (b) data visualization and (c) data upload and validation.

3.1 Query the Database from the UI

The user is able to query different available databases from the interface. The interface is illustrated in Fig. 1.

Fig. 1. User interface for queries.

Besides the main area of the UI that allows the user to enter the query, the structure of the existing databases is made available to the end-user, via the "Available databases" area on the left of the screen. Each database name functions as a dropdown, containing information regarding the structure of the databases and number of the entries that they contain. Figure 2 illustrates the content of the dropdown, when expanded.

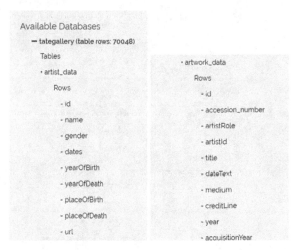

Fig. 2. List of available data collections, as provided by the application (nb. the schema of the *artwork_data* table is actually displayed below the schema of the *artist_*data table, but appears here on the right for better page space management).

User queries must be syntactically correct, in order to be validated and executed. To assist users in query formulation, relevant guidance and tips are provided on the interface, as shown in Fig. 3.

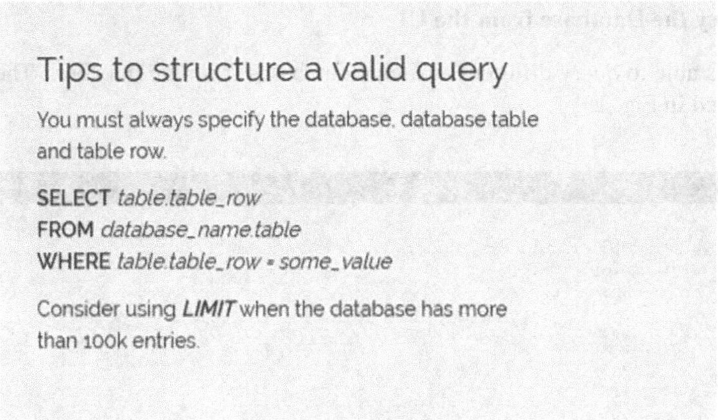

Tips to structure a valid query

You must always specify the database, database table
and table row.

SELECT *table.table_row*
FROM *database_name.table*
WHERE *table.table_row = some_value*

Consider using **LIMIT** when the database has more
than 100k entries.

Fig. 3. Instructions provided to the end-user regarding the query formulation syntax.

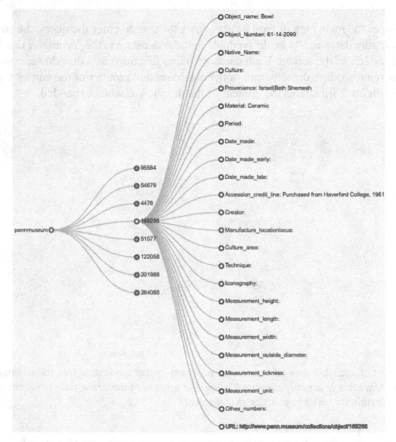

Fig. 4. Hierarchical visualization of a randomly selected item collection.

3.2 Data Visualization

Besides being able to query the databases, the user is able to visualize the results. The incorporation of visualization capabilities was deemed important, since it presents results in a more easily perceivable format, promoting user insight, and discovery of trends and patterns discovery [33].

Data visualization was implemented on top of the D3.js JavaScript library [34–36]. The impact that has the screen clutter on the user experience when the presented screen is overload with information was taken into account, in order to tune the visualization functionality. Therefore, when the user requests the visualization of the full contents of a database table, only eight random data entries from the selected data source are displayed, since the user typically wants to explore the schema and the extension of the database table. However, when user queries are evaluated and displayed, the full result set is visualized, considering that the user is interested in all records within the query result; to alleviate clutter, the user may consider limiting the records in the result using query language constructs. To present our data we have used a dendrogram [37, 38]. In the screenshots that follow, the hierarchical connection between the presented objects is illustrated; the hierarchical connection is maintained both when the visualized data corresponds to a random data selection (Fig. 4), as well as in the case when it has emerged as the result of a submitted query (Fig. 5). The query used to retrieve the dataset depicted in Fig. 5 is shown in Fig. 6.

The realization of the visualization of a new dataset entails the following steps:

- Study of the structure of the new dataset, to gain insight on the most effective way to present the information to the users.
- Design of how to form correctly a formatted string, so the D3 library can render the visualization.
- Creation of an appropriate function in the visualization controller to handle the corresponding request from the UI. In this step, the existing visualizations can be consulted, reused and tailored as needed.
- Introduce appropriate controls at UI level, which will allow the visualization implementation to be called.
- Add entry to the routes table to map the corresponding controller function and the UI.

Notably, these steps are carried out by IT staff, with the cooperation of the end-users, who will provide the requirements for the visualization.

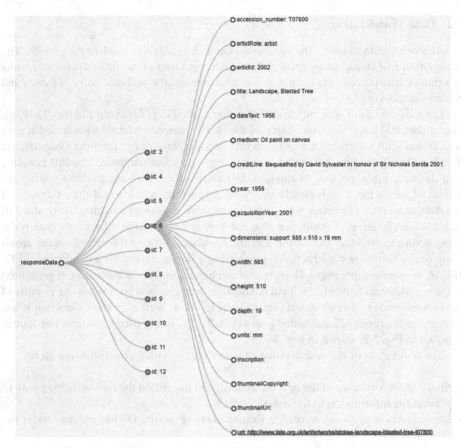

Fig. 5. Hierarchical visualization of the results of a user-provided query.

Fig. 6. User-provided query.

A sample format of a JSON string [39, 40] to be passed to the D3 visualization library, in order for a hierarchical visualization to be rendered is shown in Fig. 7.

```
{
    "name": "responsedata",
    "children": [
        {
            "name": "id5"
        },
        {
            "name": "id6",
            "children": [
                {
                    "accession_number": "T07800"
                },
                {
                    "artist_role": "artist"
                },
                {
                    "artist_id": "202"
                },
                {
                    "title": "Landscape, Blasted tree"
                }
            ]
        },
        {
            "name": "id7"
        }
    ]
}
```

Fig. 7. An excerpt from the JSON string passed to the D3 visualization library to render the tree in Fig. 5.

3.3 Data Upload and Validation

The user may populate the databases with the corresponding data, by uploading appropriately formatted files to the system. The following preprocessing steps are initially applied to the data file:

- redundant spaces from the entries are removed,
- non UTF-8 characters and character sequences are replaced with the corresponding correct one in the UTF-8 character set: for instance, the character sequence Ã© is replaced by the é character; and
- all single quotes are replaced with double quotes.

When a file is uploaded, an ETL process [41–43] is triggered that extracts the data from the given CSV file, transforms the data and then populates the corresponding database table with the data. The current implementation accepts only CSV files, while server settings regarding the maximum size of the uploaded file may be applicable.

Data uploaded to the system may have been validated to be correct and factual, or may have been harvested from diverse sources, and be in need of inspection and validation before they are made available as production data. To this end, the data that users upload is not directly inserted into the actual database but are staged into an intermediate one. Thereafter, the data validation part to is delegated to users, and performed as a crowdsourcing task: users are presented with a data panel, containing random entries from the intermediate database, and are able to vote whether the entries are factual and accurate or not. If an entry receives a sufficient number of upvotes, it is moved from the staging database to the production one, whereas if an entry is downvoted multiple times, it is deleted. To avoid user bias and assess the trustworthiness of each user's votes, some of the entries in validation panel are sourced from the main database: if the user is found to downvote entries from the main database, then the vote trustworthiness is reduced. Provisions are also available for the administrator to admit or delete all entries in a bulk fashion, should the whole of the data be deemed trustworthy/suitable (e.g. having been obtained from a reliable source) or untrustworthy/unsuitable, respectively. The UI for the file upload is shown in Fig. 8, while the UI for the data panel is illustrated in Fig. 9.

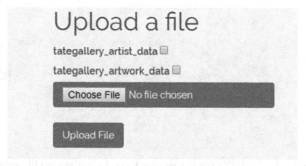

Fig. 8. User interface for file upload

Entry Validation	
id	944
name	Corker, Douglas
gender	Male
dates	1939 – 2012
yearOfBirth	1939
yearOfDeath	2012
placeOfBirth	London, United Kingdom
placeOfDeath	
url	http://www.tate.org.uk/art/artists/douglas-corker-944

Not okay   Seems fine

Fig. 9. UI for dataset validation.

The schema of the tables in the staging database is identical to the schema of the table in the production database with the exception of an extra column that is added to the staging database table, to accommodate the validation votes from the users [44, 45].

When a user uploads a CSV file, an ETL process is triggered to realize the data ingestion. Firstly, the content headers of the CSV file are checked against the schema of the database table, and subsequently all input is sanitized, checked for schema compliance and finally data are inserted in the staging database table. After the successful upload of the data, users are able to go to corresponding validation screen within the UI and vote for the presented entries. As noted above, entries in the validation panel are randomly selected either from the main database or the staging one. When the user votes, after examining whether the corresponding entry is correct or not, the following actions are taken:

- if the entry has been sourced from the main database, then an upvote will increase the user's vote trustworthiness, while a downvote will have the opposite effect.
- if the entry has been sourced from the in the staging database, an upvote or downvote will adjust the entry's score; the adjustment value is moderated by the user's vote trustworthiness. When the entry's score exceeds a predefined threshold, the entry is moved from the staging database to the main one, while if the entry's score falls below some negative threshold, it is discarded from the database.

The system provides support for the cases that an administrator uploads a trusted dataset and wants to release the data for immediate use, bypassing the validation stage. In this case, the administrator selects the relevant functionality from the UI, and-after an appropriate confirmation step- the system moves all the data from the staging database to the main one. Internally, the system performs this step by issuing SQL statements that perform bulk insertion of the staging database data to the main database, followed by statements that delete the data from the staging database.

4   System Administration Functionalities

The application has two different user levels, namely the administrator user level and the basic user level. Both user levels may submit queries to the available databases, upload data to one of the databases and visualize sample database contents and query results, using one of the available visualization methods.

Members of the administrator user class, however, have more functionalities available within the application, in comparison to basic users.

4.1   User Management

Administrator users are able to manage system users, i.e. (a) create users, (b) update users' passwords and emails, (c) change user level and (d) delete users. Figure 10 depicts the basic user management screen.

Fig. 10. User management.

4.2 Database Access Rights

The administrator is able to specify which databases users are able to query, by designating which databases are available to all users for querying, as depicted in Fig. 11. Databases may be marked as "Private" or "Public". "Private" databases are only available to administrators for curation and may be subsequently made available to the public. Moreover, a database may be made available to the public for a limited time, and then moved to private space, where it can be curated and then made again publicly available.

Move to Public

Private Databases

#	Database Name
☐	carnegie_museum
☐	cluster
☐	eattract
☐	information_schema
☐	music_site
☐	mydb
☐	mysql
☐	performance_schema
☐	phpmyadmin
☐	test
☐	testdb

Move to Private

Public Databases

#	Database Name
☐	pennmuseum
☐	tategallery

Fig. 11. Specifying database access permissions.

4.3 Check Logs

Finally, administrators have the option to check the logs of the submitted queries from all users, as Fig. 12 depicts, where erroneous, suspicious and malicious queries are marked in red. Administrators may exploit this information to offer assistance and guidance to users that submit erroneous queries, further analyze suspicious queries or ban users that submit malicious queries. Especially for users that submit a high rate of erroneous queries, the system could adapt itself by offering additional assistance through the UI, or allow/use by default query-by-example features instead of SQL. Such amenities will be considered in future releases of the system.

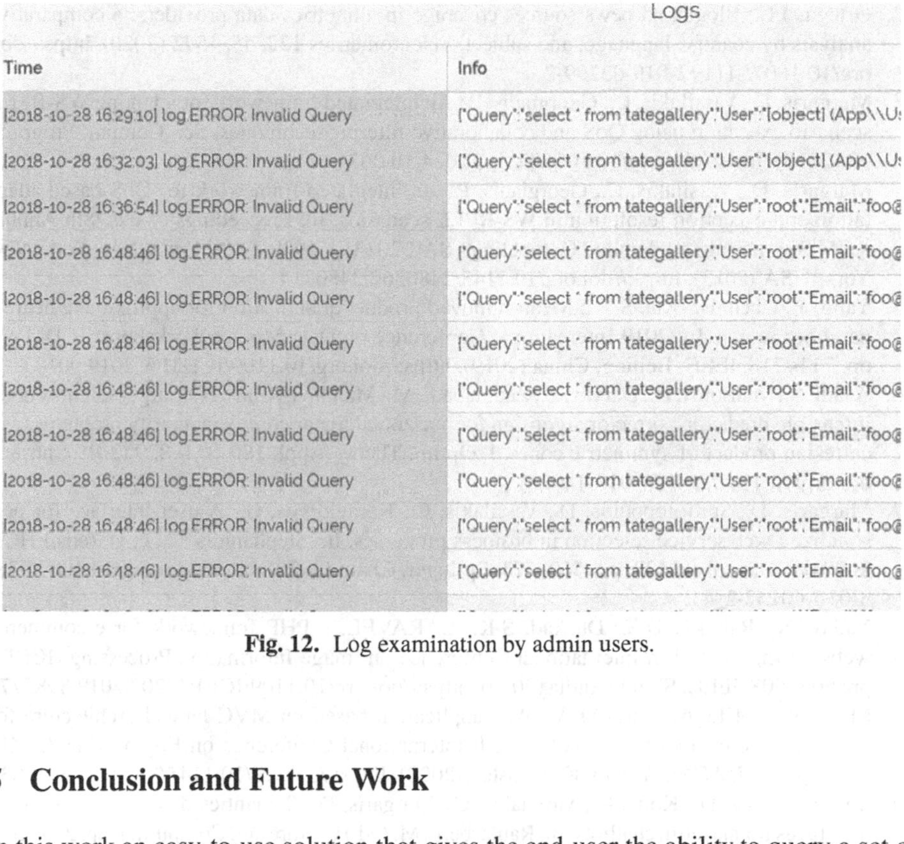

Logs	
Time	Info
[2018-10-28 16:29:10] log.ERROR: Invalid Query	['Query':'select ' from tategallery','User':'[object] (App\\U:
[2018-10-28 16:32:03] log.ERROR: Invalid Query	['Query':'select ' from tategallery','User':'[object] (App\\U:
[2018-10-28 16:36:54] log.ERROR: Invalid Query	['Query':'select ' from tategallery','User':'root','Email':'foo@
[2018-10-28 16:48:46] log.ERROR: Invalid Query	['Query':'select ' from tategallery','User':'root','Email':'foo@
[2018-10-28 16:48:46] log.ERROR: Invalid Query	['Query':'select ' from tategallery','User':'root','Email':'foo@
[2018-10-28 16:48:46] log.ERROR: Invalid Query	['Query':'select ' from tategallery','User':'root','Email':'foo@
[2018-10-28 16:48:46] log.ERROR: Invalid Query	['Query':'select ' from tategallery','User':'root','Email':'foo@
[2018-10-28 16:48:46] log.ERROR: Invalid Query	['Query':'select ' from tategallery','User':'root','Email':'foo@
[2018-10-28 16:48:46] log.ERROR: Invalid Query	['Query':'select ' from tategallery','User':'root','Email':'foo@
[2018-10-28 16:48:46] log.ERROR: Invalid Query	['Query':'select ' from tategallery','User':'root','Email':'foo@

Fig. 12. Log examination by admin users.

5 Conclusion and Future Work

In this work an easy-to-use solution that gives the end-user the ability to query a set of databases through a single and user-friendly UI was introduced. The UI provides access to a number of functionalities, including the provision of a graphical representation of the databases, the ability to upload the data to the platform and validate through a graphical interface. In order to demonstrate the capabilities of the UI, a use case with two databases (one from the Tate Gallery and one from the Penn Museum) was presented. Furthermore, users are provided with facilities to query as well as validate the available databases from the UI. We note here that there were no correlations between our two data sources due to the high degree of dissimilarity between them, both in terms of structure and in terms of content.

Our future work will focus on considering social media data for search enrichment [46–50] and recommendation accuracy [51–54], as well as personalization techniques for upgraded prediction accuracy [55–60] and personalized ranking [61–64].

References

1. Jia, F., Blome, C., Sun, H., Yang, Y., Zhi, B.: Towards an integrated conceptual framework of supply chain finance: an information processing perspective. Int. J. Prod. Econ. **219**, 18–30 (2020). https://doi.org/10.1016/j.ijpe.2019.05.013
2. Ortega, J.L.: Blogs and news sources coverage in altmetrics data providers: a comparative analysis by country, language, and subject. Scientometrics **122**, 555–572 (2020). https://doi.org/10.1007/s11192-019-03299-2
3. Margaris, D., Vassilakis, C., Georgiadis, P.: An integrated framework for adapting WS-BPEL scenario execution using QoS and collaborative filtering techniques. Sci. Comput. Program. 98 (2015). https://doi.org/10.1016/j.scico.2014.10.007
4. Margaris, D., Vassilakis, C., Georgiadis, P.: An integrated framework for QoS-based adaptation and exception resolution in WS-BPEL scenarios. In: Proceedings of the 28th Annual ACM Symposium on Applied Computing - SAC 2013. p. 1900. ACM Press, New York, New York, USA (2013). https://doi.org/10.1145/2480362.2480714
5. Yang, J., Chen, B., Xia, S.-T.: Mean-removed product quantization for approximate nearest neighbor search. In: 2019 International Conference on Data Mining Workshops (ICDMW), pp. 711–718. IEEE, Beijing, China (2019). https://doi.org/10.1109/ICDMW.2019.00107
6. Asadi, S., Mansouri, H., Darvay, Z., Zangiabadi, M., Mahdavi-Amiri, N.: Large-neighborhood infeasible predictor-corrector algorithm for horizontal linear complementarity problems over cartesian product of symmetric cones. J. Optim. Theory Appl. **180**, 811–829 (2019). https://doi.org/10.1007/s10957-018-1402-6
7. Margaris, D., Spiliotopoulos, D., Vassilakis, C., Karagiorgos, G.: A user interface for personalized web service selection in business processes. In: Stephanidis, C., et al. (eds.) HCII 2020. LNCS, vol. 12427, pp. 560–573. Springer, Cham (2020). https://doi.org/10.1007/978-3-030-60152-2_41
8. Yadav, N., Rajpoot, D.S., Dhakad, S.K.: LARAVEL: a PHP framework for e-commerce website. In: 2019 Fifth International Conference on Image Information Processing (ICIIP), pp. 503–508. IEEE, Shimla, India (2019). https://doi.org/10.1109/ICIIP47207.2019.8985771
9. Mahmood, M.T., Ashour, O.I.A.: Web application based on MVC laravel architecture for online shops. In: Proceedings of the 6th International Conference on Engineering & MIS 2020, pp. 1–7. ACM, Almaty Kazakhstan (2020). https://doi.org/10.1145/3410352.3410834
10. Spiliotopoulos, D., Kotis, K., Vassilakis, C., Margaris, D.: Semantics-driven conversational interfaces for museum chatbots. In: Rauterberg, M. (ed.) Culture and Computing, pp. 255–266. Springer International Publishing, Cham (2020). https://doi.org/10.1007/978-3-030-50267-6_20
11. Varitimiadis, S., Kotis, K., Spiliotopoulos, D., Vassilakis, C., Margaris, D.: "Talking" triples to museum chatbots. In: Rauterberg, M. (ed.) Culture and Computing, pp. 281–299. Springer International Publishing, Cham (2020). https://doi.org/10.1007/978-3-030-50267-6_22
12. Koryzis, D., Fitsilis, F., Spiliotopoulos, D., Theocharopoulos, T., Margaris, D., Vassilakis, C.: Policy making analysis and practitioner user experience. In: Stephanidis, C., Marcus, A., Rosenzweig, E., Rau, P.-P.L., Moallem, A., Rauterberg, M. (eds.) HCII 2020. LNCS, vol. 12423, pp. 415–431. Springer, Cham (2020). https://doi.org/10.1007/978-3-030-60114-0_29

13. Kouroupetroglou, G., Spiliotopoulos, D.: Usability methodologies for real-life voice user interfaces. Int. J. Inf. Technol. Web Eng. **4**, 78–94 (2009). https://doi.org/10.4018/jitwe.200 9100105

14. Margaris, D., Vassilakis, C., Georgiadis, P.: Query personalization using social network information and collaborative filtering techniques. Futur. Gener. Comput. Syst. **78**, 440–450 (2018). https://doi.org/10.1016/j.future.2017.03.015

15. Sharma, S., Rana, V.: Web search personalization using semantic similarity measure. In: Singh, P.K., Kar, A.K., Singh, Y., Kolekar, M.H., Tanwar, S. (eds.) Proceedings of ICRIC 2019. LNEE, vol. 597, pp. 273–288. Springer, Cham (2020). https://doi.org/10.1007/978-3-030-29407-6_21

16. Azhir, E., Jafari Navimipour, N., Hosseinzadeh, M., Sharifi, A., Darwesh, A.: Deterministic and non-deterministic query optimization techniques in the cloud computing. Concurr. Comput. Pract. Exp. **31**, (2019). https://doi.org/10.1002/cpe.5240

17. Sharma, M., Singh, G., Singh, R.: A review of different cost-based distributed query optimizers. Prog. Artif. Intell. **8**, 45–62 (2019). https://doi.org/10.1007/s13748-018-0154-8

18. Demidova, E., et al.: Analysing and enriching focused semantic web archives for parliament applications. Futur. Internet. **6**, 433–456 (2014). https://doi.org/10.3390/fi6030433

19. Risse, T., et al.: The ARCOMEM architecture for social- and semantic-driven web archiving. Futur. Internet. **6**, 688–716 (2014). https://doi.org/10.3390/fi6040688

20. Li, Y., Shen, Z., Li, J.: SimbaQL: a query language for multi-source heterogeneous data. In: Li, J., Meng, X., Zhang, Y., Cui, W., Du, Z. (eds.) Big Scientific Data Management, pp. 275–284. Springer International Publishing, Cham (2019). https://doi.org/10.1007/978-3-030-28061-1_27

21. Hu, X., Xu, H., Jia, J., Wang, X.: Research on distributed storage and query optimization of multi-source heterogeneous meteorological data. In: Proceedings of the 2018 International Conference on Cloud Computing and Internet of Things - CCIOT 2018, pp. 12–18. ACM Press, Singapore, Singapore (2018). https://doi.org/10.1145/3291064.3291068

22. Wu, Q., Chen, C., Jiang, Y.: Multi-source heterogeneous Hakka culture heritage data management based on MongoDB. In: 2016 Fifth International Conference on Agro-Geoinformatics (Agro-Geoinformatics), pp. 1–6. IEEE, Tianjin, China (2016). https://doi.org/10.1109/Agro-Geoinformatics.2016.7577628

23. Liu, B., et al.: A Versatile event-driven data model in HBase database for multi-source data of power grid. In: 2016 IEEE International Conference on Smart Cloud (SmartCloud). pp. 208–213. IEEE, New York, NY, USA (2016). https://doi.org/10.1109/SmartCloud.2016.28

24. Chen, Z., et al.: A multi-database hybrid storage method for big data of power dispatching and control. In: 2019 IEEE SmartWorld, Ubiquitous Intelligence & Computing, Advanced & Trusted Computing, Scalable Computing & Communications, Cloud & Big Data Computing, Internet of People and Smart City Innovation (SmartWorld/SCALCOM/UIC/ATC/CBDCom/IOP/SCI), pp. 502–507. IEEE, Leicester, United Kingdom (2019). https://doi.org/10.1109/SmartWorld-UIC-ATC-SCALCOM-IOP-SCI.2019.00127

25. Miyamoto, N., Higuchi, K., Tsuji, T.: Incremental data migration for multi-database systems based on MySQL with spider storage engine. In: 2014 IIAI 3rd International Conference on Advanced Applied Informatics. pp. 745–750. IEEE, Kokura Kita-ku, Japan (2014). https://doi.org/10.1109/IIAI-AAI.2014.151

26. Daniel, G., et al.: NeoEMF: a multi-database model persistence framework for very large models. Sci. Comput. Program. **149**, 9–14 (2017). https://doi.org/10.1016/j.scico.2017.08.002

27. Rachman, M.A.F., Santawati, G.A.P.: Database integration based on combination schema matching approach (case study: Multi-database of district health information system). In: 2017 2nd International conferences on Information Technology, Information Systems and

Electrical Engineering (ICITISEE), pp. 430–435. IEEE, Yogyakarta (2017). https://doi.org/10.1109/ICITISEE.2017.8285544

28. Phungtua-Eng, T., Chittayasothorn, S.: A multi-database access system with instance matching. In: Nguyen, N.T., Tojo, S., Nguyen, L.M., Trawiński, B. (eds.) Intelligent Information and Database Systems, pp. 312–321. Springer International Publishing, Cham (2017). https://doi.org/10.1007/978-3-319-54472-4_30

29. Xydas, G., Spiliotopoulos, D., Kouroupetroglou, G.: Modeling prosodic structures in linguistically enriched environments. In: Sojka, P., Kopeček, I., Pala, K. (eds.) TSD 2004. LNCS (LNAI), vol. 3206, pp. 521–528. Springer, Heidelberg (2004). https://doi.org/10.1007/978-3-540-30120-2_66

30. Spiliotopoulos, D., Xydas, G., Kouroupetroglou, G., Argyropoulos, V., Ikospentaki, K.: Auditory universal accessibility of data tables using naturally derived prosody specification. Univers. Access Inf. Soc. 9(2), 169–183 (2010). https://doi.org/10.1007/s10209-009-0165-0

31. Xydas, G., Spiliotopoulos, D., Kouroupetroglou, G.: Modeling improved prosody generation from high-level linguistically annotated corpora. IEICE Trans. Inf. Syst. E88-D, 510–518 (2005). https://doi.org/10.1093/ietisy/e88-d.3.510

32. Naik, S.T.: Accessing data from multiple heterogeneous distributed database systems. In: Applying Integration Techniques and Methods in Distributed Systems and Technologies: IGI Global (2019). https://doi.org/10.4018/978-1-5225-8295-3.ch008

33. Chen, C.: Information visualization. Wiley Interdiscip. Rev. Comput. Stat. 2, 387–403 (2010). https://doi.org/10.1002/wics.89

34. Dasari, V., Allen, S., Brown, S.E.: Dynamic visualization of large scale tactical network simulations. In: 2019 IEEE International Conference on Big Data (Big Data), pp. 3951–3954. IEEE, Los Angeles, CA, USA (2019). https://doi.org/10.1109/BigData47090.2019.9005641

35. Sun, Y.: Third-party library integration. In: Practical Application Development with AppRun, pp. 163–190. Apress, Berkeley, CA (2019)

36. Lu, T., Zhang, P., Li, H.: Practice teaching reform of discrete mathematics model based on D3.js. In: 2019 14th International Conference on Computer Science & Education (ICCSE), pp. 379–384. IEEE, Toronto, ON, Canada (2019). https://doi.org/10.1109/ICCSE.2019.8845409

37. Urmela, S., Nandhini, M.: Collective dendrogram clustering with collaborative filtering for distributed data mining on electronic health records. In: 2017 Second International Conference on Electrical, Computer and Communication Technologies (ICECCT), pp. 1–5. IEEE. Coimbatore (2017). https://doi.org/10.1109/ICECCT.2017.8117876

38. Arief, V.N., DeLacy, I.H., Basford, K.E., Dieters, M.J.: Application of a dendrogram seriation algorithm to extract pattern from plant breeding data. Euphytica 213, 85 (2017). https://doi.org/10.1007/s10681-017-1870-z

39. Darmawan, I., Rahmatulloh, A., Nuralam, I.M.F., Gunawan, R.: Optimizing data storage in handling dynamic input fields with JSON string compression. In: 2020 8th International Conference on Information and Communication Technology (ICoICT), pp. 1–5. IEEE, Yogyakarta, Indonesia (2020). https://doi.org/10.1109/ICoICT49345.2020.9166458

40. Pezoa, F., Reutter, J.L., Suarez, F., Ugarte, M., Vrgoč, D.: Foundations of JSON schema. In: Proceedings of the 25th International Conference on World Wide Web, pp. 263–273. International World Wide Web Conferences Steering Committee, Montréal Québec Canada (2016). https://doi.org/10.1145/2872427.2883029

41. Vyas, S., Vaishnav, P.: A comparative study of various ETL process and their testing techniques in data warehouse. J. Stat. Manag. Syst. 20, 753–763 (2017). https://doi.org/10.1080/09720510.2017.1395194

42. Biswas, N., Chattopadhyay, S., Mahapatra, G., Chatterjee, S., Mondal, K.C.: SysML based conceptual ETL process modeling. In: Mandal, J.K., Dutta, P., Mukhopadhyay, S. (eds.)

Computational Intelligence, Communications, and Business Analytics, pp. 242–255. Springer Singapore, Singapore (2017). https://doi.org/10.1007/978-981-10-6430-2_19

43. Pereira, A.P., Cardoso, B.P., Laureano, R.M.S.: Business intelligence: performance and sustainability measures in an ETL process. In: 2018 13th Iberian Conference on Information Systems and Technologies (CISTI), pp. 1–7. IEEE, Caceres (2018). https://doi.org/10.23919/CISTI.2018.8399473

44. Georgiou, M.A., Paphitis, A., Sirivianos, M., Herodotou, H.: Hihooi: A database replication middleware for scaling transactional databases consistently. IEEE Trans. Knowl. Data Eng. 1 (2020). https://doi.org/10.1109/TKDE.2020.2987560

45. Dong, L., Liu, W., Li, R., Zhang, T., Zhao, W.: Replica-aware partitioning design in parallel database systems. In: Rivera, F.F., Pena, T.F., Cabaleiro, J.C. (eds.) Euro-Par 2017: Parallel Processing, pp. 303–316. Springer International Publishing, Cham (2017). https://doi.org/10.1007/978-3-319-64203-1_22

46. Spiliotopoulos, D., Margaris, D., Vassilakis, C.: Data-assisted persona construction using social media data. Big Data Cogn. Comput. **4**, 21–21 (2020). https://doi.org/10.3390/bdcc4030021

47. Margaris, D., Vassilakis, C., Spiliotopoulos, D.: Handling uncertainty in social media textual information for improving venue recommendation formulation quality in social networks. Soc. Netw. Anal. Min. **9**, 64 (2019). https://doi.org/10.1007/s13278-019-0610-x

48. Preece, A., et al.: https://doi.org/10.1109/access.2020.2981567. IEEE Trans. Comput. Soc. Syst. **5**, 118–131 (2018). https://doi.org/10.1109/TCSS.2017.2763684

49. Aivazoglou, M., et al.: A fine-grained social network recommender system. Soc. Netw. Anal. Min. **10**, 8 (2020). https://doi.org/10.1007/s13278-019-0621-7

50. Margaris, D., Kobusinska, A., Spiliotopoulos, D., Vassilakis, C.: An adaptive social network-aware collaborative filtering algorithm for improved rating prediction accuracy. IEEE Access. **8**, 68301–68310 (2020). https://doi.org/10.1109/ACCESS.2020.2981567

51. Winter, S., Maslowska, E., Vos, A.L.: The effects of trait-based personalization in social media advertising. Comput. Hum. Behav. **114**, (2021). https://doi.org/10.1016/j.chb.2020.106525

52. Margaris, D., Vassilakis, C., Spiliotopoulos, D.: What makes a review a reliable rating in recommender systems? Inf. Process. Manag. **57**, (2020). https://doi.org/10.1016/j.ipm.2020.102304

53. Margaris, D., Spiliotopoulos, D., Vassilakis, C.: Social relations versus near neighbours: reliable recommenders in limited information social network collaborative filtering for online advertising. In: Proceedings of the 2019 IEEE/ACM International Conference on Advances in Social Networks Analysis and Mining (ASONAM 2019), pp. 1160–1167. ACM, Vancouver, B.C., Canada (2019). https://doi.org/10.1145/3341161.3345620

54. Metz, M., Kruikemeier, S., Lecheler, S.: Personalization of politics on facebook: examining the content and effects of professional, emotional and private self-personalization. Inf. Commun. Soc. **23**, 1481–1498 (2020). https://doi.org/10.1080/1369118X.2019.1581244

55. Margaris, D., Vassilakis, C.: Improving collaborative filtering's rating prediction quality in dense datasets, by pruning old ratings. In: 2017 IEEE Symposium Computer Communication, pp. 1168–1174 (2017). https://doi.org/10.1109/ISCC.2017.8024683

56. Margaris, D., Spiliotopoulos, D., Vassilakis, C., Vasilopoulos, D.: Improving collaborative filtering's rating prediction accuracy by introducing the experiencing period criterion. Neural Comput. Appl. (2020). https://doi.org/10.1007/s00521-020-05460-y

57. Wang, L., Zhang, X., Wang, R., Yan, C., Kou, H., Qi, L.: Diversified service recommendation with high accuracy and efficiency. Knowl.-Based Syst. **204**, (2020). https://doi.org/10.1016/j.knosys.2020.106196

58. Margaris, D., Vasilopoulos, D., Vassilakis, C., Spiliotopoulos, D.: Improving collaborative filtering's rating prediction accuracy by introducing the common item rating past criterion. In:

2019 10th International Conference on Information, Intelligence, Systems and Applications, pp. 1–8 (2019). https://doi.org/10.1109/IISA.2019.8900758

59. Singh, P.K., Sinha, M., Das, S., Choudhury, P.: Enhancing recommendation accuracy of item-based collaborative filtering using Bhattacharyya coefficient and most similar item. Appl. Intell. **50**, 4708–4731 (2020). https://doi.org/10.1007/s10489-020-01775-4

60. Margaris, D., Spiliotopoulos, D., Vassilakis, C.: Improving collaborative filtering's rating prediction quality by exploiting the item adoption eagerness information. In: 2019 IEEE/WIC/ACM International Conference on Web Intelligence (WI) 2019, pp. 342–347 (2019). https://doi.org/10.1145/3350546.3352544

61. Lian, D., Liu, Q., Chen, E.: Personalized ranking with importance sampling. In: Proceedings of The Web Conference 2020, pp. 1093–1103. ACM, Taipei Taiwan (2020). https://doi.org/10.1145/3366423.3380187

62. Hu, Z., Wang, J., Yan, Y., Zhao, P., Chen, J., Huang, J.: Neural graph personalized ranking for Top-N recommendation. Knowl.-Based Syst. **213**, (2021). https://doi.org/10.1016/j.knosys.2020.106426

63. Wu, B., Ye, Y.: BSPR: basket-sensitive personalized ranking for product recommendation. Inf. Sci. (Ny) **541**, 185–206 (2020). https://doi.org/10.1016/j.ins.2020.06.046

64. Liu, B., Chen, T., Jia, P., Wang, L.: Effective public service delivery supported by time-decayed Bayesian personalized ranking. Knowl.-Based Syst. **206**, (2020). https://doi.org/10.1016/j.knosys.2020.106376

Democratizing Information Visualization.
A Study to Map the Value of Graphic Design

Matteo Zallio[✉] [iD]

Department of Engineering, University of Cambridge, Trumpington Street, Cambridge, UK
mz461@cam.ac.uk

Abstract. Visual representations are a consistent component of human evolution. They are forms of concept designs using combinations of colors, patterns, and geometrical figures.

As history displays, graphical visualization has been used since early ages as a mean to transfer knowledge between human beings across generations.

Recently, visual representations became recognized by various scientists as tools to ease cognitive comprehension in various scientific fields. Therefore, visual representations are becoming important in science communication and education.

Notwithstanding the general relevance of visual representations, there is not extensive recognition of the value of graphical representation to improve communication of scientific results and the level of awareness of visual design principles among non-design-centered communities is low.

Considering these aspects, this explorative study investigates the perception of STEM researchers, without any specific visual design background, and the value of visual representations as tools to support the communication of technical and scientific knowledge among academics and a wider non-design-centered community.

To measure the user perception and the value of visual representations in daily working practice, an interpretive approach was used, and a pilot study was conducted with a group of voluntary participants recruited among research members from a well-known American institution.

Results emphasize how researchers, who included professionally executed graphical representations in their publications, reports, and grant proposals, perceived their work as more easily readable. Early findings show that visual representations can positively support scientists to share research outcomes in a more compelling, visually clear, and impactful manner, reaching a wider audience across different disciplines.

Keywords: Data visualization · Information science · Visual design · Infographics · User experience research · Democratizing information · Accessibility · Knowledge design

1 The Role of Visual Representations

Visual representation lays the foundation of its origin since the early ages of humans living on Earth.

M. M. Soares et al. (Eds.): HCII 2021, LNCS 12779, pp. 495–508, 2021.
https://doi.org/10.1007/978-3-030-78221-4_33

From prehistoric symbols in the Lascaux caves, estimated at around 17,000 years ago [1], to engraved symbols in Rome's Trajan's Column (A.D. 113) [2], to Illuminated manuscripts from the Middle Ages, beautifully hand-decorated to highlight the book's contents [3], up to visual symbols for computer-mediated communication of 21st century, such named Emoji [4], human beings established techniques to express knowledge and meaning through different visual representations.

Visual representations are a consistent component of human beings' evolution. They are a form of concept designs using combinations of colors, patterns, and geometrical figures [5].

Over the centuries, several forms of graphical visualization including drawings, photographs, diagrams, charts, tables, and many other creative forms [6], have been developed by artists, creative illustrators, scientists, designers, technologists, inventors through a mix of skills, technology, and available tools.

As history displays, graphical visualization has been used since early ages as a mean to transfer knowledge between human beings across generations. Recently, visual representations became recognized by various scientists as tools to ease cognitive comprehension in various scientific fields [7, 8].

According to Gilbert et al., graphical visualization is of great importance particularly in three aspects of the learning of science [9]. First, learning specific models that are currently used by a community of scientists such as the double-helix model of DNA, the P-N junction model of a transistor, or the visualization of a gene in biology. Second, learning to develop new qualitative models that explain an unexplored phenomenon by following a sequence of learning: to use an established model; to revise an established model; to reconstruct an established model; to construct a model de novo. Third, learning to develop new quantitative models to make a comprehensive representation available. Therefore, visual representations are greatly important in science communication and education.

Given the incremental advance in the development of scientific research, which led to high growth rates in scientific publications [10], the importance of visualizing concepts, research outcomes, and results became more understood and appreciated among the scientific community. As a matter of fact, in the last decade, several editors encouraged the scientific community to create compelling, visually attractive, and clear graphical representations [11–14].

Notwithstanding the general relevance of visual representations, there is not extensive recognition of the value of graphical representation to improve communication of scientific results and the level of awareness of visual design principles among non-design-centered communities.

The necessity to meticulously communicate complex information across several scientific fields, at a fast pace, is carrying the need to improve cross-disciplinary communicative graphical visualization strategies.

Considering these aspects, this explorative study investigates the perception of STEM researchers, with initial limited or very low awareness about visual infographic design, and the value of visual representations as tools to support the communication of technical and scientific knowledge among academics and a wider non-design-centered community.

A user experience design researcher worked for 10 months with several researchers across the Aeronautics and Astronautics Department at Stanford University to infuse a "designer mindset" and to create visual representations and graphical visualizations to help improve the communication of research findings.

To measure the user perception and the value of visual representations in daily working practice, an interpretive approach was used, and a pilot study was conducted with a group of voluntary participants recruited among research members from the same department.

2 Visual Representations as a Tool to Improve Communication

Historians assigned an important role in visual representation, particularly in early modern science [15]. Some of the most remarkable examples in this field are the extraordinary visual representation skills of Leonardo Da Vinci, an Italian polymath of the Renaissance. The visual analysis of natural processes and technological developments created by the artist and inventor was transferred on paper through compelling graphical representations. These illustrations facilitated the communication of his thoughts and complex messages to his clients [15].

More specifically, Koyré pointed out that apart from the excellent artistic quality and detailed precision of Leonardo's anatomical drawings, the artist's major aim was to truly discover the inner structure and the mechanisms of the human body to make his knowledge available to a wider audience [16]. Leonardo believed that painting and visual representations, are not only superior to the other arts but can also be trusted to represent objects and concepts and understand them better than using only verbal descriptions [16].

A further example from the Renaissance comes from the extraordinary work of Galileo Galilei, an Italian astronomer, physicist, and engineer from the 17th century. He created a series of drawings illustrating the Earth's moon to demonstrate the power of his new invention — the telescope — to his patron, Cosimo de' Medici [17].

Visual representations have been widely used to facilitate the comprehension of complex information, such as the mechanics of a human body or a complex engineering system. Therefore, it is relevant to note that the combination of science, art, and visual design makes progress and technical innovations more accessible and understandable to a wider audience.

In recent history, a variety of graphical languages and supporting tools were born. One of the most significant languages, that is still largely used for graphical representations, is the Vienna Method of Pictorial Statistics developed by Otto Neurath. Together with Marie Reidemeister and Gerd Arntz, Neurath created a new visual language to explain complex systems by using pictorial representations. In 1934 it became known as the ISOTYPE - the International System of Typographic Picture Education [18].

By looking at the literature, it is clear that a common strategy accompanying Leonardo's, Galilei's and Neurath's work was to improve the communication of findings, inventions, or simply information in a more understandable manner for a wider audience. The need of sharing knowledge and disseminate the advances of scientific research is a crucial aspect that helps to improve and develop further research among the scientific community.

The massive quantity of information and correlations between several fields of scientific knowledge [19], as well as the need from readers to gain more information in less time as possible, are key aspects to consider nowadays.

It appears that in recent years, more and more researchers perceive the need to create compelling visual representations that convey complex arrays of data in colorful displays for their publications [20]. Scientists also rely on diagrams, figures, graphs, and abstracted visual representations when problem-solving to assimilate information, perceive trends, and conceptualize spatial relationships that relate their message to peers and colleagues across disciplines [21].

Abstraction is an important technique used in the creation and interpretation of scientific illustrations [22] and together with visual design principles [23, 24], they constitute some of the auxiliary tools that could help researchers to improve the communication of research findings. To understand and map the effectiveness of these tools as an optimal solution to support scientific research communication an exploratory study was carried on.

3 Research Methodology

This exploratory pilot study is grounded in the interpretive approach to user research, where feedback was elicited and analyzed to gain empathetic understanding and map the perception of researchers on visual design as an instrument to improve communication of research.

The research process and method were defined according to the literature review findings and after several explorative conversations to understand human actions on the relevance of the topic.

A user experience design researcher worked for 10 months with several academic staff members across the Aeronautics and Astronautics Department at Stanford University, collaborating to design visual representations and data visualizations as well as to infuse a "designer mindset" aiming to improve communication of scientific results of the research group.

To measure the impact of visual representations in daily working practice, a pilot study was dispensed to a group of voluntary participants recruited among faculty, post-doctoral, Ph.D. researchers, and graduate students from the Aeronautics and Astronautics Department at Stanford University.

The study, released in English language, proposed a list of closed and open-ended questions aiming to target four specific goals: a) to investigate the pre-collaboration level of awareness on visual design, b) to understand the impact of visual design in communicating research work, c) to evaluate the learning experience that participants developed across the collaboration, d) to understand the lesson learned on effective, clear visual design communication. Best practices in creating the study were followed [25], in particular avoiding ambiguous or double-barreled questions and questions containing double negatives. For extensive information about the study refer to Zallio [26].

3.1 Participants Recruitment

Participants' recruitment was managed through an internal mailing system and an instant messaging platform normally used for communications within the group affiliates. A relatively small sample size of fourteen subjects (n = 14) who were familiar with the subject was included in the study. Notwithstanding the limited number of participants, this exploratory study could give an initial contribution to establish the presence of one or multiple factors in the use of visual design principles for graphical representations in scientific research. Participants who were involved in experimenting with new visual illustration strategies and experienced benefits of communicating research outcomes through persuasive visual illustrations were considered.

Before a full release of the study to participants, a study verification was performed with a target group of researchers. This process allowed to identify (a) whether respondents clearly understood the questions and (b) whether questions had the same meaning for all respondents.

The study was conducted following ethical manners, under the best research practice of confidentiality and informed consent. The respondents' right to confidentiality, as stated in the study description procedure, as well as the opportunity to drop out of the study at any time, were granted. The study had no time limit and participants were recommended to answer all questions. At the end of the study, participants didn't receive any compensation, and the average time for completion was six minutes.

3.2 Data Collection

The pilot study was created using an open-source platform. It consisted of a brief introduction with aim of the study, followed by a set of demographic information questions, a set of twelve closed-ended questions, and one last open-ended question. A bipolar scaling method measuring either positive or negative response to a statement was used to score certain responses.

To facilitate the choice of answers a five-point Likert Scale with symmetry of categories from a midpoint with distinctly defined linguistic qualifiers was used to guarantee that attributes were observed. Certain questions were provided with a yes and no answer or multiple selections between items.

The study was further divided into five different sections.

Section 1 focused on collecting participants' demographic data (age, gender, ethnicity). Section 2 asked questions regarding (a) familiarity with a visual design before the start of the collaboration, (b) the importance of visual design to improve research communication, (c) the potential of visual design to allow a wider community to understand complex information, and (d) how valuable was the visual design contribution to their research. Section 2 made use of ordinal data with variables ordered in categories.

Section 3 revealed a comparison between two different examples of an original design and redesigned infographic, and a series of questions aimed to capture participants' perspectives about visually compelling, clear communication of the selected examples.

These questions were important to explore if participants gained an understanding of the differences between two different representation styles of the same research item.

Section 4 questioned participants about preferred features they were considering when thinking about compelling visual design illustrations (with a multiple-choice question, based on design principles) and what constitutes a cluster of essential visual design elements for communicative graphical illustrations.

Section 5 focused on understanding how to facilitate the collaboration between designers and scientists, in terms of easing the development process of graphical representations, as well as the method to facilitate the collaboration.

4   Results

In total fourteen subjects (n = 14), ages ranged between 22 to 34 years old (M = 26.5), with one identified as female and thirteen as male, participated in the study. Their ethnicity was various and despite the small sample size, it covers several geographical areas of the world (see Table 1). The sample size and composition are strongly formed by male subjects. The statistical significance could be considered as a potential limitation of the study; however, this is an explorative pilot study that opens up future research paths. This aspect also allows reflecting on the composition of individuals working in general in STEM disciplines. A descriptive statistics approach was used to summarize and organize the characteristics of the data set.

Table 1. Participants sample and demographic data.

Variable		n	Age (years)
Sex	All	14	M 26.5
	Female	1	27
	Male	13	M 26.5
	Prefer not to say	0	0
Ethnicity	Asian/Pacific Islander/Asian Indian	4	
	White and Asian	1	
	White	1	
	Middle eastern/North African	2	

In Sect. 2 frequency was collected and specifically focused on understanding familiarity with the visual design before the start of the collaboration. Five participants (n = 5) were slightly familiar and an additional five (n = 5) were somewhat familiar with visual design principles. Only one subject was not at all familiar and one extremely familiar, whereas only two participants (n = 2) were moderately familiar.

Regarding the importance of visual design to improve the communication of research work, half of the subjects (n = 7) recognized that visual design is important to improve research communication and an additional six of them (n = 6) agreed that is very important. Only one participant expressed neutral feedback.

The majority of participants (n = 10) strongly agreed that visual design can allow a wider community across different disciplines to benefit from scientific results, and rather a small minority (n = 3) agreed. Only one subject answered with a neutral response. Detailed results are listed in Table 2 below.

Table 2. Sect. 2 results.

Question	Results				
1. Before the start of the collaboration, how familiar were you with visual design principles?	Not at all familiar	Slightly familiar	Somewhat familiar	Moderately familiar	Extremely familiar
	1	5	5	2	1
2. Based on your experience collaborating with the designer, how important do you consider visual design to improve the communication of your work?	Not at all important	Low importance	Neutral	Important	Very important
	0	0	1	7	6
3. Do you think visual design allows a wider community across different disciplines to benefit from your scientific results?	Strongly disagree	Disagree	Neither agree nor disagree	Agree	Strongly agree
	0	0	1	3	10

Section 3 of the study focused on understanding the capacity of participants to evaluate which illustration was elaborated following graphic design principles accepted by the scientific community [23, 24]. Two sets of illustrations, reported in Image 1 below, were used to analyze participants' views. First, participants were asked to select which graphical representation offers a more visually compelling (e.g., widely understandable, catches the reader's attention) and clear (e.g., readable) communication.

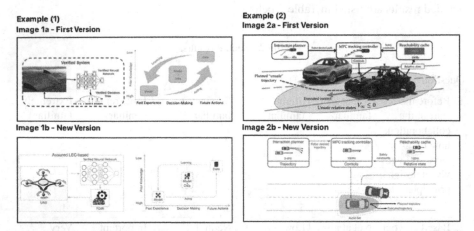

Image. 1. Illustrations 1 and 2 were submitted to participants. The above images (Image 1a and Image 2a) represent the original graphic elaborated, and the lower images (Image 1b and Image 2b) represent the updated through graphic design principles.

Regarding example 1, the majority of participants (n = 10) chose the redesigned illustration (Image 1b) and only a smaller number (n = 4) selected the original illustration.

Considering example 2, almost all of the participants (n = 13) chose the redesigned illustration (Image 2b) and only one selected the original illustration.

Section 4 of the survey was built upon the examples previously shown and participants were queried to select from a list of eight visual design principles which were the four most important features they considered when expressed their previous preference on examples 1 and 2.

The eight visual design principles were namely: geometrical balance (equal distribution within the image), contrast (make elements stand out by emphasizing differences in size, color, direction), unity (similar elements appearing to belong together), dominance (have one element as the focal point and others being subordinate), visual minimalism (the tendency to simplify and organize complex visuals, by arranging the parts into an organized, minimal system), visual clarity (how a visual design can effectively prioritize and deliver information), color balance, and hierarchy between items.

The top four ranked were namely: visual minimalism (n = 11), visual clarity (n = 10), contrast and geometrical balance respectively with half of the preferences (n = 7). Less participants selected in their top four design principles unity (n = 6), hierarchy between items (n = 6), color balance (n = 5), and dominance (n = 4).

The second question from Sect. 4 focused on identifying what essential design elements people would consider when illustrating their research projects for well-organized communication. A list of eight elements (abundance of information, minimal information, mix-use of icons and text/numbers, use only text and numbers, geometric (uniform shapes), organic (non-uniform shapes), homogeneous visual language, non-homogeneous visual language) was proposed with a bipolar question format.

Results emphasize that most of the respondents have chosen to use minimal information (n = 13), rather than the abundance of information, whereas fourteen participants were not favorable. The use of mixed icons, text, and numbers was selected by most of participants (n = 13), rather than only text and numbers, whilst fourteen participants were not favorable. In the case of geometric or organic shapes, the answers were less uniformed. Geometric shapes were the preferred choice for thirteen participants, whereas only five selected organic shapes.

A slightly similar result came out from the preference of homogeneous visual language, where thirteen respondents (n = 13) agreed and eleven (n = 11) disagreed on the use of non-homogeneous visual language.

Section 5 of the survey mainly collected data on the collaboration between designer and scientists and how to maximize it in the future. In particular, subjects were asked to rank the three most desired options regarding the exchange of information between designer and scientist.

In a pre-pandemic time, the totality of participants expressed willingness to have face to face meetings (n = 14). Almost all of them (n = 13) also selected as second option a video call system, whereas half of them (n = 7) found useful to share a folder for file exchange. Only five preferred an instant messaging system and two were favorable to an email exchange. Notable of further consideration, these results would have been probably different if collected during or after the pandemic period.

A further question explored how the best, more efficient communication of information between the scientist and the designer should happen. Three main options were available: one to one consultation (creation of an environment where the scientist explains its research to a non-expert (the design consultant) and several follow-ups with the scientist in a loop), group or team consultation (creation of an environment with the team of scientists explain their research to a non-expert (the design consultant) and several follow-ups from the team of scientists in a loop), multiple consultations (creation of an environment where a team leader scientist explains the research to a non-expert (the design consultant) and several follow-ups with members of the team in a loop).

Interestingly half of participants (n = 7) preferred a one-to-one consultation as a mean to directly connect with the designer. Fewer subjects (n = 5) opted for group or team consultation and only two were in favor of a multiple consultation approach.

5 Discussion

Research from Vogel et al. revealed that presentations using visual aids were found to be 43% more persuasive than unaided presentations [27].

In certain scientific domains, low awareness regarding the positive impact that visual design can give to improve research results communication still exists.

The early findings from this explorative study show that ahead of the collaboration between designers and scientists, a low or moderate tendency of familiarity with visual design happens between participants, (for extensive information refer to Zallio [26]).

This statement was reinforced with a further question asked in Sect. 3 of the study, that captured the capacity of participants to discern between an old-style graphic and a redesigned visual illustration, according to visual design principles. Furthermore, this section investigated which of the sample illustrations offered a more visually compelling and clear communication of the idea behind.

As the largest number of participants selected the redesigned version of the illustration both for example 1 (n = 10) and example 2 (n = 13), it is possible to identify that graphical representations created by following certain visual design principles [23, 24] offer a more visually compelling, clear communication.

These results were additionally verified by investigating which were the most important features that characterize a good visual design from the participants' perspective. Interestingly, visual minimalism, which was repeatedly chosen by eleven participants (n = 11), as well as visual clarity chosen by ten (n = 10) were highly appreciated as understandable and perceivable design principles. Geometrical balance and contrast, unity, hierarchy between items, color balance, and dominance were instead selected less frequently.

This selection has the intention to highlight potentially less understanding about the application of those principles and therefore easiness to distinguish them in visual design. Follow up discussions with subjects posed the attention to several factors, such as the ability to recognize those principles, probably an easier task for a visual designer who is constantly working with such principles, or lack of awareness regarding the specific function or clarity about their application. The factors understood from this study underline that further investigation should be done.

Noteworthy results that confirm the tendency of participants to prefer certain visual design principles were further reported in Sect. 4 of the study. What stood out was that following visual minimalism, all of respondents were against the use of excessive information and most of them were more likely to include a minimal amount of information in their visual illustrations.

In terms of visual clarity, the majority of participants preferred to use icons, with text and numbers and avoid the use of only text and numbers. These results confirm that visual minimalism and visual clarity are some of the fundamental aspects to take into account when creating visual designs.

More scattered results were reported in terms of geometric or organic shapes used for graphical illustrations. While a large preference was given for geometric illustrations, only a few participants would have chosen organic representations. This discrepancy in the result is probably given to the inner nature of the representation, personal taste, aesthetic, and context in which the representation will be published. Lastly, homogeneous visual language should be considered among different visual illustrations, in particular, the use of similar icons, colors, font, size, and geometry were recommended features.

To investigate the association between the importance of visual design to improve the communication of research work and the benefits that visual design can bring to an audience to better understand the research further analysis of questions number 2 and 3 (listed in Table 2) was done.

Almost the totality of participants selected that is important (n = 6) or very important (n = 7) to consider visual design to improve the communication of the research work. Additionally, the majority (n = 10) strongly agreed or agreed (n = 3) that visual design can allow a wider community across different disciplines to benefit from the scientific achievements. The association of these two results pose some interesting remark on the importance of visual design and illustrations to improve communication and spread scientific results to a wider community across different disciplines.

An additional aspect to consider is the fluency in graphical visualization as a highly desirable skill to support a better understanding of concepts in scientific disciplines, in particular in the learning of science.

Final remarks focused particularly on considering how to best communicate between a design professional and a potential user which doesn't necessarily have a proper knowledge or awareness of visual design.

It is important to note that the study was developed and run just at the start of the pandemic in the USA (end of March 2020), so the answers were probably influenced by still a normal behavior at work, where face to face meetings and work from office was a daily regular practice.

Early findings show that all of the participants were keen on carrying on face-to-face meetings. That was a sign that the visual contact, the ability to sketch on a whiteboard, to reiterate thoughts and update the structure of the draft illustration in real-time, in-person was greatly appreciated.

The second most ranked answer emphasized the willingness to have online meetings through video-call systems. Despite a strong preference for face-to-face meetings, participants found extremely useful to operate the collaboration through online meeting systems, already in a pre-pandemic time.

A further aspect that could overcome the necessity of one-to-one in-person meetings, is the exchange of files, sketches, and material that is produced between designer and scientist. A shared folder for file exchange was backed as a reliable solution for half of the participants, whereas others preferred instant messaging systems or email exchange.

This partially answers on how the collaboration should be developed in a pandemic and eventually a post-pandemic era. We urge to say that repeating the study at a one-year distance, after the newly established working practice, would be helpful to understand if face-to-face meetings are essential.

Furthermore, we believe that supplementary investigation should be done to more specifically comprehend the dynamics between designer and scientist, how ideas are developed during the discussion phase, and what the in-person meeting could convey in terms of creativity improvements [29].

This pilot study was of great importance to first provide an initial finding on the relevance that visual design has in strengthening the communication not only in business marketing or news information but heavily also in scientific fields such as STEM.

Second to understand how illustrations, following visual design principles, have the potential to allow a wider community, across different disciplines to better understand complex technical concepts.

A further aspect that was noted in the study is the lack of awareness that STEM scientists, in particular, have about visual design and its principles. The growing need to efficiently communicate complex information across several scientific fields is carrying the need to improve a cross-disciplinary visual design knowledge that will positively impact both the communicator and the receiver of the information. A comprehensive study organized with a larger sample size across several STEM disciplines, to further improve and consolidate the current research finding is needed. Additionally, it is suggested to target supplementary aspects such as the learning curve and experience of the non-design specialists, as well as discovering insights to develop further dissemination strategies to testify the importance of good design in visual communication.

6   Conclusion

Communication as well as receiving the information, are almost as important as the process of knowledge creation.

With this pilot study initial research was performed on visual design as a tool to improve the communication of research work. Visual design has the potential to provide an added value to communicate scientific results to a wider community across different disciplines.

Early evidence shows that visual representations positively support scientists to share research findings in a more compelling, visually clear, and impactful manner. Researchers, who included professionally executed visual illustrations in their publications, reports, and grant proposals, perceived their works as more easily readable by a wider community, with an increased impact as of its visual clarity and more likely to reach a wider audience across different disciplines. Additional research shows that visual design has the power to interprets science and translate it into a concrete artifact [28]. This initial study confirms that improving the readability of information has the potential to foster the process of democratization of knowledge across disciplines, people, and cultures and allow a wider audience to benefit from the latest, cutting-edge scientific results.

As suggested by Rolandi et al. [24], a further aspect to consider for the future is to provide essential visual design foundations to improve the creation of visual illustrations for scientific research. With this research, we sought to contribute to strengthening the value that visual design can bring to scientific research and support early findings by Rolandi et al. Fluency in graphical visualization can be considered a highly desirable skill to support a better communication of concepts in scientific disciplines, in particular in the learning of science. With relatively minimal improvements, visually compelling illustrations can considerably offer an enriched experience both to the reader, who clearly understands the concept and to the communicator, who can more easily transfer the knowledge to its audience.

Acknowledgements. The collaboration and data collection were made possible thanks to the Department of Aeronautics and Astronautics and the Autonomous Systems Laboratory at Stanford University, USA. The data analysis and article development were made possible thanks to the funding from the European Union's Horizon 2020 research and innovation programme under the

Marie Skłodowska-Curie grant agreement N° 846284, and the valuable advice from the members of the Engineering Design Centre at University of Cambridge, United Kingdom.

References

1. Leroi-Gourhan, A.: The archaeology of lascaux cave. Sci. Am. **246**(6), 104–113 (1982)
2. Packer, J.E.: The Forum of Trajan in Rome: A Study of the Monuments in Brief. University of California Press, California (2001)
3. Karkov, C.E.: Illuminated manuscripts. Med. Stud. (2016). https://doi.org/10.1093/obo/978 0195396584-0047
4. Bai, Q., Dan, Q., Mu, Z., Yang, M.A.: Systematic review of emoji: current research and future. Perspect. Front. Psychol. **10**, 2221 (2019)
5. Morriss-Kay, G.M.: The evolution of human artistic creativity. J. Anat. **216**(2), 158–176 (2010)
6. Tufte, E.R.: The Visual Display of Quantitative Information. Graphics Press, Cheshire, Connecticut (1983)
7. Wu, H.K., Shah, P.: Exploring visuospatial thinking in chemistry learning. Sci. Educ. **88**(3), 465–492 (2004)
8. Evagorou, M., Erduran, S., Mäntylä, T.: The role of visual representations in scientific practices: from conceptual understanding and knowledge generation to 'seeing' how science works. Int. J. STEM Educ. **2**(11), 1–13 (2015)
9. Gilbert, J., Reiner, M., Nakhleh, M.: Visualization: Theory and Practice in Science Education. Springer, Dordrecht, The Netherlands (2008)
10. Bornmann, L., Mutz, R.: Growth rates of modern science: a bibliometric analysis based on the number of publications and cited references. J. Assoc. Inf. Sci. Technol. **66**(11), 2215–2222 (2015)
11. Wong, B.: Points of view: Simplify to clarify. Nat. Meth. **8**(8), 611 (2011)
12. Buriak, J.: Summarize your work in 100 milliseconds or less the importance of the table of contents image. ACS Nano **5**(10), 7687–7689 (2011)
13. Kamat, P., Schatz, G.: How to make your next paper scientifically effective. J. Phys. Chem. Lett. **4**(9), 1578–1581 (2013)
14. Larson, K., Cheng, K., Chen, Y., Rolandi, M.: Proving the value of visual design in scientific communication. Inf. Des. J. **23**(1), 80–95 (2017)
15. Baldasso, R.: The role of visual representation in the scientific revolution: a historiographic inquiry. Centaurus Int. English Lang. J. Hist. Sci. Cult. Aspects. **48**(2), 69–88 (2006)
16. Koyré, A.: "Léonard de Vinci 500 Ans après", in Etudes d'Histoire de la pensée scientifique, Paris: Presses Universitaires de France, pp. 99–116 (1966)
17. Drake, S.: Galileo's first telescopic observations. J. Hist. Astron. **7**(3), 153–168 (1976)
18. Neurath, O.: International picture language. In: Paul, K. Trench, Trubner & co., ltd. edition (1936)
19. Bates, A.W.: Teaching in a Digital Age by Tony Bates Associates Ltd (2015). https://www.tonybates.ca/teaching-in-a-digital-age/
20. Yeechi, C., O'Mahony, K., Ostergren, M., Pérez-Kriz, S., Rolandi, M.: Study of interdisciplinary visual communication in nanoscience and nanotechnology. Int. J. Eng. Educ. **30**(4), 1036–1047 (2014)
21. Lynch, M.: The Production of Scientific Images: Vision and Revision in the History, Philosophy and Sociology of Science. Visual Cultures of Science: Rethinking Representational Practices in Knowledge Building and Science Communication, University Press of New England, Dartmouth College Press, NH, pp. 26–41 (2006)

22. Mishra, M.P.: The role of abstraction in scientific illustration: implications for pedagogy. J. Vis. Literacy **19**(2), 139–158 (1999)
23. Kimball, M.A.: Visual design principles: an empirical study of design lore. J. Tech. Writ. Commun. **43**(1), 3–41 (2013)
24. Rolandi, M., Cheng, K., Pérez-Kriz, S.: A brief guide to designing effective figures for the scientific paper. Adv. Mater. **23**(38), 4343–4346 (2011)
25. Kelley, K., Clark, B., Brown, V., Sitzia, J.: Good practice in the conduct and reporting of survey research. Int. J. Qual. Health Care **15**(3), 261–266 (2003)
26. Zallio M.: Democratizing information visualization. A study to map the value of graphic design to easier knowledge transfer of scientific research Extended version (2021). https://arxiv.org/abs/2101.09999
27. Vogel, D.R., Dickson, G.W., Lehman, JA.: Persuasion and the Role of Visual Presentation Support: The UM/3 M Study (1986)
28. Müller, B.: Bringing Design to Science. Science can benefit more from design than design from science (2017). https://medium.com/@borism/bringing-design-to-science-3fa653f2c149
29. Zallio, M., Berry, D.: Computer Aided Drawing software delivered through Emotional Learning. The use of Emoticons and GIFs as a tool for increasing student engagement. In: Proceedings of the 32nd International BCS Human Computer Interaction Conference (HCI 2018), Belfast, UK, 4–6 July 2018. https://doi.org/10.14236/ewic/HCI2018.75

Design Education and Practice

The Design of Online Teaching in Digital Image Creation Courses in Colleges and Universities-Based on the Short Film Production Course as an Example

Ming Cai[✉], Zhi Chen, Ziyang Li, and LiMin Wang

Art and Design, Academy, Beijing City University, Beijing, China

Abstract. In early 2020, under the influence of the global spread of novel coronavirus, colleges and universities across China have been carrying out online teaching. Taking the short film production course **in digital media art major in the Academy of Art and Design of Beijing City University** as an example, this thesis expounds the overall design of online teaching in digital image creation courses, including the research background, establishment of teaching ideas, teaching operations and the process of solving several key problems in teaching. In addition, this thesis elaborates the advantages and disadvantages of online teaching and puts forward suggestions for improvement, based on the post-class questionnaire survey and this teaching experience. The article provides a reference for the development of online teaching in digital image creation courses.

Keywords: Digital image creation courses · Short film production course · Online teaching

1 Research Background

1.1 The Full Implementation of Online Teaching

At the beginning of 2020, due to the novel coronavirus pandemic, the Ministry of Education of the People's Republic of China issued a "suspension of classes and non-suspension of learning" call, colleges and universities in China launched a comprehensive online teaching. Online teaching has quickly become the focus of attention in the education sector. Online teaching across geographical space can overcome the limitations of traditional education in space, time and educational environment, and provide excellent educational resources for users in need [1]. This new learning model will certainly develops and evolves, being accompanied by the improvement of the level of network. University educators in their respective subject areas, seriously study the law of online teaching, explore the potential of online teaching, and promote the development of information technology in higher education.

© Springer Nature Switzerland AG 2021
M. M. Soares et al. (Eds.): HCII 2021, LNCS 12779, pp. 511–522, 2021.
https://doi.org/10.1007/978-3-030-78221-4_34

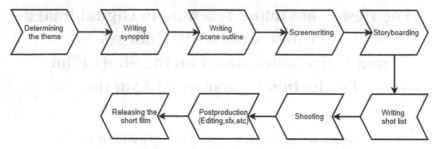

Fig. 1. Flowchart of short film creation during the course

1.2 Features of the Course

Although online teaching is imperative, it is necessary to take full account of the characteristics of the curriculum itself, and the teaching of different types of courses has its relatively unique teaching methods and teaching models. Taking the Short Film Production course as an example, the most important part of the course is that students complete the task of short film creation relatively independently [2]. From the point of view of the flowchart of short film creation (See Fig. 1), from the creative beginning to the formation of a certain scale of the script, to shooting, postproduction and release of the film, students need to continue to refine and refine on the basis of the previous stage of the finished product to achieve the ultimate goal. Obviously, it is necessary for the teacher to have a full discussion with the students, otherwise it is very easy to fall back to the initial stage and start again. In other words, the vast majority of students are repeatedly faced with the question of whether such a design is appropriate. When students and teachers basically agree, students can be more assured to move on to the next stage of creation. In other words, the teaching process of the Short Film Production course requires a lot of communication between teachers and students.

The traditional face-to-face teaching communication method has the unique advantage, because the interaction between teachers and students in the offline teaching process is very frequent and efficient. The tutoring of many details of the students' pre-creation stage and the trivial problems that arise in the process of students' independent practice can be displayed and solved through face-to-face discussion between students and teachers. Teacher Glazier, Rebecca A notes that the inherent distance imposed by online teaching and learning can make meaningful interactions between faculty and students difficult [3]. When online teaching is fully implemented in the teaching process, the non-contact communication of online teaching will undoubtedly greatly increase the cost of communication between teachers and students and the difficulty of work, which may lead to a significant reduction in the original teaching effect. Therefore, the short film production course needs to minimize the adverse effects of contactless communication in the course design.

As previously mentioned, the design of teaching should be finished before the course starts. The teaching framework would be very beneficial to later work. Here is the design framework [4] (See Fig. 2).

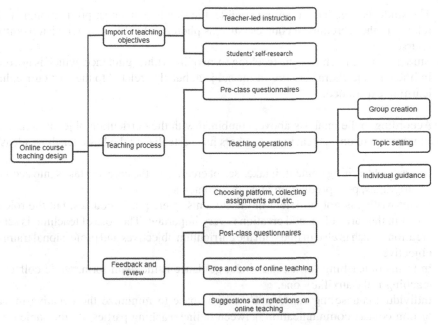

Fig. 2. Design framework of online teaching in digital image creation courses

2 Teaching Method and Process

2.1 Pre-class Questionnaires

The Short Film Production Course is a professional course in digital media art major in the Academy of Art and Design of Beijing City University, which aims to require students to lead or participate in various processes of narrative short film creation (such as storyboarding, shooting, postproduction and etc.) to produce professional-level short films. The prerequisite courses include photography, film and television editing, audio-visual language, etc., and students have developed certain short film creative skills during the pre-course period.

When it was determined that the course would adopt the online teaching method, the teachers decided to understand the students' overall situation by issuing questionnaires, mainly to investigate the general level of students' professional learning and the general problems existing in the creation stage, and then to determine teaching ideas and reasonable allocation of teaching resources in the light of the characteristics of the curriculum [5].

2.2 Establishing the Basic Teaching Ideas

The main results of the questionnaire are as follows (only part of the results):

1. The students are not clear about the short film script creation and lack of confidence

2. The students in general are more confident in shooting and post-production, may be related to the prerequisite courses (such as photography, film and television editing courses).
3. Students prefer to choose the teaching form of individual guidance, which is not only in line with the characteristics of the subject, but also related to the past curriculum learning experience.

According to the analysis above, combined with the curriculum objectives and the actual situation of online teaching, teachers have established the basic teaching ideas:

1. In terms of teaching content, it takes script creation as the core and takes into account photography, post production and other contents.
   Script writing is not sufficient in the students' prerequisite courses, but the role of script in the curriculum and creation is very important. The core of teaching is script creation, which is also in line with the curriculum objectives and professional training objectives.
2. In terms of teaching forms, individual guidance is the main form, while collective teaching is the auxiliary one.
   Individual counseling can create enough space to minimize the negative impact of non-contact communication between online teaching parties. At the same time, collective teaching is also necessary. The basic theory of creation and some reminders of creation can be conveyed to students through collective teaching. For example, Aristotle's drama theory is still of far-reaching significance to the creation of stories, which is suitable and acceptable in collective teaching [6].
3. The explanation of theory is connected with the creation of practice.
   When explaining the theory related to the course in the early stage of the course, it is necessary to link with the creative subject that the students are about to face, so as to urge the students to apply the theories they have just learned to the practice of their own creation, which requires teachers to do a good job of paving and necessary guidance work, so that students can understand and master the basic laws of creation.

2.3 Import of Teaching Objectives

Teacher-led Instruction. At the beginning of the course, the teacher explained the teaching objectives of the course in an all-round way, and made a complete explanation of the key points of the course, teaching methods, learning methods, course assignments, etc., so as to help students establish the overall idea of course learning.

Students' Self-Research. After the teacher-led explanation, students began to consciously choose the films and scripts they were interested in for study and research, and gradually found their own creative direction and formed their own creative team in the process of communication with teachers.

2.4 Specific Teaching Operations

Group Creation. Engaging in video creation is a collective creation process. In the course of short film production, teachers followed the principle of collective creation and required students to form a team freely to complete the creation task together, which was also a common practice in line with industry norms. In order to better exercise the students' comprehensive creative ability, the teachers required no more than 3 students in each group. In this way, each student would generally assume 2–3 responsibilities in the actual creative process, which met the training goal of "one specialty and multiple abilities" in the professional ability requirements.

Reasonable Topic Setting. The students are young, quick and sensitive to external things. In the early stage of the creation of video works, teachers set reasonable topics. They should not only guide the students' creative direction, make them adapt to the requirements of the industry as much as possible, but also not be too limited, resulting in similar ideas or unreasonable theme setting and other adverse consequences. The teachers helped the students to analyze the topic selection and encouraged the full communication within the group, so as to create a good creative atmosphere.

Individual Guidance. Because each group of students chose different topics and different ways to express their creativity, there were considerable differences in the following creation. The implementation of a more targeted teaching form of individual counseling could solve the problems in creation more efficiently, which was also a teaching method with higher recognition of teachers and students. It is worth mentioning that teachers can also flexibly use the online teaching platform to gather multiple groups of students to participate in the discussion on a certain problem, and do not have to stick to the teaching form of tutoring only one group at a time.

It needs to be clear that teachers can use time (in class and out of class) and space (online and face-to-face) to teach in a variety of ways (See Fig. 3).

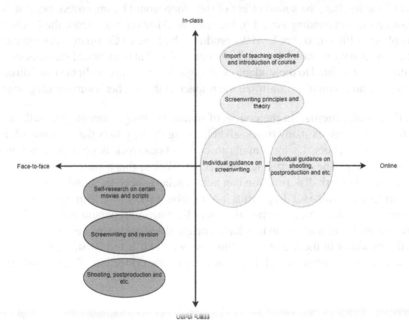

Fig. 3. Teaching arrangements in short film production course

2.5 Several Key Questions

Choice of Online Teaching Platform. Due to the need of epidemic prevention and control, people's demand for online work was surging. Many domestic software manufacturers urgently equipped their own software with the function of online conference, which provided a rich choice of online teaching platform for the education industry. After the course teaching guarantee team tested the vast majority of the same type of software on the market, combined with the specific situation of art course teaching, the teacher selected enterprise WeChat Work as the online teaching platform for short film production courses. Through the use of a semester, it is found that the platform has powerful function and high stability, which can meet the online teaching needs of this course.

Fidelity Transmission of the Sound of Video Clips. In the process of teaching, teachers generally use earphones for teaching, which can minimize the influence of teachers' surrounding sound, ensure the clarity of teachers' voice as far as possible, and also facilitate teachers to listen to students' feedback. This way is no problem for simple teaching. However, video clips are often used as a way of case teaching in short film production course. Through the interpretation and analysis of video works, it can help students to establish better image thinking and improve their creative ability. However, teachers found that the teaching platform selected by the short film production course did not support computer sound sharing, that is, when students watched the teacher's video by sharing the screen, the sound attached to the video could not be directly transmitted to the student end, but can only be transmitted to the student end through the teacher's headset, and the effect was very poor If the teacher used the microphone attached to the computer instead of the headset, the sound effect of the video would be improved, but it was easy to mix with the surrounding sound of the teacher. After repeated tests, the teacher used a microphone with a model of Um10c, produced by Lenovo Company. The microphone can be connected with headphones and other cables, so that the voice of the demonstration video can be transmitted to the students with high fidelity. The excellent sound directivity of the microphone can also minimize the impact of the teacher's surrounding sound.

Collecting Assignments. In the course of online teaching, students generally need to hand in their homework many times, and choosing the way to collect homework is also a problem for teachers. Using e-mails to collect homework is obviously not suitable for class teaching. The performance of Wechat Work in this aspect is remarkable. The use of its own network disk function can help teachers check the handing in of a certain assignment, and can also set the permissions to submit and view assignments. In addition, Baidu network disk also has the function of collecting multi person files, but the degree of convenience is limited. Leyun tool has an original design that exceeds the specification of similar products in the file name setting aspect, but it is too harsh on the upper limit of file size to be submitted, which is not suitable for the collection of video assignments.

3   Feedback and Review

3.1   Post-class Questionnaire Survey

After the course, in order to better summarize the experience of online teaching and find problems in online teaching, the teachers developed a questionnaire for all students of short film production course to fill in. It can be seen from the results of the questionnaire survey that:

The Teachers' Modification of Teaching is Effective.   Due to the change of online teaching, students have gained a great degree of freedom in learning, while teachers, as the organizers of teaching activities, have lost most of the control over teaching. In actual teaching activities, students may often go online or offline, or turn on or off the camera or microphone at any time, or leave the computer or mobile phone from time to time. Teaching activities will be affected or even interrupted due to network reasons, harassing phone calls, equipment failure, and other emergencies. Therefore, teachers need to adjust the existing teaching content. For the short film production course, the adjusted teaching content is relatively short, the content of a single explanation is reduced, the interest is enhanced, the form is more changeable and lively, the teaching of knowledge is more emphasis on fast and accurate, and the pursuit of knowledge practicality.

The Quality of Online Communication is Still Not Satisfactory.   As mentioned above, the characteristics of the course itself determine the importance of communication between teachers and students, but due to the adoption of online teaching, students generally have a certain degree of resistance to this non-contact communication. In the middle and later period of the course, the teachers had individual talks with some students, and these students complained about the low efficiency of online communication. At the same time, the students (especially those course performance comparatively low) also expressed that although the teaching arrangement of the course has left more space for communication, the process is not pleasant enough (See Fig. 4).

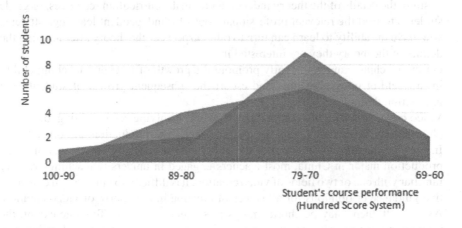

Fig. 4. Students' satisfaction survey

Obviously, students generally did not prepare well for online teaching, at least psychologically there were still many unsuitable places for online teaching [7]. This was indeed understandable. Such a comprehensive and sudden application of online teaching was a subversive change to students' usual face-to-face classroom teaching, and psychological stress was driving students to return to the traditional teaching environment. In addition, students were deeply aware of the inconvenience of life brought about by the epidemic, the negative evaluation of the quality of online teaching was also mixed with nostalgia for old learning habits and complex emotions about the yearning for a healthy and free life.

3.2 The Advantages and Disadvantages of Online Teaching in Digital Image Creation Courses

The advantages of online teaching for digital image creation courses are obvious, mainly reflected in:

1. Online teaching improves the learning efficiency of image creation theory, broadens the learning range of image creation theory, reduces the cost of learning relatively, and promotes the improvement of students' learning autonomy.

   Although the key content of the video creation course is mainly in the creative part, it is very necessary to study the theory of image creation which can guide the creation practice. In the same course as other theoretical links and practices, the theory of image creation is relatively boring, and because students' growth experience and interest points are different, different students pay attention to the theoretical part of image creation is also different. For example, some students want to learn more film directing theory, and some students want to study photography theory in combination with editing work. In practical teaching, teachers only need to make the necessary elaboration on the basic knowledge of image creation theory, and then guide students to study the details of the theory independently in the curriculum resources, or guide students to read the relevant professional books for independent learning. Students who have the ability to learn can turn to other aspects of the theory after learning the details of the theory they are interested in.

2. Online teaching can significantly promote the growth of teachers' teaching ability in the field of image creation, and escort the subsequent growth of students and graduation design.

   Video creation is a highly comprehensive work, involving screenwriting, directing, photography, filmmaking, film art, performance, post production and other fields. In view of the current situation of the cultivation of teachers and talents of video production major in China, most teachers engaged in university teaching are only familiar with one or two fields of video creation. It is difficult to put forward constructive guidance or opinions for all stages of creation in the course of video creation. As a result, there may be shortcomings in students' creation. To some extent, the implementation of online teaching promotes teachers to go out of their familiar professional fields and learn the knowledge of other fields of video creation, so as to better guide students' video creation practice.

3. Online teaching in video creation can provide direct convenience and profound practical basis for online teaching of similar courses.

As mentioned above, video creation has the characteristics of strong comprehensiveness. The research of online teaching of video creation courses will involve the guidance of the practice of screenwriting, directing, photography, filmmaking, film arts, performance, post-production and other fields and the collection and collation of curriculum resources, which can objectively provide convenient conditions and practical basis for similar courses (such as photography courses, video production software courses, audio-visual language courses, etc.), so as to gradually build an online teaching system of video creation courses.

Of course, there are drawbacks to the implementation of online teaching in video creation courses. Mainly reflected in:

1. Online communication is easy to increase the cost of communication

On-line voice or text communication is vulnerable to the network, the surrounding environment and other factors, resulting in the other party's understanding of our own information omissions or deviations, serious cases will lead to fundamental errors. In some times, it can have a severe impact on the mood of both sides of the communication, hindering follow-up work. This was also confirmed by the students in the post-class questionnaire. In this respect, traditional face-to-face communication is still the most efficient.

2. Online teaching lacks the necessary sense of ceremony

Online teaching frees up the space for learning, it seems that people can learn anytime, anywhere, but online teaching is difficult to create an alternative to offline learning needs of the atmosphere. Especially at the end of the video creation class, if the offline teaching method is adopted, the teachers will play the video works of each group on the large screen. Students can experience the same freshness and sense of accomplishment as watching their work in the cinema, and online teaching is completely unable to create a similar broadcasting environment. Video creation requires the interaction between teachers and students, as well as the interaction and sharing between students as creators of works and creators of other works. This is also a problem worthy of serious study by educators.

3.3 Suggestion and Reflections on the Online Teaching of Digital Image Creation Courses

Teaching Should Focus on Cultivating Students' Ability to Acquire and Master Knowledge Actively. It is more inappropriate to emphasize the amount of knowledge conveyed by teachers during the epidemic prevention and control period. Students can obtain a large number of text and video materials related to a certain subject and a certain course through simple keyword search on the Internet. Therefore, the teaching of knowledge itself and the teaching focusing on the amount of knowledge should seek for changes in the era of such abundant network resources, and the courses organized by schools should pay more attention to the understanding of professional knowledge and the training of executive ability. This is especially true of the course of image creation. How to let students determine their own knowledge needs, obtain the corresponding learning resources, and reasonably broaden the scope of learning according to their own situation within the limited time of teachers' guidance, so as to master the basic knowledge and application ability recognized by the industry, and continuously create professional image works, which should be a topic of more universal practical significance.

Teaching Management Should be Relatively Flexible. Under the background of the full implementation of online teaching, the teaching management of colleges and universities is easy to fall into the situation of simplification and mechanization, and the measures issued by the education management department are also easy to be across the board. However, from the professional point of view, all subjects and courses are different. The teaching management department should promote the diversification of teaching, encourage teachers to adopt various methods and forms of teaching behavior, and explore new ideas and methods of teaching reform on the premise of conforming to the form of online teaching [8]. For example, how to maintain a positive learning enthusiasm in class, how to use the camera reasonably, whether students can live their homework process online, and so on. Different stages and levels of image creation courses also need to adjust the teaching plan according to the actual situation, so as to really adapt to different courses. This is not only a test of teaching management in colleges and universities, but also a test of the educational quality and level of higher education practitioners.

The Psychological Impact of Online Teaching on Teachers. Teachers should adjust their teaching state and role change, from facing students to facing the screen, from the imparter of knowledge to the guider of knowledge [9]. Therefore, teachers should cultivate and improve their information literacy, master the basic knowledge of building an online teaching environment and other knowledge of using the Internet for professional learning; teachers should establish a classroom feedback mechanism suitable for online teaching of current courses, and pay attention to the learning effect of students at any time; teachers should also pay attention to the balance between working at home and family responsibilities. In particular, teachers should be prepared to deal with the unexpected situation in teaching at any time; teachers should also learn to calmly face the tricky questions raised by students who have roamed in the sea of the Internet. In addition, online teaching has lengthened the teaching front. Students may often discuss learning problems with teachers through the Internet, whether in or out of the course. Therefore, teachers' previous "nine to five" work rhythm may face great damage. Some teachers describe themselves as "walking on thin ice" during the online teaching for fear of making mistakes, which is obviously not conducive to the stability of education Online teaching puts forward new requirements for teachers' psychological construction.

The Psychological Impact of Online Teaching on Students. Different students face different problems. Students with poor self-control should learn to carry out online learning activities in the space of their own private life, abide by the classroom discipline of online teaching, and gradually cultivate good learning habits, instead of letting themselves go and learning in the environment of lack of supervision; students with poor independence should psychologically adapt to the great changes of learning environment and learning atmosphere in online teaching, Students need to deal with the preparation before class, classroom learning and homework independently; introverted students need to go through a period of adaptation to learn how to effectively communicate with the same group of students and teachers; students with weak learning initiative need to obtain learning resources under the guidance of teachers or with the help of students to learn from each other, step by step to cultivate the awareness and ability of autonomous learning. For those students with good learning habits and strong autonomous learning ability, the negative impact of online teaching is small.

4 Conclusion

Although online teaching is a helpless choice in an emergency situation, it is a beneficial attempt for the teaching of image creation courses. In the face of the deep application of the Internet and the exploration demand of the new teaching mode of MOOC platform in colleges and universities, the teachers who lead the online teaching of image creation courses, combined with the preliminary survey results and relying on the analysis of the teaching characteristics and teaching purpose of the course, formulate the teaching scheme in line with the actual situation, and adopted many measures, including fragmentation of teaching time, personalized teaching content, humanization of teaching requirements, etc., and successfully completed the teaching goal. In the whole process of online teaching, teachers always focus on ensuring the quality of online teaching, improving students' actual creative ability and improving students' work level, so as to minimize the negative impact of online teaching. The online teaching of short film production course will provide first-hand information for the follow-up online teaching of image creation courses and the construction of a new specialized courses information teaching system.

Acknowledgements. This research was supported by the Educational science research project of Beijing City University for program "Design enlightenment module - interactive animation" network course construction (project approval no. YJB20190735).

References

1. Yang, L.: Research on flipped classroom online teaching under the background of epidemic situation. Int. J. Educ. Econ. **3**(1), 44–47 (2020)
2. James, M.: Linton: teaching film making rather than film production. Learn. Media Technol. **3**(4), 105–110 (1977)
3. Glazier, R.A.: Making human connections in online teaching. PS: Polit. Sci. Polit. **54**(1), 175–176 (2021)
4. Guo, Z.: Exploration and practice of online scene teaching mode: taking the course of object-oriented programming as an example. Int. J. Soc. Sci. Univ. **3**(3), 142–144 (2020)
5. Schuth, H.W.: Techniques of teaching film production. J. Film Video, **21**(3), 85–87 (1969)
6. Crowe, R.D.: Classical storytelling and contemporary screenwriting: aristotle and the modern scriptwriter by brian price. J. Film Video **72**(1), 102–103 (2020)

7. Hao, J.: Online teaching in colleges and universities during the epidemic: issues and reflections. Int. J. Educ. Econ. **3**(3), 150–151 (2020)
8. Wong, J.: How will the pandemic change higher education? https://www.chronicle.com/article/How-Will-the-Pandemic-Change/248474. Accessed 21 Jan 2021
9. Morreale, S.P., Thorpe, J., Westwick, J.N.: Online teaching: challenge or opportunity for communication education scholars? Commun. Educ. **70**(1), 117–119 (2021)

Research on Practice and Teaching About Digital Media

Xiandong Cheng[1]([envelope]), Hao He[2], Ziyang Li[2], Yue Yin[1], and Shengqi Ba[3]

[1] Beijing City University, No. 269 Bei Si Huan Zhong Lu, Hai Dian District, Beijing, China
[2] Central Academy of Fine Arts, No. 8 Hua Jia Di Nan Street, Chao Yang District,
Beijing, China
[3] 314 Carshalton Road, Carshalton, England

Abstract. Nowadays, digital media has wide applications through technology and hardware that has greatly changed its professional practice and teaching in design subjects. Concepts and methodology in this area have shifted, which are influencing and interacting the design field with continuous development, therefore, arising the phenomenon of multi-directional combination in design. This change in the design field also affects on the current design education system. The barriers among subjects became indistinct whilst the design education system tends to be integrated among different subjects and professionals. Especially in digital media, this stimulates and encourages practice broadening its design process. The development of technology and design always closely associates itself with each other that the more advanced use of technology, the more sophisticated the design could be presented. Digital media design is one of the leading subjects, which benefits in technology advancement exposure. This influence of digital media design also arose the change of production relations and productive forces in design. No matter what the project is about, whether it's digital media design or other practical application of digital media, there are always new attempts for both designers and design educators. The attempts demonstrated in design process that are aiming to fasten communication speed broadens the application, thus the key message reaches out more effectively and more conveniently to its audience. This article is based on teaching experiences around digital media design, and combines the practical and teaching methods of architectural design, industrial design and experience design. It has been developed and summarized from the perspective of design project analysis, design-thinking expansion, design method research, design field combination and design tool practices. This will provide a more effective experience for design education and design practice.

Keywords: Digital media · Design practices · Design education

1 Research Background

1.1 The Digital Age

People are living in a new digital era. The continuous development and advancement of digital technology has led to the transformation and upgrading of traditional industries to digitalization. In the process of this transformation, people's

© Springer Nature Switzerland AG 2021
M. M. Soares et al. (Eds.): HCII 2021, LNCS 12779, pp. 523–532, 2021.
https://doi.org/10.1007/978-3-030-78221-4_35

life/entertainment/production/consumption etc. have quietly changed because of the influence of digitalization. Digital life/digital entertainment/digital production/digital economy, etc. They make up our daily life and digital information has changed the way people think and act. Digital technology is even evolving and improving, it is changing traditions with advanced technology and all industries are facing changes (Fig. 1).

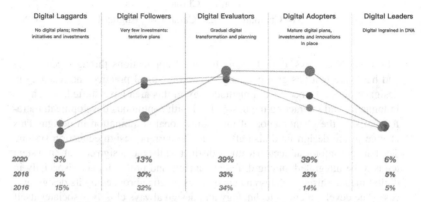

Fig. 1. Digital transformation index 2020 form: Dell technologies [1]

In the year 2020, digitalization is turning what was once an emergency technology into an everyday technology. Digital technology is becoming easier and more accurate to learn and use. So how to apply digital technology becomes a new topic for future development in every field.

1.2   Changes in Design

Design Changes with the Development of the Times

Design is for the public, good design is in line with the development of the times, the design is changing with the development of the times. Farming era/industrial era/information era/data era (intelligent era), the performance of each era is different, and the crossing of any era is not a natural transition. People know design from the industrial age, which proposed standardization/scaling/cost reduction, and design tends to point to a functional expression, or the sum of functions. In the information age, design tends to communicate and interact, product and user/user and user/product and product, and the information exchange between them. In the data era, design tends to be intelligent, design becomes more extensive, design services more precise, and designed products more lightweight (invisible).

Design's Own Properties

The design itself has the property of being "forward-looking"/"innovative". It is the property of design itself that determines that design is bound to change and update. Any design is initiated to improve or change the current situation. It is inevitable that it will change with the times and even lead the development of the field. The development of the times is itself dynamic, and it is essential to be influenced by the characteristics of the times. Changes in design also affect the transformation of design thinking/design methods/design tools. Design thinking becomes more and more open, it is no longer just to design things to look good, but more useful, and even make the usefulness become natural/invisible (users do not have to deliberately achieve the purpose of use), so that the design has life and emotion, etc.

The shift in design thinking has affected the design approach. Design methods are becoming more and more diverse and integrated, and will integrate many other areas to provide solutions. This synthesis is not an addition, it is a multiplication of changes. The design tools themselves are at the service of the designer, and for the traditional understanding of design expression (e.g. visual), it becomes more and more smart. Often, the change in design tools shifts the focus of design to design thinking and design methods.

2 The Relationship Between Digital Media and Design

2.1 The Design and Production of Digital Participation

The advancement of technology facilitates people to get better service. Digitization is an integral part of people's life, and whether you like it or not, its impact on our life will be greater in the future. After the application of the computer and Internet, the artificial intelligence has changed our life again. In terms of design and production, digitization has become the primary methods. Digital media is an important manifestation of digitization, which has changed the aspect of design and production, the application of digital technology to the aspect of design and production has become a major driving force for future development. Actually, the digital media has been involved in some processes of design and production, Taking the design of Zaha Hadid as an example, She used the data algorithms to obtain spatial structures and employed the digital 3D printing to get the architectural models as well as building materials. Zaha Hadid has explored the level of architectural form and extended her architectural experiments from abstract construction to the "new construction area". All of her design concepts seem to stem from the inherent tension in the site [2] (Fig. 2).

Sometimes, Zaha Hadid also plays this coordinate transformation game in other ways. For example, the "horizontal plane" will be reversed to form a vertical "wall".

This vertical horizontal dimension transformation has become the core architectural expression of Zaha Hadid. It not only makes the form concepts of folds/ramps/spirals to become the structural elements in the architecture, but also makes it a unique curve form element in this architecture. Through these visual elements, different elevations in the building can be smoothly transited. Indoor and outdoor can be gently transformed, and the relationship between building/base/and city can be harmoniously integrated [3]. The attempt of her design is groundbreaking, all of which can not be separated from the support of digitization (Fig. 3).

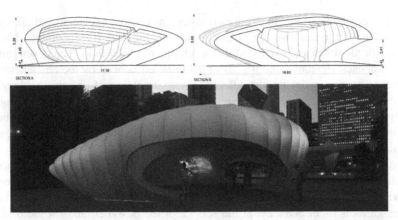

Fig. 2. Burnham Pavillion (Design by Zaha Hadid Architects) From: www.zaha-hadid.com

Fig. 3. The production line of Tesla in Shanghai from: www.jiqizhixin.com

An important symbol of the digital production is Tesla factory, which is of great cross era significance. Tesla automobile has overturned users' understanding of cars and travel, and the Tesla factory has subverted the traditional production. 47 robots scanned the assembly line in the body of Model 3 from 1,900 locations, so as to make sure the moderate design specification and keep the error within 0.15 mm [4].

In the era of industrial automation, digital intelligent operation in the manufacturing process will bring great efficiency to the whole process of production. As early as 1913, Ford has changed the manufacturing process by splitting the assembly process into 84 distinct steps, so that cars can be assembled on a single conveyor belt. This has revolutionized the manufacturing industry, cutting the assembly time of a car from 12 h to 90 min [4]. A hundred years later, Tesla American factory has tried to carry out digital automatic manufacturing after the production of Model 3, which levered the unlimited potential of automobile manufacturing once again. The methods of neural network and fuzzy control are applied to product formulation and the production scheduling, which is helpful to realize the intellectualization of manufacturing process.

2.2 The Diversified Representation of Digital Media

As an important representation of digitization, the digital media has been widely used in design. Its performance is very diverse, with rich and excellent performance in the aspect of mass entertainment/life application/and business operation. What has been realized about digital media by the public is more presented on the technical level. People are unlikely to think about the links other than the technology, but only regard it as a technical tool and presentation way. Therefore, the presentation of many digital media is only the integration of text/image/sound and pictures, which is not equal to the whole digital media. Therefore, the presentation of many digital media is only the integration of text/image/sound and pictures, which is not equal to the whole digital media.

Of course, digital media itself can also be applied to the modern art creation. The text/image/sound and other contents can be integrated through the digital media technology, so as to create objects that are easy to understand and describe. It is closely related to the design of visual art/human-computer interface/computer graphics/information communication/multimedia/Internet/digital animation/advertisement and game/virtual scene/virtual product. This unique process of digital art creation has affected the transformation of modern design from the spiritual level to humanistic care.

3 The Design of Teaching Practice

3.1 The Understanding of Modern Design and Design Teaching

The design practice and design education ought to change with the digital age, the design methods and criteria have been revised. The traditional understanding of design is the foundation of design, which divides the design into different majors at present, It is challenging to define a design project as a specialty now. In many cases, couples of professional synthesis is demanded to complete the analysis of a design problem. The opening of the design profession means that the design becomes more and more extended. Also, the boundaries between professions are becoming increasingly blurred.

In this way, as for the original design practice and design teaching, what level can the modern design truly involve in?

Introduce the design thinking into users' experience/strategy as well as more complex systems, We should break through the traditional single design itself and make the design change into a comprehensive solution, this solution is a complete information exchange cycle with the possibility of sustainability and superior development. The core of digital innovation is the design, however, the challenge is to gain insight into the users and to achieve a broader, cross-domain collaboration, That is our understanding of design.

We ought to make design understand people, rather than forcing people to understand the design. One of the fundamental principles of digital product design is UCD (User Centered Design). The opposite concept is the traditional product service centered design, this shift is a striking sign of the digital age. This is to say, the service mode has shifted from the "PC" mode where users need to find services in the past, to a "mobile" model, where the services are able to follow users wherever they go. At a word, the design has moved from a single mode of rest to a comprehensive mode of motion. The design teaching will also change accordingly, as the progress is able to be made by trying something new (Fig. 4).

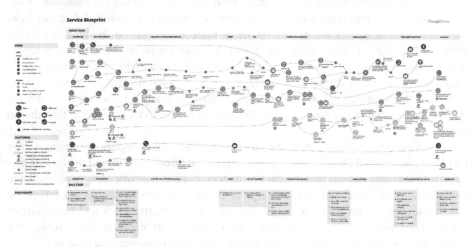

Fig. 4. ThoughtWorks uses a more contextual service blueprint to analyze the service design for a couple of specific users. From: insights.thoughtworks.cn

3.2   Design Practice

These are three examples of student works in our design teaching, three of which are very experimental works (Fig. 5 and Fig. 6).

This is a very conceptual design work. The work combines medical/Fractal Theory/interaction design/3D printing technology, by collecting the data from the patients with heart disease, the work adopts the Fractal Theory to calculate the data model. And then, get the physical object by the 3D printing of the model, this attempt is the process of materializing the information data and physically rendering the virtual data. APP is designed in the work to manage patients' information and data. This digital model makes the complex medical information easier to understand (Fig. 7).

It is also an attempt at the wearable design. It looks like a piece of jewelry or the tech hardware, it is actually a wearable device designed to treat procrastination, which can be called as "Stop Procrastination". The way to stop procrastination here is achieved via the five senses. For example, the pungent and harmless temperature will make people fidgety, the sound of metal rubbing glass is likely to make people unable to sleep at ease, all of these incentives will contribute to an end to current behavior. Using Arduino as the basis for a hardware prototype is full of creation. In addition, different sensors cooperate with APP to achieve the interaction (Fig. 8).

Fig. 5. 3D printing model (Design by Peihong Wang)

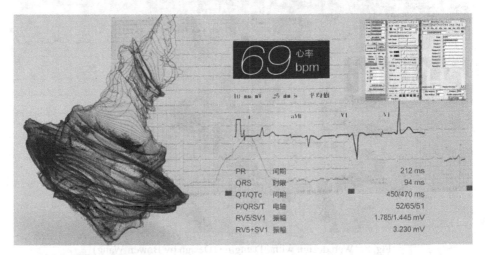

Fig. 6. ECG/fractal graphics & models (Design by Peihong Wang)

This is the design of a website. The website features the use of 3D engine, transform the original 2D vision of the website into an interactive real-time 3D social space, this is not only different from other website design, but also a new attempt of designing a website.

What have been mentioned above is a few of our attempts in design teaching practice. Although many of them are only experimental works, they still have the value to some extent. And in the course of this process, it is not just a combination of the knowledge about the design disciplines. In many cases, it is the concept and approach of the service design that truly helps students find problems, the digital media is a mean or a form of

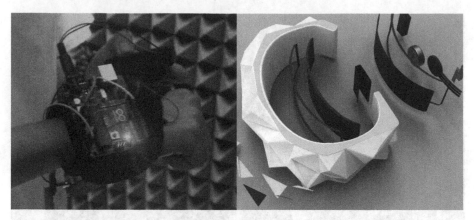

Fig. 7. Prototype design with arduino (Design by Shuyang Li)

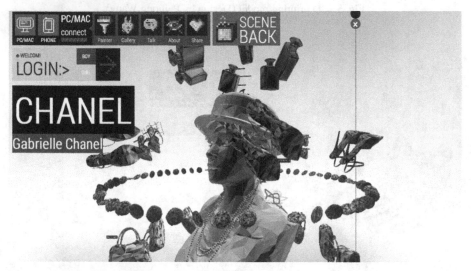

Fig. 8. Web design with 3D engine (Design by Bowen Wang)

problem-solving, the relationship among the design disciplines is complementary, at the same time, the whole design behavior ought to satisfy the setting of the subject content.

3.3 Design Principle Changes

The digital media technology brings more possibilities to design, which requires the upgrade of the design teaching. For example: the layout and characters can be presented through VR technology, which provides the important elements of the information when the users apply and experience. It is like the layout in the 2D screen within the clearly readable targets. But the layout and characters in the 3D scene under AR technology will bring greater impact on texts and overall user experience. When holographic characters are designed, 3D typeface of three-dimensional modeling may be more likely to be created; however, actually this kind of typeface will reduce the readability of texts.

2D texts within higher readability should be utilized in most cases except a few sences (such as logans, logo and so on) where 3D characters are applied; however, 3D technology is widely applied in advanced equipments and interactive applications, thus design education need search for design principles which are suitable for 3D.

The layout in Mixed Reality Technology. The text need to be clear and easy to read. The text can be on wall or superimposed on physical objects, floating together with UI.

Creation of Clear Hierarchical Structures
To improve the efficiency of conveying information, we need construct contrast and structure by using different types and weight.

Limitation of the Fonts
Use more than 2 fonts otherwise the harmony and consistency of the users experience will be destroyed, which makes it more difficult to obtain information.

Avoiding Thin Fonts
Avoid light colour or light dark colors in the size below 42pt, because slim and vertical strokes vibrates within the changes of the interface, which reduces readability. The effect will be better if modern fonts within enough line space and thickness are applied. For example, Helvetica and Arial are quite clear in normal or bold Hololens font (Fig. 9).

Fig. 9. Color contrast

Color
Emphasis the contrast between the color of the text and the interface, use dark texts in contrast to the bright background. The black is presented as transparent in color appearance system, which means users cannot see the black texts without colored background (Fig. 10).

Fig. 10. 2 m is the best distance for the users with HoloLens.

Recommended Fonts' Size

The mixed reality technology is related with 3 dimensional depth, the distance between fonts and users is need. 2 m is the best distance for the users. Generally speaking, the size of the fonts we used on PC or iPad is normally 12–32pt, however to present the fonts without dim edge in holographic environment, the recommended smallest size of the fonts from a distance of 2 m is 30 pt, which we can apply as the standard for checking the optimum size of the fonts.

Those principles are concluded from usage scenarios/software development/standards of hardware/visual design, which are different from traditional layout design.

4 Summary

The traditional design is linear, which means that you can see the head at a glance, the modern design is diverse and complex with a logical structure, rather than the chaotic system. The core of digital innovation is the design, however, the challenge is to gain insight into the users and to achieve a broader, cross-domain collaboration.

Digitalization has played a critical role and imaged many kinds of industries in 2020, taking the role of digital design to a full play is demanded for the modern design, more digital media involvement in the design is also demanded. In terms of the design, the designers should be more open-minded, apply the technology of digital media in a reasonable way. The above content is the summary of this paper. The author is willing to share and communicate with more professionals.

References

1. Dell Technologies, Digital transformation index 2020, ED (2020). https://www.delltechnolo gies.com/en-us
2. Xiao, R.: Design in digital innovation, EB, China 15 March 2018
3. Parametric design-Zaha Hadid's design ideas, EB, China 01 April 2016. https://www.zoscape. com/article-432-1.html
4. The production line of Tesla in Shanghai, EB, China 01 April 2020. https://www.jiqizhixin. com/articles/2020-04-

Experience Design Teaching Courses Linking US and China in the Context of the Covid-19 Epidemic: A Dual-End-Tutor Online and Offline Blended Teaching Case Study

Zhen Liu[1] , Guizhong Han[1]([✉]), Xiaozi Wang[1], and Donald William Carr[2]

[1] School of Design, South China University of Technology,
Guangzhou 510006, People's Republic of China
[2] School of Design, College of Visual and Performing Arts,
Syracuse University, Syracuse, NY 13244-1180, USA

Abstract. The Covid-19 epidemic promotes the rapid development of online education. Experience design course is a course that combines theory with practice. However, the efficiency of knowledge transfer is very low for simple online education. The course is set up to study whether the teaching method of a dual-end-tutor online and offline blended teaching can improve the learning effect of students in terms of across-time-zones situation. Through the course case study on the stage results and final results of the whole course, it is found that compared with the traditional online or offline teaching methods, the online and offline dual-end-tutor blended teaching method makes great improvement on students' satisfaction, knowledge mastery and result output. Therefore, in the post-epidemic era, the online and offline dual-end-tutor blended teaching method will become an important and efficient design method for user experience courses and other courses in the future.

Keywords: Covid-19 · Online course · Experience design · Dual end tutor · Blended teaching · Case study

1 Background

1.1 The Current Situation of the Covid-19 and Online Education

The Covid-19 epidemic suddenly broke out at the beginning of 2020, and people's production and living activities were forced to stop. Education, as a very important part of the functioning of society, has not been spared. Under such circumstances, everyone is seeking new teaching methods to solve students' learning problems at home. As a result, large-scale online teaching is being carried out nationwide. As an important part of Chinese education, higher education has also joined the wave of online teaching. In the development of online education in recent years, people are actively exploring various online teaching methods, such as MOOC (Massive Open Online Course) and Flipped class.

© Springer Nature Switzerland AG 2021
M. M. Soares et al. (Eds.): HCII 2021, LNCS 12779, pp. 533–543, 2021.
https://doi.org/10.1007/978-3-030-78221-4_36

MOOC is Massive Open Online Course. This mode is mainly based on classroom videos of famous schools as the way to obtain content, and put the videos, courseware and reference materials on the internet for everyone to learn [1]. The original purpose of MOOCs was to open up education and provide free higher education to as many students as possible [2].

According to the educational goal theory of Benjamin Sameul Bloon, a famous American educational psychologist, although MOOC model integrates high-quality educational resources, in terms of the realization of educational goals, MOOCs are intelligent in both knowledge and understanding, and cannot guarantee the real effect of learning. In order to solve the problems, Jonbergmann and Aaron Sams proposed the flipped classroom teaching model theory letting the students prepare the knowledge before class and then participate in the class discussion [2].

The current online education is based on online education campus that is mainly based on continuing education and in-service education, and have not had a significant impact on the teaching paradigm of university students. Since entering the internet era, great changes have taken place in the management of colleges and universities, including finance, student status, enrollment, and employment, which basically realizes the digitization and computerization of management. In comparison, the progress of educational technology in the field of teaching is relatively slow [3].

At the beginning of year 2020, students in various colleges and universities are in the winter vacation, and the sudden outbreak of the epidemic makes it impossible for students at home to go back to school, and the following courses cannot be conducted offline. In order to actively respond to the call of "Suspending Classes Without Stopping Learning", colleges and universities have launched online course education. Driven by the epidemic, online education for the students in higher education in China has made considerable progress.

1.2 Present Situation and Problems of Experience Design and Experience Design Teaching

It is generally believed that user experience is a concept put forward by Donald Norman at the end of the 20th century. With the development of science and technology, user experience also has new connotations. Norman pointed out that a successful user experience must first meet the needs of customers without harassing or annoying users. Secondly, the products provided should be concise and elegant, so that customers can use them happily and enjoy them [4].

Science and technology have brought people more product choices, and functionally satisfying products can no longer meet people's needs. Experience economy pursues the satisfaction of users' positive self-feeling and attaches importance to users' self-experience in the process of consumption. Its main characteristics are sensory, individualization and participation. The rise of experience economy makes the education of user experience design more important.

The demand for talents in the user experience industry is growing rapidly. How to systematically and effectively cultivate talents in the user experience industry has gradually become a topic and challenge for the development of the user experience industry [5].

With the increasing demand for user experience design, on the one hand, colleges and universities have gradually increased user experience courses. At present, the main mode of user experience courses is that students passively accept the service design theoretical knowledge taught by teachers and memorize it. This "passive following" learning lacks consciousness [6]. On the other hand, an good understanding of user-centered design requires a general understanding of detailed methodologies and associations, and an in-depth knowledge of a field. This kind of knowledge can not be fully mastered only by courses and books [7]. It needs to be experienced and exercised through practical projects. However, most of the current experience design is in the school, leaving the experience design part out of people's actual needs.

1.3 Course Significance

In response to the above problems, Advanced Experience Design course was opened, which adopts a teaching method of online and offline mixed and dual-teacher blended teaching.

Before learning this course of design experience, most students had not learned user experience systematically, and their previous study was only about design psychology, design methodology and other design courses. Therefore, offering this advanced design course can help students build and improve their knowledge system of user experience, and learn how to conduct user-centered user experience design.

As a graduate level class in Experience Design, the goal is to introduce students to the various elements such as complexity to specialization within design. While these challenges push tutors and students to create further definitions of roles, they have also brought everyone to point where students look to envision and then design multi-sensory experiences. As a student in experience design, they will be tasked with revisiting 'the ordinary' or 'the commonplace' so as to view these moments as opportunities for redefinition and redesign. Therefore, the class consisted of a combination of lectures, in-class discussions, team-based workshops, presentations, and critique. In the spirit of Design Thinking, emphasis was placed on the exploration of multiple solutions that would be taken to a low to medium level of fidelity in order to cover as many ideas as possible.

In the post-epidemic era, communication between different places has become difficult, and online user design experience courses have only inefficient knowledge input, and students are separated from users when designing. This advanced experience design course, which adopted the blended teaching method of online and offline dual-end tutors, aims to analyze whether such teaching method can improve students' knowledge acceptance efficiency and complete design projects with high quality through the whole course process and results.

2 Method

From November 16, 2020 to January 10, 2021, the overseas tutor of design at Syracuse University, USA, was invited by the School of Design to conduct a joint online class with Chinese tutors on the English course Advanced Experience Design for the 2020 graduate class. This course was divided into two parts, the first part was taught by Chinese tutor alone, and the second part was blended teaching by Chinese tutor and overseas tutor. After the course was over, the course case study would be conducted on the whole process of this course.

2.1 Offline Teaching Alone

Course 1–3 Offline Experience Course Knowledge Explanation. The course was taught in offline classrooms by Chinese instructors. The main content of the course was the design process led by the double diamond model, some design methods to be used in the design process, and some problems that need to be paid attention to in the use of design tools.

2.2 Blended Online and Offline Dual-End-Tutor Teaching

Due to the epidemic, overseas tutors were teaching online, while Chinese tutor was responsible for offline teaching. This part mainly focused on the practice of the theory. Firstly, some design methods were applied in practice, and then a user experience design project was completed.

Class 4 Introduced the Lesson Plan, Described the Definition and Case Study of User Experience, and Discussed in Groups. The overseas tutor first introduced the course plan and arrangement, and then explained the definition and composition of user experience design to the students through PPT. First, the overseas tutor let the students recall the most memorable things, then tell the group members, and finally the student in the group retold it to everyone, so that everyone has a deeper understanding of the user experience in life. The course assignment was to do an observation assignment in a group of three, which was to choose a place in Guangzhou to record people's voice, space and movement. Observing people and things in real life, so that students can discover and experience the actual pain points and needs, and got the design opportunity points through in-depth observation of real life, which helps students with maintaining empathy to feel the event, and recorded the event, the place, the crowd, and what they hear, see and think.

Class 5 Students Report Survey Results. The students chose a variety of places to observe according to their interests, such as the court, the pier, the department store, etc. The students reported their findings in each scenario, and the two tutors discussed with each student to find out the potential design points, so as to enhance the students' understanding of empathy and enhance their sensitivity to grasp the opportunity points.

Class 6 How Traditional Design Transforms to Experience Design and The Impact of Technology and Policies on Experience Design. Modern industrial design pays more attention to the user experience, because a good user experience will enhance the user's stickiness, and a good reputation will increase the number of users. Virtual Reality (VR), Augmented Reality (AR), holographic projection and other new technologies expand the use of traditional industrial products, making people's life more intelligent and convenient. At the same time, attention should be paid to the change and issuance of new local policies, which will also lead to new demands of people, thus generating new design points. Later, the students also expressed their views on the impact of new technology on our lives.

Class 7 Find Innovative Points of Experience Design From Traditional Stories or Traditional Culture. Traditional culture has many things that people can learn from. For example, we can get inspiration from traditional culture or apply good ideas to traditional culture so as to generate new inventions or experiences. After that, the students also expounded their views on the innovation and opportunity points of design in traditional culture.

Class 8 Demonstrate the Application of New Technologies such as Virtual Reality and Holographic Projection in Experience Design. The overseas tutor invited designers from Quantum Corporation to talk about the practical application of virtual reality and holographic projection technology in products. For example, by combining holographic projection technology with tableware, customers can interact with the environment instead of being bored when waiting for a meal. This immersive design enables customers to have a better dining experience.

Class 9–10 Re-observed Life Scenarios and Determined the Topic of Experience Design. After the previous study, the students have a deeper understanding of user experience design and more ideas. The instructor asked the students to re-select the observation location, looked for pain points and opportunities, and finally presented it in a story board. Many students had chosen a different location from the first observation, and they had gained new results. The two tutors made suggestions based on the observations of the students, and provided references for the subsequent prototype design.

Class 11–12 Discussion of the Functional Architecture and Initial Prototype of the Project. According to the observation conclusions and the suggestions of the tutors, the students summed up the pain points of users and the opportunity points of design, and gave a preliminary demonstration of the solution. Finally, tutors discussed the design scheme with the students, and put forward some suggestions for improvement.

Class 13 Final Course Presentation. Through the joint efforts of students and tutors, students reported the final project results online. All students had a complete project output. The two tutors made serious comments on the students' projects, praised the students' progress, and also pointed out the shortcomings of the projects.

3 Result

A total of nine students participated in this course. In the early research stage, they were divided into three groups to assist their own research. Finally, nine completed solutions were submitted in the form of personal assignments. The content covers the programmatic rationale and final results presentation.

3.1 Stage Result

In the topic selection stage, students chose a place to observe according to the requirements, and brought themselves into the same environment and perspective as the observation object, and truly felt the feelings of the target group in the current environment. Then students drew the storyboard and empathy map according to their observation and feelings, and visualized the observation content. In addition, students chose different design tools according to the topic, using the service blueprint, HMW analysis method, user journey map and the establishment of persona for objective analysis, from which to excavate the opportunity point of design and explore the real needs of users, as shown in Fig. 1.

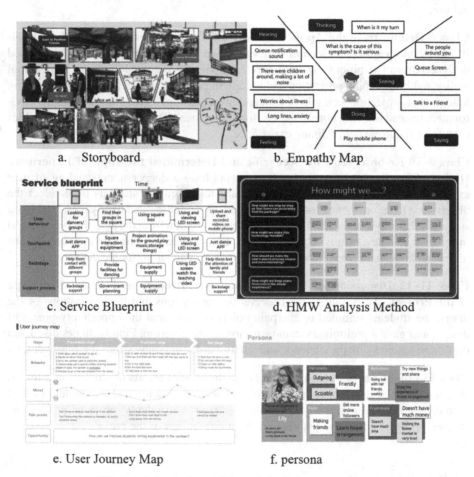

Fig. 1. Design tools used by students in the research stage

3.2 Final Result

According to the survey results, students selected different forms of achievement presentation, covering the product, software and combination of hardware and software.

They also used AR, IOT and other technologies to show new forms of experience in nine future scenarios for different spaces, such as commercial areas, hospitals, entertainment places and public spaces, as shown in Fig. 2.

Fig. 2. Final outcome program of student courses

These programs focus on issues that are very close to people's everyday lives, revisiting what people have taken for granted and identifying opportunities for new experiences.

3.3 Students' Feedback

After the class completion, a satisfaction survey questionnaire was issued to understand the students' satisfaction with this blended teaching. The full score is 5 points (1 = very dissatisfied, 5 = very satisfied). Students were asked to rate this class. The data is shown in Fig. 3. It can be seen that the students are relatively satisfied with this student-oriented online Blended Teaching form, and the score is not less than 4 points.

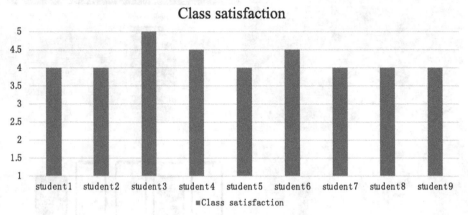

Fig. 3. Students class satisfaction

Table 1. Student feedback interview content

Feedback object	Example
For classroom forms	1. I like this teaching format very much; It is novel and interesting. I feel that I am acquiring knowledge through communication and learning to apply knowledge 2. Instead of judging our solutions with a set of standard answers, the teacher brings our perspective and helps us find information that has been overlooked. This makes me understand the people-centered core of experience design better 3. The difference with the past design professional course is quite relatively obvious, I feel the teacher is guiding me, rather than teaching me 4. Network latency has some impact. I can not timely de-termine whether the teacher is not satisfied with my answers. Without timely feedback, it is easy to doubt myself
For classroom content	1. There will be some confusion. Because of language problems, it is not very accurate to understand the task requirements 2. We will be asked to do more field research rather than desktop research, which is different from the teaching requirements experienced in the past. Prefer this requirement

In addition, students' thoughts and feelings were interviewed, as shown in after sorting (Table 1). The students' impressions of this online experience design course focused on the class form and class content. First of all, everyone feels that this form is very novel and that in the process of communicating around practical issues, they have a higher grasp of knowledge. The students all believe that language and network delay are the biggest factors affecting their learning during class.

4 Discussion

The Covid-19 epidemic has brought a wave of online education. Online education faces numerous opportunities and challenges. This online experience design course is designed for graduate students. The course includes only nine students, and a total of two tutors teach together, using Zoom software. The entire classroom is based on two-way communication rather than one-way output of knowledge by teachers.

In the traditional offline education mode, postgraduate education is dominated by self-study, and teachers play a guiding role. In this case, students first participated in offline theoretical knowledge learning before accepting online blended teaching. In this stage, the traditional teaching mode was generally followed, that is, teachers transferred knowledge in one direction. However, the difference is that teachers did not tell students all the content in detail, but told students the general framework of experience design-related knowledge, and provided curriculum outline to enable students to understand the purpose and goals of this course, and guided students to fill the framework through autonomous learning. In the subsequent research process, students selected the appropriate design tools to solve the problem according to the actual needs, and completed the understanding, application and analysis of the three levels in the understanding level, laying a good foundation for the fourth step of creating level. Research shows that this flipped classroom model based on understanding can better stimulate students' autonomous learning motivation and learning potential [8]. If all knowledge is instilled into students according to the traditional teaching mode, and they are allowed to follow the "completion" plan of the design process with the use of design tools, there is a high probability that it will not be the real needs of users. Students are also easy to fall into fixed thinking in such a mechanical design process, and it is difficult to make a truly human-centered design. Only by allowing them to observe personally in the actual scenes where users are frequently active, look at problems from the perspective of users, choose appropriate methods based on actual problems, and solve problems through their own understanding can they truly understand the meaning of experience design. At the same time, it can gradually cultivate empathy and sensitivity to insight into opportunities.

Campbell believes that for higher education, online learning focuses on the development of metacognitive, reflective and collaborative learning [9]. In the process of self-learning, students will maximize the learning effect and improve their ability most efficiently. Subject to time and space, students could communicate with professors through video only at a fixed time per week. Therefore, students must be fully prepared to consider what form they can use effectively and completely to convey the content of the program so that teachers can fully understand and give suggestions for improvement. The problems arising from this process are outside the curriculum outline, and students need to think independently to seek solutions. It is also an additional experience design training: students need to stand in the teacher's point of view to think about the best presentation of the program. Such transpositional thinking can stimulate students' empathy and also exercise students' expression ability. As a designer, empathy and expression are very important abilities.

In fact, in the process of class, the teachers did not stick to the fixed mode planned in the outline, but made adjustments according to the actual situation. The professional knowledge was transmitted to the students by the teachers according to specific problems in the process of communication and discussion between teachers and students. The study of Huang et al. [10] has also proved that online education needs to follow the "flexible teaching" and adjust the teaching mode according to the specific situation. However, it remains unchanged that the learning task should be clarified in the teaching process, and students should be encouraged to think independently based on their timely feedback, so as to promote the development of analytical thinking. This is also the point where online live education is better than MOOC education. MOOC education is still flawed in terms of interactivity. The focus of experience design education is not on content, but on practical experience. Teachers need to make different guidance according to different situations faced by each student, and timely communication is very important in this process.

There are still some shortcomings in this study. First, the number of observation samples and experiments is relatively small, and the second is that the education cost is not considered. Although the effect of this online cooperative education is remarkable, this method requires two professors to instruct online at the same time. Compared with the MOOC format, it is not suitable for large-scale promotion. Secondly, the students' language level has a certain impact on the course effect. There are also network delays and lags that are unavoidable in online education, resulting in poor communication.

5   Conclusion

This paper demonstrates the online and offline dual-end-tutor blended teaching method will become an important and efficient design method for user experience courses and other courses in the future, and highlights that 1) early and centralized theoretical input can improve students' online course efficiency; 2) blended teaching is applicable to the small-class education of postgraduates; and 3) online education should be interesting and increase interaction with students rather than simply passively listening to classes.

With the help of the network, online education enables students to easily obtain broader learning resources and more convenient way of homework display, but compared with offline education, it lacks certain interaction. Experience design education needs to maintain sufficient communication and interaction between teachers and students. Therefore, in the context of online education gradually becoming the mainstream of the epidemic, it is necessary to find a suitable way of online experience design education.

In the future, the focus of experience design education will be to emphasize the cultivation of empathy, the improvement of students' expression ability and the visualization of expression ways.

Acknowledgements. The authors wish to thank all the people who provided their time and efforts for the investigation and the **Advanced Experience Design** course, who are Peixuan Li, Changjin Li, Qi Liu, Xinqi Huang, Dan Huang, Tzu-hui Wu, and Feicai Wang. This research was supported by Guangdong Provincial Department of Science and Technology 2019-2020 "Overseas Famous Teacher" Project, and South China University of Technology Central University Basic Scientific Research and Operating Funds Project (Social Science), grant number XYZD201928.

References

1. Pan, X., Zhang, Y., Mao, M., Cui, H.: Research of online education industrial development status & product design. Sci. Technol. Ind. **13**(8), 13–16 (2013)
2. Yuan, L., Stephen, P., Ma, H.: Analysis of massive open online courses initiatives. Open Educ. Res. **19**(03), 56–62 + 84 (2013)
3. Wu, D.: The retrospect and reflection of educational technology evolution: online teaching in universities under the epidemic situation. Chin. High. Educ. Res. **04**, 1–6 + 11 (2020)
4. Ding, Y., Guo, F., Hu, M., Sun, F.: A review of user experience. Ind. Eng. Manag. **19**(04), 92–97 + 114 (2014)
5. Yang, Z., Yuan, X., Liu, Y.: An overview of the development of user experience in China. Chin. Q. **06**, 98–103 (2020)
6. Yang, M., Wang, J., Zhang, Y.: Research on teaching reform of user experience design course for industrial design specialty. Design **23**, 82–83 (2017)
7. Pan, R.: Core competence and effective educational methodologies for user experience design. Design **09**, 34–36 (2015)
8. Chen, M., Chen, S.: The class design of the flipped classroom and its implementation based on understanding. J. High. Educ. **35**(12), 63–67 (2014)
9. Keengwe, J., Kidd, T.T.: Towards best practices in online learning and teaching in higher education. MERLOT J. Online Learn. Teach. **6**(2), 533–541 (2010)
10. Huang, H., Zhang, M., Shen, Y.: Research on the core elements of running a huge scale of cyber-learning: a case study of "disrupted class, undisrupted learning" supported effectively by online education. E-education Res. **41**(3), 10–19 (2020)

Teaching Practice in the "Empathy Design Thinking" Course for Elementary School Students Grounded in Project-Based Learning

Yaru Lyu, Xiaohan Wang, Bowen Zhang, You Wang, Ming Jiang, Qi Zhang, Yiwen Zhang, and Wei Liu[✉]

Faculty of Psychology, Beijing Normal University, Beijing 100875, People's Republic of China
{yaru.lyu,wei.liu}@bnu.edu.cn, {xiaohan.wang,bowen.zhang,
202028061040,202028061014,202028061058,
202028061060}@mail.bnu.edu.cn

Abstract. This study takes the innovative education course titled "Empathy Design Thinking" developed by the User Experience Research Center of Beijing Normal University for elementary school students as an example and introduces the three major teaching processes of the course: theme exploration, design expression and prototype production. The study also examines the course theme built through the context of a "smart home", analyzes the whole process of the course using project-based teaching, shows the innovative solution design cases produced through the teamwork of four groups of students, and provides a reference for the teaching application of innovative education courses by combining the lecturers' reflections on the teaching practices in this study.

Keywords: Project-Based learning · Innovative education · Teaching practice

1 Introduction

Innovation is about breaking the mold, changing the way one thinks, and doing things in different ways. Innovation requires people to be unrestrained by traditional thinking modes, to be good at thinking, and to be bold in making breakthroughs. Building an innovative country requires innovative talent, and the cultivation of creative skills occurs through innovative education. When creativity is the core factor in talent competition, a greater number of schools and parents will focus on cultivating students' creativity. Currently, innovative education from the earliest stages of education has become a meaningful way to develop creative talent.

The "Empathy Design Thinking" course is an innovative curriculum developed specifically for Chinese elementary school students that combines the strengths of the discipline of psychology at Beijing Normal University with an interdisciplinary talent development curriculum [1–5]. Combining design, computational, and engineering thinking, innovative research methods and visual teaching toolkits are used to train students to engage in project-based learning with teamwork, using students' core attainments as a guide. This study also uses the curriculum to explore the teaching practices of project-based teaching and learning in elementary school innovation education courses.

M. M. Soares et al. (Eds.): HCII 2021, LNCS 12779, pp. 544–555, 2021.
https://doi.org/10.1007/978-3-030-78221-4_37

2   Related Work

For an individual, a nation, and even humankind to survive and progress, innovation and evolution are essential [6]. Innovation is like mutation, the biological process that keeps species evolving so they can better compete for survival [7]. To meet the challenges in the era of the knowledge economy, innovative education, the process of implementing quality education in a comprehensive way, is necessary.

As a forward-looking and innovative approach, design thinking focuses on developing and cultivating a problem-oriented mindset [8–11]. There are an increasing number of people and institutions that have experienced the creative power of design thinking [10]. The design thinking model proposed by Stanford University has been widely applied in the field of education [12, 13]. The classic design thinking model consists of five main stages: empathy, definition, ideal, prototyping, and testing [14]. This model has had a profound impact on design thinking education in the K-12 field. Among the main stages, empathy is defined as an ability that enables us to comprehend the circumstances that others are in and the perspectives taken by others, both imaginatively and effectively [15]. Design theorists and practitioners describe empathy as a crucial influencing factor in design thinking [16]. The ability to make this human connection in a meaningful way is called user-centered design, and a key component of user-centered design is empathy. The course is not intended to make students designers who develop various practical products. Instead, it aims to enable students to develop the ability to understand others and think from the perspective of others throughout the learning process.

It focuses on studying and solving the problem of cultivating pupils' creative consciousness, innovative thinking, and creative ability in basic education. Project-based learning is an inquiry activity based on the real world that requires students to solve problems and present their project results. It can help innovative education courses clarify background setting and objectives of the curriculum and help students experience learning in the real world.

Project-based learning (PBL) is a dynamic classroom approach in which students actively explore real-world problems and challenges and acquire deeper knowledge. To enable teachers to better grasp the design and implementation of projects, many experts and scholars have summarized and generalized the standards of practice for project-based learning. Among them, the Buck Institute for Education (BIE) has published a "6A" reference framework for project-based learning design in its "Handbook of Project-Based Learning": authenticity, academic rigor, applied learning, active exploration, adult connections, and assessment practices [17]. The framework provides a more detailed list of specific issues to consider in program design and is highly actionable for frontline teachers. This is a relatively comprehensive set of project-based learning design elements that has been widely used in U.S. schools, and thousands of teachers have used it to assess and improve their teaching.

The primary purpose of PBL is to create effective learning opportunities so that learners can collaborate to solve problems and create a final product. In project-based learning, tasks are assigned to students, and they create teams for group work [18]. The tasks can involve an investigation or research on a specific issue. Students collaborate with each other to support their collective learning. Students try to apply critical thinking principals by asking and refining questions, debating ideas, making predictions, collecting and analyzing data, drawing conclusions, and communicating their findings to others. PBL is a powerful teaching strategy that enhances student motivation and promotes self-directed learning.

3   Setting

In the "Empathy Design Thinking" course, the teacher creates a problem situation and asks thematic questions before class so that students can bring their questions to study videos, courseware, and other related resources. In the classroom, students work in groups to collect information, divide the work, and discuss their findings. Each group proposes its solution to the problem and creates a group presentation slide and product prototype. Throughout the teaching process, teachers help solve various problems the students encounter in the learning process and lead students back to the topic problem. This allows students to solve the issues, acquire knowledge, and improve the overall quality of their learning, thinking, and cooperation abilities.

3.1   Empathy Design Thinking Course

Developed based on years of teaching practice, the "Empathy Design Thinking" innovation education course is divided into three stages: theme exploration, design expression and prototype production. It integrates the cultivation of innovation ability into the process of "discovering-analyzing-solving" problems (Fig. 1).

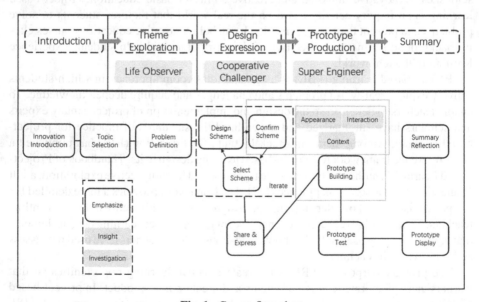

Fig. 1. Course flow chart

The first stage is the theme exploration stage. Students at the elementary level have a rich interest in exploring things but lack developed thinking paths and need to develop empathy and improve their insight. This stage requires students to put themselves in the perspective of the main character, learn about the background of the project, combine their personal life experiences to understand the feelings and behaviors of the main character, and then analyze and enrich the character's image. This helps students analyze the situation of the story from multiple perspectives, the needs and pain points of the main character, the opportunities for improvement, and other factors. At the end of this stage, students can define the most important problem that the main character needs to solve in the situation.

The second stage is the design expression stage. In traditional classrooms, individual presentations are more common, and there are fewer opportunities for teamwork. There is a need to enhance communication and interaction among students to solve problems creatively. Based on the key issues to be solved in the previous stage, students collaborate in groups to complete the task and help the main character conceive of a solution. In the process, students develop the ability to work together and communicate as a team and experience the joy of unity and cooperation.

The third stage is the prototype production stage. This phase requires students to think logically and practically and apply their thinking to real-life problems. Students will use different tools to visualize each group's creative solution, create a prototype and iterations, and share the final result. The course uses students' life experience and existing knowledge from familiar life situations and things that interest them, thus giving full play to students' self-motivation and allowing them to learn by doing.

Each stage of the course process is interlinked. Students will experience continuous divergence and convergence of thinking and obtain logical and practical outputs for the subsequent process, helping students enhance their sense of task immersion and gradually realize the transformation from thinking to practical outputs.

3.2 Mentor and Students

The teaching team included 2 mentors and 6 course assistants. The members of the team had extensive course experience and interdisciplinary backgrounds in electronic information science, industrial design, preschool education, art design, photoelectric information engineering, etc. There were 22 primary school students aged 6–11, including 13 boys and 8 girls. Mixed-age teaching was adopted in the course. Students were randomly divided into 4 groups. Each group was assisted by a teaching assistant teacher, with a teacher-student ratio of 1:3 (Fig. 2).

3.3 Project Theme

The theme of the semester's course project was "smart home", which required each group of students to produce a solution that was integrated with the home environment, met the living habits of users, and satisfied people's needs. The topic was combined with real school-enterprise cooperation projects and was dedicated to enhancing future life experience with smart homes in real situations. To align the theme of the course with

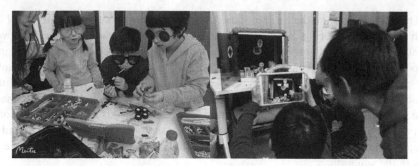

Fig. 2. Photos of the students in class

the life experience and knowledge level of elementary school students, the course development team refined the background of the theme and gave an appropriate background story in line with students' cognition. The story had three main characters in a family: a little girl (Zhang Duoduo), her mother (Sun Xiaoli), and her grandmother (Li Guilan). The keywords of the background story were as follows (Table 1).

Table 1. The keywords of the background story

Protagonist	Role	Little girl (Duoduo)	Mom (Sun Xiaoli)	Grandmother (Li Guilan)
Event (including time and location)	Character	Lively, outgoing	Calm, capable	Impatient
	Behavior	Tired of playing in the living room, goes to the refrigerator to find something to eat	Goes home after getting off work at night to be with her family	Lays in the bedroom to rest in the evening
	Emotion	Low	Low	Low
	Pain points	Too weak to open the refrigerator	Tired at work but has to be with family	The environment is too noisy to sleep
	Demand	To open the refrigerator easily	To balance work and life	To be able to sleep well

By creating story outlines, Lego scenes, stop-motion animation, and other supporting materials appropriate for students' cognitive level, the course helped students understand the background and context in which the story took place, discover the problems encountered by the main character, and analyze and solve the problems using the methods taught by the teacher in the course. Through thinking and design work, the students produce corresponding solutions. Additionally, they improve their thinking and design ability in the process.

4   Course Schedule

Through the 10-week course, the students were led to understand the thematic stories and situations of the project; recognize and master the concept, usage, and importance of innovative methods such as observation methods, user journeys, and user portraits; flexibly use the learned methods to understand the characteristics of the main character and the problems encountered in the thematic situations of the course; and complete the initial exploration and cultivation of innovation with the help of easy-to-understand and easy-to-operate paper-based teaching aids in the course. Through the exchange and discussion between teachers and students, the students inductively came up with a solution that was suitable for the background story situation and met the needs of the main character. With the help of brainstorming, design drawings, functional instructions, etc., they used a variety of teaching aids to completely express the team's design concept, provide a functional demonstration of the concept, and restore the appearance, interaction and use scenarios of the innovative solution through tools such as Lego, Techbox, ultralight clay, 3D printing, etc. Then produce a video and slidefor the final report (Table 2).

Table 2. Course process

Week	Schedule	Lecture topics	Time
1	19/9/20	Innovation introduction empathy cultivation	2 h
2	26/9/20	Cause insight thought expansion	2 h
3	3/10/20	Collaborative innovation	2 h
4	17/10/20	Solution refinement prototype design	2 h
5	24/10/20	Production practice	2 h
Break			
6	5/12/20	Course review program refinement	2 h 30 min
7	12/12/20	Introduction of visual expression and technical practice	2 h 30 min
8	19/12/20	Technology practice	2 h 30 min
9	26/12/20	Visual expression	2 h 30 min
10	2/1/21	Results report course summary	3 h

5   Case Studies

During the ten-week course, the students of each group defined the problem, sorted out and designed the solution based on the characteristics of the different main characters and the context in which the story took place, and finally, shared their innovative solutions.

5.1   Group 1 - The King Kong Gripper

The main character that the students helped was 57-year-old Grandma Li Guilan, whose eyesight is poor and who usually takes care of her 5-year-old granddaughter, Duoduo, at home. However, Duoduo always leaves her toys everywhere when she plays, and the grandmother slips and falls when she is not careful. Duoduo is still very young, but the small toy parts are a hassle to clean up. The students analyzed and discussed the backstory around what happened to the main character, hoping to help Duoduo to play happily without leaving her toys scattered on the floor, thus preventing the grandmother from falling after stepping on the toys. After a series of character insight and reasoning discussions, the students wanted to design a smart product that would help the grandmother clean up and organize Duoduo's toys scattered across the floor. Therefore, the students designed a product on their own named the King Kong Gripper. The King Kong Gripper has an intelligent start-up recognition system. When a certain number of toys are found on the floor, the machine starts running, and the robot moves next to the toys, uses its mechanical gripper to grab the toys and put them into its storage box; after picking up the toys, it moves to the location in the home where the toys are stored and places them in categories. There are no more small toys left on the floor after using the King Kong Gripper robot, and the grandmother no longer has to worry about falling (Fig. 3).

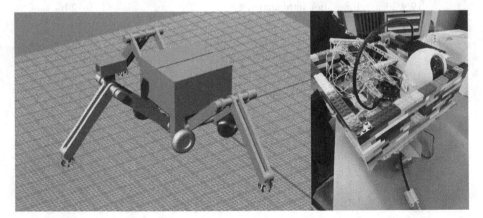

Fig. 3. The King Kong gripper

5.2   Group 2 - Multifunctional Autopen

The main character these students helped was Sun Xiaoli, a mom who is an urban, white-collar worker with a calm and competent personality but whose heavy workload makes her suffer from overtime work and feel even more overwhelmed by the need to supervise Duoduo's studies when she gets home. Through the independent exploration of the target users and situations, the students determined the reason behind the mother's behavior: she was tired from a stressful work environment and could not balance work and life.

Combining their personal experiences, the students identified a proposed solution to the problem, and they decided to help the mother better monitor Duoduo's studies. Therefore, the students designed a multifunctional automatic pen, which is mainly used in Duoduo's room. The mother can monitor Duoduo's study in real time through the pen holder's camera and send voice commands to the automatic pen. The automatic pen has wheels and wings on the pen holder; the gripper on the pen holder can move freely back and forth and grab Duoduo and pull her back to her study area. The alarm device on the automatic pen holder is linked to the camera and sends an alarm alert when Duoduo is found to be neglecting her studies. The automatic pen can switch between multiple pen tips (e.g., pencil, signature pen, watercolor pen, crayon, etc.) and between a writing implement and an eraser, reducing the distraction caused by Duoduo's frequent switching of tools while doing her homework (Fig. 4).

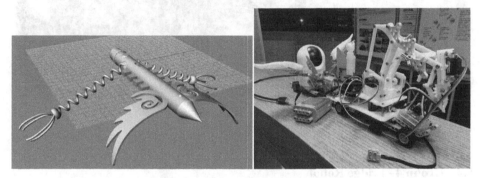

Fig. 4. Multifunctional autopen

5.3 Group 3 - Sleep Pods

These students conducted background research on the main character of the story by understanding the storyline and chose Grandma's character for an in-depth study. A character portrait of her was developed, and this led to a fuller understanding of the grandmother's daily life and behavioral motivations and insight into her pain point of low sleep quality, as she is easily awakened by the sound of children playing and noise outside the window. Through brainstorming and solution screening, the students chose a solution that was highly feasible and innovative: sleep pods. The sleep pod provides sound insulation to help the grandmother maintain good sleep and helps her get in and out of bed by lifting and lowering her into it.

After determining the solution, the students began to conceptualize what technology could be used to achieve the sleep pod's function and what shape would convey the best product appearance. In terms of functionality, they wanted to use materials that could absorb sound to reduce the impact of noise on sleep. They also wanted to add a lift to the grandmother's bed that would make it easier for her to get in and out of bed. In terms of appearance, the students created a Chinese-style scene tailored to the grandmother that was suitable for the aesthetic preferences of elderly individuals. After that, the students built the pod and a machine to simulate an automatically lifting bed. Moreover, after a group discussion, they drew three different views of the pod and created a scaled-down physical model of the sleeping pod and bedroom with help from a teaching assistant (Fig. 5).

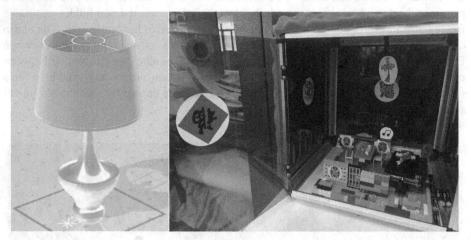

Fig. 5. Sleep pods

5.4 Group 4 - Fridge Robot

The main character that these students helped was the little girl named Duoduo. By empathizing with Duoduo based on the background of the story and observing Duoduo's life situation, they found that Duoduo's main pain points were that her mother was busy at work and could not accompany Duoduo and that when Duoduo felt hungry and wanted to retrieve food from the refrigerator, she could not open the door. The students brainstormed about these issues from Duoduo's perspective and designed a multifunctional robot refrigerator specifically for Duoduo. The refrigerator automatically adjusts its height to be accessible to Duoduo, and it has video messaging capabilities so that Duoduo can contact her mother using fingerprint recognition technology. The refrigerator can also move automatically and has a robotic arm that allows it to play with Duoduo so that she is no longer bored. Additionally, the robot is equipped with an air purification device. The students sorted the ideas they came up with according to feasibility and innovation and chose the most suitable solution on which to base their prototype sketch. From the simplest sketch to the three-view drawing, the students were able to control the product's general characteristics. The teacher helped to model the product in 3D so that the students could improve the product details. After that, the students built the robot refrigerator's body using Legos and simulated the robot's feet using a four-wheeled cart. A robotic arm was assembled using Legos, and commands were programmed to control the robot's arm, allowing it to grasp objects. The students also installed a fan on the robot's arm to show the function of air purification. The innovative design was practical from the perspective of the main character (Fig. 6).

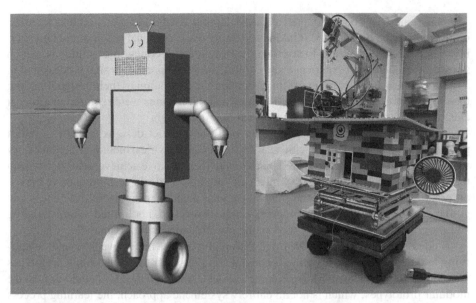

Fig. 6. Fridge robot

6   Discussion

The teaching team reflected on and summarized the course along five dimensions: course theme, learning mode, teaching team, course content, and course output, aiming to provide a reference for the teaching application of innovative education courses.

The theme of this semester's course was the intelligent transformation of future home life, so at the beginning of the course, we needed to describe the background and characteristics of the existing smart home conditions to the students. Otherwise, some children would not be clear on the relevant concepts, which would affect the direction of the program design. As an essential part of project-based teaching, the course theme should be appropriately integrated with students' background and real life experiences, the content of the theme should be specified, and students should be guided continuously during the lecture to control their learning ideas.

The course was a mixed-age class at the elementary school level, but the students had a wide range of ages and experiences. In practice, older students could lead younger students through classroom tasks, but the difference in students' levels of understanding posed a challenge to teachers' lesson planning. In subsequent courses, it is essential to ensure the completion of the same task by students of different ages or to use teaching aids that are more in line with the students' current age groups to ensure that the lesson's difficulty level is appropriate for most students.

To ensure that each group of students could complete their classroom tasks during the course, each group was assigned a teaching assistant to provide guidance. Otherwise, the individual characteristics of different teaching assistants, their communication habits, and the level of instruction of each group would affect each group's learning effect to a certain extent.

This semester's course adopted a phased approach, with the first five weeks focusing on the cultivation of students' thinking regarding discovery, analysis and problem solving. The second five weeks focused on the design and production of solutions, which allowed the students to experience and explore the whole product design process within a limited time and, to a certain extent, promoted the cultivation of their design thinking; the content of each class was self-contained, and the students were required to arrive at class on time and attend each class to avoid missing content.

The course deliverables included not only the product designs but also a report presented in the form of slide, with a variety of design activities, including product story videos. The course encouraged students to share their creative achievements on stage in the form of a mock competition, which cultivated the students' comprehensive hands-on practice, aesthetic design and public speaking abilities using useful references and guidance. The form of the final products can be diversified, not limited to only building and programming but also fully mobilizing the children's enthusiasm.

Students were encouraged to think differently during the 10-week course, identifying and defining problems, thinking about solutions, and finally, building prototypes with simple components with the help of teachers. Although the class could only make modular prototypes, which is not an entirely systematic approach, the learning process in the course mainly encouraged the thinking and operating skills of students in the second and third grades. The students achieved the goal of designing problem-solving products by starting from individual needs. The four creative concepts developed above provided a great deal of surprising inspiration for future home product improvement and concepts.

7 Conclusion

Innovative education grounded in project-based teaching is a new experience for both teachers and students, but these experiences are a sure way to meet future societal needs. Teachers in project-based education are no longer only communicators but are also guides, connecting with children in a way that inspires them and stimulates their reflective abilities during the course. Teachers need to be well prepared for the curriculum and the students' needs and to learn the skills necessary to work with the children's ideas to achieve the desired final output. Students no longer receive knowledge passively as in traditional teaching; instead, they learn independently, are inspired to learn more, and gradually develop a lifelong capacity for self-education. During the learning process, they can re-evaluate their abilities, reflect on their hobbies, and develop beneficial skills. This type of education can help students better adapt to the outside world and quickly choose an appropriate path for future societal developments.

Acknowledgments. This research is supported by the Faculty of Psychology at Beijing Normal University.

References

1. Sun, S., Teng, L.: Establishing China's first UX master program based on applied psychology perspective. In: Marcus, A., Wang, W. (eds.) DUXU 2017. LNCS, vol. 10288, pp. 767–775. Springer, Cham (2017). https://doi.org/10.1007/978-3-319-58634-2_55
2. Xin, X., Liu, W., Wu, M.: Reflecting on industrial partnered and project based master course of 'UX foundation'. In: Marcus, A., Wang, W. (eds.) DUXU 2018. LNCS, vol. 10919, pp. 148–157. Springer, Cham (2018). https://doi.org/10.1007/978-3-319-91803-7_11
3. Huang, J., Pan, W., Liu, Y., Wang, X., Liu, W.: Engineering design thinking and making: online transdisciplinary teaching and learning in a Covid-19 context. In: Markopoulos, E., Goonetilleke, R.S., Ho, A.G., Luximon, Y. (eds.) AHFE 2020. AISC, vol. 1218, pp. 159–166. Springer, Cham (2020). https://doi.org/10.1007/978-3-030-51626-0_19
4. Zhu, D., Liu, W., Lv, Y.: Reflection on museum service design based on a UX foundation course. In: Marcus, A., Wang, W. (eds.) HCII 2019. LNCS, vol. 11585, pp. 264–274. Springer, Cham (2019). https://doi.org/10.1007/978-3-030-23538-3_20
5. Lyu, Y., Liu, C., Zhu, Y.-C., Huang, J., Wang, X., Liu, W.: Study on the criteria of design of teaching toolkit for design thinking courses for lower grade students in primary school. In: Marcus, A., Rosenzweig, E. (eds.) HCII 2020. LNCS, vol. 12202, pp. 461–474. Springer, Cham (2020). https://doi.org/10.1007/978-3-030-49757-6_34
6. Serdyukov, P.: Innovation in education: what works, what doesn't, and what to do about it? J. Res. Innov. Teach. Learn. **10**(1), 4–33 (2017)
7. Hoffman, A., Holzhuter, J.: The evolution of higher education: innovation as natural selection. In: Hoffman, A., Spangehl, S. (eds.) Innovation in Higher Education: Igniting the Spark for Success, American Council on Education, pp. 3–15. Rowman & Litttlefield Publishers Inc., Lanham (2012)
8. Brenner, W., Uebernickel, F., Abrell, T.: Design thinking as mindset, process, and toolbox. In: Brenner, W., Uebernickel, F. (eds.) Design Thinking for Innovation, pp. 3–21. Springer, Cham (2016). https://doi.org/10.1007/978-3-319-26100-3_1
9. Dunne, D., Martin, R.: Design thinking and how it will change management education: an interview and discussion. Acad. Manag. Learn. Educ. **5**(4), 512–523 (2006)
10. Razzouk, R., Shute, V.: What is design thinking and why is it important? Rev. Educ. Res. **82**(3), 330–348 (2012)
11. Leifer, L., Meinel, C.: Looking further: design thinking beyond solution-fixation. In: Meinel, C., Leifer, L. (eds.) Design Thinking Research. UI, pp. 1–12. Springer, Cham (2019). https://doi.org/10.1007/978-3-319-97082-0_1
12. Edelman, J., Currano, R.: Re-representation: affordances of shared models in team-based design. In: Design Thinking, pp. 61–79. Springer, Berlin, Heidelberg (2011)
13. Leifer, L.: Design-team performance: metrics and the impact of technology. In: Evaluating Corporate Training: Models and Issues, pp. 297–319. Springer, Dordrecht (1998)
14. Plattner, H., Meinel, C., Leifer, L. (Eds.) Design Thinking: Understand–Improve–Apply. Springer Science & Business Media (2010)
15. Rogers, C.R.: Empathic: an unappreciated way of being. Counsel. Psychol. **5**(2), 2–10 (1975)
16. Kouprie, M., Visser, F.S.: A framework for empathy in design: stepping into and out of the user's life. J. Eng. Des. **20**(5), 437–448 (2009)
17. Markham, T., Larmer, J., Ravitz, J.: Project Based Learning Handbook: A Guide to Standards-Focused Project Based Learning. 2nd edn. Buck Institute for Education, Novato, CA (2003)
18. Bell, S.: Project-based learning for the 21st Century: skills for the future. Clearing House **2010**(2), 39–43 (2010)

A Study of Student Creative Thinking in User-Centred Design

Martin Maguire[✉]

School of Design and Creative Arts, Loughborough University, Leicestershire LE11 3TU, UK
m.c.maguire@lboro.ac.uk

Abstract. This paper discusses the definition of creativity in user-centred design design and considers the factors that are considered to contribute to its successful application. It reviews the stages of the creative process as described in the literature. It reports the results of a survey among design students on the tactics and methods they adopt to develop ideas during design work. These are analyzed to generate insights as well as being related back to the creative process. The study could form the basis for guiding students on how to maximize their creative thinking when carrying out project work.

Keywords: Ideation · Creativity · Student design · User-centred design · User experience design

1 Introduction

An important part of the user-centred design process or user-experience design is to be flexible and open to new ideas when identifying solutions to design problems. Yet being creative is a difficult skill to develop and ideas are often hard to generate for complex design problems. Creativity can mean different things in different areas. A parallel may be drawn between product design and the creation of product adverts. However, according to [1] the purpose of advertising design is to attract attention, break patterns, and shock or delight viewers. Consumer products are different. The goal is rarely to surprise the user, even if creating anticipation is part of many user flows. In user-centred design (UCD), creativity means making it easier for users to do things in an application and guide them towards completing their intended tasks. The idea that creativity stems from a brilliant insight is not necessarily true in UCD design [2]. For interactive consumer products to be effective, they have to be mapped to a system of ideas and insights that reflect the users' world. It can be argued that creativity in UCD design often comes about by emergence of a design, possibly based on many small innovations or improvements, meaning that the sum is greater than its individual parts.

The creative process involves uncovering users' needs. If designers do not explore their potential users' needs, the application may not be relevant. Indeed, insights gained from user interviews or observation may immediately suggest possible solutions. Users themselves may also make suggestions that can help identify innovative solutions. Creativity means solving problems that prevent product owners from finding out those

© Springer Nature Switzerland AG 2021
M. M. Soares et al. (Eds.): HCII 2021, LNCS 12779, pp. 556–566, 2021.
https://doi.org/10.1007/978-3-030-78221-4_38

features in the real world. Designers apply creative thinking to come up with better solutions for each interaction. The focus is on better, not on different for the sake of surprise and often, better means familiar. So UCD design is a chain of decisions, each of which involves comparing the pros and cons in a systematic way. Rigor is important in this process, but it should not hamper creativity. Periodic assessment during the design process helps designers come up with improved solutions.

UCD designers generate multiple options, each with a focus on one aspect of the problem to be solved or on each user requirement to be met. This is part of the process requires divergent thinking. For example, an app designer might propose two alternative view types: one as a card and one as a list. As stakeholders consider these versions, designers can generate new work that takes user feedback into account. This is called the convergent phase. Designers thus apply the cycle of divergent and convergent thinking at every level.

2 Creativity Within Design

As stated in [3], creativity is an essential element in designing, but there are multiple definitions of it and factors that influence it. The author identifies, from the literature, the factors or circumstances that contribute to the development of creative solutions. These include motivation, knowledge, and flexibility. The possession of knowledge is seen as essential to being creative and the ability to combine, order or connect information [4] (i.e., the ability to juggle scraps of knowledge to create purposeful patterns). It is often said that children can connect many ideas to each other, while adults typically connect fewer. An important model of the creative process developed by [5], is based on four processes (1) Preparation or accumulation of knowledge, (2) Incubation or transferring the task to the subconscious, (3) Illumination when two ideas come together to create a new idea, (4) Verification or implementation where the designer or developer builds on the idea and improves it to make sure that it is useful. Mental blocks are blocks against using knowledge in a flexible way [6].

The idea of the design creativity loop in the context of instructional design is introduced by [7]. This is based on the established stages of creative thinking originally developed by [5] described as: Preparation (gathering information about the situation), Problem identification (defining what the problem is), Incubation (during which the creative task is set aside and allowed to 'simmer'), Illumination (the 'eureka' moment), and Elaboration or Verification (working out the details and developing the results). The creative loop is iterative in nature and can fit into the iterative process of user-centred design, where following user research to question the challenge, user needs are identified, understanding how user-needs and the problem align, resulting in a creative brief which clearly defines the challenge based on research insights. Creation of possible solutions are then defined and tested, resulting in selection of a single solution that works and preparing it for implementation and launch.

Some key points are made by [7] about their model that reflects experience of the creative process. Firstly, that design problems are usually among the most complex and ill-structured kinds of problems encountered in practice. It is more than a series of structured problems and more than a direct application of technical skill. It is because of the poorly structured aspects that require the application of creativity. Design requires both an over-arching idea or vision [8] and the smaller scale application of creativity in a wide range of supporting design tasks. These design problems or tasks, then, present opportunities for creative thinking to occur. It is said by [9] that the design process may involve a 'drizzle' of multiple, smaller creative ideas that can add up to the larger design conception. It is therefore interesting to conduct some research into designer's experiences of generating ideas and to see if there are associations with these stages of creativity and what new insights can be gained.

3   Creativity Methods

The Design Council's Double-Diamond framework for innovation [10] emphasises the need for the generation of divergent ideas to explore the creative space to generate design concepts. Using context of use requirements, based on user, task and environmental needs, different ideas can be compared to help select the best ones to develop as a Product Design Specification (PDS) or design proposition. The Double Diamond framework refers to design methods that designers can apply in design. There is a wide range of methods and techniques for the generation of creative ideas described in the literature [e.g., 11–13].

Methods include:

Brainstorming – a group of people propose ideas. The ideas should not be criticised when presented. Rational associations, commonly used in everyday life, should be avoided, and wild ideas are welcomed. When all ideas are assembled, they are reviewed and the most suitable adopted.

Synectics – similar to brainstorming, a problem-solving methodology to help group members explore problems; retain new, often abstract, information; and develop creative solutions by breaking from existing mindsets.

Mind mapping – a type of graphic organizer that uses a diagram to visually organize ideas and concepts.

Removing mental blocks – set of techniques for problem solving such as freewriting, considering smaller tasks first, changing the environment.

High-level, detailed level switching – the designer, zooms in from a high level to the details then switches back to the high level, thus reflecting the behaviour of many good designers.

Morphological charts – a method to generate ideas in an analytical and systematic manner. Usually, the functions of the product are taken as a starting point.

Crazy eights – a fast sketching exercise that challenges people to sketch eight distinct ideas in eight minutes. The goal is for each person to push beyond their first idea, frequently the least innovative, and to generate a wide variety of solutions to the challenge.

Problem abstraction – creation of a general idea of what the problem is and how to solve it. The process guides designers to remove all specific detail and any patterns that will not help solve the problem.

Distinct concepts – here the aim is to consider the user requirements and generate 3–5 very distinct concepts stimulated by keywords (e.g. most obvious, turn problem on its head, wacky idea). Using a matrix format, each concept can be rated according to how well they meet each user, task and contextual requirement with the best concept with the highest score being taken forward.

Directions of thinking – this method is typified by Edward de Bono's 'Six thinking hats' where a group of people plan thinking processes in a detailed and cohesive way, and in doing so to think together more effectively [14].

4 Survey

To gain some insights into where creative solutions to design problems come from, a survey was conducted with undergraduate and postgraduate design students at University. Seventy-three design students responded to a survey composed of the following questions:

- At what time of day do you find that you are able to find a solution to a problem?
- Where or when is the most likely place where you will get inspiration?
- How do you normally get a design idea?
- Which ideation or creativity techniques do you find useful?

The respondents were also asked to give an example of an occasion where they had an idea or 'brainwave' for a solution to design problem. They were asked to explain what the circumstances were that gave them the idea.

4.1 Time of Day

Regarding time of day that the students found that ideas came to them, the chart below shows that nighttime was the most likely time of day for getting ideas experienced by 40% of the sample reported. Other times of day were less likely to be times when students received inspiration although morning (26%) was thought be slightly more productive than evening (21%) but more productive than the afternoon (16%) (Fig. 1).

4.2 Location or Activity

In terms of locations or activities where students found that they got inspiration, walking and exercising were most effective (55%). When studying and thinking about the problem was also reported frequently (47%). Listening to music or relaxing was the third most frequent (37%). This reflects the work of [15] whose research found that music with a positive sound can enhance cooperation, while an upbeat genre enhances cooperation to converge the ideas. The three activities: in bed (33%) watching TV or a video (26%) and being in the shower (32%) received less but significant support (Fig. 2).

Twenty-two participants (30.7%) reported other situations or activities when they found inspiration. There included being in a new environment or change of surroundings, cooking, on a long-distance journey, using social media to look at different pictures of products or forms, eating alone, kicking or bouncing a ball, talking with other people, and sitting or lying down before going to bed. It was said that ideation was often effective when doing mundane tasks where the mind wanders. As stated by one participant "It is

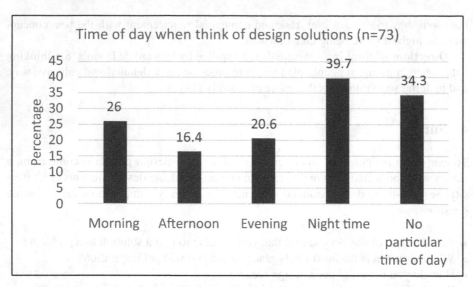

Fig. 1. Reported time of day when participants able to find a solution to a problem?

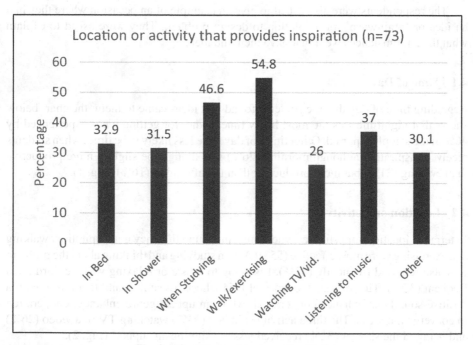

Fig. 2. Most likely place to get inspiration

this pressure free thinking that often yields the best solutions". However, the randomness of the situation was expressed by one person saying that they get ideas "Sporadically, sometimes I get inspiration out of the blue".

4.3 Methods for Generating Ideas

The participants were presented with a list of possible techniques for getting design ideas. The chart below shows the relative importance of each. Looking for sources of inspiration e.g., online or books, was the most popular (74%), followed by thinking hard about the problem (56%), asking others for suggestions (56%) and forgetting about the problem for a while (18%) (Fig. 3).

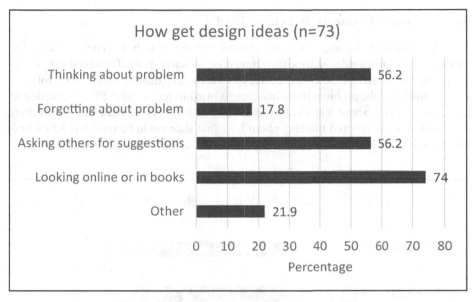

Fig. 3. How design ideas are normally generated

Twenty-two participants (22%) suggested other methods where they get design ideas. These reflect stages of the creative thinking process. A range of mental strategies are employed such as discussing with those who are new to the problem, considering user needs for similar products, looking at similar problems or existing products, leaving and returning to a problem, and using the design ideas website, Pinterest. This process of was explored by [16], who found that the incubation effects could be generated in a problem-solving task.

Following the stages of the creative process [5], preparation and problem identification activities included, thinking about the problem for the perspective of the user, learning from own experiences with the products used, writing down in notes when social situations and product usage caused annoyance. Interestingly participants tended to swap between drawing on their own experiences and considering the needs of other users. One approach reported was: *"Discover the needs of particular user groups based on my own experiences and interactions with my environment. Then projecting that onto other people and explore from there"*. Gaining inspiration through incubation was illustrated by example survey responses: *"Discussion among those who are not close to the problem will give 'out of the box' suggestions. Taking a step back from focusing, letting the task stew in the subconscious, and re-turning to it later will kick start a project"* and, *"Sometimes having discussions with others is enough to trigger a design idea, simply just talking about the topic of the project can broaden my design perspective and seeing it from another person's viewpoint, not specifically asking for suggestions".*

The idea of iteration in generating ideas was illustrated by the following response: *"I find it useful to come back to a design again and again, like putting multiple coats of paint on a wall you build up the best solution in stages".*

4.4   Ideation or Creativity Techniques Used

To help determine the use of specific mental techniques to help generate ideas, four methods were presented which the participants could select. It was found that simplifying the problem (breaking it down into parts) was the most frequently used (74%), followed by reformulating the problem (thinking about it in a different way) (52%), abstracting the problem (thinking about it at a higher level) (38%) and working backwards—assuming the problem is solved and thinking about how that state could be reached (30%). Only one person in the sample stated that they used none of these methods (Fig. 4).

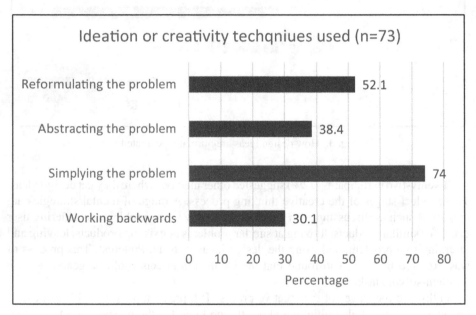

Fig. 4. Which ideation or creativity techniques that are used

Other techniques reported included building a persona and 'getting into character', seeing the bigger picture and how a design could seamlessly be integrated into a user's life, and identifying themes and brainstorming around them. A further idea was to create the worst design solution possible and work from there and use playful ways to describe the problem.

4.5 Occasions of Design Inspiration

Participants were asked to recall and give an example of an occasion when they had a bright idea for a design solution. Fifty-five of the seventy-three respondents (75%) gave an example. A few respondents indicated that ideas popped out from nowhere or just came on the spot, while others gave indications of what activity led to ideas being generated. Several themes arose from the analysis of these answers. The sections below show the main kinds of thinking or factors that correspond to the examples they gave:

Research and Examination of Similar Problems. Seven responses related to collecting ideas from similar products and researching websites and catalogues of similar products to see what features they had as a source of inspiration. An example of this approach was:

> "By using trial and error I have come up with solutions to a problem and looking at other examples of a similar problem and how that was solved. This helps to make things fall into place."

Relaxing in the Evening or Lying in Bed. Ten respondents reported being able to come up with a good idea while taking a break, lying in bed and even dreaming solutions. One response was:

> "It tends to be in the evening when I go to bed when I get proper brainwaves. I normally can't solve a problem which I have been thinking about all day but after being in bed for about 30–45 min with my eyes closed, I then somehow solve most of my issues. This normally forces me to get out of bed and I have to draw the ideas on whatever I can find."

This shows the idea of relaxation releasing the brain to process problem information and generate ideas. However, it is necessary to record the idea straightaway as was reported by another participant who dreamt of a solution:

> "I get ideas at the most random time in the most random places. Weirdest one so far was in a dream, I thought so much about the problem I dreamt a potential solution and had to immediately wake up and voice record the concept."

A detailed report was also made about how 'sleeping on an idea' helped generate a solution. This involved design of a baby monitor and the difficulty of addressing all the individual requirements of the users identified in the research and deciding to sleep on the problem.

> "I woke to thinking about the problem from a different angle, rather than trying to address all the parenting needs in one product. I designed a system that allowed for different features to be added or taken away depending on the individual parents needs. The result was a modular product that came together really well. So ultimately allowing my brain the time to process information away from the pressures of the task at hand and approaching the task from a fresh angle, worked well."

Brainstorming Ideas. Making a deliberate effort to brainstorm ideas was another tactic employed by six participants. Oner example was: *"I came up with the idea while brainstorming for a different project. One of the technologies I was looking into for the second project could be applied to the first project"*. In another example, the participant brainstormed several ideas under time pressure, and since a housemate was carrying out the same brief, they were able to identify starting points to carry out secondary research into existing problems.

Doing the Task, Immersing into the Context. The activity of thinking about the user and the context, a well-established method in user-centred design, was also found to be a creative opportunity by ten participants. As one said: *"When I was working out, and the problem was regarding the design of a working out product, being in the context was vital to identify the issues during the process and starting to find solutions."*

Another example was while doing a task, an unexpected solution arose: *"I had an idea while chatting to a friend about reducing social media usage. At the time I was holding the phone and thinking about what could stop me going on it. The idea was to make a phone case that disformed to make it uncomfortable to hold."*

Own Experiences Identifying Solutions. For seven respondents, simply using the natural world as inspiration, watching videos, doing activities unrelated to the problem helped to identify a solution. One person who was looking for a way to encourage a household to share chores came from playing games in virtual reality:

"The solution was an AR concept which involved sorting tasks using a projected hockey table, where partners can hit the pucks into their own goal or defend it if they want to accept the task. I think the brainwave came from my own personal experience of enjoying VR games and witnessing the joy that others feel when immersed in the experience with other people and their families being engaged in it too". They also reported trying to think of the opposite of housework i.e. gaming, which could be applied to the problem.

A second person found that chatting with their family helped create ideas: *"It was a family walk, and we are all chatting about different things. When you are dreaming about future you think out of the box."*

A further example came while observing their surrounding:

"I was thinking about one of the projects in my portfolio. The problem was that I had trouble with how the school monitors the form of e-hailing car operation in the campus. The problem was solved by a coincidence. I saw the security guards patrolling through the window while I was taking a shower in the evening. Finally, I decided to develop a monitor assistance system for guards to be a third party to manage e-hailing."

Lateral Thinking. Eight participants reported trying to think laterally about a problem or to look at it from different angles. For example:

"Just at night thinking of random ways to solve things that may not work in the long run but help to think of other things."

Another example given was: *"The best solutions I think come from a place of fun, when you let go of the seriousness of the problem and just start pitching ideas that are a bit ridiculous yet still on topic. I did a group design project where a lot of time was spent on ideation. Once we stopped being so serious, the good solutions start to come out because they have a more playful and thus welcoming aspect to them."*

Related to this was an approach of finding analogies: *"Often I have ideas based on analogies, for example a money saving aid, representing growth and nurturing of money in the context of growth and nurturing of plants."*

The use gamification to encourage users to stay healthy was reported, with visualisation being part of the thinking process:

"My idea was using a digital pet to visualise the health of the user. The pet would be healthy when the user is healthy and if the pet starts getting sick, the user will have to take their medicine/do exercise/any other task that they are supposed to do for their wellbeing. I thought of the idea by thinking long and hard about ways to visualise health statistics".

Thinking Past Life. Thinking about childhood experiences helped one respondent think about a modular cooking appliance designed specifically for those living in microhomes in Asia:

"I looked back onto experiences I had as a kid and walked through the issues I had growing up in Hong Kong whenever there was a celebration. There would be 30+ people all in the smallest apartment with no space to walk around. I relived memories of cousins mincing pork on their laps on a kiddie stool in the bedroom and it went from there."

5 Conclusion

This paper has reported on the process of being creative or generating ideas within the design process in the context of student work. The results from the survey show that ideas can come about in many ways. While different techniques such as brainstorming or lateral thinking can be used to successfully generate ideas, they can also come about unexpectedly while doing or thinking about something else. Interestingly while obtaining ideas when sleeping was not the most common situation for generating ideas, there were several stories of people who did get good ideas in this way. There is also evidence that thinking about a problem, researching, and experiencing the context is a good starting point for ideation. During this activity, the processes of working on a problem, forgetting about the problem, or considering it in different ways or from different angles can also help to create solutions. Being flexible in thinking seems very much the key to being creative in the design world.

Acknowledgement. The author would like to thank the students in the School of Design and Creative Arts at Loughborough University who participated in the survey reported here.

References

1. Lenard, D.: Why creativity matters in UX design, Clutch.co, July 2018. https://clutch.co/age ncies/ui-ux/resources/why-creativity-matters-in-ux-design. Accessed 7 Mar 2021
2. Weinschenk, S.: What is the role of creativity in UX design? (2018) https://www.smashingm agazine.com/2018/12/role-of-creativity-ux-design/. Accessed 7 Mar 2021
3. Chakrabarti, A.: Defining and supporting design creativity. In: International Design Conference – Design, Dubrovnik, Croatia, 15–18 May 2006, pp. 479–486 (2006)
4. Gluck, F.W.: "Big bang" management: creative innovation. McKinsley Q. **1**, 49–59 (1985)
5. Wallas, G.: Stages in the creative process. In: Rothenberg, A., Hausmann, C.R. (eds.) The Creativity Question, pp. 69–73. Duke University Press, Durham (1988)
6. Adams, J.L.: Conceptual Blockbusting: A Guide to Better Ideas, 3rd edn. Addison-Wesley, MA (1993)
7. Clinton, G., Hokanson, B.: Creativity in the training and practice of instructional designers: the design/creativity loops model. Educ. Technol. Res. Dev. **60**, 111–130 (2012)
8. Löwgren, J., Stolterman, E.: Thoughtful Interaction Design: A Design Perspective on Information Technology. MIT, Cambridge (2004)
9. Nelson, H., Stolterman, E.: The Design Way. Educational Technology Publications, Englewood Cliffs (2003)
10. Design Council: Framework for innovation. https://www.designcouncil.org.uk/news-opinion/ double-diamond-universally-accepted-depiction-design-process. Accessed 7 Mar 2021
11. Ulrich, K.T., Eppinger, S.D.: Product Design and Development, 7th edn. McGraw-Hill, New York (2019).ISBN-13: 978-1260134445
12. Pressman, A.: Design Thinking: A Guide to Creative Problem Solving for Everyone. Routledge, London (2018)
13. Soares, M.: Ergodesign Methodology for the Product Design: A User-Centered Approach. CRC Press, Taylor and Francis, Boca Raton (2021)
14. de Bono, E.: Six Thinking Hats: An Essential Approach to Business Management. Little, Brown, and Company, Boston (1985)
15. Sarinasadat, H., Hattori, Y., Miyake, Y., Nozawa, T.: Music valence and genre influence group creativity. In: Harris, D. (ed.) HCII 2019. LNCS (LNAI), vol. 11571, pp. 410–422. Springer, Cham (2019). https://doi.org/10.1007/978-3-030-22507-0_32
16. Penney, C.G., Godsell, A., Scott, A., Balsom, R.: Problem variables that promote incubation effects. J. Creat. Behav. **38**(1), 35–55 (2004)

A Brief Discussion on Design Education and Practice in the Hypermedia Era

Pu Ren, Zhe Wang, and Mingjun Yang[✉]

Beijing Institute of Graphic Communication, Beijing 102600, China
renpu@bigc.edu.cn

Abstract. The hypermedia design is becoming a mainstream of digital design works because of its contagious and communicative power. However, traditional design education is not enough to teach students the comprehensive ability to develop hypermedia works independently. Based on the design teaching practice of H5, this paper discusses the key points in designing and teaching method for hypermedia works. First, the fundamental concepts of the hypermedia and H5 are discussed from technical and application levels. Next, methodologies about the design thinking are concluded and proposed. Finally, a teaching practice case for hypermedia design is analyzed to demonstrate our points. In a word, beyond the design capability of graphic elements, the hypermedia designer needs to pay more attention to the integration of various types of multimedia including video, audio, animated and other interactable elements. Therefore, it is necessary to introduce engineering thought into the design teaching procedure.

Keywords: Hypermedia · HTML5 · Design thinking · Design education

1 Introduction

The hypermedia, also known as ultramedia, is originally an Internet technique which was expanded from the concept of hypertext. It is a form of media that is finally presented to users after the non-linear processing of the dismembering and restructuring of traditional multimedia content. The most distinctive feature of hypermedia is that all the multimedia materials can be interlinked by user interactions. Because of the rich, vivid and powerful information expressiveness, the hypermedia has fast become part of the mainstream of digital media types.

The traditional design education mainly concerns graphic elements, which could be seen from the professional curriculum in numerous art schools and institutes. Almost every student specializing in art design was taught by basic courses of planar composition, color composition and three-dimensional construction. Certainly, these courses are quite essential for students to build a good knowledge system, and to reinforce the foundation for their further study in other specialized courses. However, as the design needs to serve the community closely, our new information age has put forward much more and higher requirements to designers. Some art schools and institutes have added some technical courses to conform to the demands of times, such as Adobe software courses, basic computer courses. These skill courses undoubtedly will be of great benefit to the student for the rest of their design learning and works, but still remain in the superficial phase. Most of the existing design education schemes are not enough to cultivate synthesis talent to design hypermedia works without systematic training deeply into thinking levels.

In the following pages, we will talk about basic features of hypermedia design and the education problems, and put forward some views which are concluded from our teaching practice in the design courses.

2   Research Background

2.1   Basic Concepts

Above all, as the concept of hypermedia and H5 are both originated from information technology, it is necessary to explain the basic concepts of these two words. Technically, the hypermedia is an information organization form that utilizes interlinked blocks to manage and link multimedia information (mainly including texts, images, animations, videos, etc.). The most advantage of this structure is none-linear, which means information units could be interlinked to each other by a network instead of a single entrance and exist (see Fig. 1). The hypermedia performs much more expressive power because of the tangled and complicated associations between media elements. From this perspective, the traditional graphic design works can be regarded as a constituent part of the hypermedia [1].

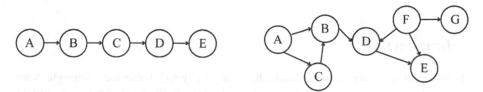

Fig. 1. Linear(left) and non-linear(right) structure forms.

Practically, with the integration of the mobile Internet, the hypermedia got much attention from commercial application fields. As a new type of communication media, the hypermedia has a superiority far beyond the traditional media. First, a hypermedia work contains much more types of media, which presents greater expressiveness. Second, a hypermedia work is often supported on the Internet, especially the mobile Internet, which reduces transmission costs and gives rise to great communication capabilities between users. Third and most important, the interaction characteristic of hypermedia brings more interestingness, which improves the users' experience. Therefore, from a practical perspective, a hypermedia application is an independent and complete design object with its own unique attributes.

The infrastructure of a hypermedia application is mainly based on the HTML5, the next generation of the Internet markup language that powers the web. Compared to earlier versions of HTML, this new version provides much more support to various multimedia types, which forms the basic architecture of a hypermedia application. However, beyond HTML5, some other Internet techniques, principally Javascript and CSS, are also essential to the hypermedia development. Technically, H5 is the abbreviation of the HTML5; while in commercial applications, H5 refers to all kinds of the hypermedia works developed by the related Internet technologies.

Due to the high popularity of mobile Internet, most H5 works are currently oriented to mobile terminals [2]. The simple H5 works are mainly used for display and marketing applications, while the complex H5 works can realize various complicated functions like mobile apps. For visual designers, it is not necessary to focus on the developing details to realize a piece of H5 work. However, it is better to change traditional design thinking for designers in the way of integrating multimedia resources.

2.2 Related Works

The research on the educational applications of hypermedia can be traced back to the time of these related technologies appeared. Begoray [1] put forward an introduction to hypermedia issues and its application areas. Almost simultaneously, researchers began to talk about the educational problems about the design and development of hypermedia. Piet [3] regarded the hypermedia design process as a gradual procedure from content into interaction design and concluded the design process into four stages: conceptual, metaphoric, structural and navigational design. Similarly, we propose a pipeline of H5 development in Sect. 3.1, which is closer to the current era.

Some other researchers have already noticed the educational problems in design teaching in the hypermedia era. Ignacio and Paloma [4] put forward a software engineering method to realize hypermedia design. John [5] explored much further for the design education in the post-digital age, and he thought the designers should be more creative and move in richer, more-humane directions to meet the requirements of the age. Meyer [6] proposed that the most valuable parts in design education are the digital perspective and process, which are unfortunately seldom taught in traditional courses. Wei [7] and Shanghai [8] put forward some countermeasures and suggestions from innovative thinking in design education. All these existing works inspired us in the research of design education problems in hypermedia era.

3 Methodology

3.1 The Pipeline of the H5 Development

In the actual commercial applications, a piece of releasable H5 work is developed by a complete team. Within such a team, the designers and developers perform their duties and collaborate with each other following an agreed designing scheme. Nevertheless, all the practice should be carried out around a unique design scheme, and it is necessary for team members to learn about partners' work for greater collaboration. Figure 2. shows the pipeline of H5 development.

The first priority of H5 development is the user requirements analysis. This is the critical stage to determine the logical functions, expression form, and even the visual style

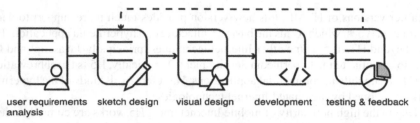

user requirements   sketch design   visual design   development   testing & feedback
analysis

Fig. 2. The pipeline of H5 development.

of the H5. The designer's task in this stage is to contribute ideas, understand customers' need, and help to make a scheme so far as practicable. Secondly, the sketch conceive stage determines the most part cost of the H5 product design and the design result. The form of the sketch is very free. Many great ideas come from a shape draft drawn on paper. The key point in this stage is to determine the story board with a clear logical path. The prototype figures can be seen as the conclusion of the sketch design and the outline of the entire development. In the third stage, designers need to create or edit all the design elements that finally presented in the H5. After that, designers can pack up all the processed material to engineers for development. The last stage is online testing. Designers and developers can adjust product details by the final operating effect, and the feedback statistics from backstage. This development approach can be seen as the *Iterative Design.*

In practice, the complex logical functions are certainly need to be realized by programming development. While with the evolution of Internet technology, some visual development toolkits are invented for H5 development. These online tools integrate common developing requirements of H5 products in the back stage and present easy visual interface for users. Therefore, designers can take the role of developers in the development stage, arrange and organize the material by themselves by these visual development toolkits.

3.2   Design Thinking

Traditional design practices and teaching methods revolve around graphic visual elements, while much more integration of various kinds of materials needs to be considered for the hypermedia design. Therefore, designers must change their design thinking in order to arrange comprehensive layout of H5.

Design Goals. There are, of course, specific goals for every H5 work according to their application scenarios. From the third-party data statistics, more than 65% commercial H5 works are used for brand display, promotion and marketing. The other unclassified ones mainly focus on functional applications, which also rely on the propagation properties of H5. Therefore, the overall design goal of H5 is to *guide the users to browse and share the pages as much as possible.*

In order to catch the users' eyes at the first sight, a good H5 application should be designed good-looking, user-friendly and amusing. This is consistent with the three-level theory proposed by famous Donald Norman [10]. According to Norman's theory, there are three design level: visceral, behavioral, and reflective. Visceral design is consistent with the human instinct pursuit of beauty. Behavioral design focuses on the using performance. Reflective design covers deep implications including culture, knowledge background, and other messages about the meaning of the product or its use. These three levels focus on different emphasis points and progress layer upon layer from the cognitive perspective.

Figure 3. shows the pyramid structure of these three targets. For a good H5 product, the basic characteristic must be visually appealing. This is also the lowest level of requirement for designers. The middle level in the pyramid is about the experience goal. As an interactive product, a good H5 should provide fluid experience for users. This point includes the appropriate interaction logic, the smooth loading state, and creative interactive forms. The ultimate goal of the H5 design comes from the reflective target. An excellent H5 work is similar to a great art work in the rethinking about the meaning of the content, and the evoked personal remembrances. This is the highest and hardest level of the goal pyramid. If an H5 work can infects users emotionally and make an association with users' life experiences tactfully, it is definitely a successful product in marketing applications.

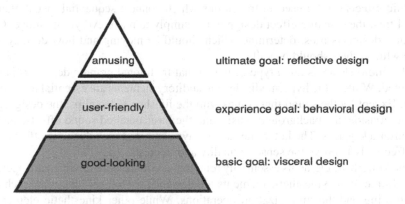

Fig. 3. Pyramid of the design goals.

Design Elements. In the development pipeline, the main task of designers is to complete the design scheme, package and deliver all the resources to the developers. In this process, applicable rules dealing with the limits induced by mobile devices, Internet transmission and ergonomic demand also need to be considered. Hereby designers create or process raw material resources in different formats. From a user-experience perspective, three types of elements are needed to be considered in the H5 design process: visual, auditory, and kinesthetic elements. Figure 4. shows these three main types and the extended types in the H5 applications. The key point is that all the elements should be designed around the interactive attribute of H5.

The visual design is far and away the most important part in the whole development process. Traditional graphic design skills can be utilized to deal with most of the visual parts [10]. However, the designers still need to tackle the new differences in the face of

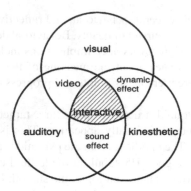

Fig. 4. Main types of the design elements.

hypermedia elements. The most notable one is that all the visual elements in H5 can be designed as dynamic effect. For one hand, human physiological nature in ocular region has determined that dynamic elements are more attractive to users. For the other hand, as the large amount of information cannot be displayed on the screen simultaneously, dynamic effects can be used in transitions which connect sequential visual elements. For all this, the dynamic effect design is not simply to make everything move. On the contrary, designers must determine which should be moving and how do they move, while which others should be still.

The audio elements are a type of media that traditional graphic designers have not contacted. While in the hypermedia design, auditory elements are essential to the overall effect. Except for the sound that comes with the finished video clips, the designers just need to consider the background music, and the basic detailed sound effects, such as a click after a keypress. The latter ones are always combined with dynamic effects, which can effectively improve the sense of quality and interests.

The kinesthetic elements essentially refer to the visual elements which are operable in H5. Some of the kinesthetic elements are designed for logical functions, such as the page-turning and the minimization operations. While other kinesthetic elements are combined with visual and auditory ones to realize the interactive effects. These visual elements should be designed as hints to suggest users how to trigger the correlative effects.

If an H5 work is just outstanding at visual and auditory parts, it can only reach the qualified requirements of the common multimedia. The reason why an excellent H5 work is not a simple presentation slide is that all the resources can be designed as interactive elements. The interactive manipulation is the foundation for the development of complex logic functions. Moreover, all the visual, auditory and kinesthetic elements should serve the functional attribute.

The most immediate challenge facing graphic designers to accomplish H5 works is to deal with various media material. Therefore, designers need to master different software tools to edit data in various format. What's more, all the processed materials are needed to be arranged according to the interactive logic, and be organized in a non-linear processing way.

Figure 5. demonstrates the non-linear processing of design elements in H5 design. The top circles with different patterns represent different multimedia sources including text, images, animations, videos, audio files, etc. In traditional linear editing way, all of these sources will be cut and reconnected into a new file. All the design elements are independent of each other. While in the non-linear editing, all these sources are disassembled and reassociate into a new file. All the design elements are closely interrelated. For example, the user can experience static image-text display and dynamic video-audio display simultaneously by a long-press operation. This characteristic of H5 determines the core difference from tradition graphic design.

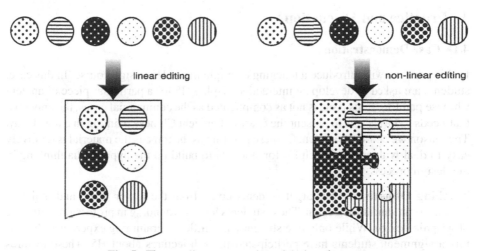

Fig. 5. The non-linear processing of design elements.

Design Principles. After having be clear the goal and operable objects, there are several principles of designing hypermedia H5 cases can been concluded.

First, the form and style should be consistent with the application targets. According to how much interactive operations an H5 application provides, it can be roughly classified into three kinds: the display type with little interaction, the guiding type with relatively more interaction, and the operating type totally concatenated by users' interactions. For example, a toy product marketing H5 could be designed as an interesting game with colorful styles; while a research questionnaire H5 may be designed with a simple and clear style.

Second, grab users' attention within a short time. Because of the application scenarios of mobile Internet, information must be delivered efficiently in H5 pages. The mobile user behavior statistics (released by Tecent company [11]) shows that users are lost as the page hierarchy deepens and the browsing time increases. Therefore, the first two pages should be designed appropriately eye-catching in visual and interactive aspects. The basic idea is to highlight the main visual element, and keep the detailed elements in order.

Third, conform to the principle of mobile interaction applications. The habits of mobile users and traditional Internet users are very different in many ways, such as the way to swipe to the next page or zoom in images on a hemline. In the stage of visual design, it is worth noting to reduce the cognitive cost, thereby increasing the interactivity for users. At the very least, simplify the operation on a single page, and keep the consistency of operations for multiple pages. In addition, the brightness of adjacent pages should not change dramatically. The design elements should be compressed as small as possible, so as to reduce the loading time and ensure the smooth interaction. There are other similar details need to be noticed for the interactive design, which cannot be covered completely in our paper.

4 Practice and Discussion

4.1 Case Demonstration

In this part, we will introduce a teaching example in our H5 design course. In this case, students are asked to develop an interactive display H5 for a particular piece of ancient Chinese painting. This issue is not as complicated as the commercial cases, the only goal that needs to be clear is to present the charm of ancient Chinese painting in a novel way. The reason we chose the ancient Chinese painting as the topic is the material is relatively easy to deal with, and it is helpful for students to build up the hypermedia thinking in the design process.

Teaching Objectives. Our target students come from the junior grade and major in Visual Communication Design. These students have a grounding in professional practice of graphic design. While only one student has a little programming experience. Before this assignment, students have participated in 48-h lectures about H5. These lectures introduced the theory of H5 design, and the developing method based on an online toolkit called *iH5* [12]. On the *iH5* platform, designers can develop a piece of H5 work by arranging the processed design elements, defining the logic flow in a visual programming way.

This course work gave the students an insight into the hypermedia design mind, and make them do comprehensive exercises on the H5 design task. For one hand, students had to think of a creative representation for Chinese paintings based on H5; for the other hand, they should practice the material processing and integration ability for H5 development.

Teaching Results. The interactive display of images and texts is the simplest form in the submitted assignments. In order to adapt to the mobile devices, pictures of traditional Chinese painting are displayed partially in a single screen, and gradually shown up in full by user's sliding interactions. In the design elements processing, objects in a Chinese painting can be cutout as graphic elements, then generated into an interactive animation together with dynamic effects. Figure 6. shows an example of the interactive dynamic effect. When the user slides the screen, the camera focuses on the red boat; then the long-press operation will trigger the moving animation which brings the scene sliding into other parts of this painting. This is a typical idea which utilizes the hypermedia thinking to disassemble source material, and reconstructs them into a new representation. The user does not just see the drawing, but visit inside the scenes in it by taking the boat.

Fig. 6. Interactive dynamic effect in H5 (frame sequence).

On this basis, students chose different 3D display methods to turn the traditional 2D images into a stereoscopic space which brought opportunities to present much more vivid details. Technically, 3D supporting is a very important improvement in the HTML5. The traditional viewing perspective of the user can only move the 2D screen plan; because of the extra Z-axis, the virtual camera can go in and out on the direction of depth. As viewed from the application, one of the most representative features of the traditional Chinese painting is the scattering perspective, which means we can rebuild space imagery by recomposing the graphic elements.

One proposed idea is to place processed graphic elements in different positions in three dimensions, and set the camera path going through these elements to create a stereoscopic parallax between objects. Figure 7. shows an example of the stereoscopic crossing effect realized by our student. By replacing the plane mountains, trees and other graphic elements at different values on z coordinate, we got a new stereo world in consistent with the original painting. Moreover, the new expression form creates much more atmosphere of the deep courtyard, and appears far-reaching in artistic conception of the work.

Another idea is utilizing the form of the panoramic roaming, which is very suitable for the long horizontal scroll of Chinese paintings. Figure 8. shows an example of the 360-degree panoramic roaming effect. When implemented, the interactive sliding operation is bind with the virtual camera in the 3D scene. The objective painting is regarded as a texture mapped on a barrel-shaped model. Moreover, the distance between the graphic elements and the virtual camera is determined by the column basal plane circumference that equals the length of the scroll. Therefore, we can place different graphic objects on varied cylinder shapes with different circumferences, thereby creating stereo parallax between different visual elements.

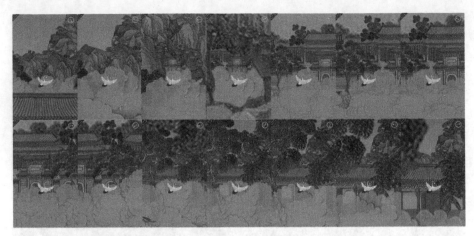

Fig. 7. Stereoscopic crossing effect in H5 (frame sequence).

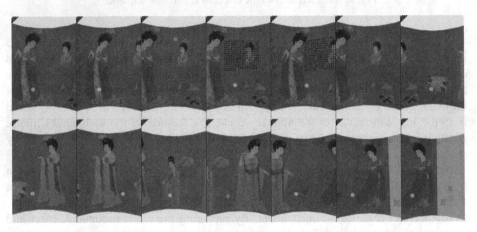

Fig. 8. Panoramic roaming effect in H5 (frame sequence).

4.2   Discussion

The basic summary of our teaching cases is that practice is better than theory teaching on the H5 design education. By designing and developing a complete work of H5 themselves, students can get a deep insight into the creative thinking and methods. In addition, several other key points of hypermedia design teaching method will be summarized as follows:

Design with Product Design Thinking. Unlike traditional media, a piece of hypermedia work is better to be defined as an Internet product. Thus, the mindset of a hypermedia designer should be closer to an Internet product manager. First, the user-centered design method should be emphasized. Second, all the design materials should be organized around interaction. Third, all the design schemes should be limited under the project feasibility analysis.

Introduce Software Engineering Methods to Design. The traditional design embraces diversity and divergent thinking, while introducing more engineering thinking is more suitable for hypermedia design. Some development modes in software engineering should be useful, such as the top-down or down-top design methods, iterative design mode, object-oriented principles and programming logic models.

Enhance Multimedia Processing Capability. It is important for H5 designers to have the ability to integrate hypermedia resources, more specifically, to disassemble material resources and restructure them into new forms. Therefore, in addition to the ability to use graphic design software, a few more instruments to edit audio and video files, to product dynamic and special effects, and to develop interactive prototype products, should be mastered by hypermedia designers. What's more, the teaching content should also cover basic graphic and image knowledge, such as concepts of pixels, screen coordinate system and so forth.

Integrate Interaction Into Traditional Design. The teaching focal and most difficult point in the hypermedia design education is to train the students' comprehensive ability to integrate all the multimedia elements, especially the interaction functions into the traditional design. Different from the linear organization, multimedia materials are structured into non-linear forms. For example, users can experience visual, audio, and dynamic effects at same time by interactive operations, and be oriented to different scenes by different choices. Therefore, interaction plays the most important and central role in the whole design process for hypermedia.

5 Conclusion

The hypermedia is not a new concept; but it's evolving continuously in the Internet era. By taking H5 as a design object, this paper discussed the basic knowledge, and proposed design thinking about the hypermedia. Taking a teaching case as an example, we analysis the concrete practice methods of hypermedia thinking. While traditional design teaching pays more attention to abstract expressions, hypermedia design needs to construct abstract creation on the basis of rational thinking. It is necessary to integrate art and technology, software and hardware, abstract and representation, sensibility and sense in hypermedia design education.

Acknowledgement. This paper is supported by the grants of the School Basic Research Key Project (BIGC): Research on the Visual Image Innovation Strategy of Beijing's Time-honored Brand Project (Number: Ea202009); Top Young Talents Cultivation Plan of Beijing Municipal Universities in 2019 (CIT&TCD201904051); and the Doctoral Research Initiation Fund of BIGC (27170120003/024).

References

1. Begoray, J.A.: An introduction to hypermedia issues and application areas. Int. J. Man-Mach. Stud. **33**, 121–147 (1990)

2. Synodinos, D.G., Avgeriou, P.: Hypermedia design for the mobile era. Int. J. Mob. Commun. **2**(3), 271–284 (2004)
3. Piet, K.: Four stages in designing educational hypermedia. Eng. Educ. Lifelong Learn. **10**, 1–4 (2000)
4. Ignacio, A., Paloma D. Applying software engineering methods for hypermedia systems. In: International Proceedings on Innovation and Technology in Computer Science Education, pp 5–8. Canterbury, UK (2001)
5. Maeda, J.: Design education in the post-digital age. Des. Manage. J. **13**(3), 79–88 (2002)
6. Meyer, M.W., Norman, D.: Changing design education for the 21st century. J. Des. Econ. Innov. **6**(1), 13–49 (2020)
7. Zhu, W.: Study of creative thinking in digital media art design education. Creative Educ. **11**(2), 77–85 (2020)
8. OuYang, S.: The creative thinking in the art design education. Int. J. Soc. Sci. Educ. Res. **3**(6), 44–48 (2020)
9. Norman, D.A.: Emotional Design: Why We Love (or Hate) Everyday Things. Basic Books, New York (2004)
10. Cristina, P., Rita, M.S.C.: Educational support for hypermedia design. Mod. Educ. Comput. Sci. **6**, 9–16 (2012)
11. Tencent Big Data. https://bigdata.qq.com/. Accessed 15 Jan 2021
12. IH5. https://www.ih5.cn/. Accessed 15 Jan 2021

Examining the Impact of Covid-19 Pandemic on UX Research Practice Through UX Blogs

Sedef Süner-Pla-Cerdà[1]([✉]) [iD], Gülşen Töre Yargın[2] [iD], Hilal Şahin[2] [iD], and Semih Danış[2] [iD]

[1] Department of Industrial Design, TED University, 06420 Ankara, Turkey
sedef.suner@tedu.edu.tr
[2] METU/BILTIR-UTEST Product Usability Unit, Department of Industrial Design, Middle East Technical University, Ankara, Turkey

Abstract. This study investigates the emerging effects of the COVID-19 pandemic on the user experience research (UXR) practices by a systematic review of the grey literature focusing on remote UXR experiences. We reviewed 49 selected blog posts which share content about post-pandemic UXR experiences, and subjected them to content analysis. The findings show that the majority of the online discussions of the UXR community evolve around the types and methods of research with an apparent focus on moderated user research and user interviews. Equally common, step-by-step research methodology has been under scrutiny by the UXR professionals, such as concerns and practical tips regarding how research is planned, conducted, how findings are analysed and insights are generated based on the specific conditions of the pandemic. Other findings include debates and discussions about remote collaboration, trustworthiness of the research, wellbeing and empathy for others, and opportunities of remote UXR during the pandemic. In the light of the findings and the literature, we discuss the future long term effects of the 'new normal' on work life and UXR, and identify the potential paths to support diverse, effective, ethical and rigorous research practices.

Keywords: User experience research · Remote user research · New normal

1 Introduction

Social distance measures enforced due to COVID-19 global outbreak have led to disruptions in our daily and professional lives. As remote work became the norm for many occupations, the way user experience research (UXR) professionals were affected is multi-faceted, as UXR often involves direct contact with and observation of users. With abrupt changes in the work life, UXR professionals had to swiftly adapt remote methods, tools and mindsets to comply with the conditions of the new normal.

While remote UXR itself is not an entirely new phenomenon, it has been new to some UXR practitioners. The pandemic conditions also obliged researchers to consider and adapt remote methods for research practices which were traditionally conducted face to face, either in natural or contrived settings. Furthermore, understanding users

© Springer Nature Switzerland AG 2021
M. M. Soares et al. (Eds.): HCII 2021, LNCS 12779, pp. 579–592, 2021.
https://doi.org/10.1007/978-3-030-78221-4_40

has gained more importance during the pandemic. First, COVID-19 creates a risky and unpredictable environment for businesses, and being close to users is vital in minimising the risk of product failure [1]. Second, digital transformation has taken charge massively, rapidly and globally in numerous aspects of life including education, work, e-commerce, and public services [2], unprecedentedly increasing the amount and diversity of users.

For these reasons, even at the dawn of the pandemic, UXR practitioners were compelled to rapidly alter their work. This shared global experience has created an online conversation space mostly through blog posts, where they share personal or institutional experiences, concerns and recommendations regarding UXR in the pandemic times. In this paper, we aim to identify (1) how professional UXR practices are affected by the pandemic conditions, and (2) how these changes were received by the UXR community. For this purpose, we conducted a systematic grey literature review focusing on online content created by UXR professionals about their remote UXR experiences. In the rest of the paper, we first present a review of the transformational effects of the pandemic on UXR, addressing mainly implications of the pandemic on digitalisation, consumer behaviour, business and work life. Second, we present the systematic review, and discuss our findings in terms of the potential implications of the new normal on UXR practice, as well as identifying the ways remote UXR could be supported in the long term.

2   UX and User Research at the Dawn of the Pandemic

The global pandemic has major effects on the worldwide economy and businesses. Although global GDP is expected to rise over the following years after the sharp decline in 2020, recovery will not be fast and uncertainty will prevail with major risks for the economy [3]. This has obvious transformational effects on the international production networks and their investment policies, where adopting technology as leverage is seen as a way to build resilience and accelerate recovery [4]. Digitalization will help to mitigate the negative effects and enhance the economy by enabling firms and industries to safeguard both their customers' and employers' health, for example through remote, touchless or robotic services [5]. Together with increased digitalisation in daily life and other effects of the pandemic, consumer behaviour and how markets responded to those has dramatically changed as well [6]. Typical alterations in consumption patterns and consumer behaviour is especially observed as behaviours like stockpiling, improvising solutions for situations complicated by the restrictions, immediate technology adoption and talent discovery [7]. In this slippery context, getting the grasp of how consumers behave and making grounded predictions on these consumption patterns would be one of the most important ways to mitigate the economic risks and ensure resiliency [1, 8]. Therefore, despite the challenges of conducting research in these difficult circumstances, instead of cancelling or postponing the current research endeavours, they should rather be channelled to explore behavioural, psychological, regional and temporal effects of the pandemic on users, as this would be a way to survive even for the most disadvantaged industries such as travelling [9].

Considering the social isolation measures and health precautions, although research is vital for industries, it became more challenging than ever. Besides the mentioned economic implications, the effects are also drastic for research areas especially requiring face-to-face human interaction and lab work compared to areas which do not necessitate those [10]. The emerging circumstances require an assessment of the risks and benefits of conducting research with human subjects and deciding on whether or not to conduct or how to conduct it [11]. Naturally, for face-to-face interaction, priority is given to medical research regarding COVID-19, though the need for understanding social, behavioural and economic impacts still remains critical and requires adaptation of current methods to remote settings. Even though organizations like UX Alliance recommend certain safety measures for face-to-face sessions with participant users [12], when the risks and benefits are assessed it is likely that the former would overrule. Therefore, it can be easily said that the majority of user research efforts will be invested in remote research.

At the turn of the pandemic, researchers in social sciences as well as UXR have urgently looked for ways to turn face-to-face research into remote one with digital tools. Among these efforts, a crowd sourced document edited by Lupton [13] doing fieldwork for social researchers summarizing digital methods for remote research and remote research tool kit compiled by the user research community in Gov.uk can be considered [14]. Despite this urge to guide researchers in remote settings, remote UXR has been previously established especially for global research, where the cost of being on site to conduct the research can be immense [15]. Remote UXR methods can be defined as research methods in which the user and the researcher are not physically in the same environment [16]. These methods can be synchronous (moderated) such as interviews and usability testing, as well as asynchronous (unmoderated) like surveys, diaries and nethnography [17]. Despite its limitations, it is known that remote UXR holds certain advantages including saving time and costs, and access to a wider audience at a global scale [18, 19]. Moreover, not being bound to a particular physical space has its own advantages in terms of providing access to participants who may not be easily invited to the research site. Therefore, through digital mediums used in remote UXR, more inclusivity can be maintained for certain research cases [20].

Despite the advantages of conducting UXR remotely with digital mediums, several limitations and challenges are also mentioned in the literature. For example, remote research might require more preparation as researchers should consider the traditions, approaches, and perceptions of the target group before determining the tools and defining the research questions [21]. During the data collection process, it may be harder to ensure in-depthness without picking up non-verbal cues as communication is mediated by digital mediums [16]. Also, it is estimated that the participants' focus would be significantly shorter, hence there is a risk that the collected data can be more superficial and straightforward [17].

There are other challenges of remote UXR which apply especially in the present pandemic context. Although it frees from physical interaction, depending solely on digital mediums restricts participant selection in terms of their tech-savviness. Young people who are more technologically ready are the most preferred group for such studies, whereas conducting research with elderly and children can be difficult as their digital literacy required for using remote mediums for participating in UXR can be low to none. For elderly, even though use of technology for remote communication, remote delivery of treatment and telemedicine are identified among the priority areas for research in the pandemic context [22], conducting remote research with them through online tools can be problematic. Therefore, alternative ways such as postal services, telephone and face-to-face interactions-with safety precautions- should be considered to ensure inclusivity [23]. For children, participatory design, as one of the common ways to study their interactions, turned into box methods such as cultural probes which do not unnecessarily add to the technology exposure of children [24]. Furthermore, even though the participants are tech-savvy, having reliable and affordable internet connections is still an issue for several groups that may affect the research quality [25].

All these mentioned conditions and transformations changed and challenged the way the UXR is conducted. Although it is yet to be seen how much of these transformations will last until after the pandemic, it can be estimated that remote UXR practices will be preferable whenever the advantages overcome the challenges. For this reason, examining the early experiences of UXR practitioners and how they tend to adjust to the new normal would enable us to identify challenges and specify further research and solution areas.

3 Global Experiences in Transitioning to Remote UX Research

In order to understand the concerns, experiences and suggestions of UXR practitioners following this unprecedented global crisis, we systematically reviewed public online content, namely grey literature, about the initial effects of COVID-19 on user research practices and initial responses of the professionals. The term 'grey literature' corresponds to the information sources which cannot be classified under highly controlled and credible formal (academic) literature. It encompasses a broad range of content such as reports, articles, books, videos, blogs and emails, and can be reviewed for a number of reasons such as lack of volume or quality of evidence in formal literature or existence of a larger body of practitioner sources which indicates an interest in the topic [26]. Knowledge in UX practice and relevant areas such as software design is often produced and disseminated in the grey literature, especially in online communities and blog posts [27, 28]. Therefore, we investigated blog posts to understand how UXR practice is affected from the pandemic conditions. In this section we will present the methodology and findings of this systematic survey.

3.1 Data Collection Procedure

Our data consists of the online content about the effects of COVID-19 on UXR practices. In the review, we loosely followed the guidelines for search process and source selection identified in [26]. Although the outbreak was recognised as a pandemic in mid-March [29], lockdowns and other social distancing measures were put into effect in many Asian countries before this date. Therefore, the search results were filtered by dates between February 15 and September 1, 2020. We reached the final data set in three consecutive steps conducted by two researchers, who are the authors of this paper (Fig. 1). First, Author 1 applied a web search via Google Search Engine by using 9 combinations of the following two keyword groups: (1) "user research", "ux research", "user experience research", and (2) "COVID-19", "pandemic", "new normal". This initial search resulted in 1071 unique content. Although the queries were repeated with the Turkish keywords,

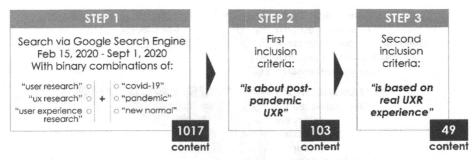

Fig. 1. Data collection procedure

they did not yield any original results. No filtering criteria was applied at this stage, other than eliminating the duplicate content.

In the second step, Author 1 reviewed these pages based on relevance, and included only those which are about UXR-related discussions in post-COVID context. This left 103 content, which were finally reviewed by both Author 1 and Author 3 to eliminate generic content and detect those that explicitly relied on real post-pandemic UXR experience. The final dataset consists of 49 pages, majority of them being blog posts (the list of sources are in Appendix A[1]).

3.2 Data Analysis

The final dataset was saved as separate text files and imported to Atlas.ti software for content analysis [30]. Three authors took part in the data analysis phase. First, Author 1 and Author 2 collaboratively coded around 20% of the pages (n = 10) to create the coding sheet and the glossary of terms. Then, Author 1 and Author 3 used this coding sheet and glossary to independently review and code for all the data. The coding process was based on nominal values. The researchers marked each page as "yes" only if the content matching with the code description is detected in it. Interrater reliability was calculated as 0.88 by using Cohen's Kappa coefficient (κ). Values between 0.8 and 1.00 are considered as "very strong" agreement [31].

3.3 Findings

The online content was grouped under eight main categories (Fig. 2 and 3). Since each category and subcategory was coded only once for each source in the code sheet, the frequencies were calculated out of 49 (find the code checklist at Appendix B). In this section, the definition and frequency of each category and subcategory is presented.

Research Types and Methods. Two issues commonly mentioned in the online content are *research types* and *research methods* (Fig. 2). A small number of content focusing on research types point out to face-to-face research experiences during pandemic including

---

Appendices are accessible as separate sheets at: https://docs.google.com/spreadsheets/d/1Al Vmp0lgYdrSBlx6tl3WFpb3_iGZFYefZM35eOQm3SQ/.

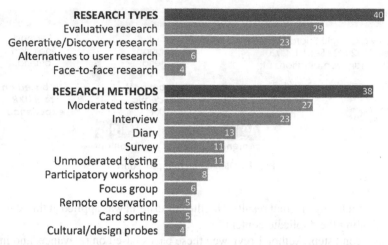

Fig. 2. Types and methods of research mentioned in blogs

safety precautions, or alternatives to user research such as desk research, marketing data or previously conducted research. Statements, experiences and suggestions regarding evaluative or generative/discovery research constitute the majority of such content.

Of all the research methods, *moderated usability testing* and *interview* were mentioned the most. These were followed by *diary*, *survey* and *unmoderated usability testing* methods, respectively. Less frequently mentioned are the methods mainly used for generative/discovery purposes, namely partici*patory workshop, focus group, remote observation, card sorting* and *cultural/design probes.*

Research Methodology. Experiences, concerns and recommendations regarding research methodology constitute the most dominant online content. These include the planning, execution, analysis and insight generation phases of the user research (Fig. 3). First of all, *care for research methodology* is mentioned as a concern which applies to remote UXR as much as it does to face to face research, although it is recommended to be flexible and open to adaptations in the methodology due to pandemic conditions (e.g. keeping certain steps shorter or longer than originally planned).

Discussions on *data analysis and synthesis of insights* are mainly concentrated around methods and tools of remote collaboration. As this phase is recommended to be conducted as a team, it is suggested to use shared files and boards which resembles face to face team meetings and workshops, collect insights via such platforms, and organise a team recap session for prioritisation and development of design roadmap.

Experiences and recommendations on planning and preparing for remote sessions are widely shared. Part of this content focuses on recommendations on *preparing for sessions* in order to have a fruitful session, such as writing step-by-step scripts, preparing instructions for participants, sharing necessary documents with participants prior to the session and pilot testing the procedure. Additionally, many sources draw attention to the need for being prepared and *planning for technical setbacks* such as internet disconnection, electricity cut, or any potential problem that can be experienced due to the device, broadband speed or network settings of the participants.

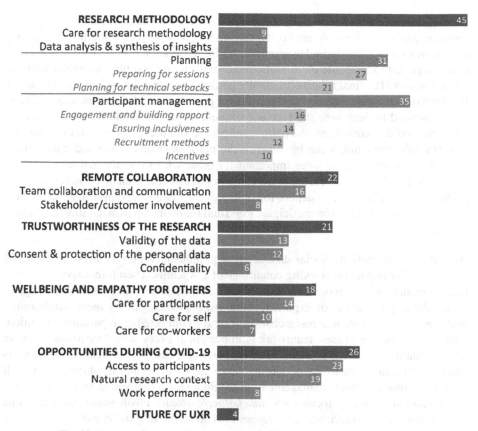

Fig. 3. Issues related to conducting remote UXR in the pandemic context

One of the most discussed content is *participant management*, including issues of rapport, inclusiveness, access and incentives. Firstly, it is assumed that *engagement and building rapport* with the participant will be more challenging in remote research compared to face to face due to lack of mimics and gestures, lack of control over the research environment which leads to disruptions by children, pets or the doorbell, and the difficulties of focusing on the study due to the domination of the pandemic over personal experiences in every aspect of lives. To overcome such challenges, it is recommended to extend warm up conversation, give more time to participants, keep the camera on to support communication with eye contact and nodding, and design interactive and fun research procedures and tools to avoid monotony. *Ensuring inclusiveness* is particularly stressed both because of the expansion of user profiles due to pandemic, and because disadvantaged groups are affected disproportionately in the times of crisis. The need for paying extra effort to include users with socio-cultural, socio-economical, generational and physical disadvantages is underlined.

For *recruitment methods*, it is recommended to collaborate with third-party agencies in addition to own participant pools of the company, with emphasis on describing a thorough and accurate target user description. Although many online usability platforms provide a participant pool, it raises concerns as monetary motivations of the pool participants may harm trustworthiness. So, it is recommended to introduce additional screening questions to access the desired user profile. As for moderated and synchronous sessions, it is suggested to schedule extra participants considering potential technical setbacks and no-shows. The final subcategory under participant management is *incentives* which involves discussions on how to compensate for participation of the users. It is generally recommended to determine the type and amount of incentive based on the impact of pandemic on the participant, the participant profile and the characteristics of research. For example, the amount can be lower as the participant saves time and travel. However, the incentive can be more important for those who were affected negatively by the pandemic. In some cases, the researchers might consider donations on behalf of the participant or tickets and vouchers for online events. Other recommendations include considering the workload on participant's end and following up to make sure the transfer was made.

Remote Collaboration. Social distancing requirements which dictates remote UXR have a similar impact on working conditions of UX teams. Therefore, experiences and recommendations on remote collaboration is often seen in the online discussions (Fig. 3). First subcategory focuses on experiences and suggestions regarding *team collaboration and communication*. As user research involves and is connected to preparation, execution, analysis and design phases, teamwork is important at every step. Discussions involve inviting team observers to sessions, team support in the case of technical problems, tools and platforms to enable teamwork during data analysis and synthesis of insights, as well as suggestions for project management, maintaining team motivation and productivity.

Second subcategory focuses on *stakeholder/customer involvement*. Similarly, this content consists of experiences and suggestions about inviting stakeholders to passively observe sessions, sharing interpreted session recordings with them to be browsed synchronously or asynchronously, and sustainable involvement and briefing of customers and stakeholders throughout the process via communication and remote collaboration tools and platforms.

Trustworthiness of Research. This category involves concerns and recommendations regarding the relevance of the collected data, research ethics and the responsibilities of the researcher in the context of the pandemic (Fig. 3). Firstly, these concerns are raised over *validity of the data*, rather than feasibility or rigour of the remote research. There appears to be discussions as to how the ambiguities emerging from the changing daily routines, habits and moods during the pandemic should be addressed in the user research process. Some question whether or not the collected user data will be meaningful in the short or long term. It is recommended to try to estimate which pandemic-related changes will be temporary or permanent in users' lives, revisit and update the aims and goals of research, and be flexible and responsive to changes.

Another important issue to be considered in remote UXR is *consent and protection of personal data*. Remote or online conduct of the research does not dismiss the obligations of researchers to properly inform participants, obtain consent and protect their data. Recommendations include assessment of research tools in terms of data security, preparing a digital consent form, retrieving written consent via e-mail or audio-recording the oral consent, and seek for legal advice when necessary. Finally, concerns about *confidentiality* are stressed particularly in remote research. On the contrary to the controlled environment of the face-to-face research where the participants are invited to use the software installed in the devices loaned by the team/company, confidentiality stands out as a prominent issue in remote research as the participants might be required to download and install the product, which may not have been released yet, and test it in their own devices. Recommendations include making non-disclosure agreement a routine procedure, using secure servers and delete prototype access links immediately after the session, or ask the participant to access remotely to the prototype which is installed in the moderator's device.

Wellbeing and Empathy. A significant part of the online content highlights the importance of being attentive to wellbeing and empathy towards the hardships caused by the pandemic conditions (Fig. 3). Many emphasised the need to *care for participants*, as people are affected by the pandemic in different ways and levels, which might have led to anxiety, stress, trauma and even mourning. Furthermore, the living conditions might be difficult and unstable; for example, in-house caring responsibilities are increased for many people, which affects their priorities and concentration. In such cases it is recommended to offer flexibility to the participant, be sensitive and use a comforting language, postpone the session if necessary, or re-examine the need for pursuing research depending on the topic and the sensitivity of the user group and consider alternative sources such as desk research.

Care for self and *care for coworkers* are also found important. It is suggested that one should be able to show the empathy and flexibility they offer others to themselves, and care for their own mental health as well. They draw attention to the globally experienced remote work, interruptions in social lives, increased domestic responsibilities, changes in routines and health issues. Accordingly, it is suggested to have realistic expectations from coworkers and themselves, be open to communicate and check in on each other.

Opportunities of Remote UXR During COVID-19 Pandemic. Almost half the content addresses the opportunities off the remote UXR as experienced during the pandemic (Fig. 3). Among those, *ease of access to participants* is placed on the top. People are believed to have more disposable time as a result of quarantines, working from home, cancelled events and no need to commute to the research venue, which led to access to a wider pool of potential participants. The flexibility of time and space helped researchers contact participants from distant cities and countries, as well as some niche user groups (e.g. executives) which were more difficult to access before. Other reasons listed are the positive attitude towards human contact (even if it is for research purposes) as opposed to social isolation, and increased motivation created by the incentives among those who were adversely impacted by the pandemic, e.g. loss of income. It is believed that this situation improved the user representation, and increased the quality of the data.

Natural research context is acknowledged as an important advantage in many of the sources. Participants are observed to be more comfortable in their own environment and be more open to communication. Furthermore, it is easier for researchers to observe issues which are impossible to detect in a contrived setting. Problems faced from connecting with personal devices, connection issues, interruptions and interactions of the users with their social and physical environment create the opportunity to observe the realistic usage setting. They share anecdotes about how the researcher could observe real time interactions, such as the discussions of family members throughout the food selection process while testing a food delivery application. Others emphasize more generic contextual factors like interruptions by pets, children, partners or business calls, as well as the artwork they hang or the music they listen to. Such observations are believed to be valuable as they increase empathy with the users. Finally, remote research is thought to have a positive impact on *work performance and efficiency*. No necessity for travel, less need for logistic planning, ease of asynchronous teamwork and the fact that all tools and research data is already digital are listed among the reasons why remote research is found to be time saving.

Future of UXR. Just like many sectors, UXR professionals too had to rapidly adapt to remote working conditions due to travel restrictions and social distance measures. Their experiences and anticipations signal the possibility of maintaining some of the remote UXR practices after the pandemic. As it presents clear advantages in terms of time and budget, it is estimated to be preferable under certain conditions, which may lead to hybrid applications by adapting the good practices of both remote and face-to-face research. Additionally, remote and flexible work practices are predicted to partially continue after the pandemic, which may include user experience researchers.

4 Discussions

Despite its limitations, the research context brought by the pandemic has even been received as serendipitous in terms of the possibilities it offers for design and research [32]. Likewise, the UXR community sees the opportunities in this context and despite challenges, they seem to be open to retain many practices even after the pandemic ends. It may be difficult to foresee as social distance measures are still in effect, and regarding practices are still unfolding. Nonetheless, our findings exhibit what has been discussed by the community as the initial response, providing generous insights into how the professional UXR practices would evolve in the foreseeable future.

Even though around half the studies mention discovery/generative research, they mainly consist of user interviews conducted with online conferencing tools or diary techniques. There is an apparent lack of methods to enrich the research with contextual data, such as observation and cultural/design probes. Additionally, moderated testing via online conferencing and screen share appears to be the dominant form of evaluative studies, with little mention of unmoderated/automated/asynchronous testing options. This may be due to the swift and compulsory shift to remote UXR by utilising and adapting their existing UXR know-how in the course of the first few months of the pandemic which we covered in our review. In order to be able to extend their remote UXR practices to the post-pandemic period, the companies will need to invest in and develop strategies for diversifying their research methods.

In terms of research methodology, session planning and participant management issues dominate the online discussions. These factors have a significant impact on the efficiency of the data collection procedure, as well as the quality of the collected data.

The major handicap of remote UXR is the low level of researcher control over the procedure. Not only that there are numerous technical issues that the researchers need to be prepared and plan for, but also remote communication poses significant disadvantages in terms of participant engagement. Such challenges impose more elaborate and meticulous preparation for the research sessions and attentiveness on the execution, a need that extends beyond the pandemic. Additionally, issues such as technology literacy and access to technology limit the researchers to work with a particular user profile. However, it should be foreseen that the digital transformation accelerated by the pandemic will continue to broaden both the number and diversity of the users. This requires developing long-term strategies and methods for a better user representation in the product development process, hence remote UXR.

Another issue that is closely related to the conditions brought by the pandemic is the opportunities for remote UXR, mainly access to a larger and more diverse user population, and conducting research in the natural context of use. In our opinion, these comments present an early optimism and should be assessed with caution. It is true to some extent that some people had more disposable time at the beginning of the pandemic due to lockdowns, disruptions in work life, and orientation to the new normal; as well as flexibility in scheduling the sessions and lack of need for travel to the research venue. We can anticipate that some of these conditions, such as the flexibility of working from home, will continue after the pandemic partly for certain user groups [33]. However, this might no longer be an advantage for remote UXR with the re-organisation of the work life in a planned and permanent fashion. Also, comments suggesting natural research context as an advantage of remote UXR share anecdotal evidence such as random and incidental observations of objects or interactions that occur within the partial camera view, rather than being conscious efforts. To be able to truly leverage the opportunity to observe contextual factors, the design of the research methodology should deliberately incorporate relevant techniques in a systematic way. Furthermore, the domestic environment cannot be considered as a "natural use context" for all products. In some cases, the natural use environment could be the workplace, school, transportation vehicle, hospital, and even outdoors. In order to amplify the benefits of integrating contextual factors in remote UXR beyond the pandemic, we need conscious efforts to find ways to accommodate remote tools and methods for various "natural" use environments. It is possible to adopt existing remote methods like diaries and cultural probes, as well as envisioning creative and effective uses of wearable and mobile technologies as data collection tools in remote UXR.

That being said, shifting the all face-to-face research venues to remote and online settings may raise the question of whether the observed phenomena and measurements are the same or not in these two settings [34]. Practitioners should pay special attention to understand the effects of remoteness and digitally mediated research on data quality. Moreover maintaining internal and external validity requires particular consideration of researchers studying behavioural and social issues as the pandemic circumstances are unprecedented, uncertain and unstable [35]. Hence, according to our findings, validity is also of concern to UXR practitioners as it is questionable whether the observed changes in user behaviour and use context are temporary or permanent. Given that the pandemic will have lasting effects which may restrict how UXR is conducted for at least a couple of years and its effects on user behaviour and psychology may continue within that time, how this poses threats to validity and trustworthiness in UXR should be examined in future studies.

According to the results of the study, the unpredictable and compelling conditions brought by the pandemic also heightened the sensitivity towards empathy with the research participants and UX practitioners, which is beneficial for the ethical code of conduct in the long term. As in many areas, digitalization in the work life has also affected the well-being of UX researchers. Although there exists many misconceptions regarding the locked-down digital work [36], conditions such as technostress [37] and zoom fatigue [38] induced by online team meetings as well as online research sessions are also valid for the practitioners in this area and require further investigation in terms of their long-term effects on employee well-being.

5   Conclusions

The online content we reviewed demonstrates a confident and optimistic attitude regarding remote UXR experiences. It should be considered that these reflect only the early reactions to the new normal, where the sense of global solidarity heightened the positive mood against the pandemic, and simply the opportunity to continue to work at this time of crisis itself was considered a blessing. Another possible reason is the business concerns as companies providing UX consultancy services needed to assure their stakeholders that they indeed can, and do continue UXR practices sufficiently enough by adopting remote research tools and methods. These limitations make it challenging to draw concrete conclusions regarding the long-term effects and the changing needs of the UXR professionals. Nevertheless, the content reflects the concerns and early experiences of the global UXR community.

Acknowledgements. This work is funded by TÜBİTAK (The Scientific and Technological Research Council of Turkey) Grant number: 120K215.

References

1. Craven, M., Liu, L., Mysore, M., Wilson, M.: COVID-19: Implications for business. McKinsey and Company Executive Briefing (2020). https://www.mckinsey.com/business-functions/risk/our-insights/covid-19implications-for-business. Accessed 08 Feb 2021
2. Dwivedi, Y.K., et al.: Impact of COVID-19 pandemic on information management research and practice: transforming education, work and life. Int. J. Inform. Manag. **55**, 102211 (2020)
3. OECD: OECD Economic Outlook, vol. 2020, no. 2. OECD Publishing, Paris (2020)
4. UNCTAD: Impact of the COVID-19 pandemic on trade and development: transitioning to a new normal. United Nations Conference on Trade and Development, Geneva (2020)
5. Grover, V., Sabherwal, R.: Making sense of the confusing mix of digitalization, pandemics and economics. Int. J. Inf. Manage. **55**, 102234 (2020)
6. Donthu, N., Gustafsson, A.: Effects of COVID-19 on business and research. J. Bus. Res. **117**, 284–289 (2020)
7. Sheth, J.: Impact of Covid-19 on consumer behavior: will the old habits return or die? J. Bus. Res. **117**, 280–283 (2020)

8. Diebner, R., Silliman, E., Ungerman, K., Vancauwenberghe, M.: Adapting customer experience in the time of coronavirus. McKinsey Company (2020). https://www.mckinsey.com/business-functions/marketing-and-sales/our-insights/adapting-customer-experience-in-the-time-of-coronavirus. Accessed 08 Feb 2021
9. Moran, K.: COVID-19 Has Changed Your Users (2020). https://www.nngroup.com/articles/covid-changed-users/. Accessed 08 Feb 2021
10. Myers, K.R., et al.: Unequal effects of the COVID-19 pandemic on scientists. Nat. Hum. Behav. 4(9), 880–883 (2020)
11. Lumeng, J.C., Chavous, T.M., Lok, A.S., Sen, S., Wigginton, N.S., Cunningham, R.M.: Opinion: a risk–benefit framework for human research during the COVID-19 pandemic. Proc. Natl. Acad. Sci. 117(45), 27749–27753 (2020)
12. UX Alliance: COVID-19 – Keep calm and Carry on Researching (2020). https://www.uxalliance.com/featured-publications/covid-19-keep-calm-and-carry-on-researching/. Accessed 08 Feb 2021
13. Lupton, D. (ed.): Doing fieldwork in a pandemic (crowd-sourced document) (2020). https://docs.google.com/document/d/1clGjGABB2h2qbduTgfqribHmog9B6P0NvMgVuiHZCl8/edit?ts=5e88ae0a. Accessed 08 Feb 2021
14. Baron, N., Petre, L.: User Research and COVID-19: crowdsourcing tools and tips for remote research (2020). https://userresearch.blog.gov.uk/2020/04/02/user-research-and-covid-19-crowdsourcing-tools-and-tips-for-remote-research/. Accessed 08 Feb 2021
15. De Boer, T.: Global user research methods. In: The Handbook of Global User Research, pp. 145–201. Morgan Kaufmann, Burlington (2010)
16. Bolt, N., Tulathimutte, T.: Remote Research: Real Users, Real Time, Real Research. Rosenfeld Media, Brooklyn, New York (2010)
17. Albert, B., Tullis, T., Tedesco, D.: Beyond the Usability Lab: Conducting Large-Scale User Experience Studies. Morgan Kaufmann, Burlington (2010)
18. Goodman, E., Kuniavsky, M., Moed, A.: Observing the User Experience: A Practitioner's Guide to User Research. Elsevier, Amsterdam (2012)
19. Marsh, S.: User Research: A Practical Guide to Designing Better Products and Services. Kogan Page Publishers, London (2018)
20. MacLeod, H., Jelen, B., Prabhakar, A., Oehlberg, L., Siek, K., Connelly, K.: Asynchronous Remote Communities (ARC) for researching distributed populations. In: Pervasive Health: Pervasive Computing Technologies for Healthcare, pp. 1–8, ICST, Belgium (2016)
21. Rubin, J., Chisnell, D.: Handbook of Usability Testing: How to Plan, Design, and Conduct Effective Tests, 2nd edn. John Wiley & Sons, New York (2008)
22. Richardson, S.J., et al.: Research with older people in a world with COVID-19: Identification of current and future priorities, challenges and opportunities. Age Aging 49(6), 901–906 (2020)
23. Hewitt, J., et al.: A multi-centre, UK-based, non-inferiority randomised controlled trial of 4 follow-up assessment methods in stroke survivors. BMC Med. 17(1), 111 (2019)
24. Antle, A.N., Frauenberger, C.: Child-computer interaction in times of a pandemic. Int. J. Child-Comput. Interact. 26, 100201 (2020)
25. Barnum, C.: Usability Testing Essentials: Ready, Set…Test!. 2nd edn. Morgan Kaufman, Amsterdam (2011)
26. Garousi, V., Felderer, M., Mäntylä, M.V.: Guidelines for including grey literature and conducting multivocal literature reviews in software engineering. Inf. Softw. Technol. 106, 101–121 (2019)
27. Kou, Y., Gray, C., Toombs, A., Adams, R.: Knowledge production and social roles in an online community of emerging occupation: a study of user experience practitioners on reddit. In: Proceedings of the 51st Hawaii International Conference on System Sciences, pp. 2068–2077. Curran Associates, Inc., Red Hook, NY (2018)

28. Melegati, J., Guerra, E., Wang, X.: Understanding hypotheses engineering in software startups through a gray literature review. Information and Software Technology, p. 106465 (2020)
29. World Health Organisation: WHO Director-General's opening remarks at the media briefing on COVID-19 (2020). https://www.who.int/director-general/speeches/detail/who-director-general-s-opening-remarks-at-the-media-briefing-on-covid-19—11-March-2020. Accessed 08 Feb 2021
30. Miles, M.B., Huberman, A.M., Saldana, J.: Qualitative Data Analysis: A Methods Sourcebook, 3rd edn. Sage, Thousand Oaks (2014)
31. McHugh, M.L.: Interrater reliability: the kappa statistic. Biochemia Med. **22**(3), 276–282 (2012)
32. Sein, M.K.: The serendipitous impact of COVID-19 pandemic: a rare opportunity for research and practice. Int. J. Inform. Manag. **55**, 102164 (2020)
33. De', R., Pandey, N., Pal, A.: Impact of digital surge during Covid-19 pandemic: a viewpoint on research and practice. Int. J. Inform. Manag. **55**, 102171 (2020)
34. Booth, T., Murray, A., Muniz-Terrera, G.: Are we measuring the same thing? Psychometric and research considerations when adopting new testing modes in the time of COVID-19. Alzheimer's & Dementia the Journal of Alzheirmer's Association (2020)
35. Fell, M.J., et al.: Validity of energy social research during and after COVID-19: challenges, considerations, and responses. Energ. Res. Soc. Sci. **68**, 101646 (2020)
36. Richter, A.: Locked-down digital work. Int. J. Inf. Manage. **55**, 102157 (2020)
37. Ayyagari, R., Grover, V., Purvis, R.: Technostress: technological antecedents and implications. MIS Quarterly, pp. 831–858 (2011)
38. Fosslien, L., Duffy, M.W.: How to combat zoom fatigue. Harvard Business Review, vol. 29 (2020)

Research on the Influence Factors of Designer's Emotion in the Design Process

Xuelin Tang[⊠], Jiapei Zou, Weiwen Chen, and Zhensheng Liu

Academy of Arts and Design, Tsinghua University, Beijing, People's Republic of China

Abstract. The emotional change of a designer may lead to a different design decision and therefore affect the outcome of the design. This paper aims to explore factors that affect the emotions of designers during the design process. To be specific, through the method of multi-level screening, three experiments were performed, including the preliminary screening of 435 emotional words, the study on the relevance of designer emotions to the design process, and the semantic similarity analysis of emotional words, after which the set of 29 frequently-used words concerning designer emotions was constructed. Further, the factors and conditions that affect the emotional state of designers were summarized based on 1069 textual messages of emotional experience in a retrospective interview. The results show that the five major factors that cause the emotional change of designers are the state and capacity of designers themselves, interpersonal interaction and evaluation, external resources and environment, progress and content of the project, and the performance and innovation of tools, while 15 minor influencing factors were identified as well. Finally, four strategies were proposed to promote positive emotions during the design process from the perspective of design organizations and designers. By studying reasons for emotional state changes of the designer, the paper proposes a new perspective of self-understanding and self-examination for designers and the achievement of this research may offer valuable guidance for the practice of emotion management in design organization.

Keyword: Emotional state · Designer · Influence factors · Emotional word set · Design process

1 Introduction

For designers, the design process is one of the main areas that require emotional input. Previous research has indicated that the emotional change of a designer may lead to a different design decision and therefore affect the outcome of the design. For instance, Desmet [1] argues that pleasant emotions have a positive influence on design practice and could help improve the quality of final design products. Dorst [2] describes the ideas or opinions that pop up during a design task as a highly emotional step that is impossible for any designer to ignore. Likewise, Ho [3] proposes that the emotional change of designers affects their ability to process information and finally results in variations in design results. Therefore, to ensure the smooth running of design projects

© Springer Nature Switzerland AG 2021
M. M. Soares et al. (Eds.): HCII 2021, LNCS 12779, pp. 593–602, 2021.
https://doi.org/10.1007/978-3-030-78221-4_41

and the high quality of design outcomes, factors that influence the emotional status of designers deserve to be further studied.

Existing studies on design-related emotions practically focus only on user perceptions of design results, with little attention paid to the personal emotional experience of designers during design practice [4], while the very few studies that explore the causes of the emotional changes mainly touch upon general components. Forlizzi [5] notes that changes in the external environment can lead to the different emotional status of designers. Based on the questionnaire survey on 120 students, Ho [6] concludes that the changes in designer emotions can partly be attributed to unexpected factors caused by technological change and those related to the external environment that are beyond the expectations of designers. It is noticeable that current exploration on factors that influence designer emotions lacks specificity and comprehensiveness, as well as recognition of high-frequency emotions in the design process. Therefore, this paper takes on the perspective of designers to explore the common types and sources of emotions that occur in the design process, aiming to provide new insights into emotion self-examination and management for designers and design organizations.

2   Study 1

To study the factors that influence designer emotions, above all it is necessary to identify those emotions that frequently appear in the design process. Therefore, in this section, the method of multistage screening was used for experimenting to retain the emotional words that frequently appear in the design process, based on which the high-frequency word set was constructed.

2.1   Method

As the study involves only Chinese designers, both the questionnaire and conversations in the experiment are in Chinese. Among the vast number of words in the Chinese language, researchers once teased out 435 words that cover almost all the emotions [7], which serves as the basis for the multistage screening in this paper. The steps are described as following (Fig. 1. Specific experimental steps).

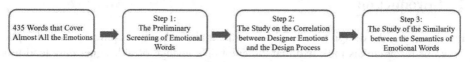

Fig. 1. Specific experimental steps

The first step is the preliminary screening of emotional words. Ambiguous or obscure words were removed from the 435 emotional words to make sure the samples studied would be semantically comprehensible and accurate. The participants include 90 Chinese designers, who come from random educational backgrounds and professional environments. The survey was conducted in the form of online questionnaire. The participants were asked to review the 435 emotional words successively to decide whether they are clear and easy to understand. They submitted their answers within two days by choosing "yes" or "no".

The second step is the study on the correlation between designer emotions and the design process. Among the emotional words in the set obtained from preliminary screening, some appear frequently in the design process due to the stimulation of various factors in the design process, while others do not. Therefore, it is necessary to screen out emotional words that are strongly associated with the design process. In this step, 84 participants were recruited, all of them are designers with experience in at least one entire project. During the experiment done separately on each, the subjects recalled the scenes during their involvement in design projects and selected those words from the remaining emotional words that they believe can be stimulated by activities related to the design process. Real-world work experience ensures a high level of validity of that judgement.

The third step is the study of the similarity between the semantics of emotional words. After two rounds of screening, some of the emotional words that remained still have problems of semantic similarity or are not precisely used for describing design emotions, making it necessary to conduct semantic analysis and clustering-based screening. Thus, a Doctor of Chinese Language and Literature and a Doctor of philosophy were responsible for screening the remaining emotional words. First, words not precisely used for describing design emotions were removed. Then, the remaining words were semantically compared in pairs and those sharing similar meanings were put in one group. In each group, the one that was selected most frequently in Step 2 was retained, while others were deleted.

2.2 Results

A total number of 90 questionnaires were obtained from Step 1. Preliminary screening was performed on the questionnaire results based on the criterion that at least 90% participants chose "yes", after which 274 easy-to-understand emotional words were left.

84 valid results were obtained from Step 2. Before proceeding to screen out the high-frequency emotional word set in the design process, this paper gave a definition to "high-frequency" first. A word is considered highly frequent when it has been selected by more than 58 times, which is to say, over 70% subjects experienced the emotion during the design process. A statistical analysis was done on valid results to obtain 70 high-frequency emotional words.

In Step 3, 7 words that are ill-suited to this study, namely, not precisely used for describing design emotions, were removed and 15 groups of similar emotional words were picked out through clustering. To ensure the conciseness of subsequent research samples, based on the results of Step 2, only the most frequent word in each group was retained.

After the screening conducted in the three steps, the condensed 29 emotions were obtained finally to form the set of high-frequency emotional words in the design process (Table 1), including 12 words of positive emotions and 17 ones of negative emotions.

Table 1. High-frequency word set of designers during the design process

Anxious	Admiring	Anticipating	Assured	Bored
Cheerful	Confused	Delighted	Depressed	Disorientated
Doubtful	Excited	Fretful	Frustrated	Gratified
Impatient	Inferior	Nervous	Powerless	Relaxing
Relieved	Regretful	Remorseful	Smug	Stressed
Touched	Unsettled	Vexed	Worried	

3 Study 2

The essence of studying factors that influence designer emotions is to externalize those emotions and to reveal their feelings and the causes of the change using emotional words and experiences. This section involves a retrospective interview on designers. Based on the statistic results, the sources of emotions were summarized and categorized.

3.1 Methodology

42 participants were recruited in this experiment, including 23 males and 19 females, all of whom are designers familiar with project processes and experience in at least one entire project. The study was performed separately in the form of structured interview. The host showed the 29 selected emotional words successively to the subjects and asked them to recall and describe the experience and event that triggered a certain emotion. A word can be skipped in the absence of related experience. The experimental process was saved in the format of audios.

After the interview was completed, all audio materials were converted into text with the method of natural language processing, and each piece of emotional experience was categorized. According to the context, the emotional words were put into the emotional category, and the causes that triggered emotions into influencing factors. Finally, the phases in which emotions appeared were categorized as project establishment, product design, design evaluation, and production preparation. The point is to highlight: in addition to the establishment, the phase of project establishment also includes the definition of design issues, judgement of design requirements, drafting of design criteria, and pre-execution analytical survey; the phase of product design includes the conception and expression of design ideas, which involve creative thinking; the phase of design evaluation primarily evaluates the design scheme and proposes suggestions for revision; the phase of production preparation is a transitional step with main activities of liaising with downstream engineers. For instance, an example of emotional experience was "I feel impatient if during model rendering my computer quits unexpectedly and start some time-consuming updates. As the causes of emotions, "quitting unexpectedly and time-consuming updating" fits into influencing factors. As the expression of design ideas, "model rendering" fits into the phase of product design, and "Impatient" into the emotional category.

3.2   Results

1,069 textual messages were acquired from the experiment. After useful information in each piece was stripped, the results of statistical analysis were as follows.

- "Anxious", "Relieved", and "Impatient" are top three words that evoke related experience, with 53, 50 and 46 emotional cases recalled respectively. By contrast, "Touched", "Regretful", and "Powerless" evoke the least number of emotional cases—30 for each (shown in Fig. 2). However, overall, each emotional word evokes the emotional experience of at least 70% (30) participants, which reflects that those emotions are indeed frequently experienced by designers.
- In the four steps of the design process, creative activities serve as a stronger stimuli of emotional experience than analytical activities do. The number of emotional cases in the phase of product design is far greater than in the other three phases, accounting for 50% of the whole design process.
- In the phase of project establishment, the most frequent emotions are "Confused", "Disorientated" and "Anxious", mainly due to lack of knowledge or unfamiliarity with external information resources. In the phase of product design, "Impatient", "Bored", and "Gratified" are the most frequent emotions, under the influence of various factors, such as the status of inspirational thinking and design capacity. In the phase of design evaluation, comments from other members on design works will cause emotions like "Delighted", "Excited", and "Frustrated". In the phase of design preparation, when part of the design work is about to end or the final design product will be unveiled, emotional words like "Anticipating" and "Unsettled" frequently appear.

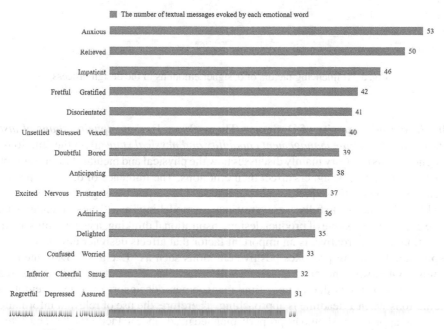

Fig. 2. The number of textual messages evoked by each emotional word

4   Discussion

4.1   Influencing Factors of Designer Emotions in the Design Process

An analysis was performed on the 1,069 pieces of emotional experience categorized as influencing factors to summarize five major categories and 15 items, which were identified as dominant influencing factors (listed in Fig. 3). Details of the discussion are presented below.

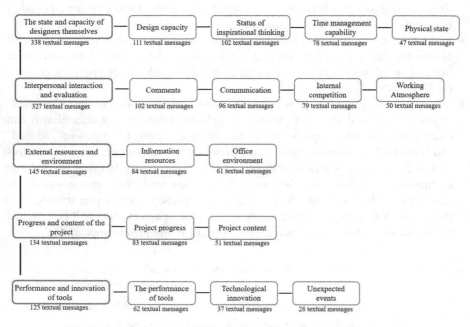

Fig. 3. Influencing factors of designer emotions in the design process

The State and Capacity of Designers Themselves. *Design capacity, status of inspirational thinking, time management capability and physical state* affect the emotions of designers. This category mainly discusses how the physical and mental state and comprehensive qualities of designers affect their emotions. The influence of design capacity is often manifested in the expressiveness of design. 111 textual messages involve information like "I'm not able to fully express my ideas in modelling" and "I cannot render out the real effects". In the stage of product design, inspirational thinking, a way of thinking that is contingent and creative, is an important factor that affects designer emotions. Active inspirational thinking provokes positive emotions such as "Excited", "Delighted" and "Smug". Otherwise, negative emotions will occur, like "Frustrated" and "Depressed". Moreover, sometimes due to poor time management, designers experience emotional fluctuations when a deadline is approaching. Therefore, the use of relevant information, tools, and approaches should be properly planned in advance to facilitate the achievement of design goals. In the textual information, the physical state of designers is related to their duration of work. After working long hours, they are likely to experience negative emotions like "Anxious" and "Depressed" that in turn affect their work efficiency.

Interpersonal Interaction and Evaluation. *Comments, communication, internal competition, and Working atmosphere* may lead to changes in designer emotions. This category mainly discusses how the connections established with other members and comments from them affect the emotions of designers. The emotional change of designers is most commonly associated with comments given on the design scheme by relevant people. Favorable comments bring positive emotions. The clearly-defined requirements and smooth communication between members provide positive emotional feedback for designers, therefore helping enhance design efficiency and outcomes. Meanwhile, the social stimuli of competition between teams makes designers feel nervous or smug. 34 textual messages mention that "I feel sort of smug when having the upper hand in the competition in my team." Working atmosphere mainly refers to the level of harmony between team members, which is positively related to positive emotions.

External Resources and Environment. *Information resources and office environment* may affect designer emotions. The lack of information related to the design project will provoke negative emotions in designers—one example is "I feel anxious when failing to get the information needed." Meanwhile, the office environment has a significant effect on designer emotions. Working in a bright, quiet and green environment can trigger positive emotions more easily.

Progress and Content of the Project. *Project progress and content* may cause changes in designer emotions as well. When the project is about to be accomplished or has arrived at a key point, there is invariably a change in designer emotions. For instance, emotional experiences like "I feel relieved after finishing reporting to the client" and "I feel delighted near the end of the project" were mentioned in the textual language. Besides, designer emotions are directly affected by the level of difficulty and fun of their tasks. 51 textual messages involve similar cases like "The boring work of organizing user data repeatedly makes me fretful", and "if the project is simple, I will be quite relaxing".

Performance of Tools and Innovation. *The performance of tools, technological innovation and unexpected events* affect the emotions of designers. This category mainly discusses the influence of the performance and status of tools on designer emotions. The conditions of design software, the operation speed of computers, the emergence of new software, and unexpected failures of design tools can provoke the different emotional experience of designers.

4.2 Strategies to Promote Positive Emotions in the Design Process

Designers who maintain positive emotions in the design process are more capable of processing information in a clear and reliable way, thinking actively and creatively, and producing design results of higher quality [8, 9]. Therefore, strategies need be developed to help designers maintain positive emotions in the design process. Based on the actual application of the research results of influencing factors, this paper puts forward four strategies to enhance positive emotions in the design process from the perspective of design organizations and designers (Fig. 4).

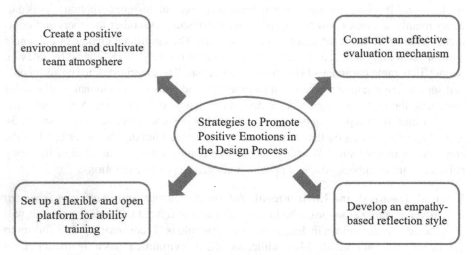

Fig. 4. Strategies to promote positive emotions in the design process

Create a Positive Environment and Cultivate Team Atmosphere. Martens [10] believes that design thinking should be completely visualized and presented in the work space. A collaborative, open work environment contributes to the development of creative thinking and the formation of positive emotions [11, 12]. Design organizations can create a proper work scenario by improving the functions of different types of space including individual space, cooperation space, production space, exhibition space and leisure space, enhancing the layout of space including flexibility, privacy and complexity, and adjusting physical elements like furniture, plants, views, sound, colors, lighting, temperature, and smell, so as to help maintain positive designer emotions. Meanwhile, it is also recommended that design organizations try to create a positive team atmosphere to promote the effectiveness and feeling of pleasure in team collaboration.

Construct an Effective Evaluation Mechanism. External evaluation is one of the factors that affect the emotions of designers. During the evaluation and decision-making of a design project, ambiguous criteria or evaluation based on subjective opinions will trigger negative emotions in the designer, such as "Disorientated", "Powerless", "Vexed" and "Confused". To ensure that the design results are scientific and objective, design organizations should strive to construct a multi-dimensional evaluation mechanism that works for the project by conducting an in-depth analysis of design goals in different phases, taking into account the diverse experiences and opinions of different roles, utilizing technologies like big data and artificial intelligence, avoiding the negative emotions of designer caused by an unreasonable evaluation mechanism.

Set up a Flexible and Open Platform for Ability Training. Design capacity and the state of inspiration have the biggest influence on the emotions of a designer, which indicates the significant effect of learning on design. Design organizations need to set up a flexible and open mechanism for ability training to ensure the flow of creativity and precise expression. For instance, regular training on software skills could be organized to help enhance proficiency with expressing tools, while polishing creative thinking skills to solve the problem of inadequate inspirational thinking. The training of these abilities contributes to the improvement of designer confidence and competence and therefore promote the formation of positive emotions.

Develop an Empathy-Based Reflection Style. While common ways to regulate emotions like distracting, self-rewarding, modifying demands, consuming physical strength, and seeking solace still work for designers, empathy-based reflection is a strategy for emotion regulation that particularly suits the needs of designers. The first step is to improve the empathy of designers, namely, their ability to share the feelings and emotions of other people, which allows them to analyze design goals at greater depths, to understand user experience and to better communicate with other project members, because designers with stronger empathy can perceive more keenly the intentions, preferences and values of others, and are able to timely regulate their own emotions and to facilitate more effective team communication. The second step is to develop an empathy-based reflection style to reflect upon relevant issues in the role of both the user and the designer, so as to obtain design experience based on a deep understanding of user experience, helping solve the problem of insufficient inspiration through the accumulation of experience. Meanwhile, the reflective mechanism will lead to a better understanding of the significance of interpersonal connections and deeper insights into the scenarios where a certain emotion can occur as well as the sources of emotions, therefore realizing the control and management of emotions.

5   Conclusion and Future Work

The study on the influencing factors of designer emotions during the design process helps designers recognize their own emotional state and the factors influencing it, while relevant strategies could be implemented to enable them to manage their emotions, which lays a foundation for quality design results. Moreover, it provides new insights to companies and design organizations, namely, paying attention to the emotional state of designers and offering more emotional support for them—after all, designers are the source of creativity.

Random experiments were conducted on a specific target group in this paper, involving a large number of experimental samples, from which authentic and valid results were obtained. Meanwhile, it should be mentioned that the current research is rather explorative, which may lead to incomplete conclusions. Plenty of previous studies take on the perspective of users to explore the relationship between user emotions and products, with rare examining the relationship between emotions and designs from the perspective of designers. Therefore, future research might focus more on the exploration of the relationship between designer emotions and design results based on the achievements of this paper.

References

1. Desmet, P.M.A.: Inspire and desire. In: Desmet, P.M.A., van Erp, J., Karlsson, M.A. (eds.) Design and emotion moves, pp. 108–127. Cambridge Scholars Publishing, Newcastle upon Tyne (2008)
2. Dorst, K., Cross, N.: Creativity in the design process: co-evolution of problem-solution. Des. Stud. **22**(5), 425–437 (2001). https://doi.org/10.1016/S0142-694X(01)00009-6
3. Ho, A.G., Siu, K.W.M.: Emotion design, emotional design, emotionalize design: a review on their relationships from a new perspective. Des. J. **15**(1), 9–32 (2012). https://doi.org/10. 2752/175630612X13192035508462
4. Sas, C., Zhang, C.: Do emotions matter in creative design? In: Proceedings of the 8th ACM Conference on Designing Interactive Systems, pp. 372–375. ACM, New York (2010). https:// doi.org/10.1145/1858171.1858241
5. Forlizzi, J., Disalvo, C., Hanington, B.: On the relationship between emotion, experience and the design of new products. Des. J. **6**(2), 29–38 (2003). https://doi.org/10.2752/146069203 789355507
6. Ho, A.G., Chau, P.W.: Understanding the capacity of emotion in decision making for designers in design process management. Int. J. Des. Manag. Prof. Pract. **10**(4), 13–24 (2016). https:// doi.org/10.18848/2325-162X/CGP/v10i04/13-24
7. Wen, S.: Study on product appearance based on emotional glossary. Tsinghua University, Beijing (2007)
8. Ye, N.: Process control. In: Wang, B. (ed.) Concurrent design of products, manufacturing processes and systems, pp. 225–246. Gordon and Breach Science Publishing, Amsterdam (1998)
9. Ho, A.G., Siu, K.W.M.: Role of designers in the new perspective of design and emotion. Des. Princ. Pract. Int. J. **4**(3), 16–24 (2010). https://doi.org/10.18848/1833-1874/CGP/v04 i03/37884
10. Martens, Y.: Unlocking creativity with the physical workspace. In: Proceedings of CIB-W70 International Conference in Facilities Management, pp. 579–588. Herriot-Watt University, Edinburgh (2008)
11. Thoring, K., Desmet, P.M.A., Badke-Schaub, P.: Creative environments for design education and practice: a typology of creative spaces. Des. Stud. **56**, 54–83 (2018). https://doi.org/10. 1016/j.destud.2018.02.001
12. Ho, A.G.: Principles of developing an effective environment for affective and pleasurable design team. In: Fukuda, S. (ed.) AHFE 2018. AISC, vol. 774, pp. 205–214. Springer, Cham (2019). https://doi.org/10.1007/978-3-319-94944-4_23

Research on the Influence of Team Members with Different Creativity Levels and Academic Background on the Collaborative Design Process

Zhengyu Wang[✉], Meiyu Zhou, and Zhengyu Shi

School of Art Design and Media, East China University of Science and Technology, No. 130, Meilong Road, Xuhui District, Shanghai, People's Republic of China

Abstract. This study will use quantitative research methods to explore the impact of the creativity and professional background of collaborative design team members on the design process development. Two experiments were carried out. First, First, subjects with different academic backgrounds were selected to participate in the Torrance Tests of Creative Thinking (TTCT). According to the test results, the subjects were divided into high, medium and low levels of creativity. Secondly, select 2 subjects at each level and set up a 6 members team to carry out a design task. Then we collect the semantic information in the experimental activities, and encode the data in time series, by structurally representing the data and information in the form of linkography, and analyze the link situation of each node and bring the node link data into the T-code parse algorithm, calculate the complexity, information (information content) and entropy data of every node. Finally, the team members' performance in the design process is evaluated from multiple dimensions according to the fluctuations and changes of experimental data.

The results showed that the level of creativity was positively related to the role of team members in collaborative design activities. In addition, teams with the same background are better than groups with different backgrounds in terms of fluency in the design process, conceptual evolution, and design direction and goals. However, from the development trend of the whole design stage, the team with different backgrounds has great development potential, and its design fluency tends to improve gradually, which is better than those with the same background in design divergence, novelty of design concept and design information implication.

This research provides a visual reference for the study of complex design activities, improves the efficiency of design cognitive computing research, and lays a foundation for future design research.

Keywords: Design cognition · Design process · Semantic link · Creativity · Collaborative design team

1 Introduction

Creativity is a uniquely human, comprehensive faculty for discovering and creating new things, the level of which is the result of a combination of factors, clearly distinguishable

M. M. Soares et al. (Eds.): HCII 2021, LNCS 12779, pp. 603–623, 2021.
https://doi.org/10.1007/978-3-030-78221-4_42

from general abilities [1], dependent on personal, cultural and organizational factors [2] and usually associated with better education and practice [3]. The development and advancement of creativity is valuable and is considered a necessary and prerequisite for invention and innovation [4].

In addition, in the current environment, as consumer product demand changes, product design needs to take into account more uncertain standards and constrained problem, which require a multidisciplinary approach to address, and product development activities evolve into innovative activities coordinated by professionals from different professional backgrounds and geographical areas. The difference of creativity level of collaborative design members has great influence on cognitive behaviors such as problem identification, planning, solving and the effect of design creativity. Therefore, it is very important to carry out related research.

At present, the research on the relationship between team members and design team creativity, team innovation performance and team organizational factor performance has attracted the attention of scholars gradually, also has formed some complete evaluation questionnaires or models. Examples include the situational outlook questionnaire [5] and the Science Team Creative Assessment Model [6]. However, most of the current design cognition research on creativity and team collaborative design has more or less some unresolved issues, which can be summarized as follows:

1. Most of the current researches focus on the factors affecting team performance, but ignore the effect of individual characteristics on membership heterogeneity.
2. Due to the lack of scientific and rigorous research methods, at present, the cognition of the design process in the field of design cognition is still at the conceptual level, and it is difficult to obtain the implicit design knowledge and functional representation data.
3. Lack of a comprehensive research framework. Most of the research is focused on the decomposition of design cognition process, which has some problems such as scattered research points and ununified research framework. In addition, there is also a lack of integrated experimental variables in terms of experimental time, questionnaire, project background, design experience, task complexity analysis, and design evaluation criteria. Moreover, there are some differences among parts of design cognition documents in the conclusion of the research.
4. Research in this area relies primarily on visual media data to study changes in the design process, such as sketches, video, hand gestures, etc. And very few of them rely on other sensory channels such as hearing and touch.

To sum up, this research will construct the multi-dimensional cognitive model of language text information and complete the deep research on the cognitive process of collaborative design team. This article discusses the following three questions: What are the differences in team design among members with different levels of creativity; What are the differences between the design performance of teams with different professional backgrounds and those with the same professional background; Whether teams with different professional backgrounds performed better in the design process than those with the same professional background; The results of this study can be used to evaluate design team members from multiple dimensions, help organizations to better configure teams, and provide a complete reference scheme for future research in this area.

2   Design Cognitive

Design is an expansive activity in which human beings realize their own ideas, plans, designs, creations, etc. [7, 8]. Design can be divided into two types, natural (intuitive) design and intentional design, according to the process from conception to result [9]. The study of the process of design from simple design concept to creative realization is the research on design cognition of a single designer or team [10].

2.1   Design of Communication Media

Design communication media is an extension of human senses and thoughts [11]. It can help designers to exchange information during the design process and enhance the effectiveness and identification of information dissemination. Therefore, the choice of design communication media has a great impact on the design details, error correction, etc. [12]. Designers rely mostly on visual media for communication, such as graphic and images [12], so visual thinking plays a key role in design cognition [13]. Design communication media is divided into traditional media and new media, which include spoken language, facial expressions, gestures, sketches, physical models, and computer models. The new media is a comprehensive concept, which includes the synthesis of five systems: text, sound, audiovisual, synthesis and channel. Many analytical tools and models have been developed, such as the tree structure genetic algorithm model for automatically generating 2-D sketches and 3-D images [14], the Digital Virtual Hybrid Modeling Tool (HIS) [15] and the VR3d sketch [16]. At present, the main research contents of design communication media mainly focus on the influence of visual media such as traditional sketch, CAD, VR-3D and digital virtual hybrid modeling on design cognitive efficiency.

2.2   Design Cognitive Features

Design can also be considered as a goal-oriented, constrained decision-making activity, and the design development process is characterized by organization, complexity and coupling [10, 17]. Design cognition also has logical characteristics, it is attached to the verification of design practice, practical features are obvious, the research difficulty is high, and the complexity of designing cognition is ubiquitous in the design process, so it has been paid much attention by the academic circles. In 2008, Zamenopoulos put forward the complexity theory of design cognition and systematically demonstrated the complex problem of designing cognition, which he thought included the following four aspects [18].

1. The complexity of design team. At present, development of design tends to multi-field cooperation, and designer's ability, background, experience etc. Have a great influence on design process.

2. The complexity of the design process. Design activities are inherently dynamic processes and their development is not regular, making it more difficult to predict their evolution [19].
3. Complexity of design content. In order to find the optimal solution during the design process, designers will constantly compare, modify, update or delete scheme according to the actual situation, which is easy to be affected by some cognitive stimulation. Therefore, the analysis and research of design content, as well as the complete acquisition of the cognitive process of the designer are put forward higher requirements.
4. Complexity of design methods. Design process faces a large number of fuzzy definition problems [20] and corresponding design methods are numerous [21]. At different design stages, designers will adopt corresponding interactive media and methods of design information according to the reality, which will make the research on design cognition equally complicated.

3 Research Methodology

3.1 Creativity Assessment

Torrance Test Scale for Creativity (TTCT) was proposed and developed in 1966 by American scholar E.P. Torrance ect. It is considered to be the most widely used and most frequently cited creativity tester [22], and has been proven to work in China [23]. In this study, four activities were selected to evaluate the creativity of subjects. In this study, four activities were selected to evaluate the creativity of the subjects. They are unusual uses (empty cans), product improvements, finished drawing and line filling. Each subject was tested for 10 min, a total of 40 min. After the questionnaire was recovered, a professional with grading experience was given a unified score, and the results showed that subjects' fluency, flexibility and originality scores were obtained (The purpose of this study is less related to precision of thinking, so this item is not considered). Convert all three scores into a standard T score [23], and add them together to get the total creativity score. Divide the high, medium, and low intervals, select the two subjects whose total scores are closest to the median value in each interval, and participate in the next round of experiments.

3.2 Computation and Visualization of Language Information

Acquisition, Analysis and Coding of Oral Information. Subjects were encouraged to express as many personal thoughts as possible during design process. At the same time, its voice information is fully recorded through recording method to obtain basic information data. In addition, the data encoding and segmentation usually consists of four steps. First, researchers need to convert the collected spoken data into text information, either manually or using computer calculations, and remove the irrelevant and social language in order to obtain basic spoken text. Second, they divide and sequentially encode the oral data text and divide design phase. Finally, recognition and localization of text information which has great influence on the design process is an important content of design cognition research.

Expression Form of Design Cognitive Information Linkography

(1) *Linkography*

The concept of linkography was first proposed by Goldschmidt ect. It is an effective tool to evaluate development of design thinking changes in design process of designers and their teams [24], with each coded node in linkography representing a single design message. If there is a high correlation between two nodes, a connection is established. Conversely, if two points are not relevant, there is no connection. In addition, if the link span between the two nodes is large, it means that there is a big difference in the concept of nodes. In team design task linkography, such link is called long link, which indicates backtracking and summarizing behavior during the design process. The judgment of short link is also related to the span of link. If there is a short linkage between nodes, it means that the design concept has an inheritance relationship between two nodes.

(2) *C-K Theory Coding*

C-K theory is generally used to distinguish C concept space from K knowledge space in design process [21]. The addition of C-K theory can expand data space contained in linkography. Through evolution of knowledge between two adjacent conceptual links, many different hidden data can be derived, such as sequence of conceptual node evolution, formation process, time period of aggregation, and design contribution of a team member (see Fig. 1).

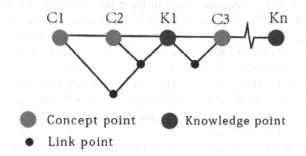

Fig. 1. C-K theory coding

Theory of Deterministic Information

(1) *Link Matrix*

Link matrix integrates the link data of stored nodes in a rectangular array arranged in form of a set of real numbers (complex numbers), which provides a basis for research or conversion of unstructured language data to structured data. Numerical values in a matrix consist of a set of numbers [0, 1] whose coding determines that they are derived from links in any node i. For example, node i is recorded as N_i, the corresponding linkage can be represented by its link vector L_i, and if it is linked to other nodes it will be recorded 1(association) in its linking vector. Otherwise, if there is no link relationship, it is recorded as 0 (no association). Among them, the node self-linking has no practical meaning, and it will be recorded as 0. In order to estimate the correlation between Ni and other coding nodes from small to large, the expression formula (1) is shown in the link vector L_i.

$$L_i = \left[l_{i1}, \ l_{i2} \ldots l_{in-1}, \ l_{in} \right] \tag{1}$$

L_i represents the link vectors of Ni, L_{i1} represents the semantic associative coding values of N_i and N_1 nodes, and in the same way, Lin represents the semantic association coding value of both N_i and N_n nodes. After completion of L_i encoding, a link vector will be formed which is the number of nodes. The combination of L_1–L_n will obtain the full link vectors and fit the complete matrix L_{nxn} formula (2) as follows:

$$L_{n \times n} = \begin{bmatrix} l_{11} \ l_{12} \ l_{13} \ \ldots \ l_{1n} \\ l_{21} \ l_{22} \ l_{23} \ \ldots \ l_{2n} \\ l_{31} \ l_{32} \ l_{33} \ \ldots \ l_{3n} \\ \vdots \ \ \vdots \ \ \vdots \ \ \vdots \ \ \vdots \\ l_{n1} \ l_{n2} \ l_{n3} \ \ldots \ l_{nn} \end{bmatrix} \tag{2}$$

In this formula, n denotes the number of nodes encoding design activity link. L_{nxn} is composed of n × n number, each of these numbers is called an element of the matrix, abbreviated as element. Number L_{xy} represents in column y of line x of the matrix L_{nxn} and it calls (x, y) element of the matrix L_{nxn}, whose coded values (0 or 1) represent a direct link between node x and node y. Its coded values (0 or 1) represent the same value of nodes x and node y. A value of 1 has a link, but when the value is 0 two things happen. The first indicates that the nodes are not linked, and the second indicates link itself. In other words, x has the same value as y and that this link is meaningless and is encoded as 0.

(2) *Analysis Algorithm of T-code*

In 2002 and 2004, Titchener put forward the theory of deterministic information in his two studies and discussed it in detail [25, 26], deterministic information theory can not only grasp the overall trend but also pay attention to the change of each node. Based on the theory, T-code [27] is combined with data link to calculate the change of entropy value of each node more accurately, and grasp the overall change trend in design process.

T-code encoding set assumes that a string is composed of a set, that symbols are used instead of specific information, and that process entropy of the information source is accurately calculated by calculating the number of steps required to construct the string. T-code string is composed of a joint splice of the front and back links in linkography in Fig. 2, and its string decomposition formula (3) is expressed as:

$$X = P_t^{K_1} P_{t-1}^{K_{t-1}} P_{t-2}^{K_{t-2}} \ldots P_1^{K_1} a \quad a \in S \tag{3}$$

In this formula, S represents the initial set of elements of a string, namely {0, 1}, p_i represents the i decomposition pattern, k_i indicates the number of times the corresponding pattern is repeated, and the original string is represented by $X_1 = a_1$, $a_2 \ldots a_n$. First, researchers need to use the elements in S to segment the initial string X_1, and the segmentation will result in string $X_2 = a_1, a_2, a_3 \ldots a_n$. The penultimate set of characters in X_2 should be selected, set to mode p_i, calculate the number of repetitions of the p_i and assign the value to k_i. Secondly, the string is continued to be segmented and a new character group is added after each pi in form of $a_k \ldots a_i, a_{i+1}$, with the exception of a_{i+1}, which is the same as other individual small string groups in this group of characters. Finally, if the string can still be partitioned, iterative computation of steps above is continued, and the resulting decomposed string is output if it is no longer partitionable, ending the computation.

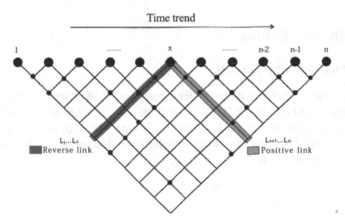

Fig. 2. T-code linkography

(3) *Complexity Calculation Analysis*
After the analysis algorithm of T-code, the basic data parameters are obtained, and then the complexity indexes (complexity (T_c), information (T_i) and entropy (T_e)) are calculated. The formula is as follows:

$$T_c = \sum_{i=1} \log_2(k_i + 1) \qquad (4)$$

$$T_i = l_i^{-1}(T_c) \qquad (5)$$

$$T_e = T_i / \|x\| \qquad (6)$$

In above three formulas, i represents decomposition times, k_i represents repetition times of pi, $\|x\|$ is length of string, T_c is complexity. It is mainly used to compute the complexity of linking nodes to other nodes. The larger value represents the more complex composition of its strings. If the node's complexity value is higher, it has more and more complex links with other nodes. T_i is the amount of information.

The higher calculated value represents the smaller distribution of characters in the string, thus supporting the greater the amount of information behind the single or multiple linked nodes that it represents, and the more complex design process. T_e is entropy. The entropy value of node represents the semantic pattern of character arrangement corresponding to inked node. The higher value represents the lower repetitive pattern and the more difficult to predict the new pattern. In the process of design, if a node has a maximum entropy value, it can be inferred and predicted that it may be a design transition concept or design transition-concept, which indicates that the concept evolves to a new stage. If a node has a minimal entropy value node, it is a concept of staged clustering or a new concept produced by it. Therefore, there may be some potential new concepts in the minimal entropy value nodes of design process. The difference between the maximum and minimum entropy in design process represents difference among the concepts.

4   Experimental Studies

4.1   Introduction to Experiments

The experimental research part of this paper is composed of two experiments. The content of Experiment 1 is to conduct TTCT creativity thinking test on subjects with different backgrounds. The purpose of test is to screen different levels of creative thinking and different background subjects for team collaborative design tasks. The experimental composition is shown in Fig. 3.

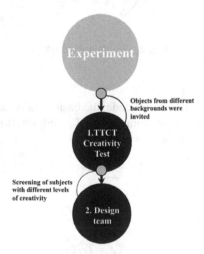

Fig. 3. Experimental composition

4.2 Experiment Subjects

1. Experiment 1 subjects
   In this research, 55 graduate students majoring in industrial design, product design and mechanical design as well as material engineering and visual communication were invited to participate in the experiment voluntarily. A total of 21 men and 34 women, aged between 22 and 27, took part in experiment for the first time. All of them had not participated in similar experiments and had never been tested for creativity. In order to carry out the experiment smoothly, subjects were given simple training before experiment 1 began, which reduced the weak basic knowledge of design and the lag in team design rhythm. After the experiment, subjects were paid a certain amount of money.
2. Experiment 2 subjects
   The data from Experiment 1 were divided into three levels of creativity and six subjects were selected (M = 23.5, SD = 1.76), including 1 male and 5 females. They will conduct team design activities with the elderly toilet seat as design theme. Prior to experiment 2, the subjects were informed of experimental process, after the end of experiment subjects can be paid a certain amount of experimental work.

4.3 Experiment Tasks and Process

1. Experiment 1 tasks
   The task of this experiment is to require the subjects to complete the four activities in Torrance Creativity Test Scale (TTCT) within 40 min. During the test, subjects were asked to answer as many questions as possible within a given time.
2. Experiment 2 tasks
   Due to the increasingly serious problem of population aging, the development of quality of life of the elderly has gradually become focus of researchers. Compared with other developed countries, however, China's products related to daily life of the elderly have not received much attention. Therefore, the design task of Experiment 2 focuses on the elderly toilets, which provides a solution to this social problem on one hand, and a basic data source for advancement of this research in the other hand. Experiment 2 is divided into three phases: initial design, intermediate design and final design. Each phase is expected to take 30 min, for a total of 90 min. Time exists only as a guide and reminder and does not interfere with the natural evolution of the team design process. Each subject is required to communicate as much as possible with other subjects during design process.

4.4 Data Analysis

Experiment 1. By the end of the test, we had obtained 60 TTCT answers, and eight invalid ones had been removed. Each questionnaire was scored and the total t scores of subjects were calculated: M = 150, SD = 28.24, as shown in Table 1.

A comparison of data from the same professional backgrounds in our previous study showed that the two groups had smaller differences in total fluency and flexibility scores, but greater variation in total creativity scores. We believe that this problem may be due

Table 1. Experiment 1 data table

Total fluency score		Total flexibility score		Total originality score		Total T scores	
M	SD	M	SD	M	SD	M	SD
37.3	9.49	28.42	7.71	38.42	12.45	150	28.24

to the different backgrounds of the subjects. In addition, as in previous studies, both the mean and standard deviation of the flexibility scores were lower than those for fluency and originality, suggesting that there was less variability in flexibility between teams from the same background and those from different backgrounds.

The subjects were divided into three groups, with a high creativity interval was $A \in [182.59, 221]$, the middle creativity interval was $B \in [144.102, 182.59]$, and the lower creativity interval was $C \in [105.61, 144.1]$, median scores of A, B and C intervals were calculated as 196.3, 158.8 and 120.3 respectively. Six target subjects were selected according to the scores and represented by A1, A2, B1, B2, C1 and C2 (Table 2).

Table 2. Team member data

	Team	High creativity subjects		Middle creativity subjects		Lower creativity subjects	
Number	6	2		2		2	
Subjects		A1	A2	B1	B2	C1	C2
Total creativity score		198.7	203.7	158.84	159.29	120.48	121.88

Experiment 2. Six subjects were selected from Experiment 1 to form a design team and carry out the experiment. The processing and coding of semantic data resulted in a total of 170 semantic nodes. Team of five experts was set up to link the relevant nodes and to code the 170 semantic nodes with C-K coding. The detailed information is shown in Table 3.

After the above analysis and coding, the obtained data are established as matrix and Python is used to convert the link information into link matrix L (170 × 170), as shown in Formula (7).

$$L_{170 \times 170} = \begin{bmatrix} 0 & 1 & 0 & 0 & \ldots & 0 \\ 1 & 0 & 0 & 0 & \ldots & 0 \\ 0 & 0 & 0 & 1 & \ldots & 0 \\ 0 & 0 & 1 & 0 & \ldots & 0 \\ \vdots & \vdots & \vdots & \vdots & \vdots & \vdots \\ 0 & 0 & 0 & 0 & \ldots & 0 \end{bmatrix} \tag{7}$$

Table 3. Experimental semantic information table

Serial number	Subject	Semantic data	Node keyword	Ck coding	Link code
1	B1	All right, come on. What do we need to do with this toilet for the elderly? Do we just make the toilet itself? Or will the rest be designed around the toilet seat as well?	Design range	K	2
2	A2	I would like to focus on the product itself, which will bring the design ideas closer together. So where do we start now?	Design range	K	1
3	C1	I think we should first consider the basic needs of the elderly, and then gradually design according to those needs	Target population needs	K	4, 6, 18, 53, 93, 112, 122
4	B1	I think we need to talk about the temperature of the toilet seat when the elderly use the toilet. You know, in the winter, the temperature of the toilet seat may be too low to stimulate the elderly, and has many adverse effects on the old people's health	Temperature requirements	C	3, 6, 18, 53, 55, 72, 93, 112, 122
…	…	…	…	…	…

(continued)

Table 3. (*continued*)

Serial number	Subject	Semantic data	Node keyword	Ck coding	Link code
42	A2	Is it better to add the lifting function?	Lifting design	C	29, 43, 87, 88, 89, 90, 123, 127, 164
43	C2	I've seen this kind of lifting and lowering, which helps the old man get up and down through the toilet seat	Lifting design	K	29, 42, 87, 88, 89, 90, 92, 94, 95, 96, 98, 99, 100, 101, 107, 123, 127
...	...	...	...	...	...
169	A2	OK, the color of toilet decided to use white	Color	K	71, 72, 168
170	C2	Then we basically completed this design, the final solution is what I just drew	Project summary	K	

4.5 Experimental Results and Analysis

Transforms the team link matrix into a linkograph, and divides the experiment into three parts according to experiment time and node linkage. First of all, we have predetermined the experimental time (90 min) and divided the design stage roughly (Initial stage of experiment: 0–30 min, Middle stage of experiment: 30–60 min, Late stage of experiment: 60–90 min).

Secondly, through the linkograph in the link situation, link distribution, link length of the situation after analysis (Figs. 4 and 5). We find that A, B, C, D and E areas are the main link areas in the design process, in which A area appears obvious short link dense phenomenon, while B area has long link phenomenon, this phenomenon indicates that the nodes in A region have generated multiple and divergent new concepts, and the concepts in B region are gradually converging. These linkage phenomena are consistent with the natural development of the design process.

During the concept elaboration phase, team members iterate over the resulting new concepts, and in the middle and later stages of the design process, some concepts may be modified, refined, or even discarded. For example, in node 50–59, team members revisited the design of night patterns, night lights, toilet cleaning, fecal detection, and remote control functions for toilets. These nodal concepts were first proposed before this section and are still linked to other nodes after it, indicating that nodes 50–59 section play a transitional role in the design phase. Based on the results of the time division in the design phase, it is concluded that the nodes 1–67 section is the initial stage of design.

The blue part of the linkograph is node 68–128. During this stage, there are clusters of short links (C area) and long links (B area), during which the design process moves towards the discussion of details. At the same time, many short connections are clustered between the nodes 87–101. It is explained that in this stage, the members have deeply discussed the concept of the incipient design, for example, node 87 discusses the selection of materials for the toilets in nodes 13 and 14 in the initial stage, and the lifting function design of toilet is proposed at this node. Many nodes since then, such as Node 88–90, 108, etc. have also carried out specific program supplement to the lifting problem. Based on the results of the time division in the design phase, it is concluded that the nodes 68–128 section is the middle stage of design.

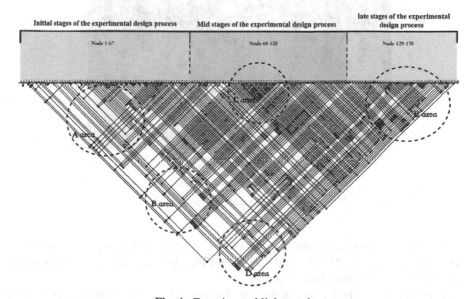

Fig. 4. Experimental linkography

After dividing the two previous phases, we find that the late stage of the design is 129–170 nodes. In this section, there are many long links and short link aggregation areas (E area) with a tendency to converge, which indicates that the team design is gradually converging and summarizing. For example, node 142 focused on the automatic opening and closing function, the cleaning function, and the touch function design of toilet. Carries out the structural deepening design for the problems in the initial and mid stages of the design, and carries out a more systematic and overall design and discussion on the single concept.

Node 164, as a summary conceptual node in the later stage of the design, summarizes the toilet tank design, one-click repair function, toilet lid opening and closing design, and button design. Compared with other nodes in this design process, this node has the most link relationship with the preceding and following nodes. In addition, node 164 is in the E area. Through observation, we found that there were many short links in area E, and there were also many long links (D area) that tended to converge between the linked nodes and the nodes in the initial and mid stages of the design. Indicates that in this area team members have carried out the final refinement and determination of the solution.

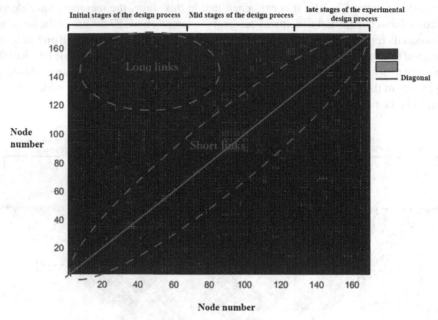

Fig. 5. Links distribution figure

Based on the above analysis, we divide the experimental design process into three parts: node 1–67, node 68–128, and node 129–170, which are the initial, mid and late stages of the experimental design process.

After calculating the team data, the data fluctuation figure is obtained, Figs. 6 and 7 show the transition from the beginning to the end of the design process, the values for each phase generally show a trend of up and down stages but a general trend towards smaller and steadier stages, however, in the initial stage of design, the overall entropy value did not fluctuate greatly, and its fluctuation shows a tendency of increasing first and decreasing later. Moreover, the average entropic value is not different from other design stages, which indicates that there are not many new concepts in this stage.

According to the information analysis in Table 4, only 32 C-code nodes were proposed by team members in the initial design stage, compared to as many as 36 K-code nodes. Through the concrete analysis of the experimental data, we find that team members have more explanatory language in the design and expression, and fail to form a better design direction in product modeling, structure, material, etc. We believe that this phenomenon may come from the different backgrounds of team members, leading to great differences in the design media (spoken language, sketching, etc.), and in terms of design emphasis, each discipline emphasizes different emphases, which may cause

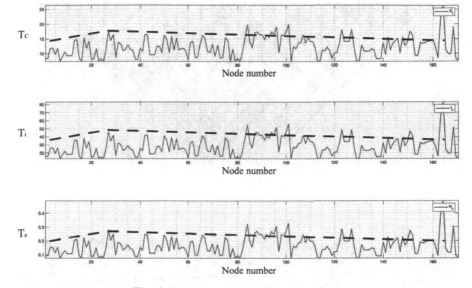

Fig. 6. Experimental data fluctuation figure

some difficulties in exploring the unity of the direction of group design at the initial stage.

In the middle and late stages of the design, the entropy tends to be flat and declining. But there is a high entropy value fluctuation interval in each of these two stages. In the middle stage of the design, the reasons for the high entropy value fluctuation section (node 82–100) are related to design backtracking. The team members begin to supplement and deepen the discussion on the new concepts that were not proposed in the previous stage, so the fluctuation of higher entropic value is also appeared. The entropy value fluctuation section (node 163–168) appeared in the later stage of the design was derived from the summing up of two concepts of previous phases by the team members.

Among all the data, node 164 has the highest entropy with value of 0.48. This node determines the design form of the water tank design, the cover design of the toilet, and the location of the cleaning function button. Nodes 16, 23, 81, 113, 114, 129 and 130 have the lowest entropy values, all lower than 0.1. The main contents of these nodes are the discussion of urinal odor, seat shape, etc. Because the content deviates from the concept of design main line, there are few links with other nodes and therefore have the lowest entropy.

From the perspective of the number of concept nodes provided, the members of group A are basically higher than those of group B and group C, and the overall trend of concept nodes numbers shows a slight downward trend after rising (Fig. 8). The number of conceptual nodes provided by members of Group A during the middle stage of design was the highest of the three phases, indicating that group A members were more active in the middle stage than in both other phases. Overall, group A has a higher number of overall concept nodes than the other two groups. The amount of information provided by group B was in the middle position, and there was little difference in the amount of

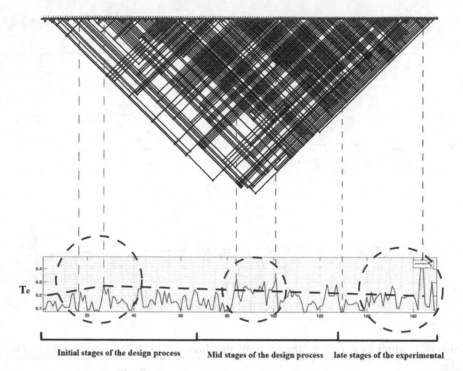

Initial stages of the design process   **Mid stages of the design process**   **late stages of the experimental**

Fig. 7. Experimental linkography and data graph

information provided by the two subjects in Group B. However, with the development of the design process, the gap between group B and group A in the middle and later stages of design is gradually widening, and the difference between groups B to group C is narrowing gradually. The overall data of group C showed a regular decreasing trend, and the two members of this group were almost the same in the number of nodes proposed.

In terms of the number of concept nodes and knowledge nodes, Group A is the highest, group B is the second highest, and group C is the lowest. In addition, all subjects provided fewer concept nodes than they provided knowledge nodes.

Combining the entropy values and concept types of the nodes proposed by the team members, we found that group A subjects were more active in team design, and presented more key creative ideas and creative ideas. Members of Group B play an important role in team design. Most of the concept nodes they propose are distributed around key nodes, and there is a link between these concept nodes and the key nodes, which can stimulate the proposal of the node or provide knowledge support for it. For example, after the key node 101 proposed the concept of lifting device design and material selection, node 102 conducted a more in-depth discussion based on the concept, and proposed an automatic lifting device, and ceramic is selected as the material of the toilet, which promotes the development the design process. In addition, most of the nodes proposed by the Group C members are knowledge nodes and the number of concept nodes is relatively small. Combined with information in Fig. 9, it is clear that the node they propose can effectively complement knowledge for the design process and also contribute to the development of design concepts.

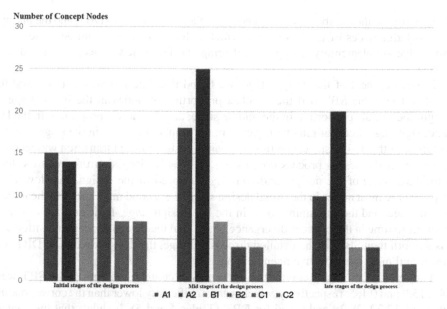

Fig. 8. The number of concept nodes of each member in different stages of the design process

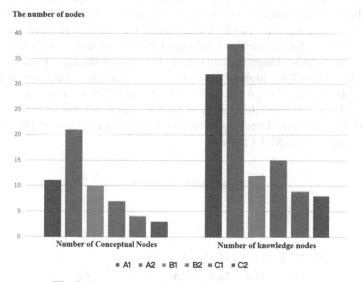

Fig. 9. The number of c-k nodes for team members

Same Background Team Versus Different Background Team. Combining the previous research data and conclusions [28], we compared the experimental data from the same background team (SBT) with those from different backgrounds team (DBT), and found that DDT produced more nodes per unit time than SBT.

In addition, the number of concept nodes of SBT is higher than DBT, and the number of knowledge nodes of DBT is higher, which indicates that this team generates more knowledge supplementary dialogues and brings up fewer new concepts in the design process.

In development of the design stage, we found that data of two teams showed the opposite trend, the SBT had the smallest proportion of nodes in the initial stage of design, the middle proportion in the middle stage, and the largest proportion in the late stage, showing a trend of gradual increase in the number of nodes in the stage with the evolution of the design stage. Overall, the team's design concept transition was smooth. However, as the design process progressed, the team's discussion time was too long in the later stage of the design, and convergence speed of the design was slow. DBT produced the most nodes in the initial design stage, the second most nodes in the middle design stage, and the minimum nodes in the late design stage. Indicates that this team spent more time in the concept divergence phase, and the design concept transition was less smooth than SBT. In the detailed discussion stage, the design rhythm of DBT was slower and more retrospective phenomenon.

The average values of complexity, information content and entropy of SBT were 8.42, 15.9 and 0.135, respectively, which were significantly lower than the corresponding values of 12.32, 28.28 and 0.166 for DBT (Tables 4 and 5). It shows that the content proposed by DBT in the design process is generally more informative and complex. This indicates that there is a strong jump between the concepts proposed by DBT.

In addition, the complexity and information content values of DBT are greater than SBT, while the entropy values of SBT are greater than DBT. Combined with the mean value and variance data of the three indicators of the two teams, we believe that SBT has more advantages in design fluency than BDT. Because the maximum and minimum entropy values of SBT are higher than DBT, and the variance of entropy values is also higher than DBT. Therefore, it indicates that SBT puts forward more design transition concepts and new concepts than DBT, and the differences between concepts are also greater. DBT has more backtracking behaviors in the design process, and the information of nodes is greater than SBT (Table 6).

Table 4. SBT experiment data

	Node							
	1	2	3	4	...	126	127	128
T_c	12.5	13	11.25	12.5	...	7	8	7
T_i	28	31.2	24.5	27.5	...	12	14.6	12
T_e	0.22	0.235	0.19	0.215	...	0.095	0.112	0.112

Table 5. DBT experiment data

	Node							
	1	2	3	4	...	168	169	170
T_c	8.2	8.2	12	12	...	19	8.4	7.5
T_i	16	16	26.5	26.5	...	52	16	13.3
T_e	0.093	0.093	0.155	0.155	...	0.308	0.095	0.075

Table 6. Comparison of team experimental data

	Maximum value		Minimum value		Average value		Variance	
	SBT	DBT	SBT	DBT	SBT	DBT	SBT	DBT
T_c	15.75	26.2	7	7.5	8.42	12.32	1.45	3.4
T_i	38.5	82.5	12	12.8	15.9	28.28	4.31	11.52
T_e	0.905	0.485	0.095	0.071	0.135	0.166	0.1	0.069

Summary. Based on the foregoing analysis, the following conclusions are drawn. In terms of the influence of members with different levels of creativity in the design process, those with higher scores on creative thinking were more active in team design, with more critical and creative ideas being put forward. The members with average scores for creative thinking have the ability to inspiration key ideas in team design and can facilitate the delivery of critical ideas. Those with relatively low scores for creative thinking played a role in promoting the smooth development of team design, and their design performance did not have a negative impact on the team design process.

In the initial and mid stages of design tasks, the number of creative points proposed by DBT is less than that of the SBT, and the design efficiency is also lower than SBT. However, in the late stage of design, this team outperformed the SBT in design efficiency.

In the aspect of design fluency, the performance of DBT in the initial and mid stages was slightly lower than SBT, but through the whole data analysis of DBT, we found that the smooth degree of their design showed a trend of increasing gradually, while SBT kept a basically unchanged trend.

In addition, although the SBT is basically better than DBT in terms of design fluency, design innovation concept and design concept evolution, the trend of development in the overall design stage shows that DBT have great potential for development. In the middle and late stage of design process, the design efficiency of DBT is obviously higher, the design fluency is gradually increased, and the concept proposed is more divergent. We believe that after many design trainings to help team members build a complete design mental model, DBT may come closer to the SBT in terms of design fluency, design innovation and design concept evolution. This team can be vastly superior to SBT in terms of innovative concept stimulation, design integrity and multi-perspective

5 Conclusion

This paper constructs a multi-dimensional cognitive model of language text information, analyzes the performance of collaborative design team in the design process by means of semantic link and calculation, provides a reference basis for complex design tasks, and improves the computing efficiency and automation level of design cognition. However, there are some limitations in this paper, such as the low number of experiments, lack of pre-experiments and the absence of comparison between experimental data and actual data. Therefore, some members had slight communication difficulties during the initial stages of the experiments due to different understanding of technical terms. This problem may affect the results of the experiment. In the next study, we will increase the number, form, and number of subjects and explore more types of team composition, such as a comparative study of design teams with or without intervention, or of teams of designers with mixed backgrounds, to provide regular findings on the impact of creativity on team design.

References

1. Kaufman, J.C., Sternberg, R.J.: The International Handbook of Creativity, vol. 52, no. 4, pp. 323–324. Cambridge University Press (2006)
2. Christiaans, H.H.C.M.: Creativity as a design criterion. Creat. Res. J. **14**(1), 41–54 (2002)
3. Sarkar, P., Chakrabarti, A.: Assessing design creativity. Des. Stud. **32**(4), 348–383 (2011)
4. Hennessey, B.A., Amabile, T.M.: Creativity. Ann. Rev. Psychol. **61**, 569–598 (2010)
5. Isaksen, S.G., Lauer, K.J., Ekvall, G.: Situational outlook questionnaire: a measure of the climate for creativity and change. Psychol. Rep. **85**(10), 665–674 (1999)
6. Zhou, Y., Zhang, J.: A Preliminary Study on the index system of high-tech Enterprise creativity evaluation. Econ. Forum **11**, 80–83 (2007). (in Chinese)
7. Goel, V.: Sketches of Thought, pp. 1–25. MIT Press, Cambridge (1995)
8. Coyne, R.: Wicked problems revisited. Des. Stud. **26**(1), 5–17 (2005)
9. Alexander, C.: Notes on the Synthesis of Form. Harvard University Press, Cambridge (1964)
10. Gero, J.S.: Design prototypes: a knowledge representation schema for design. AI Mag. **11**(4), 26–36 (1990)
11. Mcluhan, M., Lapham, L.H.: Understanding Media: the Extensions of Man. The Mit Press, Cambridge (1994)
12. Clemmensen, T., Campos, P., Orngreen, R., Pejtersen, A.M., Wong, W. (eds.): HWID 2006. IIFIP, vol. 221. Springer, Boston (2006). https://doi.org/10.1007/978-0-387-36792-7
13. Heylighen, A., Nijs, G.: Designing in the absence of sight: design cognition re-articulated. Des. Stud. **35**(2), 113–132 (2014)
14. Liu, H., Liu, X., Tang, M., Frazer, J.H.: Supporting creative configuration design in a computer-aided design environment. J. Comput. Aided Des. Comput. Graph. **15**(10), 1258–1262+1335–1336 (2003) (in Chinese)
15. Dorta, T., Prez, E., Lesage, A.: The ideation gap: hybrid tools, design flow and practice. Des. Stud. **29**(2), 121–141 (2008)
16. Rahimian, F.P., Ibrahim, R.: Impacts of VR 3D sketching on novice designers' spatial cognition in collaborative conceptual architectural design. Des. Stud. **32**(3), 255–291 (2011)
17. Ericsson, K.A., Simon, H.A.: Protocol analysis: verbal reports as data. J. Mark. Res. **23**(3), 306–307 (1986)

18. Zamenopoulos, T.: Design out of complexity: a mathematical theory of design as an universal property of organization. University College London (2008)
19. Chen, C.: Cognition Design: Cognitive Science in Design. China Building Industry Press, Sichuan (2008)
20. Cross, N.: Expertise in design: an overview. Des. Stud. **25**(5), 427–441 (2004)
21. Xu, J., Wang, X., Wang, Y., Ou, X.: The multidimensional modeling method of design cognition based on semantic link. J. Mech. Eng. **53**(15), 32–39 (2017). (in Chinese)
22. Lissitz, R.W., Willhoft, J.L.: A methodological study of the Torrance Tests of Creativity. J. Educ. Meas. **22**, 1–111 (1985)
23. Wu, J.J., Gao, Q.D., Wang, J.R., et al.: The Torrance tests of creative thinking norms-technical manual figural forms A, pp. 1–64. Yuan Liu Publishing, Taiwan (1981)
24. Goldschmidt, G.: Linkography: assessing design productivity. Cybern. Syst. 291–298 (1990)
25. Titchener, M.R.: Deterministic computation of string complexity, information and entropy. In: IEEE International Symposium on Information Theory. IEEE (2002)
26. Titchener, M.R., Nicolescu, R., Staiger, L., et al.: Deterministic complexity and entropy. Fund. Inform. **64**(1–4), 443–461 (2004)
27. EL-Khouly, T.: Creative discovery in architectural design processes: an empirical study of procedural and contextual components. London University, London (2015)
28. Wang, Z., Zhou, M., Liu, X.: The impact of different levels of creative thinking members in group collaboration based on semantic link. In: Ahram, T., Taiar, R., Colson, S., Choplin, A. (eds.) IHIET 2019. AISC, vol. 1018, pp. 240–246. Springer, Cham (2020). https://doi.org/10.1007/978-3-030-25629-6_38

User Experience Design of Navigation via Sense of Smell in Indoor Environment: A Case of Shopping Mall

Xiaozi Wang and Zhen Liu(✉)

School of Design, South China University of Technology,
Guangzhou 510006, People's Republic of China
liuzjames@scut.edu.cn

Abstract. With the development of economy, consumers' consumption mode has changed, from the material demand to the spiritual demand. People go to shopping not only to pay attention to the commodity itself, but to pay attention to the experience brought by the consumption space, i.e. the indoor environment. The experience economy is booming. Faced with the change of consumer demand, shopping malls must make corresponding changes. However, the current shopping malls in China are eager for success, and the phenomenon of homogenization and mediocrity appear. The experiential innovation that shopping malls bring needs to be appreciated, and few have been studied in user experience design of navigation via sense of smell in indoor environment. Hence, this research extracts new experience design opportunities through user observation and literature review, and proposes a wearable badge based on olfactory navigation as a potential solution to provide a reference for future shopping mall experience innovation, with a view to making future consumers can get a more immersive experience and meet the individual needs of consumers.

Keywords: User experience · Bluetooth positioning · Olfactory design · Olfactory navigation

1 Introduction

1.1 The Needs of Consumers and the Transformation of Shopping Malls in the Experience Age

In today's experience age, with the progress of urbanization and economic development, consumers' consumption patterns have also changed, from a material level to a spiritual level [1]. Most consumers go to the mall not just for shopping, but more for entertainment. In contrast to the past, customers are no longer just satisfied with a complete range of products and convenient services, but pursuing fresh and unique experiences [2]. Their needs are gradually individualized.

Therefore, Experiential Commerce is emerging. This is a multi-business combination business form based on retail. Compared with traditional commerce, it pays more

© Springer Nature Switzerland AG 2021
M. M. Soares et al. (Eds.): HCII 2021, LNCS 12779, pp. 624–636, 2021.
https://doi.org/10.1007/978-3-030-78221-4_43

attention to consumer participation, experience and feeling, and has higher requirements for consumption space and environment [3]. As the consumer space most closely related to urban development, shopping malls are the most common carrier of Experiential Commerce [3]. Scenery is the mainstream trend in the development of shopping malls today [4]. The contextualization of space can effectively induce experience [1]. Well-designed experiential shopping malls can increase sales. Therefore, how to create a scene that can bring new experiences to attract consumers has become the focus of major shopping mall design.

In the process of creating shopping space experience, space, theme and behavior are considered to be the key factors that induce experience [1]. In the design process of experiential shopping malls, the application of perceptual experience is paid attention to, but the application of vision and hearing get more attention, and the sense of smell is often ignored [5].

Experiential shopping malls in China are still in the stage of development and exploration, but some shopping malls are eager for success and copy development has appeared, which has led to the homogenization and banality of commercial buildings [2]. How to innovate the experience in the future and create a personalized consumption space to meet the growing high-level needs of consumers is a question worth considering.

1.2 The Influence of Smell and the Application of Smell Design

Among the five senses, smell has always been underestimated, and the influence of smell has been underestimated. However, stimulating or enhancing certain behaviors by dispersing odors has been verified as feasible [6]. The human nose is more flexible than imagined. Bushdid et al. found that humans can recognize about 10.000 odors [7]. Studies have also shown that there is a positive feedback between smell and spatial memory, and subjects tended to think that they were moving towards the side with higher odor concentration [8]. This shows that humans have a three-dimensional sense of smell and can obtain approximate spatial orientation information through smell.

The sense of smell can affect people's long-term memory, as well as their mood and feelings. A good smell can give a place meaning and make people remember it [9]. Due to the memory, locality and information characteristics of smell, olfactory design is proposed as a way to shape the city's characteristics [10]. Shao proposed in the paper to introduce olfactory design in the display space, balance the rendering of vision and hearing, and enhance consumers' memory and goodwill of the brand [11]. Wu and Chen also proposed in their respective papers that smell design should be added to the design of shopping spaces, breaking the single visual experience mode of traditional commercial spaces, and creating a new experiential shopping mall in the economic era [1, 5].

The application of smell in the commercial space will be a breakthrough in innovative experience.

1.3 Existing Problems of Fashion Tianhe Shopping Plaza and the Need for Research

For this project, the trendy Tianhe Commercial Plaza in Guangzhou was selected as the site for field research. Fashion Tianhe Shopping Plaza is one of the typical landscape experience shopping places in China. It is located underneath the Tianhe Sports Center in Guangzhou which is a large underground commercial plaza integrating shopping, dining, leisure, entertainment and landscape.

The observation found that the scene space created by Fashion Tianhe Shopping Plaza uses a lot of sound, light and color designs for the user's vision and hearing. However, there are few applications of scent. Even in some blocks, the exhaust is not well done, and there is an unpleasant odor, which greatly affects the entertainment experience of users.

In order to allow customers to stay for a while, shopping malls generally set up road signs to detour. However, the setting of signs in Fashion Tianhe Shopping Plaza is more confusing, and the height of the setting is unreasonable, making it harder to be viewed. At the same time, in order to allow users to better immerse themselves in the environment they create, the signs of the toilets and entrances and exits, the two "realistic" locations, are very obscure and difficult to find. However, for customers who are not familiar with this environment, the bad experience when looking for these two places will destroy their feelings about the whole experience process. Moreover, because Fashion Tianhe is located underground, the signal is weak, and mobile phone navigation is difficult to function. This not only increases the user's anxiety when finding the way, but the user's sight switches back and forth between the mobile phone and the real scene, which also greatly affects the user's scene Immersive experience.

Although complex or long movement lines can help shopping malls retain more consumers, when consumers want to leave, complex movement lines will often make consumers lose patience in the process of looking for the exit, and ultimately affect consumers' goodwill towards shopping malls. According to the peak-end rule, people's impression of an experience depends on the feeling at the peak and the end [12]. How to balance the needs of shopping malls and consumers is the key to further the experiential mall model.

Therefore, this study proposes a potential solution, which uses olfactory sense to enhance consumers' immersive experience in the shopping mall, enhance consumers' favorable degree to the shopping mall, and help consumers more clearly perceive the spatial layout around them, so as to reduce confusion and anxiety.

2 Evaluation

2.1 User Observation

According to the target group positioned by Fashion Tianhe Shopping Plaza, young people, especially students, are selected as the main observation objects. The observation time was weekend nights, and the main crowd on the scene was indeed dominated by young students. Most of them came together to play, and many people wearing traditional costumes came to the traditional scene block of fashionable Tianhe for shooting. There were also tourists who came for sightseeing. The observed behaviors are shown in Table 1.

Table 1. Customers' behavior and reason

Customer behavior	The reason
Wandering aimlessly. "Just walk around"	Users don't know where they are or what facilities are around them. Most consumers just wander around
Many consumers need mobile navigation to find the exit	The position of the ceiling sign is too high to be easily noticed; at the same time, it conflicts with the decorative sign on the ground, and it is difficult for customers to distinguish the correct direction
Turn or shake the phone to find the signal	Poor signal in underground
After walking out of the aisle where the bathroom is located, he looked blank	Each passage has multiple entrances and exits, the signs are not clear, and it is easy to go wrong to reach another block
In an attempt to figure out the direction	Doesn't know where he/she is and can't see references

In addition to on-site observation, this paper also surveyed the comments of consumers who have been to Fashion Tianhe Shopping Plaza on the forum, as shown in Table 2. After conducting desktop surveys on the Internet, netizens' forum statements confirmed the on-site observations and speculations. Netizens "complained" about getting lost in fashion Tianhe. They mentioned that entrances and exits are hard to find. Moreover, the underground shopping mall's signal is too poor, and navigation is difficult to function well. These comments from some netizens on the Internet proved that the phenomena observed were not accidental.

Table 2. What Netizens disgust about Fashion Tianhe Shopping Plaza

No.	Comments
1	Easy to get lost
2	The rotisserie is not well ventilated and smells bad
3	The signal is poor, navigation is not available
4	The toilets and exits are well hidden, especially the toilets

2.2 User Interview

In order to explore further users' needs, 5 students who like to go to shopping malls in their leisure time were interviewed. They have all been to the Fashion Tianhe Shopping Plaza and they are both 22 years old. An open interview method was used to understand their experience and feelings in the shopping mall. The questions and answers are shown in Table 3. Their answers are ranked according to the number of times mentioned.

Table 3. Users' answers of interview in the first person

Question	Answer
1. What do you think is the difference between the experience of traditional department stores and new shopping malls?	1. Traditional department stores seem to me like online stores, where everything is arranged neatly and you can quickly find things according to categories and regions. It's mostly about buying things. A shopping mall is more upscale, more like an entertainment place to me, even though it's called a shopping mall 2. Traditional department stores just feel crowded to me. Shopping malls will be more spacious 3. Most shopping malls are in the city center. It feels like there are a lot of fashion people there
2. Have you ever noticed what a shopping mall smells like?	1. K11 seems to have its own fragrance? But I think the smell is too strong for my liking 2. Most of it is perfume, right? The gourmet section is the food. But I think most of the space is full of flavor. Just create an exquisite atmosphere
3. What does a traditional department store smell like?	1. It smells like life. I don't know, it's a very realistic taste 2. The smell of raw food. Sometimes you can find the fresh area just by smelling it
4. For what purpose do you usually go to shopping malls?	1. Recreation 2. Go out with friends and go to the mall without knowing where to go. Don't worry about the weather. What's more, shopping malls have everything. It's easy to eat when you're tired
5. What factors will influence your decision whether to come back to the shopping mall next time?	1. Is the environment good? When choosing a traditional department store, they will consider the variety of goods, while shopping malls pay more attention to the environment and fun
6. Have you ever known the scene shopping mall?	1. I don't know much. But it literally means the construction of various landscapes in the mall. It's been very common in recent years
7. What was your best experience in the fashion world?	1. Complete stores. Eat, drink, and be merry 2. The scenery inside is very nice and suitable for taking photos
8. What was the worst experience?	1. It's hard to find the entrance and exit. Even walking directly from the subway is hard to find. The signs were confused. I had a good time, but I was upset when I went back 2. The ventilation of the barbecue shop in the gourmet area was not done well and the smell was bad 3. The signal is so erratic that mobile phone navigation is useless. But it feels like this is a problem for all indoor Spaces. Indoor signal is not good, navigation is not flexible

(continued)

Table 3. (*continued*)

Question	Answer
9. If you can't find your way, what do you do besides using your phone to navigate?	1. Have the courage to ask for directions 2. Go casually, when to go out with fate 3. Follow my nose and smell my way to the food court There is a lot of agreement on the function of signage: Things like Fashion Tianhe's signage are definitely wrong. But sometimes, I just don't know where to go or understand the signs exactly. The design of some signs is ambiguous. There is a lot of time do not pay attention to see the signs. There are too many eye-catching things in the mall

As can be seen from Table 3:

1. Even without a clear concept and understanding of the scenario-oriented shopping mall, users are still subconsciously pursuing a better experience environment. Because in this information age, the function of shopping mall is no longer limited to the "shopping" of the name itself, but a variety of services and functions.
2. Smell is a very personal thing. While some shopping malls have noticed the use of scent design to provide new experiences for customers, not everyone is happy with this kind of scent. Sometimes it can backfire and become a reason why some consumers choose not to come.
3. Signage may not work very well. There are so many eye-catching things in the mall that users may not see the signs if they are not paying attention. In addition, nowadays, people rely too much on mobile phone navigation. Without it, they always worry about going the wrong way, and they are not very good at telling directions.

2.3 Persona and User Journey Map

According to the observed characteristics and behaviors of the crowd, persona and user journey maps are constructed to sort out the key points and outstanding problems of users in the entire entertainment process, as shown in Figs. 1 and 2.

As shown in Fig. 2, entering the Fashion Tianhe Shopping Plaza for the first time, customers were shocked by the decoration vision. In the middle, customers came to the scene block to reach the highest surprise value. But the resulting search for an exit brings a bad end to the experience. So that consumers recall the experience, almost will have the feeling of "easy to get lost".

Zoe

21 years old,   College students ,   usually like to go to the business district for gatherings and entertainment

Traits:

Loves to play, shopping, brave to accept new things, catch up with the trend, have a certain financial foundation

Goals:

1. Relax at the mall
2. Find a place to rest and exit when you are tired
3. Can find the toilet soon

Behavior:

1. Wander aimlessly and see what is new and interesting
2. Saw the sign of the toilet just now, but now forgot where it is, but now need to go to the toilet
3. Tired and want to go home, but turn around and can't find the exit

Fig. 1. Persona

Stage	Find the entrance	Start shopping	Enter the scene block	Tired rest	Finding the exit
Doing	View mobile navigation or landmarks	Wander around to see what's new	Take a photo want to leave but found myself going around in a circle	Find a place to rest, check the route to go home later	Check mobile navigation, look for road signs and directions
Thinking	1.The landmark is too unobvious 2. The underground entrance is too hidden	1. The store products make me look dazzling. 2. I don't know where the food area is. 3. Where am I now?	1.It's so beautiful, how did I get here 2. Take a picture and record it 3. How do I leave here	1.Where is the rest area? 2. The toilet sign is so concealed	1. I was very happy, looking for an outlet made me feel bad
Feeling	😊 🙂 😣				
Pain		Users frequently watch mobile phone navigation, resulting in users not being able to immerse themselves in the scene created by the mall			The bad end of the experience ruined the good impression of the whole experience
Opportunity			Perhaps users don't need a detailed navigation but a "map" that quickly maps you to the nearest exit no matter where you are.		

Fig. 2. User journey map

2.4 Demand Analysis

This project involves merchants and users, so the needs of both parties need to be considered. From the perspective of merchants, how to create a consumer entertainment space that can make customers more immersive is a key point of competition today. New and unique experiences will mean more traffic and revenue.

From the perspective of users, most consumers now go to the mall not just for shopping, but more for a way of entertainment, wanting to get some rest in their busy lives. In contrast to the past, customers are no longer just satisfied with a complete range of products and convenient services, but are pursuing fresh and unique experiences. Most users wander aimlessly. They don't need a detailed navigation but a "map" that quickly maps them to the nearest exit no matter where you are. But if customers can perceive what's ahead, they will have more feeling control and stability, which can help them immerse themselves in the mall scene and get a better experience.

3 Solution

According to the research, a potential solution is proposed. Odor guidance can prevent consumers from switching their eyes back and forth between the phone and the environment, affecting the immersive experience. Therefore, smell navigation can make users more immersed in the scene and have a better play experience.

Concept brief:

1. A small "smell maker", users can set its scent with a mobile phone.
2. About ten meters away from the destination, the switch is triggered to release a smell to remind the user that the exit or toilet is nearby.
3. Give users more control.

3.1 Technical Principle

The main technologies and principles involved are:

1. Gas molecules are easily volatile when heated
2. Nanoporous materials can store and capture odor molecules
3. Indoor Bluetooth positioning technology iBeacon
4. Stereo olfactory navigation

Indoors or underground where the signal is unstable, the Bluetooth positioning system installs the iBeacon base station in the POI. When the user connects to the nearest iBeacon base station, the user can obtain the GPS location information of the base station and know the current location. When users enter or leave the communication range of an iBeacon base station, they will receive corresponding notification information to achieve the purpose of navigation. As long as the mobile phone can reflect the cached offline map, even if the signal is not good, the location can be sensed through the Bluetooth signal.

So in theory, when a user wears a scent maker and an odor appears, the user knows that the location indicated by the smell is nearby, and the stronger the smell, the closer the distance. In this way, users have a general understanding in their hearts and can choose their own route forward according to this information. While not telling the user exactly where they are, knowing what's ahead or around them in advance can help ease the user's anxiety. In addition, the device is worn on the user and can only be dispersed in a small area, which can satisfy the user's individual needs without disturbing others.

3.2 Flow Chart

As shown in Fig. 3, the location information sent by iBeacon is received through the Bluetooth module of the mobile phone, and then converted into a signal to adjust the heating temperature through the APP to transmit the odor navigation badge to realize the change of odor intensity and to remind the user of the distance change between the marked location.

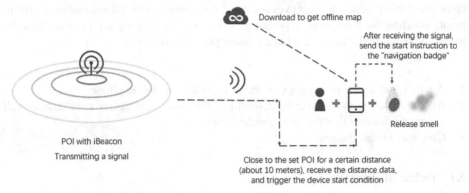

Fig. 3. Product workflow

4 Prototype Design

4.1 Dimensions

Source of inspiration for product modeling: analog signs on the map. At the same time, considering that the target population is not only women, it is designed as a gender ambiguous badge. The user can clip it on the backpack strap. The overall length is 6 cm, and the width at the widest point is 4 cm, as shown in Fig. 4.

The structure is very simple, and the main functional modules contained inside are: 1. Charging energy storage module. 2. Heating module. 3. Signal receiving module.

4.2 Rendering and Function Diagram

The rendering is shown in Fig. 5. The blue indicator light is also the master switch. After long pressing to open it, you can conduct Bluetooth combo through your mobile phone. The cover used to fix incense flakes is fixed by the way of rotating dislocation buckle, and the smell can escape through the holes on the surface of the cover. The wafer is made of nanoporous materials, and different regions store different odor molecules, corresponding to hot spots on the wafer, as shown in Fig. 6. Corresponding points need to be set through the supporting APP. And when you place it, you have to put it in the right place. Different odors can be synthesized by different temperature of hot spot and different concentration of odor molecules escaping.

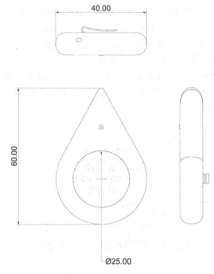

Fig. 4. Dimensions

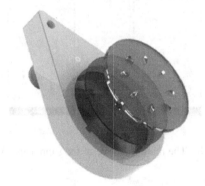

Fig. 5. Rendering of smell navigation badge

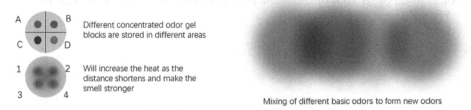

A | B Different concentrated odor gel
blocks are stored in different areas
C | D

1 | 2 Will increase the heat as the
distance shortens and make the
smell stronger
3 | 4

Mixing of different basic odors to form new odors

Fig. 6. Function diagram of heating module

The APP is only designed as a functional aid, and the original intention is not to affect the user's perception of the scene experience by paying too much attention to the phone. So the supporting APP function is very simple, only home page, setting page and map interface, as shown in Fig. 7. The main interface is shown in Fig. 8.

After connecting the device, it will automatically jump to the map interface. After searching the shopping mall that the user wants to go to, it will automatically cache the indoor map of the shopping mall (it will remind the user to cache automatically in the Wi-Fi environment). Users can then set their preferences on the Settings page to identify smells at a particular location.

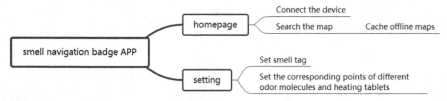

Fig. 7. APP architecture diagram

Fig. 8. The main interface of the supporting APP

Use scene concept map is shown in Fig. 9.

On the basis of the first-generation version, the curvature of the appearance has been strengthened, and the color matching of the product has been added. There are a variety of colors to choose from for the fragrant chip and shell color, as shown in Fig. 10.

Fig. 9. Use scene concept map

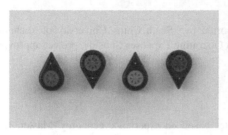

Fig. 10. Iterative modeling

5 Discussion

The current design of experiential shopping malls makes too little use of smell. Some applications are like the K11 shopping mall, which fills the whole space with a specific aroma. However, everyone has different preferences for smells, even if it is perfume, there will be some consumers do not like it. As the main consumer force, the generation born in the 90s and 00s have distinct personalities and pursue fresh and unique experiences. Giving them more options, such as setting their own scents to mark a particular mall, might be more appealing.

However, according to some existing odor manufacturing design concepts, such as the ophone designed by David Edwards [13], if the device can directly generate a variety of new odor molecules, it needs more functional components and larger volume, which is not suitable for carrying around, Therefore, the scented tablets with different basic odors proposed in this paper use the mixture of existing odor molecules to produce limited new odors in exchange for portable volume.

6 Conclusion

With the development of economy, consumers' consumption mode has changed, from the material demand to the spiritual demand. People go shopping not only to pay attention to the commodity itself, but to pay attention to the experience brought by the consumption space. The experience economy is booming. Faced with the change of consumer demand, shopping malls must make corresponding changes. However, the current shopping malls in China are eager for success, and the phenomenon of homogenization and mediocrity appear. The experiential innovation that shopping malls bring needs to be appreciated. Taking Guangzhou Fashion Tianhe Shopping Plaza as an example, this study extracted new experience design opportunities through user observation and literature review, and proposed a wearable badge based on olfactory navigation as a potential solution. This badge can emit a smell when approaching the exit of the mall or the bathroom to remind customers that these two places are nearby. And the concentration of odor is inversely proportional to the distance between the customer and the location. Customers can set the logo scent of different locations through the APP. This solution provides a reference for the innovation of shopping mall experience in the future, in order to enable future consumers to have a more immersive experience and meet the personalized needs of consumers.

Acknowledgements. This research is supported by "South China University of Technology Central University Basic Scientific Research Operating Expenses Subsidy, project approval no. XYZD201928, (x2sjC2191370)".

References

1. Wu, Z.: The analysis on shopping center based on experience economy. Master, Hunan University (2016)
2. Wang, Z., Tang, J., Feng, J., Zhang, R.: Innovative commercial design under new lifestyle-innovation of experiential shopping space. Architect. Cult. **06**, 230–231 (2020)
3. Zhen, S.: When popular business form encounters revenue balance – an analysis of the operating status of shopping center experience business form. Urban Dev. **20**, 78–79 (2012)
4. Tan, J.: Study on the type of scene of urban consumption space – a case study of shopping centers in China. City (09), 58–6 (2020)
5. Chen, S.: The research of experiential design in public space of shopping mall. Master, South China University of Technology (2012)
6. Bual, M.: Scent as a modality: study on the olfactory sense in multisensorial design. In: Ahram, T., Falcão, C. (eds.) AHFE 2020. AISC, vol. 1217, pp. 136–142. Springer, Cham (2020). https://doi.org/10.1007/978-3-030-51828-8_18
7. Bushdid, C., Magnasco, M.O., Vosshall, L.B., Keller, A.: Humans can discriminate more than 1 trillion olfactory stimuli. Science **343**(6177), 1370–1372 (2014)
8. Wu, Y., Chen, K., Ye, Y., Zhang, T., Zhou, W.: Humans navigate with stereo olfaction. Proc. Natl. Acad. Sci. **117**(27), 16065–16071 (2020)
9. Feng, R., Liu, L., Ma, D., Cheng, Q., Long, Y.: Urban smellscape - a dimension of street space quality. Time Archit. (06), 18–25 (2017)
10. Yin, M., Yang, Z., Li, G., Xu, J.: A tentative study on smell design in urban public space. City Plann. Rev. **40**(03), 58–62 (2016)
11. Shao, Z.: Study on the application of olfactory experience in the exhibition space. Nanjing University of Aeronautics and Astronautics (2019)
12. Li, C., Bao, Y.: Application of the peak-end rule in user experience research. Art Des. **2**(06), 179–181 (2011)
13. Walsh, C.: What the nose knows. https://news.harvard.edu/gazette/story/2020/02/how-scent-emotion-and-memory-are-intertwined-and-exploited/. Accessed 27 Feb 2020

Participatory Teaching Service Design and Innovation

DanDan Yu[✉], LiMin Wang, JingChuan Yao, Ning Zhang, Di Wang, and Yu Guo

Art and Design Academy, Beijing City University, Beijing, China

Abstract. This paper is about service design: the focus is on touch-points of services view as interactive events involving users and a service supplier; we mainly refer to traditional and innovative services provided by teacher and university, such as learning communication centers and cross disciplinary teaching platform services. In this paper the authors present a conceptual representation of participatory teaching shared by all services, some of that has been employed as theoretical framework in projects and didactical activities during the last few years; the proposed model supports the design of services both from the functional and formal points of view, outlining the complex correlation between students, teacher and university factors in services, highlighting some significant elements that influence the emotional experience of users, and investigating the role of the different contribution provided by the different discipline that concur in service design processes. User experience is mainly analyzed in terms of emotional and cognitive processes and it is related to perception studies. Furthermore, the paper presents a teaching model to the project of touch-points of services and some results obtained applying the presented theoretical principles to practical contexts, significantly in the field of undergraduate education of art and design; the project activities were mainly performed in art and design department of Beijing City University. Following the authors, the core element of user experience relies in the perspective adopted by a student toward himself and toward the professional study challenges posed by the course of career and the corresponding service fruition; to this purpose, service design interventions should be designed to support student in the adoption of a positive and adventurous attitude toward their state of study, reducing feeling of discouragement, boring and uncertainty often associated to frustration in learning and the unknown.

Keywords: Service design · Teaching service · Participatory teaching · Teaching model

1 Introduction

Student satisfaction levels with teaching service have become a key indicator in evaluating a university's teaching quality. As such, it has become important to realize students-centered teaching service that enhances the satisfaction of students. Universities need to adopt new and creative methods to respond to changes and redefine the role of the teacher and student in teaching processes. This paper presents the effectiveness of student participation by service design thinking for teaching processes, and aims to detail the model

© Springer Nature Switzerland AG 2021
M. M. Soares et al. (Eds.): HCII 2021, LNCS 12779, pp. 637–651, 2021.
https://doi.org/10.1007/978-3-030-78221-4_44

for a teaching service geared towards student-centered. The study proved the advantages of design thinking in identifying the diversified needs of student and coordinating their interests. Based on those, we design a teaching service mode and applied open innovation by design thinking for teaching processes. The key points include cooperation among students, the diversification of communication channels between students, capture multiple students needs, and visualization of the whole progression. Such points are principal factors that contribute to student orientation and participation, and are expected to play a conducive role in the realization of student-centered teaching service in the future.

Universities usual provide teaching services from a service supplier standpoint with a target to enhance their operational efficiency. Such a services supplier centric teaching service should not but be passive in discovering and accommodating the innate needs and problems intricate to the lives of students, as it would deprive the students of the opportunity to validate whether the teaching mode serve the teaching good. Consequently, students become unable to receive satisfaction from the teaching derived from such teaching service, and grow to mistrust their teacher and university. Such a cause and effect phenomenon could be summarized by stating that a delivery gap has occurred between university and its students. As student-centered teaching service proactively seeks out and accommodates the problems and needs of students, its process, objectives, and achievements are all based on satisfying the students, and thus reducing the delivery gap. And students participation is an effective way to increase transparency and trust. This study focused on the importance of "students' participation" to secure transparency in teaching service and overcome the delivery gap.

Design thinking was used by Tim Brown from the IDEO agency (2008) as "a discipline that uses the designer's sensibility and methods to match people's needs with what is technologically feasible and what a viable business strategy can convert into customer value and market opportunity" (Baek and Kim 2018). Therefore, we apply Participatory Design to teaching service, and the satisfaction of designing participatory services can be increased by including practices of service participants into the teaching process. In this paper, we though the description of an teaching service project of Beijing City University, the paper explores the potentials and limitations of using an ethnographic approach and Service Design Thinking to frame the service design process and interpret the complexity of services.

2 Research Context and Concepts

This paper is a project on improving students' conceptual understanding on self-designed learning roadmap. The approach for the project was a design-based research. After the needs assessment stage of the design-based research, there was the need to design and develop a teaching service system to help students self-designed learning roadmap. An embedded mixed methods design was used at this stage of the project to collect both qualitative and quantitative data for the study. During the teaching service try-out, Art and design undergraduates admitted to Beijing City University in 2018 and 2020 years was selected for the study. The total number of students was more than 600. And Digital Media Arts 1 class deeply participated in the study.

2.1 Status Quo of Teaching Services at University

In general, the teaching services available in Chinese colleges and universities "are promoted by administrative orders and are divorced from reality". There are several reasons for this. Firstly, teaching reviews and supervisions have become a formality. Secondly, support for students' learning is lacking as a result of the inadequate and low-quality application of information technology. Thirdly, support for teaching research and course reform is insufficient.

In many colleges and universities, students majoring in art and design do not specialize in a particular area of study in their first year. Instead, all students take the same foundation courses in art. It is not until they finish their first year of study that they start to choose the specific direction in which to major for the next three years. This teaching model originally sought to enable students to develop a more comprehensive knowledge before advancing into their major, so that they select the major that best suits them, inspires loyalty, and catches their interest. In practice, however, the new teaching pattern has not achieved the expected outcome, but rather it has caused considerable confusion to students vis-à-vis the selection of their courses and majors, according to research. The reason for this is that the aim of schools is not well understood by students due to the gap between the changed teaching pattern and unchanged teaching services. Thus far, selecting courses has been a "must-do" for undergraduate students, who struggle to enroll in their preferred courses. Consequently, this has become an urgent issue for universities and colleges, which unfortunately remains unsolved due to the large number of students involved.

The reform of the teaching support and service system in colleges and universities must cover a plethora of features. Firstly, the focus has to shift from teaching support to student-engaged teaching innovation. Secondly, the focus of teaching support and service must shift from teachers to students. Thirdly, the system should support not only traditional class teaching, but also online learning, student communication and the teaching service system, so as to enhance student participation.

2.2 The Status Quo of Self-cognition and Career Planning for Freshmen

Career planning is a topic of considerable concern for college students throughout their undergraduate courses. Planning a career consists involves multiple phases, rather than occurring at a single point in time. Proper career planning helps college students to better understand their own competitiveness and specialty, set clear objectives, make targeted study plans, and better shape their own future.

A 2017 study on the status quo of career planning for college students showed that 24.12% of college students have clear career goals, 68.42% are hesitant, and the remaining 7.46% do not want to make career plans, as shown in Fig. 1. Thus, the study demonstrated that most college students are undecided with regard to their career and have no plans for either their studies or life. Only 10.80% of college students surveyed possessed an in-depth understanding of their own major, while as many as 60.00% were either "fine with just not failing the course exams" or felt that course grades "don't matter at all", which shows their lack of emphasis on their studies or long-term study goals.

College students encounter various issues with regard to their career consciousness, self-cognition, career positioning, career preparation, and career pathway, which heavily affects their own development and diminishes not only their initiative to study, but also their employability. There are numerous problems with the career development courses currently available in many colleges and universities. For instance, the courses are designed from the perspective of students' employment guidance and are not tailored to each specific major. In addition, the courses often only become available immediately before graduation when students need to find a job. Thus, such courses lack subjectivity research on students and neglect their subjective initiative.

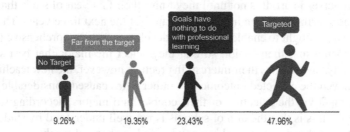

Fig. 1. Student's learning attitude

Therefore, the factors that affect the career plans of college students can be divided into two categories. The first one is the underdeveloped self-cognition of college students, while the other is their underdeveloped understanding of their social environment and career demands. Future teaching service systems should make self-cognition development and career planning available to college students throughout their undergraduate years, thereby enabling them to understand themselves, their major, and their future career demands. As a result, students would be able to match their hobbies and personal advantages to their future development, making their studies more intuitive and targeted.

2.3   The Study Situation of College Students

Since 2018, Beijing City University has implemented a Learning RoadMap Scheme for art and design majors. First-year students are offered courses in eight modules. These are design theories, design enlightenment, design performance, material experiments, design skills, design trends, art basics, sketching, and field surveys. Courses within each of the eight modules are taught by teachers from environmental design, visual communication, product design, fashion design, animation, and digital media art. This program allows students to understand the contents and career development pathways of different majors, so that they are better able to select the specific major that most suits them.

The author of this essay surveyed students majoring in art and design who enrolled in 2018 and 2020. The results indicate that 55.59% of students surveyed were hesitant with regard to their chosen major at enrollment, while 34.06% were quite clear in this area. Furthermore, 64.03% of those surveyed believe that they only had a superficial understanding of the various art and design majors of the school. The results further justify the Scheme, which allows students to first develop a better understanding of each major before making a decision. As a result, students are expected to remain loyal to their major and develop a stronger subjective initiative in their studies.

The survey also revealed some problems. For instance, although over 50% of those surveyed think that they are working hard to achieve their goals, 24.52% doubt whether what they are learning is preparing them for future work, and 19.89% are working hard on their off-campus study experiences and practices. Just less than 50% of those surveyed consider what they are learning to be exactly what they plan to do in the future, 23.43% believe that what they are learning is not very related to their future goals, 19.35% wonder whether they are moving further away from their goals, and 9.26% have no goals.In addition, 69.48% of those surveyed think that they have not developed a comprehensive understanding of their career goals since their knowledge is mainly superficial. With so many students lacking a clear goal and as many as 52.04% of those surveyed claiming they are not learning what they want to do, it is unsurprising that students are not doing well and lack the initiative to study and the motivation to overcome difficulties.

While reviewing the Study Pathway Scheme, some issues in its implementation were identified. This essay shows that, while selecting courses, students like to know not only the contents but also the form, means of practice, evaluation techniques, prior coursework and background of the teacher. Moreover, students want to know about the course teacher, including their research area, publications, and research achievements. However, the course selection system only offers course contents and students are not able to make informed choices relative to their capabilities and career development plans. As a result, the self-designed Study Pathway may not work for students as well as it could.

In order to address the above issues, it is important to improve the relevant teaching service system so that it focuses on students' development and allows them to make informed choices that take into account their capabilities, specialties and career development goals. Only in this way can students better engage in their studies and be able to formulate their own effective study scheme pathway in order to complete their undergraduate studies with more achievements.

2.4 Participatory Learning

Dewey conceived of learning as an active, fluid, and cumulative process where teachers cultivate educational experiences by giving direction to activities with which students are already engaged (Simpson 2006). Cunningham called the type of learning for which Dewey advocated "participatory learning," which could be considered as the most effective means of fostering intrinsic motivation, intelligence, the disposition for social cooperation, and an appreciation of aesthetic experience, and for helping students develop the habits of mind necessary to continually reconstruct their understanding and to direct the course of subsequent experience (Baek and Kim 2018).

According to McLoughlin and Lee (2007) in participatory learning "learners are active participants or coproducers rather than passive consumers of content, and so learning is a participatory, social process supporting personal life goals and needs." From Shen et al. (2004) participatory learning approach engages "students as active participants in the full life cycle of homework, projects, and examination." From the two definitions, it could be seen that students are basically active learners in participatory learning environment (Kucharcikova and Tokarcikova 2016, Ciobanu 2018). This is partly because students have opportunity to negotiate for the objectives, knowledge, skills, attitudes, or the teaching and learning methods of a lesson and that every student in a class has a peculiar learning style where teaching should be organised in such a way to engage him or her actively in the teaching and learning process (UNESCO 2001, AduGyamfi et al. 2020).

This essay applies participative methods to the teaching service system and the new teaching model, including student participation and student centricity. This system also features different student participation methods for different touch points, so that students can develop a stronger subjective initiative and participate more actively. By having the right to choose the contents, methods and focus of their own study according to their own free will, students are more likely to take their studies seriously.

3   Service Model and Design Principles

As with the general problems in our society, one must consider that the problems with teaching service are also complicated. Complication in teaching service originates from the disparate needs of the students. As the scale of students and teaching service expands, so continually does the complication of needs. Therefore, to understand the varied interests of students and obtain balance through adjustment, a new process or methodology for problem-solving is necessary. Changes in university activity requires not only organizational changes, but also a new service model that supports such changes.

This essay adds student participation to the design and implementation of the student-centered teaching service system, and reforms the current teaching evaluation system, supervision management system, and teaching support system, based on the diverse and complex needs of students. This study was conducted based on the following questions.

– What is the teaching service model?
– What are the principles that must be considered for teaching service?
– What are the advantages of using Participatory Design in teaching process?
– What is the efficacy of utilizing participatory teaching service model?

3.1   Teaching Service Model

Professor Dorothy Barton at the Harvard Business School proposed the concept of "T-type" talent in 1995, pointing out that individuals need to develop not only professional expertise (longitudinal) but also the ability to wisely apply the right knowledge in extensive backgrounds (horizontal). Only such individuals can form the backbone of successful companies. Numerous colleges and universities that teach art and design in China are attempting to apply an interdisciplinary approach to cultivating individuals, including through courses, experience, practice, research, and life. At the same time, they are incorporating various kinds of knowledge, capabilities, space and resources in order to form an ecological system for personal growth. In response to such a complex ecological system, this essay proposes a new teaching service system, which serves students

Fig. 2. The teaching service model

in their studies and life from four aspects. The four modules are: Vocational Cognition, Professional Cognition, Self-Knowledge, and Social Cognition, as shown in Fig. 2.

Vocational Cognition. The Vocational Cognition module allows students to understand the contents, requirements, procedures, status and social networks of future careers, as well as the status of companies and the development of industries. This module originally consisted of courses, social practices and lectures, most of which involve unidirectional teaching and are of limited quality due to the background and scope of the teachers and experts involved. The proposed teaching service enlarges the scope of its services in order to activate the social resources and activities of students themselves, thereby allowing them to get in touch with persons of interest through Second Class and sharing sessions. At the same time, they can access the latest information with which to develop their career goals.

Professional Cognition. The Professional Cognition module provides students with insights into scopes, prospects, teaching features, cultivation abilities, leading figures, design works, teachers' information, and relevant software, among other information, for all the majors available. The module is realized through the Learning RoadMap Scheme and enhances the study service platform in the new service system. The teaching information system, course-selection system, hybrid teaching system, laboratory system, library system, and credit and grade management system are newly designed and integrated through the experience design method and big-data analysis. The new system enhances the user experience for students and provides easier access to teaching service information, so that they can design their own suitable Study Pathway.

Self-Knowledge. The Self-Knowledge module allows students to review comments from their teachers, classmates and wider society. Their grades across various courses also help them to understand their own advantages and disadvantages. The evaluation system is regularly updated to include comments from students, industrial experts and society, so as to expand the channels through which students may display their works. Consequently, students can develop their self-knowledge and gain the motivation to study.

Social Cognition. The Social Cognition module allows students to enrich their extracurricular life and acquire various social skills by experiencing different approaches to life and discovering their own potential and interests. Through volunteer work, students are also able to develop a better understanding of the manner in which society functions and prevailing social rules. This module is achieved by courses in theme design, projects, public optional courses and Second-Classes.

3.2 The Design Principles of Teaching Service

As the concept of teaching service is wide-ranging, and as the viewpoints, needs, and objectives of teaching service have changed with the times, a variety of definitions exist. Teaching service is the process through which the university distributes learning resource in order to solve students' problems and form a more ideal learning environment. And teaching service refers to the comprehensive set of activities by the university to supply resources and services to students, aiming to satisfy students desires. And Teaching services are the tangible and intangible products that a university supplies to its students. Based on the above explanation, we think that the following principles are the design principles of teaching services system.

1. Student-centered teaching service
   The teaching service design will be centered on students, with a particular focus on the individual differences between students. The service will help students to explore their goals and develop their subjective initiative vis-à-vis their studies. As a result, the experience and quality of existing teaching will be enhanced.
2. Participative-study-driven teaching service
   Through this service, students will actively participate in the development of their study plan, the design of course contents and progress, the organization of extracurricular practices, and their selection of study activities. Moreover, students will also engage in the development of the teaching service design.
3. Make teaching service sustainable by using appropriate communication activities
   By diversifying the support groups available to students, by including their classmates, parents, off-campus students, graduates, frontline workers in target industries, and leading figures in those industries, students will engage in multi-point and multi-tier communication. At the same time, this will promote the sustainable development of the service system.
   By utilizing participatory service design in teaching service processes, university would reinforce their interactions with students and redefine the relationship, while simultaneously deriving drastic organizational changes. Such changes trigger two-way communication between universities and students, as well as contribute to an enhanced student initiative. Teaching service processes with a high student initiative

also have a high value towards the teaching quality, provide highly satisfactory services, and enhance the outcome of professional teaching. As such, the use of participatory teaching service in teaching processes is significant.

4   Design Framework and Process

The project study dealt with students at Beijing City University majoring in arts and design as design targets in its attempt to identify the causes for the delivery gap that emerged when supporting their education, and to propose a solution accordingly. This essay utilizes the service design method to improve the existing teaching service system. Students are chosen as the ultimate audience and student participation forms the main design means. They participate in the design of not only the service design system, but also all the touchpoints within. In 2003, the educator Boettcher proposed four effective study factors. These are the learner, teaching personnel, knowledge, and the environment. In this project, the design team views students as stakeholders, as shown in Fig. 3. Together, they form an interlinked and interacting service system that centers on learners and is linked with implicit and explicit services. The student-participative teaching service system features four different types of touchpoints, as shown in Fig. 4. These are "Insight, Interaction, Task, and Forum". This system not only focuses on the individual emotional feelings of students, but also emphasizes the activation of their subjective initiative, so that they actively plan their own studies and life and make adjustments accordingly. Thus, the system helps to enhance the teaching service quality and construct a complete teaching service design model.

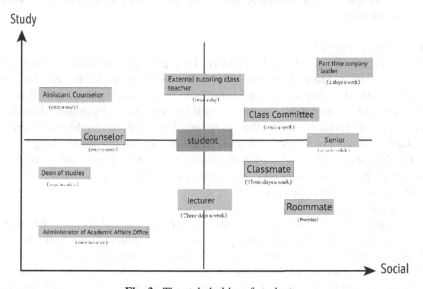

Fig. 3. The stakeholder of student

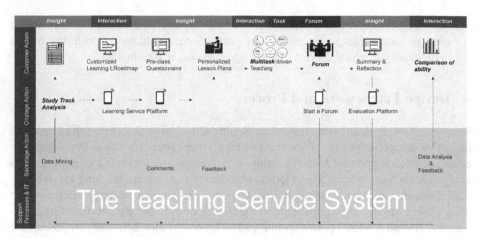

Fig. 4. The blueprint of the teaching service system

4.1 Insight

The complex and changing demands of students are attained from two channels. The first is communication through social activities in order to understand their needs and ideas. The second is a digital service platform based on big data, which analyses the study track of students online so as to understand their knowledge, capability index, hobbies and interests, and study habits.

The system is based on a student-participative teaching service system, which is available throughout their undergraduate years. The study process can be divided into three components:

- Before each semester
  The basic data of students are first analyzed using big-data techniques. Then, a questionnaire is offered to students when they select their courses, so that they can provide feedback on what they expect and want from the course. Su et al. (2010) note that the participatory approach to learning considers knowledge by doing. Moreover, the participatory approach requires that designers of instructions should involve end users in the design process. Consequently, users are partners and their knowledge is valued in the design process (Baek and Kim 2018). Therefore, students are engaged in the design of the courses they take, and teachers can tailor the course to make it suit students in different semesters.
- During each semester
  The system offers information on courses, exhibitions, and lectures, based on the study progress of students. Offline discussions and communication can also be spurred through the platform. Both students and teachers can establish their own project groups on the teaching service platform and recruit classmates, seniors, and designers from different subject backgrounds for the purpose of completing interdisciplinary tasks.
- After each semester
  The system focuses on course grades and evaluations. Course grade composition and evaluation techniques are reconstructed. Course grades are broken down into

different capability components, such as design performance, team communication, design innovation, and practice. Teachers grade students based on the different capabilities they have demonstrated in their work. Consequently, the relevant capabilities obtained in different courses are calculated for students and presented in a visually-friendly manner. Students therefore clearly know their strengths and weaknesses. At the same time, students can also match their own abilities with those of the professional requirements presented in the system, and learn in a more specific manner. A proportion of their grades may also come from the comments of spectators on social media or at offline exhibitions. Participatory approach is practical and collaborative, reflective in process, and purposefully in bridging the gap between theory and practice in a classroom. Reflection is an important feature of the participatory approach (Pain et al. 2011, TrauthNare and Buck 2011, Kucharcikova and Tokarcikova 2016). After each engagement using the participatory approach, there should be at least fifteen minutes roundup (reflection) which has the potential of slowing down instruction but it is important to help get to the target (Pain et al. 2011, AduGyamfi et al. 2020). Therefore, the questionnaire rating, which used to be based on teachers' teaching attitude and quality, is reformed. Now, the system is based on empowering students to review the capabilities they have developed from each course so that they may reflect on the courses taken. The summary of an inductive lesson should return to the generalizations derived from the discovery lesson and reinforce those that are most salient. Often, it is useful to ask the visitors, themselves, to summarize what they have discovered.

4.2 Interaction

The interaction component of the system mainly involves interactions of students with others, the digital system, and the study environment. Each interaction is a touchpoint between students and the teaching service system.

The rise of Web 2.0 sites and the subsequent advent of social media platforms has brought forth a shift toward more participatory and interactive media experiences. Some distinctions and limitations (i.e., time and space) of traditional education can wane in online spaces, where participatory cultures grow through informal learning. The social network is first introduced into students' study system so as to establish links between students and others taking the same major both nationally and internationally. Students may initiate a discussion on a topic, establish project teams, collect ideas through brainstorming, collect user study data, or seek help on this social platform. Use the platform is reducing distinctions among groups like administrators and teachers, administrators and students, and students and teachers, among other groups. Minimal evidence exists that social media has transcended national, racial, or class lines to bring people of different experiences together for the common good. Students can engage in democratic school governance dialog with teachers and administrators using a school hashtag, and parents can engage in class content discussions with students and teachers. Social media allow students to engage with digital pen pals to grow as cosmopolitan global students. New media have made participatory learning possible

In terms of human-machine interaction, the information that students want to know about each course is offered during course selection. Such information includes coursework exhibitions, course evaluations, introductions to teachers, schedules, other students who have taken the course, and course design. It is especially noteworthy that a group-selection function has been introduced to the course-selection system, which has been designed following in-depth interviews with students. Based on the interviews, it is revealed that an important factor in course selection is being able to take a course with one's friends. Furthermore, based on the author's experience, attending classes with friends helps to enhance attendance rates and attention paid in class. Hence, this function is expected to further enhance students' initiative, which is especially important in the first few years following enrollment, when students remain undecided in their major. Such unintentional courses may bring about unexpected possibilities and opportunities.

In terms of student-space interaction, the SECI model proposed by Ikujiro Nonaka and Hirotaka Takeuchi in 1995 in Innovation to Win informs the system developed in this essay. This model views knowledge as a dynamic activity instead of a goal. Knowledge creation is accomplished through four steps. These are "S(Socialization)", "E(Externalization)", "C(Combination)" and "I(Internalization)", which are jointly achieved by many people. The space within which these people communicate with each other and have activities is known as "Ba", or "shared space that creates interconnectivity". Originating Ba emphasizes open organizational design and enables individuals to talk and communicate directly. Interacting/Dialoguing Ba emphasizes being open to new ideas and frank discussions for the purpose of converting implicit knowledge into explicit knowledge and creating both new knowledge and value. Cyber/Systemizing Ba refers to interactions in the virtual world, instead of the real world. New explicit knowledge is combined with existing information and knowledge so as to create fresh explicit knowledge and construct a knowledge framework. Exercising Ba emphasizes practice through observations or rehearsal under the guidance of experienced teachers, so as to apply and assimilate real-life or simulated explicit knowledge. One's studies should be seen as using one's vision, experience and understanding to apply conceptualized things into the real-life world, instead of merely accumulating more knowledge (Gao et al. 2015). Hence, discussion and cooperation are integrated into the teaching space and the tradition of teachers talking and students listening is broken. This system encourages teaching where students have practical operations and teachers fully engage students in discussions. A platform for student organization and discussion is created where they can create knowledge and coordinate with one another.

4.3 Task

Countless studies have proven that listening does not lead to learning. In fact, the vast majority of what is told to us is forgotten within a few short hours. These same studies do demonstrate, however, that learning and retention are strongest when there are opportunities for participation and dialogue (AduGyamfi et al. 2020). This is exactly consistent with the rules of art and design majors. Most of their courses consist primarily of discussions and guided practices. However, as more and more students study art and design, the time that a student receives effective information and help continues to shrink. For instance, in Beijing City University, the size of each art and design major class has reached 30–35 students. In the case of independent homework, if it takes 10 min for each student to engage in independent training or develop a presentation, then it takes almost six hours to mark the homework of a whole class. Thus, in a whole day of homework, one student receives effective information for only 10 min. When a student is waiting for their turn, they may choose to engage in other students' discussion, but this also takes too long and can cause some to experience boredom. In order to address this issue, courses can be decomposed into their requirements. In some credit hours, all the students in a class need to be present, but in others, only certain groups of students may need to be present; the teacher and/or senior students could teach together; or students could conduct an off-campus survey and visit on their own. Thus, students could notice enhanced class efficacy and teachers could control the class atmosphere more easily. Such class tasks drive students in their study at different phases, and helps students to better engage in forming task goals. After students develop a clear understanding of the study goals for each credit hour or off-campus survey, they develop a stronger sense of responsibility, which helps to improve the teaching quality.

Participatory learning makes use of tasks (Landcare Research 2002, Ciobanu 2018) which are defined as the day's problems and processes which are the ways people work together in solving the problem and the instruction is an evolving one which cannot be considered as a single event and takes time as a process (AduGyamfi et al. 2020). This is to say that participatory instruction is a complex process and teacher and students can participate, construct, and coordinate classroom processes.

4.4 Forum

Dewey (1916) believed that participatory learning experiences in school should be interconnected with democratic experiences. In discussing the importance of individuals' reconciling their interests with others in a pluralistic society, Dewey wrote, "Democracy is more than a form of government; it is primarily a mode of associated living, of conjoint communicated experience" (Baek and Kim 2018).

Communication is a vital means and form of study. Furthermore, communication is a crucial capability for students when engaging with classmates, teachers, clients and users. At the same time, communication is important for reaching an agreement with others or compromising. According to UNESCO (2001), group discussions are a useful participatory instructional tool, through which students learn to agree, disagree, and have mutual respect for the views of other students in a safe atmosphere (Ciobanu 2018, AduGyamfi et al. 2020). Students might also enrich their knowledge through communication, explore new possibilities, and seize new opportunities. Hence, students need to take the initiative to participate in their own studies, which is made possible through our social platform and offline activities.

Participatory instruction takes advantage of the students'' existing experiences (Omol-lo et al. 2017) and encourages students to share their respective experiences with other students (UNESCO 2001). Landcare Research (2002) found that since individual as well as group experiences the world in different ways, it is important to involve people on a subject or topic in order to share their respective experiences, activities, and understanding on the subject or topic (Liu et al. 2013, AduGyamfi et al. 2020).

In our teaching service system, students participate in discussion activities in groups. These activities can involve course teaching, optional courses, or Second-Class. Second-Class is a common teaching method in colleges and universities, which takes place alongside professional courses. Usually, schools ask students to obtain enough Second-Class credits beyond those obtained in their major courses. Examples include cultural activities, volunteering activities, and collective movie-watching activities, which can enrich students' extracurricular life and develop their sense of social responsibility. Moreover, through extracurricular topic discussions in Second-Class credits, it is possible to encourage more students to participate and have fun.

In the early phase of implementation, credits were used to encourage students to engage in group discussions or practices. These activities can be online or offline. Online group discussions are mainly initiated by teachers or students themselves. Online discussions can engage students as well as off-campus students, off-campus experts, international students, and international peers. Offline discussions are mainly conducted among on-campus students, teachers and external consultants. In initiating online activities, it is possible to set the time, number of participants, designated spare classrooms or public discussion spaces, or the format. Three primary types of activities have been predetermined.

The first type is project activities. Teachers and students can initiate group activities through a practice project. The activity can suit anyone who is interested, regardless of their level of study or major.

The second type is a fixed-theme activity. An example of this is a reading party, where the initiator may formulate the reading list. Students can then choose any activity they are interested in and join the relevant discussion.

The third type is the self-determined activity. Typically, this involves students or teachers initiating an activity based on course demand or their own studies. Students may invite other students, be they on-campus students or off-campus students, in order to capture more ideas.

According to John Seely Brown, in a good university, students have the opportunity to enter and access various different groups. At the same time, Brown believed that, the "face-to-face teaching and service" of peer support, collective study and thought sharing could never be replaced by network technology. Designers must examine the new possibilities that integrate innovation design, so as to promote and accelerate such reform. This essay seeks to create an innovation study space for students by fully utilizing tangible and intangible elements in the environment for the purpose of developing more reasonable service context awareness. Consequently, societal demand vis-à-vis college and university development can be better met, which is expected to become an inevitable trend in the future.

This teaching service framework was in the form of participatory teaching and learning approach comprising Insight, Interaction, Task, and Forum. The results showed that there was an improvement in students "conceptual understanding of designing their own learning roadmap". It is, therefore, recommended that arts and design educators and researchers should use the framework in large-scale research to assure the education community the efficacy of it in developing conceptual change in students.

5 Conclusion and Future Work

We have introduced the case of how is it possible to innovate and make initiative for students of arts and design using participatory methods. The study extracted the strengths of participatory methods by design thinking used in teaching service system through the case study, and then identified four kinds of touchpoints for student-centered teaching service. Applying the derived service to teaching processes is contribute to reducing the delivery gap of the teaching service and achieving student centered teaching services.

The thinking student is "Active", who makes a personal, inner and abstract reflection effort, which is given the opportunity to learn knowledge by understanding, storing and applying them personally. Our teaching service model wishes to teach students able to solve any unexpected problem situation and who are willing to develop their full potential. During the teaching service, we have to make student an active participant in their own learning process prepared to acquire knowledge through their own effort, by engaging the thinking, communication and mobilizing all intellectual functions. Knowledge, skills and experience that students thus obtain, are a more memorable and easier to apply in the future of their profession even personal life. In conclusion, it is important to emphasize the need for participatory teaching and teaching service. The content of this study, in which theory and practice coexist, will contribute to the promotion and improvement of similar studies in the future. Furthermore, it will contribute to realizing teaching and teaching service innovation based on its participation.

References

AduGyamfi, K., Ampiah, J.G., Agyei, D.D.: Participatory teaching and learning approach: a framework for teaching redox reactions at high school level. Int. J. Educ. Pract. **8**(1), 106–120 (2020)

Baek, S., Kim, S.: Participatory public service design by Gov. 3.0 design group, sustainability, 18 January 2018

Gao, B., Wu, R., Shi, Y., Liu, Y.: Service design practice for university innovative learning, creation and design, pp. 77–81 (2015)

Ciobanu, N.R.: Active and participatory teaching methods. Eur. J. Educ. **1**(2), 69–72 (2018)

Sangiorgi, D., Clark, B.: Toward a participatory design approach to service design. In: Participatory Design Conference 2014 (2004)

Traina, I., Fracasso, A.: Tips for teaching the "service design thinking" to students of higher education institutions. Sci. Res. **3**(8), 1 (2016)

Toikkanen, T., Keune, A., Leinonen, T.: Designing Edukata, a participatory design model for creating learning activities. In: Van Assche, F., Anido, L., Griffiths, D., Lewin, C., McNicol, S. (eds.) Re-engineering the Uptake of ICT in Schools, pp. 41–58. Springer, Cham (2015). https://doi.org/10.1007/978-3-319-19366-3_3

Fan, X., Huang, W.: Finding and solving: the teaching practice innovation and realization based on service design idea, vol. 281. ZhuangShi (2016)

Tang, L., Chang, Y.: A new training mode for design talents based on service design concept. China Acad. J. Electron. Publishing House (2017)

Ying, H., Wang Qin, D., Xing, C.S.: Practice and thinking of classroom teaching mode based on heuristic service design. China Acad. J. Electron. Publishing House **330**, 76–79 (2020)

Gao, B.: Exploration and practice of "three-dimensional T-shaped" service design education in the college of design and innovation. In: Creation and Design, pp. 81–85. Tongji University (2017)

Research on Course Experience Optimization of Online Education Based on Service Encounter

Chuqiong Zhang and Chang Xiao[✉]

South China University of Technology, Guangzhou 510006, People's Republic of China
xiaocsd@scut.edu.cn

Abstract. Under the influence of COVID-19, online education booms in its scale. Quite a lot of teachers and students lack experience in online courses, leading to poor course experience and other problems. This dissertation takes the CAID experimental course as the research object, finding out the influencing factors of online course experience based on the Service Encounter Theory, identifying the key service touch-points according to the Peak-End Rule. We Summarize the online course experience model. Then build an online flipped classroom model, so as to provide ideas for experience optimization of online courses in universities.

Keywords: Online course · Course experience · The Service Encounter Theory · The Peak-End Rule

1 Introduction

With the development of Internet + education, online class has developed rapidly. An outbreak of COVID-19 accelerate the transformation of traditional face-to-face teaching to online course in spring 2020. Everyone takes classes online, promoting the modernization of education, on the other hand, quite a lot of teachers and students lack experience in online courses, leading to poor course experience. The experimental course with practical operation is facing new challenges.

With the traditional teaching mode changing to the online mode, the contact mode between teachers and students has changed significantly. The influence of this change on students' course experience is an important basis to verify the effectiveness of the change of curriculum model. Since the 1990s, scholars have proposed that the product of education should be teaching service [1]. Over the years, with universities facing the challenge in globalization and commercialization, the view of higher education as a service has get more attention. The products offered by universities are the result of educational activities and processes—Students make advances in knowledge, Capacity, morality, physical and psychological health. Universities and their staff are the providers of services, while students are the recipients of services [2]. Therefore, this study intends to find the service touch-points of online courses under the research paradigm of the Service Encounter Theory, and construct the experience model of online courses by judging the key service touch-points.

© Springer Nature Switzerland AG 2021
M. M. Soares et al. (Eds.): HCII 2021, LNCS 12779, pp. 652–665, 2021.
https://doi.org/10.1007/978-3-030-78221-4_45

2 Aim and Objectives

Aim. To improve the efficiency of teacher-student collaboration and reduce cognitive overload in the transformation of the teaching model, improve the course experience, and provide reference for universities to promote the construction of online courses in the modernization of education.

Objectives. To analysis the contact mode between students and teachers for offline courses and online courses in universities, identify the service touch-points of online course, find out the key factors that affect the online teaching experience using the Peak-End Rule, propose countermeasure for optimization, construct online courses system model.

3 Methods and Approaches

3.1 Methods

Literature Review. The research status of the Service Encounter Theory and the Peak-End Rule are summarized and the value of their application in educational activities is discussed. The Service Encounter Theory is used to describe the scene of online courses and capture the service touch-points of online courses, so as to improve the experience of online courses by optimizing the service touch-points.

Survey. During the research, we use the methods such as observation, questionnaire, interview, case study, to collect the problems existing in the online courses of design experimental courses, to make a scientific analysis of the status. In order to define the touch-points between teachers and students, and the experience change during the class process, teachers and students were investigated through in-depth interviews and questionnaires, so that the positions, views and tendencies to be expressed in this dissertation are more authentic and representative.

Case Study. This dissertation takes the CAID experiment course as the research object, which was a course for undergraduates in the School of Design of South China University of Technology in spring 2020. Combined with the method of the Service Encounter Theory, representative exploration is carried out.

3.2 Theoretical Research

The Service Encounter is a concept in the field of management, which put forward by Shostack [3]. He associated customer satisfaction with the contact between customers and services, and believed that the contact is the key factor affecting satisfaction. After that, the Service Encounter Theory has been widely applied to explain the key influencing factors such as customer satisfaction of receiving electronic services and employee performance in online service enterprises and their influencing conditions [4].

The Service Encounter Theory takes service touch-point as its research unit. Touch-point refers to the point of contact between the customer and the service provider, equipment, environment and system in the process of receiving service, including tangible and intangible touch-points. Tangible touch-points refer to the contact of physical entities, face-to-face contact between people and man-machine interaction, etc. Intangible touch-points refer to emotional or cognitive experiences. The most painful needs of customers can be identified through the service touch-points, to help users to quickly complete the task at the right time and improve the user experience. Scholars have summarized various models to construct the interaction process of customer and service touch-points, including theater model [5], service interaction model [6], service contact system model [7], etc.

The identification and optimization of service touch-points is the key to improve the service system experience. In the design research, the story-board and user experience map are important way to build a clear service process and visually show the service touch-points.

In order to apply the Service Encounter Theory to assist the complex service system to find the key indicators, the research should focus on the construction of touch-points. Zhou Yan [8] took the study of children with autism, researched the touch-points in the process of slow disease management services, built the autism slow disease management applications, and then summarized a set of methods of touch-points built. She proposed that researcher carry out the identification, refining, assessment, remodeling of the touch-points, in the process of strengthening positive touch-points, eliminating the negative touch-points, creating a new touch-point, blending touch-points, to derive the strategy of service system design.

Since there are many touch-points in the process of service experience and the actual resources used to support the service are limited, the research of service experience optimization based on the Peak-End Rule to identify the key touch-points has attracted the attention of the academic community. Psychologist Daniel Kahneman proposes the Peak-End Rule, which states that people's memories of an experience are determined by two key factors: the peak and the end of the experience. Both positive peaks and negative peaks are remembered by the experiencer. In other words, the experiencer only remembers the experience at the peak and the end, and the proportion of positive and negative experiences, the length of both types of experiences, has little effect on either memory or feeling. The rule is applied to three main areas of research. Economists use the hypothesis model and the Peak-End Rule to carry out reasoning and dynamic pricing [9, 10]. Scholars in the field of management use the Peak-End Rule as an analytical aid to improve management methods [11]. Scholars in the field of design analyze the needs and experience of users in the service process with the method of qualitative research, and identify the key touch-points based on the Peak-End Rule in combination with the data of quantitative research, so as to provide references for the design of service experience. Hong Xinhui etc. [12] used the service design method to identify the touch-points, then the overall feeling of each touch-point was assigned subjectively in combination with Likter method, and confirmed the key touch-points by the Peak-End Rule, so as to eliminate the negative key touch-points of children atomization treatment services and optimize the positive key touch-points and end experience.

3.3 Case Study

This project followed the whole curriculum of the undergraduate course of Computer Aided Industrial Design in the School of Design, South China University of Technology, From March to May, 2020. Under the call of the Ministry of Education to keep learning while classes are suspended. This course is urgently transferred from face-to-face teaching to online teaching. Tencent Classroom is used as the teaching platform, which is a typical case of course transformation under the university scene. In order to determine the impact of online courses on students' class experience, this research conducted in-depth interviews with teachers and a questionnaire survey among 37 students, then conducted study and analysis on the online experiment course experience of design discipline. The research process of this topic is shown in Fig. 1 below.

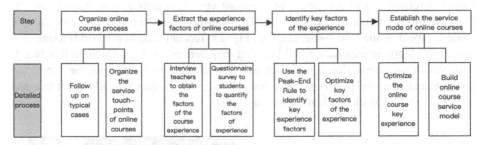

Fig. 1. Research flow chart.

Analysis of the Characteristics of Design Curriculum. The purpose of the graphic design experimental course is to help students master the basic operation and application of software, dig deep into the hidden tricks behind the tools, skilled use software for standardized design [13]. Through literature review and interview, it is found that there are three main characteristics of design experiment teaching compared with the traditional teaching method of theoretical subjects.

Firstly, the learning of design software has focused on procedures. If one step is not clearly seen, it is difficult for the students to follow up with the teacher, leading to a bad course experience. Especially in the course of 3D modeling, students who lack spatial imagination will take a long time to think. Therefore, preview before class and review after class have a great influence on the teaching effect.

Secondly, after class, students need to spend a long time to practice skills and complete coursework, which tests students' self-consciousness. Such public basic courses are generally taught in large classes, and the large number of students leads to less interaction between teachers and students. In this case, if students encounter problems, it is difficult to get timely guidance from teachers.

Thirdly, CAID experimental courses are mainly open to the undergraduate students of design discipline, and the content is focused on basic teaching, with little involvement in cutting-edge technology. As new concepts and technologies emerge in endlessly in the field of design. It is necessary to expand extracurricular knowledge. The course software is numerous and miscellaneous. If the traditional teaching method is adopted, the students will completely rely on the teachers to teach, then they won't learn deeply.

Selection of Teaching Platform. According to the desktop survey, Online teaching platform mainly includes the following 7 kinds: Online open course platform (MOOC, XuetangX, Bay Area Colleges, etc.), Virtual simulation experiment platform, network teaching platform (Rain Classroom, Tencent Classroom, Bb, etc.), Video interactive platform (Tencent meeting, Zoom, CCtalk, Panopto, etc.), social media platform (QQ, WeChat, etc.), Online Office Software (DingTalk, etc.), and the teaching platform independently developed by the school.

In this study, Rhinoceros software is the main learning software in the CAID experimental class. Different from other theoretical courses, it requires high operability and interaction in the teaching process. Due to the development of the epidemic and the limited time of the course, teachers need to quickly modify the teaching model and get familiar with the platform functions. After comparison, we chose Tencent Classroom, which is related to QQ account. The superfast version is easy to operate, without the lag time of the Internet. It supports sign-in, hand-up interaction in class, and multiple students speak at the same time, etc. (see Fig. 2). Tencent Classroom builds a one-stop immersive learning experience. All learning experiences, such as watching live broadcast, watching videos, doing exercises and downloading materials, can be completed in the client in a one-stop immersive way. The screen is automatically recorded, and students can look back and learn after class [14].

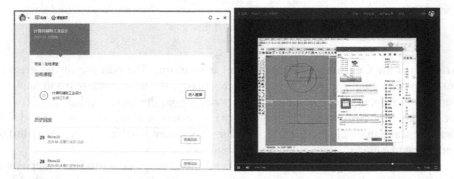

Fig. 2. Tencent Classroom online teaching interface.

The Teaching Model of Online Courses. Based on the Service Encounter Theory, taking the service encounter system model of Gronroos as a reference, the service model of online courses is constructed (see Fig. 3). In the online course, the service provider is the teacher and the service recipient is the student. What makes them connected are devices such as mobile phones, computers and Internet environments such as WiFi and video. The service process takes the course assessment standards, teaching model, and the platform operation mode as the operation system. At the same time, intangible service touch-points such as emotional communication and participation will be generated. During the whole process, there is no direct contact between students and teachers, or students and students, due to the lack of common physical space.

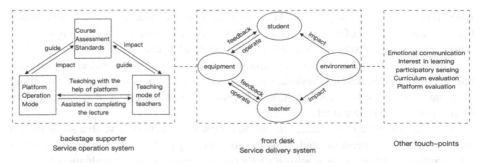

Fig. 3. Service model for online courses.

Combined with the service model, this dissertation summarizes the main behaviors of students in online courses before class (a–c points), in class (d–g points) and after class (h–l points).

a. Students receive learning materials released by teachers on the platform and review them in advance.
b. Students debug equipment and networks, test videos and microphones to create a good course environment.
c. Students turn on the video function to call the roll, and confirm their entry into the course.
d. Students operate the software follow up with the teacher.
e. Students click on the microphones to answer the teacher's question.
f. Students input text or voice to raise questions, and teachers answer them.
g. Students use computers to complete course exercises and submit them to the teacher for review.
h. Students watch replays of courses to consolidate their knowledge.
i. Students search for information and expand their knowledge.
j. Students have problems, then ask their teachers or classmates.
k. Students use computers to complete homework.
l. Students take the final examination.

Since the main purpose of teaching activities is to promote students' study and development. Teacher as service providers, whose main behavior of the online course model is also to serve students, will not be explained separately.

3.4 User Interview

In order to investigate teachers' experience in online courses, this study interviewed three teachers and sorted out their evaluation on the practical effect of online courses.

In the design experimental course, the progress of students in software learning varies greatly. The progress can be quickly identified in face-to-face teaching through inspection, so that students with fast progress can be assigned new tasks, and students with slow progress can be provided key guidance. However, teachers cannot directly see the operation process of all students on the Tencent Classroom. Only outgoing students who encounter questions will actively communicate with teachers.

On the other hand, the auxiliary functions of Tencent Classroom, including playback and release course reference materials in advance, help teachers to shorten the teaching time and extend the time for Q&A, which also improves the effect of teacher-student interaction to a certain extent.

In terms of the learning effect of online courses, teachers believe that students can master the basic content through classes and watching replays, but the details need to be improved. Although the teaching mode has changed, the main evaluation index of course is still the performance of students' interaction in the class and the quality of assignment. In the final score distribution of the course, the proportion of more than 70 points increased compared with the face-to-face teaching before, and the proportion of more than 90 points decreased. Thanks to the function of Tencent Classroom's automatic screen recording and playback, students' learning time has become longer.

Based on the above analysis, online course has its advantages compared with the traditional face-to-face teaching, but also has some disadvantages. In the subsequent teaching practice, it is necessary to make further planning based on the characteristics of the subject, strengthen interaction and optimize details, in order to achieve better results.

3.5 Questionnaire

In order to further investigate the application effect of online teaching of design experimental course under the flipped classroom model, this study investigates students' experience evaluation of online course model through questionnaires.

Questionnaire Design. In terms of questionnaire design, Likert Scale was adopted and combined with the Service Encounter Theory to analyze the 12 activities before, during and after online courses. The students' satisfaction was investigated from five dimensions of "very satisfied", "satisfied", "general", "dissatisfied" and "very dissatisfied", and the data was analyzed.

Questionnaire Analysis. The questionnaire survey was issued to all students of the research course, and 34 valid questionnaires were collected. To quantify the student experience, the proportion of "very satisfied" and "satisfied" were defined as positive experiences, the proportion of "general" was defined as insensate experiences, the proportion of "dissatisfied" and "very dissatisfied" were defined as negative experiences. The advantages and disadvantages of the online course model are summarized based on the statistical analysis of the questionnaire data (see Fig. 4).

A. Experience Before Class. Students' satisfaction at the pre-class stage shifted from high to low. The main reason is that online courses are not bound by location, reducing commuting time and making classes easier to start. However, the facilities and network conditions of online courses are not as good as students' expectations. This is mainly due to the fact that teachers and students in online courses are scattered in different environments, and the performance of network or equipment cannot be guaranteed uniformly, which makes different students have different experience in class.

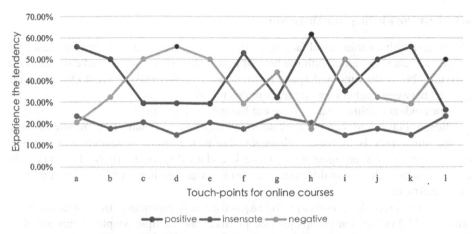

Fig. 4. Satisfaction curve of online course touch-points.

B. Experience During Class. In the age of the Internet, students themselves are more inclined to communicate with teachers online. In this survey, 58.82% of students tend to communicate with teachers through QQ group or WeChat group, 11.76% of them tend to choose QQ or WeChat, only 26.47% Prefer face-to-face communication. Students prefer group chatting to one-to-one communication. On the one hand, online courses cater to the needs of students who tend to communicate with teachers online, so they promote the interactive experience. On the other hand, only online communication leads to a sense of distance between teachers and students, which increases the cost of communication. At the same time, the decentralized class model leads to students being easily disturbed by other things, and their self-discipline becomes worse. At this node, the maximum negative experience occurs.

C. Experience After Class. Online courses provide students with a variety of ways to actively study, and this flipped classroom model enabled the students in the case to get a better learning experience. 58.82% of students said it was a positive experience for teachers to post the cases and models of the next class through QQ group in advance. There was a positive maximum of experience in the use of replay of course video. It showed that the implementation of flipped classroom under the model of online courses has a good effect on students' course experience.

D. Overall Experience Evaluation. As for the overall evaluation of the course, 85.29% of the students chose "very good", 11.76% of them chose "good". Between online course and traditional face-to-face teaching, 76.47% of students choose the former.

4   Results and Discussion

This dissertation summarizes the needs and experience of teachers and students in online courses through sorting out the above research results, then identifies the existing problems, and hopes to put forward optimizing strategies in the future research.

4.1 List the Findings for Discussion

Compared with the traditional face-to-face courses, online courses expand the teaching scene and teaching model with the help of new technologies, which make the teaching activities break the time and space restrictions, and also make a great change in the contact between teachers and students in this teaching service.

For students, online courses have the following characteristics:

Before class, there is no space constraint, students don't have to commute to class, so the study time is increased. However, due to the strong dependence of physical environment such as equipment and network, and the dispersed form of class makes the conditions of each student different. The result is that non-human factors interfere with the learning effect.

During class, online courses provide a good mode of communication for teachers and students. QQ or WeChat groups provide platform for multiple people to chat together. Students can ask personalized questions at any time, all voices can be heard and have the opportunity to be answered. In addition, the platform information is available to everyone so that students can quickly find common problems and reduce the frequency of repeated questions to teachers. But in most cases, students were asked to turn off the video after the roll call in consideration of the Internet speed. In the absence of place constraints, students' consciousness of attending class is significantly reduced. Only Online Communication also creates a sense of distance between students and teachers and classmates, which leads to less emotional communication and lower experience.

After class, online courses provide a lot of convenience for promoting students' independent study. The playback function allows students to review lectures multiple times, which is especially useful for design experimental course. Convenient online communication channels also enable students to consult teachers at any time after class.

In conclusion, online courses increase the frequency of contact between teachers and students. This model has both advantages and disadvantages, which need to be further explored and clarified.

4.2 Identify the Problems

To further clarify the experience evaluation of students under the online course mode, we draw the user experience map (see Fig. 5) from the perspectives of behaviors, thoughts, emotions and pain points and opportunity points, combine with the online course service model (see Fig. 3) based on the Service Encounter Theory, and the student experience tendency judged by data from user interviews and questionnaires.

4.3 Key Point of Concepts

As can be seen from the user experience map, there are 12 touch-points between students and teachers in the online course service. These touch-points are important nodes that affect students' online course experience. Service experience is affected by many factors such as environment, service providers, and the resources supporting service experience are limited. Compared to the average whole-process customer experience management,

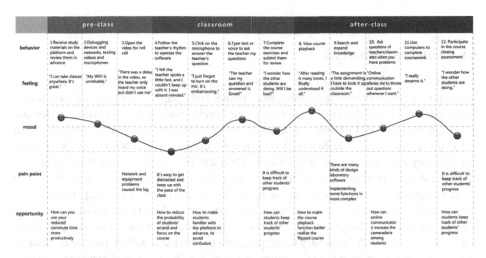

Fig. 5. User experience map.

applying the Peak-End Rule to service design and experience management, and focusing limited resources on the experience management of peak-points and end-point of customer contact, higher service performance can be achieved with the same or fewer resources.

From the experience map, the positive peak of online course experience is in the behavior of watching the replay of the course after class. This function can be used for students to review the content of the class for many times, and to learn and practice the important and difficult points repeatedly. This is especially useful for design experimental course. To some extent, it alleviates students' anxiety caused by not keeping up with the teacher's progress in the course.

The negative peak of the experience is in the behavior of falling behind the pace of the course due to desertion and other reasons. Although online courses are organized by the same teacher at a fixed time, they lack the constraints of offline classroom atmosphere and lack of supervision from teachers due to the internet lag, which makes self-discipline the worst node of online course experience. So how does an online course ensure that students are focused and following the teacher's progress throughout the course is a key touch-point in the entire experience.

The end point of contact is the final examination at the end of the course. In this node, because students only interact with teachers and classmates online, there is a time difference in getting guidance from teachers and less contact with classmates, so they cannot judge their own progress ranking among classmates, which leads to poor experience such as confusion.

The above three points are the key touch-points to explore the influence of online course transformation on course experience in universities. In the follow-up online course development, key research and design should be done.

5   Modeling

5.1   Optimize Service Process

A good online course experience should have the basic functions of offline courses, and enhance the positive experience touch-points and optimize the negative experience touch-points. On the basis of the previous research, this dissertation summarizes the user experience model of online courses (see Fig. 6). First of all, online courses are in the exploratory stage. The first part of students' course experience is not the lecture, but the operation and use of the platform. Operational experience, such as debugging equipment and opening video, is the basic evaluation element. Secondly, teachers and students carry out teaching activities on the platform, and the cognitive experience, such as the teaching rhythm, course playback, and answering effect, is perceived by students. The improvement of this experience not only depends on the ability of service providers, but also improves with the ability of the platform to provide auxiliary functions. Finally, the distance between people in the online mode makes the emotional experience worse, which requires online courses to create more ways of interaction between teachers and students and classmates as much as possible on the premise of satisfying the basic functions.

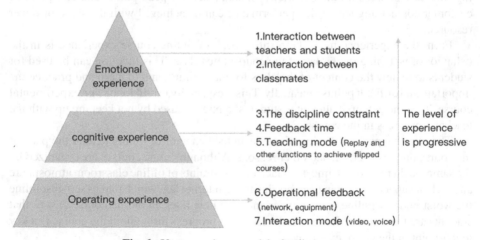

Fig. 6. User experience model of online courses.

The three key service touch-points in this research belong to the level of cognitive experience, so the service process of online courses should be optimized from the two levels of operational experience and cognitive experience.

In terms of course playback, the platform should have the function of recording screen and annotating key links to assist teachers to record the teaching process and annotate the key parts, so that students can improve efficiency when looking back. The teacher should make the modeling case into courseware for students to review.

In terms of attention, the platform should have the function of showing the status of students in class. For example, capturing the mouse track of students can be used by teachers to judge the progress of students' operation, and help teachers to ensure that the time left for students to practice matches the time required by students' actual operation. Adopt the flipped classroom model [15]. Realize the change from focusing on teacher teaching to student learning. Promote students' active exploration and active discovery of knowledge and the reconstruction of the learned knowledge. Shorten the time of lecture, increase the time of experimental operation, problem thinking, group discussion and teacher's guidance, and improve students' learning enthusiasm.

In terms of examine, the platform should have the function of integrating the data of students' asking questions, answering questions, operating time and so on, which can be used as the basis for daily assessment. Students can master their daily study status. At the same time, a homework database should be established for students to learn and communicate with each other, so as to quantify the learning effect of students and make them have a more specific learning experience.

5.2 Building Service Patterns

By analyzing the model of CAID experimental course to carry out online courses based on Tencent Classroom and QQ, this study obtains the strategy of optimizing online course experience. The flipped classroom model is applied to the online course model of design experimental courses. It can be summarized as follows: pre-class—classroom—after-class—flipping—opening (see Fig. 7).

The flipped classroom model of online courses is a reform of teaching methods. Before class, 3D models and other learning materials were released on the platform, and students previewed through video, PPT, and completed the learning tasks online, so as to make good preparations for improving the quality of the class. During class, the teachers shorten the time of lecture, increase the time of experimental operation, problem thinking, group discussion and teacher's guidance. Teachers improved their own level through students' feedback. After class, students watched replay, PPT and other relevant materials to lay a solid foundation. Students who found good tutorial and materials could recommend them in QQ group to help teachers enrich the teaching content, improve the teaching materials, improve the teaching methods and improve the teaching level.

Under the background of epidemic prevention, online experimental teaching can help teachers break through the shackles of traditional classroom teaching mode and transcend the limitations of time and space. Through the combination of online teaching platform and flipped classroom model, the experimental teaching methods and means are enriched, the subject is more interesting, the time for students to immerse themselves in learning is prolonged, the subjective initiative of students is improved, and the teaching is more practical and exploratory. These characteristics can overcome the problems caused by transferring design experiment course to online course, and improve the course experience.

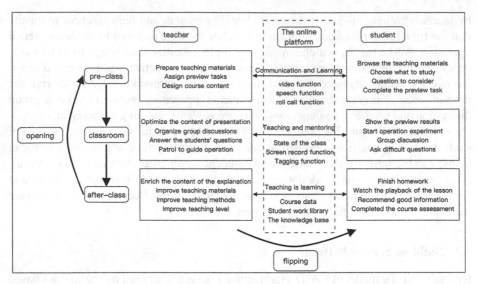

Fig. 7. Model of flipped classroom system for online courses

6 Conclusions

This dissertation sorts out touch-points between teachers and students in design course under the online teaching mode, by tracking a design experimental course, and investigating the actual experience and needs of teachers and students. Thus, the influencing factors of online design course experience are found out, and the Peak-End Rule is used to reshape the touch-points of the teaching process, enhance the positive service touch-points, weaken the negative service touch-points, and integrate the relevant service touch-points, so as to construct the online course experience model. According to the model, the process optimization countermeasures are put forward, the online flipped classroom model for online courses is built, which provide references for optimizing the online course experience in colleges and universities.

Acknowledgment. This work was supported by a grant from the South China University of Technology Education Reform Project (Y1190391).

References

1. Hill, F.: Managing service quality in higher education: the role of the student as primary consumer. Qual. Assur. Educ. **3**(3), 10–21 (1995)
2. Halliay, S.V., Davies, B., Philippa, W., Ming, L.: A dramaturgical analysis of the service encounter in higher education. J. Mark. Manage. **24**, 47–68 (2008)
3. Shostack, G.L.: Planning the Service Encounter. Lexington Books, Lexington (1985)
4. Jeffrey, A.M.: 40 must-read theories for management and organization studies. Peking University Press, Beijing (2017). Xu, S.Y., Li C.P. (translate)

5. Grove, F., Bitner, M.J.: Dramatizing the service experience: a managerial approach. In: Advances in Service Marketing and Management, no. 1, pp. 91–121 (1992)
6. Fan, X.C.: Quality of service management: interaction process and interaction quality. Nankai Manag. Rev. **1**, 8–12 (1999)
7. Gronroos, C.: Service Management and Marketing. Lexington Books, Lexington (1990)
8. Zhou, Y.: Research on application design of chronic disease management based on service touch point. Shandong University, Shangdong (2019)
9. De, M.P., Estelami, H.: Applying the peak-end rule to reference prices. J. Prod. Brand Manag. (2013)
10. Nasiry, J., Popescu, I.: Dynamic pricing with loss-averse consumers and peak-end anchoring. Oper. Res. **59**, 1361–1368 (2011)
11. Zeng J.Q., Yuan, Y., Zhang, J.: Research on Customer Experience Management of Telecom Operators. Journal of Beijing University of Posts and Telecommunications (Social Science Edition) (2013).
12. Hong, X.H., Zhan, X.T.: Design and research of improving children's nebulization service experience based on peak-end law. Design (2018)
13. Shi, R.: Research on teaching strategy of network broadcast course – taking the practical course photoshop graphic design as an example. Comput. Prod. Circ. (2020)
14. China's online education platform user big data report - Tencent Classroom data chapter (2020). http://report.iresearch.cn/report_pdf.aspx?id=3516. Accessed 15 Feb 2021
15. Zhang, X., Zhang, C., Xu, Q.: Application of "flipped classroom+" mixed teaching mode in software engineering course teaching. University Education (2020)

Author Index